Paragraphs
& Essays

Paragraphs & Essays

with MULTICULTURAL READINGS

Sixth Edition

Lee Brandon
Mount San Antonio College

D. C. HEATH AND COMPANY
Lexington, Massachusetts Toronto

Address editorial correspondence to:

D. C. Heath and Company
125 Spring Street
Lexington, MA 02173

Acquisitions Editor: Paul A. Smith
Developmental Editor: Linda M. Bieze
Production Editor: Bryan Woodhouse
Designer: Cornelia Boynton
Production Coordinator: Richard Tonachel
Permissions Editor: Margaret Roll
Cover: Photograph © Morley Baer

For permission to use copyrighted materials, grateful acknowledgment is made to the copyright holders listed on page TC1, which is hereby considered an extension of this copyright page.

Copyright © 1994 by D. C. Heath and Company.

Previous editions copyright © 1990, 1983, 1979, 1975, and 1969 by D. C. Heath and Company.

All rights reserved. No part of this publication may be reproduced or transmitted in any form or by any means, electronic or mechanical, including photocopy, recording, or any information storage or retrieval system, without permission in writing from the publisher.

Published simultaneously in Canada.

Printed in the United States of America.

International Standard Book Number: 0-669-29790-9

10 9 8 7 6 5 4 3 2

To P. Joseph Canavan (1915–1992)

colleague, mentor, fellow writer, friend

Preface

Intended for use in developmental and college writing courses that deal with paragraph and essay writing, *Paragraphs & Essays*, 6th Edition, is based on the principles that writing is a recursive process, that writing instruction should be linked to reading, and that good writing and critical thinking are intrinsically bound together. This book addresses developmental paragraph writing and essay writing together because they often share the same patterns; whether an idea is developed into a paragraph or an essay is often determined by the extent of the explanation and the quantity of the evidence. Of course, in college writing, need for that explanation and evidence will be determined by the nature of the assignment and the anticipated needs of the audience, as well as by the capacity of the writer. Addressing both the paragraph and the essay in one text provides a broad base that allows instructors to adjust the lengths and types of various assignments (subject to time constraints and to the needs of a given class at a particular point in the semester). Some instructors will no doubt choose to concentrate on the paragraph (perhaps finishing the semester with a few essays), whereas others will begin with shorter assignments and rather rapidly move the students to the essay. *Paragraphs &Essays* accommodates such flexibility.

A Comprehensive and Flexible Textbook

While retaining the basic framework that made *Paragraphs and Themes* (the title of previous editions) an enduring textbook, I have incorporated certain significant changes and refinements in all the main aspects of instruction. The result is a comprehensive and flexible textbook. Writing instruction includes explanations, examples, and exercises, in forms ranging from the sentence, to the essay, to the documented paper. Readings include paragraphs, essays, short stories, poems, and even a song with music. Contemporary cartoons lighten the atmosphere while making instructional points. The number of exemplary paragraphs from both professional and classroom sources (more than sixty essays and more than a hundred paragraphs) make it unnecessary for instructors to assign a separate reader while allowing for varying reading assignments from class to class and from semester to semester.

Writing

My approach to writing instruction begins with the premise that each student writer has ideas to express. Those ideas, though apparent to the student writer, must be "decoded" by using a writing process to conceptualize and present them to the reader. To define this process, I have coined the acronym **DCODE** (pronounced "décode"): **Delve, Concentrate, Organize, Draft** (with revision), and **Edit**. DCODE is presented for the developmental paragraph in Chapter 1 and for the essay in Chapter 2, and is integrated throughout the book. This system gives form to what most instructors teach—freewriting, brainstorming, clustering, writing of the topic sentence or thesis, organizing by outline or outline substitute, writing and revising, and editing. It is flexible enough for instructors to vary assignments and approaches, yet structured enough to guide student writers in an orderly way through the writing forms and purposes presented in Chapters 3–13. Those chapters include both generic and reading-related assignments for writing paragraphs, essays, and journal entries. An alternate Thematic Table of Contents arranges material for idea-related treatment and is specifically keyed to instruction and assignments in simple textbook-based documented writing in Chapter 14, which also provides instruction in using the library and writing a short research paper. Every chapter includes an analysis of a brief piece of writing from a professional source and the step-by-step production of a student paragraph or essay. In each of the first fourteen chapters, students can see how another student moved from the inception of an idea, through the stages of the writing process, to the final draft.

Handbook for Revising and Editing

Chapter 15, the handbook, has a new section on revision using **cluess** (**c**oherence, **l**anguage, **u**nity, **e**mphasis, **s**upport, and **s**entence structure), complete with exercises on both the developmental paragraph and the essay. The section on fundamentals (stressing editing) features two exercises for each topic, one with answers in the Answer Key and one without answers. Exercises have been simplified in several instances, and more sentence writing is included in this edition. Taking Tests and Making Application (writing letters of application and résumés) are among the new handbook sections. Instruction is supported in the *Instructor's Guide* with a quiz on each topic. A separate section entitled Brief Guide for ESL Students focuses on special problems through explicit instruction, cross-references, and an exercise.

Readings

The readings are varied in content, form, and perspective, reflecting cultural diversity in the broadest sense and the thoughts of both men and women. Each of the first fourteen chapters includes numerous paragraphs and essays that have been selected for three reasons: to stimulate ideas for discussion, to stimulate ideas for reading-related writing, and to provide models for forms of discourse. The readings are supported by vocabulary highlights where appropriate, by guide questions for both writing and discussion, and by teaching suggestions and reading quizzes in the *Instructor's Guide*.

Critical Thinking

Critical thinking underpins both the reading and writing components. Chapter 13 introduces critical thinking explicitly, highlighting such matters as fact and opinion, inductive and deductive thought, logical fallacies, and kinds of evidence. Throughout the book, guide questions for readings are both implicitly and explicitly concerned with critical thinking. Writing instruction, keyed especially to reading assignments, requires the same critical-thinking principles as does reading.

Collaborative Learning

This book readily adapts to collaborative learning. The Applications for Critical Reading and Discussion questions are linked to both form and idea, so that reading, thinking, and writing become the basis for useful and stimulating discussion. The **DCODE** approach to writing provides a highly accessible and comprehensive framework for students engaged in peer editing.

Acknowledgments

Reviewers: I am grateful to the following instructors who have reviewed this text: Herbert Karl Green, Jr., Camden County College; Ida R. Page, Durham Technical Community College; Elisabeth Leyson, Fullerton College; Wayne Rambo, Camden County College; Joseph Szabo, Mercer County Community College; Virginia Schilt, Mt. San Antonio College; and Daniel M. E. Landau, Santa Monica College. Thanks also to the faculty at Mt. San Antonio College who reviewed this text and suggested readings to me: Pamela Arterburn, Keith Cole, Debra Farve, Jean Garrett, and Julian Medina. I am also grateful to the students at Mt. San Antonio College and the California Institution for Women who reacted helpfully to early drafts of the manuscript and contributed thirty-five paragraphs and essays to this book.

D. C. Heath and Company: Thanks also to the staff at D. C. Heath and Company: Margaret Roll, Senior Permissions Editor; Paul A. Smith, Senior Acquisitions Editor; Linda Bieze, Developmental Editor; Bryan Woodhouse, Senior Production Editor; Cornelia Boynton, Senior Designer; and Paul Durantini, Sales Representative.

Family: Finally, I am grateful to my family for their encouragement and humor: my son Kelly, daughter-in-law Jeanne, and grandson Shane; my daughter Erin and son-in-law Michael; and especially my wife Sharon.

LEE BRANDON

Contents

1 Using a Pattern of Strategies to Write Paragraphs: DCODE 1

Developmental Paragraph Defined 2
    Example of Form A 3
    Example of Form B 3
The DCODE Process 3
    Delve 4
        Freewriting ■ *Brainstorming* ■ *Clustering*
    Concentrate 8
    Organize 10
        Clustering 10 ■ *Outlining 10*
    Draft 16
        Coherence ■ *Language* ■ *Unity* ■ *Emphasis* ■ *Support* ■ *Sentence Structure*
    Edit 18
*Byron Jackson, "Make Me a Traffic Cop" 18

Types of Paragraph Writing 23
    Critical Reading, Critical Thinking, Critical Writing 23
*Judith Ramsay, "Causes of Mental Illness" 23
    Outlining Reading Material 24
    Summary 25
        Using DCODE in Summary Writing 25
    Reaction 26
    Spin-Off 27
        Using DCODE in Writing Reaction Statements 27
Writing a Journal 27

WORKSHEET: Writing in DCODE 29

EXERCISES 6, 7, 8, 9, 10, 11, 13, 15, 18, 23, 26

2 Using a Pattern of Strategies to Write Essays: DCODE 31

Essay Defined 32
Jim Ellis, "Forever Elvis" 32

*student essay

Special Paragraphs within the Essay 32
    Introductions 34
        Direct Statement of Thesis ■ *Background* ■ *Definition* ■ *Quotation* ■ *Shocking Statement and Questions* ■ *Questions and a Definition*
    Conclusions 36
        Example

Michael W. Fox, "What Is Your Pet Trying to Tell You?" 38

Writing the Essay 41
    Delve 42
        Freewriting ■ *Brainstorming* ■ *Clustering*
    Concentrate 43
    Organize 44
    Draft 45
    Edit 48

*Leah, "Razor Wire Sweat Lodge" 51

WORKSHEET: Writing in DCODE 57

EXERCISES: 36, 38, 39, 40, 55

3 Narration: Moving Through Time 59

Narrative Defined 60

Purposes and Forms 60

Narrative Technique 61
    Order 61
    Verb Tense 61
    Point of View 62
    Description 63
    Dialogue 64

The Reading Connection 65

Helen Keller, "Language Set Me Free" 65

Luis Torres, "Los Chinos Discover el Barrio" 66

Elizabeth Wong, "The Struggle to Be an All-American Girl" 68

Maya Angelou, "Cotton-Picking Time" 70

Tim Rutten, "Face to Face with Guns and the Young Men Who Use Them" 72

The Reading Connection from Classroom Sources 74

*James Hutchinson, "Pain Unforgettable" 74

*Jack Mullins, "The Customer Is Always Right" 78

*Sandra Pei, "Love Happened" 79

Suggested Topics for Writing Narratives 80

6 Functional Analysis: Examining the Components   145

Functional Analysis Defined   146
    Moving from Subject, to Principle, to Division, to Relationship   146
    Order   147

The Reading Connection   148

IRWIN RUBENSTEIN, "The Living Cell"   148

RICHARD FORD, "The Boss Observed"   149

RAYMOND KENDALL, "The Sonata"   150

LEWIS GROSSBERGER, "A Big Wheel"   151

WILLIAM HELMREICH, "Optimism, Tenacity Lead Way Back to Life"   153

KESAYA E. NODA, "Growing Up Asian in America"   155

The Reading Connection from Classroom Sources   161

*CYRUS NORTON, "Magic Johnson"   161

*ANGELA DESARRO, "The Success of 'Roseanne' "   164

*ALLISON UDELL, "Ben Franklin, Renaissance Man"   165

Suggested Topics for Writing Functional Analysis   167
    General Topics   167
    Reading-Related Topics   167

Writer's Checklist   168

Journal-Entry Suggestions   169

WORKSHEET: Writing in DCODE   171

EXERCISES: 148, 149, 150, 151, 153, 155, 160, 164, 165

7 Process Analysis: Writing About Doing   173

Process Analysis Defined   174
    Two Types of Process Analysis: Directive and Informative   174
    Blending Process Analysis with Other Forms   175

Considering the Audience   176
    Knowledge   176
    Attitude   176

Working with the Stages   176
    Preparation   176
    Steps   176
    Order   176

The Reading Connection 177

FLORENCE H. PETTIT, "How to Sharpen a Knife" 177
JENNIFER MCBRIDE YOUNG, "Gonna Rock To-o-n-i-i-ight!" 178
ANN AND MYRON SUTTON, "Nature on the Rampage" 179
L. RUST HILLS, "How to Eat an Ice-Cream Cone" 180
RACHEL CARSON, "The Birth of an Island" 181
BRUCE JAY FRIEDMAN, "Eating Alone In Restaurants" 183
CARL WILGUS, "Conserving Energy as You Ski" 185
W. S. MERWIN, "Unchopping a Tree" 187
MALCOLM X AND ALEX HALEY, "The Autobiography of Malcolm X" 190

The Reading Connection from Classroom Sources 192

*MAYSIM MONDEGARAN, "Sabzi Polo Mahi" 193
*A. DEL TURCO, "Popping the Cork" 197
*JOHN L. TILLMAN, "Making a Perfect Paper Airplane" 199

Suggested Topics for Writing Process Analysis 200
    General Topics 200
    Reading-Related Topics 202

Writer's Checklist 203

Journal-Entry Suggestions 204

WORKSHEET: Writing in DCODE 205

EXERCISES: 177, 178, 179, 180, 181, 182, 185, 187, 190, 192, 197, 199

8 Analysis by Causes and Effects: Determining Reasons and Outcomes 207

Analysis by Causes and Effects Defined 208

Determining Your Purpose 208

Composing the Topic Sentence or Thesis 209

Considering Kinds of Causes and Effects 209
    Primary or Secondary 209
    Immediate or Remote 209

Evaluating the Importance of Sequence 210
    Order 210

Introducing Ideas and Working with Patterns 210

The Reading Connection 212

JOHN BROOKS, "The Effects of the Telephone" 212

A. J. P. TAYLOR, "Causes of World War II" 213

MARTIN LUTHER KING, JR., "Back of the Bus" 214

RACHEL CARSON, "Arsenic for Everyone" 215

ANASTASIA TOUFEXIS, "What Happens to Steroid Studs?" 216

SHARON BERNSTEIN, "Multiculturalism: Building Bridges or Burning Them?" 217

DAVID LEVINE, "I'm Outta Here" 220

NORMAN COUSINS, "Who Killed Benny Paret?" 224

The Reading Connection from Classroom Sources 225

*AIDA GONZALES, "Death by Gangbanging" 225

*ANGELA DeSARRO, "No Secrets to Her Success: Reba McEntire" 226

*JAMIE MORGAN, "Kick Me" 228

Suggested Topics for Writing Analysis of Causes and Effects 234

    General Topics 234
    Reading-Related Topics 235

Writer's Checklist 236

Journal-Entry Suggestions 237

WORKSHEET: Writing in DCODE 239

EXERCISES: 211, 212, 213, 214, 215, 216, 217, 220, 223, 225, 226, 227

9 Classification: Establishing Groups   241

Classification Defined 242

    Observing Classification in Action 242
    Applying a Principle That Fits the Purpose 243
    Avoiding Overlap 243
    Working with Good Topics, Average Topics, and Bad Topics 243

Writing Classification Using DCODE 245

    Delve 245
        Freewriting ■ *Brainstorming* ■ *Clustering*
    Concentrate 246
    Organize 247
    Draft 247

Working with Simple and Complex Forms 247

The Reading Connection 249

FREDERICK B. KNIGHT, "Maslow's Classification of Motives" 249

GLENN R. CAPP, "Listen Up!" 250

MORTIMER J. ADLER, "Kinds of Book Owners" 251

JOHN CUBER, "Kinds of Scientific Findings" 252

MARY ANN HOGAN, "Why We Carp and Harp" 253

LOUISE DUDLEY AND AUSTIN FARICY, "Musical Instruments: Blowing, Bowing, and Beating" 256

The Reading Connection from Classroom Sources 258

*JERRY LOPEZ, "Types of Night Clubbers" 258

*ANGELA DESARRO, "Three Kinds of Siblings" 259

*MARGE TANNER, "Types of Fly Fighters" 261

Suggested Topics for Writing Classifications 266
    General Topics 266
    Reading-Related Topics 267

Writer's Checklist 268

Journal-Entry Suggestions 268

WORKSHEET: Writing in DCODE 269

EXERCISES: 244, 249, 250, 251, 252, 253, 256, 258, 259, 260

10 Comparison and Contrast: Showing Similarities and Dissimilarities 271

Comparison and Contrast Defined 272

Generating Topics and Working with the 4 P's 272
    Purpose 272
        Informative ■ *Persuasive*
    Using Clustering as a Technique for Finding Points 273
    Pattern 274
    Presentation 276

Analogy 278

Charles Prebish, "Heavenly Father, Divine Goalie" 279

Suggested Topics for Writing Analogy 279

The Reading Connection 280

JOSEPH WOOD KRUTCH, "The Desert and the Jungle" 280

ALISON LURIE, "Pink Kittens and Blue Spaceships" 281

LOUISE DUDLEY AND AUSTIN FARICY, "The Temple and the Cathedral" 282

ASHLEY MONTAGU, "The Natural Superiority of Women" 283

SUZANNE BRITT, "Neat People vs. Sloppy People" 284

GARY SOTO, "Looking for Work" 286

RICHARD RODRIGUEZ, "Private Language, Public Language" 290

The Reading Connection from Classroom Sources 294

*Jennifer Jeffries, "Two Loves: Puppy and True" 295

*Ray Sinclair, "Sam and Woody" 299

*Vanessa Capili, "Men and Women: More Equal Than the Same" 301

Suggested Topics for Writing Comparison and Contrast 303

    General Topics 303
    Reading-Related Topics 304

Writer's Checklist 306

Journal-Entry Suggestions 306

WORKSHEET: Writing in DCODE 307

EXERCISES: 279, 280, 281, 282, 283, 284, 286, 290, 294, 299, 301

11 Definition: Clarifying Terms   309

Definition Defined 310

Simple Definitions 310

    Dictionary Entries 310
    Techniques for Conveying Simple Definitions 311
    Avoiding Common Problems 313

Extended Definitions 314

    Purpose 314
    Techniques for Development 315
    Order 317
    Introduction and Development 317

The Reading Connection 318

Robert H. Dalton, "Personality" 318

Morris Tepper, "Tornado" 319

Paul Mussen and Mark Rosenzweig et al., "Conformity" 320

Ray Jenkins, "Georgia on My Mind" 321

Richard Rodriguez, "Does America Still Exist?" 322

Polingaysi Qoyawayma (Elizabeth Q. White), "The Hopi Way" 325

Jo Goodwin Parker, "What Is Poverty?" 327

The Reading Connection from Classroom Sources 330

*Jeri Linda White, "Prison Slang" 330

*Linda Wong, "Going Too Far" 332

*Michelle Proctor, "Perspectives on Motivation" 335

Suggested Topics for Writing Extended Definitions 337
      General Topics 337
      Reading-Related Topics 338

Writer's Checklist 339

Journal-Entry Suggestions 339

WORKSHEET: Writing in DCODE 341

EXERCISES: 312, 313, 316, 318, 319, 320, 321, 322, 325, 327, 330, 331, 335

12 Literary Analysis: Reacting to Stories   343

Why We Read Fiction 344
      Reading Literature 344
Writing About Literature 344
      Setting 344
      Conflict 345
      Characters 345
      Plot 345
      Theme 345
      Point of View 346
      Analysis 346
Finding Topics for Literary Analysis 346
      Analytical Analysis 346
      Speculative Analysis 347
Writing Literary Analysis with DCODE 347

The Reading Connection 348

WILLIAM CARLOS WILLIAMS, "The Use of Force" 348
*MICHAEL FULTON, "More Than Just a House Call" 352
*GLORIA MENDEZ, "Out of His Element" 355
*JANET PETERSON, "The Use of Self-Analysis" 356
TONI CADE BAMBARA, "Raymond's Run" 357
IRWIN SHAW, "The Girls in Their Summer Dresses" 363
EDGAR ALLAN POE, "The Tell-Tale Heart" 367
ANONYMOUS, "Frankie and Johnny" 370
ROBERT BROWNING, "My Last Duchess" 372
EDWIN ARLINGTON ROBINSON, "Richard Cory" 373
W. H. AUDEN, "The Unknown Citizen" 374

Suggested Topics for Writing About Literature 376
      Analytical Topics 376
      Imaginative Topics 377

Contents xxi

Writer's Checklist 379

Journal-Entry Suggestions 379

WORKSHEET: *Writing in DCODE* 381

EXERCISES: 348, 351, 355, 356, 357, 362, 366, 370, 372, 373, 374

13 Argumentation: Persuading, Arguing, and Thinking Critically — 383

Persuasion and Argumentation Defined 384
    Purpose 384
    The Problem and Your Proposition 384
    Your Audience 385
    Components of Your Paper 385
    Organizational Plan 385
    Appropriate Kinds of Evidence 386
    Inductive and Deductive Reasoning 387
    Logical Fallacies 389

The Reading Connection 393
LOUIS NIZER, "How About Low-Cost Drugs for Addicts?" 393
TIPPER GORE, "Curbing the Sexploitation Industry" 395
ED ANGER, "Make Docs Wheel and Deal Like Used Car Salesmen!" 397

The Reading Connection from Classroom Sources 398
*ERIC MILLER, "A New Wind Blowing" 398
*ANGELA DESARRO, "Right to Die" 405

Suggested Topics for Writing Argumentation 406
    General Topics 406
    Reading-Related Topics 407

Writer's Checklist 408

Journal-Entry Suggestions 409

WORKSHEET: *Writing in DCODE* 411

EXERCISES: 391, 392, 393, 395, 397, 398, 399, 405

14 Using the Textbook and Library Sources: Writing the Documented Paper — 413

Two Types of Documented Writing 414
    The Library-Based Documented Paper 414
    The Textbook-Based Documented Paper 414

Working with the Thematic Table of Contents   415

Suggested Topics Related to Areas in the Thematic Table of Contents   415

DCODE Application   416

Basic Documentation   416

The Presentation   417

The Library Catalog   418

General Encyclopedias and Biographical Dictionaries   418

Specialized Reference Works   418

> *The Sciences* ■ *The Social Sciences* ■ *The Humanities* ■ *Periodical Indexes and Bibliographies* ■ *Indexes to Articles and Reviews in Popular Magazines* ■ *How to Use the Reader's Guide to Periodical Literature* ■ *Microfilm Resources and Computerized Information Services*

The Research Paper   421

> Background: The Research Assignment   422
> Circumstances of Composition   422
> Preliminary Bibliography and Works Cited   422
>> *Books* ■ *Articles in Periodicals* ■ *A Work in an Anthology* ■ *An Article in an Encyclopedia* ■ *Government Publications* ■ *Published Proceedings of a Conference* ■ *A Lecture, Speech, or Address* ■ *A Personal Interview*
> Documenting   425
>> *References to Articles and Single-Volume Books* ■ *References to Works in an Anthology* ■ *References to Works of Unknown Authorship* ■ *References in Block Quotations*

Researching and Writing   428

> Plagiarism   430
> Sample Research Paper   431
>> *Use and Documentation of Sources* ■ *Content and Organization*

Writer's Checklist   442

WORKSHEET: Writing in DCODE   443

EXERCISES: 441

15 Revising and Editing: A Handbook   H1

Revising   H2

> Coherence   H2
>> *Overall Plan* ■ *Transitional Words and Expressions* ■ *Pronoun Reference* ■ *Repetition of Key Words and Ideas* ■ *Consistent Point of View*
> Language   H5
>> *Usage* ■ *Tone* ■ *Diction*
> Unity   H8
> Emphasis   H8

Placement ■ *Repetition*
>Support   H9
>Sentence Structure   H10

Writer's Revision Checklist   H14
>*Coherence* ■ *Language* ■ *Unity* ■ *Emphasis* ■ *Support* ■ *Sentence Structure*

Parts of Speech   H16
>*Nouns* ■ *Pronouns* ■ *Verbs* ■ *Adjectives* ■ *Adverbs* ■ *Prepositions* ■ *Conjunctions* ■ *Interjections*

Verbs and Subjects   H24
>Verbs   H24
>>*Basic Principles* ■ *Other Considerations* ■ *Variations in Type and Location*

Sentence Problems   H28
>Fragments   H28
>>*Dependent Clauses as Fragments* ■ *Phrases as Fragments* ■ *Fragments as Word Groups Without Subjects or Without Verbs*
>
>Comma Splices and Run-Togethers   H30

Types of Sentences   H36
>Clauses   H37
>Simple Sentences   H37
>Compound Sentences   H37
>Complex Sentences   H38
>Compound-Complex Sentences   H38
>Punctuation Tips   H39
>Summary   H39

Sentence Combining   H42
>Coordination   H42
>>*Relevant Punctuation*
>
>Subordination   H43
>>*Relevant Punctuation*
>
>Coordination and Subordination   H45
>>*Relevant Punctuation*
>
>Other Methods of Combining Ideas   H46

Balance in Sentence Writing   H49
>Basic Principles of Parallelism   H49
>Signal Words   H50
>Combination Signal Words   H50

Verbs   H53
>Community Dialects and Standard Usage   H53
>Regular and Irregular Verbs   H55
>>*Regular Verbs* ■ *Irregular Verbs*
>
>"Problem" Verbs   H58
>Subject-Verb Agreement   H61
>Consistency in Tense   H65
>Active and Passive Voice   H66
>Strong Predication   H67

Pronouns   H68

Case   H68
- Subjective Case ■ Objective Case ■ Techniques for Determining Case

Pronoun-Antecedent Agreement   H72
- Agreement in Person ■ Agreement in Number ■ Agreement in Gender

Pronoun Reference   H76

Modifiers   H79

Adjectives and Adverbs   H80
- Selecting Adjectives and Adverbs ■ Identifying and Correcting Common Problems with Adjectives and Adverbs ■ Dangling and Misplaced Modifiers

Punctuation and Capitalization   H88

End Punctuation   H88
- Periods ■ Questions Marks ■ Exclamation Points

Commas   H89
- Commas to Separate ■ Commas to Set Off

Semicolons   H93

Quotation Marks   H96
- Punctuation with Quotation Marks

Italics   H97
Dashes   H97
Colons   H98
Parentheses   H99
Brackets   H99
Capitalization   H99
Apostrophes   H101
Hyphens   H102

Spelling   H105

Frequently Misspelled Words   H108
- Confused Spelling/Confusing Words

Brief Guide for ESL Students   H112

Using Articles in Relation to Nouns   H112
Rules   H112
Sentence Patterns   H113
Verb Endings   H114
Idioms   H114
Suggestions for ESL Writers   H115

EXERCISES: H5, H15, H22, H23, H26, H27, H33, H34, H35, H39, H40, H46, H47, H51, H52, H58, H59, H60, H63, H64, H66, H67, H70, H71, H74, H75, H77, H78, H83, H85, H87, H91, H92, H94, H95, H102, H104, H105

APPENDIX A1

Taking Tests   A1
    Objective Tests   A1
    Subjective or Essay Tests   A2
Making Application   A2
    Letter of Application   A2
    Résumé   A3

ANSWER KEY AK1

TEXT CREDITS TC1

NAME AND TITLE INDEX IN1

SUBJECT INDEX IN4

Thematic Table of Contents

(For use with combined forms of discourse. Instructions for documented paragraphs and essays are in text Chapter 14, pages 414–417.)

Sexism
"Why Not Ms. and Mr.?" 125
"The Fighting, Founding Mothers" 133
"Growing Up Asian in America" 155
"Pink Kittens and Blue Spaceships" 281
"The Natural Superiority of Women" 283
"Men and Women: More Equal Than the Same" 301
"The Girls in Their Summer Dresses" 363
"Frankie and Johnny" 370
"My Last Duchess" 372
"Curbing the Sexploitation Industry" 395

Exploitation
"Cotton-Picking Time" 70
"A Shack of Misery" 97
"She Came a Long Way" 109
"Back of the Bus" 214
"Looking for Work" 286
"What Is Poverty?" 327
"My Last Duchess" 372
"Curbing the Sexploitation Industry" 395

Cultural Issues
"Razor Wire Sweat Lodge" 51
"Los Chinos Discover el Barrio" 66
"The Struggle to Be an All-American Girl" 68
"Cotton-Picking Time" 70
"Rules of the Game" 99
"Growing Up Asian in America" 155
"The Autobiography of Malcolm X" 190
"Multiculturalism: Building Bridges or Burning Them?" 217
"Looking for Work" 286
"Does America Still Exist?" 322
"The Hopi Way" 325
"Raymond's Run" 357

Violence
"Face to Face with Guns and the Young Men Who Use Them" 72
"Optimism, Tenacity Lead Way Back to Life" 153
"Who Killed Benny Paret?" 224
"Death by Gangbanging" 225
"Kick Me!" 228
"Frankie and Johnny" 370
"My Last Duchess" 372
"Curbing the Sexploitation Industry" 395

Show Business
"The Boss Observed" 149
"A Big Wheel" 151
"The Success of 'Roseanne'" 164
"Gonna Rock To-o- N-i-i-ight" 178
"No Secrets to Her Success: Reba McEntire" 226
"Sam and Woody" 299
"Curbing the Sexploitation Industry" 395

Prison Life
"Razor Wire Sweat Lodge" 51
"Cops Can Be Human" 132
"The Autobiography of Malcolm X" 190
"Kick Me!" 228
"Types of Fly Fighters" 264
"Prison Slang" 330

Education
"Cheating Is Not Worth the Bother" 135
"The Autobiography of Malcolm X" 190
"Multiculturalism: Building Bridges or Burning Them?" 217
"I'm Outta Here!" 220
"Looking for Work" 286
"Private Language, Public Language" 290

Environment and Health
"Causes of Mental Illness" 23
"She Came a Long Way" 109
"The Cancer Puzzle" 147
"Arsenic for Everyone" 215
"What Happens to Steroid Studs?" 216
"How About Low-Cost Drugs for Addicts?" 393
"Make Docs Wheel and Deal Like Used Car Salesmen!" 397
"A New Wind Blowing" 398

Psychology
"Personal Space" 120
"Optimism, Tenacity Lead Way Back to Life" 153
"Maslow's Classification of Motives" 249
"Going Too Far" 332
"Perspectives on Motivation" 335
"The Use of Force" 348
"Richard Cory" 373
"Right to Die" 405

Love
"Two Loves: Puppy and True" 295
"Raymond's Run" 357
"The Girls in Their Summer Dresses" 363
"Frankie and Johnny" 370
"My Last Duchess" 372

Sports
"On the Ball" 88
"Babe Ruth" 89
"Magic Johnson" 161
"Nature on the Rampage" 179
"Conserving Energy as You Ski" 185
"Who Killed Benny Paret?" 224
"Heavenly Father, Divine Goalie" 279

Paragraphs & **Essays**

Using a Pattern of Strategies to Write Paragraphs: DCODE

> "If I had to limit all my remarks about paragraph writing to seven words, I would say, "State your topic sentence and support it."
> — Professor Virginia Schilt

Writers' strike.

QUESTIONS FOR FOCUS:
Keep the following questions in mind as you read the chapter. After you have finished your reading, see if you can answer them.

What is a developmental paragraph? What are the parts of a topic sentence? What does each part do? What is support? What does **DCODE** mean? How can you use it to help you write effective paragraphs?

Developmental Paragraph Defined

Defining the word *paragraph* is no easy task, because there are different kinds of paragraphs: introductory, developmental, transitional, and concluding. Each is a short unit of material based on a single idea. The developmental paragraph, which concerns us here, is a multisentence unit that expands on an idea. You can use it in two ways: (1) as a complete answer to a short writing assignment and (2) as a middle or body paragraph in an essay. The following paragraph both defines and illustrates the developmental paragraph.

> The developmental paragraph contains three parts: the subject, the topic sentence, and the support. The *subject* is what you will write about. It is likely to be broad and must be focused or qualified for specific treatment. The *topic sentence* contains both the subject and the treatment, meaning what you will do with the subject. It carries the central idea to which everything else in the paragraph is subordinated. For example, the first sentence of this paragraph is a topic sentence. Even when not stated, the topic sentence as an underlying concept unifies the paragraph. The *support* is the evidence and/or reasoning by which a topic sentence is developed. It comes in several basic patterns and serves any of the four forms of discourse for purposes of communication:
>
> narration (What happened?)
> description (What does it look like?)
> exposition (What does it mean?)
> argumentation (What should we believe?)
>
> These forms of discourse, which are usually combined in thought and writing, will be presented with both student and professional examples in Chapters 3–13. The developmental paragraph, therefore, is a group of sentences, each with the function of stating or supporting a single, controlling idea that is contained in the topic sentence.

topic sentence
support

support

support

restated topic sentence (with the complete definition)

Usually the developmental paragraph will be indented only one time: however, you will note in your reading that some writers, especially journalists, indent more than once in developing a single idea. That arrangement, called a *paragraph unit*, is fairly common in magazine and newspaper articles but less so in college writing. Two effective forms of conventional paragraph structure are shown in Figure 1.1.

FIGURE 1.1 Effective Paragraph Structures

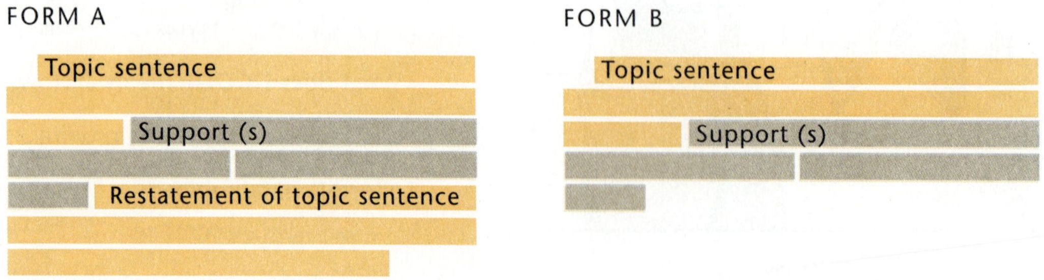

FORM A
- Topic sentence
- Support (s)
- Restatement of topic sentence

FORM B
- Topic sentence
- Support (s)

Example of Form A

> <mark>For some viewers, the world of the soap and their own daily lives begin to blur.</mark> Early in my research, I encountered one such fan. At a local supermarket, I picked up *Soap Opera Digest*, a magazine that offers weekly synopses of soap plots and articles about the stars. The cashier, in her late teens, quickly spotted the magazine I had hidden between the detergent and the broccoli. Its cover featured a famous couple from ABC's popular soap, "General Hospital." As she rang up the items, the cashier commented, "I think Grant and Celia will work it out, don't you?" Stunned, I nodded. She bagged my groceries and continued her monologue on Grant and Celia's marital problems, offering suggestions and advice. Imperceptibly, I had slipped into the curious world of the soap opera. The cashier simply assumed that I too was a "resident" of "General Hospital"'s fictional Port Charles.

topic sentence

support (extended example)

restatement (by implication)

Ruth Rosen, "Search for Yesterday"

Example of Form B

> <mark>Viewers frequently confuse the character with the actor.</mark> An actress who played the wicked Lisa on "As the World Turns" for sixteen years is punched by an irate viewer in front of Manhattan's Lord & Taylor department store. CBS finds that viewers send carefully wrapped "Care" packages to actors who play impoverished characters. An actress on "All My Children" reports that fans begin their letters by addressing her and then imperceptibly slip into accusatory condemnations of her character's actions. When Julie, in "Days of Our Lives," wonders whether to have an abortion, actress Susan Hayes receives pictures of fetuses in the mail.

topic sentence
support (example)

support (example)

support (example)

support (example)
Ruth Rosen, "Search for Yesterday"

The DCODE Process SEE PG. 105

DCODE (pronounced "decode," as in "decoding your ideas") is a systematic process for writing. In this chapter, it will be applied to developmental paragraphs; in the next chapter, it will be applied to writing essays. Flexible enough to accommodate different kinds of assignments, **DCODE** provides a set of strategies that will help you in generating topics and in developing them for effective paragraphs and essays.

The **DCODE** writing process has five stages:

- **D** *Delve:* Freewrite, brainstorm, and cluster in order to generate and investigate topics.
- **C** *Concentrate:* Narrow your topic and state your topic sentence or thesis.
- **O** *Organize:* Develop an outline or a section of the **Delve** cluster.
- **D** *Draft:* Write, rewrite, and revise as many times as necessary for **c**oherence, **l**anguage, **u**nity, **e**mphasis, **s**upport, and **s**entence structure (**cluess**).
- **E** *Edit:* Correct problems in **c**apitalization, **o**missions, **p**unctuation, and **s**pelling (**cops**).

The **DCODE** writing process is central to writing paragraphs and essays. **DCODE** helps you move naturally from exploring relevant ideas and generating a topic; to stating a topic sentence or thesis precisely; to organizing the material; to writing, rewriting, and revising; and finally to editing. It also allows for recursive movement: you can go back and forth as you rework your material. In short, **DCODE** systematizes what you as a good writer should do. Paying attention to its components will remind you of the importance of writing as a process. Initially, you may approach **DCODE** somewhat mechanically, but as you become accustomed to its logical progression, through the useful repetition provided by the worksheets at the ends of chapters, you will begin following it with natural ease.

Keep in mind that one of the most useful features of **DCODE** is its *flexibility*. You can emphasize, deemphasize, or even delete strategies according to the needs of your assignments.

Let's examine the stages of **DCODE** in detail.

Delve

When you begin to write, your thinking may be rigid, perhaps because you are a bit uncomfortable with your writing assignment. **Delve** is designed to loosen, stimulate, and sharpen your thoughts as it generates topics. It also moves toward the formulation of a topic sentence or thesis while perhaps even suggesting some divisions for further development. **Delve** means "to investigate vigorously and thoroughly." Using the following strategies in sequence will help you in your writing.

One strategy you can use in this stage is *freewriting*, an exercise that its originator, Peter Elbow, has called "babbling in print." In freewriting, you write without stopping, letting your ideas tumble forth. You do not concern yourself with the fundamentals of writing, such as punctuation and spelling. This strategy is especially useful in generating or further exploring topics. Where you start depends on your assignment: working with original topics, working from a restricted list of topics, or working with reading-related topics. If you are at a loss for words on your subject, write in a comment such as "I don't know what is coming next" or "blah, blah, blah," and continue when relevant words come. In doing this exercise, you will shake loose ideas of all kinds to look at on paper. You will get an impression of how much you know and of what your interests are. If practically nothing worthwhile emerges, perhaps it is time to freewrite another topic.

Another strategy is *brainstorming*. Begin by applying the Who? What? Where? When? Why? and How? questions to your subject. Then let your mind run free as you jot down answers in single words or lists. Some of the questions will be more important than others, depending on the purpose of your writing. For example, if you are writing about the causes of some situation, the Why? question could be more important than the others; if you are concerned with how to do something, the How? question would predominate. Sometimes, in order to focus on a particular form of writing, another question will be added to the brainstorming "basic six." If you are writing in response to something you have read (as you will be doing frequently in assignments from this book), confine your thinking to ideas appropriately related to that content. Whatever your focus for questions, the result is likely to be a long list of ideas that will provide information for the next strategy of **Delve**.

Still another technique of exploration is *clustering* (also called *mapping*). Begin by "double bubbling" your topic (writing it down and drawing a double circle around it). Then, in response to the question, What comes to mind?, single-bubble other ideas on spokes radiating out from the hub, which contains the topic. Any bubble can lead to another bubble or bubbles in the same fashion.

Freewriting, brainstorming, and clustering will help you to generate topics and explore their potential.

Following is an example of how one student, Byron Jackson, completed the **Delve** stage for an assignment to write a paragraph. Because the instructor asked him to organize and write a paper around personal experience and to use a few examples, he picked something that interested him, "bad drivers." (He is a freeway driver.) His exploration of that idea took this form:

Freewriting

Everyday when I drive to school I see bad drivers. Sometimes I'm mad. Sometimes I'm irritated. Sometimes I'm scared. I think someone should do something about them. The drunk drivers are the worst. They should be put away. But a lot of the other should be getting tickets too. Some of the drivers are worse than others. Make me a cop, a super-cop, a Rambo cop, and I'll go after the worst. Maybe I'd just go after the ones that bother me. Some bad drivers cause a lot of accidents and get people all angry. Take the tailgaters for example. And what about the drivers that go into the emergency lanes on the freeways to pass when there's a jam. And then you've got the lane changers and the people that don't signal and those that keep going and turning left when the light turns red. Then you've got the people that drive too fast and too slow. And you've got the ones that don't stop for pedestrians. All kinds of bad drivers are out there—young, old, male, female, insane, drunk, angry, and rushed.

Brainstorming

Who?	bad drivers; me as a cop
What?	driving recklessly, unsafely; a cop's job
Where?	on every roadway
When?	all the time
Why?	hurried, disrespectful, self-centered, hostile
How?	lane changing, driving illegally in diamond lane, not signaling, passing on the shoulder, tailgating, turning left on red, rolling stop, speeding, driving while intoxicated

Clustering

Now try your hand at the **Delve** stage of **DCODE**. Begin with a topic such as a type of music, an author, a book, a career, an influence (parents, siblings, peers, teachers, preachers, one experience), a peeve, a problem (money, health, love), or something else, all pending your instructor's approval. You can use the space provided or, because this activity begins a series of **DCODE** writing strategies, you may instead use the blank writing worksheet (at end of this chapter), which you can tear out and submit with the drafts of your paragraph.

EXERCISE 1

Freewrite on your topic.

EXERCISE 2

Brainstorm your topic.

        Who?

        What?

        Where?

        When?

        Why?

        How?

EXERCISE 3

Develop a cluster on your topic.

Concentrate

Now you are ready to concentrate on a precise idea, one that emerges from the **Delve** stage, in which you explore the possibilities of working with a topic. As you move from freewriting to brainstorming to clustering, you will discover subject material that you can develop successfully as a unit—in this instance, a paragraph. The idea is likely to be at the beginning of a cluster section. It takes form here as an assertion or controlling purpose. Try to state it in one sentence, which is called a *topic sentence* for a paragraph. Keep in mind what you want to say and to whom—to what audience. The extent to which you present and explain your topic and the language you use will depend on your content, so phrase your topic sentence with the expected development in mind. The topic sentence will indicate the subject (what you are concerned with generally) and the treatment of that subject (what aspect of it you intend to discuss).

Each of the following examples is based on Byron Jackson's bad topic, what he'd like to do with certain types of drivers, but the first two are flawed.

A narrow factual statement will not bear development.

WRONG: <u>Unsafe lane changing</u> <u>is illegal.</u>
    Subject   Treatment (too narrow)

A broad or vague statement cannot be easily developed.

WRONG: <u>Bad drivers</u> <u>are bad citizens.</u>
    Subject Treatment (broad, vague)

An effective topic sentence leads naturally to development. It indicates a topic and shows how it will be treated.

The treatment may be factual:

RIGHT: <u>Driving speed</u> <u>can be correlated with the rate and severity of accidents.</u>
    Subject   Treatment

The treatment may be an opinion:

RIGHT: <u>Traffic officers</u> <u>should concentrate on citing the worst offenders.</u>
    Subject   Treatment

In some topic sentences, especially in published writing, the subject and treatment may seem to merge or they may be reversed in order, but you should always be able to separate these parts in your thinking.

EXERCISE 4

Mark the following statements for subject (S) and treatment (T), and label each as E (effective) or I (ineffective). The effective ones are those you can easily relate to supporting evidence. In those you can say, "This statement is true because . . . [often for several reasons]." The ineffective statements are too broad, too vague, or too narrowly factual. (See the Answer Key for answers.)

EXAMPLE: <u>Basketball</u> <u>is an interesting sport.</u> (I)
     Subject   Treatment

1. Students who cheat in school may be trying to release certain pressures.

2. Shakespeare is an Elizabethan writer.

3. The quarterback in football and the general of an army are alike in significant ways.

4. Animals use color chiefly for protection.

5. Portland is a city in Oregon.

6. The life of the ocean has distinct realms.

7. Rome has a glorious and tragic story.

8. Boston is the capital of Massachusetts.

9. The word *macho* has a special meaning to the Hispanic community.

10. The history of plastics is exciting.

EXERCISE 5

Mark the following statements for subject (S) and treatment (T), and label each as E (effective) or I (ineffective). The effective ones are those you can easily relate to supporting evidence. In those you can say, "This statement is true because . . . [often for several reasons]." The ineffective statements are too broad, too vague, or too narrowly factual.

1. The lesson I learned in the first grade about honesty is one that I will never forget.

2. Robbers seldom target doughnut shops, even late at night.

3. Lincoln was assassinated at the Ford Theater.

4. The dictionary has an interesting history.

5. The world is a place of many contrasts.

6. Rap music can be classified on the basis of the intent of the writers/composers.

7. Los Angeles is one of the largest cities in the world.

8. What I've seen while working in a fast-food place has made me lose my appetite.

9. My physical education teacher is called "coach."

10. Count Dracula's reputation is based on his activities as a "night person."

After working with several versions of how to discuss bad drivers, Byron Jackson came up with this topic sentence:

<u>Make me a cop,</u> <u>and I'll crack down on certain types of drivers</u>.
    Subject   **Treatment**

EXERCISE 6

Convert your topic idea into a well-defined topic sentence that includes both the subject and the treatment. For this exercise, label the parts.

Organize

This step involves some patterned writing. These patterns may be as simple as a modified cluster section taken from the **Delve** stage or as carefully structured as a topic outline. The objective is to organize the ideas you have generated in the order that best supports the topic idea. Through experimentation, you will find the **Organize** strategy that fits your way of thinking and working. Again, direct your work toward your anticipated audience; consider how many people comprise the audience, how much the audience knows, and what attitudes the audience is likely to have about your topic.

Clustering

This strategy in the **Organize** phase is usually one modified section of the more broad-based cluster from the **Delve** phase. This one section is extended or otherwise modified so as to reflect the development of the topic sentence in **Concentrate**. Going back and forth within **DCODE** while ultimately moving forward illustrates the true nature of writing.

Although typically writers either cluster or outline, in this instance, Byron Jackson has decided to do both. Here is his cluster on his topic sentence. It is almost the same as one section of his **Delve** cluster.

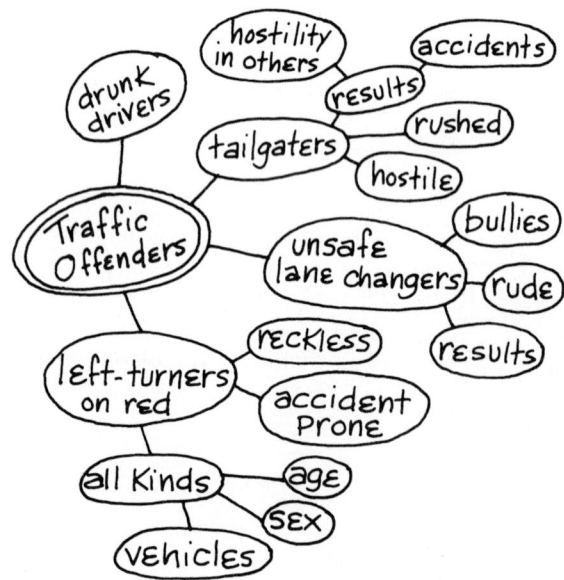

Outlining

The outline is a pattern for showing the relationship of ideas. Use it to demonstrate the framework of a reading passage or to show the organization of a piece of writing. In writing about a piece of writing, both uses may merge.

The two main forms are the *sentence outline* (each entry is a complete sentence) and the *topic outline* (each entry is a key word or phrase). The topic outline is more common for both paragraph and essay writing.

The placement of words (with indentation), punctuation, and number and letter sequences are important to clear communication. The outline is not basically a creative effort. We do not read it expecting to be surprised by form and content, as we do a poem. We go to the outline for information, and we expect to find ideas easily. Unconventional marks (circles, squares, half parentheses) and items out of order are distracting and therefore undesirable in an outline. The standard form is as easily mastered as a nonstandard form, and it is well worth your time to learn it. Outlining is not difficult; here is the pattern:

Main idea (will usually be the topic sentence for the paragraph or the thesis for the essay)

   I. Major support
      A. Minor support
         1. Details (specific information of various kinds)
         2. Details
      B. Minor support
         1. Details
         2. Details
  II. Major support
      A. Minor support
      B. Minor support
         1. Details
         2. Details
         3. Details

The pattern is flexible and can have any number of levels and parts.

EXERCISE 7

Using your reason and imagination, fill in the parts of this outline. It is more detailed than one for a typical paragraph; therefore, each roman-numeral section might frame a paragraph, or the three might serve for three separate paragraphs of development in an essay. (See the Answer Key for possible answers.)

                                            Subject   Treatment

TOPIC SENTENCE: <u>The successful Buzzard Breath concert</u> <u>had all the important components to satisfy fans.</u>

I. Songs

  A. Variety

    1.

    2.

  B. Themes

    1. Love

    2. War

    3.

    4.

II. Staging

    A. Sound

        1.

        2.

    B.

        1. Stuffed buzzards

        2. Simulated carrion

    C.

        1. Strobes

        2. Spots

III. Artists

    A.

        1. Feathers

        2. Chains

        3. Leather

    B.

        1. Simulated buzzard-bashing with guitars

        2.

    C. Talent

        1.

        2. Playing

            a.

            b.

    D. Choreography

        1.

        2.

        3.

EXERCISE 8

Name a movie and, using your reason and imagination, fill in the parts of this outline. It is more detailed than one for a typical paragraph; therefore, each roman-numeral section might frame a paragraph, or the three might serve for three separate paragraphs of development in an essay. Do not be bound by the capital letter and arabic numeral parts; add or subtract as needed.

TOPIC SENTENCE: _____ **Subject** has all the **Treatment** important components to satisfy the movie goers.

I. Acting (names of actors or roles they play, followed by their traits such as behavior, delivery of lines, appearance)

    A.

        1.

        2.

    B.

        1.

        2.

II. Story (major scenes showing plot development or other pattern of suspense)

    A.

        1.

        2.

    B.

        1.

        2.

    C.

        1.

        2.

    D.

        1.

        2.

III. Special effects (stunts, chases, marvels of lighting, sound, etc.)

   A.

      1.

      2.

   B.

      1.

      2.

IV. Theme (main point being made or significance of the work as seen in such aspects as behavior of character[s], thoughts expressed through words or pattern of action)

   A.

   B.

Continuing to work with the topic of what he would do with certain types of bad drivers, Byron Jackson also completed a topic outline for the **Organize** stage of **DCODE**. Although it covers the same areas as the cluster, the outline is more detailed and more carefully structured.

    I. Drunks
   II. Unsafe lane changers
      A. Character
         1. Rude
         2. Bullying
      B. Results
         1. Accidents
         2. People upset
  III. Left-turners on red
      A. Attitude
         1. Self-centered
         2. Putting self above law
      B. Kinds
         1. Age
         2. Sex
      C. Results
         1. Collisions
         2. Mass irritation
  IV. Tailgaters
      A. Motives
         1. Hostility
         2. Rushed
      B. Effects
         1. Accidents
         2. People upset
            a. My reaction
            b. Bumper-sticker evidence

EXERCISE 9

Complete a cluster or a topic outline, or both a cluster and a topic outline, as directed by your instructor.

Draft

Draft is the stage of the process in which your writing begins to assume its final form. Use your cluster diagram or outline to help you develop the sentences of your paragraph or the paragraphs of your essay into a first draft. In addition, here are some ideas to consider as you draft and revise. The first letter of each word forms the acronym **cluess**, though you need not complete these parts in any order or even work on them one at a time. (All of these parts are discussed in detail in Chapter 15.)

Coherence

Coherence is progression of ideas, with each idea leading logically and smoothly to the next. It is achieved by numbering parts or otherwise indicating time (*first, second, third; then, next, soon,* and so on), giving directions (spatial, as in "To the right is a map, and to the left of that map is a bulletin board"), using transitional words (*however, otherwise, therefore, similarly, hence, on the other hand, then, consequently, accordingly, thus*), using demonstrative pronouns (*this, that, those*), and moving in a logical or emphatic order (through functional stages, from the least important to the most important or from the most important to the least important).

Language

Language here means the appropriate usage, tone, and diction. *Usage* refers to the level of language appropriate for your topic, your writing task, and your audience; it can be formal or informal, and should be standard (educated) language rather than nonstandard. *Tone* refers to your attitude toward your subject and your audience. Like speech, writing can project a tone as diverse as playful, serious, objective, sarcastic, cautionary, and loving. *Diction* pertains to word choice appropriate for your writing as it addresses a particular audience; word choice will convey your ideas clearly and concisely, usually avoiding slang and cliches.

Unity

You carefully wrote the topic sentence at the **Concentrate** stage of **DCODE**. Now go back and rephrase the rest of the paragraph as necessary. Everything in your passage should be related and subordinate to your topic statement. Repetition of a key word or phrase can make the unity even more apparent.

Emphasis

Emphasize important ideas by using *position* (the most emphatic parts of a work are the beginning and the end), *repetition* (repeat key words and phrases), and *isolation* (a short, direct sentence among longer ones will usually command attention).

Support

Support is the material that backs up, justifies, or validates your topic sentence or thesis. Work carefully with the material from the **Organize** step to ensure that your ideas are well supported. If the paragraph or essay is skimpy and your ideas thin, you probably are generalizing and not explaining how you arrived at your conclusions. Use details and examples;

Using a Pattern of Strategies to Write Paragraphs: DCODE   17

indicate parts and discuss relationships; explain why your generalizations are true, logical, and accurate. Your reader can't accept your ideas unless he or she knows by what reasoning or use of evidence you developed them.

Sentence Structure

Be sure that your sentences are complete (not fragments) and that you have not incorrectly combined word groups that could be sentences (comma splices and run-togethers). Consider using different types of sentences and different sentence beginnings. (Chapter 15 offers specific instruction on these concerns.)

Write as many drafts as necessary, revising as you go for all the aspects of effective writing. Don't confuse revising with editing (the final stage of the writing process), and get bogged down in fixing such things as spelling and punctuation. In the drafting and revising phase, focus on rewording your material for good sentence and paragraph structure. After you have finished drafting and revising, use **cluess** as a checklist to make sure that you have revised thoroughly. (All of these matters of revision are presented with discussion and exercises in Chapter 15.)

Following is Byron Jackson's first draft, with marks for revision.

If I were a Traffic Cop
~~Rambo Traffic Cop~~

If I were
~~Make me~~ a traffic cop, and I'll crack down on certain types of drivers. ~~First off are the~~ *My primary target would be* drunks. I'd *arrest* ~~zap~~ them *immediately* off ~~the highways right off~~, and any cop would. But what I'm really ~~talking~~ *concerned* about ~~is~~ *are* the jerks of the highway. Near *of my hit list* *unsafe* the top are the ~~up-tight~~ lane changers, ~~for example,~~ this morning when I was driving to school, ~~I saw several~~. I could of carved at least a couple notches in a vilation pad, and I wasn't even cranky. They cut off ~~people~~ *other drivers* and force their way in, ~~and~~ *ing* leav~~e~~ behind upset and ~~hurt~~ *injured* people. Then there's the left-turn bullies the ones that keep moving out when the yellow turn to red. They come in all ages and sexes, ~~they can be young or old, male or female.~~ Yesterday, I saw this female in a pick-up *barrel* right out into the teeth of a red light. She had a baby on board~~.~~, *and* She had lead in her foot~~.~~, She had evil in her eye. She was hostile and self-centered~~.~~, *t*aking advantage of others. She knew that the facing traffic would probably not pull out and risk a head-on crash. The key word there is probably but many times people with a green light do move out and colide with the left turn bullies. ~~Third~~ *Fourth*, I'd *z*~~s~~ap the tailgaters. No one goes fast enough for these

18 CHAPTER 1

~~guys~~ them. I'm not alone in this peeve. Many of my fellow drivers agree. One bumper sticker reads, "Stay back. I chew tobacky." And James Bond sprayed cars that chased him. Since the first is ~~dirty~~ unsanitary and the second ~~is against the law~~ illegal, if I had the ~~clout~~ authority of a ~~Rambo~~ cop I'd just ~~rack~~ issue up a lot of tailgater tickets. ~~But there's a lot of road demons out there.~~ These types of road demons would feel my wrath. But Maybe it's good I'm not a traffic cop, Rambo or otherwise, cause traffic cops are suppose to inforce hundreds of laws. I don't know if I'd have time cause ~~I have my own pet peeves in mind.~~ I'd be concentrating on this private list of obnoxious drivers.

EXERCISE 10

Using your own paper, write the first draft of your paragraph. Then revise it for coherence, language, emphasis, unity, support, and sentence structure (**cluess**).

Edit

Edit, the final stage of the process, involves a careful examination of your work. This stage is represented by the acronym **cops**: look for basic problems such as **c**apitalization, **o**missions, **p**unctuation, and **s**pelling. These points will also be addressed in detail in Chapter 15. Before preparing the final draft to hand in, read your paper aloud to discover oversights and awkwardness of expression.

This is Byron Jackson's second draft with the marks for editing.

If I Were a Traffic Cop

If I were a traffic cop, I'd crack down on certain types of drivers. My primary target would be drunk drivers. I'd arrest them immediately, and any cop would. But the jerks of the highway are what I'm really concerned about here. Near the top of my hit list are the unsafe lane changers. They cut off other drivers and force their way in, leaving behind upset and injured people. This morning when I was driving to school, I could have carved at least a couple of notches into a citation pad, and I wasn't even cranky. Then there are the left-turn bullies, the ones that keep moving out when the yellow turns to red. They come in all ages and sexes. Yesterday, I saw this female in a pickup barrel right out into the teeth of a red light. She had a baby on board, lead in her foot, and evil in her eye. She was hostile and self-centered, taking advantage of others. She knew that the facing traffic would probably not pull out and risk a head-on crash. The key word there is "probably," but many times people with a green light do move out and collide with the left-turn bullies. Fourth, I'd zap the tailgaters. No one goes fast enough for them. Many of my fellow drivers agree. One bumper sticker reads, "Stay back. I chew tobacky." And James Bond sprayed oil on cars that chased him. Since the first is unsanitary and the second illegal, if I had the authority of a traffic cop, I'd just issue a lot of tailgater tickets. These four types of road demons would feel my wrath. But maybe it's good I'm not a traffic cop, Rambo or otherwise, because traffic cops are supposed to enforce hundreds of laws. I don't know if I'd have time because I'd be concentrating on this private list of obnoxious drivers.

Following is an uninterrupted sequential copy of the first stages of Byron Jackson's writing, this time using this book's standard Worksheet: Writing in DCODE. Observe how the material moved from general idea to completed paragraph, though at times it doubled back to redirect and regroup. This material is followed by the final draft of his paragraph.

WORKSHEET
Writing in DCODE

NAME: Byron Jackson

SECTION: _____ CHAPTER: _____ DATE: _____

Delve   Generate your topic, or ideas for your topic, by delving into your subject area through:

- *Freewriting*—writing sentence after sentence, nonstop and spontaneously.
- *Brainstorming*—jotting down answers to Who? What? Where? When? Why? and How? and then listing words and phrases in relation to those answers.
- *Clustering*—connecting bubbled ideas with lines to show strings of relationships, producing each new bubble item in response to the question, What comes to mind?
- *Combining* any of these approaches, as directed by your instructor.

Freewriting

    Everyday when I drive to school I see bad drivers. Sometimes I'm mad. Sometimes I'm irritated. Sometimes I'm scared. I think someone should do something about them. The drunk drivers are the worst. They should be put away. But a lot of the other should be getting tickets too. Some of the drivers are worse than others. Make me a cop, a supercop, a rambo cop, and I'll go after the worst. Maybe I'd just go after the ones that bother me. Some bad drivers cause a lot of accidents and get people all angry. Take the tailgaters for example. And what about the drivers that go into the emergency lanes on the freeways to pass when there's a jam. And then you've got the lane changers and the people that don't signal and those that keep going and turning left when the light turns red. Then you've got the people that drive too fast and too slow. And you've got the ones that don't stop for pedestrians. All kinds of bad drivers are out there--young, old, male, female, insane, drunk, angry, and rushed.

Brainstorming

    Who?   bad drivers; me as a cop
    What?   driving recklessly, unsafely; a cop's job
    Where?   on every roadway
    When?   all the time
    Why?   hurried, disrespectful, self-centered, hostile
    How?   lane changing, driving illegally in diamond lane, not signaling, passing on the shoulder, tailgating, turning left on red, rolling stop, speeding, driving while intoxicated

Clustering

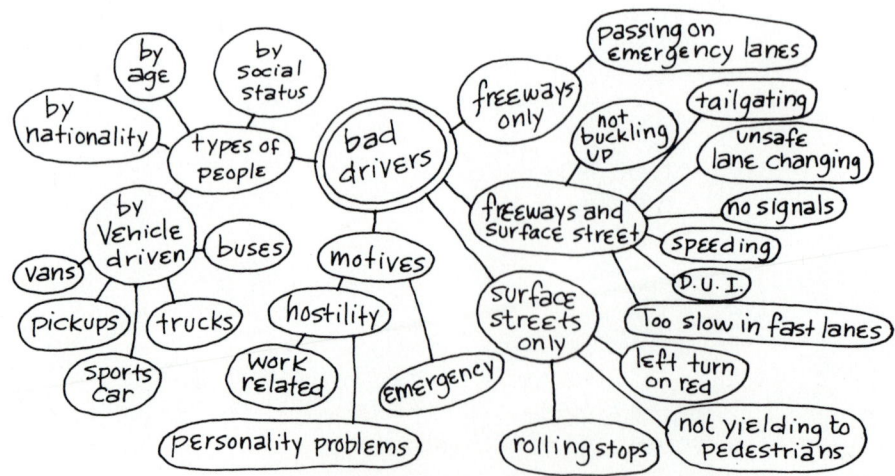

WORSHEET: Writing in DCODE   21

Concentrate Concentrate your work by stating your topic in one sentence that is not too broad, narrow, or vague to be developed. Base this sentence (which may become the topic sentence for your paragraph or the thesis for your essay) on an idea emerging from the **Delve** stage. You may have to try several statements here before you formulate one that is best for your writing task. Be sure that your final statement covers your assignment or intent and specifies both your subject (what you are writing about) and treatment (what aspect you will focus on). Label the *subject* and *treatment* parts.

<u>If I were a traffic cop</u> <u>I'd crack down on certain types of drivers</u>.
      Subject   Treatment

Organize Complete an outline or a cluster, as directed by your instructor. The cluster should be a section from, or a refined version of, the **Delve** clustering. Regardless of the strategy you use, the organizational pattern should indicate a division of your topic into parts that will, in turn, be further subdivided for support as necessary to address a particular audience on your concentrated topic.

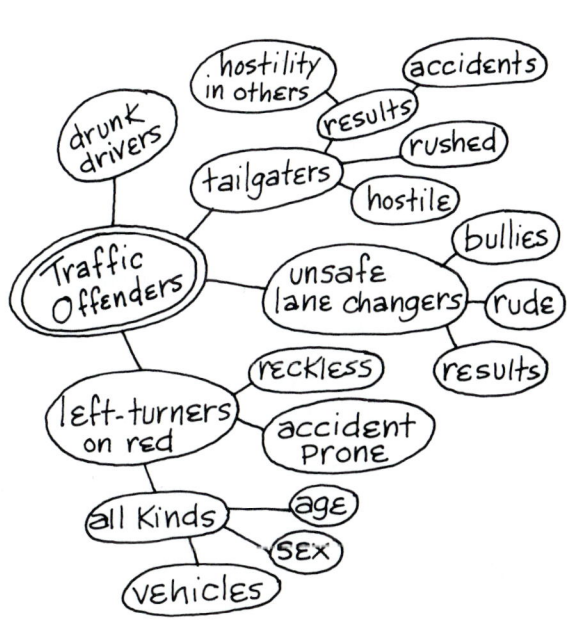

```
I.   Drunks
II.  Unsafe lane changers
     A. Character
        1. Rude
        2. Bullying
     B. Results
        1. Accidents
        2. People upset
III. Left-turners on red
     A. Attitude
        1. Self-centered
        2. Putting self above law
     B. Kinds
        1. Age
        2. Sex
     C. Results
        1. Collisions
        2. Mass irritation
IV.  Tailgaters
     A. Motives
        1. Hostility
        2. Rushed
     B. Effects
        1. Accidents
        2. People upsetcv
           a. My reaction
           b. Bumper sticker
              evidence
```

Draft On separate paper, write and then revise your assignment as many times as necessary for **c**oherence, **l**anguage (usage, tone, and diction), **u**nity, **e**mphasis, **s**upport, and **s**entence structure (**cluess**).

Edit Correct problems in fundamentals such as **c**apitalization, **o**missions, **p**unctuation, and **s**pelling (**cops**). Before writing the final draft, read your paper aloud to discover oversights and awkwardness of expression.

Final Draft

If I Were a Traffic Cop
Byron Jackson

If I were a traffic cop, I'd crack down on certain types of drivers. My primary target would be drunk drivers. I'd arrest them immediately, and any cop would. But the jerks of the highway are what I'm really concerned about here. Near the top of my hit list are the unsafe lane changers. They cut off other drivers and force their way in, leaving behind upset and injured people. This morning when I was driving to school, I could have carved at least a couple of notches in a citation pad, and I wasn't even cranky. Then there are the left-turn bullies, the ones that keep moving out when the yellow turns to red. They come in all ages and sexes. Yesterday, I saw this female in a pickup barrel right out into the teeth of a red light. She had a baby on board, lead in her foot, and evil in her eye. She was hostile and self-centered, taking advantage of others. She knew that the facing traffic would probably not pull out and risk a head-on crash. The key word there is "probably," but many times people with a green light do move out and collide with the left-turn bullies. Fourth, I'd zap the tailgaters. No one goes fast enough for them. Many of my fellow drivers agree. One bumper sticker reads, "Stay back. I chew tobacky." And James Bond sprayed oil on cars that chased him. Since the first is unsanitary and the second illegal, if I had the authority of a traffic cop, I'd just issue a lot of tailgater tickets. These four types of road demons would feel my wrath. But maybe it's good I'm not a traffic cop, Rambo or otherwise, because traffic cops are supposed to enforce hundreds of laws. I don't know if I'd have time because I'd be concentrating on this private list of obnoxious drivers.

EXERCISE 11

Write another draft of your paragraph and edit it for **c**apitalization, **o**missions, **p**unctuation, and **s**pelling (**cops**). Then write your final draft. Finally, collect all your materials and arrange them in **DCODE** sequence.

Types of Paragraph Writing

So far the writing you have considered, in both the student examples and your assignments, has been of a personal nature. The content derives from direct and indirect experience (reading and listening), and often involves opinion. Mastering this kind of writing is important, because you do have something to say. Most college writing tasks, however, will require you to evaluate and to reflect on what you read, rather than write only about personal experience. You will be expected to read, think, and write. The writing part in these circumstances is commonly called reading related. It includes:

- the *summary* (main ideas in your own words);
- the *reaction* (usually meaning how it relates specifically to you, your experiences and attitudes but also often the critique, involving the worth and logic of a piece); and
- the *spin-off* (a smaller form of the reaction, in that it takes one aspect of the reading and develops a parallel experience, or simply one that has an interesting connection to the piece of writing).

These kinds of writing have certain points in common; they all:

- originate as a response to something you have read;
- indicate, to some degree, content from that piece; and,
- demonstrate a knowledge of the piece of writing.

Critical Reading, Critical Thinking, Critical Writing

Because reading is such an important ingredient in this reading-related writing process, it is useful to consider how reading, thinking, and writing go together, how they are similar, and how ability in one strengthens ability in the others. The comments and marks on the following essay will help you understand the connection between writing and reading. The underlining and annotations show the basic types of organization already presented in this chapter. Following the essay is a topic outline. All three techniques—underlining to indicate main and supporting ideas, annotating to indicate importance and relevance to the task at hand, and outlining to show the relationship of ideas and the underlying structure—aid reading, thinking, and writing.

Far more is known about the symptoms of mental illness and how to treat them than about the causes. <u>But it is known that these problems often don't have a single cause.</u>	*causes of mental illness—main idea (thesis)*
<u>Some types</u> of <u>mental illness,</u> or <u>at least a predisposition</u> toward them, <u>can be inherited.</u> For example, depression is more likely to occur in a <u>person</u> with a <u>family history</u> of	*1. inherited depression in family*

depression. Similarly, a child with a schizophrenic parent may be more likely to develop schizophrenia than a child with nonschizophrenic parents.

schizophrenia in family

But though there may be inherited differences in susceptibility to mental illness, some triggering factors, perhaps environmental stress or a particular set of circumstances, must be present for mental illness to manifest itself. For example, one study showed that each of 40 depressed patients had suffered several personal problems in the year preceding breakdown. These included a threat to sexual identity, moving to another community, physical illness, and death of a loved one.

2. triggering factors

personal problems such as

Chemical changes in the body also have to do with how the mind functions. Exactly what these changes are and know they work isn't fully understood. Some mental disorders (known as organic psychoses) are caused by physical problems. Among the possible causes of organic psychoses are congenital defects, prenatal injury, hardening of the arteries in the brain, brain tumors and infections, and severe alcoholism. Glandular disturbances and certain nutritional deficiencies can also produce psychotic symptoms.

3. chemical changes

physical problems such as

Emotional disturbances are also related to how the individuals feel about themselves and the world around them. For example, those who are constantly criticized can develop an exaggerated feeling of guilt. They come to expect everyone will find fault with them and even punish them. Or, if as youngsters they were repeatedly neglected and reprimanded, they may have grown up expecting trouble and rejection. They may have developed a protective reaction of verbally attacking another before the other criticized them. Or perhaps they remain detached and aloof from other people so as not to give others a chance to reject them. For some people these painful feelings are successfully buried till they run into a crisis situation—for example, the loss of a job or the breakup of a marriage—when the feelings surface again.

4. feelings: self, others

guilt

hostile

detached

Judith Ramsey, "Causes of Mental Illness"

Outlining Reading Material

After reading, underlining, and annotating the piece, the next step could be to outline. If the piece is well organized, you should be able to reduce it to a simple outline so that you can, at a glance, see the relationship of ideas (sequence, relative importance, and interdependence).

Ramsay's piece can be outlined very easily:

Causes of Mental Illness

I. Inherited, at least predisposition for
    A. From family with depression
    B. From a parent with schizophrenia
II. Trigger factor
    A. Environmental stress
    B. Circumstances
        1. Sexual identity crisis
        2. Physical illness
        3. Death of a loved one

  III. Chemical changes
    A. Congenital defects
    B. Brain tumors
    C. Glandular disturbances
  IV. Emotional disturbances
    A. Abuse
    B. Neglect

Summary

Your instructor may ask you to summarize a piece of reading. If so, the outline will serve as an excellent prelude to your task, because it shows the main ideas and their most basic support. In the summary, concentrate on those main ideas, putting them into your own words while usually reducing the piece by more than two-thirds. You can use your summary as part of a larger work, such as a research paper. When your summary is derived from an original source, you are obliged to credit that source on your paper. This credit can usually be done informally on a simple class assignment by indicating the title and author, and it can be done formally by parenthetical citations (explained in Chapter 14), which are usually just the author's surname and the page number following the summarized passage.

 The following rules will guide you in writing effective summaries. The summary

1. is usually about one-third the length of the original, though it will vary depending on the content of the original.
2. begins with the main idea (as in developmental paragraphs) and proceeds to cover the major supporting points in the same sequence as the source, always in complete sentences.
3. changes the wording without changing the idea.
4. does not evaluate the content or give an opinion in any way (even if you see an error in logic or fact).
5. does not add ideas (even if you have an abundance of related information).
6. does not refer directly to the writing (do not write, for example, "the author says").
7. does not include any personal comments by the author of the summary (therefore, do not use I) and
8. seldom uses quotations (but if so, always with quotation marks).

Using DCODE in Summary Writing

Because you are summarizing specified material, you will not need to generate your topic. Moreover, the development is contained in the material you are summarizing. Therefore, you can skip the **Delve** section of **DCODE** and go directly to the material. After you read, underline, and annotate it, you can work with the other stages of **DCODE**:

 Delve: Probably skip

 Concentrate: Indicate the gist of the topic sentence for the paragraph
  or of the thesis (main purpose, main point) for the essay.

 Organize: Make a simple outline of the material.

 Draft: Complete with revisions.

 Edit: Complete.

EXERCISE 12

Apply the rules of summary writing to the following summary of "Causes of Mental Illness." Mark the instances of poor summary writing by using numbers from the preceding list.

   One cause of mental illness can be heredity, traceable back to families with depression and especially to schizophrenic parents. I know that to be true because of some family problems I have. Then the writer says that another cause is circumstantial in that mental illness may be brought on by various kinds of stress. I wish the author had given more statistics on this point. A third is how chemical changes in the body also have to do with how the mind functions. These chemical changes can be linked to physical problems, glandular disturbances and certain nutritional deficiencies. Finally low self-esteem can cause emotional problems, although it seems to me this is one point that's difficult to prove. Persons who have been neglected or abused will often withdraw or become hostile.

The following paragraph is an example of an effective summary:

   Mental illness has at least four causes. One can be heredity, traceable to families with depression and especially schizophrenic parents. Another cause is circumstantial in that mental illness may be brought on by various kinds of stress. A third cause is chemical, which can be linked to physical problems, glandular problems, and dietary problems. Finally, low self-esteem can cause emotional problems. Persons who have been neglected or abused often withdraw or become hostile.

Reaction

The reaction paragraph is another kind of reading-related writing. Some reactions require evaluation with a critical-thinking emphasis. Some focus on a simple discussion of the content presented in the reading and include summary material. Others concentrate on your experiences as related to the content of the passage.
   The following paragraph is an example of a student statement of reaction to "Causes of Mental Illness."

   The article "Causes of Mental Illness" makes sense from my perspective because it does not try to simplify a complex problem. The introductory paragraph points out that "the symptoms of mental illness . . . often don't have a single cause." That admission is perhaps the best insight in the article. The four causes—heredity, stress, chemical, and abuse—often occur in combination. The people I have known with mental illness cannot be diagnosed easily, for they all have complicated backgrounds. For example, a physical problem can cause both stress and low self-esteem. And a person with family mental problems must be concerned about more than heredity problems. That person must also deal with stress and probably with neglect or other forms of abuse. If single causes were the issue, treatment would be much simpler.

Spin-off

The spin-off, a shorter form of the reaction statement, takes one aspect of the reading and develops a parallel experience or one that has an interesting connection to the piece of writing. The following example shows how one student personalized a spin-off response to the reading "Causes of Mental Illness."

> One statement in "Causes of Mental Illness" gave me a better understanding of my friend. He is normal in relationships that are well established. With me he is at ease, and we laugh and joke a lot. But when he is around strangers, something seems to snap. He will find points of disagreement and focus on them aggressively until I am embarrassed. Sometimes he will bring up topics about religion or politics in an opinionated way that shuts off all discussion. At first I couldn't understand this Jekyll-and-Hyde behavior, but then I learned that he was self-conscious and afraid of being criticized, so he just launched a first attack. Fortunately in the last year he has become much more successful in his work; hence, he has higher self-esteem. The result is a noticeable improvement in his behavior with strangers.

Using DCODE in Writing Reaction Statements

As noted previously, you should use **DCODE** flexibly by emphasizing, deemphasizing, and deleting strategies according to the needs of your assignments.

Critical Evaluations: If you are evaluating some specific ideas stated in your reading, then your topic is pretty well defined for you, and you can perhaps dispense with **Delve** (the discovery stage) and move to **Concentrate**, followed by **Organize**, **Draft** (with revision), and **Edit**.

Spin-off and Other Personal Reactions and Inventions: In these forms, the full range of strategies will probably be useful.

Writing a Journal

Your journal entries are likely to be concerned primarily with the relationship between the reading material and you—your life experiences, your views, your imagination. The reading material will give you something of substance to write about, but you will be writing especially for yourself, developing confidence and ease in writing, so that writing becomes a comfortable part of your everyday activities, as speaking already is.

These journal entries will, in a sense, be part of your intellectual diary, recording what you are thinking about a certain issue. They will be of use in helping you understand the reading material, in helping you develop your writing skills, in uncovering ideas that can be used on other assignments, and in helping you think more clearly and imaginatively. Because these entries are of a more spontaneous nature than the more structured writing assignments, organization and editing are likely to be of less concern.

Each journal entry should be clearly dated and, if reading related, should specify the title and author of the subject piece.

In order to provide a little whimsical variety, along with the each chapter's suggestions for reading-related journal entries, I have included some bizarre headlines from the tabloid newspaper *Weekly World News*, which regularly features pieces such as "Woman Gives Birth to Chimp in Sperm Bank Mishap" and "Elvis Sighted on Mars." Thus mixed with your more conventional entries might be a few in which you elaborate on some preposterous ideas. (I trust that you will be able to exercise your imagination without being corrupted by the fanciful illogic of tabloid journalism!)

Even if your instructor wants you to concentrate on what you read for your journal writing, he or she might not want you to be restricted to the material in this text. Fortunately, you are surrounded by reading material in newspapers, magazines, and, of course, textbooks from other courses. These topics can serve you well (especially if you want to begin your journal writing now). Explicit suggestions for journal entries will begin with Chapter 3 and continue for the following nine chapters.

WORKSHEET
Writing in DCODE

NAME:_____

SECTION:_____ CHAPTER:_____ DATE:_____

Delve   Generate your topic, or ideas for your topic, by delving into your subject area through:

- *Freewriting*—writing sentence after sentence, nonstop and spontaneously.
- *Brainstorming*—jotting down answers to Who? What? Where? When? Why? and How? and then listing words and phrases in relation to those answers.
- *Clustering*—connecting bubbled ideas with lines to show strings of relationships, producing each new bubble item in response to the question, What comes to mind?
- *Combining* any of these approaches, as directed by your instructor.

WORKSHEET: Writing in DCODE

Concentrate   Concentrate your work by stating your topic in one sentence that is not too broad, narrow, or vague to be developed. Base this sentence (which may become the topic sentence for your paragraph or the thesis for your essay) on an idea emerging from the **Delve** stage. You may have to try several statements here before you formulate one that is best for your writing task. Be sure that your final statement covers your assignment or intent and specifies both your subject (what you are writing about) and treatment (what aspect you will focus on). Label the *subject* and *treatment* parts.

Organize   Complete an outline or a cluster, as directed by your instructor. The cluster should be a section from, or a refined version of, the **Delve** clustering. Regardless of the strategy you use, the organizational pattern should indicate a division of your topic into parts that will, in turn, be further subdivided for support as necessary to address a particular audience on your concentrated topic.

Draft   On separate paper, write and then revise your assignment as many times as necessary for **c**oherence, **l**anguage (usage, tone, and diction), **u**nity, **e**mphasis, **s**upport, and **s**entence structure (**cluess**).

Edit   Correct problems in fundamentals such as **c**apitalization, **o**missions, **p**unctuation, and **s**pelling (**cops**). Before writing the final draft, read your paper aloud to discover oversights and awkwardness of expression.

Using A Pattern of Strategies to Write Essays: DCODE

2

> Writing is easy. All you do is stare at a blank sheet of paper until drops of blood form on your forehead.
> — Gene Fowler
>
> My objective is to make the drops of blood smaller.
> — Lee Brandon (author of this book)

Poorly planned diner holdup.

What is an essay? How are the developmental paragraph and the essay often similar? What is a thesis? How does one use **DCODE** in writing an essay?

31

Essay Defined

The essay is as difficult to define as the paragraph, but the paragraph definition gives us a framework. Consider the definition from Chapter 1:

> The developmental paragraph is a group of sentences, each with the function of stating or supporting a controlling idea called the topic sentence.

The main parts of the developmental paragraph are the topic sentence (subject and treatment), support (evidence and reasoning), and, often, the restated topic sentence at the end. Now let's use that framework for the essay:

> The essay is a group of paragraphs, each with the function of stating or supporting a controlling idea called the thesis.

The main parts of the essay are:

Introduction: carries the thesis, which states the controlling idea—much like the topic sentence for a paragraph but on a larger scale.

Development: evidence and reasoning—the support.

Transition: points out divisions of the essay (seldom used in the short essay).

Conclusion: an appropriate ending—often a restatement of or reflection on the thesis.

Thus, considered structurally, the paragraph is often an essay in miniature. That does not mean that all paragraphs can grow up to be essays or that all essays can shrink to become paragraphs. For college writing, however, a good understanding of the parallel between well-organized paragraphs and well-organized essays is useful. As you learn the properties of effective paragraphs—those with strong topic sentences and strong support—you also learn how to organize an essay, if you just magnify the procedure.

Recall the developmental paragraphs on soap operas from Chapter 1. Following is another paragraph that is similarly organized, with a topic sentence, the development, and the restatement of the topic sentence, in this example on the fans of Elvis. The annotations show how it could also have been developed into a whole essay if the author, Jim Miller, had wanted to amplify his supporting ideas.

A messiah, a jester, a reckless jerk—or a soulful singer from the Deep South—Elvis at different times to different people was all these things. <mark>His fans mirror every facet of their idol</mark>. "I liked him because of his looks," says Sue Scarborough, forty-nine, of Lexington, Kentucky, as she waits with her husband to tour Graceland. "He didn't put on airs," says Jeff Graff, twenty, of Cleveland, Ohio. "He went out of his way to help people." "I met him in 1960 when I was twelve years old," says Billie Le Jeune of

topic sentence (subject and treatment)

support 1

support 2

support 3

Memphis, who visits Graceland once or twice a month: "He asked me what my favorite subject was." On the pink fieldstone wall outside Graceland, which for years has functioned as an unauthorized bulletin board, the graffiti runs like this: ELVIS IS LOVE; I DID DRUGS WITH ELVIS; and most cryptic of all—ELVIS DIDN'T DESERVE TO BE WHITE.

support and reflection on topic sentence

Jim Miller, "Forever Elvis"

By taking a bit of license to fabricate, one can easily expand this into a short essay. The fabricated parts are in parentheses.

Good King Elvis

A messiah, a jester, a reckless jerk—or a soulful singer from the Deep South—Elvis at different times to different people was all these things. His fans mirror every facet of their idol.

introductory paragraph

thesis

For some fans the attraction is appearance. "I liked him because of his looks," says Sue Scarborough, forty-nine, of Lexington, Kentucky, as she waits with her husband to tour Graceland. (She grins good-naturedly at her husband and give him an affectionate nudge in the ribs when he says, "My wife really likes Elvis, but I'm not jealous because he is dead—I think." Her response tells all: "My husband's a good man at drivin' a truck and fishin' for bass, but no one'll ever paint his picture on velvet.")

topic sentence
paragraph of development 1 from support 1

(For others, Elvis was a king with a common touch and humanitarian instincts.) "He didn't put on airs," says Jeff Graff, twenty, of Cleveland, Ohio. "He went out of his way to help people." (His friend nods his head in agreement. "Elvis must've given away a hundred Cadillacs in his day." Others in line break-in to tell stories about the generosity of this good man who once walked among them.)

topic sentence
paragraph of development 2 from support 2

(The speakers at Graceland who get the most attention are those who actually met Elvis and have information about his basic goodness.) "I met him in 1960 when I was twelve years old," says Billie Le Jeune of Memphis, who visits Graceland once or twice a month: "He asked me what my favorite subject was." (A few others have stories equally compelling. The crowd listens in awe.)

topic sentence
paragraph of development 3 from support 3

(Along with these talkers at Graceland are the writers, who sum up the range of Elvis's qualities.) On the pink fieldstone wall outside Graceland, which for years has functioned as an unauthorized bulletin board, the graffiti runs like this: ELVIS IS LOVE; I DID DRUGS WITH ELVIS; and most cryptic of all—ELVIS DIDN'T DESERVE TO BE WHITE.

topic sentence reflecting
concluding paragraph reflecting on introductory paragraph and thesis

Ponder that fanciful expansion with our definition in mind: "The essay is a group of paragraphs, each with the function of stating or supporting a controlling idea called the thesis." Note that the introduction carries the thesis, complete with subject and treatment; the developmental paragraphs collectively support the thesis, and each, in turn, has a topic sentence and support; the conclusion recalls the introduction and, in fact, illustrates the thesis.

Like the paragraph, the essay may also assume different patterns. It may be principally one form of discourse: narration, description, exposition, or argumentation. Or it may be a combination, varying from paragraph to paragraph and even within paragraphs. But no matter what its pattern is, it will be unified around a central idea, the thesis. The *thesis* is the assertion or controlling purpose to which all other parts of the essay will be subordinate and supportive. As with the paragraph, the main point, here the thesis, will almost certainly be stated, usually in the first paragraph, and again, more frequently than not, at the end of the essay. The essay on Elvis illustrates this pattern.

The only difference in concept between the topic sentence and the thesis is one of scope: the topic sentence unifies and controls the content of the paragraph, and the thesis does the same for the essay. Because the essay is longer and more complex than the typical paragraph, the thesis may suggest a broader scope and may more explicitly indicate the parts.

Special Paragraphs Within the Essay

Developmental paragraphs were discussed extensively in Chapter 1, and paragraphs of transition (usually short and simple structure) are almost never needed in short essays; but the paragraphs of introduction and conclusion bear some attention.

Introductions

An introductory paragraph or introductory paragraph unit (a number of paragraphs at the beginning of the essay whose purpose is to introduce the subject) has various functions, including gaining reader interest, indicating or pointing toward the thesis, and moving the reader smoothly into the body paragraphs, the developmental paragraphs. The introductory methods are varied. They include:

1. a direct statement of the thesis,
2. background,
3. definition of term(s),
4. quotation(s),
5. a shocking statement,
6. question(s), and
7. a combination of two or more of this list.

You should not decide that some of the methods are good and some are bad. Indeed, all are valid, and the most common one is the last, the combination. Use the approach that best fits each essay. Resist the temptation to find a pat introduction to use for each essay you write.

In each of the following examples, the thesis is quite explicit, and it comes naturally from the whole context of one or more of the recommended methods of introduction. Notice that in some of the theses, the subject and the treatment are not easily separated in space.

Direct Statement of Thesis

Anyone on the road in any city near midnight on Friday and Saturday is among dangerous people. They're not the product of the witching hour; they're the product of the "happy hour." They're called drunk drivers. ==These threats to our lives and limbs need to be controlled by federal laws with strong provisions.==

Background

In one five-year period in California (1982–1987), 215,000 people were injured and 43,000 were killed by drunk drivers. Each year, the same kinds of figures come in from all our states. The state laws vary. The federal government does virtually nothing. Drunk driving has reached the point of being a national problem of huge proportions. ==This slaughter of innocent citizens should be stopped by following the lead of many other nations and passing federal legislation with strong provisions.==

Definition

Here's a recipe. Take two thousand pounds of plastic, rubber, and steel, pour in ten gallons of gas, and start the engine. Then take one human being of two hundred pounds of flesh, blood, and bones, pour in two glasses of beer in one hour, and put him or her behind the wheel. Mix the two together, and the result may be a drunken driver ready to cause death and destruction. ==This problem of drunk driving can and should be controlled by federal legislation with strong provisions.==

Quotation

The National Highway Traffic Safety Administration has stated that 50 percent of all fatal accidents involve intoxicated drivers and that "75 percent of those drivers have a Blood Alcohol Content of .10 or greater." That kind of information is widely known, yet the carnage on the highways continues. ==This problem of drunk driving should be addressed by a federal law with strict provisions.==

Shocking Statement and Questions

Almost 60,000 Americans were killed in the Vietnam War. What other war kills more than that number each year? Give up? It's the war with drunk drivers. The war in Vietnam ended about two decades ago, but our DUI war goes on, and the drunks are winning. ==This deadly conflict should be controlled by a federal law with strong provisions.==

Questions and a Definition

What is a drunk driver? In California it's a person with a Blood Alcohol Content of .8 or more who is operating a motor vehicle. What do those drivers do? Some of them kill. Every year more than 60,000 people nationwide die. Those are easy questions. The difficult one is, What can be done? <u>One answer is clear:</u> <u>drunk drivers</u> <u>should be controlled by federal laws with strong provisions.</u>   subject / treatment } thesis

Although the preceding methods are effective, some others are ineffective because they are too vague to carry the thesis or because they carry the thesis in a mechanical way. The mechanical approach may have merit in directness and explicitness, but it usually disengages the reader's imagination and interest.

> AVOID: The purpose of this essay is to write about the need for strong national laws against drunk driving.
>
> AVOID: I will now write a paper about the need for strong national laws against drunk driving.

The length of an introduction can vary, but the typical one for a student essay is about three to five sentences. If your introduction is shorter than three, be certain that it conveys all that you want to say. If it is longer than five, be certain that it only introduces and does not attempt to expand upon ideas, a function reserved for the developmental paragraphs; a long and complicated introduction may make your essay top heavy.

EXERCISE 1

Pick one of the following theses (altering it a bit to suit your own ideas, if you like) and write at least three introductions for it, each one featuring a different method. Underline the thesis in each paragraph, and label the subject and treatment parts.

1. Marriages come in different shapes and sizes.

2. Career choices are greatly influenced by a person's background.

3. *Friendship* is just one word, but friends are of different kinds.

4. The spirit of sports has been corrupted by money.

5. Sexual harassment at work often goes unreported for some very practical reasons.

Conclusions

Your *concluding paragraph* should give the reader the feeling that you have said all that you want to say about your subject. Like introductory paragraphs, conclusions can be quite varied. Some effective ways of concluding a paper are:

- Conclude with a final paragraph or sentence that is a logical part of the body of the paper; that is, it functions as part of the support. In this case, the paper requires no formal conclusion. This form is more common in the published essay than in the student essay.

    > One day he hit me. He said he was sorry and even cried, but I could not forgive him. We got a divorce. It took me a while before I could look back and see what the causes really were, but by then it was too late to make any changes.

    Maria Campos, From an essay on divorce

- Conclude with a restatement of the thesis in slightly different words, perhaps pointing out the significance and/or making applications.

    > Don't blame it on the referee. Don't even blame it on the fight managers. Put the blame where it belongs—on the prevailing mores that regard prize fighting as a perfectly proper enterprise and vehicle of entertainment. No one doubts that many people enjoy prize fighting and will miss it if it should be thrown out. And that is precisely the point.

    Norman Cousins, From an essay on boxing

- Conclude with a review of the main points of the discussion—a kind of summary. This will be appropriate only if the complexity of the essay necessitates a summary.

    > And that's *why*. Now you know. Let me just add, before taking a well-deserved nap, that I doubt that Merv and his minions set out to design "Wheel of Fortune" around the Big V Principle or analyzed the economy. I think they just happened, by instinct, experience—and good luck—to hit on a formula that would make it the state-of-the-art eighties game show. A formula that sucks the viewer through the screen and into that dazzling dreamscape—Vanna's Nirvana—where he is transformed from a nullity, a hapless anonymous bozo, a nobody from nowhere, to the only being now worth being: a Winner. Someone possessed of wealth, luck, and maybe more important, television exposure. Someone, in short, who finally exists. You know, a big wheel.

    Lewis Grossberger, From an essay on "Wheel of Fortune"

- Conclude with an anecdote related to the thesis.

    > Over the harsh traffic sounds of motors and horns and blaring radios came the faint whang-whang of a would-be musician with a beat-up guitar and a money-drop hat turned up at his feet. It all reminded me of when I had first experienced the conglomeration of things that now assailed my senses. This jumbled mixture of things both human and nonhuman was, in fact, the reason I had come to live here. Then it was different and exciting. Now it was the reason I was leaving.

    Brian Maxwell, From an essay on leaving Los Angeles

- Conclude with a quotation related to the thesis.

    > Fifty percent of all fatal traffic accidents involve intoxicated drivers, according to the National Highway Traffic Safety Administration. Cavenaugh and Associates, research specialists, say that drunk drivers killed 119,000 people in the five-year period from 1982 through 1986. They go on to say that intoxicated drivers cost us somewhere between eleven and twenty-four billion dollars each year. It is time to give drunk drivers a message: "Stay off the road. You are costing us pain, injury, and death, and no one has the right to do that."

    Daniel Humphries, From an essay on drunk driving

There are also many ineffective ways of concluding a paper; do not conclude with:

- a summary when a summary is unnecessary.

- a complaint about the assignment or an apology about the quality of the work.

- an afterthought—that is, adding something that you forgot to discuss in the body of the paper.

- a tagged conclusion—for example, using *In conclusion, To conclude*, or *I would liked to conclude this discussion*.

- a conclusion that raises additional problems that should have been settled during the discussion.

The conclusion is an integral part of the essay and is often a reflection of the introduction. If you have trouble with the conclusion, reread your introduction, and work for a roundness or completeness in the whole paper.

EXERCISE 2

Consider the relationships of the introduction and conclusion and answer the questions.

introduction

When I come home from work in the evening, I sometimes like to relax by playing my flute while my dog, Benji, and wolf, Tiny, enjoy a good howl. Neighbors who might glimpse me harmonizing with my companions sometimes smile patronizingly. Few know that, by joining in this canine duet, I am actually communicating with my animals and deepening my friendship with them. For, although our dogs and cats share our homes and affections, most of us know very little about communicating with them.

As a veterinarian trained in animal psychology, I have studied cats and dogs for almost 20 years, trying to learn how they communicate, to better understand their wants and needs. I am convinced that we could respond to their needs more readily and could control them more successfully if, by learning to recognize and interpret their expressions and postures, we could learn how to communicate with them more effectively. In short, we could develop deeper, more satisfying relationships with them. . . .

conclusion

As you can see, the body language and facial expressions of dogs and cats are remarkably similar to those of humans, and they depict a similar range of emotions. The more we understand our pets' behavior, emotions, and intentions, the better our relationships with them will be. Above all, through understanding their ways, we can better appreciate them as sensitive, intelligent beings. We can then treat them with the respect that all of the creatures great and small under our stewardship deserve.

Michael W. Fox, "What Is Your Pet Trying to Tell You?"

1. What is the thesis? Write it here, and mark the subject and treatment parts.

2. What is the relationship between the introduction and the conclusion (such as restatement, review, anecdote, or quotation)?

EXERCISE 3

introduction

Confusion prevails on the issue of smoking in public places. Both smokers and nonsmokers are confused and would like the problem solved. On the one side are many of those who, because of preference or addiction, desire to smoke. On the other side are primarily those who do not smoke and do not want to breathe the smoke of those who do. Laws vary from community to community; businesspersons wonder about what is morally right and what price they may eventually have to pay in relation to this issue. For all the right reasons, the solution has become quite clear. It is time for the federal government to pass a law restricting smoking in public.

conclusion

Powerful lobbies for tobacco companies are on the other side. But on the side of restriction is logic, honesty, and an abundance of scientific information. On the side of restriction is also a large group of smokers who are unable or unwilling to quit smoking but see the rightness of such a proposal. A new wind is blowing across the nation—and it is smoke-free, at least in public places.

1. What is the thesis? Write it here, and mark the subject and treatment parts.

2. What is the relationship between the introduction and the conclusion (such as restatement, review, anecdote, or quotation)?

EXERCISE 4

introduction

One of the main thrusts in "The Use of Force" is point of view. The narrator, a doctor, tells his own story, a story about his encounter with an uncooperative patient but also—and mainly—a story about the narrator's transformation from a mature, rational person to someone of a lower order who has lost considerable self-respect. This transformation happens in stages of attitudinal change that occur during his arrival, his early attempt at obtaining cooperation, his losing his self-control, and his reflection on his behavior.

conclusion

The use of force has two effects in this story. The girl resents the force and becomes alternately defensive and offensive. The doctor uses force and becomes so caught up in the physical and emotional conflicts that he is responding to the wrong motive for acting. It is the point of view that highlights the doctor's feeling of guilt in retrospect. This feeling comes across much more poignantly because this story is, after all, a confessional.

1. What is the thesis? Write it here, and mark the subject and treatment parts.

2. What is the relationship between the introduction and the conclusion (such as restatement, review, anecdote, or quotation)?

EXERCISE 5

Select one of the introductions you wrote in Exercise 1, consider how you would develop your support, and write a brief conclusion to match it.

Writing the Essay

Having examined the essay—the parts and the whole—you are now ready for the main concern of this chapter: how to write an essay. For this task we naturally turn to the system introduced in detail in the first chapter: **DCODE**.

Because the well-organized paragraph so closely resembles the essay in organization and concept, the **DCODE** approach to the two differs only in the extent of its application. The following presentation contains a concise statement of the **DCODE** principles and an illustration of how they are used in student work.

- **D**   *Delve:* Freewrite, brainstorm, and cluster in order to generate and investigate topics.
- **C**   *Concentrate:* Narrow your subject and state your topic sentence or thesis.
- **O**   *Organize:* Develop an outline or a section of the **Delve** cluster.
- **D**   *Draft:* Write, rewrite, and revise as many times as necessary for **c**oherence, **l**anguage, **u**nity, **e**mphasis, **s**upport, and **s**entence structure (**cluess**).
- **E**   *Edit:* Correct problems in **c**apitalization, **o**missions, **p**unctuation, and **s**pelling (**cops**).

The **DCODE** writing process is central to writing paragraphs and essays. It helps you move naturally from exploring relevant ideas and generating a topic; to stating a topic sentence or thesis precisely; to organizing the material; to writing, rewriting, and revising; and, finally, to editing. It also allows for recursive movement: you can go back and forth as you rework your material. In short, **DCODE** systematizes what you as a good writer should do. Paying attention to its components will remind you of the importance of writing as a process.

Keep in mind that one of the most useful features of **DCODE** is *flexibility*. You can emphasize, deemphasize, or even delete strategies according to the needs of your assignments.

Our student writer, Leah, is an inmate at a California prison where she is enrolled in a small, low-cost college program. Her assignment was to write a personal essay of 500–800 words. Her instructor suggested that she concentrate on a recent development or event at the prison that had changed her life, for better or worse.

Numerous topics interested her. There was the problem of overcrowding: she lived in an institution built for 900 inmates, and the population was now 2,200. She also considered education. After spending some time in routine prison work and aimless activities, she had discovered school and found it highly satisfying. And then there was the accomplishment made by her Native American (they referred to themselves as American Indians and Native Americans interchangeably) friends at the prison. After years of arguing their case, they finally convinced the institution to build a sweat lodge for their religious purposes, and it was now in operation. That was a subject she knew well, and it was one for which she held the most enthusiasm. She was ready to proceed, knowing that the **DCODE** system would provide her with strategies and give her direction.

Delve

Freewriting

First Leah started freewriting, which enabled her to probe her memory and to measure her inclinations. She would write without stopping, letting her ideas tumble forth in order to liberate and associate the many thoughts she had had on the subject of "sweat lodge."

> For several years I have wanted to worship in the way that I did when I was on the reservation. These people here at prison were discriminating against me, I thought. I knew that the other people here could go to the chaplain and to the chapel and they could do so without people complaining or going to any bother. I didn't know why they did not allow me to follow my own religious preference. Then I talked to the other Indian sisters here at prison and they told me that they had been working for many years to get a sweat lodge. I started working with them. It took years of work, but it is worth it for now we have a sweat lodge where we can go for our ceremonies. It makes me feel good. I look forward to it. I have used it once a week for most of the last year. When I am nervous and when things are tense on the prison grounds, I think about the sweat lodge and just thinking about it gives me some peace. Then when I go there and sweat for a period of time I seem to feel that I am leaving the prison grounds and I am at peace with the universe. It is a ceremony that is important to me and also to the prison. We even have women who are not Indians who are interested and we teach them about Indian ways and we all learn from what we do. What else is there to say. I could go on and on. That is what I have to say. I love the sweat lodge which we call the sweats. I think it is the most important thing in my life now. I used to be bitter toward the prison for denying me my rights, but now I am even at peace with them—most of the time. I remember when we were trying to get approval and . . .

Brainstorming

After setting up a useful framework of questions, she let herself free-associate with tentative answers.

Who?	American Indian inmates and others
What?	sweat lodge—how it was started—the politics—the ceremonies
Where?	California Institution for Women—off the yard
When?	1989, before, after, long time in planning and building
Why?	spiritual, physical, self-esteem, educational

Clustering

Next Leah was ready for some more precise structuring of her thoughts, which would take the form of clustering. She began with a double circle enclosing her topic. Then, in response to the question What comes to mind? she bubbled in ideas on spokes radiating out from the hub. She knew that she was covering more than she could include in her essay, but she wanted to see her topic presented broadly so she could focus her work and proceed. Leah's first bubble cluster is shown in Figure 2.1.

FIGURE 2.1 Leah's First Bubble Cluster

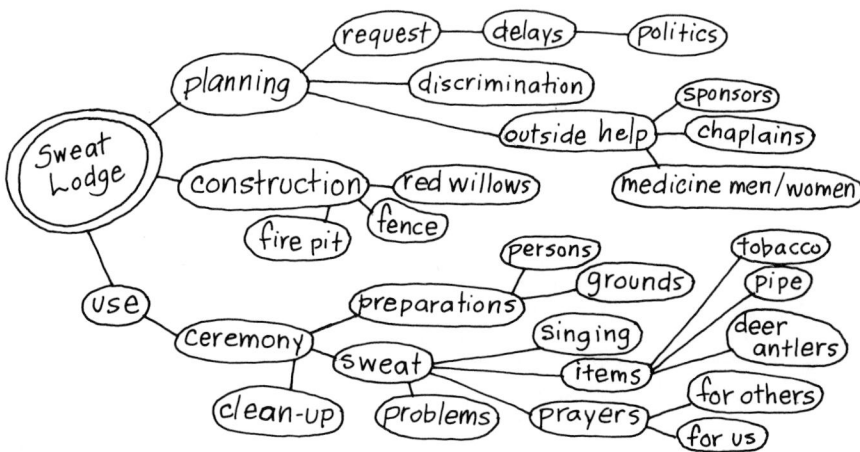

Concentrate

Now Leah was ready to focus, concentrating on one aspect of her larger topic that could be reasonably developed in an essay of 500–800 words. She also wanted to establish a direction for the essay that would target her audience, who knew little about her topic. It would be necessary to explain her topic in detail so that uninformed readers could easily understand. Moreover, she would avoid any Native American word that her audience might not know. Although the sweat lodge was developed in an atmosphere of controversy in which she and others often had to be persuasive, she anticipated that her readers of this essay would be open-minded and interested. She would simply inform them about her experience with the sweat lodge, giving a personal perspective. She would also have to avoid using prison slang, because this essay was for an assignment in a college writing class.

The third attempt at writing the **Concentrate** statement produced a subject and its treatment that pleased her. It would become her thesis.

> I want to explain how we use the sweats and why.
>
> Using the prison sweat lodge involves specific practices which contribute to my well-being.

I want to discuss the prison sweat lodge, what we do in the preparation period, what we do when we're inside for the ceremony, and what we do afterwards.   *subject treatment*

Organize

Leah's next task was to organize her material. For this strategy, she went back to her **Delve**-stage clustering, which she had divided into Planning, Construction, and Use. She had already decided in the **Concentrate** stage that she wanted to work with the "use" aspect and to explain it from her perspective. Therefore, she focused on only one part of the cluster. Her refined bubble cluster is shown in Figure 2.2.

FIGURE 2.2 Leah's Refined Bubble Cluster

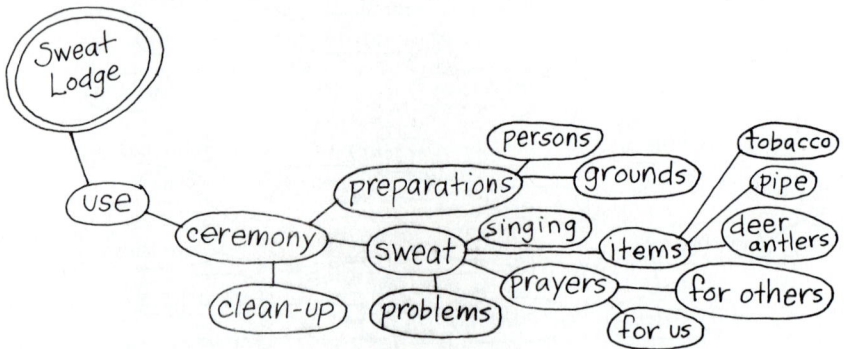

She might have started to write a first draft on that point, but instead she decided she wanted to recall and organize more detail, so she began an outline. She used her own memory and private reference sources for information. Had she been working on a reading-related topic, she would have gone back to the reading. Had she been working on a topic subject to research, she would have consulted library sources.

The outline shows a relationship of ideas, suggesting divisions of the essay according to her thesis and now indicating support. The divisions are Preparation, Ceremony, and Completion. Those items are her roman-numeral headings.

I want to discuss the prison sweat lodge, what we do in the preparation period, what we do when we're inside for the ceremony, and what we do afterwards.   *subject treatment* } *thesis*

    I. Preparation period
        A. Fasting
            1. Duration
            2. Only water
        B. Heat rocks
            1. Thirty to fifty
            2. Build fire
        C. Set up lodge
            1. Permission from sponsor
            2. Cover framework

II. The ceremony
   A. Movement
      1. Going and coming
      2. Passing sacred objects
   B. Establishing attitude
   C. Sweating
   D. Praying and singing
   E. Purification rites
      1. Tobacco ties
      2. Sage
      3. Sweet grass
III. Completing the ceremony and site restoration
   A. Personal
      1. Water down
      2. Eat and drink
      3. Change
   B. Site
      1. Remove and store blankets
      2. Move rocks

Draft

At this point Leah was ready to draft her essay, revising as she went. After completing the first draft, she began revising. She marked problems, but she was mainly concerned with **cluess:**

coherence	one idea leading smoothly to the next
language	usage, tone, and diction
unity	using the thesis to unify the essay parts and the topic sentences to unify the developmental paragraphs
emphasis	principally, repetition of words and phrases and placement of key parts at the beginning or ending of units
support	presenting evidence and reasoning in relation to the thesis and topic sentences
sentence structure	especially, using a variety of beginnings and types, along with avoiding fragments, comma splices, and run-togethers

Razor Wire Sweat Lodge

My tribe is ~~I am a~~ Pomo ~~Indian~~, one ~~tribe~~ of *twenty-one represented* ~~many here~~ on the prison grounds. I have *always* had tremendous interest in my *Ancestors* ~~Ancestry~~ and *in* their customs, and the cultures of all Indian tribes. The sacred sweat ceremonies, I've found to be one of the most interesting. *Cultural practices.* Many women of *other* ~~all~~ races here in the facility have also taken interest and found peace *Other benefits* → *Rewrite* within themselves from participating in the sweats. I want to discuss the prison sweat lodge, what we do in the preparation period, what we do when we're inside for the ceremony, and what we do afterwards.

The first step to sweating ~~is~~ [In our prison facility] the preparation period. [Rewrite for stronger Topic sentence] Before anyone can sweat there are many requirements ~~in~~ [concerning] what we wear, ~~how we are instructed (depending on how many times we've gone)~~, and how we act. [For] Twenty-four hours before the sweat, we fast. ~~We can only drink~~ [Participants should drink only] water or juices, but if someone has health problems, we will excuse them. [coherence] The lava rocks have to [heat] in the fire approximately three hours before we start sweating. The fire has to be built just right in a little house shape. ~~Putting~~ [We put] all the rocks in the middle with the wood standing like a teepee around them; then the paper [is] stuffed between and around the wood. [Organize / Be more concise] Once there's a good fire going, then we ~~start~~ tend to the sweat lodge itself. Since we have no tarp to put on the sweat lodge, the state has provided us with plenty of blankets. The blankets have to cover the seat lodge fully. We put at least three layers of blankets on the sweat lodge. We make sure we leave about eight inches of blanket around the bottom of the sweat lodge. ~~Around~~ [By] this time some women have started making their tobacco ties. These ties are used for ~~putting~~ [sending] your prayer on. We ~~'ve got~~ [must] to [coherence] make sure the sponser is somewhere by the sweat lodge at all times. ~~Also about~~ [As for] the rock, we use thirty to fifty of them, it depends on their size and how many women are sweating that day. Then the women are told to change into only muu muus; the state provides them also. Then we're ready to go inside. The preparation period is very important ~~and~~ [but] everyone looks forward to it being over.

Once everyone is inside the sweat lodge, there are certain things ~~you~~ [we] must do. ~~The way we enter is first we~~ enter counter clockwise, and [once] inside we ~~maintain everything~~ [conduct all parts of the ceremony] we do counter clockwise. There are four rounds in the sweat, which last [each] about twenty to thirty minutes ~~each~~. We stress that no one ^should break our circle inside the sweat lodge, but it ~~is possible~~ sometimes happens. Some women can't handle the heat inside [coherence] we never make them stay. The praying and singing is in the Sioux language since our outside sponsor [Rephrase] is Sioux. Not everyone has to sing or pray. Its up to ~~them~~ the individual. As someone finishes a prayer ~~they say for all their relations~~ she mentions all her relatives, then the next person prays. Before ~~anyone~~ we ~~even~~ enter(s) the sweat ~~they~~ we have to make sure they have peace [Agr] and good feelings with all other members. The tobacco ties hang over our heads in the sweat or around our necks. Also we ^take in sage with us and smudge ourselves with it. for purification After each round, new hot rocks are brought in. As these [verb tense] rocks are place(d) in the fire, sweet grass is put on them. ~~All~~ What we do inside the sweat lodge is not only for [Be more concise] ourselves, but ~~for~~ through our prayers, for others. We maintain ourselves with humility during the whole sweat.

When the sweat is over, we enter the final phase. We come out and throw our tobacco ties in^to the fire pit. The^n ~~first thing~~ we ~~do is~~ hose ourselves down with plenty of cold water. The refreshments are opened and someone goes after food. Once we've eaten and changed our cloths, we start taking down the sweat. The blankets have to be taken off the same way they were put on and folded up ~~good~~ carefully. The left-over wood has to be put away and ~~on both~~ the blankets must be covered. and the wood ~~we put their covers~~. Any garbage that's been left around is thrown in^to the dumpster. Then we lock the gate and bid our farewells until the next weekend. A^fter [move to end] its all over, ~~you~~ we ~~really~~ feel physically ~~a sense of~~ refresh(ed)ness and clean~~liness~~ and peaceful~~ness~~.

Using ~~The~~ sweat lodge is a custom of most~~ly all~~ Indian tribes. Certain Indian tribes go about it differently ~~than~~ from [Rewrite] others, but once they're all inside everyone feels of one whole being. All three of the steps I've gone through are helpful for a successful sweat ceremony. ~~Many of us~~ Each week we members look forward to these ceremonies ~~every week~~. They help us cope better with the prison system.

Edit

The final stage was exceedingly important, for Leah knew that after completing the other drafts and doing the revision, a writer can be tempted into laziness. That condition may cause the writer to neglect such fundamentals as **c**apitalization, **o**missions, **p**unctuation, and **s**pelling **(cops)**, thereby spoiling an otherwise strong project. She had already marked some of the **cops** items during the drafting and revising. She read the paper aloud twice to be sure that it flowed well and that she had no awkward phrases. Then she examined it with care. Here is the draft she edited.

```
                    Razor Wire Sweat Lodge
     My Indian tribe is Pomo, one of twenty-one represented
at this prison. I have always had tremendous interest in
my Ancestors and their customs, and in the cultures of all
Indian tribes. The sacred sweat ceremony has always been
at the center of my life. Here at prison it has taken on a
special meaning. In fact, many women of other races here
have also found peace within themselves as a result of
participating with me and other American Indians in the
sweats. Each Saturday we have a routine: we make
preparations, we sweat, and we conclude with a post-sweat
activity.
     Before we sweat, we must prepare ourselves and the
facility. For twenty-four hours before the sweat, we fast.
We do not eat anything and drink only water or juices, but
if someone has a health problem, we will excuse her. As
for clothing we wear simple, loose dresses such as the
prison-issued muu-muus. We bring tobacco ties, sage
leaves, sweet grass, and sometimes a pipe. Preparing the
facility is more complicated than preparing ourselves.
About thirty-five lava rocks must be heated in a fire
approximately three hours before we start sweating. The
wood for the fire has to be placed in a tepee shape around
the pile of rocks and ignited. Once the fire is hot, we
tend to the sweat lodge itself. Since we have no tarp to
put on the sweat lodge frame, the state provides us with
blankets. We use these to cover the lodge fully draping it
```

with about three layers and leaving an opening to the East. Finally we are ready to go inside. The preparation period is very important, but everyone looks forward to its being over.

From this point on through the ceremony, everything must be done according to rules. First we enter counterclockwise, and once inside we conduct all parts of the ceremony counterclockwise. There are four rounds in the sweat, each of which lasts about twenty to thirty minutes. We stress that no one should break our circle inside the sweat lodge, but it sometimes happens. Some women can't handle the steam and the heat, so we never make them stay. Those who do stay are free to participate in the singing and praying or not. The four rounds are similiar. For each, six hot rocks are brought in, and six dippers of water are poured onto the rocks. The number six indicates the four directions and the sky and the ground. As someone finishes a prayer (usually in Sioux because our sponser is a Sioux) she mentions her relatives, for this ceremony is also for others. Then another person follows. As sweet grass burns outside on the fire, we sit in the hot steam and rub sage leaves on our bodies for purification. We maintain ourselves with humility during the whole sweat.

When the sweat is over, we enter the final phase. We come out and throw our tobacco ties into the fire pit, and the smoke takes our prayers to the sky. Then we hose ourselves down with plenty of cold water, and open the refreshments we brought. Once we've eaten and changed our cloths we start dismantling the sweat. The blankets have to be taken off the same way they were put up and then folded carefully. The left-over wood has to be put away, and the blankets and wood must be covered. Any garbage that's been left around is thrown into the dumpster. Then we lock the gate to our facility and bid farwell.

Using a sweat lodge is a custom of most Indian tribes. Certain Indian tribes go about it differently from others, but in here when we are together in the lodge, we feel like one whole being. Each week we look forward to this ceremony. It helps us cope better with the prison system. After its over, we feel refreshed, clean, and peaceful.

Following is an uninterrupted, sequential copy of Leah's writing process, this time using the standard Worksheet: Writing in DCODE. Observe how the material moved from general idea to completed essay, though at times it doubled back to redirect and regroup. The worksheet is followed by the final draft of her essay, annotated for thesis and topic sentences.

WORKSHEET
Writing in DCODE

NAME: Leah

SECTION: _____ CHAPTER: _____ DATE: _____

Delve Generate your topic, or ideas for your topic, by delving into your subject area through:

- *Freewriting*—writing sentence after sentence, nonstop and spontaneously.
- *Brainstorming*—jotting down answers to Who? What? Where? When? Why? and How? and then listing words and phrases in relation to those answers.
- *Clustering*—connecting bubbled ideas with lines to show strings of relationships, producing each new bubble item in response to the question, What comes to mind?
- *Combining* any of these approaches, as directed by your instructor.

Freewriting

For several years I have wanted to worship in the way that I did when I was on the reservation. These people here at prison were discriminating against me, I thought. I knew that the other people here could go to the chaplain and to the chapel and they could do so without people complaining or going to any bother. I didn't know why they did not allow me to follow my own religious preference. Then I talked to the other Indian sisters here at prison and they told me that they had been working for many years to get a sweat lodge. I started working with them. It took years of work, but it is worth it for now we have a sweat lodge where we can go for our ceremonies. It makes me feel good. I look forward to it. I have used it once a week for most of the last year. When I am nervous and when things are tense on the prison grounds, I think about the sweat lodge and just thinking about it gives me some peace. Then when I go there and sweat for a period of time I seem to feel that I am leaving the prison grounds and I am at peace with the universe. It is a ceremony that is important to me and also to the prison. We even have women who are not Indians who are interested and we teach them about Indian ways and we all learn from what we do. What else is there to say. I could go on and on. That is what I have to say. I love the sweat lodge which we call the sweats. I think it is the most important thing in my life now. I used to be bitter toward the prison for denying me my rights, but now I am even at peace with them--most of the time. I remember when we were trying to get approval and . . .

Brainstorming

    Who?   American Indian inmates and others
    What?   sweat lodge--how it was started--the politics--the ceremonies
    Where? California Institution for Women--off the yard
    When?   1989, before, after, long time in planning and building
    Why?   spiritual, physical, self-esteem, educational

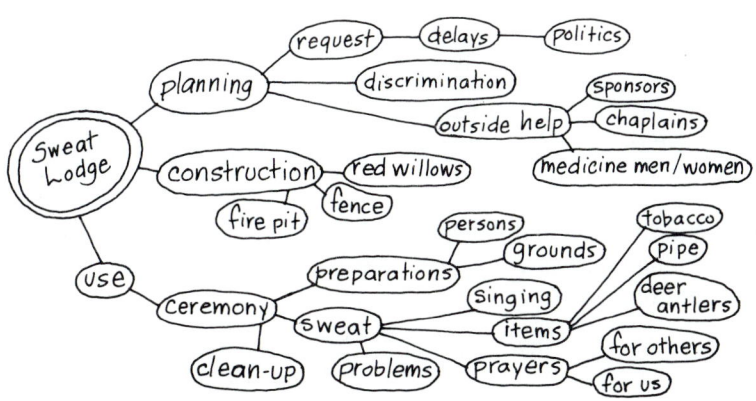

Concentrate Concentrate your work by stating your topic in one sentence that is not too broad, narrow, or vague to be developed. Base this sentence (which may become the topic sentence for your paragraph or the thesis for your essay) on an idea emerging from the **Delve** stage. You may have to try several statements here before you formulate one that is best for your writing task. Be sure that your final statement covers your assignment or intent and specifies both your subject (what you are writing about) and treatment (what aspect you will focus on). Label the *subject* and *treatment* parts.

```
I want to explain how we use the sweats and why.
Using the prison sweat lodge involves specific practices which contribute
to my well-being.
                                subject
I want to discuss the prison sweat lodge, what we do in the preparation
period, what we do when we're inside for the ceremony, and what we do
afterwards.                        treatment
```

Organize Complete an outline or a cluster, as directed by your instructor. The cluster should be a section from, or a refined version of, the **Delve** clustering. Regardless of the strategy you use, the organizational pattern should indicate a division of your topic into parts that will, in turn, be further subdivided for support as necessary to address a particular audience on your concentrated topic.

```
I.   Preparation period
     A. Fasting
        1. Duration
        2. Only water
     B. Heat rocks
        1. Thirty to fifty
        2. Build fire
     C. Set up lodge
        1. Permission from sponsor
        2. Cover framework
II.  The ceremony
     A. Movement
        1. Going and coming
        2. Passing sacred objects
     B. Establishing attitude
     C. Sweating
     D. Praying and singing
     E. Purification rites
        1. Tobacco ties
        2. Sage
        3. Sweet grass
III. Completing the ceremony and
     site restoration
     A. Personal
        1. Water down
        2. Eat and drink
        3. Change
     B. Site
        1. Remove and store
           blankets
        2. Move rocks
```

Draft On separate paper, write and then revise your assignment as many times as necessary for **c**oherence, **l**anguage (usage, tone, and diction), **u**nity, **e**mphasis, **s**upport, and **s**entence structure (**cluess**).

Edit Correct problems in fundamentals such as **c**apitalization, **o**missions, **p**unctuation, and **s**pelling (**cops**). Before writing the final draft, read your paper aloud to discover oversights and awkwardness of expression.

Final Draft

Razor Wire Sweat Lodge
Leah

My Indian tribe is Pomo, one of twenty-one represented at this prison. I have always had tremendous interest in my ancestors and their customs, and in the cultures of all Indian tribes. The sacred sweat ceremony has always been at the center of my life. Here at prison it has taken on a special meaning. In fact, many women of other races here have also found peace within themselves as a result of participating with me and other American Indians in the sweats. ==Each Saturday we have a routine: we make preparations, we sweat, and we conclude with a post-sweat activity.== *thesis*

==Before we sweat, we must prepare ourselves and the facility.== *topic sentence* For twenty-four hours before the sweat, we fast. We do not eat anything and drink only water or juices, but if someone has a health problem, we will excuse her. As for clothing we wear simple, loose dresses such as the prison-issued muu-muus. We bring tobacco ties, sage leaves, sweet grass, and sometimes a pipe. Preparing the facility is more complicated than preparing ourselves. About thirty-five lava rocks must be heated in a fire approximately three hours before we start sweating. The wood for the fire has to be placed in a tepee shape around the pile of rocks and ignited. Once the fire is hot, we tend to the sweat lodge itself. Since we have no tarp to put on the sweat lodge frame, the state provides us with blankets. We use these to cover the lodge fully, draping it with about three layers and leaving an opening to the east. Finally we are ready to go inside. The preparation period is very important, but everyone looks forward to its being over.

==From this point on through the ceremony, everything must be done according to rules.== *topic sentence* First we enter counterclockwise, and once inside we conduct all parts of the ceremony counterclockwise. There are four rounds in the sweat, each of which lasts about twenty to thirty minutes. We stress that no one should break our circle inside the sweat lodge, but it sometimes happens. Some women can't handle the steam and the heat, so we never make them stay. Those who do stay are free to participate in the singing and praying or not. The four rounds are similar. For each, six hot rocks are brought in, and six dippers of water are poured onto the rocks. The number six indicates the four directions and the sky and the ground. As someone finishes a prayer (usually in Sioux because our sponsor is a Sioux) she mentions her relatives, for this ceremony is also for others. Then another person follows. As sweet grass burns outside on the fire, we sit in the hot steam and rub sage leaves on our bodies for purification. We maintain ourselves with humility during the whole sweat.

==When the sweat is over, we enter the final phase.== We come out and throw our tobacco ties into the fire pit, and the smoke takes our prayers to the sky. Then we hose ourselves down with plenty of cold water and open the refreshments we brought. Once we've eaten and changed our clothes, we start dismantling the sweat. The blankets have to be taken off the same way they were put up and then folded carefully. The left-over wood has to be put away, and the blankets and wood must be covered. Any garbage that's been left around is thrown into the dumpster. Then we lock the gate to our facility and bid farewell.

topic sentence

Using a sweat lodge is a custom of most Indian tribes. Certain Indian tribes go about it differently from others, but in here when we are together in the lodge, we feel like one whole being. Each week we look forward to this ceremony. It helps us cope better with the prison system. After it's over, we feel physically refreshed, clean, and peaceful.

EXERCISE 6

Select one of the following theses, and complete the Worksheet: Writing in DCODE. Alter the topic if you like, even by taking the opposite position. Your instructor may also ask you to go beyond the initial stages (**DCO**).

1. That date (marriage, class, game, job) was a disaster (success).

2. I will never forget my first experience in racial prejudice (cruelty to animals, inhumanity).

3. The kind of music I listen to reflects the kind of person I would like to be.

4. A preoccupation with a single activity or concern throws life out of balance.

5. The importance of student government is often overlooked.

6. A death in the family can teach one a great deal about life.

7. The way a person drives reveals his or her personality.

8. The way I drive depends upon my mood.

9. The way I keep my room (car, house, yard, desk) is a reflection of the way I think (regard life).

10. One of my most embarrassing moments has become only a humorous recollection in retrospect.

WORKSHEET
Writing in DCODE

NAME:_____

SECTION:_____ CHAPTER:_____ DATE:_____

Delve   Generate your topic, or ideas for your topic, by delving into your subject area through:

- *Freewriting*—writing sentence after sentence, nonstop and spontaneously.
- *Brainstorming*—jotting down answers to Who? What? Where? When? Why? and How? and then listing words and phrases in relation to those answers.
- *Clustering*—connecting bubbled ideas with lines to show strings of relationships, producing each new bubble item in response to the question, What comes to mind?
- *Combining* any of these approaches, as directed by your instructor.

WORKSHEET: Writing in DCODE

Concentrate Concentrate your work by stating your topic in one sentence that is not too broad, narrow, or vague to be developed. Base this sentence (which may become the topic sentence for your paragraph or the thesis for your essay) on an idea emerging from the **Delve** stage. You may have to try several statements here before you formulate one that is best for your writing task. Be sure that your final statement covers your assignment or intent and specifies both your subject (what you are writing about) and treatment (what aspect you will focus on). Label the *subject* and *treatment* parts.

Organize Complete an outline or a cluster, as directed by your instructor. The cluster should be a section from, or a refined version of, the **Delve** clustering. Regardless of the strategy you use, the organizational pattern should indicate a division of your topic into parts that will, in turn, be further subdivided for support as necessary to address a particular audience on your concentrated topic.

Draft On separate paper, write and then revise your assignment as many times as necessary for **c**oherence, **l**anguage (usage, tone, and diction), **u**nity, **e**mphasis, **s**upport, and **s**entence structure (**cluess**).

Edit Correct problems in fundamentals such as **c**apitalization, **o**missions, **p**unctuation, and **s**pelling (**cops**). Before writing the final draft, read your paper aloud to discover oversights and awkwardness of expression.

Narration: Moving Through Time

3

> " The art of writing is the art of applying the seat of the pants to the seat of the chair.
>
> — M. H. Vorse

What does *narrative* mean ? What is at the heart of all narratives ? What are the five parts of the narrative ? What are some simple forms of the narrative ? What are the main purposes of the narrative in college writing ?

Narrative Defined

In our everyday lives, we tell stories and invite other people to do so by asking questions such as "What happened at work today?" and "What did you do last weekend?" We are disappointed when the answer is "Nothing much." We may be equally disappointed when a person doesn't give us enough details—or maybe gives us too many and spoils the effect. After all, we are interested in people's stories and in the people who tell them. We like the narrative.

What is the narrative? *The narrative is an account of an incident or a series of incidents that make up a complete and significant action.* Each narrative has five properties:

- *setup,* which may be quite brief or even implied, but always gives the necessary setting or situation for the action ("It was a Saturday afternoon in the park.");
- *conflict,* which is at the heart of each story ("when this mugger came up and grabbed my purse.");
- *struggle,* which adds action to the conflict, though it need not be physical engagement ("He yanked and I yanked back, and then I kicked him in the groin.");
- *outcome,* which is merely the result of the struggle ("He ran away, and I smirked."); and
- *meaning,* which is a significance and may be deeply philosophical or simple, stated or implied ("Don't mess with me!").

These components are present in some way in all of the many forms of the narrative.

Purposes and Forms

Narratives primarily inform or persuade, although they may also entertain. They make up many of the examples we use in explaining ideas, and they engage a reader's feelings and intellect as we persuade readers to accept our views. Narratives can be used in brief paragraph statements and throughout the essay: the introduction, the developmental paragraphs, and the conclusion.

Narratives come in different lengths and forms. Parts of short stories, novels, essays, ballads, and plays are narrative. Anecdotes and jokes are often purely narrative.

When Mark Twain was reminded of his reputation for always bothering people with his questions and observations—in short, for being a gadfly or a pest—he had this to say:

> I was always told that I was a sickly and precarious and tiresome and uncertain child, and lived mainly on allopathic medicines during the first seven years of my life. I asked my mother about this, in her old age—she was in her eighty-eighth year—and said:

> "I suppose that during all that time you were uneasy about me?"
> "Yes, the whole time."
> "Afraid I wouldn't live?"
> After a reflective pause—ostensibly to think out the facts—"No—afraid you would."

Thus instead of saying, "People have always regarded me as a pain in the posterior," Mark Twain told a story. His brief story is one kind of narrative, called an *anecdote*. Usually based on truth, and often experience, anecdotes frequently illustrate points and set a tone in speeches and writings.

Our conversations are filled with narratives, too. Speakers use story-based jokes to relax and engage the audience. Comedians make up stories purely for the sake of entertainment, making no significant point:

> Ugly! I was such an ugly kid my parents once took me on a vacation because they didn't want to kiss me goodbye.

> Ugly! When people called me that, I went to the dictionary to see what it meant, and I saw my picture.

But even these jokes—in, let's say, an essay about the idea "self-consciousness during youth"—could be used effectively to inform by entertaining.

Everywhere people inform, persuade, and entertain with the narrative.

Narrative Technique

Order

Narratives almost always move in chronological order. The progressive action, of course, carries that idea, but transitional words that suggest time change—such as *then, later, soon, finally, last,* and *now*—are also useful. Furthermore, you can specify time change directly by using such phrases as "the next day," "after ten minutes had passed," and "when the smoke had cleared," for example.

Because description is so frequently an ally of narration, you may combine references to space as a technique for giving order to your writing. Space references include the specific noting of movement from place to place by using words such as *here, there,* and *beyond*.

Verb Tense

Because most narratives relate experience in time order, the verb tense is more likely to be past (She *walked* into the room) than present (She *walks* into the room), though you can use either. An unnecessary change in tense may distract or confuse readers.

Two generalizations may be useful as you work with verb tense.

- Most narratives (often summaries) taken from literature are written in *present tense*.

> Tom Sawyer *pretends* that painting the fence *is* a special pleasure. His friends *watch* him eagerly. He *talks* and *displays* his joy. They *pay* him to do his work.

- Most historical events and personal experiences are written in *past tense*.

> The Battle of Gettysburg *was* the decisive encounter in the Civil War. Although General Lee, the Confederate general in charge of the overall strategy, *was* a wise and experienced man, he *made* some tactical blunders that *led* to a devastating victory by the Union forces.

> We *walked* down the path to the well-house, attracted by the fragrance of the honeysuckle with which it *was covered*. Someone *was* drawing water and my teacher *placed* my hand under the spout. As the cool stream *gushed* over one hand she *spelled* into the other the word *water*, first slowly, then rapidly.

Helen Keller, *The Story of My Life*

Although Helen Keller chose the conventional past tense for verbs in the last passage, in a different context, she might have chosen the present tense for a sense of immediacy.

The two main points about tense are:

- The generalizations about verb tense selection (using past for the historical and personal and using present for fiction) are useful.

- The change of verb tense in a passage should be made only when the change is needed for clarity and emphasis.

Point of View

Point of view shows the writer's relationship to the material, the subject, and it usually does not change within a passage.

If you are conveying personal experience, the point of view will be *first person,* which can be either involved (a participant) or detached (an observer). The involved perspective uses *I* more prominently than the detached does.

If you are presenting something from a distance, geographical or historical (for example, telling a story about George Washington), the point of view will be *third person*, and the participants will be referred to as "he," "she," and "they."

In the following paragraph the author is present but uninvolved other than as another member of the audience (and even then she is mainly watching the audience). The annotation indicates narrative parts and tense change. Transitional words (those indicating the order of time) are italicized.

> A slick-haired Russian M.C. announced B. B. King ("A great Negritanski musician"), and *then* King was onstage with his well-known guitar—Lucille—and a ten-man ensemble. *As* King and the ensemble swung into "Why I Sing the Blues," <u>one could sense the puzzlement of the Russian audience.</u> "Negro" music to them meant jazz or spirituals, but this was something else. Also, <u>there was the question of response.</u> B. B. King is a great, warm presence when he performs, and he asks his audiences to pour themselves out to him in return. King teases his audiences, urging them to clap along, to whistle, to hoot their appreciation, like the congregations in the Southern churches in which he grew up. But to Russians, such behavior suggests a lack of <u>culture and an almost frightening disorder.</u> Though obviously impressed, the audience *at first* kept a respectful silence *during* the

conflict introduced

tense change with a reason: King as a person, aside from the narrative, is discussed in the present tense

conflict dealt with

numbers, as it might at the symphony. (Only the foreigners shouted and stomped out the beat; we found the Russians around us staring at us open-mouthed.) *Then* King played an irresistible riff, stopped, and leaned toward the audience with his hand cupped to his ear. The audience caught on and began to clap. King changed the beat, and waited for the audience to catch up. *Then* he changed it again. *Soon* the whole place was clapping along to "Get Off My Back, Woman," and there were even a few timid shouts and <u>whistles</u>. King, who has carried the blues to Europe, Africa, and the Far East, had broken the ice one <u>more time</u>.

conflict dealt with

conflict dealt with

outcome

Andrea Lee, "The Blues Abroad"

Description

A good descriptive writer presents material so that the perceptive reader can read and reexperience the writer's ideas. One device important to that writer is imagery. Images can be perceived through the senses (sight, sound, taste, smell, and touch). A good descriptive writer also gives specific details and presents concrete particulars (actual things) in a convincing way. We read, we visualize, we identify, and *zap!*—connection with a narrative account.

In the following paragraphs the images are italicized to emphasize how the author has made us see, hear, smell, touch, and see. Also note the other specific details.

> Before she had quite arisen, she *called* our names and *issued* orders, and *pushed* her large feet into homemade slippers and *across* the *bare lye-washed wooden floor* to *light* the coal-oil lamp.
>
> The *lamplight* in the Store gave a *soft* make-believe feeling to our world which made me want to *whisper* and walk about on tiptoe. The *odors* of onions and oranges and kerosene had been *mixing* all night and wouldn't be disturbed until the wooded slat was removed from the door and the early morning air forced its way in with the bodies of people who had walked miles to reach the pickup place.

Maya Angelou, "Cotton-Picking Time"

Note the use of specific information in the next paragraph.

> On one recent Saturday afternoon a Latino fifth-grader, wearing the same type of hightop tennis shoes I wore as a 10-year-old on that same street corner, strode up to Señor Farrillas' snow-cone pushcart. The kid pulled out a pocketful of dimes and bought two *raspadas*. One for himself, and one for his school chum—a Vietnamese kid. He was wearing hightops, too. They both ordered strawberry, as I recall.

Luis Torres, "Los Chinos Discover el Barrio"

Torres presents the material so you can visualize it. Try to picture this, instead: "The other day I saw a youngster buy a refreshment for himself and his friend." Of course, that is what happened, but very little narrative/descriptive communication takes place in this abbreviated version. In Torres's account, you know when and where the action took place. You know what the kids were wearing, and you know that the author (point of view as technique) identifies with the kids. They buy strawberry *raspadas* from Señor Farrillas. The Latino kid pays for the *raspadas* with "a pocketful of dimes." Did you ever, as a kid, put your hand in the pocket of some tight jeans and tried to pull out those dimes with a balled fist? We identify, and the imagery registers. We may not have visited that street corner in reality, but vicariously we take a trip with Torres.

Dialogue

Good dialogue should sound like speech but should be represented so that it is not as uninspiring and common as our conversation ordinarily is. *Dialogue is used purposefully in narration to characterize, particularize, and support ideas.* It shows us how people talk and think, as individuals or as representatives of society. The dialogue should not be eloquent unless the speaker is an eloquent person. Rather, the dialogue should be appropriate for the speaker and the purpose of the narrative. Usually the statements will be brief. Not every narrative will require dialogue.

Note in the following paragraph the economy of the selections. The language will ring true to Asian immigrants and those who have been around Asian immigrants. It is starkly realistic, yet sympathetically engaging in context so that we are convinced of its authenticity and drawn into the story. This passage is from an essay included in this chapter: "The Struggle to Be an All-American Girl" by Elizabeth Wong. As narrator, she was present when the utterances in this paragraph were made.

> My brother was even more fanatical than I about speaking English. He was especially hard on my mother, criticizing her, often cruelly, for her pidgin speech—smatterings of Chinese scattered like chop suey in her conversation. "It's not 'What it is,' Mom," he'd say in exasperation. "It's 'What *is* it, what *is* it!'" Sometimes Mom might leave out an occasional "the" or "a," or perhaps a verb of being. He would stop her in mid-sentence: "Say it again, Mom. Say it right." When he tripped over his own tongue, he'd blame it on her: "See, Mom, it's all your fault. You set a bad example."

Elizabeth Wong, "The Struggle to Be an All-American Girl"

Before turning to your own writing of narratives, let's look at a range of narratives, some composed by professional writers and some by students. These examples will show you different forms and different techniques, and they will furnish you with subject material for your own writing in paragraphs, essays, and journals.

The Reading Connection

EXERCISE 1

Demonstration

Helen Keller was a remarkable person. With the help of her teacher and companion, Anne Sullivan, she conquered the handicaps of blindness and deafness and became one of the most famous and admired persons of her time. Here she writes about perhaps the most important constructive event in her life.

Language Set Me Free*
HELEN KELLER

One day, while I was playing with my new doll, Miss Sullivan put my big rag doll into my lap also, spelled "d-o-l-l" and tried to make me understand that "d-o-l-l" applied to both. Earlier in the day we had had a tussle over the words "m-u-g" and "w-a-t-e-r." Miss Sullivan had tried to impress it upon me that "m-u-g" is *mug* and that "w-a-t-e-r" is *water*, but I persisted in confounding the two. In despair she had dropped the subject for the time, only to renew it at the first opportunity. I became impatient at her repeated attempts and, seizing the new doll, I dashed it upon the floor. I was keenly delighted when I felt the fragments of the broken doll at my feet. Neither sorrow nor regret followed my passionate outburst. I had not loved the doll. In the still, dark world in which I lived there was no strong sentiment of tenderness. I felt my teacher sweep the fragments to one side of the hearth, and I had a sense of satisfaction that the cause of my discomfort was removed. She brought me my hat, and I knew I was going out into the warm sunshine. This thought, if a wordless sensation may be called a thought, made me hop and skip with pleasure.

2   We walked down the path to the well-house, attracted by the fragrance of the honeysuckle with which it was covered. Someone was drawing water and my teacher placed my hand under the spout. As the cool stream gushed over one hand she spelled into the other the word *water*, first slowly, then rapidly. I stood still, my whole attention fixed upon the motions of her fingers. Suddenly I felt a misty consciousness as of something forgotten—a thrill of returning thought; and somehow the mystery of language was revealed to me. I knew then that "w-a-t-e-r" meant the wonderful cool something that was flowing over my hand. That living word awakened my soul, gave it light, hope, joy, set it free! There were barriers still, it is true, but barriers that could in time be swept away.

* title by the author of this book

APPLICATIONS FOR CRITICAL READING AND DISCUSSION

1. What is the main conflict?
    between Helen Keller and language use (as taught by Miss Sullivan)

2. Items for annotation:
    a. Circle the first indication of conflict and mark it with a *C*.
    b. Mark the struggle with a vertical line and an *S*.

c. If the struggle contains multiple parts (often indicated by time breaks or place changes), mark them by underlining key sentences and using numbers.
d. Circle the outcome of the struggle and mark it with an *O*.
e. If the author states the meaning of the narrative passage, circle it and mark it with an *M*.

3. Is the order based on time, space, or both?
    both

4. Is the main purpose to inform or to persuade?
    inform

EXERCISE 2

Cautious optimism characterizes the following essay by Luis Torres, who chronicles the cultural changes of this East Los Angeles neighborhood. Note how the concluding scene reflects back on the introductory scene. If, after you have finished reading the piece, you are not certain whether it is optimistic or pessimistic, reread the first and last paragraphs again.

Vocabulary Preview: Write short definitions for these words as they are used in the contexts of the following passage. (The paragraph numbers are given in parentheses.) Be prepared to use the words in your own sentences.

depicted (1)

simmering (2)

Chicano (3)

animated (3)

disparaging (5)

los gringos y la raza (15)

ostensibly (15)

chinos (15)

barrio (17)

enclave (17)

Los Chinos Discover el Barrio
LUIS TORRES

1   There's a colorful mural on the asphalt playground of Hillside Elementary School, in the neighborhood called Lincoln Heights. Painted on the beige handball wall, the mural is of life-sized youngsters holding hands. Depicted are Asian and Latino kids with bright faces and ear-to-ear smiles.

2   The mural is a mirror of the makeup of the neighborhood today: Latinos living side-by-side with Asians. But it's not all smiles and happy faces in the Northeast Los Angeles community, located just a couple of miles up Broadway from City Hall. On the surface there's harmony between Latinos and Asians. But there are indications of simmering ethnic-based tensions.

3   That became clear to me recently when I took a walk through the old neighborhood—the one where I grew up. As I walked along North Broadway, I thought of a joke that comic Paul Rodriguez often tells on the stage. He paints the picture of a young Chicano walking down a street on L.A.'s Eastside. He comes upon two Asians having an animated conversation in what sounds like babble. "Hey, you guys, knock off that foreign talk. This is America—speak Spanish!"

4   When I was growing up in Lincoln Heights 30 years ago most of us spoke Spanish—and English. There was a sometimes uneasy coexistence in the neighborhood between brown and white. Back

then we Latinos were moving in and essentially displacing the working-class Italians (to us, they were just *los gringos*) who had moved there and thrived after World War II.

5   Because I was an extremely fair-skinned Latino kid I would often overhear remarks by gringos in Lincoln Heights that were not intended for Latino ears, disparaging comments about "smelly wetbacks," and worse. The transition was, for the most part, a gradual process. And as I recall—except for the slurs that sometimes stung me directly—a process marked only occasionally by outright hostility.

6   A trend that began about 10 years ago in Lincoln Heights seems to have hit a critical point now. It's similar to the ethnic tug-of-war of yesteryear, but different colors, different words are involved. Today Chinese and Vietnamese are displacing the Latinos who, by choice or circumstance, had Lincoln Heights virtually to themselves for two solid generations.

7   Evidence of the transition is clear.

8   The bank where I opened my first meager savings account in the late 1950s has changed hands. It's now the East-West Federal Bank, an Asian-owned enterprise.

9   The public library on Workman Street, where I checked out *Charlotte's Web* with my first library card, abounds with signs of the new times: It's called "La Biblioteca del Pueblo de Lincoln Heights," and on the door there's a notice advising that the building is closed because of the Oct. 1 earthquake; it's written in Chinese.

10 The white, wood-frame house on Griffin Avenue that I once lived in is now owned by a Chinese family.

11 What used to be a Latino-run mortuary at the corner of Sichel Street and North Broadway is now the Chung Wah Funeral Home.

12 A block down the street from the funeral home is a *panaderia*, a bakery. As I would listen to radio reports of the U.S. war in faraway Indochina while walking from class at Lincoln High School, I often used to drop in the *panaderia* for a snack.

13 The word *panaderia*, now faded and chipped, is still painted on the shop window that fronts North Broadway. But another sign, a gleaming plastic one, hangs above the window. The sign proclaims that it is a Vietnamese-Chinese bakery. The proprietor, Sam Lee, bought the business less than a year ago. With a wave of his arm, he indicates that *La Opinion*, the Spanish-language daily newspaper, is still for sale on the counter. Two signs hang side-by-side behind the counter announcing in Spanish and in Chinese that cakes are made to order for all occasions.

14 Out on North Broadway, Fidel Farrillas sells *raspadas* (snow-cones) from his pushcart. He has lived and worked in Lincoln Heights "for 30 years and a pinch more," he says, his voice nearly whistling through two gold-framed teeth. He has seen the neighborhood change. Twice.

15 Like many older Latinos he remembers the tension felt between *los gringos y la raza* years ago—even though most people went about their business ostensibly coexisting politely. And others who have been around as long will tell an inquiring reporter scratching away in his notebook, "We're going out of our way to treat the *chinos* nice—better than the *gringos* sometimes treated us back then." But when the notebook is closed, they're likely to whisper, "But you know, the thing is, they smell funny, and they talk behind your back, and they are so arrogant—the way they're buying up everything in our neighborhood."

16 Neighborhood transitions can be tough to reconcile.

17 It isn't easy for the blue-collar Latinos of Lincoln Heights. They haven't possessed much. But they had the barrio, "a little chunk of the world where we belonged," as one described it. There may be some hard times and hard feelings ahead as *los chinos* continue to make inroads into what had been an exclusively Latino enclave. But there are hopeful signs as well.

18 On one recent Saturday afternoon a Latino fifth-grader, wearing the same type of hightop tennis shoes I wore as a 10-year-old on that same street corner, strode up to Señor Farrillas' snow-cone pushcart. The kid pulled out a pocketful of dimes and bought two *raspadas*. One for himself, and one for his school chum—a Vietnamese kid. He was wearing hightops, too. They both ordered strawberry, as I recall.

APPLICATIONS FOR CRITICAL READING AND DISCUSSION

1. What is the main conflict?

2. Items for annotation:
   a. Circle the first indication of conflict and mark it with a *C*.
   b. Mark the struggle with a vertical line and an *S*.
   c. If the struggle contains multiple incidents (often indicated by time breaks or place changes), mark them by underlining key sentences and using numbers.
   d. Circle the outcome of the struggle and mark it with an *O*.
   e. If the author states the meaning of the narrative passage, circle it and mark it with an *M*.

3. Is the order based on time, space, or both?

4. Is the main purpose to inform or to persuade, or are they equally important?

EXERCISE 3

The title of the reading may suggest that Elizabeth Wong would experience success if she became the All-American Girl. But then, the question is, Would she as an adult enjoy what she had wanted as a child? Another question comes to mind: Must one relinquish one's own cultural identity in order to assume another cultural identity?

Vocabulary Preview: Write short definitions for these words as they are used in the contexts of the following passage. (The paragraph numbers are given in parentheses.) Be prepared to use the words in your own sentences.

stoically (1)

defiant (3)

maniacal (3)

kowtow (5)

pedestrian (7)

chaotic (8)

pidgin (9)

The Struggle to Be an All-American Girl
ELIZABETH WONG

1 It's still there, the Chinese school on Yale Street where my brother and I used to go. Despite the new coat of paint and the high wire fence, the school I knew 10 years ago remains remarkably, stoically the same.

2 Every day at 5 P.M., instead of playing with our fourth- and fifth-grade friends or sneaking out to the empty lot to hunt ghosts and animal bones, my brother and I had to go to Chinese school. No amount of kicking, screaming, or pleading could dissuade my mother, who was solidly determined to have us learn the language of our heritage.

3 Forcibly, she walked us the seven long, hilly blocks from our home to school, depositing our defiant tearful faces before the stern principal. My only memory of him is that he swayed on his heels like a palm tree, and he always clasped his impatient twitching hands behind his back. I recognized him as a repressed maniacal child killer, and knew that if we ever saw his hands we'd be in big trouble.

4 We all sat in little chairs in an empty auditorium. The room smelled like Chinese medicine, and imported faraway mustiness. Like ancient

mothballs or dirty closets. I hated that smell. I favored crisp new scents. Like the soft French perfume that my American teacher wore in public school.

5   Although the emphasis at the school was mainly language—speaking, reading, writing—the lessons always began with an exercise in politeness. With the entrance of the teacher, the best student would tap a bell and everyone would get up, kowtow, and chant, *"sing san ho,"* the phonetic for "How are you, teacher?"

6   Being ten years old, I had better things to learn that ideographs copied painstakingly in lines that ran right to left from the tip of a *moc but,* a real ink pen that had to be held in an awkward way if blotches were to be avoided. After all, I could do the multiplication tables, name the satellites of Mars, and write reports on "Little Women" and "Black Beauty." Nancy Drew, my favorite book heroine, never spoke Chinese.

7   The language was a source of embarrassment. More times than not, I had tried to disassociate myself from the nagging loud voice that followed me wherever I wandered in the nearby American supermarket outside Chinatown. The voice belonged to my grandmother, a fragile woman in her seventies who could outshout the best of the street vendors. Her humor was raunchy, her Chinese rhythmless, patternless. It was quick, it was loud, it was unbeautiful. It was not like the quiet, lilting romance of French or the gentle refinement of the American South. Chinese sounded pedestrian. Public.

8   In Chinatown, the coming and goings of hundreds of Chinese on their daily tasks sounded chaotic and frenzied. I did not want to be thought of as mad, as talking gibberish. When I spoke English, people nodded at me, smiled sweetly, said encouraging words. Even the people in my culture would cluck and say that I'd do well in life. "My, doesn't she move her lips fast," they would say, meaning that I'd be able to keep up with the world outside Chinatown.

9   My brother was even more fanatical than I about speaking English. He was especially hard on my mother, criticizing her, often cruelly, for her pidgin speech—smatterings of Chinese scattered like chop suey in her conversation. "It's not 'What it is' Mom," he'd say in exasperation. "It's 'What *is* it, what *is* it, what *is* it!'" Sometimes Mom might leave out an occasional "the" or "a," or perhaps a verb of being. He would stop her in mid-sentence: "Say it again, Mom. Say it right." When he tripped over his own tongue, he'd blame it on her: "See, Mom, it's all your fault. You set a bad example."

10   After two years of writing with a *moc but* and reciting words with multiples of meanings, I finally was granted a cultural divorce. I was permitted to stop Chinese school.

11   I thought of myself as multicultural. I preferred tacos to egg rolls; I enjoyed Cinco de Mayo more than Chinese New Year.

12   At last, I was one of you; I wasn't one of them.

13   Sadly, I still am.

APPLICATIONS FOR CRITICAL READING AND DISCUSSION

1. What is the main conflict?

2. Items for annotation:
   a. Circle the first indication of conflict and mark it with a *C*.
   b. Mark the struggle with a vertical line and an *S*.
   c. If the struggle contains multiple incidents (often indicated by time breaks or place changes), mark them by underlining key sentences and using numbers.
   d. Circle the outcome of the struggle and mark it with an *O*.
   e. If the author states the meaning of the narrative passage, circle it and mark it with an *M*.

3. Is the order based on time, space, or both?

4. Is the main purpose to inform or to persuade?

EXERCISE 4

In this narrative passage from her celebrated book *I Know Why the Caged Bird Sings,* Maya Angelou introduces you to people and situations from her childhood. She also introduces you to a full range of her emotions, from reverential love to bitter anger. Early mornings and late evenings frame the passage, but they represent more than just the time of day.

Cotton-Picking Time
MAYA ANGELOU

1 Each year I watched the field across from the Store turn caterpillar green, then gradually frosty white. I knew exactly how long it would be before the big wagons would pull into the front yard and load on the cotton pickers at daybreak to carry them to the remains of slavery's plantations.

2 During the picking season my grandmother would get out of bed at four o'clock (she never used an alarm clock) and creak down to her knees and chant in a sleep-filled voice, "Our Father, thank you for letting me see this New Day. Thank you that you didn't allow the bed I lay on last night to be my cooling board, nor my blanket my winding sheet. Guide my feet this day along the straight and narrow, and help me to put a bridle on my tongue. Bless this house, and everybody in it. Thank you, in the name of your Son, Jesus Christ, Amen."

3 Before she had quite arisen, she called our names and issued orders, and pushed her large feet into homemade slippers and across the bare lye-washed wooden floor to light the coal-oil lamp.

4 The lamplight in the Store gave a soft make-believe feeling to our world which made me want to whisper and walk about on tiptoe. The odors of onions and oranges and kerosene had been mixing all night and wouldn't be disturbed until the wooded slat was removed from the door and the early morning air forced its way in with the bodies of people who had walked miles to reach the pickup place.

5 "Sister, I'll have two cans of sardines."

6 "I'm gonna work so fast today I'm gonna make you look like you standing still."

7 "Lemme have a hunk uh cheese and some sody crackers."

8 "Just gimme a coupla them fat peanut paddies." That would be from a picker who was taking his lunch. The greasy brown paper sack was stuck behind the bib of his overalls. He'd use the candy as a snack before the noon sun called the workers to rest.

9 In those tender mornings the Store was full of laughing, joking, boasting and bragging. One man was going to pick two hundred pounds of cotton, and another three hundred. Even the children were promising to bring home fo' bits and six bits.

10 The champion picker of the day before was the hero of the dawn. If he prophesied that the cotton in today's field was going to be sparse and stick to the bolls like glue, every listener would grunt a hearty agreement.

11 The sound of the empty cotton sacks dragging over the floor and the murmurs of waking people were sliced by the cash register as we rang up the five-cent sales.

12 If the morning sounds and smells were touched with the supernatural, the late afternoon had all the features of the normal Arkansas life. In the dying sunlight the people dragged, rather than their empty cotton sacks.

13 Brought back to the Store, the pickers would step out of the backs of trucks and fold down, dirt-disappointed, to the ground. No matter how much they had picked, it wasn't enough. Their wages wouldn't even get them out of debt to my grandmother, not to mention the staggering bill that waited on them at the white commissary downtown.

14 The sounds of the new morning had been replaced with grumbles about cheating houses, weighted scales, snakes, skimpy cotton and dusty rows. In later years I was to confront the stereotyped picture of gay song-singing cotton pickers with such inordinate rage that I was told even by fellow Blacks that my paranoia was embarrassing. But I had seen the fingers cut by the mean little

cotton bolls, and I had witnessed the backs and shoulders and arms and legs resisting any further demands.

15   Some of the workers would leave their sacks at the Store to be picked up the following morning, but a few had to take them home for repairs. I winced to picture them sewing the coarse material under a coal-oil lamp with fingers stiffening from the day's work. In too few hours they would have to walk back to Sister Henderson's Store, get vittles and load, again, onto the trucks. Then they would face another day of trying to earn enough for the whole year with the heavy knowledge that they were going to end the season as they started it. Without the money or credit necessary to sustain a family for three months. In cotton-picking time the late afternoons revealed the harshness of Black Southern life, which in the early morning had been softened by nature's blessing of grogginess, forgetfulness and the soft lamplight.

APPLICATIONS FOR CRITICAL READING AND DISCUSSION

1. What is the main conflict?

2. Items for annotation:
   a. Circle the first indication of conflict and mark it with a *C*.
   b. Mark the struggle with a vertical line and an *S*.
   c. If the struggle contains multiple incidents (often indicated by time breaks or place changes), mark them by underlining key sentences and using numbers.
   d. Circle the outcome of the struggle and mark it with an *O*.
   e. If the author states the meaning of the narrative passage, circle it and mark it with an *M*.

3. Is the order based on time, space, or both?

4. Is the main purpose to inform or to persuade?

5. Name the different feelings expressed or implied by the author.

EXERCISE 5

Tim Rutten is a journalist, but this is one article that was not assigned by his editor. Instead, it came to him under the cover of darkness in the form of two menacing individuals with drawn guns. Had the action developed in a slightly different direction, his life could have ended as an obituary statistic, and this account would have been written (much more sketchily) by someone else.

Vocabulary Preview: Write in short definitions for these words as they are used in the contexts of the following passage. (The paragraph numbers are given in parentheses.) Be prepared to use the words in your own sentences.

cohabitation (1)

precludes (1)

scan (3)

contriving (5)

solicitous (35)

essential (41)

Face to Face with Guns and the Young Men Who Use Them
TIM RUTTEN

1 My wife was out that Wednesday evening and, too tired to cook, I decided on one of those small self-indulgences civilized cohabitation often precludes: pizza and a televised hockey game. I phoned for the pizza and was told I could pick it up in 20 minutes.

2 Ours is an older Spanish-style house with a detached garage at the back of the property. You have to step out on the sidewalk, then through a gate to reach the steps leading up to the service porch door.

3 Like most city-dwellers, I'm cautious. I scan the street and sidewalk for anything—or anyone—unusual before pulling into the garage. That night was no exception. But, as I walked out of the garage, pizza in hand, a burly, stubble-cheeked young man in a stocking cap and dark nylon windbreaker stepped out of the tall shrub at the edge of the parkway and put the barrel of his pistol between my eyes.

4 "Give it up, mother—————," he snarled. "Give it up."

5 "Hey," I said, "just take it." As I spoke, I set the cardboard pizza box on the lip of the planter that runs along the sidewalk toward our gate, contriving as I did so to toss my house keys into a nearby rose bush.

6 "Where's your money? Where's your money?" he barked.

7 "It's in my wallet. It's in my wallet," I said.

8 By that time, he had slid around behind me, put his gun to the back of my neck and begun to go through my pants pockets.

9 "Where's your wallet?" he asked. Perhaps he was nervous; perhaps he thought I was slow. Everything he said during our encounter was repeated; instinctively, I did the same.

10 "It's in my back pocket."

11 I felt it being snatched away.

12 "Where's the rest of your money?"

13 "I don't have any more money. That's it."

14 "Where's your watch?"

15 "Here, on my wrist," I replied, extending my left arm sideways.

16 At that moment, his companion appeared. He was shorter and rather slight. He had a thin mustache and wore a denim jacket. In his left hand was an outsize blue steel revolver. Even in that dim light, his dark eyes glinted like polished glass, and his arms and legs twitched unexpectedly, as if attached to unseen wires.

17 "This one," I thought, "is going to kill me."

18 "Where's the watch? Where's the watch?" he hissed. And then, his voice rising: "Stop looking at us. Stop looking at us."

19 He may have been loaded, but he wasn't stupid. I've been around enough criminal trials to know that one of the reasons victims of armed

attacks are seldom able to firmly identify their assailants is that their attention naturally focuses on the guns, rather than on the people holding them. In those brief moments, I made a conscious effort to note what I could of this pair's faces.

20   "I'm not looking at you," I lied, bending my head forward as the big one ripped the watch from my wrist.

21   "Get down. Get down," the thin one snarled. And, as I went to my knees, he grabbed my glasses and tossed them onto the parkway lawn.

22   "Down. Down," he said.

23   By that time, I was flat on my face on the sidewalk. I felt its grit against my forehead. I felt the big one's gun at the back of my head and the thin one's revolver at my left temple.

24   I took a deep breath and thought, "I am going to die."

25   I thought of my wife and of my soul.

26   "This is going to kill Leslie." And then: "Lord, have mercy on me, a sinner."

27   "What's this?" the big one growled.

28   I rolled my head to the right, feeling, as I did, the barrels of their guns digging into my head.

29   "It's a pizza," I said.

30   "We'll take it," the big one snapped.

31   And, suddenly—wallet, watch and pizza in hand—they were off in a clatter of footsteps down the darkened street.

32   I turned to see their shadows get into a car and speed away.

33   I had been spared, but by what? Mercy? A short attention span? Hunger?

34   "Good Lord," I thought, "to have your life saved by a pizza. How peculiar. I saw eternity; they saw food."

35   I got to my feet, fished around for the house keys, let myself in and called 911. The operator took a quick description of the robbers and said a police car would arrive shortly. I poured myself a stiff drink and, in less than five minutes, two efficient, solicitous uniformed officers of the Los Angeles Police Department were there. They took a report and told me that the "important thing" was that nobody had been hurt.

36   "But geez," one officer said as they left, "taking your pizza—that's rough."

37   I agreed.

38   A few days later, a Wilshire Division detective telephoned to collect additional details. He said my description of the pair's methods suggested they might be the same men who had committed a number of robberies in the neighborhood over the past few months. He asked whether I was willing to go down to the station and look through mug books.

39   So, early on last Monday's gray morning I sat in the bustling detectives' room at the Wilshire station looking through album-sized books entitled "Parolees" and "Robbery #10," "Robbery #11" and "Robbery #12." Most of the pictures were of young men—some of them defiant, some of them dazed, some of them obviously frightened; an astonishing number of them actually were children.

40   To turn those pages and study the photographs there is to be borne along on a melancholy current that, like that of Blake's dreary Thames, seems to "mark in every human face, marks of weakness, marks of woe."

41   Together, these young men are indeed a kind of river—one that is out of control, one that is gnawing at the foundations of things we hold essential: our freedom to move about; the fruits of labor; our own lives and those of the people we hold dear. Some day, all of us will have to confront this river at its source and plumb the depths of it discontent.

42   For the moment, all we can do is look at mug shots and stick our fingers in the dike.

APPLICATIONS FOR CRITICAL READING AND DISCUSSION

1. What is the main conflict?

2. Items for annotation:
   a. Circle the first indication of conflict and mark it with a *C*.
   b. Mark the struggle with a vertical line and an *S*.
   c. If the struggle contains multiple incidents (often indicated by time breaks or place changes), mark them by underlining key sentences and using numbers.
   d. Circle the outcome of the struggle and mark it with an *O*.
   e. If the author states the meaning of the narrative passage, circle it and mark it with an *M*.

3. Is the order based on time or space?

4. Is the main purpose to inform or to persuade?

The Reading Connection from Classroom Sources

EXERCISE 6

Demonstration Using the DCODE Worksheet

Working in heavy industry as a laborer often carries the risk of personal injury because one is surrounded by potentially harmful equipment and substances. Those who work in such jobs are aware of the jeopardy and comfort themselves by noting that accidents seldom occur. But they do occur, suddenly and unexpectedly. Student James Hutchinson knows, for he was a victim of a painful accident.

WORKSHEET
Writing in DCODE

NAME: James Hutchinson

SECTION: _____   CHAPTER: _____   DATE: _____

Delve   Generate your topic, or ideas for your topic, by delving into your subject area through:

- *Freewriting*—writing sentence after sentence, nonstop and spontaneously.
- *Brainstorming*—jotting down answers to Who? What? Where? When? Why? and How? and then listing words and phrases in relation to those answers.
- *Clustering*—connecting bubbled ideas with lines to show strings of relationships, producing each new bubble item in response to the question, What comes to mind?
- *Combining* any of these approaches, as directed by your instructor.

Freewriting

On the evening swing shift at the tire recapping plant where I was working we were recapping large off road tires. I had to head the rubber in a large tank filled with boiling, steaming water. When I started working there, I gave a lot of thought to all of the heavy equipment and the substances around me, but later I became used to them and I just did my job. But on that day something terrible happened. While the platform was in the up position, the chain that lowers it into the tank snapped. This sent the heavy platform loaded with strips of rubber into the tank. That sent the steaming waster out in waves, and it hit me above the waste and on the backside. It took my break away and I passed out. I could only stand there and scream. Then I fell down and waited for the medics to arrive. I'll never forget it. It was the most painful thing that I have ever experienced.

Brainstorming

    Who? me, co-workers, paramedics
    What? accident, boiling water
    Where? tire recapping plant
    When? Jan. 1986
    Why? defective equipment
    How? equipment broke and spilled galls of boiling water on me
    Conflict? survival in industrial accident
    Meaning? greatest pain I ever experienced

Clustering

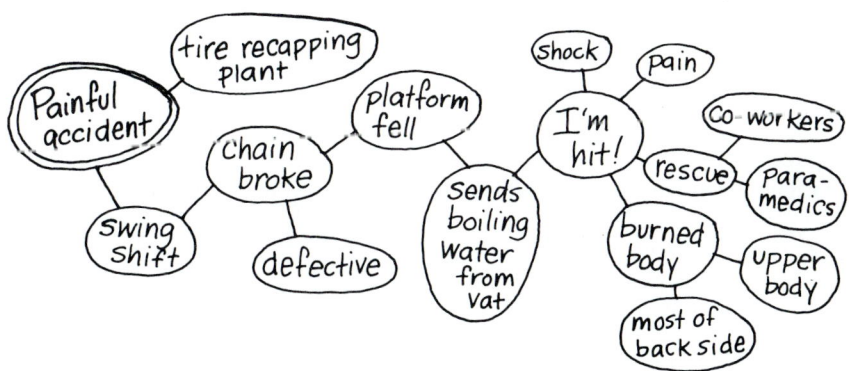

WORKSHEET: Writing in DCODE

Concentrate Concentrate your work by stating your topic in one sentence that is not too broad, narrow, or vague to be developed. Base this sentence (which may become the topic sentence for your paragraph or the thesis for your essay) on an idea emerging from the **Delve** stage. You may have to try several statements here before you formulate one that is best for your writing task. Be sure that your final statement covers your assignment or intent and specifies both your subject (what you are writing about) and treatment (what aspect you will focus on). Label the *subject* and *treatment* parts.

              subject   treatment

<u>The greatest pain I ever experienced came as the result of a work accident in which I received severe burns.</u>

Organize Complete an outline or a cluster, as directed by your instructor. The cluster should be a section from, or a refined version of, the **Delve** clustering. Regardless of the strategy you use, the organizational pattern should indicate a division of your topic into parts that will, in turn, be further subdivided for support as necessary to address a particular audience on your concentrated topic.

```
I.   Chain broke
     A. Defective equipment
     B. No warning

II.  Platform falls
     A. Drops rubber strips
     B. Strips crash into vat

III. Boiling water surges
     A. Sudden
     B. No time to react

IV.  Water burned me
     A. Above waist
     B. Backside

V.   People helped
     A. Co-workers
     B. Paramedics

VI.  Terrible pain
     A. Then
     B. Always in memory
```

Draft On separate paper, write and then revise your assignment as many times as necessary for **c**oherence, **l**anguage (usage, tone, and diction), **u**nity, **e**mphasis, **s**upport, and **s**entence structure (**cluess**).

Edit Correct problems in fundamentals such as **c**apitalization, **o**missions, **p**unctuation, and **s**pelling (**cops**). Before writing the final draft, read your paper aloud to discover oversights and awkwardness of expression.

Rough Draft (Revision and Edit)

While working the swing shift at a tire recapping plant ⊙ I had a terrible accident. I was recapping large off-road tires. I had to heat raw rubber in a large tank ~~filled with boiling water~~ prior to feeding the rubber into an extruder. While the lowering platform was in the up position ⊙ the chain snap(p)ed ⊙ sending the ^heavy platform into the tank. This ~~created~~ caused a huge wave of steaming water to ~~fly~~ surge out of the tank. The wave of water hit me just above the waist(e) on the backside. The sudden pain took by breath away. I could not move ⊙ because my cloth(e)s were steaming ⊙ I could only stand there and scream. Co-workers ran to me ^my aid and tore my clothes off ⊙ ^taking skin As they did ⊙ skin came off too. I lay ^face down on the ^plant floor ^naked ~~in shock~~, shaking ~~and waited for the paramedics to arrive.~~ for what seemed like an eternity until the paramedics arrived to transport me to the hospital. The painful experience is still with me as a nightmare memory.

Final Draft

Pain Unforgettable
James Hutchinson

One evening in 1986 while I was working the swing shift at the General Tire Recapping Plant, I experienced the greatest pain of my life due to a terrible accident. I was recapping large off-road tires. Raw rubber was heated in a large tank prior to it being fed into an extruder. While the lowering platform was in the up position, the chain snapped, sending the heavy platform crashing down into the tank. This caused a huge wave of steaming water to surge out of the tank. Unfortunately, I was in its path. The wave hit me just above the waist on my backside. The sudden pain took my breath away. I could not move because my clothes were steaming; I could only stand there and scream. Co-workers ran to my aid and stripped the hot clothing from my body, taking skin as they did. I lay face down on the plant floor, naked and shaking for what seemed an eternity until the paramedics arrived to transport me to the hospital. The painful experience is still with me as a nightmare memory.

EXERCISE 7

When the manager of a business must choose between being fair to an employee or risking bad public relations, the employee may have to lose face—and a considerable portion of his or her paycheck.

> The Customer Is Always Right
> Jack Mullins
>
> "The customer is always right" is a saying that took on new meaning for me soon after I acquired my first job, as attendant in a gas station. It was a Union station, and the manager regularly reminded us workers that we were "Minutemen" and that cheerful, fast service was our reputation. After all, he was bucking the trend toward all self-service stations. I soon developed a routine for quick service—insert nozzle, start gas, check oil, clean windshield, stop gas, remove nozzle, collect money or process credit card. At times the unexpected would occur and upset my routine. The "unexpected" on this occasion was a co-worker telling me he couldn't work the next day, and I would have to work a double shift. The result was that I skipped one part of my routine: the gas had cut off automatically, but I did not remove the nozzle. After I looked at the pump tab, collected the money, and gave the change, the customer headed out. I had just turned to walk away when I heard the sounds of metal against metal, the snap of the hose, and the gushing of gas. Immediately the manager appeared and shut off the main gas valve. Then the customer was out of his car, pointing to a shallow, two-inch scratch in his paint job—a faded paint job that already had several much larger scratches. The manager apologized, said I was new, and promised "we" would pay when the customer brought in an estimate. After the customer left, the manager explained that I would pay out of my wages, and I certainly didn't object. But a few days later, the customer returned with an estimate for three hundred and forty-two dollars. The manager didn't blink as he wrote out a check. After the man left, the manager said to me, "It's public relations. I couldn't argue with him." I worked for more than a month to pay for the scratch. "The customer is always right" may be a necessary slogan, but at times the customer may be partly wrong.

APPLICATIONS FOR CRITICAL READING AND DISCUSSION

1. What is the main conflict?

2. Items for annotation:
    a. Circle the first indication of conflict and mark it with a *C*.
    b. Mark the struggle with a vertical line and an *S*.
    c. If the struggle contains multiple incidents (often indicated by time breaks or place changes), mark them by underlining key sentences and using numbers.
    d. Circle the outcome of the struggle and mark it with an *O*.
    e. If the author states the meaning of the narrative passage, circle it and mark it with an *M*.

3. Is the order based on time, space, or both?

4. Is the main purpose to inform or to persuade?

EXERCISE 8

Sandra Pei was born in Singapore, and though she lives contentedly in America, she fondly remembers her relatives "back home." There, in the traditional Chinese culture, the family had tremendous influence in all matters, even marriage. The prospects for a loveless marriage were there, but sometimes, beautifully, "love happened," even following great disappointment.

Love Happened
Sandra Pei

Love in our dreams may be something that takes place in a moment, at first sight. We meet the gaze of someone across a crowded room and that's it—for life. For most people falling in love for life is much less spectacular. It may even follow disappointments. My Uncle George and Aunt Hua had that experience, and they are the leading characters in my favorite love story of all time.

Uncle George lived in Singapore when he fell deeply in love. At least he thought so. As a member of a traditional Chinese family, he worked hard and established himself in business before he would permit himself to think about marriage. When he was thirty, he was finally secure, and ready; so he started looking around and discovered that just next door was a beautiful young single woman. They exchanged glances, and being sure that he was in love, he asked his parents to talk to her parents about a wedding.

In about two months, the arrangements had been made and Uncle George was content. He would have his beautiful bride, and life would be perfect. He worked with his family and made all the plans for a new house. He never talked directly to the girl, but he continued to look at her as she worked about her house, often accompanied by her older, plain sister.

On the day of the wedding, Uncle George was very happy, and when the music played, he entered the temple to accept his bride. As he joined her at the alter, he shyly turned to look at her lovely face. But to his consternation, he saw instead the plain sister. Someone had switched brides, and he was furious in his protest.

The families quickly called a conference to solve the problem, and tea was served amid much talking and even yelling. The other family had switched brides with the permission of Uncle George's family. They all wanted the older daughter to get married first. They argued and argued and argued with Uncle George. The prospective bride was tearful and embarrassed. Uncle George gave in and married the plain daughter, *Hua*.

The word *Hua* means flower in Chinese, and that's what she was, a flower that as Uncle George's wife, blossomed and, to him, became very beautiful. They have had a loving marriage for more than thirty years now. To Uncle George love was not something that he saw; it was something that happened—with a little help.

APPLICATIONS FOR CRITICAL READING AND DISCUSSION

1. What is the main conflict?

2. Items for annotation:
   a. Circle the first indication of conflict and mark it with a *C*.
   b. Mark the struggle with a vertical line and an *S*.
   c. If the struggle contains multiple incidents (often indicated by time breaks or place changes), mark them by underlining key sentences and using numbers.
   d. Circle the outcome of the struggle and mark it with an *O*.
   e. If the author states the meaning of the narrative passage, circle it and mark it with an *M*.

3. Is the order based on time or space,?

4. Is the main purpose to inform or to persuade?

Suggested Topics for Writing Narratives

Notice that each of the suggested topics that follows concerns the writing of a narrative that has meaning beyond the story itself; in other words, the narrative will be used to inform or persuade in relation to a clearly stated idea.

General Topics

1. Write a narrative based on a topic sentence such as this: "One experience showed me what _____ (pain, fear, anger, love, sacrifice, dedication, joy, sorrow, shame, pride) was really like."

2. Write a simple narration about a fire, a riot, an automobile accident, a rescue, shoplifting, or some other unusual happening that you witnessed.

3. Write a personal-experience paper about falling in love, cheating (or being tempted to cheat), receiving important recognition, being betrayed or abandoned, or becoming independent.

4. Most families have stories they tell at family gatherings about funny, strange, or even bizarre occurrences pertaining to themselves or relatives. Retell one of these stories.

5. Write a personal-experience paper about an occurrence that was so poignant that you will never forget it or the surrounding circumstances and environment. You might consider moments of extreme happiness or sorrow. You might write about the occasion when you learned of the death of someone close to you or the death of a celebrity. You should discuss where you were, what you were doing, what the surroundings were, how others reacted, and how you reacted.

6. Write a narrative that supports (or opposes) the idea of a familiar saying such as one of these:

You never know who a friend is till you need one.	Never give advice to a friend.
A bird in the hand is worth two in the bush.	If it isn't broken, don't fix it.
It isn't what you know, it's who you know.	Nice guys finish last.
A fool and his money are soon parted.	Every person has a price.

A person who is absent is soon forgotten.

Better to be alone than to be in bad company.

A person in a passion rides a mad horse.

Borrowing is the mother of trouble.

A person who marries for money earns it.

The person who lies down with dogs gets up with fleas.

You get what you pay for.

Haste makes waste.

The greatest remedy for anger is delay.

A person full of himself is empty.

To forget a wrong is the best revenge.

Money is honey, my little sonny,
And a rich man's joke is always funny.

Reading-Related Topics

"Language Set Me Free"

1. This passage is an epiphany—a moment that reveals an important truth (through setup, incident, and understanding). Helen Keller went through that one experience, and her life was transformed. Using this passage as a model, write your own epiphany about the first time you knew or understood something about a concept such as love, caring, or family. Or write about the first time you realized you could read or learn another language.

"Los Chinos Discover el Barrio"

2. Write a narrative about changes in your neighborhood.

3. Write a narrative about an incident that reflected cultural tension in your school or neighborhood.

"The Struggle to Be an All-American Girl"

4. As a reflection on this piece, discuss one event that reveals how you or someone you know has (1) lost non-American family cultural identity, (2) become closer to non-American family cultural identity, or (3) achieved a blend of identity with non-American family culture and American culture.

5. Write a narrative in which you found your cultural values challenged.

6. Write a narrative in which you reveal the differences between generations in your family or that of a family you know.

"Cotton-Picking Time"

7. The author reveres her grandmother, as illustrated in the first part of this passage. Using that as a model, write a narrative in which you show your admiration for someone.

8. Write a narrative in which you present another group of workers who are exploited in the fields, factories, or streets.

"Face to Face with Guns and the Young Men Who Use Them"

9. If you have been mugged, threatened, or assaulted, give a narrative account of the incident, using this article as a model. Unify your writing around one feeling, such as anger or fear.

"Pain Unforgettable"

10. Use this student narrative for a model as you develop Suggestion 1 under the preceding "General Topics" section.

"The Customer Is Always Right"

11. Write your own narrative in which you discuss how you have had to lose face in order to achieve company goals in public relations. For subject material, you might want to consider incidents involving company return and refund policies.

"Love Happened"

12. Write a narrative about an unusual or chance encounter that led to a satisfying relationship or about a blind date that "worked out."

13. Write a narrative about a marriage based on something other than love but that turned to love.

"The Blues Abroad"

14. Using the paragraph on B. B. King as a model for organization, write a narrative account of the first few minutes of a concert you attended, showing how the audience became involved in the event, or present the factors that negatively influenced the audience so it did *not* become involved.

15. Pretend that you are a Russian music lover at the B. B. King concert in Moscow and write a narrative about how you became involved in the audience response.

Writer's Checklist

Apply these ideas to your writing as you work with **DCODE**.

1. Consider personal experience for good subject material.
2. Develop your ideas so there is actually a plot structure in segments from conflict to outcome.
3. Remember that most narratives are presented in chronological order; space order can also provide coherence.
4. Use dialogue when appropriate.
5. Use specific descriptions. Make your readers experience—see, smell, taste, hear, touch—vicariously.
6. Give details concerning action.
7. Be consistent with point of view and verb tense.
8. Keep in mind that most narratives written as college assignments will have an expository purpose (they explain a specified idea).
9. Consider working with a short time frame for short writing assignments. The scope would usually be no more than one incident of brief duration for one paragraph. For example, writing about an entire graduation ceremony might be too complicated, but concentrating on the moment when you walked forward to receive the diploma or the moment when the relatives and friends come down on the field could work very well.

 **Journal-Entry Suggestions**

1. Select some of the unused "Reading-Related Topics" suggestions above and use them for journal topics.

2. Write a reaction to one or more "Reading Connection" selections. Agree, disagree, apply the statements to your own experiences, indicate the value of such statements, or explain why your were surprised, shocked, disgusted, pleased, or whatever, by the material.

3. Invent statements (using narration if appropriate) to support headlines from *Weekly World News*:

    "Hang Glider Attacked by Kill-Crazy Eagle!"
    "Woman Whips Tough Trucker in Arm Wrestling Match—So He Kills Himself!"
    "Farmer Shoots 23-lb. Grasshopper!"
    "Your Pet May Be a Space Alien!"
    "You May Be a Space Alien!"
    "Bride's Kisses Make 80 Guests Sick!"
    "Man Jailed for Snoring!"
    "Mystery of the Mummy's Curse Solved!"
    "Psychic Pops Popcorn with His Mind!"
    "Snowbound Motorist Eats His Own Clothes!"

WORKSHEET
Writing in DCODE

NAME:_____

SECTION:_____ CHAPTER:_____ DATE:_____

Delve Generate your topic, or ideas for your topic, by delving into your subject area through:

- *Freewriting*—writing sentence after sentence, nonstop and spontaneously.
- *Brainstorming*—jotting down answers to Who? What? Where? When? Why? and How? and then listing words and phrases in relation to those answers.
- *Clustering*—connecting bubbled ideas with lines to show strings of relationships, producing each new bubble item in response to the question, What comes to mind?
- *Combining* any of these approaches, as directed by your instructor.

WORKSHEET: Writing in DCODE

Concentrate   Concentrate your work by stating your topic in one sentence that is not too broad, narrow, or vague to be developed. Base this sentence (which may become the topic sentence for your paragraph or the thesis for your essay) on an idea emerging from the **Delve** stage. You may have to try several statements here before you formulate one that is best for your writing task. Be sure that your final statement covers your assignment or intent and specifies both your subject (what you are writing about) and treatment (what aspect you will focus on). Label the *subject* and *treatment* parts.

Organize   Complete an outline or a cluster, as directed by your instructor. The cluster should be a section from, or a refined version of, the **Delve** clustering. Regardless of the strategy you use, the organizational pattern should indicate a division of your topic into parts that will, in turn, be further subdivided for support as necessary to address a particular audience on your concentrated topic.

Draft   On separate paper, write and then revise your assignment as many times as necessary for **c**oherence, **l**anguage (usage, tone, and diction), **u**nity, **e**mphasis, **s**upport, and **s**entence structure (**cluess**).

Edit   Correct problems in fundamentals such as **c**apitalization, **o**missions, **p**unctuation, and **s**pelling (**cops**). Before writing the final draft, read your paper aloud to discover oversights and awkwardness of expression.

Description: Moving Through Space

4

> "My task... is, by the power of the written word, to make you hear, to make you feel—it is, before all, to make you see. That—and no more—is everything.
>
> —Joseph Conrad

What does the word *description* mean? What is the difference between objective and subjective description? What do you do in order to achieve emphasis in descriptive writing? What is point of view? What is the main basis for establishing order in descriptive writing?

Defining Description

Description means the use of words to represent the appearance or nature of something. Often called a word picture, description attempts to present its subject for the mind's eye. In doing so, it does not merely become an indifferent camera; instead, it selects details that will convey a good depiction. Just what details the descriptive writer selects will depend on several factors, especially the type of description and the dominant impression in the passage.

Types of Description

On the basis of treatment of subject material, description is customarily divided into two types: objective and subjective.

Effective objective description presents the subject clearly and directly as it exists outside the realm of feelings. If you are explaining the function of the heart, the characteristics of a computer chip, or the renovation of a manufacturing facility, your description would probably feature specific, impersonal details. Most technical and scientific writing is objective in that sense. It is likely to be practical and utilitarian, making little use of speculation and poetic technique.

Effective subjective description is also concerned with clarity and it may be direct, but it conveys a feeling about the subject and sets a mood while making a point. Because most expression involves personal views, even when it explains by analysis, subjective description (often called "emotional description") has a broader range of uses than objective description.

Descriptive passages can have a combination of objective and subjective description; only the larger context of the passage will reveal the main intent. The following description of a baseball begins with objective treatment and then moves to subjective.

> It weighs just over five ounces and measures between 2.86 and 2.94 inches in diameter. It is made of a composition-cork nucleus encased in two thin layers of rubber, one black and one red, surrounded by 121 yards of tightly wrapped blue-gray wool yarn, 45 yards of white wool yarn, 53 more yards of blue-gray wool yarn, 150 yards of fine cotton yarn, a coat of rubber cement, and a cowhide (formerly horsehide) exterior, which is held together with 216 slightly raised red cotton stitches. Printed certifications, endorsements, and outdoor advertising spherically attest to its authenticity. Like most institutions, it is considered inferior in its present form to its ancient archetypes, and in this case the complaint is probably justified; on occasion in recent years it has actually been known to come apart under the demands of its brief but rigorous active career. Baseballs are assembled and hand-stitched in Taiwan (before this year the work was done in Haiti, and before 1973 in Chicopee, Massachusetts), and contemporary pitchers claim that there is a tangible variation in the size and feel of the balls that now come into play in a single game; a true peewee is treasured by hurlers, and its departure from the premises, by fair means or foul, is secretly mourned. But never mind: any baseball

is beautiful. No other small package comes as close to the ideal in design and utility. It is a perfect object for a man's hand. Pick it up and it instantly suggests its purpose; it is meant to be thrown a considerable distance—thrown hard and with precision. Its feel and heft are the beginning of the sport's critical dimensions; if it were a fraction of an inch larger or smaller, a few centigrams heavier or lighter, the game of baseball would be utterly different. Hold a baseball in your hand. As it happens, this one is not brand-new. Here, just to one side of the curved surgical welt of stitches, there is a pale-green grass smudge, darkening on one edge almost to black—the mark of an old infield play, a tough grounder now lost in memory. Feel the ball, turn it over in your hand; hold it across the seam or the other way, with the seam just to the side of your middle finger. Speculation stirs. You want to get outdoors and throw this spare and sensual object to somebody or, at the very least, watch somebody else throw it. The game has begun.

objective treatment moving to subjective treatment

Roger Angell, "On the Ball"

The following subjective description, also on the subject of baseball, is designed to move the emotions while informing.

The Babe was a bundle of paradoxes. Somehow one of the most appealing things about him was that he was neither built, nor did he look like an athlete. He did not even look like a ballplayer. Although he stood six feet two inches and weighed 220 pounds, his body was pear-shaped and even when in tip-top condition he had a bit of a belly. His barrel always seemed too much for his legs, which tapered into a pair of ankles as slender almost as those of a girl. The great head perched upon a pair of round and unathletic shoulders, presented a moon of a face, the feature of which was the flaring nostrils of a nose that was rather like a snout. His voice was deep and hoarse, his speech crude and earthy, his ever-ready laughter a great, rumbling gurgle that arose from the caverns of his middle. He had an eye that was abnormally quick, nerves and muscular reactions to match, a supple wrist, a murderous swing, and a gorgeously truculent, competitive spirit.

the following details relate to the paradoxes

note the emotional appeals, the subjective approach

Paul Gallico, "Babe Ruth"

Techniques of Descriptive Writing

As a writer of description, you will need to focus your work so as to emphasize a single point, establish a perspective from which to describe your subject, and position the details for coherence. The terms for these considerations are *dominant impression, point of view,* and *order*.

Dominant Impression

See if you can find the dominant impression in this functional description:

Please help me find my dog. He is a mongrel with the head of a poodle and the body of a wolf hound, and his fur is patchy and dingy-gray. He has only three legs, but despite his arthritis, he uses them pretty well to hobble around and scratch his fleas and mange. His one seeing eye is cloudy, so he runs with his head sideways. He ragged, twisted ears enable him to hear loud sounds, which startle his troubled nervous system and cause him to howl pitifully. If you give him a scrap of food, he will gum it up rapidly and try to wag his broken tail. He answers to the name of Lucky.

Of course, the dominant impression, what is being emphasized, is "misery," not "lucky." Linked closely to purpose, the dominant impression derives from a pattern of details, often involving repetition of one idea with different particulars. Word choice is of paramount importance, and that choice depends on the situation of your writing, which in turn involves your purpose for writing and your audience—two inseparable factors.

If you are eating hamburgers in a restaurant, and you say to your companion, "This food is good," your companion may understand all he or she needs to understand on the subject. After all, your companion can see you sitting there chewing the food, smacking your lips, and wiping the sauce off your chin. But if you write that sentence on a piece of paper and mail it to someone, your reader may be puzzled. Although you may know the reader fairly well, your reader may not know the meaning of "good" (to eat, to purchase for others, to sell), and "this food" (What kind? Where is it? How is it special? How is it prepared? What qualities does it have?).

In order to convey your main concern effectively to readers, you will have to give some sensory impressions, and you may use figures of speech. These sensory impressions, collectively called *imagery*, refer to that which can be experienced by the senses—what we can see, smell, taste, hear, and touch. The figures of speech involve comparisons of unlike things that, nevertheless, have something in common. We will discuss these techniques in more detail following the student work.

The imagery in this passage is italicized.

Sitting here in Harold's Hefty Burgers at midnight, I am convinced that I am eating the ultimate form of food. The *buns* are *feathery soft* to the touch but *heavy* in the hand and *soggy* inside. As I take a full-mouth, no-nonsense bite, the *melted cheese* and *juices cascade* over my fingers and make little *oil slicks* on the *vinyl table* below. I *chew noisily* and happily like a puppy at a food bowl, stopping occasionally to flush down the *rich, thick taste* of *spicy animal fat* with a *swig* from a *chilled mug* of *fizzing root beer* that *prickles* my *nose*. Over at the grill, *the smell of frying onions creeps away stealthily on invisible feet* to conquer the neighborhood, turning hundreds of ordinary *citizens* like me into drooling, stomach growling, fast food addicts, who *trudge* in from the *night like the walking dead* and *call out* the same order, time after time. "Hefty Burger." "Hefty Burger." "Hefty Burger."	topic sentence dominant impression image (touch) images (sight) image (sound) image (taste) image (taste) image (smell) figure of speech image (sight) image (sound) Dale Scott, "Hefty Burger"

note movement through time and space

In reading Dale's enthusiastic endorsement of the Hefty Burger, the reader will have no trouble in understanding the idea that Dale liked the food. Through *imagery*, Dale has involved the reader in what he has seen, smelled, heard, tasted, and touched. He has also used *figures of speech*, including these examples:

Simile: *a comparison using like or as*	"chew noisily like a puppy"
Metaphor: *a comparison using word replacement*	"feathery [instead of 'delicately'] soft"
Personification: *an expression giving human characteristics to something not human*	"smell of frying onions creeps out stealthily on invisible feet to conquer" [instead of "spreads to entice"]

Subjective description is likely to make more use of imagery, figurative language, and words rich in associations than does objective description. But just as a fine line cannot always be drawn between the objective and the subjective, a fine line cannot always be drawn between word choice in one and in the other. However, we can say with certainty that whatever the type of description, careful word choice will always be important. Consider these points about precise diction:

General and Specific Words / Abstract and Concrete Words

To move from the general to the specific is to move from the whole class or body to the individual(s); for example:

General	Specific	More Specific
food	hamburger	Hefty Burger
mess	grease	oil slicks on table
drink	soda	mug of root beer
odor	smell from grill	smell of frying onions

Words are classified as abstract or concrete depending on what they refer to. *Abstract words* refer to qualities or ideas: *good, ordinary, ultimate, truth, beauty, maturity, love.* *Concrete words* refer to a substance or things; they have reality: *onions, grease, buns, tables, food.* The specific concrete words, sometimes called *concrete particulars*, often support generalizations effectively and convince the reader of the accuracy of the account.

Never try to give all of the details in description; instead, be selective, picking only those that you need to project a dominant impression, always taking into account the knowledge and attitudes of your readers. To reintroduce an idea from the beginning of this chapter, description is not photographic. If you wish to describe a person, select the traits that will project your intended dominant impression. If you wish to describe a landscape, do not give all the details that you might find in a picture; on the contrary, pick the details that support your intended dominant impression. That extremely important dominant impression is directly linked to your purpose and is created by the judicious choice and arrangement of images, figurative language, and revealing details.

Point of View

Point of view shows the writer's relationship to the subject, thereby establishing the perspective from which the subject is described. It rarely changes within a passage. Two terms usually associated with fiction writing, *first person* and *third person*, also pertain to descriptive writing.

If you want to convey personal experience, your point of view will be *first person*, which can be either involved (a participant) or uninvolved (an observer). The involved perspective uses *I* more prominently than the uninvolved. Student Dale Scott's essay, "Hefty Burgers," uses first person, involved.

If you want to present something from a detached position, especially from geographical or historical distance (see "Babe Ruth" and "On the Ball"), your point of view will be *third person,* and you will refer to your subjects by name or by third-person pronouns such as *he, she, him, her, it, they,* and *them,* without imposing yourself as an *I* person.

Order

The point of view you select may indicate or even dictate the order in which you present descriptive details. If you are describing your immediate surroundings while taking a walk (first person, involved), the descriptive account would naturally follow spatially as well as chronologically—in other words, by space and time.

- For space, give directions to the reader, indicating *next to, below, under, above, behind, in front of, beyond, in the foreground, in the background, to the left,* or *to the right*.

- For time, use words such as *first, second, then, soon, finally, while, after, next, later, now,* and *before.*

Some descriptive pieces, such as the one on Babe Ruth, may follow an idea progression for emphasis and not move primarily through space or time. Whatever appropriate techniques you use will guide your reader and thereby aid coherence.

The three factors—dominant impression, point of view, and order—work together in a well-written description.

The dominant impression of the paragraph "On the Ball" is of an object remarkably well-designed for its purpose. The point of view is third person, and the order of the description moves from the core of the baseball outward.

The paragraph "Babe Ruth" emphasizes the idea of paradox (something that appears to be a contradiction). The details are presented from a detached point of view (third person) and appear in order from physique, to overall appearance, to behavior. The details show a person who wasn't built like an athlete and didn't look like an athlete yet is one of the most famous athletes of all time. Collectively those details emphasize "Ruth, the paradox."

Dale Scott's paragraph "Hefty Burger" can also be evaluated for all three factors:

- *Dominant impression:* good food (images, figurative language, other diction). The reader experiences the incident vicariously because of the diction. The general and abstract have been made clear by use of the specific and the concrete. Of course, not all abstract words need be tied to the concrete, nor do all general words need be transformed to the specific. As you describe, use your judgment to decide which words fit your purposes—those needed to enable your audience to understand your ideas, and to be persuaded or informed.

- *Point of view:* first person, involved

- *Order:* spatial, from restaurant table to grill, to outside, and back to restaurant

EXERCISE 1

Improve the following sentences by supplying specific and concrete words. Use images when they serve your purpose.

> EXAMPLES: The animal was restless and hungry.
> The gaunt lion paced about the cage and chewed hungrily on an old shoe.

1. The fans were happy.
2. She was in love.
3. Confusion surrounded him.
4. The traffic was congested.
5. The dessert impressed the diner.
6. The woman liked her date.
7. The salesman was obnoxious.
8. The room was cluttered.
9. His hair was unkempt.
10. The room smelled bad.

The Reading Connection

EXERCISE 2

Demonstration

This descriptive paragraph is from *Pilgrim at Tinker Creek,* a Pulitzer Prize–winning book (1974). By using a careful selection of details, Annie Dillard gives her impressions of mysteries lurking in Tinker Creek. But even with her perceptive eyes and ears, she can only be a stranger curiously observing the surface level of darkness.

Strangers to Darkness*
ANNIE DILLARD

But shadows spread, and deepened, and stayed. After thousands of years we're still strangers to darkness, fearful aliens in an enemy camp with our arms crossed over our chests. I stirred. A land turtle on the bank, started, hissed the air from its lungs and withdrew into its shell. An uneasy pink here, an unfathomable blue there, gave great suggestion of lurking beings. Things were going on. I couldn't see whether that sere rustle I heard was a distant rattlesnake, slit-eyed, or a nearby sparrow kicking in the dry flood debris slung at the foot of a willow. Tremendous action roiled

*title by author of this book

the water everywhere I looked, big action, inexplicable. A tremor welled up beside a gaping muskrat burrow in the bank and I caught my breath, but no muskrat appeared. The ripples continued to fan upstream with a steady, powerful thrust. Night was knitting over my face an eyeless mask, and I still sat transfixed. A distant airplane, a delta wing out of nightmare, made a gliding shadow on the creek's bottom that looked like a stingray cruising upstream. At once a black fin slit the pink cloud on the water, shearing it in two. The two halves merged together and seemed to dissolve before my eyes. Darkness pooled in the cleft of the creek and rose, as water collects in a well. Untamed, dreaming lights flickered over the sky. I saw hints of hulking underwater shadows, two pale splashes out of the water, and round ripples rolling close together from a blackened center.

APPLICATIONS FOR CRITICAL READING AND DISCUSSION

1. State the dominant impression in a word or phrase.
   > darkness (with mysterious action)

2. Circle key words that support the dominant impression.

3. What is the point of view—first or third person?
   > first

4. What is the order—time, space, emphasis, or a combination?
   > time with some space

5. Make boxes around the words that indicate order based on movement through space or time.

   Examples for space: *next to, below, under, above, behind, in front of, beyond, in the foreground, in the background, to the left,* and *to the right.*

   Examples for time: *first, second, then, soon, now, finally, next, while, after,* and *before.*

6. Underline the topic sentence or thesis. If one is not stated, supply a brief one here.

EXERCISE 3

Some creatures are defined more by their behavior than their appearance. A cat is such an animal. Many writers have been fascinated by the cat: its self-reliance, its smugness, its other-dimensional staring, its tranquility, its gracefulness, its curiosity, its self-centeredness, its capacity to play with prey or keeper or simply objects. Certainly Mark Twain knew the cat well. This description focuses on movement rather than on physical characteristics.

The Cat
MARK TWAIN

The cat sat down. Still looking at us in that disconcerting way, she tilted her head first to one side and then the other, inquiringly and cogitatively, the way a cat does when she has struck the unexpected and can't quite make out what she had better do about it. Next she washed one side of her face, making such an awkward and unscientific job of it that almost anybody would have seen that she was either out of practice or didn't know how. She stopped with the one side, and looked bored, and as if she had only been doing it to put in the time, and wished she could think of something else to do to put in some more time. She sat a while, blinking drowsily, then she hit an idea, and looked as if she wondered she hadn't thought of it earlier. She got up and went visiting around among the furniture and belongings, sniffing at each and every article, and elaborately examining it. If it was a chair, she examined it all around, then jumped up in it and sniffed all over its seat and its back; if it was any other thing she could examine all around, she examined it all around; if it was a chest and there was room for her between it and the wall, she crowded herself in behind there and gave it a thorough overhauling; if it was a tall thing, like a washstand, she would stand on her hind toes and stretch up as high as she could, and reach across and paw at the toilet things and try to rake them to where she could smell them; if it was the cupboard, she stood on her toes and reached up and pawed the knob; if it was the table she would squat, and measure the distance, and make a leap, and land in the wrong place, owing to newness to the business; and, part of her going too far and sliding over the edge, she would scramble, and claw at things desperately, and save herself and make good; then she would smell every thing on the table, and archly and daintily paw everything around that was movable, and finally paw something off, and skip cheerfully down and paw it some more, throwing herself into the prettiest attitudes, rising on her hind feet and curving her front paws and flirting her head this way and that and glancing down cunningly at the object, then pouncing on it and spatting it half the length of the room, and chasing it up and spatting it again, and again, and racing after it and fetching it another smack—and so on and so on; and suddenly she would tire of it and try to find some way to get to the top of the cupboard or the wardrobe, and if she couldn't she would look troubled and disappointed; and toward the last, when you could see she was getting her bearings well lodged in her head and was satisfied with the place and the arrangements, she relaxed her intensities, and got to purring a little to herself, and praisefully waving her tail between inspections—and at last she was done—done, and everything satisfactory and to her taste.

APPLICATIONS FOR CRITICAL READING AND DISCUSSION

1. State the dominant impression in a word or phrase.

2. Circle key words that support the dominant impression.

3. What is the point of view—first or third person?

4. What is the order—time, space, emphasis, or a combination?

5. Make boxes around the words that indicate order based on movement through space or time.

   Examples for space: *next to, below, under, above, behind, in front of, beyond, in the foreground, in the background, to the left,* and *to the right.*

   Examples for time: *first, second, then, soon, now, finally, next, while, after,* and *before.*

6. Underline the topic sentence or thesis. If one is not stated, supply a brief one here.

EXERCISE 4

In this passage a Native American gives his reaction at Christmastime to the area where he grew up on a Chippewa reservation. He is reacquainted with much more than the environment. His thoughts move both outward and inward as he returns home after a long absence.

Blue Winds Dancing
THOMAS S. WHITECLOUD

Christmas Eve comes in on a north wind. Snow clouds hang over the pines, and the night comes early. Walking along the railroad bed, I feel the calm peace of snow-bound forests on either side of me. I take my time; I am back in a world where time does not mean so much now. I am alone; alone but not nearly so lonely as I was back on the campus at school. Those are never lonely who love the snow and the pines, never lonely when the pines are wearing white shawls and snow crunches coldly underfoot. In the woods I know there are the tracks of deer and rabbit; I know that if I leave the rails and go into the woods, I shall find them. I walk along feeling glad because my legs are light and my feet seem to know that they are home. A deer comes out of the woods just ahead of me and stands silhouetted on the rails. The North, I feel, has welcomed me home. I watch him and am glad that I do not wish for a gun. He goes into the woods quietly, leaving only the design of his tracks in the snow. I walk on. Now and then I pass a field, white under the night sky, with houses at the far end. Smoke comes from the chimneys of the houses, and I try to tell what sort of wood each is burning by the smoke; some burn pine, others aspen, others tamarack. There is one from which comes black coal smoke that rises lazily and drifts out over the tops of the trees. I like to watch houses and try to imagine what might be happening in them.

Description: Moving Through Space

APPLICATIONS FOR CRITICAL READING AND DISCUSSION

1. State the dominant impression in a word or phrase.
   I am back into a world where time does not mean so much now.

2. Circle key words that support the dominant impression.
   I am alone;

3. What is the point of view—first or third person?
   first

4. What is the order—time, space, emphasis, or a combination?
   Time, emphasis, space

5. Make boxes around the words that indicate order based on movement through space or time. *I take my time; go into; I walk; I watch*

   Examples for space: *next to, below, under, above, behind, in front of, beyond, in the foreground, in the background, to the left,* and *to the right.*

   Examples for time: *first, second, then, soon, now, finally, next, while, after,* and *before.*

6. Underline the topic sentence or thesis. If one is not stated, supply a brief one here.
   I feel the calm peace of snow-bound forests on either side of me.

EXERCISE 5

This descriptive passage comes from *The Plum Pickers,* a novel about Hispanic migrant workers. Here, Manuel, a farmworker, looks around his "shack of misery" and considers each detail. He naturally asks, What is such a shack good for?

A Shack of Misery
RAMOND BARRIO

Manuel studied the whorls in the woodwork whirling slowly, revealed in the faint crepuscular light penetrating his shack. His cot was a slab of half-inch plywood board twenty-two inches wide and eight feet long, the width of the shack, supported by two two-by-four beams butted up against the wall at both ends beneath the side window. The shack itself was eight by twelve by seven feet high. Its roof had a slight pitch. The rain stains in the ceiling planks revealed the ease with which the rain penetrated. Except for two small panes of glass exposed near the top, most of the window at the opposite end was boarded up.

A single, old, paint-encrusted door was the only entry. No curtains. No interior paneling. Just a shack. A shack of misery. He found he was able to admire and appreciate the simplicity and the strength of the construction. He counted the upright studs, level, two feet apart, the double joists across the top supporting the roof. Cracks and knotholes aplenty, in the wall siding, let in bright chinks of light during the day and welcome wisps of clear fresh air at night. The rough planking of the siding was stained dark. The floor was only partly covered with odd sections of plywood. Some of the rough planking below was exposed, revealing cracks leading down to the cool black earth beneath. A small thick table was firmly studded to a portion of the wall opposite the door. A few small pieces of clear lumber stood bunched together, unsung, unused, unhurried, in the far corner. An overhead shelf, supported from the ceiling by a small extending perpendicular arm, containing some boxes of left-over chemicals and fertilizers, completed the furnishings in his temporary abode.

2   It was habitable.
3   He could raise his family in it.
4   If they were rabbits.

APPLICATIONS FOR CRITICAL READING AND DISCUSSION

1. State the dominant impression in a word or phrase.

2. Circle key words that support the dominant impression.

3. What is the point of view—first or third person?

4. What is the order—time, space, emphasis, or a combination?

5. Make boxes around the words that indicate order based on movement through space or time.

    Examples for space: *next to, below, under, above, behind, in front of, beyond, in the foreground, in the background, to the left,* and *to the right.*

    Examples for time: *first, second, then, soon, now, finally, next, while, after,* and *before.*

6. Underline the topic sentence or thesis. If one is not stated, supply a brief one here.

EXERCISE 6

This passage is taken from *The Joy Luck Club*, a novel of sixteen tales that reflect author Amy Tan's childhood in San Francisco. Here, in brief narrative and rich descriptive treatment, she reveals a young girl's ties to her community and her mother.

Vocabulary Preview: Write short definitions for these words as they are used in the contexts of the following passage. (The paragraph numbers are given in parentheses.) Be prepared to use the words in your own sentences.

curio (4)

imparted (4)

saffron (6)

eluded (6)

pungent (6)

embossed (6)

festive (6)

deftly (7)

grotto (8)

cuttlefish (7)

Rules of the Game
AMY TAN

1. I was six when my mother taught me the art of invisible strength. It was a strategy for winning arguments, respect from others, and eventually, though neither of us knew it at the time, chess games.

2. "Bite back your tongue," scolded my mother when I cried loudly, yanking her hand toward the store that sold bags of salted plums. At home, she said, "Wise guy, he not go against wind. In Chinese we say, Come from South, blow with wind—poom!—North will follow. Strongest wind cannot be seen."

3. The next week I bit back my tongue as we entered the store with the forbidden candies. When my mother finished her shopping, she quietly plucked a small bag of plums from the rack and put it on the counter with the rest of the items.

4. My mother imparted her daily truths so she could help my older brothers and me rise above our circumstances. We lived in San Francisco's Chinatown. Like most of the other Chinese children who played in the back alleys of restaurants and curio shops, I didn't think we were poor. My bowl was always full, three five-course meals every day, beginning with a soup full of mysterious things I didn't want to know the names of.

5. We lived on Waverly Place, in a warm, clean, two-bedroom flat that sat above a small Chinese bakery specializing in steamed pastries and dim sum. In the early morning, when the alley was still quiet, I could smell fragrant red beans as they were cooked down to a pasty sweetness. By daybreak, our flat was heavy with the odor of fried sesame balls and sweet curried chicken crescents. From my bed, I would listen as my father got ready for work, then locked the door behind him, one-two-three clicks.

6. At the end of our two-block alley was a small sandlot playground with swings and slides well-shined down the middle with use. The play area was bordered by wood-slat benches where old-country people sat cracking roasted watermelon seeds with their golden teeth and scattering the husks to an impatient gathering of gurgling pigeons. The best playground, however, was the dark alley itself. It was crammed with daily mysteries and adventures. My brothers and I would peer into the medicinal herb shop, watching old Li dole out onto a stiff sheet of white paper the right amount of insect shells, saffron-colored seeds, and pungent leaves for his ailing customers. It was said that he once cured a woman dying of an ancestral curse that had eluded the best of American doctors. Next to the pharmacy was a printer who specialized in gold-embossed wedding invitations and festive red banners.

7. Farther down the street was Ping Yuen Fish Market. The front window displayed a tank crowded with doomed fish and turtles struggling

to gain footing on the slimy green-tiled sides. A hand-written sign informed tourists, "Within this store, is all for food, not for pet." Inside, the butchers with their bloodstained white smocks deftly gutted the fish while customers cried out their orders and shouted, "Give me your freshest," to which the butchers always protested, "All are freshest." On less crowded market days, we would inspect the crates of live frogs and crabs which we were warned not to poke, boxes of dried cuttlefish, and row upon row of iced prawns, squid, and slippery fish. The sanddabs made me shiver each time; their eyes lay on one flattened side and reminded me of my mother's story of a careless girl who ran into a crowded street and was crushed by a cab. "Was smash flat," reported my mother.

8   At the corner of the alley was Hong Sing's, a four-table café with a recessed stairwell in front that led to a door marked "Tradesmen." My brothers and I believed the bad people emerged from this door at night. Tourists never went to Hong Sing's since the menu was printed only in Chinese. A Caucasian man with a big camera once posed me and my playmates in front of the restaurant. He had us move to the side of the picture window so the photo would capture the roasted duck with its head dangling from a juice-covered rope. After he took the picture, I told him he should go into Hong Sing's and eat dinner. When he smiled and asked me what they served, I shouted, "Guts and duck's feet and octopus gizzards!" Then I ran off with my friends, shrieking with laughter as we scampered across the alley and hid in the entryway grotto of the China Gem Company, my heart pounding with hope that he would chase us.

9   My mother named me after the street that we lived on: Waverly Place Jong, my official name for important American documents. But my family called me Meimei, "Little Sister." I was the youngest, the only daughter. Each morning before school, my mother would twist and yank on my thick black hair until she had formed two tightly wound pigtails. One day, as she struggled to weave a hard-toothed comb through my disobedient hair, I had a sly thought.

10 I asked her, "Ma, what is Chinese torture?" My mother shook her head. A bobby pin was wedged between her lips. She wetted her palm and smoothed the hair above my ear, then pushed the pin in so that it nicked sharply against my scalp.

11 "Who say this word?" she asked without a trace of knowing how wicked I was being. I shrugged my shoulders and said, "Some boy in my class said Chinese people do Chinese torture."

12 "Chinese people do many things," she said simply. "Chinese people do business, do medicine, do painting. Not lazy like American people. We do torture. Best torture."

APPLICATIONS FOR CRITICAL READING AND DISCUSSION

1. State the dominant impression in a word or phrase.

2. Circle key words that support the dominant impression.

3. What is the point of view—first or third person?

4. What is the order—time, space, emphasis, or a combination?

5. Make boxes around the words that indicate order based on movement through space or time.

   Examples for space: *Next to, below, under, above, behind, in front of, beyond, in the foreground, in the background, to the left,* and *to the right.*

   Examples for time: *first, second, then, soon, now, finally, next, while, after* and *before.*

6. Underline the topic sentence or thesis. If one is not stated, supply a brief one here.

7. Give one example of each of the five images: sight, sound, smell, taste, and touch.

EXERCISE 7

The typical person might try not to see the details in certain unsavory places such as a filthy, dilapidated subway station. Not Gilbert Highet. Instead, here he observes the scene and even enjoys it—almost.

Subway Station
GILBERT HIGHET

Standing in a subway station, I began to appreciate the place—almost to enjoy it. First of all, I looked at the lighting: a row of meager electric bulbs, unscreened, yellow, and coated with filth, stretched toward the black mouth of the tunnel, as though it were a bolt hole in an abandoned coal mine. Then I lingered, with zest, on the walls and ceiling: lavatory tiles which had been white about fifty years ago, and were now encrusted with soot, coated with the remains of a dirty liquid which might be either atmospheric humidity mingled with smog or the result of a perfunctory attempt to clean them with cold water; and, above them, gloomy vaulting from which dingy paint was peeling off like scabs from an old wound, sick black paint leaving a leprous white undersurface. Beneath my feet, the floor was a nauseating dark brown with black stains upon it which might be stale oil or dry chewing gum or some worse defilement; it looked like the hallway of a condemned slum building. Then my eye traveled to the tracks, where two lines of glittering steel—the only positively clean objects in the whole place—ran out of darkness into darkness above an unspeakable mass of congealed oil, puddles of dubious liquid, and a mishmash of old cigarette packets, mutilated and filthy newspapers, and the débris that filtered down from the street above through a barred grating in the roof. As I looked up toward the sunlight, I could see more débris sifting slowly downward, and making an abominable pattern in the slanting beam of dirt-laden sunlight. I was going on to relish more features of this unique scene: such as the advertisement posters on the walls—here a text from the Bible, there a half-naked girl, here a woman wearing a hat consisting of a hen sitting on a nest full of eggs, and there a pair of girl's legs walking up the keys of a cash register—all scribbled over with unknown names and well-known obscenities in black crayon and red lipstick; but then my train came in at last, I boarded it, and began to read. The experience was over for the time.

APPLICATIONS FOR CRITICAL READING AND DISCUSSION

1. State the dominant impression in a word or phrase.

2. Circle key words that support the dominant impression.

3. What is the point of view—first or third person?

4. What is the order—time, space, emphasis, or a combination?

5. Make boxes around the words that indicate order based on movement through space or time.

   Examples for space: *Next to, below, under, above, behind, in front of, beyond, in the foreground, in the background, to the left,* and *to the right.*

   Examples for time: *first, second, then, soon, now, finally, next, while, after* and *before.*

6. Underline the topic sentence or thesis. If one is not stated, supply a brief one here.

EXERCISE 8

Sound is one dimension of your environment, wherever you are. If you live in a noisy neighborhood or a noisy household, you become accustomed to sounds. You may even come to notice them only by their absence. James Tuite, a reporter and freelance writer, largely puts other images aside and concentrates on one—sound.

Vocabulary Preview: Write short definitions for these words as they are used in the contexts of the following passage. (The paragraph numbers are given in parentheses.) Be prepared to use the words in your own sentences.

muted (1)	arrogant (7)
inaudible (2)	precocious (8)
restive (2)	taunts (8)
raucous (4)	vibrant (9)
tentative (5)	perpetuate (10)

The Sounds of the City
JAMES TUITE

1 New York is a city of sounds, muted sounds and shrill sounds; shattering sounds and soothing sounds; urgent sounds and aimless sounds. The cliff dwellers of Manhattan—who would be racked by the silence of the lonely woods—do not hear these sounds because they are constant and eternally urban.

2 The visitor to the city can hear them, though, just as some animals can hear a high-pitched whistle inaudible to humans. To the casual caller to Manhattan, lying restive and sleepless in a hotel twenty or thirty floors above the street, they tell a story as fascinating as life itself. And back of the sounds broods the silence.

3   Night in midtown is the noise of tinseled honky-tonk and violence. Thin strains of music, usually the firm beat of rock 'n' roll or the frenzied outbursts of the discotheque, rise from ground level. This is the cacophony, the discordance of youth, and it comes on strongest when nights are hot and young blood restless.

4   Somewhere in the canyons below there is shrill laughter or raucous shouting. A bottle shatters against concrete. The whine of a police siren slices through the night, moving ever closer, until an eerie Doppler effect* brings it to a guttural halt.

5   There are few sounds so exciting in Manhattan as those of fire apparatus dashing through the night. At the outset there is the tentative hint of the first-due company bullying his way through midtown traffic. Now a fire whistle from the opposite direction affirms that trouble is, indeed, afoot. In seconds, other sirens converging from other streets help the skytop listener focus on the scene of excitement.

6   But he can only hear and not see, and imagination takes flight. Are the flames and smoke gushing from windows not far away? Are victims trapped there, crying out for help? Is it a conflagration, or only a trash-basket fire? Or, perhaps, it is merely a false alarm.

7   The questions go unanswered and the urgency of the moment dissolves. Now the mind and the ear detect the snarling, arrogant bickering of automobile horns. People in a hurry. Taxicabs blaring, insisting on their checkered priority.

8   Even the taxi horns dwindle down to a precocious few in the gray and pink moments of dawn. Suddenly there is another sound, a morning sound that taunts the memory for recognition. The growl of a predatory monster? No, just garbage trucks that have begun a day of scavenging.

9   Trash cans rattle outside restaurants. Metallic jaws on sanitation trucks gulp and masticate the residue of daily living, then digest it with a satisfied groan of gears. The sounds of the new day are businesslike. The growl of buses, so scattered and distant at night, becomes a demanding part of the traffic bedlam. An occasional jet or helicopter injects an exclamation point from an unexpected quarter. When the wind is right, the vibrant bellow of an ocean liner can be heard.

10 The sounds of the day are as jarring as the glare of a sun that outlines the canyons of midtown in drab relief. A pneumatic drill frays countless nerves with its rat-a-tat-tat, for dig they must to perpetuate the city's dizzy motion. After each screech of brakes there is a moment of suspension, of waiting for the thud or crash that never seems to follow.

11 The whistles of traffic policemen and hotel doormen chirp from all sides, like birds calling for their mates across a frenzied aviary. And all of these sounds are adult sounds, for childish laughter has no place in these canyons.

12 Night falls again, the cycle is complete, but there is no surcease from sound. For the beautiful dreamers, perhaps, the "sounds of the rude world heard in the day, lulled by the moonlight have all passed away," but this is not so in the city.

13 Too many New Yorkers accept the sounds about them as bland parts of everyday existence. They seldom stop to listen to the sounds, to think about them, to be appalled or enchanted by them. In the big city, sounds are life.

*The drop in pitch that occurs as a source of sound quickly passes by a listener.

APPLICATIONS FOR CRITICAL READING AND DISCUSSION

1. State the dominant impression in a word or phrase.

2. Circle key words that support the dominant impression.

3. What is the point of view—first or third person?

4. What is the order—time, space, emphasis, or a combination?

5. Make boxes around the words that indicate order based on movement through space or time.

   Examples for space: *Next to, below, under, above, behind, in front of, beyond, in the foreground, in the background, to the left,* and *to the right.*

   Examples for time: *first, second, then, soon, now, finally, next, while, after* and *before.*

6. Underline the topic sentence or thesis. If one is not stated, supply a brief one here.

The Reading Connection from Classroom Sources

EXERCISE 9

Demonstration Using the DCODE Worksheet

Regardless of where you live, you are familiar with storms. In southern California, the most famous and the most dreaded storms are the fierce wind storms that come howling in from the desert—the Santa Anas.

The following essay is developed using the **DCODE** Worksheet.

WORKSHEET
Writing in DCODE

NAME: Juanita Rivera

SECTION: _____ CHAPTER: _____ DATE: _____

Delve   Generate your topic, or ideas for your topic, by delving into your subject area through:

- *Freewriting*—writing sentence after sentence, nonstop and spontaneously.
- *Brainstorming*—jotting down answers to Who? What? Where? When? Why? and How? and then listing words and phrases in relation to those answers.
- *Clustering*—connecting bubbled ideas with lines to show strings of relationships, producing each new bubble item in response to the question, What comes to mind?
- *Combining* any of these approaches, as directed by your instructor.

Freewriting

    I remember the Santa Anas from early childhood. They are strong hot winds that come in from the desert over the mountains and through the passes and down the canyons and across the foothills and across the LA basin before finally moving out to sea. They can come at any time of the year but mainly they come in the early spring and in late fall and early winter. I know it has something to do with high pressure in the desert and low pressure over the sea. Once the Santa Anas start they last for a long time, maybe several days. The winds blow over trees and damage houses and kick up dust. Blow. Blow. Blow. I can remember the sound from when I was just a kid. Dogs would run away and grown-ups would get grouchy.

Brainstorming

    Who? people in LA
    What? Santa Anas
    Where? LA
    When? several times every year
    Why? air pressure
    How? blowing wildly

Clustering

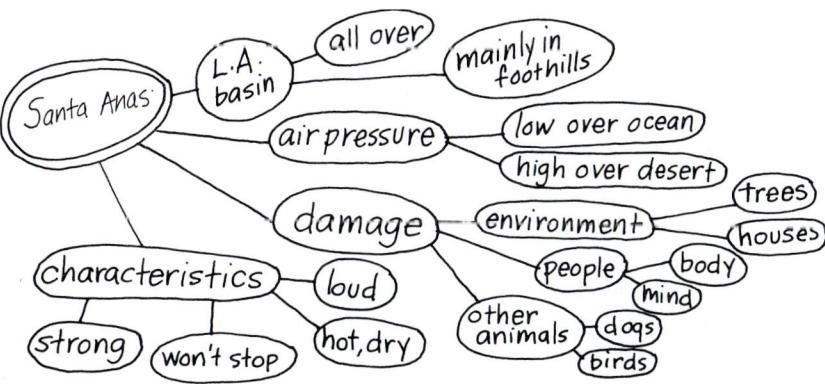

105

WORKSHEET: Writing in DCODE

Concentrate   Concentrate your work by stating your topic in one sentence that is not too broad, narrow, or vague to be developed. Base this sentence (which may become the topic sentence for your paragraph or the thesis for your essay) on an idea emerging from the **Delve** stage. You may have to try several statements here before you formulate one that is best for your writing task. Be sure that your final statement covers your assignment or intent and specifies both your subject (what you are writing about) and treatment (what aspect you will focus on). Label the *subject* and *treatment* parts.

<u>The Santa Anas</u> <u>are the "devil winds."</u>
    subject   treatment

Organize   Complete an outline or a cluster, as directed by your instructor. The cluster should be a section from, or a refined version of, the **Delve** clustering. Regardless of the strategy you use, the organizational pattern should indicate a division of your topic into parts that will, in turn, be further subdivided for support as necessary to address a particular audience on your concentrated topic.

```
    I.   Movement
         A.  From desert
         B.  To foothills
         C.  To flatlands
         D.  To coast
    II.  Characteristics
         A.  Hot
         B.  Dry
         C.  Relentless
    III. Effects
         A.  Environment
             1. Trees
             2. Houses
         B.  Animals
             1. Dogs
             2. Birds
         C.  Human beings
```

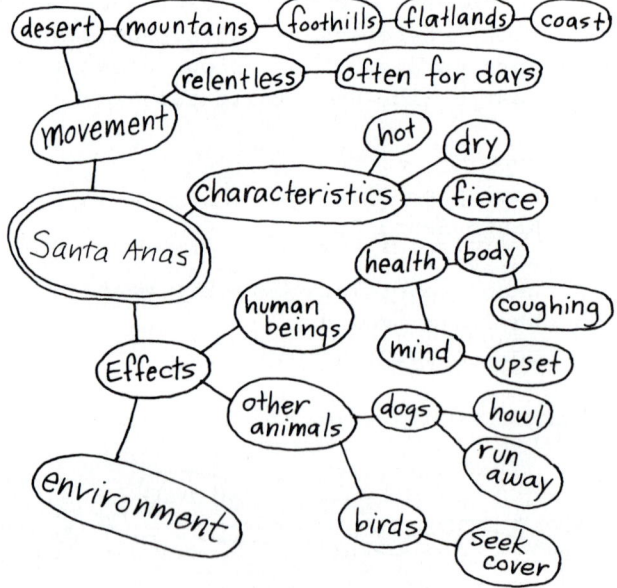

Draft   On separate paper, write and then revise your assignment as many times as necessary for **c**oherence, **l**anguage (usage, tone, and diction), **u**nity, **e**mphasis, **s**upport, and **s**entence structure (**cluess**).

Edit   Correct problems in fundamentals such as **c**apitalization, **o**missions, **p**unctuation, and **s**pelling (**cops**). Before writing the final draft, read your paper aloud to discover oversights and awkwardness of expression.

Rough Draft

The **Draft** and **Edit** stages are combined here. Some of the corrections are identified in the margin.

```
                The Santa Anas
```

In the L. A. basin, everyone [people] knows why the Santa Anas are called the "devil winds." ~~Coming~~ [They come] in from the des~~s~~ert [sp.] searing hot like the breath of a blast furnace, tumbling over the mountain ranges and ~~blowing~~ [streaking] down the canyons. ~~Everywhere~~ [Pitilessly they] destroy~~ing~~ and disrupt~~ing~~. Trees are stripped of foliage, broken, and toppled. Fire[s] that start in the foothills [may] become fire storms and ~~hit~~ [bombard] the downwind areas with smoke, ash, and burning embers. But even without fire, the winds pick up [sand, dirt, and] debris and send ~~it~~ [them] [down on the flatlands] toward the ocean as a hot, dry, dirty tide going out. All the time the ~~winds~~ [Santa Anas] are relentless, humming, [howling,] and whining through ~~wires and fences,~~ [yards] ~~howling in crevices~~ [and], rattling and rippling loose shingles~~, moaning and groaning through the trees~~. Palms fronds ~~make noises~~ [slap and clatter]. Dogs howl and [often] panic and run away; birds hunker down in wind breaks; and human beings mostly stay inside, ~~fighting~~ [wiping up] the dust, coughing, and ~~complaining~~ [getting grumpy]. The devil winds earn their reputation.

	topic sentence
	fragment/sp
	diction
	fragment
	diction
	make more specific
	tighten up
	delete repeated idea
	diction
	punctuation
	diction

Final Draft

Words that support the dominant impression of "devil winds" are circled. Most are images of sight and sound.

```
                The Santa Anas
                Juanita Rivera
```

    In the L.A. Basin, people know why the Santa Anas are called the "devil winds." They come in from the desert searing hot like the breath of a blast furnace, tumbling over the mountain ranges and streaking down the canyons. Pitilessly they destroy and disrupt. Trees are stripped of foliage, broken, and toppled. Fires that start in the foothills may become fire storms and bombard the downwind areas with smoke, ash, and burning embers. But even without fire, the winds pick up sand, dirt, and debris and send them toward the ocean as a hot, dry, dirty tide going out. All the time the Santa Anas are relentless, humming, howling, and whining through yards, and rattling and rippling loose shingles. Palm fronds slap and clatter. Dogs howl and often panic and run away; birds hunker down in wind breaks; and human beings mostly stay inside, wiping up the dust, coughing, and getting grumpy. The devil winds earn their reputation.

topic sentence

order by space from desert to mountains to flatlands to coast/ also time of movement

repeated topic idea

EXERCISE 11

A first experience can be vivid and memorable. Here student Ed Fee describes his first scuba dive in the Caribbean Sea.

Underwater Paradise
Ed Fee

On my first scuba dive in the Caribbean, I was taken by the beauty of the tropical fish and coral reefs. I had no idea how pretty everything under water really is. From the surface, it was as if I were looking at a painting with every color of the spectrum. The water had so many shades of blue from the color of the sky on a bright and sunny day to the deepest shade of blue, which resembled the heavens on a full moonlit night. Upon my first glance, the coral looked like a labyrinth with multicolored graffiti of soft and fluorescent colors and sharp edges with an occasional plant protruding from the side. These plants were swaying gently back and forth in the current like ballerinas dancing on a stage. Descending toward the coral reefs, I observed these plants more closely. Their shape and color resembled an orange maple leaf during autumn with the veins of the leaf being a soft violet color. Later I discovered it was called a gorgonian, very common among Caribbean reefs. Getting even closer to this labyrinth of coral, I noticed the floors of the passageways were of a brilliant white fine grain sand that looked like freshly fallen snow. In these passageways were thousands upon thousands of fish with multitudes of vibrant colors. One such fish was an imperial angelfish. Its body of a neon blue and bright yellow stripes running from its head to its tail made it stand out among all the other fish. Another fish that caught my eye was a coral trout, with different shades of red and yellow, like a volcano that had just erupted, and little powder blue dots covering the entire body made it the most beautiful. There are so many pretty things to see in the Caribbean waters that it would take a year to describe all that I saw. The best thing to do is to see this beautiful paradise and get a first hand look for yourself.

APPLICATIONS FOR CRITICAL READING AND DISCUSSION

1. State the dominant impression in a word or phrase.

2. Circle key words that support the dominant impression.

3. What is the point of view—first or third person?

4. What is the order—time, space, emphasis, or a combination?

5. Make boxes around the words that indicate order based on movement through space or time.

   Examples for space: *Next to, below, under, above, behind, in front of, beyond, in the foreground, in the background, to the left,* and *to the right.*

   Examples for time: *first, second, then, soon, now, finally, next, while, after* and *before.*

6. Underline the topic sentence or thesis. If one is not stated, supply a brief one here.

EXERCISE 12

Some descriptions can deliver a message without preaching. This one, by student Shontel Jasper, never says directly that tobacco is an addictive drug and that a person who smokes may die a horrible death as a consequence. But the indirect message carried by the descriptions says all of that and more.

She Came a Long Way
Shontel Jasper

Eyelids closed, she lay in the white hospital bed in the intensive care ward, her lungs filling with water and collapsing. In three days she would be dead, but she wouldn't go easily. She would go out as she had lived, for she had no choice.

She could have been an aged poster child for emphysema and lung cancer. Her face was drawn around her skull, her head was hairless from chemotherapy, the lines around her eyes revealed years of squinting through tobacco smoke, and her lips were dry and flaky like scales of a dead fish lying in the sun. A thin plastic belt hung loosely under her slack jowls like a necklace and the pendant was a clear plastic plug with a hole in it. The plug had been inserted into an incision in the woman's throat to aid her in breathing, and the air now whistled in and out irregularly. At the head of her bed stood an oxygen bottle like a cold and impersonal sentinel.

The nurse had just checked off items on the chart and left the room. Slowly, warily, the patient opened her eyes, and seeing no one in the room, immediately began her caper. Because of her shallow, rapid breathing, she was a study in slow movement. First there was a faint stirring under the sheet and then the sound of crackling cellophane. Then her hands emerged, holding a crumpled pack of Camels, from which she took a crooked cigarette before putting the remainder back under the covers. Next she removed the thin book of matches from her pillowcase. With the cigarette and matches clutched in her right hand, she fingered the control button to raise the head of her bed to almost ninety degrees. Laboriously she swung her legs over the edge of the mattress, and choked back a fit of wheezy coughing that made the plug sound like a toddler playing a penny whistle.

Heading for the rest room, she knew exactly what she would do, because she had done it before. After closing the door behind herself, she turned on the exhaust fan. She then popped the insert from the plug and licked the paper at the end of her cigarette. When she raised her chin, the raw flesh showed through the transparent plastic, looking

like a gill slit, into which she placed her cigarette and
pinched the plastic around the part she had just licked.
With trembling hands she scratched a match to flame and
raised it awkwardly toward the cigarette. Instinctively she
looked above the commode for a mirror, but there was none.
The hospital doesn't want patients in this ward to see
their own images.

   At last the moment of enjoyment had arrived. After
taking a deep drag and removing the cigarette, she
coughed, and the smoke streamed out of the hole and
billowed. It looked white and vaporous as if she were an
internal-combustion engine with a blown head gasket. She
held her chin high, and lined up the hole carefully to
receive the treat once more.

APPLICATIONS FOR CRITICAL READING AND DISCUSSION

1. State the dominant impression in a word or phrase.

2. Circle key words that support the dominant impression.

3. What is the point of view—first or third person?

4. What is the order—time, space emphasis, or a combination?

5. Make boxes around the words that indicate order based on movement through space or time.

    Examples for space: *Next to, below, under, above, behind, in front of, beyond, in the foreground, in the background, to the left,* and *to the right.*

    Examples for time: *first, second, then, soon, now, finally, next, while, after* and *before.*

6. Underline the topic sentence or thesis. If one is not stated, supply a brief one here.

Suggested Topics for Writing Description

General Topics

Objective Description

Give your topic some kind of frame. As you develop your purpose, consider the knowledge and attitudes of your readers. You might be describing a lung for a biology instructor, a geode for a geology instructor, a painting for an art instructor, or a comet for an astronomy instructor. Or maybe you could pose as the seller of a object such as a desk, a table, or a bicycle. Try the following topics:

1. A simple object, such as a pencil, a pair of scissors, a cup, a sock, a dollar bill, a coin, ring, notebook.

2. A human organ, such as a heart, liver, lung, or kidney.

3. A visible part of your body, such as a toe, a finger, an ear, a nose, an eye.

4. A construction, such as a room, a desk, a chair, a commode, a table.

5. A mechanism, such as a bicycle, a tricycle, a wagon, a car, a motorcycle, a can opener, a stapler.

Subjective Description

The following topics should also be presented in the context of a purpose other than writing a description. Your intent can be as simple as giving a subjective reaction to your subject, such as found in "Strangers to Darkness" and "A Shack of Misery." But unless you are dealing with one of those topics that you can present reflectively or a topic as interesting in itself as the one in "On the Ball," you will usually need some kind of situation. The narrative frame (something happening) is especially useful in providing order and vitality to writing. "Rules of the Game" describes several scenes from childhood, each one revealing a relationship between narrator and environment. "She Came a Long Way" shows a woman struggling to have one more cigarette. Here are three possibilities for you to consider:

1. Personalize a trip to a supermarket, a stadium, an airport, an unusual house, a mall, the beach, a court, a church, a club, a business, the library, or the police station. Deal with a simple conflict in one of those places, while emphasizing descriptive details.

2. Pick a high point in any event, and describe it as it lasts for only a few seconds. Think about how a scene can be captured by a video camera, and then give focus by applying the dominant impression principle, using the images of sight, sound, taste, touch, and smell that are relevant. The event might be a ball game, a graduation ceremony, a wedding ceremony, a funeral, a dance, a concert, a family gathering, a class meeting, a rally, a riot, a robbery, a fight, a proposal, or a meal. Focus on a body of subject material that you can cover effectively in the passage you write.

3. Pick a moment when you were angry, sad, happy, confused, lost, rattled, afraid, courageous, meek, depressed, or elated. Describe how the total context of the situation contributed to your feeling.

Reading-Related Topics

"On the Ball"

1. Describe another item that seems perfect in design and function—one that has been around for a long time and is regarded as a standard or a classic—perhaps a piece of sports equipment, a tool, an item of clothing, or a toy.

"Babe Ruth"

2. Describe another famous athlete or an entertainer who doesn't look or act the part.

"The Cat"

3. Describe your pet engaged in typical behavior.

"A Shack of Misery"

4. Have you ever been confined to a hospital bed or to your own room by illness or injury? If so, did you find yourself studying the designs on the ceiling and walls, counting squares, finding designs in the cracks in the plaster, and generally making a detailed study of your environment? Write a description about such a setting. The same approach could be applied to any place in which you have lived, were stranded (maybe inside a car?), camped, were detained, or stayed with a friend.

"Blue Winds Dancing"

5. Describe your return to an area after a considerable passage of time, showing how the surroundings bring back warm feelings for neighborhood and family—or maybe feelings that are at best bittersweet.

"Subway Station"

6. Select an area that is regarded as unsightly, and describe it in detail.

"Rules of the Game"

7. Describe your neighborhood as it was when you were growing up. Populate it with one or more of the people (not necessarily family members) who influenced you. Limit your description in time or place, and unify it around a dominant impression.

"The Sounds of the City"

8. Concentrate on sound imagery to reveal the nature of one location. Try closing your eyes while you make mental notes. Or perhaps you could wear a blindfold while being led by a classmate.

"The Santa Anas"

9. Describe a local weather situation that has a dramatic influence on your community. It might be a chinook, tornado, hurricane, blizzard, dust storm, flood, or drought.

"She Came a Long Way"

10. Describe a scene in which one person is involved in self-destructive behavior. Consider other addictions and excesses such as overeating, overexercising, and overworking.

Writer's Checklist

1. Use a dominant impression to unify your description.
2. Select your point of view (first, involved or observer/third) with care, and be consistent.
3. To promote coherence, impose a plan for order by space, time, or emphasis.
4. In objective description, use direct, practical language, and (usually) appeal mainly to the sense of sight.
5. In emotional description, appeal to the reader's feelings, especially through the use of figurative language and images of sight, sound, smell, taste, and touch.
6. Use specific and concrete words if appropriate.

Journal-Entry Suggestions

1. Select some ideas from "Reading-Related Topics" and use them for brief journal entries.
2. If you have had experiences similar to those covered in the exemplary paragraphs and essays in this chapter, give your reactions; discuss similarities, dissimilarities, and insights.
3. Invent descriptions to support headlines from *Weekly World News*:

    "Sliced Onion Screams in Pain" "Shocking First Photo of Space Alien Baby"
    "Blimp Scared UFO Away from Stadium" "Incredible Powder Made from Chicken Wings Cures All!"
    "Pearl Bracelet Found in Oyster" "Psychic Cooks Food with the Power of His Mind!"
    "Amazing Kitty Says More Than 100 Words" "Meet the World's First Singing Pig"
    "Music Makes Plants Grow Like Crazy!" "Kissing Couple Bursts into Flames!"
    "Flying Dragons Attack Villagers!" "Baby Born Singing Christmas Carols"

WORKSHEET
Writing in DCODE

NAME:_____

SECTION:_____ CHAPTER:_____ DATE:_____

Delve   Generate your topic, or ideas for your topic, by delving into your subject area through:

- *Freewriting*—writing sentence after sentence, nonstop and spontaneously.
- *Brainstorming*—jotting down answers to Who? What? Where? When? Why? and How? and then listing words and phrases in relation to those answers.
- *Clustering*—connecting bubbled ideas with lines to show strings of relationships, producing each new bubble item in response to the question, What comes to mind?
- *Combining* any of these approaches, as directed by your instructor.

Concentrate   Concentrate your work by stating your topic in one sentence that is not too broad, narrow, or vague to be developed. Base this sentence (which may become the topic sentence for your paragraph or the thesis for your essay) on an idea emerging from the **Delve** stage. You may have to try several statements here before you formulate one that is best for your writing task. Be sure that your final statement covers your assignment or intent and specifies both your subject (what you are writing about) and treatment (what aspect you will focus on). Label the *subject* and *treatment* parts.

Organize   Complete an outline or a cluster, as directed by your instructor. The cluster should be a section from, or a refined version of, the **Delve** clustering. Regardless of the strategy you use, the organizational pattern should indicate a division of your topic into parts that will, in turn, be further subdivided for support as necessary to address a particular audience on your concentrated topic.

Draft   On separate paper, write and then revise your assignment as many times as necessary for **c**oherence, **l**anguage (usage, tone, and diction), **u**nity, **e**mphasis, **s**upport, and **s**entence structure (**cluess**).

Edit   Correct problems in fundamentals such as **c**apitalization, **o**missions, **p**unctuation, and **s**pelling (**cops**). Before writing the final draft, read your paper aloud to discover oversights and awkwardness of expression.

Exemplification: Illustrating Ideas

5

> "Like a picture, a specific, vivid example may be worth a thousand words of explanation.
> — a wise, anonymous professor

What is the purpose of examples? What are the differences among specific, typical, and hypothetical examples? What are some good sources of examples? How can examples be organized?

Surveying Exposition

With this chapter on exemplification, we turn to *exposition*, a form of writing that explains as its main purpose. This and the following seven chapters will explore these questions:

Exemplification	Can you give me an example or examples of what you mean?
Functional Analysis	How do the parts work together?
Process Analysis	How do I do it? How is it done?
Classification	What types of things are these?
Comparison and Contrast	How are these similar and dissimilar?
Definition	What does this term mean?

In most informative writing, these various methods of organizing and developing thought are used in combination, with one method dominating according to the writer's purpose for explaining. The other forms of discourse can be used in combination with these. You have already learned that narration and description are frequently used for expository purposes. In Chapter 14 you will see how persuasive and expository writing are often blended, becoming interdependent.

Exemplification

Exemplification Defined

Exemplification is simply using examples to develop ideas. We all know of the effectiveness of examples. In the 1992 presidential campaign, the candidates made much use of this technique. On one occasion, Ross Perot announced he had received thousands of letters from supporters. Then he offered an example. He made the example specific and concrete by reading the letter and stating the supporter's name. He made his example even more specific and concrete by showing a photograph of the supporter, a young girl he called "the future of America." If she had been there, he might have held her up as a live, specific, concrete example, squirming and protesting in embarrassment, before the audience of reporters and photographers. His technique worked, at least in one way: we remember the event.

You will, of course, note that the previous paragraph used an example to explain the effectiveness of examples. In fact, glance back at the paragraph and try to imagine how it could be developed well without an example.

All perceptive readers appreciate and even expect well-chosen examples. One recurring complaint English instructors hear from instructors in other departments is that student writers use generalizations without support. These unsupported generalizations are likely to be uninteresting, unclear, and unconvincing.

Consider these two statements on the same subject.

> College coaches know the importance of finding talented athletes for intercollegiate sports programs, and they know all the techniques for attracting such athletes to their schools. Ironically, one technique is the appeal to the athletes' desire for an education. To that end, the coaches will highlight the tutorial help and other learning assistance that are available in their schools. Some of these athletes have learning disabilities, some of them were not serious students in high school, and some attended inferior schools. Unfortunately some of these athletes are promised more than will be delivered. The school will make millions on its athletic program, but the athletes will be neglected as students.

Dull, isn't it? Now read another version.

> As any coach knows, the outcome of a season is often determined before the opening tip-off of the first game. It begins with the high school players recruited by the school. A single talented player can be worth hundreds of thousands of dollars to a college—and, indirectly, to a coach. The NCAA prohibits recruiters from offering money to prospective players. But many student athletes say recruiters offered them cash, cars and jewelry. For some young players, and especially for their families, the promise of educational help can swing their decision. It is not only the larger schools that have problems.
>
> Take the case of Reggie Ford. As a 6-ft. 4-in. senior at Marion High School in rural South Carolina three years ago, Reggie was an All-State center. More than a dozen universities salivated over his 22-points-a-game average. They paid little mind to his scant 2.0 grade-point average. It was Bob Battisti, coach of Northwestern Oklahoma State University, who persuaded Reggie to attend his school. What won him over, said Reggie, was Battisti's promise that a tutor would be available to help him through the difficult academic times ahead. "I knew I wasn't no A student," explains Reggie. For the Ford family, it was a shining moment. They are poor. Reggie's mother is disabled from a car accident, his father from a stroke. Reggie was the first member of his family to go to college.
>
> Initially, the coaches were attentive. Reggie remembers they joked with him and invited him into their homes. But each time Reggie asked about a tutor, he was put off. Then he injured his knee, and everything changed, he said. The coaches ignored him, and the invitations dried up. His grades dropped; the scholarship was withdrawn. "After I hurt my knee, it seemed like they were trying to tell me there wasn't much I could do for them, so I got up and left," says Reggie. Now 21, he lives with his family in South Carolina and is collecting unemployment.

Ted Gup, "Foul"

One example here in the second version makes the topic idea come alive. The second and following paragraphs in this unit support the idea by using an example. The subject of the example is named. With this kind of development, we are more likely to be interested, informed, and convinced, and we are more likely to remember.

Sources of Examples

For the personal essay, the best source of examples is your own knowledge. If you know your subject well, from either reading or experience, you will be able to recall many examples through your writing strategies of freewriting, brainstorming, and clustering. Good examples are likely to come from something you know well. If you have worked in a fast-food restaurant, you probably have dozens of stories about activities there. Some of these stories might be appropriate for illustrating a topic on human behavior. Although a reader has not shared an experience with a writer, he or she will almost certainly be able to judge and appreciate its authenticity. Professional writers working outside their specialties often interview (and sometimes pay) ordinary individuals in order to obtain concrete particulars to color and enliven their work. Television crime show writers, for instance, regularly collect information from police officers.

A more academic topic, such as one on a novel, might be researched by scrutinizing the book itself for incidents, statements, or descriptions. A history topic might be researched in a textbook or in library sources.

Connecting Examples with Purpose

Examples, by their very definition, are functional. They are representative of something, or they illustrate something. In purpose, they may explain, convince, or amuse. The connection between this purpose and the example must be clear. If your example is striking, yet later your reader can remember the example but not the point being illustrated, then you have failed in your basic task. Writing good exemplification begins with a good topic sentence or thesis.

BROAD: People seeking plastic surgery have various motives.

Subject   *Treatment*

FOCUSED: Some people seeking plastic surgery are driven by irrational emotional needs that can never be met.

In the following paragraph on essentially that focused idea, the author uses an example effectively by stating the purpose (topic sentence), connecting it with the example, and restating the purpose while relating it, in turn, directly to the example.

Leigh Lachman, a plastic surgeon in Manhattan, notes that "some patients are never satisfied." One of his clients, a 45-year-old woman, came to him for a facelift, then a nose job, and then a breast reduction. She now insists that her breasts are too small and she wants them augmented. Then she plans to get an eye-lift. She started bringing in friends to see Lachman. "Her attitude seems to be that she's bringing me business, so I should continue to operate on her," Lachman says. "These kinds of patients can be very difficult to help, because it becomes obvious that they want more than a surgical correction can provide."

topic sentence

extended example

restatement of topic sentence

Holly Hall, "Scalpel Slaves"

Examples: Kinds, Choices, Patterns

Specific

"Take the case of Reggie Ford" begins the paragraph on exploitation of student-athletes. "One of his clients, a 45-year-old woman, came to him for a facelift" highlights the paragraph on plastic surgery. Both examples are specific and concrete. The first names a person and discusses him for several paragraphs; the second refers directly to a woman and in a short paragraph discusses her in relation to the topic sentence. Each example illustrates an idea and fulfills a purpose. The examples are effective because readers can see the subjects as both individuals and as representatives of groups. Each is interesting and appropriate. Specific examples can be powerful tools in writing to explain and persuade.

We can write about our own experiences:

> For example, as I bent over outside my house this morning to pick up my newspaper, I closed my eyes and listened, and the whole neighborhood seemed to be transformed into an Indianapolis pit stop: next door the out-of-tune pickup rumbled, across the street the diesel Mercedes clicked and clanged, from up the street a motorcycle roared and popped, and all of those sounds were cemented by the undercurrent of sound from passing cars and the hum of traffic in the distance.

Typical

The typical differs from the specific in that it is not an actual experience. We could write about the same noise pollution problem in this way:

> We are surrounded by noise pollution. For example, every morning as people drive to work, the city takes on the dimension of sound of hundreds of thousands of internal combustion engines.

You get the point, for you have also heard that sound. The example is a description written in a collective sense: it is any morning in any big city; therefore, it is typical, average.

Hypothetical

Another kind of example is the hypothetical. At times we will offer an example that is presented in an "imagine that" or "what if" posture. In other words, we make up something and offer it to the reader, who understands that it is contrived, made up, for the purpose of discussion. An author could write,

> Let's say, for example, that traffic is in gridlock, and one driver moves out on the shoulder of the road and tries to go around the stationary cars. Some other drivers blow their horns and shout. Another swings her car out to block the progress of the offender.

That specific incident did not occur, but the author wants us to consider it as if it did for the sake of discussion, and we comply.

Following is a sample paragraph containing typical and hypothetical examples.

> If there are distance problems when engaged in conversation, then there are clearly going to be even bigger difficulties where people must work privately in a shared space. Close proximity of others, pressing against the invisible boundaries of our personal body-territory, makes it difficult to concentrate on non-social matters. Flatmates, students sharing a study, sailors in the cramped quarters of a ship, and office staff in crowded workplaces, all have to face this problem. They solve it by "cocooning." The use a variety of devices to shut themselves off from the others present. The best possible cocoon, of course, is a small private room—a den, a private office, a study or a studio—which physically obscures the presence of other nearby territory-owners. This is the ideal situation for non-social work, but the space-sharers cannot enjoy this luxury. Their cocooning must be symbolic. They may, in certain cases, be able to erect small physical barriers, such as screens and partitions, which give substance to their invisible Personal Space boundaries, but when this cannot be done, other means must be sought. One of these is the "favored object." Each space-sharer develops a preference, repeatedly expressed until it becomes a fixed pattern, for a particular chair, or table, or alcove. Others come to respect this, and friction is reduced. This system is often formally arranged (this is my desk, that is yours), but even where it is not, favored places soon develop. Professor Smith has a favorite chair in the library. It is not formally his, but he always uses it and others avoid it. Seats around a mess-room table, or a boardroom table, become almost personal property for specific individuals. Even in the home, father has his favorite chair for reading the newspaper or watching television. Another device is the blinkers-posture. Just as a horse that over-reacts to other horses and the distractions of the noisy race-course is given a pair of blinkers to shield its eyes, so people studying privately in a public place put on pseudo-blinkers in the form of shielding hands. Resting their elbows on the table, they sit with their hands screening their eyes from the scene on either side.

typical

hypothetical

hypothetical

typical

Desmond Morris, "Personal Space"

No specific person is mentioned in this paragraph. Instead, typical and hypothetical examples take their place as if they were real. We recognize them. In these instances, we may identify with them. Even "Professor Smith" is a made-up name for a made-up situation. But they have served the author well in supporting his contentions about people, space, and privacy. In some instances, it may be difficult to distinguish the typical from the hypothetical examples.

Choosing the Kinds

Whether you use the specific, the typical, or the hypothetical example will depend on your purpose, your audience, and the context. No firm rules can apply here; you must consider the complete situation, reflect on the properties of each example, and exercise judgment. However, keep in mind that a specific example dealing with a concrete particular that the reader can conceptualize is a powerful aid in developing ideas.

Number and Arrangement

Exemplification can be used with single or multiple examples. The section on exploitation of student-athletes uses only one example and extends it through several paragraphs. The paragraph on plastic surgery also uses only one example but extends it just within the paragraph. The paragraph on personal space uses several hypothetical examples. Certainly there are no formulas regarding the number of examples you should employ. However, short essays of five paragraphs are often developed with three examples presented in the middle three paragraphs, and one example is sometimes extended and presented in logical three-paragraph units in the same kind of essay. These organizational patterns can also be applied to simple paragraphs, although you should always think about what examples you need rather than select a design before you work with your ideas.

Order

Once you have selected examples, proceed to work on the order in which you will relate the extended example or in which you will present the multiple examples.

The three basic ways of establishing order—time, space, and emphasis—also apply here. The extended example may be a narrative account; therefore, **time** order (using words such as *next, then, soon, later, last, finally*) will be appropriate. When movement is a component of the example, **space** references (*up, down, left, right*) are used. The third method, **emphasis,** simply means that one point leads to the next in logical thought. The paragraph on private space does that. Emphasis may move from the general to the specific, from the specific to the general, or from the least important to the most important. In this regard, a writer who has two extraordinary examples and two others that are good but not spectacular might lead with a lively one to attract attention, use the two serviceable ones for conventional support, and finish with the remaining lively one for emphasis. You should experiment. Consider what principles apply if any. Experiment with your outline or your cluster; rework the organization in your drafts as you go back and forth in your recursive writing.

The Reading Connection

EXERCISE 1

Demonstration

Mix together an imaginative person, a large chamber, and some dead animals, and what do you have? A very unusual occupation. This is the way it goes: This person, Jeff, purchased a chamber used for freeze-drying vegetables, but he would not use it for that purpose. He had asked himself the question, What do people like better than eating vegetables (freeze-dried or otherwise)? Of course, they like the companionship of their pets better than eating vegetables. The problem with pets is that most do not live as long as their human owners. Jeff had the solution and a use for his chamber: He would freeze-dry the pets—for a price.

Freeze-Dried Memories
PAT JORDAN

Jeff will freeze-dry just about anything. But most of his business is in freeze-drying the deceased pets of distraught owners. Cats. Dogs. Birds. Snakes. Lizards. Hamsters. Even alligators. Currently, he has about 30 such pets in his chamber, undergoing a freeze-drying process that will take three to six months, depending on the size of the pet. Jeff charges about $400 to freeze-dry small pets and about $1,800 for large pets like the two Doberman pinschers sitting completely still in the softly humming chamber. The dogs are bathed in a mysterious yellow light and surrounded by a Noah's Ark menagerie of other perfectly serene-looking pets, all of which would probably be at one another's throats if still alive. A chipmunk, its tiny paws held out as if to receive a nut, is standing in front of a cat, which in turn is crouched beside one of the Dobermans. Farther back in the chamber, the second Doberman is surrounded by some small dogs and dozens of cats, cockatiels, cockatoos, snakes and lizards. In their freeze-dried state, all the animals look eerily alive in their natural poses, except that they are stock-still and their wide eyes are unblinking.

APPLICATIONS FOR CRITICAL READING AND DISCUSSION

1. What is the idea being supported? State it here, and circle it (if stated directly) in the passage.
   ```
   Jeff will freeze-dry just about anything.
   ```

2. Is this exemplification based on single or multiple examples?
   ```
   multiple
   ```

3. Underline the examples.

4. Is each example specific, typical, or hypothetical? Label each one in the margin using the letters *S*, *T*, or *H*.

5. What is the organization of the examples—time, space, emphasis, or a combination?
    `space`

6. List some words that indicate order.
    `in front of, beside me, farther back`

EXERCISE 2

To human beings, cannibalism is a heinous act. But in the larger animal kingdom, it is a way of life—and death. Shark behavior offers a good example. Sharks, not well known for their gentleness of disposition or overall niceness, practice cannibalism. Where does it all start, you might ask? How about in the womb?

Cannibalism in Sibling Rivalry
DESMOND MORRIS

Sharks provide the most gruesome example of this type of behavior [cannibalism] in nature. For young sand sharks and mackerel sharks the struggle for survival starts early. Although it is hard to believe, these predatory fish produce cannibal embryos. At the onset of pregnancy, the female's body contains a dozen or so small fetuses, but as these start to grow they begin to prey on one another while they are still in her oviduct. Already well equipped with sharp teeth, the bigger and stronger embryos tear to pieces and devour the younger ones. As other eggs start to develop, these too are gobbled up until, in the end, there is only one large, well fed embryo left, stuffed with its unborn brothers and sisters. With no more siblings on which to dine, the survivor then changes its position in the oviduct, triggering its own birth.

APPLICATIONS FOR CRITICAL READING AND DISCUSSION

1. What is the idea being supported? State it here, and circle it (if stated directly) in the passage.

2. Is this exemplification based on single or multiple examples?

3. Underline the examples.

4. Is each example specific, typical, or hypothetical? Label each one in the margin using the letters *S*, *T*, or *H*.

5. What is the organization of the examples—time, space, emphasis, or a combination?

6. List some words that indicate order.

EXERCISE 3

When a parent is busy with the workaday world, quality time becomes compensation for the toddler starved for parental company. But when there is no time for quality time, what then? The answer is "quality absence," which can be provided with an electronic toy named Dozzzy.

Baby Nag-a-Lot
TIME MAGAZINE

For children whose parents rarely make it home in time to tell bedtime stories, Lewis Galoob offers Dozzzy ($60), a blue-pajamaed doll stuffed with a tape recorder that is activated when a child squeezes its hand. The doll supervises the bedtime ritual: "Did you remember to brush your teeth?" and "Is the light turned out?" As it asks about the child's day, the questions are punctuated with suggestive yawns. To spare the batteries, a microprocessor tells the doll to turn itself off once the child falls asleep and stops squeezing the toy. The bedtime companion comes in two forms—a baby bear or a baby human—each with bright eyes that double as a night-light and little electric lips that flicker as it speaks.

APPLICATIONS FOR CRITICAL READING AND DISCUSSION

1. What is the idea being supported? State it here, and circle it (if stated directly) in the passage.

2. Is this exemplification based on single or multiple examples?

3. Underline the examples.

4. Is each example specific, typical, or hypothetical? Label each one in the margin using the letters *S*, *T*, or *H*.

5. What is the organization of the examples—time, space, emphasis, or a combination?

EXERCISE 4

Who gets top billing when a heterosexual couple is introduced? Does the order of introduction make a difference? Francine Frank and Frank Ashen, two linguists, maintain that the choice reflects attitudes about sex roles. They have examples to support their point.

> ### Why Not "Ms. and Mr."?
> FRANCINE FRANK AND FRANK ASHEN
>
> First let us consider what the last members of the following groups have in common: Jack and Jill, Romeo and Juliet, Adam and Eve, Peter, Paul and Mary, Hansel and Gretel, Roy Rogers and Dale Evans, Tristan and Isolde, Guys and Dolls, Abelard and Heloise, man and wife, Dick and Jane, Burns and Allen, Anthony and Cleopatra, Sonny and Cher, Fibber Magee and Molly, Ferdinand and Isabella, Samson and Delilah, and Stiller and Meara. That's right, it is a group of women who have been put in their place. Not that women must always come last: Snow White gets to precede all seven dwarfs, Fran may follow Kukla, but she comes before Ollie, Anna preceded the King of Siam, although it must be noted that, as colonialism waned, she was thrust to the rear of the billing in "The King and I." Women with guns are also able to command top billing, as in Frankie and Johnny, and Bonnie and Clyde. The moral is clear: a woman who wants precedence in our society should either hang around with dwarfs or dragons, or shoot somebody. "Women and children first" may apply on sinking ships, but it clearly doesn't apply in the English language.

APPLICATIONS FOR CRITICAL READING AND DISCUSSION

1. What is the idea being supported? State it here, and circle it (if stated directly) in the passage.

2. Is this exemplification based on single or multiple examples?

3. Underline the examples.

4. Is each example specific, typical, or hypothetical? Label each example in the margin using the letters *S, T,* or *H.*

5. What is the organization of the examples—time, space, emphasis, or a combination?

6. Is the purpose mainly to persuade or to inform?

EXERCISE 5

Some would call the problems of mental health among the young an epidemic. "The Institute of Medicine estimates that as many as 7.5 million children—12% of those below the age of 18—suffer from some form of psychological illness." Anastasia Toufexis, a feature writer for *Time*, uses examples, references, quotations, and explanations to provide an assessment of the mental condition of youth in America.

Vocabulary Preview: Write in short definitions for these words as they are used in the contexts of the following passage. (The paragraph numbers are given in parentheses.) Be prepared to use the words in your own sentences.

divulge (1)

turmoil (2)

anguish (3)

psyches (3)

autistic (4)

manic-depressive (9)

daunting (10)

myriad (11)

promiscuity (11)

extracurricular (14)

Struggling for Sanity
ANASTASIA TOUFEXIS

The dozen telephone lines at the cramped office of Talkline/Kids Line in Elk Grove Village, Ill., ring softly every few minutes. Some of the youthful callers seem at first to be vulgar pranksters, out to make mischief with inane jokes and naughty language. But soon the voices on the line—by turns wistful, angry, sad, desperate—start to spill a stream of distress. Some divulge their struggles with alcohol or crack and their worries about school and sex. Others tell of their feeling of boredom and loneliness. Some talk of suicide. What connects them all, says Nancy Helmick, director of the two hot lines, is a sense of "disconnectedness."

2   Such calls attest to the intense psychological and emotional turmoil many American children are experiencing. It is a problem that was not even recognized until just a decade ago. Says Dr. Lewis Judd, director of the National Institute of Mental Health: "There had been a myth that childhood is a happy time and kids are happy go lucky, but no age range is immune from experiencing mental disorders." A report prepared last year by the Institute of Medicine estimates that as many as 7.5 million children—12% of those below the age of 18—suffer from some form of psychological illness. A federal survey shows that after remaining constant for 10 years, hospitalizations of youngsters with psychiatric disorders jumped from 81,500 to about 112,000 between 1980 and 1986. Suicides among those ages 15 to 19 have almost tripled since 1960, to 1,901 deaths in 1987. Moreover, the age at which children are exhibiting mental problems is dropping: studies suggest that as many as 30% of infants 18 months old and younger are having difficulties ranging from emotional withdrawal to anxiety attacks.

3   What is causing so much mental anguish? The sad truth is that a growing number of American youngsters have home lives that are hostile to healthy emotional growth. Psyches are extremely fragile and must be nourished from birth. Everyone starts out life with a basic anxiety about survival. An attentive parent contains that stress by making the youngster feel secure and loved.

4   Neglect and indifference at such a crucial stage can have devastating consequences. Consider the case of Sid. (Names of the children in this story have been changed.) When he was three months old, his parents left him with the maid while they took a five-week trip. Upon their return, his mother noticed that Sid was withdrawn, but she did not do anything about it. When Sid was nine

months old, his mother left him again for four weeks while she visited a weight-loss clinic. By age three, Sid had still not started talking. He was wrongly labeled feeble-minded and borderline autistic before he received appropriate treatment.

5   As children mature within the shelter of the family, they develop what psychologists call a sense of self. They acquire sensitivities and skills that lead them to believe they can cope independently. "People develop through a chain," observes Dr. Carol West, a child psychotherapist in Beverly Hills. "There has to be stability, a consistent idea of who you are."

6   The instability that is becoming the hallmark of today's families breeds in children insecurity rather than pride, doubts instead of confidence. Many youngsters feel guilty about broken marriages, torn between parents and households, and worried about family finances. Remarriage can intensify the strains. Children may feel abandoned and excluded as they plunge into rivalries with stepparents and stepsiblings or are forced to adjust to new homes and new schools. Children from troubled homes used to be able to find a psychological anchor in societal institutions. But no longer. The churches, schools and neighborhoods that provided emotional stability by transmitting shared traditions and values have collapsed along with the family.

7   Such disarray hurts children from all classes; wealth may in fact make it harder for some children to cope. Says Hal Klor, a guidance counselor at Chicago's Lincoln Park High School: "The kids born into a project, they handle it. But the middle-class kids. All of a sudden—a divorce, loss of job, status. Boom. Depression."

8   Jennifer shuttled by car service across New York City's Central Park between her divorced parent's apartments and traveled by chartered bus to a prep school where kids rated one another according to their family cars. "In the eighth grade I had panic attacks," says Jennifer, now 18. "That's when your stomach goes up and you can't leave the bathroom and you get sweaty and you get headaches and the world closes in on you." Her world eventually narrowed so far that for several weeks she could not set foot outside her home.

9   The children who suffer the severest problems are those who are physically or sexually abused. Many lose all self-esteem and trust. Michele, 15, who is a manic-depressive and an alcoholic, is the child of an alcoholic father who left when she was two and a mother who took out her rage by beating Michele's younger sister. When Michele was 12, her mother remarried. Michele's new stepbrother promptly began molesting her. "So I molested my younger brother," confesses Michele. "I also hit him a lot. He was four. I was lost; I didn't know how to deal with things."

10 At the same time, family and society are expecting more from kids than ever before. Parental pressure to make good grades, get into college and qualify for the team can be daunting. Moreover, kids are increasingly functioning as junior adults in many homes, taking on the responsibility of caring for younger siblings or ailing grandparents. And youngsters' own desires—to be accepted and popular with their peers, especially—only add to the strain.

11 Children express the panic and anxiety they feel in myriad ways: in massive weight gains or losses, in nightmares and disturbed sleep, in fatigue or listlessness, in poor grades or truancy, in continual arguing or fighting, in drinking or drug abuse, in reckless driving or sexual promiscuity, in stealing and mugging. A fairly typical history among disturbed kids, says Dr. L. David Zinn, co-director of Northwestern Memorial Hospital's Adolescent Program, includes difficulty in school at age eight or nine, withdrawal from friends and family and persistent misbehavior at 10 or 11 and skipping school by 15. But the most serious indication of despair—and the most devastating—is suicide attempts. According to a report issued in June by a commission formed by the American Medical Association and the National Association of State Boards of Education, about 10% of teenage boys and 18% of girls try to kill themselves at least once.

12 Despite the urgency of the problems, only 1 in 5 children who need therapy receives it; poor and minority youngsters get the least care. Treatment is expensive, and even those with money and insurance find it hard to afford. But another reason is that too often the signals of distress are missed or put down to normal mischief.

13 Treatment relies on therapeutic drugs, reward and punishment, and especially counseling—not just of the youngster but of the entire family. The goal is to instill in the children a feeling of self-

worth and to teach them discipline and responsibility. Parents, meanwhile, are taught how to provide emotional support, assert authority and set limits.

14   One of the most ambitious efforts to reconstruct family life is at Logos School, a private academy outside St. Louis that was founded two decades ago for troubled teens. Strict rules governing both school and extracurricular life are laid out for parents in a 158-page manual. Families are required to have dinner together every night, and parents are expected to keep their children out of establishments or events, say local hangouts or rock concerts, where drugs are known to be sold. Parents must also impose punishments when curfews and other rules are broken. Says Lynn, whose daughter Sara enrolled at Logos: "My first reaction when I read the parents' manual was that there wasn't a thing there that I didn't firmly believe in, but I'd been too afraid to do it on my own. It sounds like such a cop-out, but we wanted Sara to be happy."

15   As necessary and beneficial as treatment may be, it makes better sense to prevent emotional turmoil among youngsters by improving the environment they live in. Most important, parents must spend more time with sons and daughters and give them the attention and love they need. To do less will guarantee that ever more children will be struggling for sanity.

APPLICATIONS FOR CRITICAL READING AND DISCUSSION

1. What is the idea being supported? State it here, and circle it (if stated directly) in the passage.

2. Is this exemplification based on single or multiple examples?

3. Underline the examples.

4. Is each example specific, typical, or hypothetical? Label each example in the margin using the letters *S, T,* or *H.*

5. What is the organization of the examples—time, space, emphasis, or a combination?

6. Are most of the examples used *in place of* statistics or *along with* statistics?

EXERCISE 6

The central example in this essay on violence by youth concerns a sixteen-year-old who killed a teenage neighbor for a nickel. Journalist Nancy Traver discusses the causes and effects of this senseless act and relates it to a problem for society.

Vocabulary Preview: Write in short definitions for these words as they are used in the contexts of the following passage. (The paragraph numbers are given in parentheses.) Be prepared to use the words in your own sentences.

caesarean (5)

horrific (7)

allegedly (7)

aggravated (13)

flourish (13)

Children Without Pity
NANCY TRAVER

1   Like a child whose mother scolds him for knocking over a glass of milk, Anthony Knighton has his excuses ready. He was just playing. It was an accident. He didn't know the gun was loaded. It could have happened to anyone. Then he admits he shot a pregnant girl because she wouldn't give him a nickel.

2   His trouble started when he went out to buy cigarettes at a corner grocery in his hometown of Deerfield Beach, Florida, on Aug. 13, 1990. The store sold then two for a quarter, and Knighton, then 16, had only 20¢ in his books. So on the way he stopped to ask a neighbor, Schanell Sorrells, 13, for a nickel. Schanell said she didn't have one. He shouted, "Give it over." She refused.

3   Knighton drew a .22-cal. revolver out of his belt, jabbed it into her swollen belly and pulled the trigger. The bullet ripped through her unborn baby's head. Schanell managed to stagger to the room she shared with her mother and four siblings in a boardinghouse in one of the oldest, most dangerous neighborhoods of Deerfield Beach. As she collapsed on a bed, Knighton took a nickel from her room, strolled back to the store and calmly bought two Kools.

4   There were witnesses, but Knighton persuaded them to tell police that Schanell had been injured in a drive-by shooting. He ordered her 15-year-old sister (also pregnant) to hide his gun in a plastic bag full of baby toys. As he rode to Broward General Medical Center in Fort Lauderdale with Schanell and her mother, he told attendants that he was a friend of the family and had nothing to do with the girl's injuries.

5   Doctors delivered the baby by emergency ceasarean. The infant took several breaths, then died; the mother survived and went home to live with her family. Knighton meanwhile slipped away from the hospital and made his way to his father's house near Pompano Beach, where he hoped to hide out for a while. But his father persuaded him to turn himself in, and the boy was charged as an adult with second-degree murder and aggravated battery. He eventually pleaded guilty to third-degree murder and in April 1991 was sentenced to four years in the Indian River Correctional Institution, a medium-security juvenile facility in Vero Beach. Last week, with a felony record, a sixth-grade education, no skills, a bus ticket and $100 from the state, Knighton left prison after serving two years.

6   Knighton's crime is a statistic—an isolated act in a nation where the number of those under 18 who were arrested for murder has climbed 93% over the past decade, while similar arrests among adults grew by only 10%. Among black juveniles, the murder arrest rate rose 145%, compared with 48% among whites. Police chiefs around the country point to another frightening trend: the increase in savage, senseless murders, the kind that occur over a scuffle in a school playground, a pair of sneakers, a romance gone sour. Like

Anthony Knighton who pulled a gun in a squabble over a piece of change, many teenagers no longer use their fists or feet to settle disputes. Instead, they open fire.

7   Newspapers are so filled with reports of such crimes that all but the most horrific lose their power to shock. In Madison, Indiana, four teenage girls doused 12-year-old Shanda Sharer with gasoline and burned her alive in January because she was "trying to steal the affections of another girl." Henry ("Little Man") James, 19, opened fire into a passing car on a Washington-area interstate because he felt "like busting somebody." The somebody turned out to be a 32-year-old woman driving home from work. In Los Angeles two teenage sisters allegedly killed an elderly neighbor while another sister allegedly played a stereo to drown out the screams. They have denied all charges.

8   In the inner cities, where weapons are treated like household appliances, the lessons in cruelty usually start at home. Psychologist Charles Patrick Ewing, author of *Kids Who Kill*, has found that many young people committing seemingly motiveless killings were themselves sexually or physically abused. "To brutalize another human being, a youngster has to have been brutalized himself," he says. Ewing finds that teenage murderers often don't recall, or won't admit, that they were once victims. "A street tough would rather go to the gas chamber than admit to having been beaten or sodomized by a male relative."

9   Anthony Knighton has only vague memories of beatings by his father, a roofer who now lives in Deerfield Beach. His sharpest memories of childhood are of neglect more than fear. After his mother died when he was three, Knighton, the youngest of six children, shuttled among various relatives in Georgia and Florida. By the time he as 15, he had moved 30 times. "It seemed like nobody cared about me," he says, "so I guessed I had to do for myself." Joyce Moore, 27, a cousin who lives in Delray Beach, Florida, recalls that "people would say he could come live with them, but he better not ask for no clothes or money or nothing, 'cause they weren't gonna give it." Why should it come as a surprise, psychologists ask, that children thus passed around have a hard time developing any sense of identity or stability? A child who doesn't know where he is going to live from one month to the next is bound to stay focused on his immediate needs—like a cigarette or a new pair of shoes, no matter what it takes to get them.

10   Knighton never had much chance of being rescued, even if someone had bothered to try. By the time he entered sixth grade, he had attended seven schools. Frank Scalise, director of guidance counseling at Deerfield Beach Middle School, said Knighton came to class only 12 days that year. Truant officers were dispatched to find him, but the family had no address. "He wasn't in school long enough for anybody to get next to him, help him or counsel him," says Scalise. "Then he dropped out, and we never saw him again."

11   Knighton was 14 and living with his father when he began selling crack cocaine. A year later, he was stealing cars and running a $1,000-a-day drug operation. His life savings—what he called his "bank account"—was $30,000 worth of crack and a gold Cadillac. As the boy began making big money, he became a target himself. That inspired him to get his first gun. Weapons were so plentiful that he never had to buy one but simply borrowed from friends. Openly proud of the firearms he has used, Knighton smiles fondly as he recalls each one. "When I was 14, I started out with a .25 automatic, then got me a .38 snub-nosed, then a 12-gauge shotgun, a .45 automatic and a 9-mm. But my last gun—and my best gun—was a baby Uzi."

12   When everyone has a gun, every argument carries the potential for deadly violence. The FBI reports that in 1990 nearly 3 out of 4 juvenile murderers used guns to commit their crimes. "A gun in the hands of a 14-year-old is much more dangerous than in the hands of a 41-year-old," says James Fox, dean of Northeastern University's College of Criminal Justice. "He has little investment in his life, and he doesn't know the meaning of death."

13   Knighton does know a lot about the criminal-justice system. At 16, he had been in juvenile custody 19 times, charged with aggravated assault, auto theft, robbery, drug possession, escape and contempt of court. Knighton was sent to the Better Outlook Center, a halfway house for juvenile offenders in a Miami suburb. Staff members recall Knighton as hostile and angry at first; later he began to flourish under the

supervision of caring adults. "Anthony thought it was heaven," says superintendent Jounice Morris. "It was his first glimpse of stability." Morris, who gave him the nickname "Peanut," recalls that Knighton had the reading ability of a nine-year-old. She says his sister visited him only once during the months he spent at the halfway house; no other relative appeared. "It was clear he'd been passed around from pillar to post, sharing apartments with 12 or 13 other people," Morris said. "There was nobody there for him—there had never been."

14 After the murder, when Knighton landed in the Indian River prison, he worked on a cleanup crew six hours a day. Until state budget cuts forced the prison to eliminate its teachers' salaries, he took high school classes. Because he was considered cooperative and well behaved, Knighton had nearly two years shaved off his sentence. He does not know where his father and siblings now live, but he still keeps in touch with the staff at Better Outlook. In a letter to Morris, Knighton wrote, "I think about that baby I killed, and it hurts real bad."

15 Criminologists predict that the population of young offenders will explode in the decade to come. Just as crime began to surge in the late '60s, when the postwar baby-boom generation reached its teens and early 20s, the children of those baby boomers are committing their first offenses. And for many of them, pulling out a gun is just a funny game with the little girl on the corner.

APPLICATIONS FOR CRITICAL READING AND DISCUSSION

1. What is the idea being supported? State it here, and circle it (if stated directly) in the passage.

2. Is this exemplification based on single or multiple examples?

3. Underline the examples.

4. Is each example specific, typical, or hypothetical? Label each example in the margin with the letters *S*, *T*, or *H*.

5. What is the organization of the examples—time, space, emphasis, or a combination?

6. Does the article imply that there is a solution to the problem of "Children Without Pity"? Explain.

The Reading Connection from Classroom Sources

EXERCISE 7

The author of this paragraph occasionally had heard that "there are good cops and bad cops," but she had a bias against all police that was difficult to overcome. Then a correctional officer, without shirking his duties, surprised her enough so that she reexamined her thinking and even made him the main example in a writing assignment in a college class at the prison where she was incarcerated.

```
                    Cops Can Be Human
                  Janet Larue (Pseudonym)
     After spending six months in a county jail where no cop
ever said anything nice to me, I wasn't expecting to meet
any here in the state prison that I would call "human."
Then I met correctional officer Jenkins (we refer to them
as "cops"). First of all, he called me by my given name
when I moved in, something that I hardly ever heard; even
the other inmates use last names or nicknames most of the
time. He was doing it for all the women, even if he was
calling them down for doing something wrong. Later after
we'd gone to our rooms and he'd locked us in, he came
around again for lights out. Instead of yelling at us to
turn our lights out, he had a little song that went
"Goodnight, Marge. Goodnight, Linda. Goodnight, Beverly.
It's time to kill the lights." He'd go on and on down the
hall, working in lots of names. Then that night when he was
checking the rooms, he didn't make a big deal of it. The
cops are supposed to check twice each night after we go to
bed and "see flesh," and some of them make a lot of noise
with their flashlights till they can see more flesh than
they have to. But Officer Jerkins just moved along, quietly
checking us, so we usually didn't know he'd been there.
Most cops are not like Officer Jenkins, but he was enough
to make me feel better about human beings in general. He
got us to cooperate by being good instead of bad.
```

APPLICATIONS FOR CRITICAL READING AND DISCUSSION

1. What is the idea being supported? State it here, and circle it (if stated directly) in the passage.

2. Is this exemplification based on single or multiple examples?

3. Underline the examples.

4. Is each example specific, typical, or hypothetical? Label each example in the margin with the letters *S*, *T*, or *H*.

5. What is the organization of the examples—time, space, emphasis, or a combination?

6. List some words that indicate order.

EXERCISE 8

Some people are surprised to discover that among the soldiers who fought gallantly in the War of Independence were numerous women. Mary Hayes, who once had a cannonball sail between her knees and tear her dress, actually received a veteran's pension. U.S. history student Maxine Johnson provides some good examples here to support her topic sentence.

> The Fighting, Founding Mothers
> Maxine Johnson
> People argue a lot about the prospects of women in the military fighting in combat, but in the War of Independence, several women distinguished themselves in combat situations. In 1775, Paul Revere got the main credit for riding to warn the Patriots that the British were coming on a military move on Concord and Lexington, Massachusetts. The fact is that although he did warn some Patriots, he was stopped by the British. Who did get through? Several people, including Sybil Ludington, a teenage woman who fearlessly rode her horse like the wind. Another famous woman was known as Molly Pitcher. Her real name was Mary Hayes. She went with her husband to the battlefield, where she brought the men pitchers of water (hence her nickname) and helped load the cannon her husband fired. When her husband was shot at the Battle of Monmouth in 1778, she took over the cannon and fought bravely. At the end of the battle, won by the Patriots, she carried a wounded man for two miles. More than two hundred years ago, these women proved that their gender can be soldiers in every sense.

APPLICATIONS FOR CRITICAL READING AND DISCUSSION

1. What is the idea being supported? State it here, and circle it (if stated directly) in the passage.

2. Is this exemplification based on single or multiple examples?

3. Underline the examples.

4. Is each example specific, typical, or hypothetical? Label each example in the margin with the letters *S*, *T*, or *H*.

5. What is the organization of the examples—time, space, emphasis, or a combination?

EXERCISE 9

Demonstration Using the DCODE Worksheet

Lara Olivas, the student author of this piece "Cheating Is Not Worth the Bother," calls herself an expert in cheating—not because she is a cheater, but because she has seen cheating take place for most of her life. What is the best reason for not cheating: that the cheater might get caught—or that the cheater doesn't learn? The main reason she gives is neither. Read on.

WORKSHEET
Writing in DCODE

NAME: Lara Olivas

SECTION: _____ CHAPTER: _____ DATE: _____

Delve   Generate your topic, or ideas for your topic, by delving into your subject area through:

- *Freewriting*—writing sentence after sentence, nonstop and spontaneously.
- *Brainstorming*—jotting down answers to Who? What? Where? When? Why? and How? and then listing words and phrases in relation to those answers.
- *Clustering*—connecting bubbled ideas with lines to show strings of relationships, producing each new bubble item in response to the question, What comes to mind?
- *Combining* any of these approaches, as directed by your instructor.

Freewriting:
    Cheating is a fact of life at most--maybe all--schools. It starts in the early grades with students looking at other papers and then it gets more complicated. Some people don't do it and a few maybe never have, but I have and I just wasn't up to it. It made me all nervous and I felt bad about what I was doing and I knew I wasn't learning anything. I think many students go through that. Some students just keep on doing it and never stop. For some it's reading plot summaries and Cliff Notes and stuff and for others its more complicated. I've seen kids write all over their bodies. I remember this one girl that hid her notes in a loose fitting blouse and then there was this boy that bought a research paper and almost went crazy using it.

Brainstorming:
    Who? cheating students--me--students I've known--have heard about
    What? cheating--plagiarism, copying
    Where? all schools--schools I've attended
    When? recent past to now
    Why? lazy, insecure, unprincipled
    How? buying work, looking

Clustering:

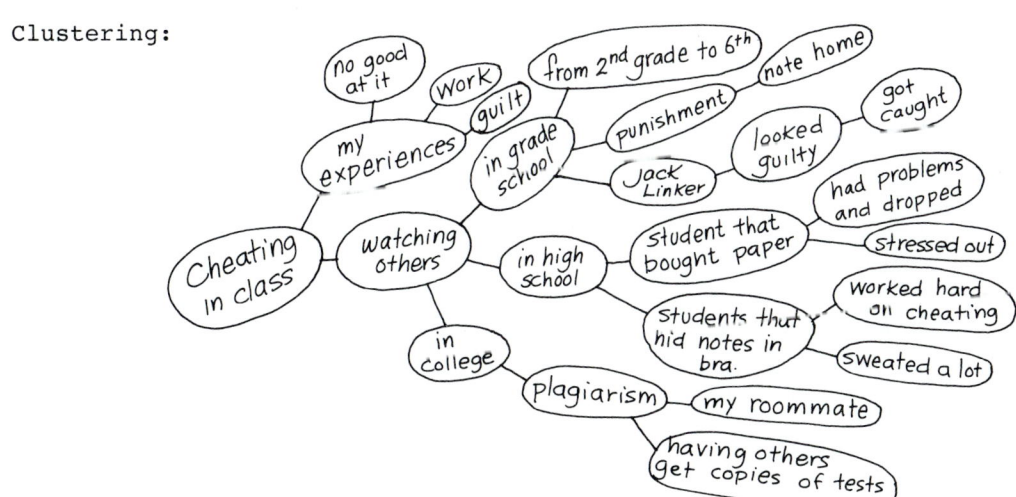

WORKSHEET: Writing in DCODE

Concentrate Concentrate your work by stating your topic in one sentence that is not too broad, narrow, or vague to be developed. Base this sentence (which may become the topic sentence for your paragraph or the thesis for your essay) on an idea emerging from the **Delve** stage. You may have to try several statements here before you formulate one that is best for your writing task. Be sure that your final statement covers your assignment or intent and specifies both your subject (what you are writing about) and treatment (what aspect you will focus on). Label the *subject* and *treatment* parts.

<u>subject</u>   <u>treatment</u>
<u>Cheating students</u> <u>often put themselves under more stress than honest students</u>.

Organize Complete an outline or a cluster, as directed by your instructor. The cluster should be a section from, or a refined version of, the **Delve** clustering. Regardless of the strategy you use, the organizational pattern should indicate a division of your topic into parts that will, in turn, be further subdivided for support as necessary to address a particular audience on your concentrated topic.

    I. Student who bought paper
        A. Had trouble with form
            1. Prewriting
            2. Drafts
        B. Had trouble with quality
        C. Drops class
   II. Student with cheat cards
        A. Had a system
        B. Sometimes under suspicion
        C. Experienced stress

Draft On separate paper, write and then revise your assignment as many times as necessary for **c**oherence, **l**anguage (usage, tone, and diction), **u**nity, **e**mphasis, **s**upport, and **s**entence structure (**cluess**).

Edit Correct problems in fundamentals such as **c**apitalization, **o**missions, **p**unctuation, and **s**pelling (**cops**). Before writing the final draft, read your paper aloud to discover oversights and awkwardness of expression.

First Draft

    I ~~know dozens of~~ [Knew many] students ~~that~~ [who] took college prep classes all the way through high school and never ~~even~~ got ~~close~~ to reading a ~~book~~ [novel] in ~~a~~ [an] English class. They read Cliff'~~s~~Notes or Monarch Notes or they copied work from other people who did. But ~~it wasn't~~ [they weren't cheating] just [in] English classes. They had systems of cheating in every class. It became a way of life. They were always ~~working~~ [conniving] deals and scheming. I'm not that pure. I've tried cheating, but I soon ~~decided~~ [rejected] ~~that it wasn't for me.~~ I didn't learn that way and ~~felt rotten about myself later~~ [lost my self-esteem]; I ~~ran a chance of~~ [also feared] getting caught; and ~~most of all~~ I discovered that most of the time cheating was ~~more work that it was worth~~ [hard, stressful work]. So I never became, like some of my friends, a master cheater~~.~~ [but] I did become a master ~~watcher~~ [observer of cheaters,] because students almost always ~~pick up~~ [see] more than teachers do. The fact is cheaters get all stressed out with the bother. What I learned was that cheaters ~~a~~ often put themselves under more stress than honest students.

    Even the student who pays for ~~some~~ [school] work can ~~get stressed out~~ [become a victim of]. I remember ~~this~~ [a junior] student in my ~~advanced~~ composition class~~.~~ [who] ~~He~~ needed a research paper, so he ~~made a connection~~ [found a source] and bought one for seventy-five dollars. ~~He finally dropped the class after spending more time on his paper than I did on mine.~~ ~~The first trouble~~ [His first problem] was that he had to turn it in in stages: the topic, the working bibliography, [the] ~~note~~ cards, the outline, the rough draft, and the final. ~~So~~ [Therefore,] he went to the library and started working backwards. [Of course] ~~He~~ couldn't turn in ~~just~~ [only] the bib cards actually used in the paper, [and next] he had to make ~~out~~ note cards for the ~~footnoted stuff~~ [material he would be documenting] and ~~then~~ [After] make ~~out~~ more. ~~Having all kinds of trouble. Then finally~~ he realized that the paper [bought] ~~was an "A" paper, and~~ [of quality, whereas] he, ~~since we was~~ [had been] a "C" student ~~even with the cheating would attract the teacher's attention~~. So he went to [his source and] ~~this party where~~ he bought the paper and ~~he was told~~ he could change sentence structure, and so on [to make the paper weaker].

Then, during my senior year a female student became another subject for my study in cheating. ~~there was this girl~~ in Biology 4. She was sitting next to me, so I could see everything she did. She kept her cheat cards ~~sheets~~ in her bra. This is the way she did it. On the day of the test, she would wear a loose-fitting blouse or dress. Sometimes she'd have to fiddle around down there to get the cheat cards ~~sheet~~ to pop into place. Her writing was tiny. ~~If you want to know how~~ because I know about the writing, ~~it's simple.~~ One day the teacher left the room and she just took a card out ~~the sheet out~~ and used it openly. Then when the instructor wasn't watching, she would slump ~~hunch~~ her shoulders like a buzzard sleeping and stoop so she could look down the front of her own dress. If the instructor stared ~~looked~~ at her when she was looking down, she would blow inside her dress as if ~~like~~ she were ~~was~~ trying to cool off her bosom or something. ~~and~~ Then she would smile at the instructor and shake her head and pucker her lips to how hot it was. Her strategy worked because she did perspire due to the stress. The tests were mainly on muscles and bones and weren't that difficult. She probably worked harder in rigging ~~her~~ the cheat a cards ~~sheets~~ on her underwear ear than I did in memorizing information.

There were dozens of other examples ~~s~~—the writing on seats, hands, arms, legs, and cuffs; ~~and~~ the ~~signals~~ signals, hand, blinks, and coughs; and the plagiarism of all kinds. There were even ~~the~~ classes where cheating would never be caught because some. ~~The~~ teachers ~~who~~ didn't watch carefully during the tests and others ~~those who~~ didn't read carefully later. But for the most part, the cheaters were the ones who had the most anxiety and often the ones who ~~that~~ did the most work. ~~The~~ work that was never directed toward learning.

Final Draft

Cheating Is Not Worth the Bother
Lara Olivas

I knew many students who took college prep classes all the way through high school and never read a book in an English class. They read Cliff Notes or Monarch Notes, or they copied work from other people who did. But they weren't cheating just in English classes. They had systems of cheating in every class. Cheating became a way of life. They were always conniving and scheming. I'm not that pure. I've tried cheating, but I soon rejected it. I didn't learn that way, and I lost my self-esteem. I also feared getting caught; and I discovered that most of the time cheating was hard, stressful work. So I never became, like some of my friends, a master cheater, but I did become a master observer of cheaters because students almost always see more than teachers do. What I learned was that cheaters often put themselves under more stress than honest students. *[thesis]*

    Even the student who pays for school work can become a victim of stress. I remember a student in my junior composition class who needed a research paper, so he found a source and bought one for seventy-five dollars. The first trouble was that he had to submit the work in stages: the topic, the working bibliography, the note cards, the outline, the rough draft, and the final. Therefore, he went to the library and started working backwards. Of course, he couldn't turn in only the bib cards actually used in the paper, and next he had to make out note cards for the material he "would be" documenting, and even make out more. After having all kinds of trouble, he realized that the bought paper was of "A" quality, whereas he had been a "C" student. He went back to his source and was told he should change the sentence structure and so on to make the paper weaker. Finally he dropped the class after spending more time on his paper than I did on mine. *[topic sentence / specific example / order by time]*

    Then during my senior year, a female student in Biology 4 became another subject for my study in cheating. She was sitting next to me, so I could see everything she did. She kept her cheat cards in her bra. This is the way she did it. On the day of the test, she would wear a loose-fitting blouse or dress. Then when the instructor wasn't watching, she would hunch her shoulders like a buzzard sleeping and slump so she could look down the front of her own dress. Sometimes she'd have to fiddle around down there to get the cheat card to pop into place. Her writing was tiny. I know about the writing because one day the teacher left the room, and she just took a card out and used it openly. If the instructor stared at her when she was looking down, she would blow inside her dress as if she were trying to cool off her bosom or something. Then she would smile at the instructor and shake her head and pucker her lips to show how hot it was. Her strategy worked because she did perspire due to the stress. The tests were mainly on muscles and bones and weren't that difficult. She probably worked harder in rigging the cheat cards on her underwear than I did in memorizing information. *[topic sentence / specific example / order by time]*

    There were dozens of other examples--the writing on seats, hands, arms, legs, and cuffs; the hand signs, blinks, and coughs; and the plagiarism of all kinds. There were even the classes where cheating would never be caught because some teachers didn't watch carefully during the tests, and others didn't read carefully later. But for the most part, the cheaters were the ones who had the most anxiety and often the ones who did the most work--work that was never directed toward learning. *[cluster of examples]*

APPLICATIONS FOR CRITICAL READING AND DISCUSSION

1. What is the idea being supported? State it here, and circle it (if stated directly) in the passage.

   Cheaters often put themselves under more stress than honest students.

2. Is this exemplification based on single or multiple examples?

   multiple

3. Underline the examples.

4. Is each example specific, typical, or hypothetical? Label each example in the margins with the letters *S*, *T*, or *H*.

   specific

5. What is the organization of the examples—time, space, emphasis, or a combination?

   time

6. Is the purpose to persuade or to inform?

   persuade

Suggested Topics for Writing Exemplification

General Topics

1. Television commercials are often amusing [or misleading, irritating, sexist, racist, useless, etc.].
2. Rap music often carries important messages [or makes me sick, brings out the best in people, brings out the worst in people, degrades women, promotes violence, presents reality, appeals to our better instincts, tells funny stories, etc.].
3. A part-time job can offer more than just the money.
4. Rock groups don't have to be sensational in presentation and appearance to be popular.
5. A person can be an environmentalist in everyday life.
6. Many people who consider themselves law-abiding citizens break laws on a selective basis.
7. Television news is full of stories of violence, but we can also find acts of kindness in everyday life.
8. If you consider what people wear and eat, you can draw some valid conclusions about their attitudes toward life.
9. Car salespeople behave differently depending on the kind of car they are selling and the kind of customer they have.
10. Too many of us are preoccupied with material things.

11. The popularity of a certain [specify it] sitcom [or movie] tells how most people view women [or certain races, nationalities, or social classes].
12. An experience that seems devastating at the time it occurs may seem funny later.
13. We too often get caught up in jealousy, pettiness, and self-centeredness in our daily lives.
14. The best present I ever received was one that cost almost nothing.
15. The kinds of toys people buy for their children tell us much about the prevailing value system in society.
16. People who do not have a satisfying family life will find a family relationship somewhere else.
17. One painful experience reminded me of the importance of human rights [student rights, worker rights, gender rights, etc.].
18. Sexual harassment doesn't have to include touching.
19. Drug abuse, including alcohol abuse, may be present with those who seem to be functioning well.
20. Country music appeals to some of our most basic concerns.
21. A funny incident or statement can relieve a lot of tension.
22. The shoes a person wears can reveal his or her personality.

Reading-Related Topics

"Scalpel Slaves"

1. Develop a topic on hypochondria (a psychological condition in which a person believes that he or she is ill) by giving examples of person you know who have made sickness a way of life.

"Personal Space"

2. Develop a topic on using body language to discourage unwanted advances, interruptions of any sort, conversations, introductions, and so on.

"Baby Nag-a-Lot"

3. Develop a topic on using toys, television, or other devices as a substitute for parents.

"Struggling for Sanity"

4. Borrow the main idea from this essay, use it for your topic sentence or thesis, and develop it with your own examples.

"Children Without Pity"

5. Borrow the main idea from this essay, use it for your topic sentence or thesis, and develop it with your own examples.

"Cops Can Be Human"

6. Adapt this topic on the character of police personnel to a local situation involving an occupational group (teachers, preachers, doctors, bus drivers, salespeople, and so on), and develop it by using an example or examples.

"The Fighting, Founding Mothers"

7. Use an example or examples to develop a topic about the involvement of Native Americans or African Americans in the War of Independence (or with any underrepresented or misrepresented group in any war or movement).

"Cheating Is Not Worth the Bother"

8. Use the main idea as your topic sentence or thesis and develop it, with your own example(s), for a paragraph or an essay.

 **Writer's Checklist**

Apply the following ideas to your writing as you work with **DCODE**. Later, as a peer editor (a student reviewing another student's work) or as a participant in collaborative work, apply the same ideas to the material you work with.

1. Pick the kind of example that will best support your ideas; don't overlook the power of the specific example (name, place, etc.).
2. Don't overlook personal experience as a source of good examples.
3. Select an example or examples that are representative and interesting.
4. Consider how much your audience knows about your example or examples and how they are likely to react to them.
4. Establish and maintain a clear relationship between the supporting example or examples and the main idea.
5. In the extension of an example or in the use of several examples, consider order of presentation, such as time, space, emphasis, and logic.

 **Journal-Entry Suggestions**

1. Select some of the unused "Reading-Related Topics" writing suggestions and use them for journal topics.
2. Write a reaction to one or more reading selections. Agree, disagree, apply the statements to your own experiences, indicate the value of such statements, and explain why you were surprised, shocked, disgusted, pleased, or whatever, by the material.
3. Invent statements (examples if appropriate) to support headlines from *Weekly World News*:
    "U.S. Navy Captures Monster in Lake Michigan"
    "Goldfish Gets Run Over by 18-Wheeler—and Survives"
    "Fortune Cookies for Gamblers"
    "Dopey Dolphin Falls in Love with a Surfboard"
    "Man Fired over Spilled Coffee"
    "Kissing Couple Bursts into Flames"
    "Ritzy Restaurant Raided by Hungry Apes"
    "Docs Deliver Baby Frozen for 600 Years"
    "Ouija Board Nabs Killer"
    "Gramps Grows New Set of Teeth"

WORKSHEET
Writing in DCODE

NAME: _____

SECTION: _____ CHAPTER: _____ DATE: _____

Delve   Generate your topic, or ideas for your topic, by delving into your subject area through:

- *Freewriting*—writing sentence after sentence, nonstop and spontaneously.
- *Brainstorming*—jotting down answers to Who? What? Where? When? Why? and How? and then listing words and phrases in relation to those answers.
- *Clustering*—connecting bubbled ideas with lines to show strings of relationships, producing each new bubble item in response to the question, What comes to mind?
- *Combining* any of these approaches, as directed by your instructor.

WORKSHEET: Writing in DCODE

Concentrate Concentrate your work by stating your topic in one sentence that is not too broad, narrow, or vague to be developed. Base this sentence (which may become the topic sentence for your paragraph or the thesis for your essay) on an idea emerging from the **Delve** stage. You may have to try several statements here before you formulate one that is best for your writing task. Be sure that your final statement covers your assignment or intent and specifies both your subject (what you are writing about) and treatment (what aspect you will focus on). Label the *subject* and *treatment* parts.

Organize Complete an outline or a cluster, as directed by your instructor. The cluster should be a section from, or a refined version of, the **Delve** clustering. Regardless of the strategy you use, the organizational pattern should indicate a division of your topic into parts that will, in turn, be further subdivided for support as necessary to address a particular audience on your concentrated topic.

Draft On separate paper, write and then revise your assignment as many times as necessary for **c**oherence, **l**anguage (usage, tone, and diction), **u**nity, **e**mphasis, **s**upport, and **s**entence structure (**cluess**).

Edit Correct problems in fundamentals such as **c**apitalization, **o**missions, **p**unctuation, and **s**pelling (**cops**). Before writing the final draft, read your paper aloud to discover oversights and awkwardness of expression.

Functional Analysis: Examining the Components

> "Whatever we conceive well, we express clearly.
> — Nicolas Boileau

"This next one goes out to all those who have ever been in love, then become engaged, gotten married, participated in the tragic deterioration of a relationship, suffered the pains and agonies of a bitter divorce, subjected themselves to the fruitless search for a new partner, and ultimately resigned themselves to remaining single in a world full of irresponsible jerks, noncommittal weirdos, and neurotic misfits."

What does *functional analysis* mean? How does one avoid the selection of unequal parts in functional analysis? How does one organize functional analysis?

Functional Analysis Defined

If you need to explain how something works or exists as a unit, you will write a *functional analysis.* You will break down your subject into its parts and explain how each part functions in relation to the operation or existence of the whole.

Moving from Subject, to Principle, to Division, to Relationship

Almost anything can be analyzed for function—for example, how the parts of the ear work in hearing, how the parts of the eye work in seeing, or how the parts of the heart work in pumping blood throughout the body. Subjects such as these are all approached with the same systematic procedure.

Step 1. Begin with something that is a unit.
Step 2. State the principle by which that unit functions.
Step 3. Divide the unit into parts according to that principle.
Step 4. Discuss each of those parts in relation to the unit.

This is the way you might apply that procedure to a leaf:

Unit	leaf
Principle of function	food manufacturer
Parts based on the principle	(1) the blade (including the food-making cells, the veins, and the molecules of chlorophyll) and (2) the the petiole (the stalk by which the leaf is attached to the stem of the plant)
Discussion	an explanation of how each part contributes to the manufacturing of food

A leaf can represent still another unit as a concept. You could say a leaf is a beautiful object. In this case, you would follow the same procedure, but the particulars would be different.

Unit	leaf
Principle of function	beautiful object
Parts based on the principle	texture, shape, color
Discussion	an explanation of how the three parts function together to produce that which we call "beautiful object"

Those two approaches are equally valid. But if we mix them by applying more than one principle at a time, we will have an illogical functional analysis. For example, if we say that a leaf has a blade, a petiole, and the eye-catching color of a ripe tangerine, we will have trouble in performing a functional analysis.

The important point here is that subjects can often be considered from different perspectives according to function. A sound analysis must begin with that function clearly in mind. Institutions such as churches, governments, families, and schools can have different functions. So can art forms such as short stories, poems, plays, novels, and songs. A particular woman can be analyzed according to all her functions collectively as an entity, or, more likely, according to a particular function—independent individual, worker, family member, wife, mother, or friend.

Order

Your organizational pattern for the functional analysis will vary, depending on the nature of the unit. Following are some considerations:

Time	Something may function in a sequential fashion, one thing naturally leading to another, as you would analyze a legislature passing a law.
Space	If you were analyzing a baseball team in the fielding or defensive mode, you might begin with the pitcher and move to the catcher and then through the infield to the outfield.
Emphasis	The word *function* means working or moving toward an end, and the sequence (time) often provides order or coherence, but in some instances the parts will all function simultaneously. In that case, you may want to move from the most important to the least important or, more likely, from the least important to the most important. Although the first part of any passage receives special attention, the last is the most emphatic.
Combination	Time and space, especially, can be combined for order.

In the following short essay, Robert F. Weaver explains how cancer cells (unit) function as destructive units (principle) because they have certain characteristics (equivalent to parts): (1) lack of control over growth, (2) tendency to invade, and (3) ability to pass the malignant properties on to their offspring through cell division. Consider the use of the last paragraph, which clearly states the divisions of the subject and covers the relationship of those divisions. The order of the parts, time, is dictated by the progressive nature of cancer cells.

> Why can we prevent polio with relatively simple vaccines, cure pneumonia with antibiotics, and yet make only modest inroads against cancer? One reason is that cancer is not one disease, but many. The human body contains more than a hundred different types of cells, and each of these can go awry in its own distinctive way. The cancer puzzle is a whole series of puzzles. On the other hand, we recognize certain characteristics common to most cancer cells. The most obvious trait of these savage cells is that they run amok. They go out of control. Consider, for example, what happens when you cut a finger accidentally. Very quickly the cells around the incision receive a signal to divide more rapidly and heal the wound. Then, as soon as they accomplish the job, another

principle of functioning unit
part 1

note the time order through parts 1, 2, and 3

signal tells them to slow down. Normal cells always obey this slow-down sign, preserving an exquisite balance between old cells dying and new cells appearing.

But renegade cancer cells no longer obey. They continue to divide without control until their voracious appetites overwhelm their host.

<u>Cancer cells show a distressing ability to invade the tissues around them, disrupting them and robbing them of food.</u> <u>Worse, they metastasize, or spread.</u> For instance, cancer cells may break off from a bone tumor, migrate through the bloodstream, and establish new tumors in the lungs. Once a tumor has metastasized, the cancer is much harder to treat. This points to the importance of frequent physical examinations and prompt attention to the seven warning signals publicized by the American Cancer Society.

These two characteristics of cancer cells—lack of control over growth and tendency to invade—imply a third quality: the ability of cancer cells to pass the malignant properties on to their progeny, cell division after cell division.

part 2

part 3

restated principle with specific information

Robert F. Weaver, "The Cancer Puzzle"

The Reading Connection

EXERCISE 1

Demonstration

Surely no one else could think of a more concise way of writing a functional analysis than Irwin Rubenstein has in this short paragraph. The explanation is clear, direct, and informative.

The Living Cell
IRWIN RUBENSTEIN

A *thin covering* encloses each cell. Within the covering is a jellylike fluid called *cytoplasm*. This fluid contains many tiny structures. Each structure has a job to do, such as producing energy. Most cells have a structure called the *nucleus*, which is the cell's control point. The nucleus contains the cell's *genetic program*, a master plan that controls almost everything the cell does. The entire living substance that makes up the cell is often called *protoplasm*.

APPLICATIONS FOR CRITICAL READING AND DISCUSSION:

1. What is the unit?
    ```
    cell
    ```

2. What is the principle by which that unit functions? In other words, what does the unit do or represent from this perspective? Write the answer here, and circle the passage that states or suggests the principle.
    ```
    living substance
    ```

3. What are the parts that make up the unit according to this principle? Underline them in the text, and write them here.
    ```
    (1)  thin covering (cell wall)
    (2)  cytoplasm
    (3)  nucleus
    ```

4. What is the order of the parts (time, space, emphasis, or a combination)?
    ```
    space--from the cell wall in
    ```

EXERCISE 2

In this brief paragraph unit of functional analysis, Richard Ford tries to encapsulate the characteristics that make Bruce Springsteen a top entertainer. In discussing the components for greatness, Ford goes well beyond the realm of superficial performance.

The Boss Observed
RICHARD FORD

Springsteen's excellence is right there. The best he writes and sings and plays does what rock 'n' roll always has: advances an observable world where the heart's sometimes bad transactions are standard and unprofound. Then, through his songs' complex little beauties and surprises, he dignifies small feelings with the gravity of real emotion, defines innocence in terms new to it, makes rote gestures seem heartbreaking, and gives a voice of consequence to the unlistened to. It's what poets sometimes do.

2   Revealing the exquisite where it hasn't been known before can, of course, add up to less than art. It can add up to a lot of baloney—pretension and sentimentality played too loud. But Springsteen, who plays both loud and soft, instead writes music that's ascendant and urgent, surprising and unusually sweet for rock 'n' roll. His lyrics are discursive, quirky, intimate, and exotic, but never mysterious. All this comes fronted by a street-tough persona that seems robust and sincere, unrestrained, poignant, savvy—a street kid you'll listen to.

3   And these are only the simple niceties. What gives Springsteen's music its texture, its feeling of underpinning, and what defeats sentimentality, at least most of the time, is Springsteen's—I guess you'd call it extensive *voice*: his fine instinct for what a song might possibly be about, as in, say, "Spirit in the Night"; his music's ease at drawing our notice pleasingly to its own formal parts; and the almost literary way all his songs interest us in what he *knows*, as much as how he can perform musically.

APPLICATIONS FOR CRITICAL READING AND DISCUSSION

1. What is the unit?

2. What is the principle by which that unit functions? In other words, what does the unit do or represent from this perspective? Write the answer here, and circle the passage that states or suggests the principle.

3. What are the parts that make up the unit according to this principle? Underline them in the text, and write them here.

4. What is the order of the parts (time, space, emphasis, or a combination)?

EXERCISE 3

Using a prescribed form is common in all the arts. The sonata, as analyzed here, may seem somewhat mechanical with its four sequential parts, but with development it can become a beautiful work with an imaginative, seamless flow.

The Sonata
RAYMOND KENDALL

A sonata is an instrumental composition with two or more movements with contrasts both in tempo and key, but related in thought. The usual four-movement sonata begins with a brilliant *allegro*, and the second movement is slow, rhythmic, and lyrical (*andante, adagio,* or *largo*).

The third movement is usually light and graceful, and may be in dance form, or a *scherzo*. The *finale* (last movement) is in quick, bright tempo. Symphonies, string quartets, and long works for solo instruments use this sonata form.

APPLICATIONS FOR CRITICAL READING AND DISCUSSION

1. What is the unit?

2. What is the principle by which that unit functions? In other words, what does the unit do or represent from this perspective? Write the answer here, and circle the passage that states or suggests the principle.

3. What are the parts that make up the unit according to this principle? Underline them in the text, and write them here.

4. What is the order of the parts (time, space, emphasis, or a combination)?

EXERCISE 4

A successful game show may appear to be something that happens in an almost free form because it appears to be simple and superficial in every way. Lewis Grossberger knows better. He says that whether the planners set up this show with shrewd calculation or not, the success can be explained. The explanation can be found in a process called, of course, functional analysis.

Vocabulary Preview: Write in short definitions for these words as they are used in the context of the following passage. (The paragraph numbers are given in parentheses.) Be prepared to use the words in your own sentences.

debuted (1)

subtle (2)

illusion (3)

surrogates (5)

relegated (5)

morbid (6)

ambiance (7)

primal (7)

benign (8)

sophisticates (9)

minions (10)

nullity (10)

A Big Wheel
LEWIS GROSSBERGER

When the nighttime "Wheel of Fortune" debuted, the slot was occupied by magazine shows like "Entertainment Tonight" and "PM Magazine." The conventional wisdom was that only older women—not the bigger-spending eighteen-to-forty-five mixed audience advertisers drool for—watched gamers. But "Wheel" took off. Soon it was on 163 stations, in many cities twice a day. It was huge.

2   Obviously, night gave "Wheel" bigger audience potential than day had. More sets are on at night. (Daytime "Wheel" pulls a measly 8 million faces.) But night alone doesn't explain the show's hegemony. What does explain it is the subtle but powerful wonder ingredient all successful game shows have, but none so purely as "Wheel of Fortune." It starts with a V, like Vanna. It's called Vicariousness.

3   Vicariousness. "Wheel of Fortune" creates the illusion for the hard-working, treadmill-trotting Middle American yearner (the show's greatest strength is outside the major media markets) that he or she is in the big game. Viewers don't exactly identify with the contestants; they *become* the contestants.

4   Look at the elements of the show.

5   *The Players:* Unlike the dramatized big domes of the fifties, "Wheel" contestants are ordinary folk who serve as the viewers' surrogates. In the whoopee-cushion seventies, game-show contestants screamed, bounced, and wet themselves, but in the we-mean-business eighties, Americans are

cooler and less likely to appear in public dressed as yams. "Wheel" subtly de-emphasizes its contestants, who seem interchangeable. Pat introduces these undemonstrative, low-profile types with the briefest possible questioning, then the camera quickly moves off them and zooms in on the game. With the contestants relegated to the background, the viewer can put himself in their place and play. And when a winner goes prize picking, we see only a small head shot in a corner of the screen; the main focus is on the merchandise. Even if undefeated, a contestant is booted out after three days. No stars are born here. (Which is why there's no chance "Wheel of Fortune" is rigged—the producers don't care who wins.) In your fantasy, you are the star.

6   *The Game:* Both games promise easy success, one through luck, the other skill. The wheel—hypnotic, alluring, symbolic of nearly everything—is luckier than a roulette wheel, since it can yield only two bad outcomes: BANKRUPT or LOSE A TURN. Any other spin wins. Nice odds. The word puzzle is simple but compelling—it gets easier as you play, because more letters fill in. (No Gloomy Gus, Merv discarded the morbid scoring system of the original hangman, which utilizes a stick figure dangling from a gallows. Like casino owners, game-show proprietors want you to be cheery.) As Pat Sajak noted, viewers often solve the puzzle before contestants. With the whole family watching, someone at home is almost bound to. The result: You feel happy, excited, superior. You're chalking up wins. You're on a roll.

7   *The Payoff:* During play, the wheel-whirling contestants (and, by extension, the viewers) are given credit. A nice touch. Who doesn't love credit? It's like betting on someone else's tab. And when you win, you don't win mere cash or some preordained prize. You go *shopping*! A brilliant touch. Shopping may be the ultimate thrill in this commodity-crazed era, an actual addiction for some. And it doesn't hurt "Wheel," in the yuppie department, either. Merv himself once said, "It's like being let loose on Rodeo Drive." As the winner shops, the camera lovingly roves around the prize showcase, as though the viewers' own eyeballs have been let loose amid the VCRs, Isuzu pickups, Tahitian vacations, and ceramic Dalmatians. "Wheel's" ambiance blends the organized excitement of the casino with the primal pull of the department store.

8   *The Cast:* Game-show hosts are permitters and forgivers. Their benign presence signals that it's okay to indulge your greed, just in case some shred of conscience or old-fashioned values intrudes to make you feel guilty for craving wealth without work. Pat Sajak is today's kind of authority figure: casual, low-key, jocular, even a bit irreverent. Dignified and well dressed, he could be a yuppie cleric, lawyer, or doctor. He could switch jobs with Ronald Reagan and little would change. Merv has said Pat is like everyone's son-in-law. He must have meant everyone's fantasy son-in-law.

9   And Vanna? Pat Sajak likes to say that Vanna's silence gives her a mysterious air. But there isn't any mystery. Her personality shines through without benefit of speech. She's a *cheerleader*. Your own personal cheerleader. Her most vital function is not really her letter turning (artistic though it is) but her clapping! She is forever clapping for the contestants (all of them—Vanna is impartial). Despite her glitzy outfits, which sophisticates find tacky but most Americans probably find glamorous, she's a throwback to the kind of simple, sunny, apple-pie-sexy, all-American girl next door who'd be content to stay on the sidelines cheering for someone else. Vanna knows what she's doing, sort of. When I asked if she'd been a cheerleader in high school, she said, "Of course. Who would have ever thought I'd still be a cheerleader?"

10 And that's *why*. Now you know. Let me just add, before taking a well-deserved nap, that I doubt that Merv and his minions set out to design "Wheel of Fortune" around the Big V Principle or analyzed the economy. I think they just happened, by instinct, experience—and good luck—to hit on a formula that would make it the state-of-the-art eighties game show. A formula that sucks the viewer through the screen and into that dazzling dreamscape—Vanna's Nirvana—where he is transformed from a nullity, a hapless anonymous bozo, a nobody from nowhere, to the only being now worth being: a Winner. Someone possessed of wealth, luck, and, maybe more important, television exposure. Someone, in short, who finally exists. You know, a big wheel.

APPLICATIONS FOR CRITICAL READING AND DISCUSSION

1. What is the unit?

2. What is the principle by which that unit functions? In other words, what does the unit do or represent from this perspective? Write the answer here, and circle the passage that states or suggests the principle.

3. What are the parts that make up the unit according to this principle? Underline them in the text, and write them here.

4. What is the order of the parts (time, space, emphasis, or a combination)?

EXERCISE 5

If you were almost murdered dozens of times and if most of your family and hundreds of thousands of your race were tortured and slaughtered in places such as the one in which you were incarcerated, what traits would you need for survival? And then if you did survive, what would you need in order to reclaim your life after the ordeal we now call the Holocaust?

Vocabulary Preview: Write in short definitions for these words as they are used in the context of the following passage. (The paragraph numbers are given in parentheses.) Be prepared to use the words in your own sentences.

siege (1)

stereotypical (3)

anecdotal (3)

succumb (3)

constitute (4)

inflicted (5)

adversity (5)

assertive (7)

assimilation (10)

debilitating (11)

sustenance (12)

Optimism, Tenacity Lead Way Back to Life
WILLIAM HELMREICH

Accounts of tragedy and catastrophe have been much in the news: hurricanes in Florida and Hawaii, the siege of Sarajevo, famine in Somalia and Sudan. The media focus tends to be on death and destruction and the terrible aftereffects on human beings. This is not surprising, but there are other, more hopeful, lessons to be learned from calamity.

2 I have spent the last six years traveling the United States, from New York to California, from Wisconsin to Mississippi, hearing from hundreds of people who lived through the greatest horror

of the 20th Century, the Holocaust. I was curious as to how the lives of these Jews had turned out and whether they were able to recover from their terrible experiences.

3 The results, when compared with the stereotypical anecdotal accounts of survivors who succumb to depression, anxiety and hopelessness, were highly surprising. While many survivors did have these serious emotional problems, the great majority did not. They led relatively normal lives, holding down jobs, having and raising children and contributing to the communities in which they settled. Some, such as Rep. Tom Lantos (D-Burlingame); Abraham Resnick, former vice mayor of Miami; Maj. Gen. Sidney Shachnow and the director of the Anti-Defamation League, Abraham Foxman, achieved considerable fame in their chosen fields. Others, not so well-known, became musicians, tailors, businessmen, teachers and farmers.

4 Naturally, all of the survivors are still affected, even haunted, by what happened to them. But they also constitute, on the whole, a community whose members display a zest for life and who have faith in the future.

5 How did they do it, I wondered? How, after experiencing betrayal and unspeakable cruelty in the Nazi death camps and elsewhere in Europe, were the survivors able to learn to live again, trust again, love again, and bring children into a world that had inflicted such pain on them? The answers contain lessons for everyone who goes through crisis and adversity, be it loss of a loved one, crippling illness, natural disaster or even a job reversal.

6 Most of the survivors who succeeded in rebuilding their lives possessed several traits:

7 First was flexibility, a willingness to adapt to new situations, much like what faces the survivors of Hurricanes Andrew and Iniki. In addition, there was a need to be assertive—a recognition that help given by others would be temporary and that ultimately they were on their own. Related to this was tenacity, an approach to life that refused to accept initial setbacks as the status quo.

8 One of the most crucial survivor characteristics was optimism. More than not thinking about the past, it reflected a certain mind-set. Alex Gross, a real estate developer who survived Auschwitz and Buchenwald, later lost his only son, at 14, in a farming accident. When he saw the mangled body, he resolved never to reveal the details of the death to his wife. Alas, that was not the end of Gross's woes. Nine years later his wife was murdered. Despite this double tragedy, Alex Gross has remarried and is active in his community. He is a survivor.

9 Survivors who did well were intelligent. This trait, which includes "street smarts," amounts to an ability to think quickly, analyze a situation and act. Another key feature was distancing ability, the capacity to view the Holocaust as a unique event requiring certain behavior that was appropriate then but not now. This was accompanied by group consciousness, the forging of a common bond with others who shared their tragedy.

10 Related to this was a more subtle trait, assimilation of the knowledge that they survived. This amounted to using the fact that one has prevailed over hardship as a source of strength. Of equal significance was finding meaning in one's life. For some it was their work, for others religion, and for many it was the bonds of love within the family structure.

11 Finally, there was courage. Simply continuing with life was an act of bravery. Specifically, however, it took many forms—fighting back from debilitating illness, taking risks in business or standing up to bigotry.

12 Those who have lived through the riots in Los Angeles or the siege in Sarajevo, those who have lived through earthquakes, hurricanes and floods, can draw strength and sustenance from Hitler's survivors. The reason is that the success story of the survivors is not one of remarkable people. Rather, it is one of just how remarkable people can be.

APPLICATIONS FOR CRITICAL READING AND DISCUSSION

1. What is the unit?

2. What is the principle by which that unit functions? In other words, what does the unit do or represent from this perspective? Write the answer here, and circle the passage that states or suggests the principle.

3. What are the parts that make up the unit according to this principle? Underline them in the text, and write them here.

4. What is the order of the parts (time, space, emphasis, or a combination)?

EXERCISE 6

Who are you? Can you classify yourself with a single word? Kesaya E. Noda has grown up Asian in America, but she needs several words to characterize herself because her identity has many facets.

Vocabulary Preview: Write in short definitions for these words as they are used in the context of the following passage. (The paragraph numbers are given in parentheses.) Be prepared to use the words in your own sentences.

perpetuated (1)

devastated (15)

arduously (18)

gait (22)

pluralism (32)

spontaneous (32)

harangued (32)

harassed (32)

affirmation (34)

encounter (34)

Growing Up Asian in America
KESAYA E. NODA

Sometimes when I was growing up, my identity seemed to hurtle toward me and paste itself right to my face. I felt that way, encountering the stereotypes of my race perpetuated by non-Japanese people (primarily white) who may or may not have had contact with other Japanese in America. "You don't like cheese, do you?" someone would ask. "I know your people don't like cheese." Sometimes questions came making allusions to history. That was another aspect of the identity. Events that had happened quite apart from the me who stood silent in that moment connected my face with an incomprehensible past. "Your parents were in California? Were they in those camps during the war?" And sometimes there were phrases or nicknames: "Lotus Blossom." I was sometimes addressed or referred to as racially Japanese, sometimes as Japanese-American, and sometimes as an Asian woman. Confusions and distortions abounded.

2   How is one to know and define oneself? From the inside—within a context that is self-defined from a grounding in community and a connection with culture and history that are comfortably accepted? Or from the outside—in terms of messages received from the media and people who are often ignorant? Even as an adult I can still see two sides of my face and past. I can see from the inside out, in freedom. And I can see from the outside in, driven by the old voices of childhood and lost in anger and fear.

I Am Racially Japanese

3   A voice from my childhood says: "You are other. You are less than. You are unalterably alien." This voice has its own history. We have indeed been seen as other and alien since the early years of our arrival in the United States. The very first immigrants were welcomed and sought as laborers to replace the dwindling numbers of Chinese, whose influx had been cut off by the Chinese Exclusion Act of 1882. The Japanese fell natural heir to the same anti-Asian prejudice that had arisen against the Chinese. As soon as they began striking for better wages, they were no longer welcomed.

4   I can see myself today as a person historically defined by law and custom as being forever alien. Being neither "free white," nor "African," our people in California were deemed "aliens, ineligible for citizenship," no matter how long they intended to stay here. Aliens ineligible for citizenship were prohibited from owning, buying, or leasing land. They did not and could not belong here. The voice in me remembers that I am always a *Japanese*-American in the eyes of many. A third-generation German-American is an American. A third-generation Japanese-American is a Japanese-American. Being Japanese means being a danger to the country during the war and knowing how to use chopsticks. I wear this history on my face.

5   I move to the other side. I see a different light and claim a different context. My race is a line that stretches across ocean and time to link me to the shrine where my grandmother was raised. Two high, white banners lift in the wind at the top of the stone steps leading to the shrine. It is time for the summer festival. Black characters are written against the sky as boldly as the clouds, as lightly as kites, as sharply as the big black crows I used to see above the fields in New Hampshire. At festival time there is liquor and food, ritual, discipline, and abandonment. There is music and drunkenness and invocation. There is hope. Another season has come. Another season has gone.

6   I am racially Japanese. I have a certain claim to this crazy place where the prayers intoned by a neighboring Shinto priest (standing in for my grandmother's nephew who is sick) are drowned out by the rehearsals for the pop singing contest in which most of the villagers will compete later that night. The village elders, the priest, and I stand respectfully upon the immaculate, shining wooden floor of the outer shrine, bowing our heads before the hidden powers. During the patchy intervals when I can hear him, I notice the priest has a stutter. His voice flutters up to my ears only occasionally because two men and a woman are singing gustily into a microphone in the compound, testing the sound system. A pre-recorded tape of guitars, samisens, and drums accompanies them. Rock music and Shinto prayers. That night, to loud applause and cheers, a young man is given the award for the most *netsuretsu*—passionate, burning—rendition of a song. We roar our approval of the reward. Never mind that his voice had wandered and slid, now slightly above, now slightly below the given line of the melody. Netsuretsu. Netsuretsu.

7   In the morning, my grandmother's sister kneels at the foot of the stone stairs to offer her morning prayers. She is too crippled to climb the stairs, so each morning she kneels here upon the path. She shuts her eyes for a few seconds, her motions as matter of fact as when she washes rice. I linger longer than she does, so reluctant to leave, savoring the connection I feel with my grandmother in America, the past, and the power that lives and shines in the morning sun.

8   Our family has served this shrine for generations. The family's need to protect this claim to identity and place outweighs any individual claim to any individual hope. I am Japanese.

I Am a Japanese-American

9   "Weak." I hear the voice from my childhood years. "Passive," I hear. Our parents and grandparents were the ones who were put into those

camps. They went without resistance, they offered cooperation as proof of loyalty to America. "Victim," I hear. And, "Silent."

10 Our parents are painted as hard workers who were socially uncomfortable and had difficulty expressing even the smallest opinion. Clean, quiet, motivated, and determined to match the American way; that is us, and that is the story of our time here.

11 "Why did you go into those camps?" I raged at my parents, frightened by my own inner silence and timidity. "Why didn't you do anything to resist? Why didn't you name it the injustice it was?" Couldn't our parents even think? Couldn't they? Why were we so passive?

12 I shift my vision and my stance. I am in California. My uncle is in the midst of the sweet potato harvest. He is pressed, trying to get the harvesting crews onto the field as quickly as possible, worried about the flow of equipment and people. His big pickup is pulled off to the side, motor running, door ajar. I see two tractors in the yard in front of an old shed; the flatbed harvesting platform on which the workers will stand has already been brought over from the other field. It's early morning. The workers stand loosely grouped and at ease, but my uncle looks as harried and tense as a police officer trying to unsnarl a New York City traffic jam. Driving toward the shed, I pull my car off the road to make way for an approaching tractor. The front wheels of the car sink luxuriously into the soft, white sand by the roadside and the car slides to a dreamy halt, tail still on the road. I try to move forward. I try to move back. The front bites contentedly into the sand, the back lifts itself at a jaunty angle. My uncle sees me and storms down the road, running. He is shouting before he is even near me.

13 "What's the matter with you?" he screams. "What the hell are you doing?" In his frenzy, he grabs his hat off his head and slashes it through the air across his knee. He is beside himself. "Don't you know how to drive in sand? What's the matter with you? You've blocked the whole roadway. How am I supposed to get my tractors out of here? Can't you use your head? You've cut off the whole roadway, and we've got to get out of here."

14 I stand on the road before him helplessly thinking, "No, I don't know how to drive in sand. I've never driven in sand."

15 "I'm sorry, uncle," I say, burying a smile beneath a look of sincere apology. I notice my deep amusement and my affection for him with great curiosity. I am usually devastated by anger. Not this time.

16 During the several years that follow I learn about the people and the place, and much more about what has happened in this California village where my parents grew up. The issei, our grandparents, made this settlement in the desert. Their first crops were eaten by rabbits and ravaged by insects. The land was so barren that men walking from house to house sometimes got lost. Women came here too. They bore children in 114-degree heat, then carried the babies with them into the fields to nurse when they reached the end of each row of grapes or other truck-farm crops.

17 I had no idea what it meant to buy this kind of land and make it grow green. Or how, when the war came, there was no space at all for the subtlety of being who we were—Japanese-Americans. Either/or was the way. I hadn't understood that people were literally afraid for their lives then, that their money had been frozen in banks; that there was a five-mile travel limit; that when the early evening curfew came and they were inside their houses, some of them watched helplessly as people they knew went into their barns to steal their belongings. The police were patrolling the road, interested only in violators of curfew. There was no help for them in the face of thievery. I had not been able to imagine before what it must have felt like to be an American—to know absolutely that one is an American—and yet to have almost everyone else deny it. Not only deny it, but challenge that identity with machine guns and troops of white American soldiers. In those circumstances it was difficult to say, "I'm Japanese-American." "American" had to do.

18 But now I can say that I am a Japanese-American. It means I have a place here in this country, too. I have a place here on the East Coast, where our neighbor is so much a part of our family that my mother never passes her house at night without glancing at the lights to see if she is home and safe; where my parents have hauled hundreds of pounds of rocks from fields and arduously planted Christmas trees and blueberries, lilacs, asparagus, and crab apples, where my father still dreams of angling a stream to a new bed so that he can dig a pond in the field and fill it with

water and fish. "The neighbors already came for their Christmas tree?" he asks in December. "Did they like it? Did they like it?"

19 I have a place on the West Coast where my relatives still farm, where I heard the stories of feuds and backbiting, and where I saw that people survived and flourished because fundamentally they trusted and relied upon one another. A death in the family is not just a death in a family; it is a death in the community. I saw people help each other with money, materials, labor, attention, and time. I saw men gather once a year, without fail, to clean the grounds of a ninety-year-old woman who had helped the community before, during, and after the war. I saw her remembering them with birthday cards sent to each of their children.

20 I come from a people with a long memory and a distinctive grace. We live our thanks. And we are Americans. Japanese-Americans.

I Am a Japanese-American Woman

21 Woman. The last piece of my identity. It has been easier by far for me to know myself in Japan and to see my place in America than it has been to accept my line of connection with my own mother. She was my dark self, a figure in whom I thought I saw all that I feared most in myself. Growing into womanhood and looking for some model of strength, I turned away from her. Of course, I could not find what I sought. I was looking for a black feminist or a white feminist. My mother is neither white nor black.

22 My mother is a woman who speaks with her life as much as with her tongue. I think of her with her own mother. Grandmother had Parkinson's disease and it had frozen her gait and set her fingers, tongue and feet jerking and trembling in a terrible dance. My aunts and uncles wanted her to be able to live in her own home. They fed her, bathed her, dressed her, awoke at midnight to take her for one last trip to the bathroom. My aunts (her daughters-in-law) did most of the care, but my mother went from New Hampshire to California each summer to spend a month living with Grandmother, because she wanted to and because she wanted to give my aunts at least a small rest. During those hot summer days, mother lay on the couch watching the television or reading, cooking foods that Grandmother liked, and speaking little. Grandmother thrived under her care.

23 The time finally came when it was too dangerous for Grandmother to live alone. My relatives kept finding her on the floor beside her bed when they went to wake her in the mornings. My mother flew to California to help clean the house and make arrangements for Grandmother to enter a local nursing home. On her last day at home, while Grandmother was sitting in her big, overstuffed armchair, hair combed and wearing a green summer dress, my mother went to her and knelt at her feet. "Here, Mamma," she said. "I've polished your shoes." She lifted Grandmother's legs and helped her into the shiny black shoes. My Grandmother looked down and smiled slightly. She left her house walking, supported by her children, carrying her pocket book, and wearing her polished black shoes. "Look, Mamma," my mom had said, kneeling. "I've polished your shoes."

24 Just the other day, my mother came to Boston to visit. She had recently lost a lot of weight and was pleased with her new shape and her feeling of good health. "Look at me, Kes," she exclaimed, turning toward me, front and back, as naked as the day she was born. I saw her small breasts and the wide, brown scar, belly button to pubic hair, that marked her because my brother and I were both born by Caesarean section. Her hips were small. I was not a large baby, but there was so little room for me in her that when she was carrying me she could not even begin to bend over toward the floor. She hated it, she said.

25 "Don't I look good? Don't you think I look good?"

26 I looked at my mother, smiling and as happy as she, thinking of all the times I have seen her naked. I have seen both my parents naked throughout my life, as they have seen me. From childhood through adulthood we've had our naked moments, sharing baths, idle conversations picked up as we moved between showers and closets, hurried moments at the beginning of days, quiet moments at the end of days.

27 I know this to be Japanese, this ease with the physical, and it makes me think of an old Japanese folk song. A young nursemaid, a fifteen-year-old girl, is singing a lullaby to a baby who is strapped to her back. The nursemaid has been sent as a servant to a place far from her own home. "We're the beggars," she says, "and they

are the nice people. Nice people wear fine sashes. Nice clothes."

> If I should drop dead,
> bury me by the roadside!
> I'll give a flower
> to everyone who passes.
>
> What kind of flower?
> The cam-cam-camellia [*tsun-tsun-tsubaki*]
> watered by Heaven:
> alms water.

28 The nursemaid is the intersection of heaven and earth, the intersection of the human, the natural world, the body, and the soul. In this song, with clear eyes, she looks steadily at life, which is sometimes so very terrible and sad. I think of her while looking at my mother, who is standing on the red and purple carpet before me, laughing, without any clothes.

29 I am my mother's daughter. And I am myself.
30 I am a Japanese-American woman.

Epilogue

31 I recently heard a man from West Africa share some memories of his childhood. He was raised Muslim, but when he was a young man, he found himself deeply drawn to Christianity. He struggled against his inner impulse for years, trying to avoid the church yet feeling pushed to return to it again and again. "I would have done *anything* to avoid the change," he said. At last, he became Christian. Afterwards he was afraid to go home, fearing that he would not be accepted. The fear was groundless, he discovered, when at last he returned—he had separated himself, but his family and friends (all Muslim) had not separated themselves from him.

32 The man, who is now a professor of religion, said that in the Africa he knew as a child and a young man, pluralism was embraced rather than feared. There was "a kind of tolerance that did not deny your particularity," he said. He alluded to zestful, spontaneous debates that would sometimes loudly erupt between Muslims and Christians in the village's public spaces. His memories of an atheist who harangued the villagers when he came to visit them once a week moved me deeply. Perhaps the man was an agricultural advisor or inspector. He harassed the women. He would say: "Don't go to the fields! Don't even bother to go to the fields. Let God take care of you. He'll send you the food. If you believe in God, why do you need to work? You don't need to work! Let God put the seeds in the ground. Stay home."

33 The professor said, "The women laughed, you know? They just laughed. Their attitude was, 'Here is a child of God. When will he come home?'"

34 The storyteller, the professor of religion, smiled a most fantastic tender smile as he told this story. "In my country, there is a deep affirmation of the oneness of God," he said. "The atheist and the women were having quite different experiences in their encounter, though the atheist did not know this. He saw himself as quite separate from the women. But the women did not see themselves as being separate from him. 'Here is a child of God,' they said. 'When will he come home?'"

APPLICATIONS FOR CRITICAL READING AND DISCUSSION

1. What is the unit?

2. What is the principle by which that unit functions? In other words, what does the unit do or represent from this perspective? Write the answer here, and circle the passage that states or suggests the principle.

3. What are the parts that make up the unit according to this principle? Underline them in the text, and write them here.

4. What is the order of the parts (time, space, emphasis, or a combination)?

 **The Reading Connection from Classroom Sources**

EXERCISE 7

Demonstration Using the DCODE Worksheet

Magic Johnson is perhaps the most-talked-about basketball player of all time. Arguably no one else put more energy and enthusiasm into the game. It is difficult to separate the different facets of his reputation as person and player. Student Cyrus Norton concentrates on the qualities of Magic's greatness as a player.

WORKSHEET
Writing in DCODE

NAME: Cyrus Norton

SECTION: _____ CHAPTER: _____ DATE: _____

Delve   Generate your topic, or ideas for your topic, by delving into your subject area through:

- *Freewriting*—writing sentence after sentence, nonstop and spontaneously.
- *Brainstorming*—jotting down answers to Who? What? Where? When? Why? and How? and then listing words and phrases in relation to those answers.
- *Clustering*—connecting bubbled ideas with lines to show strings of relationships, producing each new bubble item in response to the question, What comes to mind?
- *Combining* any of these approaches, as directed by your instructor.

```
Freewriting
        Magic Johnson was the greatest I've ever seen in the NBA. He was always
   moving, always thinking, always smiling. I've seen him lots of times at the
   Forum. He was the greatest player in lots of ways. He was great at shooting
   the ball and when the team needed a basket, he was usually the one that got
   the ball. If he hadn't been so unselfish he would have scored even more
   points, but he seemed to love passing the ball as much as shooting it. He
   was famous for his no-look passes that almost always hit their mark. Then
   he used a lot of energy on rebounds and many times he was in double digets,
   which isn't so surprising when you think that he was six feet and nine
   inches tall with a strong body.

Brainstorming
        Who: Magic Johnson
        What: great basketball player
        Where: the NBA
        When: for more than ten years
        Why: love of game and great talent
        How: shooting, passing, rebounding, leading

Clustering
```

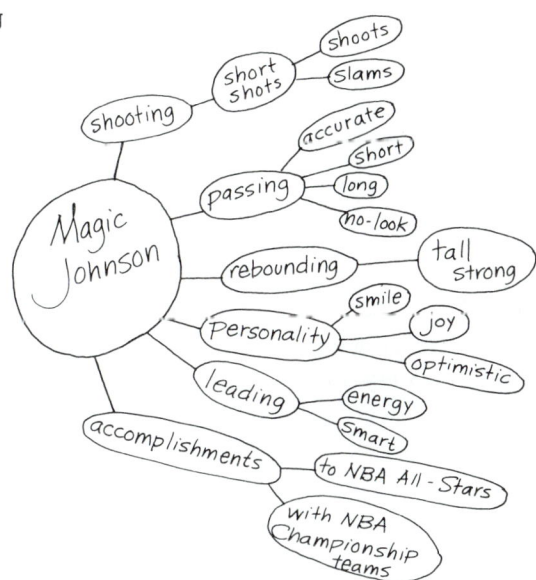

161

WORKSHEET: Writing in DCODE

Concentrate Concentrate your work by stating your topic in one sentence that is not too broad, narrow, or vague to be developed. Base this sentence (which may become the topic sentence for your paragraph or the thesis for your essay) on an idea emerging from the **Delve** stage. You may have to try several statements here before you formulate one that is best for your writing task. Be sure that your final statement covers your assignment or intent and specifies both your subject (what you are writing about) and treatment (what aspect you will focus on). Label the *subject* and *treatment* parts.

```
         subject                              treatment
Magic Johnson was a great NBA star because he was excellent in shooting,
passing, rebounding, and leading.
```

Organize Complete an outline or a cluster, as directed by your instructor. The cluster should be a section from, or a refined version of, the **Delve** clustering. Regardless of the strategy you use, the organizational pattern should indicate a division of your topic into parts that will, in turn, be further subdivided for support as necessary to address a particular audience on your concentrated topic.

```
    I.   Shooting
         A.  Short shots
         B.  Long shots
         C.  Free throws
    II.  Passing
         A.  No-look
         B.  Precise
    III. Rebounding
         A.  Tall
         B.  Rugged
    IV.  Leading
         A.  Energy
         B.  Spirit
```

Draft On separate paper, write and then revise your assignment as many times as necessary for **c**oherence, **l**anguage (usage, tone, and diction), **u**nity, **e**mphasis, **s**upport, and **s**entence structure (**cluess**).

Edit Correct problems in fundamentals such as **c**apitalization, **o**missions, **p**unctuation, and **s**pelling (**cops**). Before writing the final draft, read your paper aloud to discover oversights and awkwardness of expression.

First Draft

Magic Johnson

Some ~~NBA~~ *National Basketball Association* players are good because they ~~are good~~ *have a special talent* in one area such as shooting, passing, or rebounding. Magic Johnson was great because he ~~was good~~ *had talent* in all of those ~~things~~ *areas* and more. As a shooter few have ~~ever been able to do what he could~~ *equaled him*. He could slam, shovel, hook, and fire from three-point range~~.~~*,* *all with deadly accuracy.* ~~When it came to~~ *As for* free throws, he led all NBA players in shooting percentage in 1988–89. ~~Then he averaged~~ *While averaging* more than twenty points per game, he helped others become stars. As the point guard *(the quarterback of basketball)* he was always near the top in the league in a*s*sists and was famous for his "no-look" passes*,* ~~W~~*w*hich often surprised even his teammates with their precision. A top rebounding guard is unusual, but Magic, ~~standing~~ at six feet nine inches ~~tall~~, could bump sh*o*lders and ~~jump~~ *leap* with anyone. These three qualities made him probably the most spectacular triple-double threat of all time. *"Triple-double" means reaching two digits in scoring, assists, and rebounding.* Magic didn't need more for greatness in the NBA, but he had more. ~~H~~*h*e was also an inspirational team leader (with his everlasting smile and boundless energy). ~~Always believing~~ *He always believed* in himself and his team. When his team was down by a point and three seconds *remained on the clock* ~~were left,~~ *the fans* ~~you always~~ looked for Magic to get the ball. Then ~~you~~ *they* watched as "he dribbled once, *he* faded, *he* leaped, *he* twisted, and *he* hooked one in from twenty *feet*!" ~~That was Magic.~~ *That was magic.*

Final Draft

Magic Johnson
Cyrus Norton

Some National Basketball Association (NBA) players are good because they have a special talent in one area such as shooting, passing, or rebounding. **Magic Johnson was great because he had talent in all of those areas and more.** As a shooter few have ever equaled him. He could slam, shovel, hook, and fire from three-point range—all with deadly accuracy. As for free throws, he led all NBA players in shooting percentage in 1988–89. While averaging more than twenty points per game, he helped others become stars. As the point guard (the quarterback of basketball), he was always near the top in the league in assists and

topic sentence

Part 1: shooter

Part 2: passes

was famous for his "no-look" passes, which often surprised even his teammates with their precision. A top rebounding guard is unusual in professional basketball, but Magic, at six feet nine inches, could bump shoulders and leap with anyone. These three qualities made him probably the most spectacular triple-double threat of all time. "Triple-double" means reaching two digits in scoring, assists, and rebounding. Magic didn't need more for greatness in the NBA, but he had more. With his everlasting smile and boundless energy, he was also an inspirational team leader. He always believed in himself and his team. When his team was down by a point and three seconds remained on the game clock, the fans looked for Magic to get the ball. Then they watched as "he dribbled once, he faded, he leaped, he twisted, and he hooked one in from twenty feet!" That was magic. That was Magic.

Part 3: rebounding

Part 4: leader

APPLICATIONS FOR CRITICAL READING AND DISCUSSION

1. What is the unit?
   Magic Johnson

2. What is the principle by which that unit functions? In other words, what does the unit do or represent from this perspective? Write the answer here, and circle the passage that states or suggests the principle.
   great basketball player

3. What are the parts that make up the unit according to this principle? Underline them in the text, and write them here.
   shooting, passing, rebounding, leading

4. What is the order of the parts (time, space, emphasis, or a combination)?
   emphasis

EXERCISE 8

Television sitcoms come and go—rapidly. Occasionally one comes along and sticks. It has what is commonly called "chemistry," meaning that all parts work together to form a successful unit. "Roseanne" is such a show. Offbeat, outrageous, funny, and wonderfully disconnected at times, it apparently reminds its audience of just how complicated and yet simple life really is and how people have to be able to laugh at adversity. Although not created by a formula, nevertheless, it can be examined as a unit made up of indispensable, interlinking parts. Student Angela DeSarro discusses those parts.

The Success of "Rosanne"
Angela DeSarro

Each of the great television sitcoms has its own appeal. Somehow all parts of the show come together, and something magical happens. In "Roseanne," the parts are story reality, language, and talent. "Roseanne"'s story lines deal with the reality that many American families face day to day. People like to see a show that tells them they're not alone in their daily struggles of trying to make ends meet. Unlike many other shows, "Roseanne" story lines don't have "Beaver Cleaver" endings. For example, in one episode, Becky runs off, marries her boyfriend, and then comes back and asks Roseanne and Dan for forgiveness at the end of the show. Roseanne forgives her, but Dan doesn't. Another component of the "Roseanne" show is the quality of the language in the scripts. Along with the fresh, unique story lines, the characters "whip off" a steady supply of hilarious one-liners. The final part is the great ensemble cast. Roseanne Arnold, John Goodman, Laurie Metcalf, Sara Gilbert, and the other talented actors are terrific as individuals, and they have a chemistry among them that really works. These three qualities blended together smoothly make for good entertainment and create one of the all-time great sitcoms.

APPLICATIONS FOR CRITICAL READING AND DISCUSSION

1. What is the unit?

2. What is the principle by which that unit functions? In other words, what does the unit do or represent from this perspective? Write the answer here, and circle the passage that states or suggests the principle.

3. What are the parts that make up the unit according to this principle? Underline them in the text, and write them here.

4. What is the order of the parts (time, space, emphasis, or a combination)?

EXERCISE 9

One of the most famous and best-loved figures in American history is Benjamin Franklin. Those with only a superficial knowledge of him may think of his experiment with electricity by using the kite and the key and of his printing of *Poor Richard's Almanac*, but his accomplishments extended well beyond those. According to Allison Udell, Benjamin Franklin was our country's first and greatest Renaissance man.

Ben Franklin, Renaissance Man
Allison Udell

Anyone who doesn't know the definition of *Renaissance man* would do well to study Benjamin Franklin. When he died in 1790 at the age of eighty-four, he was acknowledged for greatness in numerous areas of endeavor. In short, he was a multi-genius, and each area of his accomplishments registered more than almost any other person of his time. Putting the areas together made him probably the greatest Renaissance man that America has ever produced.

One side to Benjamin Franklin was his education. Although he went to school for only two years, he was curious, energetic, and determined. He educated himself through reading, and learned six languages. By the age of twenty-four he opened his own print shop, first publishing a newspaper, then *Poor Richard's Almanac*. His *Autobiography* is still read for its brilliance of style.

He was also an inventor and scientist. Almost everyone has heard of his experimentation with electricity, and of his invention of bifocals, the lightning rod, the Franklin stove, and the school chair. Other scholars still read his studies of ocean currents and soil improvement. In his middle years he was elected to the prestigious group of scientists called the Royal Society of London.

His work in planning took two directions. In urban life, he planned a hospital, a library, the postal system, the city police, and the city fire department. These institutions were successful and became the models for other cities and even countries. The second direction occurred just before the War of Independence during the French and Indian War. At the request of people in government, he designed strategy that was enormously successful.

His involvement as a patriot during the War of Independence was still another area of accomplishment. An acknowledged leader, he signed the Declaration of Independence and later helped write the Constitution, which he also signed. During the war, he served the patriot colonists as the Minister to France. There he arranged for financial and military support from the French, helped negotiate the Treaty of Peace with Great Britain, and now is regarded as probably the most successful diplomat in the history of America.

Renaissance man means "one who is an expert in several different areas of endeavor." For these more than two hundred years we have found no better example than Benjamin Franklin.

APPLICATIONS FOR CRITICAL READING AND DISCUSSION

1. What is the unit?

2. What is the principle by which that unit functions? In other words, what does the unit do or represent from this perspective? Write the answer here, and circle the passage that states or suggests the principle.

3. What are the parts that make up the unit according to this principle? Underline them in the text, and write them here.

4. What is the order of the parts (time, space, emphasis, or a combination)?

Suggested Topics for Writing Functional Analysis

General Topics: Some of the following topics are too broad for a short writing assignment and should be narrowed. For example, "a wedding ceremony," could be narrowed to a particular "José and Maria's wedding ceremony."

1. An organ in the human body
2. A machine such as an automobile, a computer, a camera
3. A city administration, a governmental agency, a school board, a student council
4. A ceremony—wedding, graduation
5. A holiday celebration, a pep rally, a sales convention, a religious revival
6. An offensive team in football (any team in any game)
7. A family, a relationship, a gang, a club, a sorority, a fraternity
8. A religion, a church
9. A musical instrument
10. A school class
11. A singer, a musical group, or an actor (any celebrity)
12. An album, a performance, or a song
13. A movie, a television program, a video game
14. Any well-known person—athlete, politician, criminal, writer
15. A specific meal, dish, drink

Reading-Related Topics

"The Cancer Puzzle"

1. Write about another disease, such as AIDS.

"The Living Cell"

2. Select another organic unit from the field of biology and discuss the parts.

"The Boss Observed"

3. Select another prominent entertainer and discuss the characteristics that have brought success to him or her.

4. Select a song by Springsteen or some other entertainer, and explain how it functions by discussing its parts, such as words, music, arrangement, performance, and special effects.

"The Sonata"

5. Pick a piece of music in sonata form (by Beethoven or Mozart, perhaps) and discuss it according to the simple explanation in this paragraph.

"A Big Wheel"

6. Select and analyze another quiz program.

7. Analyze Pat Sajak or Vanna White as performers on "Wheel of Fortune."

"Optimism, Tenacity Lead Way Back to Life"

8. Write a functional analysis about a challenging experience you or someone you know has had. Use three or more of the characteristics discussed in this essay.

"Growing Up Asian in America"

9. Write a functional analysis in which you discuss your own or someone else's origin(s). "Origin(s)" here may mean nationality, culture, region (part of the country), or a combination of two or more of these. Use this essay as a pattern.

"Magic Johnson"

10. Pick one of Magic's traits, and analyze it functionally in detail.

11. Choose another sports figure for a study in functional analysis.

The Success of "Roseanne"

12. Write a functional analysis of another successful television program. Concentrate on Roseanne as a character for a study in functional analysis.

13. Instead of working with a "successful sitcom" as a subject, begin with Dan and Roseanne's functional family, and analyze it.

"Ben Franklin, Renaissance Man"

14. Pick another outstanding figure from history, and analyze him or her. Do some research in an encyclopedia or a textbook.

Writer's Checklist

Apply these ideas to your writing as you work with **DCODE**. Later as a peer editor, apply the same ideas to the material you evaluate.

1. Take into account how much your typical reader knows about your subject.

2. State the principle on which the subject is divided; this statement will usually be in the topic sentence for the paragraph or the thesis for the essay.

3. Indicate the parts clearly.

4. Present the parts in an order that will promote coherence (time, space, emphasis, or a combination).

5. State or clearly imply how the parts function in relation to the operation or existence of the whole subject.

Journal-Entry Suggestions

1. Select some of the unused "Reading-Related Topics" suggestions, and use them for journal topics.

2. Write a reaction to one or more "Reading Connection" selections. Agree, disagree, apply the statements to your own experiences, indicate the value of such statements, or explain why you were surprised, shocked, disgusted, pleased, or whatever, by the material.

3. Invent statements (using functional analysis, if appropriate) to support headlines from *Weekly World News*:

    "1950s Airliner Lands with 92 Skeletons on Board!"
    "Bandit Uses a Cucumber to Rob 16 Banks!" (Veggie-packing varmint ate the evidence after each holdup.)
    "Robin Hood Had Bad Breath!"
    "Dead Ventriloquist Speaks from Beyond the Grave—Through Wooden Dummy!"
    "Incredible Pet Fish Can Tell When Earthquakes Will Strike!"
    "Pet Dog Swallows Man's False Teeth!"
    "My Husband Has Turned into a Frog!" (He croaks, catches flies, and hops around the yard.)
    "Hot-Rodding Hearse Roars to Funeral at 86 M.P.H.!" (Death wish is fulfilled.)
    "Pigs Get Drunk and Tear Up Town!"
    "Judge Lowers the Boom on No-Show Groom!"

WORKSHEET
Writing in DCODE

NAME:_____

SECTION:_____ CHAPTER:_____ DATE:_____

Delve   Generate your topic, or ideas for your topic, by delving into your subject area through:

- *Freewriting*—writing sentence after sentence, nonstop and spontaneously.
- *Brainstorming*—jotting down answers to Who? What? Where? When? Why? and How? and then listing words and phrases in relation to those answers.
- *Clustering*—connecting bubbled ideas with lines to show strings of relationships, producing each new bubble item in response to the question, What comes to mind?
- *Combining* any of these approaches, as directed by your instructor.

WORKSHEET: Writing in DCODE

Concentrate   Concentrate your work by stating your topic in one sentence that is not too broad, narrow, or vague to be developed. Base this sentence (which may become the topic sentence for your paragraph or the thesis for your essay) on an idea emerging from the **Delve** stage. You may have to try several statements here before you formulate one that is best for your writing task. Be sure that your final statement covers your assignment or intent and specifies both your subject (what you are writing about) and treatment (what aspect you will focus on). Label the *subject* and *treatment* parts.

Organize   Complete an outline or a cluster, as directed by your instructor. The cluster should be a section from, or a refined version of, the **Delve** clustering. Regardless of the strategy you use, the organizational pattern should indicate a division of your topic into parts that will, in turn, be further subdivided for support as necessary to address a particular audience on your concentrated topic.

Draft   On separate paper, write and then revise your assignment as many times as necessary for **c**oherence, **l**anguage (usage, tone, and diction), **u**nity, **e**mphasis, **s**upport, and **s**entence structure (**cluess**).

Edit   Correct problems in fundamentals such as **c**apitalization, **o**missions, **p**unctuation, and **s**pelling (**cops**). Before writing the final draft, read your paper aloud to discover oversights and awkwardness of expression.

Process Analysis: Writing About Doing

7

> " Writing and rewriting are a constant search for what it is one is saying.
> — John Updike

"No, NO, Bob! I believe you have the instructions confused with those of the harmonica!"

What is process analysis? What is the difference between directive and informative process analysis? Why is audience so important to this form of writing? What is the usual order in process analysis, and what can be done to promote coherence?

Process Analysis Defined

If you have any doubt about the frequency of the use of process analysis, just think about how many times you have heard people say, "How do you do it?" or "How is [was] it done?" Even when you are not hearing those questions, you are posing them yourself when you need to make something, cook a meal, assemble an item, take some medicine, repair something, or figure out what happened. In your college classes, you may have to discover how osmosis occurs, how a rock changes form, how a mountain was formed, how a battle was won, or how a bill goes through the legislature.

If you need to explain how to do something or how something is (was) done, you will write a paper of *process analysis*. You will break down your topic into stages, explaining each so that your reader can duplicate or understand the process.

Do not underestimate the complexity of this form because of its directness. Try this scenario:

> Someone calls you on the phone and says he needs to tie a tie. You try to explain. Even though you have tied ties hundreds of times and have become proficient in the art, you find yourself fumbling with words. If the person were here, you could demonstrate with a tie. You could stand behind him while he looks in a mirror. He could ask questions the moment something goes awry. Your hand moves to your neck in pantomime as you try to recall the steps. Your confidence shaken, you ask him to hold the phone. You hurriedly get a tie from the closet. You put your phone on speaker and say, "Drape the tie around your neck with the fat end on your right. Then you . . ."

Try another scenario, this time without a phone and without props:

> You have to write instructions on how to tie shoes and put the instructions in the mail—or maybe on your instructor's desk. [Use your imagination to complete this.]

Two Types of Process Analysis: Directive and Informative

The questions How do I do it? and How is (was) it done? will lead you into two different types of process analysis—directive and informative.

Directive process analysis explains how to do something. As the name suggests, it gives directions and tells the reader how to do something. It says, for example, "Read me, and you can bake a pie (tune up your car, read a book, write an essay, take some medicine)." Because it is presented directly to the reader, it usually addresses the reader as "you," or it implies the "you" by saying something such as, "First [you] purchase a large, fat wombat, and then [you] . . ." In the same way, this textbook addresses you or implies "you" because it is a long how-to-do-it (directive process analysis) statement.

Informative process analysis explains how something is (was) done by giving data (information). Whereas the directive process analysis tells you what to do in the future, the informative process analysis tells you what has occurred or what is occurring. If it is something in nature, such as the formation of a mountain, you can read and understand the process by which something was done, but, of course, you would not be able to make a mountain. If it is how Harry Truman won the presidential election in 1948, you could learn from what happened and perhaps apply your knowledge, but you could not duplicate the experience. Even if the subject is a scientific experiment and you could duplicate the experience, the stress would still be on your *understanding* the process, not on your *doing* the process. Therefore, instead of addressing the reader ("you"), the writer of informative process analysis either discusses his or her own experience (using I), or addresses the subject material by using third-person words such as *he, she, they, it,* or *an individual*. For example:

Directive: When you encounter a person at a party who starts to tell jokes with racial slurs, you should take certain steps. First, you should not laugh at the jokes, even though you may embarrass that person. Then . . .

Informative: Last weekend at a party, a man started telling racial jokes. I decided it was time to take a stand, and I developed some strategies I intend to use from now on. First, I didn't laugh at his jokes. Then . . .

Directive process analysis and informative process analysis are sometimes combined, especially in longer works, such as this book, and in personalized paragraphs and essays, in which the writer tells "how to" but also discusses his or her experiences.

Blending Process Analysis with Other Forms

The directive and informative types of process analysis often overlap with other forms of discourse presented in this book. These are some examples:

Definition: If you need to explain what a taco is, you may decide to simply recite a recipe, which would include the ingredients and their transformation into a dish.

Persuasion: As a persuasive statement, you could present the steps for getting adequate exercise in relation to good health.

Narration: You could explain how your neighborhood has changed.

Cause and effect: You could explain why the United States became involved in the Vietnam conflict, stage by stage.

Functional analysis: You could explain how an ocean wave functions, one thing leading to another.

In fact, a single form of discourse is seldom used alone, although one may be dominant. That is our concern here: the use of directive or informative process analysis as the dominant form to satisfy a how-to or how-it-is-done purpose.

Considering the Audience

Knowledge

Your audience's knowledge about the topic will determine the depth of your explanation. If you are trying to explain how to tune a car to readers who have never worked on a car or learned anything about gasoline engines, your task is much larger than if you were addressing readers who were somewhat knowledgeable. In explaining to the poorly informed, avoid technical words, provide definitions, and go into more detail about the location of parts, the use of tools, and the need for certain precautions.

Attitude

Equally important to knowledge in many cases is the attitude of your audience—that is, how they feel about your topic. Your audience may be open and even eager for the instruction, or uninterested, or even hostile. Anticipate the likely reaction to your subject, and write with the appropriate tone as you attempt to inform or persuade. (See Tone section in Chapter 15.)

Working with the Stages

Preparation

In this first stage of the directive type of process analysis, list the materials or equipment needed for the process and discuss the necessary setup arrangements. For some topics, this stage will also provide technical terms and definitions. The degree to which this stage is detailed will depend on both the subject itself and the expected knowledge and experience of the projected audience.

The informative type of process analysis may begin with background or context rather than with preparation. For example, a statement explaining how mountains form might begin with a description of a flat portion of the earth made up of plates that are arranged like a jigsaw puzzle.

Steps

The actual process will be presented here. Each step must be explained clearly and directly, and phrased to accommodate the audience. The language, especially in directive process analysis, is likely to be simple and concise; however, avoid dropping words such as *and, a, an, the,* and *of,* and thereby lapsing into "recipe language." The steps may be accompanied by explanations about why certain procedures are necessary and how not following directions carefully can lead to trouble.

Order

The order will usually be chronological (time based) in some sense. Certain words are commonly used to promote coherence: *first, second, third, then, soon, now, next, finally, at last, therefore, consequently,* and—especially for informative process analysis—words used to show the passage of time such as hours, days of the week, and so on.

The Reading Connection

EXERCISE 1

Demonstration of Directive Process Analysis

The simplest tasks are often the most poorly done because we assume that we know how to do them and do not seek instruction. Florence H. Pettit explains here how to sharpen a knife properly, and what we learn reminds us that we could probably take lessons on performing any number of everyday chores.

How To Sharpen A Knife
FLORENCE H. PETTIT

If you have never done any whittling or wood carving before, the first skill to learn is how to sharpen your knife. You may be surprised to learn that even a brand-new knife needs sharpening. Knives are never sold honed (finely sharpened), although some gouges and chisels are. It is essential to learn the firm stroke on the stone that will keep your blades sharp. The sharpening stone must be fixed in place on the table, so that it will not move around. You can do this by placing a rubber inner tube or a thin piece of foam rubber under it. Or you can tack four strips of wood, if you have a rough worktable, to frame the stone and hold it in place. Put a generous puddle of oil on the stone—this will soon disappear into the surface of a new stone, and you will need to keep adding more oil. Press the knife blade flat against the stone in the puddle of oil, using your index finger. Whichever way the cutting edge of the knife faces is the side of the blade that should get a little more pressure. Move the blade around three or four times in a narrow oval about the size of your fingernail, going *counterclockwise* when the sharp edge is facing right. Now turn the blade over in the same spot on the stone, press hard, and move it around the small oval *clockwise*, with more pressure on the cutting edge that faces left. Repeat the ovals, flipping the knife blade over six or seven times, and applying lighter pressure to the blade the last two times. Wipe the blade clean with a piece of rag or tissue and rub it flat on the piece of leather strop at least twice on each side. Stroke *away* from the cutting edge to remove the little burr of metal that may be left on the blade.

APPLICATIONS FOR CRITICAL READING AND DISCUSSION

1. What type of process analysis (informative or directive) is used?
    directive

2. To what type of audience (well informed, moderately informed, or poorly informed on the topic) does the writer direct this selection?
    poorly informed

3. What is the prevailing tone (objective, humorous, reverent, argumentative, cautionary, playful, ironic, ridiculing) of this selection?
    objective

4. Draw a line at the point at which the preparation (materials, setup, explaining words, and so on) ends and the steps begin.

5. Write numbers in the margin to indicate the steps or stages in the process.
   `Treat the preparation as a single stage.`

6. Circle any transitional words indicating time or other progression (*first, second, then, soon, now, next, after, before, when, finally, at last, therefore, consequently*, and—especially for the informative process analysis—words used to show the passage of time, such as hours, days of the week, and so on).

7. Is the author trying to inform or to persuade?
   `inform`

EXERCISE 2

Demonstration of Informative Process Analysis

The author says that when we go to a rock concert, something almost mythical happens. The rock star becomes a mysterious figure who awes us. We, in turn, are transformed into another being (barbaric? destructive?) in order to fulfill some psychic needs.

Gonna Rock To-o- N-i-i-ight!
JENNIFER MCBRIDE YOUNG

[margin notes: 1 either or, 2, 3]

Many rock musicians consciously work to maintain the aura of mystery surrounding themselves. Typically, they walk on stage and proceed to sneer at or completely ignore the audience. If a star is especially articulate, he may yell, "A-a-all ri-i-ight! Gonna rock to-o- ni-i-ight!" He cannot use the vocabulary of the common man, for fear of being mistakenly identified as such. Besides, a few well-timed thrusts of the hips communicate the message just as well. The audience responds wildly to this invitation, and the concert is off to a good start. The performer has successfully gauged the mood of the spectators; now his task is to manipulate it, through his choice of material and through such actions as dancing, prancing, foot-stomping, and unearthly screaming. His movements, gestures, and often, his bizarre clothing, high heels, and make-up deliberately violate accepted standards of conduct and appearance. He can afford to take chances and to risk offending people; after all, as every good student of mythology knows, deities are not bound by the same restrictions as mere mortals. The Dionysus figure on the stage tempts us to follow him into the never-never land where inhibitions are nonexistent.

2 Initially, the audience may be content to allow the performer alone to defy civilized constraints. We rebel vicariously; the smashing of instruments onstage perhaps serves as a catharsis for our own destructive impulses. As the intensity and excitement of the concert mount, however, the audience is drawn into the act. People begin to sing along, clap, yell, dance, or shake their fists. This is a particularly favorable setting for the release of tensions by the timid. No one can hear their screams (the music is too loud) and no one can see the peculiar movements of their bodies (the hall is dark, and the strange smoke reduces visibility—everyone's eyes are glued to the stage anyhow). The rock god has successfully asserted his power over our bodies, and now all that remains is for him to master our minds and our imaginations.

[margin note: This paragraph interprets and elaborates upon the first paragraph.]

APPLICATIONS FOR CRITICAL READING AND DISCUSSION

1. What type of process analysis (informative or directive) is used?
   ```
   informative for each paragraph
   ```

2. To what type of audience (well informed, moderately informed, or poorly informed on the topic) does the writer direct this selection?
   ```
   well informed to moderately informed
   ```

3. What is the prevailing tone (objective, humorous, reverent, argumentative, cautionary, playful, ironic, ridiculing) of this material?
   ```
   ironic
   ```

4. Draw a line at the point at which the preparation (materials, setup, explaining words, and so on) ends and the steps begin.

5. Write numbers in the margin to indicate the steps or stages in the process.

6. Circle any transitional words indicating time or other progression (*first, second, then, soon, now, next, after, before, when, finally, at last, therefore, consequently,* and—especially for the informative process analysis—words used to show the passage of time, such as hours, days of the week, and so on).

EXERCISE 3

If you are about to die under tons of snow, ice, and debris and you have, say, one chance in thousands to live, what do you do? The Suttons offer steps that will at least increase your odds for survival.

Nature on the Rampage
ANN AND MYRON SUTTON

If you're caught: get moving! Ski or snowshoe as fast as you possibly can to the edge of the avalanche. Get rid of all of your accessories, or as many as you can, and do it at once—ski poles, pack, snowshoes, whatever you have. When the avalanche overtakes you, swim! This sounds ridiculous, but it's the best thing you can do to avoid being sucked under. Swim for your life, lying on your back if possible and with your feet downhill. Of course, you may have no choice, and the avalanche may tumble you whither it wishes, but do what you can to stay on the surface. Cover your mouth and nose—suffocation is easy in dry-snow avalanches. If you do get pulled under, make a supreme effort to widen a little airspace around you just as you come to a stop, and do it instantly! The snow may harden, pack and freeze almost at once. Then pray for help, and remember that the great Houdini made a living proving how long man could survive in tight and nearly airless spaces if he remained calm and confident and didn't panic. How to avoid panic in an avalanche is your problem.

APPLICATIONS FOR CRITICAL READING AND DISCUSSION

1. What type of process analysis (informative or directive) is used?

2. To what type of audience (well informed, moderately informed, or poorly informed on the topic) does the writer direct this selection?

3. What is the prevailing tone (objective, humorous, reverent, argumentative, cautionary, playful, ironic, ridiculing) of this selection?

4. Draw a line at the point at which the preparation (materials, setup, explaining words, and so on) ends and the steps begin.

5. Write numbers in the margin to indicate the steps or stages in the process.

6. Circle any transitional words indicating time or other progression (*first, second, then, soon, now, next, after, before, when, finally, at last, therefore, consequently,* and—especially for the informative process analysis—words used to show the passage of time, such as hours, days of the week, and so on).

EXERCISE 4

Our simple behavior may seem absurd when examined with solemn deliberation. Here, L. Rust Hills explains how to eat an ice-cream cone, even when things go wrong. Perhaps this piece is so successful because the author describes techniques and behavior (with a bit of exaggeration) that we are all familiar with but have not really considered.

How to Eat an Ice-Cream Cone
L. RUST HILLS

Grasp the cone with the right hand firmly but gently between thumb and at least one but not more than three fingers, two-thirds of the way up the cone. Then dart swiftly away to an open area, away from the jostling crowd at the stand. Now take up the classic ice-cream-cone-eating stance: feet from one to two feet apart, body bent forward from the waist at a twenty-five-degree angle, right elbow well up, right forearm horizontal, at a level with your collarbone and about twelve inches from it. But don't start eating yet! Check first to see what emergency repairs may be necessary. Sometimes a sugar cone will be so crushed or broken or cracked that all one can do is gulp at the thing like a savage, getting what he can of it and letting the rest drop to the ground, and then evacuating the area of catastrophe as quickly as possible. Checking the cone for possible trouble can be done in a second or two, if one knows where to look and does it systematically. A trouble spot some people overlook is the bottom tip of the cone. This may have been broken off. Or the flap of the cone material at the bottom, usually wrapped over itself in that funny spiral construction, may be folded in a way that is imperfect and leaves an opening. No need to say that through this opening—in a matter of perhaps thirty or, at most, ninety seconds—will begin to pour hundreds of thousands of sticky molecules of melted ice cream. You know in this case that you must instantly get the paper napkin in your left hand under and around the bottom of the cone to stem the forthcoming flow, or else be doomed to eat the cone far too rapidly. It is a grim moment. No one wants to eat a cone under that kind of pressure, but neither does anyone want to end up with the bottom of the cone stuck to a messy napkin. There's one other alternative—one that takes both skill and courage: Forgoing any cradling action, grasp the cone more firmly between thumb and forefinger and extend the other fingers so that they are out of the way of the dripping from the bottom, then increase the waist-bend angle from twenty-five to thirty-five degrees, and then eat the cone, *allowing* it to drip out of the bottom onto the ground in front of you! Experienced and thoughtful cone-eaters enjoy facing up to this kind of sudden challenge.

APPLICATIONS FOR CRITICAL READING AND DISCUSSION

1. What type of process analysis (informative or directive) is used?

2. To what type of audience (well informed, moderately informed, or poorly informed on the topic) does the writer direct this selection?

3. What is the prevailing tone (objective, humorous, reverent, argumentative, cautionary, playful, ironic, ridiculing) of this material?

4. Draw a line at the point at which the preparation (materials, setup, explaining words, and so on) ends and the steps begin.

5. Write numbers in the margin to indicate the steps or stages in the process.

6. Circle any transitional words indicating time or other progression (*first, second, then, soon, now, next, after, before, when, finally, at last, therefore, consequently,* and—especially for the informative process analysis—words used to show the passage of time, such as hours, days of the week, and so on).

EXERCISE 5

We usually think of birth in a biological sense, but Rachel Carson describes a different kind—a geological birth. It requires no coach, no midwife, no obstetrician. And unless you can live for thousands or even millions of years, you can't witness the whole process. Nevertheless, it is a process, and it can be described in steps.

The Birth of an Island
RACHEL CARSON

The birth of a volcanic island is an event marked by prolonged and violent travail: the forces of the earth striving to create, and all the forces of the sea opposing. The sea floor, where an island begins, is probably nowhere more than about fifty miles thick—a thin covering over the vast bulk of the earth. In it are deep cracks and fissures, the results of unequal cooling and shrinkage in past ages. Along such lines of weakness the molten lava from the earth's interior presses up and finally bursts forth into the sea. But a submarine volcano is different from a terrestrial eruption, where lava, molten rocks, gases, and other ejecta are hurled into the air through an open crater. Here on the bottom of the ocean the volcano has resisting it all the weight of the ocean water above it. Despite the immense pressure of, it may be, two or three miles of sea water, the new volcanic cone builds upward toward the surface in flow after flow of lava. Once within reach of the waves, its soft ash and tuff are violently attacked, and for a long period the potential island may remain a shoal, unable to emerge. But, eventually, in new eruptions, the cone is pushed up into the air and a rampart against the attacks of the waves is built of hardened lava.

APPLICATIONS FOR CRITICAL READING AND DISCUSSION

1. What type of process analysis (informative or directive) is used?

2. To what type of audience (well informed, moderately informed, or poorly informed on the topic) does the writer direct this selection?

3. What is the prevailing tone (objective, humorous, reverent, argumentative, cautionary, playful, ironic, ridiculing) of this material?

4. Draw a line at the point at which the preparation (materials, setup, explaining words, and so on) ends and the steps begin.

5. Write numbers in the margin to indicate the steps or stages in the process.

6. Circle any transitional words indicating time or other progression (*first, second, then, soon, now, next, after, before, when, finally, at last, therefore, consequently,* and—especially for the informative process analysis—words used to show the passage of time, such as hours, days of the week, and so on).

EXERCISE 6

Have you ever felt self-conscious about being alone in a congregation in which others had companions? Bruce Jay Friedman tells you how to deal with the situation to build your confidence and even "turn the tables" on the group people.

Vocabulary Preview: Write short definitions for these words as they are used in the context of the following passage. (The paragraph numbers are given in parentheses.) Be prepared to use the words in your own sentences.

inconspicuous (1)	discreetly (14)
hors d'oeuvre (7)	desolate (15)
gaucho (10)	conviviality (17)
suffice (10)	riveted (17)
promenade (13)	eccentric (22)
imperiously (14)	audacious (24)

Eating Alone in Restaurants
BRUCE JAY FRIEDMAN

1 Hunched over, trying to be inconspicuous as possible, a solitary diner slips into a midtown Manhattan steakhouse. No sooner does he check his coat than the voice of the headwaiter comes booming across the restaurant.

2 "Alone again, eh?"

3 As all eyes are raised, the bartender, with enormous good cheer, chimes in: "That's because they all left him high and dry."

4 And then, just in case there is a customer in the restaurant who isn't yet aware of the situation, a waiter shouts out from the buffet table: "Well, we'll take care of him anyway, won't we fellas!"

5 *Haw, haw, haw,* and a lot of sly winks and pokes in the ribs.

6 Eating alone in a restaurant is one of the most terrifying experiences in America.

7 Sniffed at by headwaiters, an object of scorn and amusement to couples, the solitary diner is the unwanted and unloved child of Restaurant Row. No sooner does he make his appearance than he is whisked out of sight and seated at a thin sliver of a table with barely enough room on it for an hors d'oeuvre. Wedged between busboy stations, a hair's breadth from the men's room, there he sits, feet lodged in a railing as if he were in Pilgrim stocks, wondering where he went wrong in life.

8 Rather than face this grim scenario, most Lonely Guys would prefer to nibble away at a tuna fish sandwich in the relative safety of their high-rise apartments.

9 What can be done to ease the pain of this not only starving but silent minority—to make dining alone in restaurants a rewarding experience? Absolutely nothing. But some small strategies *do* exist for making the experience bearable.

Before You Get There

10 Once the Lonely Guy has decided to dine alone at a restaurant, a sense of terror and foreboding will begin to build throughout the day. All the more reason for him to get there as quickly as possible so that the experience can soon be forgotten and he can resume his normal life. Clothing should be light and loose-fitting, especially around the neck—on the off chance of a fainting attack during the appetizer. It is best to dress modestly, avoiding both the funeral-director-style suit as well as the bold, eye-arresting costume of the gaucho. A single cocktail should suffice; little sympathy will be given to the Lonely Guy who tumbles in, stewed to the gills. (The fellow who stoops to putting morphine in his toes for courage does not belong in this discussion.) En route to the restaurant, it is best to play down dramatics, such as swinging the arms pluckily and humming the theme from *The Bridge on the River Kwai.*

Once You Arrive

11 The way your entrance comes off is of critical importance. Do not skulk in, slipping along the walls as if you are carrying some dirty little secret. There is no need, on the other hand, to fling your coat arrogantly at the hatcheck girl, slap the headwaiter across the cheeks with your gloves and demand to be seated immediately. Simply walk in with a brisk rubbing of the hands and approach the headwaiter. When asked how many are in your party, avoid cute responses such as "Jes lil ol' me." Tell him you are a party of one; the Lonely Guy who does not trust his voice can simply lift a finger. Do not launch into a story about how tired you are of taking out fashion models, night after night, and what a pleasure it is going to be to dine alone.

12 It is best to arrive with no reservation. Asked to set aside a table for one, the restaurant owner will suspect either a prank on the part of an ex-waiter, or a terrorist plot, in which case windows will be boarded up and the kitchen bombswept. An advantage of the "no reservation" approach is that you will appear to have just stepped off the plane from Des Moines, your first night in years away from Marge and the kids.

13 All eyes will be upon you when you make the promenade to your table. Stay as close as possible to the headwaiter, trying to match him step for step. This will reduce your visibility and fool some diners into thinking you are a member of the staff. If you hear a generalized snickering throughout the restaurant, do not assume automatically that you are being laughed at. The other diners may all

have just recalled an amusing moment in a Feydeau* farce.

14. If your table is unsatisfactory, do not demand imperiously that one for eight people be cleared immediately so that you can dine in solitary grandeur. Glance around discreetly and see if there are other possibilities. The ideal table will allow you to keep your back to the wall so that you can see if anyone is laughing at you. Try to get one close to another couple so that if you lean over at a 45-degree angle it will appear that you are a swinging member of their group. Sitting opposite a mirror can be useful; after a drink or two, you will begin to feel that there are a few of you.

15. Once you have been seated, and it becomes clear to the staff that you are alone, there will follow The Single Most Heartbreaking Moment in Dining Out Alone—when the second setting is whisked away and yours is spread out a bit to make the table look busier. This will be done with great ceremony by the waiter—angered in advance at being tipped for only one dinner. At this point, you may be tempted to smack you forehead against the table and curse the fates that brought you to this desolate position in life. A wiser course is to grit your teeth, order a drink and use this opportunity to make contact with other Lonely Guys sprinkled around the room. A menu or a leafy stalk of celery can be used as a shield for peering out at them. Do not expect a hearty greeting or a cry of "huzzah" from these frightened and browbeaten people. Too much excitement may cause them to slump over, curtains. Smile gently and be content if you receive a pale wave of the hand in return. It is unfair to imply that you have come to help them throw off their chains.

16. When the headwaiter arrives to take your order, do not be bullied into ordering the last of the gazelle haunches unless you really want them. Thrilled to be offered anything at all, many Lonely Guys will say, "Get them right out here" and wolf them down. Restaurants take unfair advantage of Lonely Guys, using them to get rid of anything from withered liver to old heels of roast beef. Order anything you like, although it is good to keep to the light and simple in case of a sudden attack of violent stomach cramps.

*A French writer of comedies.

Some Proven Strategies

17. Once the meal is under way, a certain pressure will begin to build as couples snuggle together, the women clucking sympathetically in your direction. Warmth and conviviality will pervade the room, none of it encompassing you. At this point, many Lonely Guys will keep their eyes riveted to the restaurant paintings of early Milan or bury themselves in a paperback anthology they have no wish to read.

18. Here are some ploys designed to confuse other diners and make them feel less sorry for you.

19. • After each bite of food, lift your head, smack your lips thoughtfully, swallow and make a notation in a pad. Diners will assume you are a restaurant critic.

20. • Between courses, pull out a walkie-talkie and whisper a message into it. This will lead everyone to believe you are part of a police stake-out team, about to bust the salad man as an international dope dealer.

21. • Pretend you are a foreigner. This is done by pointing to items on the menu with an alert smile and saying to the headwaiter: "Is good, no?"

22. • When the main course arrives, brush the restaurant silverware off the table and pull some of your own out of a breastpocket. People will think you are a wealthy eccentric.

23. • Keep glancing at the door, and make occasional trips to look out at the street, as if you are waiting for a beautiful woman. Half-way through the meal, shrug in a world-weary manner and begin to eat with gusto. The world is full of women! Why tolerate bad manners! Life is too short.

The Right Way

24. One other course is open to the Lonely Guy, an audacious one, full of perils, but all the more satisfying if you can bring it off. That is to take off your dark glasses, sit erectly, smile broadly at anyone who looks in your direction, wave off inferior wines, and begin to eat with heartiness and enormous confidence. As outrageous as the thought may be—enjoy your own company.

Suddenly, titters and sly winks will tail off, the headwaiter's disdain will fade, and friction will build among couples who will turn out to be not as tightly cemented as they appear. The heads of other Lonely Guys will lift with hope as you become the attractive center of the room.

25 If that doesn't work, you still have your fainting option.

APPLICATIONS FOR CRITICAL READING AND DISCUSSION

1. What type of process analysis (informative or directive) is used?

2. To what type of audience (well informed, moderately informed, or poorly informed on the topic) does the writer direct this selection?

3. What is the prevailing tone (objective, humorous, reverent, argumentative, cautionary, playful, ironic, ridiculing) of this material?

4. Draw a line at the point at which the preparation (materials, setup, explaining words, and so on) ends and the steps begin.

5. Write numbers in the margin to indicate the steps or stages in the process.

6. Circle any transitional words indicating time or other progression (*first, second, then, soon, now, next, after, before, when, finally, at last, therefore, consequently*, and—especially for the informative process analysis—words used to show the passage of time, such as hours, days of the week, and so on).

EXERCISE 7

When you go skiing, do you sometimes become fatigued and want to retire to the inn? Are you the one who lags, pretending to tighten your equipment, when you are actually buying some time for rest? Carl Wilgus has some suggestions.

Vocabulary Preview: Write in short definitions for these words as they are used in the context of the following passage. (The paragraph numbers are given in parentheses.) Be prepared to use the words in your own sentences.

monitor (1)

phenomenon (1)

metronome (6)

cadence (7)

Conserving Energy as You Ski
CARL WILGUS

One day a few years ago, as I rode one of the chairs at Sun Valley, it occurred to me that there were quite a number of people standing still on the slope below. Throughout the rest of that season I continued to monitor this phenomenon, and the results were almost always the same— lots of people standing. I could think of only four possible reasons that skiers would stop so often: 1) their equipment or clothing needed attention; 2) the view was too good to pass up; 3) they were waiting for other skiers, to regroup; or 4) they were tired and needed a rest.

2   Watching what skiers did when they stopped led me to believe that the last reason was the most common one. But how could so many people be so badly out of shape? After all, skiing as practiced by the average intermediate skier is not all that strenuous. I couldn't figure it out.

3   Later that season, a possible answer came when I was giving a lesson to a high school athlete. His name was Phil, and he stood about 6'1" and weighed about 170 pounds. He told me that he played on both the varsity football and basketball teams and that he was in good shape, but that when it came to skiing, he could only make a few turns before he ran out of gas. On closer inspection, his problem was obvious. He would start out nicely, but with each turn his stance would get lower and lower until, after a half-dozen turns, he would be squatting over his skis. This unnatural position would cause his thighs to burn, and he'd have to stop frequently to give himself a rest.

4   After this experience, I started looking around, and it became clear that most skiers work much harder on the slopes than they need to. Whether they burn up too much energy physically or mentally, the result is the same—a loss of ski time because they have to stop and rest so frequently. What was needed were ways to help conserve energy.

5   For Phil, the way to conserve energy was to learn to *let go* between turns. I had him make some turns as if he were the Tin Man from *The Wizard of Oz*—stiff and unbending. Then I had him pretend he was the Scarecrow—loose and floppy. Phil discovered for himself through this process that being totally stiff resulted in early fatigue while being as loose as a goose resulted in sloppy turns. The next step was to combine the elements of tension and relaxation, to learn to vary them and to find a middle ground. Once Phil got the idea of a brief moment of relaxation between turns, he found that he could cover longer distances on the mountain without stopping.

6   Another useful exercise for conserving energy while skiing is to exhale as you make a turn and to inhale between turns. This can be helpful for several reasons. Some skiers hold their breath when they ski, and, as a result, they not only run out of oxygen but end up tightening their muscles, putting even more strain on the system. Another advantage of this exercise is that good timing and rhythm are incorporated in your skiing as breathing and turning become coordinated. This natural, easy, consistent tempo can create a metronome effect that is energy-conserving. It can be especially valuable toward the end of the day when you are tired and your major concern is to get off the hill safely.

7   If coordinating your breathing with your turning doesn't appeal to you, try humming or singing. These will also develop a cadence that will improve timing and conserve energy.

8   Psychologically, what these exercises do is divert attention from self-defeating behavior to refocus on timing and rhythm—two very important parts of relaxed, natural skiing. They also help reduce anxiety, tension, and frustration, all of which add to fatigue.

9   Tuning in to the sound of your skis is another tool you can use to conserve energy. Allow your attention to focus on the intensity and duration of the sound you hear as the edges bite the snow. In general, the harsher the sound, the more effort is being expended. See if you can produce moments of almost total silence between turns. This will indicate that you are not only releasing the edges of your skis but also releasing the tension in your body, allowing yourself a moment of relaxation. This will help you ski longer distances without stopping.

10 Many novice skiers work much harder than necessary because they keep their attention too close to the body. This is like driving a car while staring at the hood ornament. Stress and anxiety, as well as the need for physical effort, will diminish if you'll focus your attention on some fixed point down the slope. Then ski toward that point while maintaining easy—not strained—eye contact with it.

11 As we have been made all too aware lately in this country, the more energy we conserve now, the more we'll have for the future. The same holds true for skiing. So take the Soft Path of energy conservation as you ski. You'll not only be able to make longer non-stop runs, but you'll have more energy to burn on the dance floor.

APPLICATIONS FOR CRITICAL READING AND DISCUSSION

1. What type of process analysis (informative or directive) is used?

2. To what type of audience (well informed, moderately informed, or poorly informed on the topic) does the writer direct this selection?

3. What is the prevailing tone (such as objective, humorous, reverent, argumentative, cautionary, playful, ironic, ridiculing) of this material?

4. Draw a line at the point at which the preparation (materials, setup, explaining words, and so on) ends and the steps begin.

5. Write numbers in the margin to indicate the steps or stages in the process.

6. Circle any transitional words indicating time or other progression (*first, second, then, soon, now, next, after, before, when, finally, at last, therefore, consequently,* and—especially for the informative process analysis—words used to show the passage of time, such as hours, days of the week, and so on).

EXERCISE 8

W. S. Merwin—poet, essayist, teacher—takes us backward. Instead of chopping a tree, the usual kind of topic in an exercise in directive process analysis, he explains how to unchop. Unchopping becomes a metaphor for the impossible dream of undoing our destructive acts.

Vocabulary Preview: Write in short definitions for these words as they are used in the context of the following passage. (The paragraph numbers are given in parentheses.) Be prepared to use the words in your own sentences.

simulate (1)

panoply (3)

bole (3)

complementary (3)

fixative (3)

translucent (5)

subcutaneous (5)

thoroughfares (5)

struts (6)

joinery (6)

Unchopping a Tree
W. S. MERWIN

Start with the leaves, the small twigs, and the nests that have been shaken, ripped, or broken off by the fall; these must be gathered and attached once again to their respective places. It is not arduous work, unless major limbs have been smashed or mutilated. If the fall was carefully and correctly planned, the chances of anything of the kind happening will have been reduced. Again, much depends upon the size, age, shape, and species of the tree. Still, you will be lucky if you can get through this stage without having to use machinery. Even in the best of circumstances it is a labor that will make you wish often that you had won the favor of the universe of ants, the empire of mice, or at least a local tribe of squirrels, and could enlist their labors and their talents. But no, they leave you to it. They have learned, with time. This is men's work. It goes without saying that if the tree was hollow in whole or in part, and contained old nests of bird or mammal or insect, or hoards of nuts or such structures as wasps or bees build for their survival, the contents will have to be repaired where necessary, and reassembled, insofar as possible, in their original order, including the shells of nuts already opened. With spiders' webs you must simply do the best you can. We do not have the spider's weaving equipment, nor any substitute for the leaf's living bond with its point of attachment and nourishment. It is even harder to simulate the latter when the leaves have once become dry—as they are bound to do, for this is not the labor of a moment. Also it hardly needs saying that this is the time for repairing any neighboring trees or bushes or other growth that may have been damaged by the fall. The same rules apply. Where neighboring trees were of the same species it is difficult not to waste time conveying a detached leaf back to the wrong tree. Practice, practice. Put your hope in that.

2   Now the tackle must be put into place or the scaffolding, depending on the surroundings and the dimensions of the tree. It is ticklish work. Almost always it involves, in itself, further damage to the area, which will have to be corrected later. But as you've heard, it can't be helped. And care now is likely to save you considerable trouble later. Be careful to grind nothing into the ground.

3   At last the time comes for the erecting of the trunk. By now it will scarcely be necessary to remind you of the delicacy of this huge skeleton. Every motion of the tackle, every slight upward heave of the trunk, the branches, their elaborately reassembled panoply of leaves (now dead) will draw from you an involuntary gasp. You will watch for a leaf or a twig to be snapped off yet again. You will listen for the nuts to shift in the hollow limb and you will hear whether they are indeed falling into place or are spilling in disorder—in which case, or in the event of anything else of the kind—operations will have to cease, of course, while you correct the matter. The raising itself is no small enterprise, from the moment when the chains tighten around the old bandages until the bole hangs vertical above the stump, splinter above splinter. Now the final straightening of the splinters themselves can take place (the preliminary work is best done while the wood is still green and soft, but at times when the splinters are not badly twisted most of the straightening is left until now, when the torn ends are face to face with each other). When the splinters are perfectly complementary the appropriate fixture is applied. Again we have no duplicate of the original substance. Ours is extremely strong, but it is rigid. It is limited to surfaces, and there is no play in it. However the core is not the part of the trunk that conducted life from the roots up into the branches and back again. It was relatively inert. The fixative for this part is not the same as the one for the outer layers and the bark, and if either of these is involved in the splintered section they must receive applications of the appropriate adhesives. Apart from being incorrect and probably ineffective, the core fixative would leave a scar on the bark.

4   When all is ready the splintered trunk is lowered onto the splinters of the stump. This, one might say, is only the skeleton of the resurrection. Now the chips must be gathered, and the sawdust, and returned to their former positions. The fixative for the wood layers will be applied to chips and sawdust consisting only of wood. Chips and sawdust consisting of several substances will receive applications of the correct adhesives. It is as well, where possible, to shelter the materials from the elements while working. Weathering makes it harder to identify the smaller fragments. Bark sawdust in particular the earth lays claim to very quickly. You must find your own ways of coping with this problem. There is a certain beauty, you will notice at moments, in the pattern of the chips as they are fitted back into place. You will wonder to what extent it should be described as natural, to what extent man-made. It will lead you on to speculations about the parentage of beauty itself, to which you will return.

5   The adhesive for the chips is translucent, and not so rigid as that for the splinters. That for bark and its subcutaneous layers is transparent and runs into the fibers on either side, partially dissolving them into each other. It does not set the sap flowing again but it does pay a kind of tribute to the preoccupations of the ancient thoroughfares. You could not roll an egg over the joints but some of the mineshafts would still be passable, no doubt. For the first exploring insect who raises its head in the tight echoless passages.

The day comes when it is all restored, even to the moss (now dead) over the wound. You will sleep badly, thinking of the removal of the scaffolding that must begin the next morning. How you will hope for sun and a still day!

6   The removal of the scaffolding or tackle is not so dangerous, perhaps, to the surroundings, as its installation, but it presents problems. It should be taken from the spot piece by piece as it is detached, and stored at a distance. You have come to accept it there, around the tree. The sky begins to look naked as the chains and struts one by one vacate their positions. Finally the moment arrives when the last sustaining piece is removed and the tree stands again on its own. It is as though its weight for a moment stood on your heart. You listen for a thud of settlement, a warning creak deep in the intricate joinery. You cannot believe it will hold. How like something dreamed it is, standing there all by itself. How long will it stand there now? The first breeze that touches its dead leaves all seems to flow into your mouth. You are afraid the motion of the clouds will be enough to push it over. What more can you do? What more can you do?

7   But there is nothing more you can do.
8   Others are waiting.
9   Everything is going to have to be put back.

APPLICATIONS FOR CRITICAL READING AND DISCUSSION

1. What type of process analysis (informative or directive) is used?

2. To what type of audience (well informed, moderately informed, or poorly informed on the topic) does the writer direct this selection?

3. What is the prevailing tone (objective, humorous, reverent, argumentative, cautionary, playful, ironic, ridiculing) of this material?

4. Draw a line at the point at which the preparation (materials, setup, explaining words, and so on) ends and the steps begin.

5. Write numbers in the margin to indicate the steps or stages in the process.

6. Circle any transitional words indicating time or other progression (*first, second, then, soon, now, next, after, before, when, finally, at last, therefore, consequently,* and—especially for the informative process analysis—words used to show the passage of time, such as hours, days of the week, and so on).

7. If we assume that the process here is an impossible one, then what is the message?

8. What do the last two sentences in paragraph 4 mean?

EXERCISE 9

You are probably familiar with the life of Malcolm X. Here he focuses on, arguably, the most important step he ever took: the beginning of his serious education, one that was self-administered under difficult conditions in a maximum security prison.

Vocabulary Preview: Write short definitions for these words as they are used in the context of the following passage. (The paragraph numbers are given in parentheses.) Be prepared to use the words in your own sentences.

articulate (2)

immensely (9)

mammal (9)

inevitable (11)

feigned (17)

The Autobiography of Malcolm X
MALCOLM X AND ALEX HALEY

It was because of my letters that I happened to stumble upon starting to acquire some kind of a homemade education.

2   I became increasingly frustrated at not being able to express what I wanted to convey in letters that I wrote, especially those to Mr. Elijah Muhammad.* In the street, I had been the most articulate hustler out there—I had commanded attention when I said something. But now, trying to write simple English, I not only wasn't articulate, I wasn't even functional. How would I sound writing in slang, the way I would *say* it, something such as, "Look, daddy, let me pull your coat about a cat, Elijah Muhammad—"

3   Many who today hear me somewhere in person, or on television, or those who read something I've said, will think I went to school far beyond the eighth grade. This impression is due entirely to my prison studies.

4   It had really begun back in the Charlestown Prison, when Bimbi† first made me feel envy of his stock of knowledge. Bimbi had always taken charge of any conversation he was in, and I had tried to emulate him. But every book I picked up had few sentences which didn't contain anywhere from one to nearly all of the words that might as well have been in Chinese. When I just skipped those words, of course, I really ended up with little idea of what the book said. So I had come to the Norfolk Prison Colony still going through only book-reading motions. Pretty soon, I would have quit even these motions, unless I had received the motivation that I did.

5   I saw that the best thing I could do was get hold of a dictionary—to study, to learn some words. I was lucky enough to reason also that I should try to improve my penmanship. It was sad. I couldn't even write in a straight line. It was both ideas together that moved me to request a dictionary along with some tablets and pencils from the Norfolk Prison Colony school.

6   I spent two days just riffling uncertainly through the dictionary's pages. I'd never realized so many words existed! I didn't know *which* words I needed to learn. Finally, just to start some kind of action, I began copying.

7   In my slow, painstaking, ragged handwriting, I copied into my tablet everything printed on that first page, down to the punctuation marks.

8   I believe it took me a day. Then, aloud, I read back, to myself, everything I'd written on the tablet. Over and over, aloud, to myself, I read my own handwriting.

9   I woke up the next morning, thinking about those words—immensely proud to realize that not only had I written so much at one time, but I'd written words that I never knew were in the world. Moreover, with a little effort, I also could remember what many of these words meant. I reviewed the words whose meanings I didn't

---

*the Black Muslims' founder and leader   †a fellow inmate he met in 1947, at Charlestown State Prison

remember. Funny thing, from the dictionary first page right now, that "aardvark" springs to my mind. The dictionary had a picture of it, a long-tailed, long-eared, burrowing African mammal, which lives off termites caught by sticking out its tongue as an anteater does for ants.

10 I was so fascinated that I went on—I copied the dictionary's next page. And the same experience came when I studied that. With every succeeding page, I also learned of people and places and events from history. Actually the dictionary is like a miniature encyclopedia. Finally the dictionary's A section had filled a whole tablet—and I went on into the B's. That was the way I started copying what eventually became the entire dictionary. It went a lot faster after so much practice helped me to pick up handwriting speed. Between what I wrote in my tablet, and writing letters, during the rest of my time in prison I would guess I wrote a million words.

11 I suppose it was inevitable that as my word-base broadened, I could for the first time pick up a book and read and now begin to understand what the book was saying. Anyone who has read a great deal can imagine the new world that opened. Let me tell you something: from then until I left that prison, in every free moment I had, if I was not reading in the library, I was reading on my bunk. You couldn't have gotten me out of books with a wedge. Between Mr. Muhammad's teachings, my correspondence, my visitors—usually Ella and Reginald*—and my reading of books, months passed without my even thinking about being imprisoned. In fact, up to then, I never had been so truly free in my life.

12 The Norfolk Prison Colony's library was in the school building. A variety of classes was taught there by instructors who came from such places as Harvard and Boston universities. The weekly debates between inmate teams were also held in the school building. You would be astonished to know how worked up convict debaters and audiences would get over subjects like "Should Babies Be Fed Milk?"

13 Available on the prison library's shelves were books on just about every general subject. Much of the big private collection that Parkhurst† had willed to the prison was still in crates and boxes in the back of the library—thousands of old books. Some of them looked ancient: covers faded, old-time parchment-looking binding. Parkhurst, I've mentioned, seemed to have been principally interested in history and religion. He had the money and the special interest to have a lot of books that you wouldn't have in general circulation. Any college library would have been lucky to get that collection.

14 As you can imagine, especially in a prison where there was heavy emphasis on rehabilitation, an inmate was smiled upon if he demonstrated an unusually intense interest in books. There was a sizable number of well-read inmates, especially the popular debaters. Some were said by many to be practically walking encyclopedias. They were almost celebrities. No university would ask any student to devour literature as I did when this new world opened to me, of being able to read and *understand*.

15 I read more in my room than in the library itself. An inmate who was known to read a lot could check out more than the permitted maximum number of books. I preferred reading in the total isolation of my own room.

16 When I had progressed to really serious reading, every night at about ten P.M. I would be outraged with the "lights out." It always seemed to catch me right in the middle of something engrossing.

17 Fortunately, right outside my door was a corridor light that cast a glow into my room. The glow was enough to read by, once my eyes adjusted to it. So when "lights out" came, I would sit on the floor where I could continue reading in that glow.

18 At one-hour intervals the night guards paced past every room. Each time I heard the approaching footsteps, I jumped into bed and feigned sleep. And as soon as the guard passed, I got back out of bed onto the floor area of that light-glow, where I would read for another fifty-eight minutes—until the guard approached again. That went on until three or four every morning. Three or four hours of sleep a night was enough for me. Often in the years in the streets I had slept less than that.

*his sister and brother †a millionaire interested in the prison rehabilitation program

APPLICATIONS FOR CRITICAL READING AND DISCUSSION

1. What type of process analysis (informative or directive) is used?

2. To what type of audience (well informed, moderately informed, or poorly informed on the topic) does the writer direct this selection?

3. What is the prevailing tone (objective, humorous, reverent, argumentative, cautionary, playful, ironic, ridiculing) of this material?

4. Draw a line at the point at which the preparation (materials, setup, explaining words, and so on) ends and the steps begin.

5. Write numbers in the margin to indicate the steps or stages in the process.

6. Circle any transitional words indicating time or other progression (*first, second, then, soon, now, next, after, before, when, finally, at last, therefore, consequently*, and—especially for the informative process analysis—words used to show the passage of time, such as hours, days of the week, and so on).

7. What parallel do you see between the stages of Malcolm X's self-education and a typical formal school education?

The Reading Connection from Classroom Sources

EXERCISE 10

Demonstration of Directive Process Analysis Using the DCODE Worksheet

Many of us reclaim our ethnic origin at our New Year as we celebrate by eating a meal that is intended to bring us happiness, peace, and prosperity for the next twelve months. For Maysim Mondegaran, the meal is Sabzi Polo Mahi, and each phase of the preparation and cooking is done with care and feeling. Reading her paragraph will make you hungry. Notice how her paragraph includes both directive and informative elements.

WORKSHEET
Writing in DCODE

NAME: Maysim Mondegaran

SECTION: _____ CHAPTER: _____ DATE: _____

Delve   Generate your topic, or ideas for your topic, by delving into your subject area through:

- *Freewriting*—writing sentence after sentence, nonstop and spontaneously.
- *Brainstorming*—jotting down answers to Who? What? Where? When? Why? and How? and then listing words and phrases in relation to those answers.
- *Clustering*—connecting bubbled ideas with lines to show strings of relationships, producing each new bubble item in response to the question, What comes to mind?
- *Combining* any of these approaches, as directed by your instructor.

Freewriting:
   Some of my fondest memories about Iran are on the way we celebrated the Iranian New Year. It was a joyous time for all the family. The sons and daughters and parents and grandparents would get together whenever possible and we would have a special meal. I say special meal because it was always the same. I can remember it so well. The meal is called Sabzi Polo Mahi referring to the fish and vegetables and rice that are prepared together. But it was more than just a meal. Each part of the meal had to be of the best quality we could obtain and my mother knew just how to find, buy, and prepare it.

Brainstorming:
   Who? my family in Iran
   What? New Year's meal
   Where? Iran
   When? old, continuing tradition
   Why? celebration of the New Year
   How? obtaining the food/
        preparing the food

Clustering:

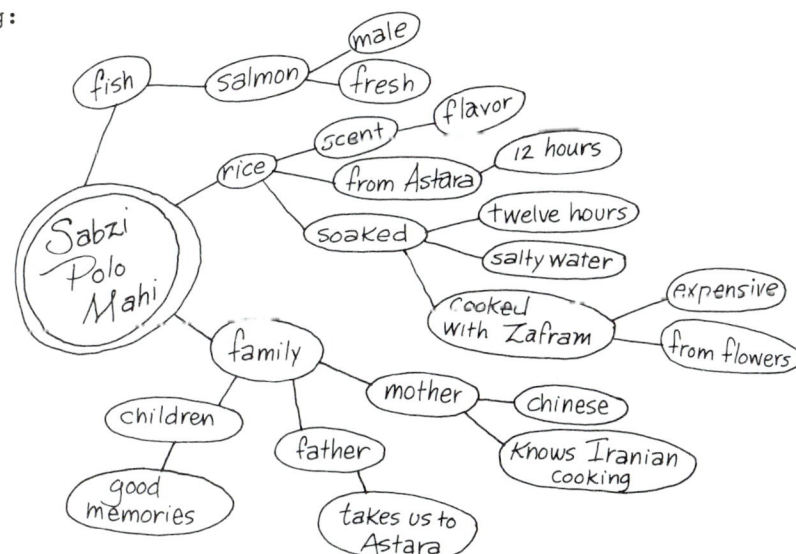

193

WORKSHEET: Writing in DCODE

Concentrate   Concentrate your work by stating your topic in one sentence that is not too broad, narrow, or vague to be developed. Base this sentence (which may become the topic sentence for your paragraph or the thesis for your essay) on an idea emerging from the **Delve** stage. You may have to try several statements here before you formulate one that is best for your writing task. Be sure that your final statement covers your assignment or intent and specifies both your subject (what you are writing about) and treatment (what aspect you will focus on). Label the *subject* and *treatment* parts.

         Subject   Treatment

<u>In order to make Sabzi Polo Mahi properly</u>, <u>you need to know how to pick the right ingredients and how to cook them.</u>

Organize   Complete an outline or a cluster, as directed by your instructor. The cluster should be a section from, or a refined version of, the **Delve** clustering. Regardless of the strategy you use, the organizational pattern should indicate a division of your topic into parts that will, in turn, be further subdivided for support as necessary to address a particular audience on your concentrated topic.

```
    I. Preparation                II. Cooking
       A. Picking the fish            A. Fish
          1. Fresh                       1. Baked
          2. Salmon                      2. Flaky, white, juicy
          3. Male                     B. Rice
       B. Picking the rice               1. Soaked for twelve hours
          1. Appearance                  2. Boiled
          2. Scent                       3. Drained
          3. Where found              C. Vegetables
       C. Vegetables                     1. Stir-fried
          1. Leafy                       2. Steamed with rice
          2. Garlic                   D. Seasoning
       D. Picking the seasoning          1. Butter
          1. Butter                      2. Saffron
          2. Saffron
```

Draft   On separate paper, write and then revise your assignment as many times as necessary for **c**oherence, **l**anguage (usage, tone, and diction), **u**nity, **e**mphasis, **s**upport, and **s**entence structure (**cluess**).

Edit   Correct problems in fundamentals such as **c**apitalization, **o**missions, **p**unctuation, and **s**pelling (**cops**). Before writing the final draft, read your paper aloud to discover oversights and awkwardness of expression.

First Draft

Sabzi Polo Mahi

In Iran the ~~new year is celebrated~~ N Y comes at the beginning of ~~every~~ spring. ~~It is a custom for all parents to invite their children and serve a dish~~ Families like to celebrate it with a meal called Sabzi Polo Mahi which means fish with vegetable rice. The preparation is as important as the cooking. In order to make this special dish one must first know how to ~~prepare and~~ and pick the right fish, rice, vegetables, and seasoning. ~~and then prepare them.~~ ~~Although the best fishes are usually caught at that time of the year, it is best to know how to select a fish.~~ A fresh fish is required for the main part of the meal. ~~A fresh fish must~~ It should have shiny, bright eyes, nonsticky light grey skin, and pale pink meat. ~~The~~ Salmon ~~fish~~ is ~~usually~~ recommended. In my family we usually buy ~~a Salmon fish which~~ one that weighs about eight ~~8~~ kilograms. It is best to pick a male fish because the meat is more tender and tastier than that of the female. The males always have several black round dots that look like moles on top of their heads. Second, the rice must be ~~from Astara, which is located~~ excellent, and the best is grown in Astara, in ~~the~~ northern ~~part of~~ Iran. ~~It must be long and have a good scent.~~ Although my mother is Chinese, she likes to follow the Iranian custom, so every now and then we drive six hours to Astara and buy several big bags of Astarian rice with long grains and a good scent. ~~She refuses to use any other kind of rice.~~ To get the best results, the rice must be soaked in salty water for twelve hours before it is cooked. When the rice is almost through soaking, ~~At the end of the soaking period,~~ the fish is placed in the oven preheated to about 350 degrees and ~~and~~ baked. From time to time it should be basted. The baking time will vary, depending on the size of the fish. It is cooked ~~done~~ when the flesh is white and flaky. While the fish is cooking, the rice should be boiled and drained. While the rice is draining, ~~Meanwhile the rice is about done, and~~ the vegetables should be prepared. The vegetables (in my family mainly a leafy green ones like spinach) are chopped fine and stir-fried with garlic. After the vegetables are done, ~~and the rice is drained,~~ they should be combined with the rice and steamed so that the flavors mix. After they are steamed, melted butter and ground saffron mixed with a few drops of water are poured over them.

Saffron is made of the stamens of a very sensitive flower
which can grown only in certain parts of the world. ~~It~~ Saffron has
a bright yellow color and a ~~special~~ rich flavor. My mother buys
it raw and grinds it∧ for this meal. ~~She then mixes it with~~
~~a few drops of water.~~ This is one of my favorite dishes,
and I just can't wait to go back home next year.

Final Draft

At last the Sabzi Polo Mahi is ready – the succulent baked fish and the mixture of the spicy green vegetables and the rice, now made vibrant yellow and flavorful by the saffron and butter.

Sabzi Polo Mahi
Maysim Mondegaran

In Iran, families like to celebrate the beginning of the New Year each spring with a meal called Sabzi Polo Mahi, which means fish with vegetables and rice. The preparation is as important as the cooking. In order to make this special dish, one must (first) know how to pick the right fish, rice, vegetables, and seasoning. A fresh fish is required for the main part of the meal. It should have shiny bright eyes, nonsticky light grey skin, and pale pink meat. Salmon is recommended. In my family we usually buy one that weighs about eight kilograms. It is best to pick a male fish because the meat is more tender and tastier than that of the female. The males always have several black round dots that look like moles on top of their heads. (Second,) the rice must be excellent, and the best is grown in Astara, in Northern Iran. Although my mother is Chinese, she likes to follow the Iranian custom, so every now and then we drive six hours to Astara and buy several big bags of Astarian rice with long grains and a good scent. To get the best results, the rice must be soaked in salty water for twelve hours before it is cooked. When the rice is almost through soaking, the fish is placed in the oven preheated to about 350 degrees and baked. (From time to time) it should be basted. The baking time will vary, depending on the size of the fish. It is done when the flesh is white and flaky but still moist. (While) the fish is cooking, the rice should be boiled and drained. (While) the rice is draining, the vegetables should be prepared. The vegetables (in my family, mainly leafy green ones like spinach or parsley) are chopped fine and stir-fried with garlic. (After) the vegetables are done, they should be combined with the rice and steamed so that the flavors mix. (After) they are steamed, melted butter and ground saffron mixed with a few drops of water are poured over them. Saffron has a bright yellow color and a rich flavor. My mother buys it raw and grinds it specially for this meal. (At last) the Sabzi Polo Mahi is ready--the succulent baked fish and the mixture of spicy green vegetables and rice, (now) made vibrant yellow and flavorful by the saffron and butter. This is one of my favorite dishes, and I look forward to the next time when I can have it with my family.

APPLICATIONS FOR CRITICAL READING AND DISCUSSION

1. What is the type of process analysis (informative or directive) is used?
   ```
   informative/directive
   ```

2. To what kind of audience (well informed, moderately informed, or poorly informed on the topic) does the writer direct this selection?
   ```
   poorly informed
   ```

3. What is the prevailing tone (objective, humorous, reverent, argumentative, cautionary, playful, ironic, ridiculing) of this material?
   ```
   thoughtful, almost reverent
   ```

4. Draw a line at the point at which the preparation (materials, setup, explaining words, and so on) ends and the steps begin.
   ```
   at line 19
   ```

5. Use numbers in the margin to indicate the steps or stages in the process.

6. Circle any transitional words indicating time or other progression (*first, second, then, soon, now, next, after, before, when, finally, at last, therefore, consequently,* and—especially for the informative process analysis—words used to show the passage of time, such as hours, days of the week, and so on).

EXERCISE 11

The author gives you a scenario. Your mission, should you choose to accept it, is to open a bottle of champagne while a host of friends watch. Are you fearful that you might not perform with grace? If the answer is yes or if you are just a bit hesitant, A. Del Turco provides the directions you need.

```
              Popping the Cork
                 A. Del Turco
   All of the guests have arrived. Everyone has been
seated at the dinner table. Light conversation abounds.
Amid all of the explanations of what everyone "does," your
wife leans over to you and speaks the words of doom: "Why
don't you open the champagne?" All conversation ceases.
Suddenly you are aware of seven pairs of eyes, all looking
at you. Each guest in turn mentally sizes you up. "Is he
man enough?" "Will he embarrass himself again this year?"
"Did they really have to re-carpet?" There it sits, ten
feet away, smugly chilling in an ice bucket. The enemy.
Relax. Opening a good bottle of champagne is not an ordeal
once you know how. The necessary materials are few. All
that is needed is an ice bucket, a table napkin, a little
bravery, and some patience. To start, do yourself a favor
by choosing a good champagne. Well-chilled good champagnes
won't explode, while bad champagnes are potentially
embarrassing. The wine should be chilled in the ice bucket
for at least twenty minutes. This is done to reduce
pressure in the bottle and allow for an uneventful
```

opening. First, remove the bottle from the bucket and quickly dry it. Wrap the table napkin around the neck of the bottle. This affords you a better grip. Next remove the neck wrapping to expose the wire basket. Removing the wire basket is the first tricky bit. The basket can be removed by twisting the wire braid counterclockwise six turns. This is an international standard among champagne vintners. Then pull the table napkin over the cork. This is done, once again, to allow for a better grip. Now comes the fun part. At the bottom of the champagne bottle is a deep indentation. This is not a manufacturing defect; it is called the "punt." Hold the bottle in your left hand by the punt. With your right, grip the cork between thumb and forefinger. Gently begin rocking the cork back and forth, slowing pulling at the cork. Soon the cork will begin to loosen and move more quickly. This is a critical point in the opening. Slow it down! Hold the cork back and slowly work it out of the neck. If the cork is removed properly, only the slightest sign should be heard. From the champagne--not you.

APPLICATIONS FOR CRITICAL READING AND DISCUSSION

1. What type of process analysis (informative or directive) is used?

2. To what type of audience (well informed, moderately informed, or poorly informed on the topic) does the writer direct this selection?

3. What is the prevailing tone (objective, humorous, reverent, argumentative, cautionary, playful, ironic, ridiculing) of this material?

4. Draw a line at the point at which the preparation (materials, setup, explaining words, and so on) ends and the steps begin.

5. Write numbers in the margin to indicate the steps or stages in the process.

6. Circle any transitional words indicating time or other progression (*first, second, then, soon, now, next, after, before, when, finally, at last, therefore, consequently,* and—especially for the informative process analysis—words used to show the passage of time, such as hours, days of the week, and so on).

EXERCISE 12

John Tillman has a special interest in engineering, and here his expertise shows as he explains how to use simple materials to do something we have all dreamed about: building a perfect paper airplane. Follow the directions, and you'll get a lot of admiring glances. This approach is guaranteed.

```
              Making a Perfect Paper Airplane
                       John L. Tillman
```
   Most people know how to make a paper airplane. Generally, these paper airplanes end up looking like a sleek delta-winged fighter, but there are other types. What you are about to read is a set of directions for making an unusual paper airplane that most people would claim, some adamantly, to be unflyable.

   At the outset, you must gather the necessary materials. A standard piece of notebook paper, preferably one with squared corners and no holes for binder rings, is the most essential item. If you are a novice paper airplane maker, use a pen or pencil and a ruler at least as long as the diagonal corner-to-corner length of the paper.

   Now the construction can begin. First set the piece of paper flat on a desk or table in front of you with the long dimension of the paper's rectangular shape facing side to side. Using a pencil and ruler, draw a line diagonally across the paper from the lower left hand corner to the upper right hand corner, as you face it. Grab the upper left hand corner and pull it up and toward your lower right, creating a fold along the line you have drawn.

   After you have made the fold, take the paper and slightly rotate the paper clockwise so that the long flat edge is on top and the sawtooth edge is facing you. Next, using the ruler and pencil, draw a line parallel to the top long flat edge, about one-third to one-half inch below the top edge. Fold the paper along this line, bringing the top edge up, over and toward you. Where this now former top edge is now located is your next fold line; fold again as described in the preceding sentence. Once again, repeat this fold sequence for a third and last time. What you now have should look like a sawtooth pattern facing you with a laterally extended flat leading edge at the top. Take the left and right ends of this leading edge and bend them up toward the ceiling. Continue bending these ends until they start coming together, forming a circle. Push these two ends together into one another, connecting them and creating an object that looks like a crown. If necessary, work with this crown-like object so that the leading edge is as perfectly round as you can get it.

   What you now have is an aerodynamically viable object. With the leading edge facing forward and away from you, and the leading edge connection facing up toward the ceiling, place your index and middle fingers in the middle and on top of the sawtooth trailing edge. Your thumb should naturally fall into place on the bottom of the

```
          trailing edge. Lifting your hand so that the forward
          circular part of this paper airplane is facing well above
          the horizon, flick you wrist from up to forward, letting
          it go with a firm shove. A forceful throw is not
          necessary. If it does not fly straight (a gentle curve is
          permissible), check to see if either the circular leading
          edge or the trailing sawtooth shaped wing is warped. If
          they aren't circular when looking at it in a fore-aft
          direction, bend it or play around with it until it is.
          Happy flying.
```

APPLICATIONS FOR CRITICAL READING AND DISCUSSION

1. What type of process analysis (informative or directive) is used?

2. To what type of audience (well informed, moderately informed, or poorly informed on the topic) does the writer direct this selection?

3. What is the prevailing tone (objective, humorous, reverent, argumentative, cautionary, playful, ironic, ridiculing) of this material?

4. Draw a line at the point at which the preparation (materials, setup, explaining words, and so on) ends and the steps begin.

5. Write numbers in the margin to indicate the steps or stages in the process.

6. Circle any transitional words indicating time or other progression (*first, second, then, soon, now, next, after, before, when, finally, at last, therefore, consequently,* and—especially for the informative process analysis—words used to show the passage of time, such as hours, days of the week, and so on).

Suggested Topics for Writing Process Analysis

General Topics: The directive and informative topics that follow are not separated. The topics on history (such as "battle" and "election") and natural phonomena (such as "earthquake" and "hurricane") are purely informative and cannot be switched. However, each "how-to" directive topic can be transformed into a "how-it-was-done" informative topic by personalizing it and explaining stage by stage how you, someone else, or a group did something. For example, you could write a directive process analysis about how to deal with a sexually aggressive person or an informative process analysis paper about how you or someone else dealt with a sexually aggressive person. Keep in mind that the two types are often blended, especially in the personalized approach. Many of these topics will be more interesting to you and your readers if they are personalized.

Many of these topics must not only be made more specific but must also be narrowed. Writing about how to play baseball is too broad; writing about how to throw a curve ball may be manageable.

1. How to make a commercial for a product you invent
2. How to plant corn, radishes, and so on
3. How to tie a tie, knot a rope, or tie shoe strings
4. How to sleep without falling out of your seat
5. How to concentrate during a lecture
6. How some natural phenomenon happened: an earthquake, hurricane, glacier, thunderstorm
7. How a child acquires prejudice
8. How to learn about another culture
9. How they lost the battle, game
10. How to end a relationship without hurting feelings
11. How to put something together—a swing set, a bicycle, a table, a model
12. How to collect rocks, coins, stamps, autographs, baseball cards
13. How to make a flag of the United States (or other country)
14. How to win in a video game, a card game, an argument
15. How to obtain tickets for a sold-out concert or a baseball game
16. How to pass a test for a driver's license
17. How to fix your own hair, nails, face
18. How to get a job at _____
19. How to cook a _____
20. How to eat _____
21. How to deal with a person who is angry, sexually aggressive, controlling
22. How to forgive, forget, assert yourself
23. How to pretend you are well, sick, happy, satisfied
24. How to deal gracefully with a jerk, bore, bigot, sexist, racist
25. How to mend a broken relationship, a tangible object such as a vase
26. How to offer constructive criticism
27. How to play a sport
28. How to reduce sibling rivalry
29. How to play a musical instrument
30. How to drive your parents, sibling, roommate, teacher, or boss crazy
31. How to diet
32. How to awaken yourself (or someone else) in the morning
33. How to perform a magic trick
34. How a machine, an engine, or part of an engine works
35. How to make a videotape or take a photograph
36. How to end a telephone conversation that is unwelcome or that has gone on too long

Reading-Related Topics

Several of these topics can be developed as either directive or informative process analysis. Concentrate on one purpose.

"How to Sharpen a Knife"

1. Use this selection as a model to write about another task that seems simple, such as cleaning an oven or snow-sealing your boots.

"Gonna Rock To-o- n-i-i-ight!"

2. Apply this pattern of behavior to a rock concert you have seen; work with the same stages and steps in an informative process analysis.

"Nature on the Rampage"

3. Explain how to increase your chances for survival in a tornado, a hurricane, an earthquake, a fire in a high-rise building, an airplane crash, or a flood.

"How to Eat an Ice-Cream Cone"

4. Explain how to eat another food such as pizza, Chinese food (using chopsticks), fried chicken, Arabic food, or watermelon.

"The Birth of an Island"

5. Use this paragraph as a guide to writing about some other transformation in the earth sciences: an alluvial plain, a beach, a mountain lake, and so on.

"Eating Alone in Restaurants"

6. Discuss what you do when you are pressured into doing a dance you don't know.

7. Explain what you do when you are with your current steady companion and an old boyfriend or girlfriend appears.

8. Explain what you do when you encounter someone who knows you, but whom you don't remember.

9. Discuss what you do when someone serves you food you can't eat because of your diet, the type of food, or the quality of the food.

"Conserving Energy as You Ski"

10. Use this selection as a model to write about conserving energy in another sport, such as swimming, tennis, or basketball.

"Unchopping a Tree"

11. Write about unkilling an animal (of your choice).

12. Write about undivorcing a person, uncrashing a car, unshooting a person, unstabbing a person, unAIDSing a person, unflooding an area, undeveloping an area, unburning something, unmugging a victim, unmarrying a person, or unliving an experience.

"The Autobiography of Malcolm X"

13. Read Malcolm X's complete autobiography, and write about one other phase of his life (perhaps his becoming a Muslim or his altering his philosophy somewhat in his last few years), again in an informative process analysis.

14. Using this material as a model, write about your own experiences in self-education (academic, vocational, social, or recreational).

"Sabzi Polo Mahi"

15. Write about a special holiday dish prepared in your home. Follow Maysim's lead in discussing the source and quality of the foods, and try to capture her warmth of tone.

"Popping the Cork"

16. Discuss how to perform a specialty, such as barbequeing a steak, carving a turkey, making a toast, or flambéeing cherries jubilee.

"Making a Perfect Paper Airplane"

17. Use this essay as a model in explaining how to make an oragami item or a different style of paper airplane.

 **Writer's Checklist**

Apply these ideas to your writing as you work with **DCODE**. Later, as a peer editor, apply the same ideas to the material you evaluate.

1. Decide on whether your process analysis type is mainly directive or informative, and be appropriately consistent in using pronouns and other designations:

    - Use second person for the directive as you address the reader (*you, your*);

    - Use first person for the informative; do not address the reader (use *I*); or

    - Use third person for the informative; do not address the reader (use *he, she, it, they, them, individuals,* the name of your subject).

2. In explaining the stages and using technical terms, take into account whether your audience will be mainly well informed, moderately informed, or poorly informed.

3. Explain reasons for procedures whenever you believe explanations will help.

4. Select an appropriate tone (such as objective, humorous, argumentative, cautionary, playful, ironic, ridiculing), and be consistent.

5. Use transitional words indicating time or other progression (such as *first, second, then, soon, now, next, after, before, when, finally, at last, therefore, consequently,* and—especially for the informative process analysis—words used to show passage of time, such as hours, days of the week, and so on).

6. Avoid recipe language; in other words, do not drop *the, a, an,* or *of*.

7. Indicate major stages by main headings on your outline or main bubbles in your cluster.

 **Journal-Entry Suggestions**

1. Select some of the unused "Reading-Related Topics" suggestions, and use them for journal topics.

2. Write a reaction to one or more "Reading Connection" selections. Agree, disagree, apply the statements to your own experiences, indicate the value of such statements, or explain why your were surprised, shocked, disgusted, pleased, or whatever, by the material.

3. Invent statements (using process analysis, if appropriate) to support headlines from *Weekly World News:*

    "Best Man Swallows Ring and Ruins Wedding!"
    "Robot Waiter Goes Berserk and Makes Shambles of Restaurant!"
    "Man Gives Wife Necklace Every Year—Made from His Toenails!"
    "I Won the World's Biggest Brat Contest!"
    "Flying Pig Shot Down over Indonesia!"
    "Underwater Empire Discovered!"
    "Pregnant Lizard Stops Traffic!"
    "World's 1st UFO Detector!" (costs $29.95)
    "Dead Husband's Dentures Still Talk!"

WORKSHEET
Writing in DCODE

NAME:_____

SECTION:_____ CHAPTER:_____ DATE:_____

Delve Generate your topic, or ideas for your topic, by delving into your subject area through:

- *Freewriting*—writing sentence after sentence, nonstop and spontaneously.
- *Brainstorming*—jotting down answers to Who? What? Where? When? Why? and How? and then listing words and phrases in relation to those answers.
- *Clustering*—connecting bubbled ideas with lines to show strings of relationships, producing each new bubble item in response to the question, What comes to mind?
- *Combining* any of these approaches, as directed by your instructor.

WORKSHEET: Writing in DCODE

Concentrate   Concentrate your work by stating your topic in one sentence that is not too broad, narrow, or vague to be developed. Base this sentence (which may become the topic sentence for your paragraph or the thesis for your essay) on an idea emerging from the **Delve** stage. You may have to try several statements here before you formulate one that is best for your writing task. Be sure that your final statement covers your assignment or intent and specifies both your subject (what you are writing about) and treatment (what aspect you will focus on). Label the *subject* and *treatment* parts.

Organize   Complete an outline or a cluster, as directed by your instructor. The cluster should be a section from, or a refined version of, the **Delve** clustering. Regardless of the strategy you use, the organizational pattern should indicate a division of your topic into parts that will, in turn, be further subdivided for support as necessary to address a particular audience on your concentrated topic.

Draft   On separate paper, write and then revise your assignment as many times as necessary for **c**oherence, **l**anguage (usage, tone, and diction), **u**nity, **e**mphasis, **s**upport, and **s**entence structure (**cluess**).

Edit   Correct problems in fundamentals such as **c**apitalization, **o**missions, **p**unctuation, and **s**pelling (**cops**). Before writing the final draft, read your paper aloud to discover oversights and awkwardness of expression.

Analysis By Causes And Effects: Determining Reasons and Outcomes

8

> "Originality doesn't mean saying what no one has ever said before; it means saying exactly what you think yourself.
> — James Stephen

What is the meaning of analysis by causes and effects ? What are subject, emphasis, and purpose used for in writing ? What are the different kinds of causes and effects ? On what three principles can order (organization) be established ?

"Lemme guess. . . . You were a test-tube baby, right?"

Analysis by Causes and Effects Defined

Causes and effects deal with reasons and results; they are sometimes discussed together and sometimes separately. Like other forms of writing to explain, writing about causes and effects is basic to your thought processes. The shortest, and arguably the most provocative, poem in the English language—"I/Why?"—poses a causal question. Children are preoccupied with delightful and often exasperating "why" questions. Daily we encounter matters of causes and effects. The same subject may raise questions for both:

The car won't start. Why? *(cause)*

The car won't start. What now? *(effect)*

At school, from the biology lab to the political science classroom, and at work, from maintaining relationships to changing procedures, causes and effects are pervasive.

Determining Your Purpose

Your purpose in analyzing by causes and/or effects will probably be to inform or persuade. Usually your work will emphasize either causes or effects. Your initial exploration of ideas (the **Delve** stage of **DCODE**) will allow you to decide on that purpose and emphasis, as is appropriate for accommodating your interests and background and for meeting the assignment.

Freewriting on an idea that appeals to you will reveal your knowledge and interest, perhaps along with some possibilities for development.

Brainstorming will give you more specific information. In this strategy you should emphasize the *why?* part (for causes) and add a *what happened?* or *what happens?* part (for effects).

Then comes the most important strategy in your exploration of ideas: the *clustering*. For causes and effects, begin with a double bubble for your subject (the situation, circumstance, or trend), and then arrange bubbles to the left for causes and to the right for effects. Consider the partial cluster on "Joining a Gang" shown in Figure 8.1. You will note that "Joining a Gang" is not the effect; it is the subject. As a subject, it can have both causes and

FIGURE 8.1 A Partial Cluster

effects, which are both sets of emphases. Thus the *subject* is what you are writing about; your *emphasis* will be on causes, effects, or a combination of both; and your *purpose* will be to inform or persuade.

It is at this point in your writing that you will decide whether your topic should mainly inform or mainly persuade. If you intend to inform, your tone should be coolly objective. If you intend to persuade, your tone should be subjective, even biased. You will take into account the views of your audience as you phrase your ideas. You will also take into account how much your audience understands about your topic and develop your ideas accordingly.

Composing the Topic Sentence or Thesis

Now that you have ideas lined up on either side of the double bubble, you are ready to focus on causes, on effects, or, occasionally, on both.

Your **Concentrate** statement might be one of causes: "People join gangs for three main reasons." Later, as you use the idea as a topic sentence in a paragraph or a thesis in an essay, you might rephrase it to make it less mechanical allowing it to become part of the flow of your discussion. If you wanted to personalize the work—thereby probably making it more interesting—you could write about someone you know who joined a gang. And you could use the same basic framework indicating why this person joined a gang.

Your selection of a topic sentence or thesis takes you to the next writing phase: organization (the **Organize** stage in **DCODE**). There you need to consider three closely related points.

Considering Kinds of Causes and Effects

Both causes and effects can be primary or secondary, immediate or remote.

Primary or Secondary

Primary means "major," and *secondary* means "minor." A primary cause may be sufficient to bring about the situation (subject). For example, infidelity may be a primary (and possibly sufficient by itself) cause of divorce for some people but not for others, who regard it as secondary. In another example, if Country X is attacked by Country Y, the attack itself, as a primary cause, may be sufficient to bring on a declaration of war. But a diplomatic blunder regarding visas for workers may be of secondary importance and, through significant, certainly not sufficient to start a war over.

Immediate or Remote

Causes and effects often occur at a distance in time from the situation. The immediate effect of sulfur in the atmosphere may be atmospheric pollution, but the long-range, or remote, effect may be acid rain. The immediate cause of the greenhouse effect may be the depletion of the ozone layer, whereas the long-range, or remote, cause is the use of CFCs (commonly called freons, which are found in such items as Styrofoam cups). The ultimate cause may be the people who use the products containing freons.

Evaluating the Importance of Sequence

The sequence in which events occur(red) may or may not be significant. When you are dealing with several sequential events, determine whether the sequence of events has causal connections. Specifically, does one cause bring about another?

Consider this sequence of events: Joe's parents get divorced, and Joe joins a gang. We know that one reason for joining a gang is family companionship. Therefore, we may conclude that Joe joined the gang in order to satisfy his needs for family companionship, which he lost when his parents were divorced. But if we do so, we may have reached a wrong conclusion, because Joe's joining the gang after the family breakup does not necessarily mean that the two events are related. Maybe Joe joined the gang because of drug dependency, low self-esteem, or a need for protection. In examining the whole situation, we may discover that other members of his family, going through the same family turmoil, did *not* join gangs.

In each case, examine the connections. To assume that one event following another is caused by the other is called a *post hoc* ("after this") fallacy. An economic depression may occur after a president takes office, but that does not automatically mean that the depression was caused by the new administration. It might have occurred anyway, perhaps in an even more severe form. (See Chapter 13 for more information on flawed reasoning.)

Order

The order of the events you discuss in your paper will be based on time, space, emphasis, or a combination:

- *Time:* If, as in the case of a paper discussing the causes and effects of upper atmospheric pollution, one stage leads to another, your paper would be organized best by time.

- *Space:* In some instances causes and effects are best organized by their relation in space. For instance, the causes of an economic recession could be discussed in terms of local factors, regional factors, national factors, and international factors.

- *Emphasis:* Some causes and effects may be more important than others. For instance, if some causes of divorce are primary (perhaps infidelity and physical abuse) and others are secondary (such as annoying habits and laziness), a paper about divorce could be organized from secondary to primary in order to emphasize the most important causes.

In some instances, more than one factor (such as time and emphasis) may be linked; in that case, select the order that best fits what you are trying to say, or combine orders.

Introducing Ideas and Working with Patterns

The introduction of your topic, whether in a topic sentence and its appropriate context for a paragraph or in an introductory paragraph with a thesis for an essay, will almost certainly perform two functions:

1. *Discuss your subject.* For example, if you are writing about the causes or effects of divorce, begin with a statement about divorce as a subject.

2. *Indicate whether you will concentrate on causes or effects or combine them.* That indication should be made clear early in the paper. Concentrating on one—causes or effects—does not mean you will not mention the other; it only means you will emphasize one of them.

The most likely pattern for your work is one of those shown in Figure 8.2.

FIGURE 8.2 Patterns for Paragraph and Essay

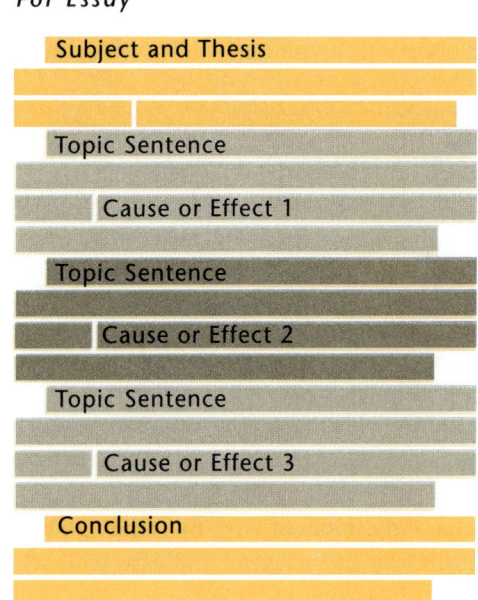

EXERCISE 1

Complete the following cluster on teenage parenthood. Then select three primary causes or three primary effects that could be used in writing a paragraph or an essay.

Causes   **Effects**

Primary causes   Primary effects

1. _____   1. _____

2. _____   2. _____

3. _____   3. _____

# The Reading Connection

EXERCISE 2

Demonstration

We are surrounded by mechanisms that are so integrated into our way of life that we take them for granted. The telephone is one of those mechanisms. Occasionally, our telephone service is out of order and we feel as devastated as if a member of our body has been severed. In the following paragraphs, John Brooks discusses effects that may not have occurred to you but will leave you nodding your head in agreement.

The Effects of the Telephone
JOHN BROOKS

1   What has the telephone done to us, or for us, in the hundred years of its existence? A few effects suggest themselves at once. It has saved lives by getting rapid word of illness, injury, or famine from remote places. By joining with the elevator to make possible the multistory residence or office building, it has made possible—for better or worse—the modern city. By bringing about a quantum leap in the speed and ease with which information moves from place to place, it has greatly accelerated the rate of scientific and technological change and growth in industry. Beyond doubt it has crippled if not killed the ancient art of letter writing. It has made living alone possible for persons with normal social impulses; by so doing, it has played a role in one of the greatest social changes of this century, the breakup of the multi-generational household. It has made the waging of war chillingly more efficient than formerly. Perhaps (though not provably) it has prevented wars that might have arisen out of international misunderstanding caused by written communication. Or perhaps—again not provably—by magnifying and extending irrational personal conflicts based on voice contact, it has caused wars. Certainly it has extended the scope of human conflicts, since it impartially disseminates the useful knowledge of scientists and the babble of bores, the affection of the affectionate and the malice of the malicious.

2   But the question remains unanswered. The obvious effects just cited seem inadequate, mechanistic; they only scratch the surface. Perhaps the crucial effects are evanescent and unmeasurable. Use of the telephone involves personal risk because it involves exposure; for some, to be "hung up on" is among the worst of fears; others dream of a ringing telephone and wake up with a pounding heart. The telephone's actual ring—more, perhaps, than any other sound in our daily lives—evokes hope, relief, fear, anxiety, joy, according to our expectations. The telephone is our nerve-end to society.

3   In some ways it is in itself a thing of paradox. In one sense a metaphor for the times it helped create, in another sense the telephone is their polar opposite. It is small and gentle—relying on low voltages and miniature parts—in times of hugeness and violence. It is basically simple in times of complexity. It is so nearly human, recreating voices so faithfully that friends or lovers need not identify themselves by name even when talking across oceans, that to ask its effects on human life may seem hardly more fruitful than to ask the effect of the hand or the foot. The Canadian philosopher Marshall McLuhan—one of the few who have addressed themselves to these questions—was perhaps not far from the mark when he spoke of the telephone as creating "a kind of extra-sensory perception."

APPLICATIONS FOR CRITICAL READING AND DISCUSSION

1. What is the subject (a situation, circumstance, or trend) at the center of this discussion?
   ```
   use of the telephone
   ```

2. Circle the sentence that most clearly indicates the author's intention of writing about cause, effect, or a combination.

3. Is this passage concerned more with causes, effects, or a combination?
   ```
   effects
   ```

4. Underline the sentences that indicate the specific causes or effects.

5. In what order (time, space, emphasis, or combination) are the parts presented?
   ```
   emphasis
   ```

6. Is the author's purpose mainly to inform or to persuade?
   ```
   inform
   ```

EXERCISE 3

Textbooks in history deal especially with causes and effects. Authors such as A. J. P. Taylor look back with historical perspective and sort out causes and effects in the long sweep of human events. This passage from *Civilization Past and Present* contains a concise account of the causes of World War II. It is the kind of passage you might underline heavily if you were using this author's textbook.

Causes of World War II
A. J. P. TAYLOR

What caused the second World War? There can be many answers: German grievances against the peace settlement of 1919 and the failure to redress them; failure to agree on a system of general controlled disarmament; failure to accept the principles of collective security and to operate them; fear of communism and, on the Soviet side, of capitalism, cutting across ordinary calculations of international policy; German strength, which destroyed the balance of power in Europe, and the resentment of German generals at their previous defeat; American aloofness from European affairs; Hitler's inordinate and unscrupulous ambition—a blanket explanation favored by some historians; at the end, perhaps only mutual bluff. The question of its immediate outbreak is easier to answer. The House of Commons forced war on a reluctant British government, and the government dragged an even more reluctant French government in their train. The British people accepted the decision of Parliament and government without complaint. It is impossible to tell whether they welcomed it or whether they would have preferred some other outcome. Argument was almost stilled once the war had started, and, if doubts existed, they were kept in the shadows.

APPLICATIONS FOR CRITICAL READING AND DISCUSSION

1. What is the subject (a situation, circumstance, or trend) at the center of this discussion?

2. Circle the sentence that most clearly indicates the author's intention of writing about cause or effect, or a combination.

3. Is this passage concerned more with causes, effects, or a combination?

4. Underline the sentences that indicate the specific causes or effects.

5. In what order (time, space, emphasis, or combination) are the parts presented?

6. Is the author's purpose mainly to inform or to persuade?

EXERCISE 4

One common response to injustice experienced personally is, "I'm sick and tired of this, and I'm not going to take it anymore." Rosa Parks felt that way—for herself and collectively for those who came before her—and she didn't move to the back of the bus. In this paragraph by Martin Luther King, Jr., the famed civil rights leader, we get an account of one of the key incidents that incited the civil rights movement in the United States.

Back of the Bus
MARTIN LUTHER KING, JR.

On December 1, 1955, an attractive Negro seamstress, Mrs. Rosa Parks, boarded the Cleveland Avenue Bus in downtown Montgomery. She was returning home after her regular day's work in the Montgomery Fair—a leading department store. Tired from long hours on her feet, Mrs. Parks sat down in the first seat behind the section reserved for whites. Not long after she took her seat, the bus operator ordered her, along with three other Negro passengers, to move back in order to accommodate boarding white passengers. By this time every seat in the bus was taken. This meant that if Mrs. Parks followed the driver's command she would have to stand while a white male passenger, who had just boarded the bus, would sit. The other three Negro passengers immediately complied with the driver's request. But Mrs. Parks quietly refused. The result was her arrest.

APPLICATIONS FOR CRITICAL READING AND DISCUSSION

1. What is the subject (a situation, circumstance, or trend) at the center of this discussion?

2. Circle the sentence that most clearly indicates the author's intention of writing about cause or effect, or a combination.

3. Is this passage concerned more with causes, effects, or a combination?

4. Underline the sentences that indicate the specific causes or effects.

5. In what order (time, space, emphasis, or combination) are the parts presented?

6. Is the author's purpose mainly to inform or to persuade?

EXERCISE 5

More than thirty years ago, Rachel Carson wrote the following passage in *Silent Spring*, a book that awakened the world to the interrelationship and interdependence of all living things. Her point was simple: once poisons enter the food chain in significant quantity, all life is threatened. Here we learn about a small range of destructive effects.

Arsenic for Everyone
RACHEL CARSON

An arsenic-contaminated environment affects not only man but animals as well. A report of great interest came from Germany in 1936. In the area about Freiberg, Saxony, smelters for silver and lead poured arsenic fumes into the air, to drift out over the surrounding countryside and settle down upon the vegetation. According to Dr. Hueper, horses, cows, goats, and pigs, which of course fed on this vegetation, showed loss of hair and thickening of the skin. Deer inhabiting nearby forests sometimes had abnormal pigment spots and precancerous warts. One had a definitely cancerous lesion. Both domestic and wild animals were affected by "arsenical enteritis, gastric ulcers, and cirrhosis of the liver." Sheep kept near the smelters developed cancers of the nasal sinus; at their death arsenic was found in the brain, liver, and tumors. In the area there was also "an extraordinary mortality among insects, especially bees. After rainfalls which washed the arsenical dust from the leaves and carried it along into the water of brooks and pools, a great many fish died."

APPLICATIONS FOR CRITICAL READING AND DISCUSSION

1. What is the subject (a situation, circumstance, or trend) at the center of this discussion?

2. Circle the sentence that most clearly indicates the author's intention of writing about cause or effect, or a combination.

3. Is this passage concerned more with causes, effects, or a combination of both?

4. Underline the sentences that indicate the specific causes or effects.

5. In what order (time, space, emphasis, or combination) are the parts presented?

6. Is the author's purpose mainly to inform or to persuade?

EXERCISE 6

Youth take steroids because they want the Rambo look. But they get much more than muscles in their steroids effects package—and what they get, no one wants.

What Happens to Steroid Studs?
ANASTASIA TOUFEXIS

But the drug-enhanced physiques are a hazardous bargain. Steroids can cause temporary acne and balding, upset hormonal production and damage the heart and kidneys. Doctors suspect they may contribute to liver cancer and atherosclerosis. Teens, who are already undergoing physical and psychological stresses, may run some enhanced risks. The drugs can stunt growth by accelerating bone maturation. Physicians also speculate that the chemicals may compromise youngsters' still developing reproductive systems. Steroid users have experienced a shrinking of the testicles and impotence. Dr. Richard Dominguez, a sports specialist in suburban Chicago, starts his lectures to youths with a surefire attention grabber: "You want to shrink your balls? Take steroids."

2 Just as worrisome is the threat to mental health. Drug users are prone to moodiness, depression, irritability and what are known as "roid rages." Ex-user Darren Allen Chamberlain, 26, of Pasadena, Calif., describes himself as an "easy-going guy" before picking up steroids at age 16. Then he turned into a teen Terminator. "I was doing everything from being obnoxious to getting out of the car and provoking fights at intersections," he says. "I couldn't handle any kind of stress. I'd just blow. You can walk in my parents' house today and see the signs—holes in doors I stuck my fist through, indentations in walls I kicked." Chamberlain grew so despondent, he recalls, that he "held a gun to my head once or twice." Others have succeeded in committing suicide. Warns Aaron Henry, 22, a St. Charles, Mo., drug counselor whose adolescent dependence on steroids drove him close to physical and mental ruin: "When you put big egos and big dreams together with steroids, that's a nasty combination."

APPLICATIONS FOR CRITICAL READING AND DISCUSSION

1. What is the subject (a situation, circumstance, or trend) at the center of this discussion?

2. Circle the sentence that most clearly indicates the author's intention of writing about cause or effect, or a combination.

3. Is this passage concerned more with causes, effects, or a combination of both?

4. Underline the sentences that indicate the specific causes or effects.

5. In what order (time, space, emphasis, or combination) are the parts presented?

6. Is the author's purpose mainly to inform or to persuade?

EXERCISE 7

Some educators have begun to rethink courses because they fear that emphasizing ethnic pride increases divisiveness. Should schools emphasize separate ethnic-studies courses or should they weave information about each group into traditional courses? Sharon Bernstein, a *Los Angeles Times* reporter, presents a spectrum of views on those questions.

Vocabulary Preview: Write in short definitions for these words as they are used in the context of the following passage. (The paragraph numbers are given in parentheses.) Be prepared to use the words in your own sentences.

inclusive (4)

chauvinism (5)

assimilation (8)

particularism (8)

pluralism (8)

curricula (11)

diverse (11)

chronicles (12)

boycotting (13)

poignantly (15)

Multiculturalism: Building Bridges or Burning Them?
SHARON BERNSTEIN

1 Multiculturalism—the notion that ethnic and cultural groups in the United States should preserve their identities instead of fusing them in a melting pot—has become a byword in education in Los Angeles and other cities. But now, educators at the elementary, secondary and university levels are rethinking that idea—and worrying that past efforts to teach multiculturalism may have widened the ethnic divisions they were meant to close.

2 Fearing that the current approach—which relies largely on ethnic studies courses and the recognition of special holidays and heroes—may have unintentionally isolated students from each other, teachers and academics are gingerly beginning to question the way multiculturalism has been taught. "I think many people, especially in the post–Rodney King era, are beginning to realize that we can't just study ourselves as separate groups," said Ronald Takaki, ethnic studies professor at UC [University of California at] Berkeley. "We've gone beyond the need to recover identity and roots, and now we're realizing that our paths as members of different groups are crisscrossing each other."

3 Not that these educators have abandoned multiculturalism as a concept. Nor do they suggest schools are solely to blame for ethnic tensions in society and on campus. But, in growing numbers, they are struggling to better define multiculturalism's goals and ways to teach it.

4 At present, many courses either focus entirely on one ethnic population or teach a standard history and throw a few ethnic names into the

mix. The new approach would teach events as they had happened—as interconnected and inclusive history that changed lives in every ethnic group, and was also changed by all of those groups. The discussion is so new that it has barely begun to show up in the pages of education journals. But it is gaining speed among teachers, administrators and university professors, many who were surprised to discover that others are voicing the same concerns.

5   Even students, searching for reasons why violence erupted recently at North Hollywood High School and other campuses in the Los Angeles Unified School District, suggested that some youngsters have misunderstood lessons about ethnic pride, developing ethnic chauvinism instead. "They teach you that you have to identify with your own group," said Karina Escalante, a senior at Cleveland High School in Reseda, where African-American and Latino students clashed last year [1991]. She said students receive conflicting messages that teach them pride in their ethnic identities but not how those identities can and should mesh with others in society. "They tell you to keep with your own. Then they tell you to go out and mix. They should have a program that says: 'Yes, you should identify yourself but then you have to go out and mix.'" Educators in the Los Angeles district say they are particularly troubled and point to the violence that broke out in October [1992] between African-American and Latino students at North Hollywood and Hamilton high schools.

6   Esther Taira, the resource teacher who in 1986 spearheaded the development of a multicultural curriculum for the district's high schools, said she would design her course very differently today. "We do have ethnic-specific courses, but they do not create the bridges we need," said Taira, whose course is an elective offered only in some schools. "Even when we do talk about more than one group, we tend to focus on similarities, and that ignores the problems in the streets. It is the differences that are the issues."

7   Among youngsters, feelings of isolation can start early. In Christine Toleson's fifth-grade and Marcia Klein's sixth-grade classes at Pacoima Elementary School, where the walls are festooned with posters in English and Spanish, students said they felt happy and proud when the school celebrated holidays or held "appreciation days" for their ethnic group. most students said they remembered discussing their heritage in class. But very few students raised their hands when asked whether they remembered discussing the culture of a different ethnic group. "On Martin Luther King Day, they were celebrating black people," said Gerardo Nunez, a Latino fifth-grader. "I went over there. Other people were not my color. I felt all alone."

8   Originally, the term multiculturalism was used by minority activists in the mid-1980s who rejected assimilation. They believed that students should be taught about their ethnic and cultural backgrounds, which would bolster their pride and preserve their cultural identities. Within the movement, two competing theories developed. One, called particularism, emphasized separate ethnic studies courses, such as Chicano studies or black studies. The other, pluralism, recommended that information about each group be woven into traditional courses. By far, the particularists have dominated, bringing to campuses not only special ethnic studies courses but clubs, dormitories and celebrations that have ethnic themes. For example, a typical class in a multicultural program would be "a course that an African-American student can take which gives him a sense of identity," said Deborah Dash Moore, director of the American Culture program at Vassar College in Poughkeepsie, N.Y., and an organizer of a recent conference on ways to teach American studies. "It gives him a cultural connection with others, respect for his past, and a sense of knowing where he fits within a larger society of which he can be proud."

9   The new movement finds particularists and pluralists moving toward a middle ground, where instead of treating each ethnic group separately, elements from all their histories are woven into discussions of particular topics. "I'm in the movement toward bringing them together," said Los Angeles Board of Education member Warren Furutani, an advocate of ethnic studies who was formerly the program coordinator at UCLA's Asian American Studies Center. "Because it means people can understand their own experience, but bring it together with other people's experiences."

10 Raising questions about multiculturalism has been difficult for educators, in part because the

movement has come under intense criticism from conservatives such as Dinesh D'Souza, of the American Enterprise Institute, whose book, *Illiberal Education: the Politics of Race and Sex on Campus,* reached the *New York Times* bestseller list. "Many people are very defensive, and have been put on the defensive by attacks by conservatives," Vassar's Moore said. "They feel that there is no room for them to be self-reflective, self-critical, that if they do some critical thinking they are playing into the hands of people who really want to destroy the entire enterprise."

11 In the Los Angeles public schools, teachers at all levels are encouraged to talk about the different cultures represented by their students. Most schools conduct festivals or hold special assemblies or parties to celebrate such holidays as the birthday of Martin Luther King Jr. or Cinco de Mayo, which marks the day Mexico defeated French forces in the Battle of Puebla. In addition, the district has developed for high schools elective ethnic studies classes—including African-American studies, Mexican-American studies and courses about Asian and Jewish concerns. From kindergarten on up, the reading and history curricula include stories and information about diverse cultures.

12 Cultural Awareness, the class developed by Taira, explores similarities between ethnic groups and discusses the contributions of a number of cultures. But Taira said if she were designing that course today, she would take pains to interweave the lives and experiences of members of different ethnic groups. Sharing her concerns, Takaki, the UC Berkeley professor, said he wished he had made his 1989 book *Strangers from a Different Shore*—which chronicles Asian immigration to the United States—more inclusive. In schools and at universities, they and others said, even courses that spotlight several ethnic groups tend to treat each group separately. A course might highlight African-Americans one week, Korean-Americans the next, and so on.

13 And, experts said, most students tend to take only the classes that relate to the group to which they belong. In Los Angeles, administrators said, many schools offer only those courses that relate to the majority of their student populations. In such a climate, even the celebration of ethnic holidays has caused problems, with one group believing that another got more attention or boycotting another group's festivities, said Casey Browne, who heads the peer counseling program at North Hollywood High. "To some extent I think we bring on racial tensions when we celebrate one holiday over another," Browne said. "Some schools do a better job on certain holidays than they do on others, and then the other kids feel left out." Such problems have developed, said Bernadine Lyles, the school district's multicultural education unit adviser, because "the climate was not prepared" for students to want to celebrate the cultures of others. She noted that a framework for multicultural education adopted by the school board last spring emphasizes "activities that would bring groups together, rather than those activities that might look like separation."

14 In the new course that Taira is developing, lessons are organized around historical themes instead of ethnicity. If the subject is American agriculture, Taira said, the teacher might discuss how farming and ranching affected the lives of black African slaves, Chinese and Mexican immigrants and poor whites who worked as sharecroppers—all within broader contexts such as family farms or the plantation economy of the South. "There has been a drawing back from the notion that we just have to add more African-Americans, or add more Latinos, as well as the notion that we have to focus on victims," Moore said. "People are in a complex relationship with each other. They may be victims in one set of relationships and served in others."

15 Students sum up the situation most poignantly—and appear to offer the most hope. After last month's racial brawl at North Hollywood High, senior Pele Keith called out to a group of African-American and Latino students who were arguing about the events of that troubled day. "They say brown pride, but look, I'm just as brown as she is," Pele, an African-American, said, placing her arm alongside the arm of a Latino friend, Patti Martinez. "Look at that," Patti sang out in reply, "the same color."

APPLICATIONS FOR CRITICAL READING AND DISCUSSION

1. What is the subject (a situation, circumstance, or trend) at the center of this discussion?

2. Circle the sentence that most clearly indicates the author's intention of writing about cause or effect, or a combination.

3. Is this passage concerned more with causes, effects, or a combination?

4. Underline the sentences that indicate the specific causes or effects.

5. In what order (time, space, emphasis, or combination) are the parts presented?

6. Is the author's purpose mainly to inform or to persuade?

7. Is this article mainly pessimistic or optimistic?

EXERCISE 8

Every day, three thousand students give up on high school—for good. They push open the doors and walk out. Turn their backs on it. Drop out. Now what?

Vocabulary Preview: Write in short definitions for these words as they are used in the context of the following passage. (The paragraph numbers are given in parentheses.) Be prepared to use the words in your own sentences.

epidemic (10)

sibling (11)

symptom (12)

potential (8)

obsolete (9)

I'm Outta Here!
DAVID LEVINE

Think about it. In some ways it seems perfect. Quit school. Just say No—no more pressure, no more stupid rules, no more deadlines, no more uncaring teachers, no more snobby, clique-conscious peers. Nearly every high school student has imagined what it would be like.

2   Beth Kierny* did more than imagine. A few months into her senior year at Columbia High School, in East Greenbush, New York, she dropped out of school.

3   Beth is a shy eighteen-year-old with dark, curly hair who hated getting up early for classes. She was spending most of her time "gypping," leaving the building (or never showing up) and hanging out with her friends instead. Her parents didn't know; she was having problems with them and had moved in with her boyfriend, Dave, who had dropped out a few years earlier. When Beth found out she had missed so many days that she couldn't take her exams, she figured: Why not just leave?

*Names with asterisks have been changed.

4   She thought it would be great. She'd just get a job like Dave, sleep in later, work at some cool place instead of sitting in boring classes, and lead an easier, more interesting life.

5   But without a diploma, Beth found it difficult to get a job. She had to finally settle for one at the Hessmart gas station a few miles down Route 20. Being the youngest and newest employee, she got stuck working the worst shifts. Often she had to get up even earlier than she had to for school—sometimes she had to be *at work* by 7:00 A.M. Or she'd have to work the midnight shift, which was scary because you never knew if the place might get held up. Or she'd have to work weekends, when her friends were all out partying.

6   The money was terrible—at minimum wage she cleared maybe $90 a week—and she couldn't afford a car, so she had to take cabs to and from work, which cost almost ten bucks a day. That didn't leave much for her share of the $425 a month in rent on their small apartment behind the Burger King.

7   And if Dave, a part-time carpenter, found himself out of work, things were really tight. They were weeks and weeks late with the rent and got letters from the landlord threatening eviction (they'd already been thrown out of another place only a few months earlier). The bills wouldn't stop coming. The electricity was turned off. The telephone was disconnected. She and Dave fought all the time, mostly about money, sometimes about stupid things.

8   Then spring came, and her friends still in school were talking about the prom and the parties, and she found herself left out. Then came graduation, with its class rings and college plans and yearbooks, and Beth felt like a total outsider. She was more depressed than she'd ever been in her life.

9   Like many students, Beth thought that school was hard and the world outside of school would be easier. Instead, she found that the world outside of school was hard, too.

10 Everyone knows kids like Beth, who for one reason or another believe they can't handle school and decide to quit. What you might not realize is that all those kids add up to a dropout epidemic. Every day, up to three thousand kids leave school—that's between thirty and sixty busloads of students. Although the estimates vary, about half a million leave each year. The national graduation rate, which has been dropping for years, is now 71 percent, meaning nearly one in three students don't finish school. In some urban areas, the dropout rate can be over 50 percent. While the majority of high school dropouts—60 percent—are white and do not live in cities, minorities as a group are hardest hit: Hispanic students, for example, have a dropout rate more than twice the national average. One recent study found that one in four black guys will drop out, while one in five black girls will. A 1988 study found that 62 percent of Hispanic students dropped out, along with 53 percent of black students and 42 percent of Native American students. Overall, boys are only slightly more likely to drop out than girls.

11 Within this larger puzzle are the individual pieces—the reasons why kids quit school. According to the Department of Education, there are six things that put students at higher risk. They include having a dropout sibling, coming from a single-parent family, coming from a household with an income below $15,000, being home alone more than three hours a day, not speaking English well, and having parents who didn't finish high school. What makes any student actually quit is harder to assess. Caroline Abbott, sixteen, who lives in Charlotte, North Carolina, never stopped going to school entirely, she just missed a lot of days. "I'd sit home, go to a friend's house," she says. "A good friend of mine dropped out, and I wanted to, too. I just wanted to be with her."

12 "Poor attendance is a symptom, not the disease," says Joseph Markham, director of pupil personnel services for the Albany City School District, in New York. And these days there are many diseases.

13 A student's initial trouble may come from parents' marital problems, domestic violence, drug or alcohol use, or physical abuse. For Darrell Maynard,* now a tenth grader in Columbia, South Carolina, it was moving when he was in the eighth grade. "I didn't know no one," he says. So he started to hang out, and soon after that he began to sell drugs. He says he didn't like doing it. "It was kind of scary, really," Darrell says. "Other students looked at us as gangsters, and the teachers were afraid to get involved." But he felt as if he had nothing else in his life. "My mom keeps foster kids," he says. "She wasn't paying attention to me: My dad was away all week working." Eventually, he was caught with a machete in school and got kicked out. "When my dad found out, he said I had to go to work every day with him. I didn't want that."

14   Curt Niedrach, seventeen, is a junior at Jackson Alternative School, in Jackson Township, New Jersey. All of his closest friends have dropped out. "They didn't think about how it was really going to be outside of school," he says. "They want to be free, but they don't think about what they're losing. Mostly, they don't want to be organized or deal with other people's deadlines, like showing up for class. Also, no one wants to get hassled if they don't follow every little rule." Edwin Soto, a sophomore at Bayard Ruskin High School, in New York City, has a lot of friends who've dropped out, too. "A typical day in their lives is getting up about 10:00 A.M., then finding each other and all the other guys from around the way," he says. "They try to gather as much money as possible to buy weed and go to the park to hang out. Later on, they head to pick up their girlfriends at school. After that, they go back to the park to hang out some more."

15   Some students leave school because they feel as if nobody cares. "Classes were too big, with thirty-five or more students in them," says Heather Murphy, seventeen, from Miami, who dropped out when she was fourteen. "I wasn't getting anything from my school in return for going. Teachers didn't have time for me, so why should I go?" Given the size and impersonal nature of some public high schools, finding help can be hard. Forty percent of the girls who drop out every year leave because they're pregnant. Other students quit because they feel its a way of sparing themselves the failure.

16   Take Caroline. In eighth grade everything was great: honor roll, cheerleading. She loved school, had lots of friends. Everyone told her that high school would be great, too. But it wasn't. "I hated it," she says. "They weren't friendly people. I wasn't interested in the classes." Caroline's ex-boyfriend—who had left the state—came back to the town. She couldn't keep her mind on school.

17   Still, she was trying, really trying. But when she failed algebra, something in her snapped. "You think, I'm trying so hard, I must be doing well, then one thing turns it all around. So I thought, Well, forget it. Why try so hard and accomplish nothing? I thought I was just dumb. So I just stopped trying. I gave up."

18   "To think that all dropouts or potential dropouts leave school because they aren't smart enough to hack it is to miss the point," says John K. Dougherty, Ph.D., president of alternative education for the state of New Jersey. Many kids lack motivation, and they aren't getting enough support at home to overcome that. Absenteeism pushes them further behind, so they can't perform well when they do show up at school. The discouragement spirals.

19   Some of the blame for the high dropout rate must fall on the schools themselves. Unfortunately, much of traditional education is uninspiring, and some experts believe it's simply obsolete. Teachers aren't paid well, and budget and staff cuts have left them unsupported. Classes are regularly overcrowded, and, too often, quiet or uninvolved kids are overlooked.

20   Schools are trying to adapt and respond to the crisis. Cities In Schools, Inc. (CIS), a national organization designed to get dropout-prone students into personalized programs that address their problems, believes that schools have to do more than educate. CIS president Bill Milliken says that what's needed is a sense of community, a sense that adults really care. He says schools should abandon the system of churning out graduates on an assembly line and bring the resources to the kids. "You have to build the community," he says. "If they don't have positive relationships at home and have negative ones on the street, then we have to build positive ones for them at school."

21   There's no denying that a high school diploma opens doors; staying in school and graduating extends the range of options of what you can do with your life. It's also a fact that the consequences of dropping out are severe and the prospects for dropouts are bleak. According to the National Dropout Prevention Center, less than 50 percent of dropouts find jobs when they leave school. When they do, they earn 60 percent less than high school graduates (over a lifetime, that adds up to $250,000). They are not accepted into military service and are 50 percent more likely to be on welfare. Eighty-eight percent of female dropouts under age thirty who head households live in poverty.

22   More than half of Curt Niedrach's friends are now enrolled in a GED (general equivalency diploma) program. Beth Kierny is also going for her GED, but she's afraid that even this might not be good enough. "A lot of jobs want a diploma, not a GED," she says. Things are better with her parents—they're talking again, at least—but the

pressures of her life still don't let up. She and Dave are looking for their third place to live in eighteen months. "It's hard, because a lot of places don't want to rent to kids," she says.

23   Because she's taking classes again, Beth has had to quit her job at the Hessmart and support herself with baby-sitting jobs. She's making even less money than she was before. Dave has decided to join the army. Beth, because she doesn't yet have a GED, can't.

24   There just aren't many options. "You have to finish school to get a decent job and to afford a car. You can't make it on minimum wages, working at gas stations or restaurants on weekends," she says. "You just can't."

APPLICATIONS FOR CRITICAL READING AND DISCUSSION

1. What is the subject (a situation, circumstance, or trend) at the center of this discussion?

2. Circle the sentence that most clearly indicates the author's intention of writing about cause or effect, or a combination.

3. Is this passage concerned more with causes, effects, or a combination?

4. Underline the sentences that indicate the specific causes or effects.

5. In what order (time, space, emphasis, or combination) are the parts presented?

6. Is the author's purpose mainly to inform or to persuade?

7. What is the purpose of the examples in this essay?

8. Considering that this essay was published in *Seventeen* magazine, explain how the examples are appropriate.

EXERCISE 9

Benny Paret was killed in the ring. Obviously the other fighter killed him. But is it that simple, or do others bear responsibility? Norman Cousins looks around and finds other causes—millions of them.

Vocabulary Preview: Write in short definitions for these words as they are used in the context of the following passage. (The paragraph numbers are given in parentheses.) Be prepared to use the words in your own sentences.

fledgling (1)

colossus (2)

feinting (3)

hemorrhage (8)

concussion (8)

Who Killed Benny Paret?
NORMAN COUSINS

1 Sometime about 1935 or 1936 I had an interview with Mike Jacobs, the prize-fight promoter. I was a fledgling reporter at that time; my beat was education but during the vacation season I found myself on varied assignments, all the way from ship news to sport reporting. In this way I found myself sitting opposite the most powerful figure in the boxing world.

2 There was nothing spectacular in Mr. Jacobs' manner or appearance; but when he spoke about prize fights, he was no longer a bland little man but a colossus who sounded the way Napoleon must have sounded when he reviewed a battle. You knew you were listening to Number One. His saying something made it true.

3 We discussed what to him was the only important element in successful promoting—how to please the crowd. So far as he was concerned, there was no mystery to it. You put killers in the ring and the people filled your arena. You hire boxing artists—men who are adroit at feinting, parrying, weaving, jabbing, and dancing, but who don't pack dynamite in their fists—and you wind up counting your empty seats. So you searched for the killers and sluggers and maulers—fellows who could hit with the force of a baseball bat.

4 I asked Mr. Jacobs if he was speaking literally when he said people came out to see the killer.

5 "They don't come out to see a tea party," he said evenly. "They come out to see the knockout. They come out to see a man hurt. If they think anything else, they're kidding themselves."

6 Recently, a young man by the name of Benny Paret was killed in the ring. The killing was seen by millions; it was on television. In the twelfth round, he was hit hard in the head several times, went down, was counted out, and never came out of the coma.

7 The Paret fight produced a flurry of investigations. Governor Rockefeller was shocked by what happened and appointed a committee to assess the responsibility. The New York State Boxing Commission decided to find out what was wrong. The District Attorney's office expressed its concern. One question that was solemnly studied in all three probes concerned the action of the referee. Did he act in time to stop the fight? Another question had to do with the role of the examining doctors who certified the physical fitness of the fighters before the bout. Still another question involved Mr. Paret's manager; did he rush his boy into the fight without adequate time to recuperate from the previous one?

8 In short, the investigators looked into every possible cause except the real one. Benny Paret was killed because the human fist delivers enough impact, when directed against the head, to produce a massive hemorrhage in the brain. The human brain is the most delicate and complex mechanism in all creation. It has a lacework of millions of highly fragile nerve connections. Nature attempts to protect this exquisitely intricate machinery by encasing it in a hard shell. Fortunately, the shell is thick enough to withstand a great deal of pounding. Nature, however, can protect man against everything except man himself. Not every blow to the head will kill a man—but there is always the risk of concussion and damage to the brain. A prize fighter may be able to survive even repeated brain concussions and go on fighting, but the damage to his brain may be permanent.

9 In any event, it is futile to investigate the referee's role and seek to determine whether he should have intervened to stop the fight earlier. That is not where the primary responsibility lies. The primary responsibility lies with the people who pay to see a man hurt. The referee who stops a fight too soon from the crowd's viewpoint can expect to be booed. The crowd wants the knockout; it wants to see a man stretched out on the canvas. This is the supreme moment in boxing. It is nonsense to talk about prize fighting as a test of boxing skills. No crowd was ever brought to its feet screaming and cheering at the sight to two men beautifully dodging and weaving out of each other's jabs. The time the crowd comes alive is when a man is hit hard over the heart or the head, when his mouthpiece flies out, when the blood squirts out of his nose or eyes, when he wobbles under the attack and his pursuer continues to smash at him with pole-axe impact.

10 Don't blame it on the referee. Don't even blame it on the fight managers. Put the blame where it belongs—on the prevailing mores that regard prize fighting as a perfectly proper enterprise and vehicle of entertainment. No one doubts that many people enjoy prize fighting and will miss it if it should be thrown out. And that is precisely the point.

APPLICATIONS FOR CRITICAL READING AND DISCUSSION

1. What is the subject (a situation, circumstance, or trend) at the center of this discussion?

2. Circle the sentence that most clearly indicates the author's intention of writing about cause or effect, or a combination.

3. Is this passage concerned more with causes, effects, or a combination?

4. Underline the sentences that indicate the specific causes or effects.

5. In what order (time, space, emphasis, or combination) are the parts presented?

6. Is the author's purpose mainly to inform or to persuade?

7. Why do you think he doesn't bring up the argument that the fighters choose to take their chances in the ring?

8. Should anyone who freely chooses to participate in a public "sporting" spectacle be allowed to do so? What if the combatants were equipped with lethal weapons (more than fists)?

The Reading Connection from Classroom Sources

EXERCISE 10

Senseless as we may think joining a gang is, everyone who does has reasons. Here are some for one individual, told from an unusual perspective.

                    Death by Gangbanging
                    Aida Gonzales (pseudonym)
        He was one of seventeen killed in one gangbanging
        weekend in a place called "the city of angels." Lying
        there in the casket, he looked peaceful, as he left behind
        a world of violence and turmoil. Sorting out the causes of

his becoming a gang member is not easy. He got off to a bad start because his father was a gang member. Once when a very naive teacher tried to tell the father that his son might be a gang member, he said, "My kid's not a gang member. He's just a wanna be. I'm a gang member." The young man idolized his father, and when his father was killed at a party, the family tradition of gang membership didn't die. A few years later the young man would resent the stepfather who came into his home, and, in turn, the stepfather was unkind. Then the fights started between the neighborhood gang and the young man. Finally he laughed and said, "If you can't beat'em, join'em." And he did. He said he found family and protection there. He wasn't bad. Deep down he had good feelings, and he could be funny and warm. He just had too much going against him. I should know. I'm his mother.

APPLICATIONS FOR CRITICAL READING AND DISCUSSION

1. What is the subject (a situation, circumstance, or trend) at the center of this discussion?

2. Circle the sentence that most clearly indicates the author's intention of writing about cause or effect, or a combination.

3. Is this passage concerned more with causes, effects, or a combination?

4. Underline the sentences that indicate the specific causes or effects.

5. In what order (time, space, emphasis, or combination) are the parts presented?

6. Is the author's purpose mainly to inform or to persuade?

EXERCISE 11

Some entertainers have a set of qualities that work together to produce greatness. As the author here says, there's no secret to the success of Reba McEntire. The causes are obvious to anyone who watches and listens.

> No Secrets to Her Success: Reba McEntire
> Angela DeSarro
> Good singers can be found anywhere, even in a local lounge or pizza parlor, but great singers are rare. They have the "something special" qualities that just seem to work together. Country singer Reba McEntire is definitely one of the greats, and to me the reasons are obvious: voice, songs, and style. Her voice is like no other. Her Oklahoma "twangy" accent is known by everyone in country music. She is able to jump from note to note and cover two

octaves with ease. Her voice is rich and sensitive, yet powerful. When Reba sings, she takes up all the oxygen in the room. The songs she sings are another cause of her greatness. Her lyrics deal with the issues that really touch the heart, inspire the mind, and make even the men cry. Her song "Is There Life Out There?" encourages women and men everywhere to follow their dreams, no matter what they may be. After that song came out, Reba got thousands of letters from people, thanking her for writing such an encouraging song during difficult times. The final cause of her greatness is her style, one that is all its own, from her spunky attitude right down to her steel-toed boots. This fiery redhead really knows how to get the crowd going. She has been performing for about twenty years, has produced about twenty albums, and is still going strong. With all those qualities, Reba McEntire will be around for a long, long time.

APPLICATIONS FOR CRITICAL READING AND DISCUSSION

1. What is the subject (a situation, circumstance, or trend) at the center of this discussion?

2. Circle the sentence that most clearly indicates the author's intention of writing about cause or effect, or a combination.

3. Is this passage concerned more with causes, effects, or a combination?

4. Underline the sentences that indicate the primary causes or effects.

5. In what order (time, space, emphasis, or combination) are the parts presented?

6. Is the author's purpose mainly to inform or to persuade?

EXERCISE 12

Demonstration Using the DCODE Worksheet

Victims of abuse do not always feel sorry for themselves. They also do not always protect others who are being abused. These are shocking conclusions reached by Jamie Morgan,* a victim who now looks at herself thoughtfully.

*pseudonym

WORKSHEET
Writing in DCODE

NAME: Jamie Morgan

SECTION: _____ CHAPTER: _____ DATE: _____

Delve   Generate your topic, or ideas for your topic, by delving into your subject area through:

- *Freewriting*—writing sentence after sentence, nonstop and spontaneously.
- *Brainstorming*—jotting down answers to Who? What? Where? When? Why? and How? and then listing words and phrases in relation to those answers.
- *Clustering*—connecting bubbled ideas with lines to show strings of relationships, producing each new bubble item in response to the question, What comes to mind?
- *Combining* any of these approaches, as directed by your instructor.

Freewriting:

    I guess you could call me a first-hand expert at physical child abuse because I've been a victim and I've dished it out. When I was a kid, my dad used to beat on me all the time--well mainly when he was drunk which was most of the time. He liked to throw things at me--all kinds of things like ash trays and beer cans and the TV remote control. When he missed he'd chase me down and pound on me, but I outsmarted him by dodging into whatever he throwed. He beat on me and I beat on my brother Joey. I guess I thought I deserved being beat and so did my brother, but he didn't have anyone to beat on so he started cutting himself and I ended up with men that were beaters. Now I'm trying to understand things and change.

Brainstorming:

    Who? me
    What? physical abuse
    Where? home
    When? when I was growing up
    Why? crazy father
    How? beating, throwing things
    What happened? I felt I deserved the beatings, but I still abused my brother

Clustering:

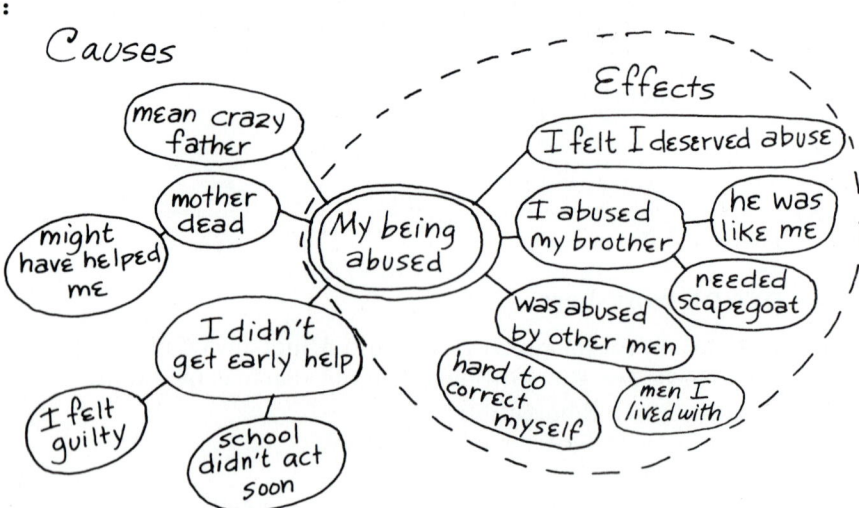

WORKSHEET: Writing in DCODE

Concentrate   Concentrate your work by stating your topic in one sentence that is not too broad, narrow, or vague to be developed. Base this sentence (which may become the topic sentence for your paragraph or the thesis for your essay) on an idea emerging from the **Delve** stage. You may have to try several statements here before you formulate one that is best for your writing task. Be sure that your final statement covers your assignment or intent and specifies both your subject (what you are writing about) and treatment (what aspect you will focus on). Label the *subject* and *treatment* parts.

<u>A person that gets beat on everyday</u>   <u>may feel she deserves it, but she may still beat on others.</u>

    subject   treatment

Organize   Complete an outline or a cluster, as directed by your instructor. The cluster should be a section from, or a refined version of, the **Delve** clustering. Regardless of the strategy you use, the organizational pattern should indicate a division of your topic into parts that will, in turn, be further subdivided for support as necessary to address a particular audience on your concentrated topic.

I. Was injured
   A. Physical
   B. Psychological
II. Felt guilty
III. Became abuser
   A. Abused my brother
   B. Felt good about it
IV. Found other abusive relationships

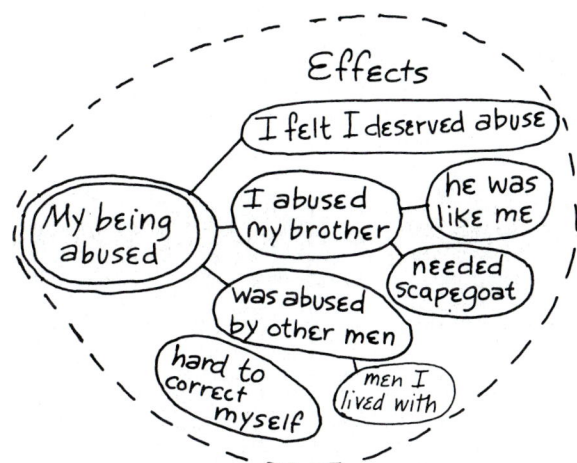

Draft   On separate paper, write and then revise your assignment as many times as necessary for **c**oherence, **l**anguage (usage, tone, and diction), **u**nity, **e**mphasis, **s**upport, and **s**entence structure (**cluess**).

Edit   Correct problems in fundamentals such as **c**apitalization, **o**missions, **p**unctuation, and **s**pelling (**cops**). Before writing the final draft, read your paper aloud to discover oversights and awkwardness of expression.

First Draft

Kick Me!

I can identify with people who were physically abused as ~~kids~~ children. I ~~was~~ am one of them~~.~~ and I've got all kinds of scars. I was in prison. I was surrounded by people with a background ~~like~~ similar to mine. They were ~~like me.~~ L They were trying to leave a ~~way~~ whole pattern of thinking and behavior behind. One woman filed a grievance against a guard ~~that~~ who had struck her ~~a lot~~ numerous times. When the Watch Commander read the statement, he said, "You didn't fill in this part that says, 'Action Requested?'" ~~She talked right back.~~ Her answer was immediate. "I want people to stop beating me unless I deserve it." ~~She was~~ A former victim of child abuse, she was taking an important step. The final one would ~~happen~~ occur when she stopped believing that she should be beaten for any reason. Some people might think that understanding is simple, but it isn't. First ~~you have~~ one has to understand what happens ~~when you get~~ to a person who gets beat on every day.

When I was a little kid, my father used to beat me--in ways I don't want to describe ~~right now~~ just yet. Abuse was a normal part of my life. He ~~mainly threw~~ especially liked to throw things like ashtrays, books, the TV remote control, and beer cans (usually with beer in them). Sometimes he'd say how sorry he was and how I got him all upset. It was always my fault. Then if he missed, he'd get even madder and chase me down and pound me with his fists. Naturally I ~~figgered~~ figured out it would be better to be hit with a flying object tha~~t~~n to be pounded, so I learned to move toward whatever he threw. He never seemed to catch on. I'd lunge toward something like an ashtray, and it'd hit me--fleshy parts like my seat were the best targets--and then I'd cry, and he'd stop.

Of course, I believed it was my fault. Whenever he hit me, however he did it, I knew I deserved it, if not for the immediate mischief, for something else--I was wicked. I always felt more guilt than anger~~,~~. My life was full of guilt-producing ~~stuff~~ incidents. I rec~~ie~~eived bad grades in school. I embarassed [r] him in front of his friends. If [f] got in his way around the house. The food I cooked was never as good as that cooked by my mother, who'd disappeared two years after I was born--which was another source of guilt because she probably didn't like me. There were plenty of reasons for me to feel guilty, [and] I didn't neglect any of them.

But I wasn't the only one around the house who felt guilty. My little brother ~~with~~ [had] his share of guilt feelings. For him, it was not my father he had to watch out for. My father thought Joey could do no wrong[.] I was the one ~~that~~ [who] beat Joey. When my father was out, I slapped Joey around and threw things--ashtrays, books, hair brushes, whatever I had. Pretty soon I had me [a] little whiner to pick on, so I could feel better. I even had him apologizing, acting mousier than I ever did, and even cutting on himself.

Finally [when] I went to school with bruises for the hundredth time, a teacher took me to the principal, and I told all. The result was juvenile hall, [f]ollowed by a half-dozen foster homes and a pattern of beating by adults in all kinds of situations--even by men I lived with.

Being abused is bad. It made me feel guilty. It made me want to be abused. And it made me want to be an abuser. Now I'm working on undoing the pattern of thinking that I've had all these years. I want to take the "Kick me" sign off my back and replace it with one that reads "Kiss me." But right now I'm ~~all all~~ [so] mixed up in changing, ~~and~~ [that] if someone ~~was to~~ [did] kiss me, I don't know whether I'd kick or kiss back.

Final Draft

Kick Me!
Jamie Morgan (pseudonym)

I can identify with people who were physically abused as children. I am one of them, and I've got all kinds of scars. When I was in prison, I was surrounded by people with a background similar to mine. Like me, they were trying to leave a whole pattern of thinking and behavior behind. Here in prison, a woman I know filed a grievance against a guard who had struck her numerous times. When the Watch Commander read the statement, he said, "You didn't fill in this part that says, 'Action Requested?'" Her answer was immediate. "I want people to stop beating me unless I deserve it." A former victim of child abuse, she was taking an important step. The final one would occur when she stopped believing that she should be beaten for any reason. Some people might think that understanding is simple, but it isn't. First, one has to understand what happens to a person who gets beat on every day.

When I was a little kid, my father used to beat me--in ways I don't want to describe just yet. Abuse was a normal part of my life. He especially liked to throw things such as ashtrays, books, the TV remote control, and beer cans (usually with beer in them). Then if he missed, he'd get even madder and chase me down and pound me with his fists. Naturally I figured out it would be better to be hit with a flying object than to be pounded, so I learned to move toward whatever he threw. He never seemed to catch on. I'd lunge toward something like an ashtray, and it'd hit me--fleshy parts like my seat were the best targets--and then I'd cry, and he'd stop. Sometimes he'd say how sorry he was and how I got him all upset. It always was my fault.

Of course, I believed it was my fault. Whenever he hit me, however he did it, I knew I deserved it, if not for the immediate mischief, for something else--I was wicked. I always felt more guilt than anger. My life was full of guilt-producing incidents. I received bad grades in school. I embarrassed him in front of his friends. I got in his way around the house. The food I cooked was never as good as that cooked by my mother, who'd disappeared two years after I was born--which was another source of guilt because she probably didn't like me. There were plenty of reasons for me to feel guilty, and I didn't neglect any of them.

But I wasn't the only one around the house who felt guilty. My little brother had his share of guilt feelings. For him, it was not my father he had to watch out for. My father thought Joey could do no wrong. I was the one who beat Joey. When my father was out, I slapped Joey around and threw things--ashtrays, books, hair brushes, whatever I had. Pretty soon I had me a little whiner to pick on, so I could feel better. I even had him apologizing, acting mousier than I ever did, and even cutting on himself.

Finally, when I went to school with bruises for the hundredth time, a teacher took me to the principal, and I told all. The result was juvenile hall, followed by a half-dozen foster homes and a pattern of beating by adults in all kinds of situations--even by men I lived with.

Being abused is bad. It made me feel guilty. It made me want to be abused. And it made me want to be an abuser. Now I'm working on undoing the pattern of thinking that I've had all these years. I want to take the "Kick me" sign off my back and replace it with one that reads "Kiss me." But right now I'm all so mixed up in changing that if someone did kiss me, I don't know whether I'd kick or kiss back.

APPLICATIONS FOR CRITICAL READING AND DISCUSSION

1. What is the subject (situation, circumstance, or trend) that is at the center of this discussion?
   being abused

2. Circle the sentence that most clearly indicates the author's intention of writing about cause, effect, or a combination.

3. Is this passage concerned more with causes, effects, or a combination?
   effects

4. Underline the sentences that indicate the specific causes or effects.
   See outline.

5. In what order (time, emphasis, or combination) are the parts presented?
   time

6. Is the author's purpose mainly to inform or to persuade?
   inform

Suggested Topics for Writing Analysis by Causes and Effects

General Topics

Regard each of the following items as a subject (situation, circumstance, or trend) that has causes and effects. Then use the **Delve** strategies to determine whether you will concentrate on causes, effects, or a combination. You can probably write a more interesting, well-developed, and, therefore, successful paper on a topic you have personalized. For example, a discussion about a young person you know who contemplated, attempted, or committed suicide is probably a better topic idea than a general discussion on the broad topic. If you do not personalize the topic, you will probably have to do some basic research to supply details for development.

1. Youth suicide
2. Drug addiction
3. Failing or passing a test or a course
4. Disease (particular one)
6. Fire (specify)
7. War (gang or international)
8. Poverty
9. Crime
10. Inflation
11. Unemployment
12. Divorce
13. Marriage
14. Attending or completing college
15. Having or getting a job
16. Change in policy or administration
17. Change in coaches, teachers, office holder(s)
18. Alcoholism
19. Gambling
20. Moving to another country, state, or home
21. Youth runaways
22. Punishment
23. Abuse
24. Loving care
25. Loneliness
26. Dieting
27. Exercise
28. Lies

29. Manners (good or bad)
30. Grooming
31. Language use
32. Popularity of a certain TV program or song
33. Belief in astrology, UFOs, ghosts, aliens from outer space, immortality of Elvis
34. Success of a particular car, motorcycle, or other product
35. Early marriage
36. Teenage parenthood

Reading-Related Topics

"The Effects of the Telephone"

1. Write about the effects that not having a telephone would have on your life.
2. Write about one time when your telephone was out of order and the inconvenience that followed.
3. Write about the loss of (or a time in your life when you did not have) an appliance, such as a washing machine, dryer, or refrigerator, that you take for granted.

"Causes of World War II"

4. Write a piece about the causes of another war you have studied or are studying in a history class.
5. Write about the causes of any dispute between political parties, schools, towns, neighborhoods, gangs, or individuals.

"Back of the Bus"

6. If you are familiar with the civil rights struggle, write about some of the effects of it.
7. Write about a time when you decided to take a stand on an issue because you felt you or others were not being treated fairly.
8. Write about some other person in history who decided to stand up for his or her beliefs.

"Arsenic for Everyone"

9. Write about the causes or effects of other environmental problems, such as acid rain or the greenhouse effect.

"What Happens to Steroid Studs?"

10. Write a piece about the causes or effects on someone you know who has used or is using steroids.
11. Write a piece about the effects of other drugs such as tobacco, heroin, cocaine, marijuana, LSD, or alcohol on someone your know, or do a more detailed study on the effects on users and addicts generally (obtain an informational pamphlet from your library or the American Heart or the American Lung Association).

"Multiculturalism: Building Bridges or Burning Them?"

12. Write an analysis by causes or effects in which you argue for having culturally specific programs. Make the setting a school you know.

13. Write an analysis by effects or causes in which you argue against having culturally specific programs. Make the setting a school you know.

14. Write about an ethnic incident (riot, fight, demonstration, rally) in terms of causes or effects.

"I'm Outta Here"

15. Write a causes or effects paper about someone you know who has dropped out of school.

16. Write an effects paper to some imaginary person who is thinking about dropping out of school.

"Who Killed Benny Paret?"

17. Write a paper of causal analysis about anyone who has been killed or permanently disabled in a high-risk sport, such as hockey, football, or auto racing.

18. This essay is written in a persuasive tone with a certain point of view. If you disagree with the author, rewrite it (maintaining the same basic pattern of causes) with a different view and perhaps a different tone.

"Death by Gangbanging"

19. Write a causal analysis about someone you know who joined a gang.

20. Write about the effects of gang membership on someone you know.

21. Write about the effects of a gang's presence in a neighborhood.

22. Write about the effects of gangs on society.

"No Secrets to Her Success: Reba McEntire"

23. Write about the causes of the success of some other person of distinction.

24. Write about a highly successful person whose life has been changed drastically by that success.

"Kick Me"

25. Write about a similar case of abuse by concentrating on either the causes or the effects.

Writer's Checklist

Apply the following ideas to your writing as you work with **DCODE**. Later, as a peer editor, apply the same ideas to the material you evaluate.

1. State your subject (situation, circumstance, or trend) specifically.

2. Clearly indicate your intention of writing about causes, effects, or a combination, and repeat key words, such as *causes, effects, reasons, results, consequences,* and *outcomes.*

3. In selecting the causes or effects, or both, for the main thrust of your paper, usually select immediate over remote and primary over secondary causes and effects.

4. Organize your work for coherence by using the principles of time, space, or emphasis.

5. Be consistent in tone (how you want to treat your topic and your readers—objectively, humorously, persuasively, indignantly, or ironically).

6. Avoid pitfalls in logic such as the *post hoc* fallacy (A follows B; therefore, A is caused by B).

Journal-Entry Suggestions

1. Select some of the unused "Reading-Related Topics" suggestions, and use them for journal topics.

2. Write a reaction to one or more "Reading Connection" selections. Agree, disagree, apply the statements to your own experiences, indicate the value of such statements, or explain why you were surprised, shocked, disgusted, pleased, or otherwise, by the material.

3. Invent statements (using analysis by causes or effects if appropriate) to support headlines from *Weekly World News*:

    "Ostrich KO's a Pair of Crooks!"
    "Man Shines Light in One Ear and It Comes Out the Other!"
    "Dinosaur People! (Scientists' World Stunned by Shocking Discovery of Ancient Remains)"
    "A Space Alien Attacked Me and Tried to Mate with My Weed Eater!"
    "Real-Life Mutant Ninja Turtle Found in Paris Sewer!"
    "Animal Lovers Miffed over Pig Kissing"
    "Blabbermouth Parrot Sued by Neighbor—for Slander!"
    "Mom Eats Spaghetti Through Her Nose!"
    "World War II Bomber Found on Moon"
    "Girl Moons Traffic and Gets Hit by Car"

WORKSHEET
Writing in DCODE

NAME:_____

SECTION:_____ CHAPTER:_____ DATE:_____

Delve   Generate your topic, or ideas for your topic, by delving into your subject area through:

- *Freewriting*—writing sentence after sentence, nonstop and spontaneously.
- *Brainstorming*—jotting down answers to Who? What? Where? When? Why? and How? and then listing words and phrases in relation to those answers.
- *Clustering*—connecting bubbled ideas with lines to show strings of relationships, producing each new bubble item in response to the question, What comes to mind?
- *Combining* any of these approaches, as directed by your instructor.

Concentrate   Concentrate your work by stating your topic in one sentence that is not too broad, narrow, or vague to be developed. Base this sentence (which may become the topic sentence for your paragraph or the thesis for your essay) on an idea emerging from the **Delve** stage. You may have to try several statements here before you formulate one that is best for your writing task. Be sure that your final statement covers your assignment or intent and specifies both your subject (what you are writing about) and treatment (what aspect you will focus on). Label the *subject* and *treatment* parts.

Organize   Complete an outline or a cluster, as directed by your instructor. The cluster should be a section from, or a refined version of, the **Delve** clustering. Regardless of the strategy you use, the organizational pattern should indicate a division of your topic into parts that will, in turn, be further subdivided for support as necessary to address a particular audience on your concentrated topic.

Draft   On separate paper, write and then revise your assignment as many times as necessary for **c**oherence, **l**anguage (usage, tone, and diction), **u**nity, **e**mphasis, **s**upport, and **s**entence structure (**cluess**).

Edit   Correct problems in fundamentals such as **c**apitalization, **o**missions, **p**unctuation, and **s**pelling (**cops**). Before writing the final draft, read your paper aloud to discover oversights and awkwardness of expression.

Classification: Establishing Groups

9

> "You don't write because you want to say something; you write because you've something to say."
> — F. Scott Fitzgerald

Animal fast-food joints

How is classification defined? Why is the difference between subject and principle in the process of classifying? What is the most common problem of developing classification? What strategy associated with **Delve** is likely to indicate your principle for establishing classes?

Classification Defined

To explain by classification, you place persons, places, things, or ideas into groups or classes based on similar and dissimilar characteristics.

Observing Classification in Action

Consider this situation. Joe is taking a class, and his instructor tells him to write a paper of personal experience. He says he can't think of anything worth writing about. His instructor asks Joe if he works. Joe says yes he does; he works in a department store as a salesperson. His instructor suggests that Joe write about his customers. Deep in thought, Joe begins. On an extremely bad day, he might write this:

> 3,042 Customers
>
> I have been working at my job for three weeks now, and I have had three thousand and forty-two customers. The first one was a woman. She said she was only looking, and she didn't buy anything. The next person was a young man, and he also said he was a looker, and he didn't buy anything either. Then the third one was shopping for sales, and she went through the merchandise and picked out three sales items and bought them. The fourth one was looking for a specific item; I showed it to her and she bought it. The fourth, a young girl, was also a looker. The fifth one . . .

Joe (on a bad day)

Of course, if Joe were to write that way, he would produce a very long and very boring paper, and the instructor would be sorry he or she made the suggestion. On a better day, Joe might write this:

> Sorting Them Out
>
> I've had several kinds of customers at my job at May Company. Specifically, I can divide most of them into three classes: the looking shoppers, the sales shoppers, and the special-item shoppers. The largest class is the *looking shoppers*. One can see them wandering around all over the store as if they were lost or maybe out for exercise. They stop for discoveries here and there, but they don't want to be bothered by salespersons. They're pretty harmless, except sometimes they bump into each other. And quite infrequently they buy something. The next class, the *sales shoppers*, are the ones who have read the advertisements. They may even be carrying an advertisement with them, matching pictures and numbers with items. If a salesperson can help them get to the merchandise before someone else does, they're grateful; otherwise, get out of their way. They are single-minded and ruthless. Beware of verbal assaults and vicious bodily contact at the sales tables. The last group is my favorite. It is the *special-item shoppers*. They know what they want, but they would like good quality and a good price. They are usually friendly, and they are appreciative of good service. On a given day, one person may move from one group to another, and when the person does, his or her behavior changes. After serving more than three thousand customers, I can identify and classify them almost immediately.

the classification
class 1

class 2

class 3

Joe (on a good day)

The difference between the two efforts is remarkable. The first considered thousands of persons and discussed some of them (before being mercifully cut off) without producing any discernible order or meaning. The second classified the persons according to a single principle, and the reader can follow the logical arrangement and the meaning of the presentation.

If Joe wanted to polish his skills in writing a paper of classification, he could write about the arrangement of items in the department store. *Department*, as a word, suggests that items are being grouped according to similar and dissimilar characteristics: footwear, underwear, jewelry, perfume, sports equipment, and so on.

Applying a Principle That Fits the Purpose

The purpose of a paper of classification is to inform or to persuade. The principle on which the division of the classes is based must fit that purpose. Joe wanted to inform the reader (purpose) about the different types of customers according to their motives (principle). Therefore, the purpose and the principle are quite similar. Had he wanted to persuade the reader, let's say, to avoid working in department stores because of the stress related to dealing with customers, he might have used the idea of stress-provoking customers as a principle and classified certain unsavory customers as thieves, manipulators, and bullies. Those three classes would be discussed according to their capacity for producing stress on the salespersons.

The key to organization in the second example paragraph is found in Joe's application of the principle in relation to the subject. Again, the purpose is to inform, and the principle is the intention of the customers—why they come to the store. In the first paragraph, there is no intention. In the second, the three intentions are (1) looking, (2) sale hunting, and (3) special purchasing. Most customers would fit into those classes.

Avoiding Overlap

After a disastrous beginning, Joe might have stumbled around a bit in applying the principle of classification. He might have come up with four classes: (1) looking, (2) sale hunting, (3) special purchasing, and (4) being informed. Although a certain percentage of customers are informed in various ways, item number 4 is out of place because it is not based on the principle of intention. In his groups there would be a problem of overlapping because members of the other groups could also be informed. Overlapping is the most common problem in developing a classification.

Working with Good Topics, Average Topics, and Bad Topics

The preceding subhead, demonstrates an ineffective set of classes. It is colorless, flat, insipid, boring, unimaginative, and monotonous. It requires no thought to write and no thought to read, and it requires no effort to forget. Topics with two extremes and a middle position are almost always destined for dullness. Consider some more bad ideas: fast runners, slow runners, and average runners; intelligent thinkers, unintelligent thinkers, and average thinkers; good hamburgers, bad hamburgers, and average hamburgers. Who would want to read material based on those ideas? But what about *intelligence* based on the kind of thinking that is employed:

academic intelligence (raw IQ), commonsense intelligence (good practical judgment), and street-smart intelligence (cunning)?

When you write classifications, try to look at subjects in new ways. If you are a hairdresser, you might write about your customers as dogs: some pretty and lovable like the cocker spaniel, some growly and assertive like the doberman, and some feisty and temperamental like the poodle. Instead of writing about different kinds of marriages by giving general and abstract terms, you could label the marriages using the names of well-known television entertainers or programs such as "a Cosby (Huxtable) marriage," "a Roseanne marriage," and "a Bundy marriage."

Spontaneous, free-ranging thinking in the **Delve** stage of the writing process should give you plenty of original ideas. Make comparisons, use examples, and indulge in free associations.

Try some of the following patterns for consistency of an applied principle. You may want to add a bit of clustering to this activity.

EXERCISE 1

Mark the sets of classes as **OK** or **OL** (overlapping) for items 1–5. Circle parts that are overlapping.

Subject	Principle	Classes
Example: community college students	intentions	vocational academic transfer specialty needs hardworking
1. airline flights	passenger seating	first class business coach
2. country singers	clothing trademark	hat overalls decorative costume expensive
3. schools	ownership	private religious public
4. faces	shape	round square oval beautiful broad long
5. dates	behavior	sharks clams jellyfish cute octopuses

Complete the categories for items 6–10.

6. waitresses   style of serving   Lucy Ricardo

7. baseball fans   according to   _____
                         where they sit

8. dancers   _____   _____

9. intelligence   _____   _____

10. walkers (men or women)   mannerisms   _____

Writing Classification Using DCODE

Delve

In the development of a paragraph or essay of classification, the **Delve** stage will take you from the initial exploration of your subject, to your choice of principle, to the tentative selection of your classes.

If you are going to relate your classes to ideas in movies, television programs, or books, consider your audience. Shared experience provides a rich foundation for communication, but if your readers have never heard of Roseanne, for example, a reference to her realistically wacky world will not register. In some instances, you may estimate that some audience members are familiar with your supporting material and some are not; the solution might be to include more explanation than if all members were familiar with it.

Freewriting

After deciding on a subject (by assignment, from a list, or from a consideration of your interests, knowledge, and experiences), freewrite; write nonstop and spontaneously so as to open up all channels of your memory and imagination. Then read through what you have written before you narrow your focus to the next strategy. Let's say your subject is bosses, and you freewrote about different types of bosses: young and old, intelligent and unintelligent, handsome and plain, open-minded and closed-minded, and so on. You had a lot to say about how the bosses treated their employees.

Brainstorming

Here you move closer to some of the specifics of your topic by answering the key questions and by free-associating with them.

Who?   bosses—based on about ten I've known
What? the way they treat employees—management style
Where? at work—sometimes moving to social situations
When? management situations—shows up mainly in problem solving
Why?   to do their jobs—to fulfill ambition
How?   in various ways—dictatorial, democratic, buddy-friendly, manipulative

Looking at that information, you might surmise that your answers to How? lead to some potentially good material, especially since you also developed these ideas while freewriting. You tentatively decide on a principle for your paper of classification:

Subject: bosses

Principle: management style

With the classes still not named specifically, you move to the last **Delve** strategy.

Clustering

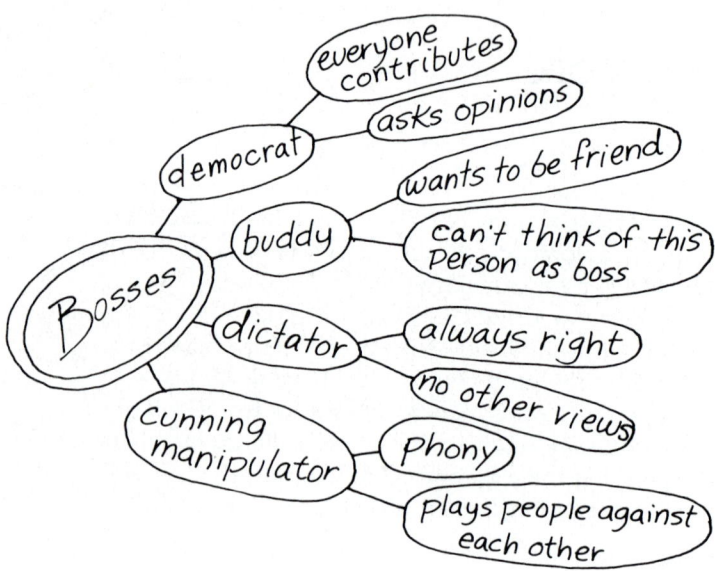

The clustering should confirm your choice of the principle and guide you to the set of classes you will need to state in the next stage. The cluster may reveal that the classification exists through more than one level, a pattern that will be developed further in the **Organize** stage.

Concentrate

Now your development moves into sharp focus with a simple, single sentence that states subject, principle, and classes. This statement may be rather mechanical and may need to be smoothed out for inclusion as a topic sentence in your paragraph or a thesis in your essay. The classes will become main parts of the outline or cluster that follows. Here is the basic statement for the topic sentence or thesis:

<u>subject</u>
<u>Bosses</u> maintain control mainly though the use of one of these

<u>principle</u>　　　　　　　　　<u>classes</u>
<u>management styles:</u> <u>dictator, cunning manipulator, buddy, and democrat.</u>

Organize

Your writing is now moving from the larger idea as the subject to the controlling principle, and finally to the supporting classes, which provide structure and sequence. Consider how this outline provides a skeletal structure for the topic sentence or thesis on the management styles of bosses:

I. Dictator
    A. Uses fear
    B. Issues commands
II. Cunning manipulator
    A. Devious
    B. Turns people against each other
III. Buddy
    A. Wants to be friends
    B. Loses respect
IV. Democrat
    A. Treats others with respect
    B. Works with consensus

Draft

The main parts (classes) of your outline become main parts of support. If you are writing a paragraph, the main parts of the outline become the sentences that support the topic sentence. If you are writing an essay, the main parts of the outline will probably become paragraphs of development. You will develop these parts by explaining their characteristics, traits, or qualities. They may be supported by authoritative statements, statistics, or details. These parts can often be made more emphatic and colorful by giving examples and by referring directly to other relevant data.

Working with Simple and Complex Forms

The outline shown for the **Organize** stage is typical for most paragraphs and essays, but more complicated arrangements exist, especially in published sources. Two main patterns prevail: the simple and the complex. A subject that is presented with one principle of classification is called *simple*. Here is an example presented in the standard class-by-class arrangement:

> Though at times there was considerable social mobility, (medieval society) conventionally consisted of three classes: the <u>nobles</u>, the <u>peasants</u>, and the <u>clergy</u>. Each of these groups had its own (task) to perform. Since the <u>vassals</u> usually gave military service to their lord in return for their fiefs, the nobles were primarily fighters, belonging to an honored society distinct from the peasant people—freemen, villeins, and serfs. In an age of physical violence, society obviously would accord first place to the man with the sword rather than to the man with the hoe. The <u>peasants</u> were the workers; attached to the manors, they produced the crops and did all the menial labor. The Church drew on both the noble and the peasant classes for the <u>clergy</u>. Although the higher churchmen held land as vassals under the feudal system, the clergy formed a class which was considered separate from the nobility and peasantry.

subject
classes
principle
development of classes

T. Walter Wallbank et al., "Medieval Society"

The classifications that are based on one principle and then subgrouped by another related principle are called *complex.* This is a typical example:

There are two principal types of glaciers: the continental and the valley. The continental glaciers are great sheets of ice, called ice caps, that cover parts of continents. The earth has two continental glaciers at present: one spreads over most of Greenland and one over all of Antarctica save for a small window of rock and the peaks of several ranges. The Greenland ice sheet is over 10,000 ft. thick in the central part and covers an area of about 650,000 sq. miles. The Antarctic sheet has been sounded, in one place at least, to a depth of 14,000 ft., and it spreads over an area of 5,500,000 sq. miles. This is larger than conterminous United States in the proportion of 5 1/2: 3. It is calculated to store 7 million cu. miles of ice, which if melted would raise the ocean level 250 ft.	subject main class main class I principle
Valley glaciers are ice streams that originate in the high snow fields of mountain ranges and flow down valleys to warmer climates, where they melt. Some break up into icebergs and eventually melt in the ocean. In certain places the valley glaciers flow down the mountain valleys to adjacent plains and there spread out as lobate feet. These are called expanded-foot glaciers. Generally the sprawling feet of several valley glaciers coalesce to form one major sheet, and this is called a piedmont glacier.	main class II subclass A (conventional) subclass B subclass C

Notice that the valley glacier is subdivided:

```
Continental ─────────── Valley
                           │
        ┌──────────────────┼──────────────────┐
   conventional      expanded foot         piedmont
```

A. J. Eardley, "Glaciers: Types and Subtypes"

As you can see, glaciers are of two types based on their location (with implications for size): (1) the continental glacier, such the huge one in the Antarctic, and (2) the valley glacier. The valley glacier can be subdivided into the conventional valley glacier, flowing straight; the expanded-foot glacier, which spreads out; and the piedmont glacier, which is made up of several expanded–foot glaciers. This is the way this information could be organized in a simple outline:

    I. Continental glacier
   II. Valley glacier
       A. Conventional
       B. Expanded-foot
       C. Piedmont

This outline on glaciers could be cut down to the "valley glacier" part and developed into a paragraph or an essay. Moving in the other direction, we can say that almost all classifications can be part of a higher level of classification. For example, glaciers are one type of earth-altering process. (Others are earthquakes, volcanoes, and wind erosion.)

Most papers of classification will be simple (based on one principle) in concept, informative in purpose, and class by class in organization. Those matters are stressed in this chapter.

The Reading Connection

EXERCISE 2

Demonstration

In his *Introduction to General Psychology,* Knight shows how a famous psychologist groups the various human needs.

Maslow's Classification of Motives
FREDERICK B. KNIGHT

A comprehensive classification of motives has been formulated by Maslow. He has proposed a theory of motivation in which motives are classified according to the basic needs underlying the motives. Needs are classified into five groups or levels and arranged in a hierarchy of pre-potency. This arrangement means that "the appearance of one need usually rests on the prior satisfaction of another, more pre-potent need." The five groups of needs, listed in descending order of their pre-potency, are as follows:

1. *Physiological needs*. This group includes the need for food, for water, for oxygen, for constant temperature, etc.

2. *Safety needs*. These needs are concerned with seeking safety and avoiding pain, threats, and danger.

3. *Love needs*. These needs give rise to the desire to belong, to be wanted, to be loved by friends, relatives, and family.

4. *Esteem needs*. These needs give rise to the desire for self-respect, strength, achievement, adequacy, prestige, attention, and appreciation.

5. *Self-actualization needs*. This group is characterized by saying that one must do what one can do.

APPLICATIONS FOR CRITICAL READING AND DISCUSSION

1. Circle the subject (what is being classified) the first time it appears in the piece of writing. Write it here.
    motives

2. What is the principle of the classification (on what basis is the classifying being done)?
    basic needs

3. Underline the classes the first time each appears.

4. State the topic sentence or thesis (the author's exact words or your own phrasing).
    He has proposed a theory of motivation in which motives are classified according to the basic needs underlying the motives.

5. Translate the basic parts of the classification into a brief topic outline. Each roman-numeral part will be a class.

```
    I.   Physiological needs
    II.  Safety needs
         A. Avoiding pain
         B. Avoiding threats
         C. Avoiding danger
    III. Love needs
         A. To belong
         B. To be wanted
         C. To be loved
    IV.  Esteem needs
    V.   Self-actualization needs
```

6. Is the main purpose to inform or to persuade?
    inform

EXERCISE 3

As you address your audience, they may all be looking at you attentively, but Glenn R. Capp points out that equal gazing does not mean equal listening.

Listen Up!
GLENN R. CAPP

Listeners can be classified into four groups: (1) Some do not listen; they "tune the speaker out" and think of matters foreign to the speaker's subject. They get little from a speech. (2) Some only half-listen; their spasmodic listening fluctuates all the way from careful attention to no attention. They understand fragments of the speech but they do not see the idea as a whole. (3) Some listen with passive acceptance; they accept all the speaker says without question. Because of their lack of discrimination, they add little to what the speaker says from their own experiences. (4) Some listen with discrimination; this critical type of listener gets the most from a speech.

APPLICATIONS FOR CRITICAL READING AND DISCUSSION

1. Circle the subject (what is being classified) the first time it appears in the piece of writing. Write it here.

2. What is the principle of the classification (on what basis is the classifying being done)?

3. Underline the classes the first time each appears.

4. State the topic sentence or thesis (the author's exact words or your own phrasing).

5. Translate the basic parts of the classification into a brief topic outline. Each roman-numeral part will be a class.

6. Is the main purpose to inform or to persuade?

EXERCISE 4

The author discusses three kinds of book owners, but only one kind that truly owns books. If you have a collection of books, where would you be placed in this three-group classification?

Kinds of Book Owners
MORTIMER J. ADLER

There are three kinds of book owners. The first has all the standard sets and best-sellers—unread, untouched. (This deluded individual owns woodpulp and ink, not books.) The second has a great many books—a few of them read through, most of them dipped into, but all of them as clean and shiny as the day they were bought. (This person would probably like to make books his own, but is restrained by a false respect for their physical appearance.) The third has a few books or many—every one of them dog-eared and dilapidated, shaken and loosened by continual use, marked and scribbled in from front to back. (This man owns books.)

APPLICATIONS FOR CRITICAL READING AND DISCUSSION

1. Circle the subject (what is being classified) the first time it appears in the piece of writing. Write it here.

2. What is the principle of the classification (on what basis is the classifying being done)?

3. Underline the classes the first time each appears.

4. State the topic sentence or thesis (the author's exact words or your own phrasing).

5. Translate the basic parts of the classification into a brief topic outline. Each roman-numeral part will be a class.

6. Is the main purpose to inform or to persuade?

EXERCISE 5

Many people use the words *laws, theories,* and *hypotheses* interchangeably. John Cuber shows that they are separate classes.

Kinds of Scientific Findings
JOHN CUBER

Scientific findings when stated in words are usually classified into *laws, theories,* and *hypotheses*. If the evidence indicates that the finding is clearly established, and can be stated definitely without too many "ifs, ands and provideds," then it is called a "law." Examples are the "Law of Falling Bodies" in physics, "Boyle's Law" in chemistry, the "Law of Diminishing Returns" in economics. Discoveries which are probably true, but for which the evidence is not quite so conclusive, are usually called "theories." It is necessary to emphasize, however, that a theory is not a guess, it is not "a notion spun out of thin air" but is a truth for which there exists considerable but not final and conclusive evidence. Finally, there are "hypotheses." A hypothesis is an idea about which we are not yet sufficiently certain to permit us to call it a law or a theory, but there is, nevertheless, some evidence to support it. An idea usually does not remain a hypothesis very long. It is usually soon tested and if found true becomes a theory or a law, if found to be false is discarded. This may, of course, take a long time.

APPLICATIONS FOR CRITICAL READING AND DISCUSSION

1. Circle the subject (what is being classified) the first time it appears in the piece of writing. Write it here.

2. What is the principle of the classification (on what basis is the classifying being done)?

3. Underline the classes the first time each appears).

4. State the topic sentence or thesis (the author's exact words or your own phrasing).

5. Translate the basic parts of the classification into a brief topic outline. Each roman-numeral part will be a class.

6. Is the main purpose to inform or to persuade?

EXERCISE 6

Nag. Nag. Nag. Stop! Stop! Stop! We know nagging, don't we? After all, we've heard so much that we're experts, right? Maybe not. Listen to what this expert says about types of naggers. She points out that in this sophisticated world, some people specialize in certain kinds of nagging.

Vocabulary Preview: Write in short definitions for these words as they are used in the context of the following passage. (The paragraph numbers are given in parentheses.) Be prepared to use the words in your own sentences.

crescendoing (1)

timbre (1)

advocacy (adj.) (6)

purveyors (8)

demolition (9)

status quo (9)

escalates (10)

scenario (12)

stalemate (12)

paradoxical (13)

Why We Carp and Harp
MARY ANN HOGAN

Bring those dishes down from your room! Put those scissors away. . . . I told you not to smoke in the kitchen and you shouldn't be smoking anyway! Take your feet off the table! Why do I have to tell you again and again. . . ?! The hills are alive with the sound of nagging—the gnawing, crescendoing timbre of people getting in each other's face. Parents nag children, wives nag husbands, husbands nag wives, friends nag friends . . . "*Use* your fork . . . *Stop* spending money like water . . . *Can't* you be ready on time? . . . *Act* like an adult. . . ." Nagging, of course, has been around since the first cave husband refused to take out the cave garbage. But linguists, psychologists and other scholars are just now piecing together what nagging really is, why we do it, and how to stop it before we nag each other to death.

2   Common perception holds that a nag is an unreasonably demanding wife who carps at a long-suffering husband. But in truth, nagging is universal. It happens in romances, in families, in businesses, in society—wherever people gather and one person wants another to do something he or she doesn't want to do. "It's a virus. You pick it

up through kissing, shaking hands and standing in crowded rooms with people who have perfect children, wonderful husbands and sterilized homes," says humor columnist Erma Bombeck, whose family members nag her as artfully as she nags them. "It makes you feel good—like you're getting something done. Most of us want perfection in this world," she adds.

3   Thus, doctors can nag patients to lose their potbellies; accountants can nag timid clients to buy low; bosses can nag workers to get things done on time; special interest groups can nag the public to save the planet and send money, and the government can nag everyone to pay their taxes on time, to abstain from drink if they're pregnant and, while they're at it, to Buy American. And when the going gets desperate, the desperate get nagging: Our recession-plagued nation, experts say, could be headed for a giant nag jag.

4   "When people are generally dissatisfied, they tend to harp at other people more," says Bernard Zilbergeld, a Bay Area psychologist. Naggers tend to fall into four categories—friendly, professional, social and domestic—that range from the socially acceptable to the toxic.

5   The Friendly Ones are proud of their art. "My sisters call me a nag, but that's not necessarily a bad thing," says Bari Brenner, a 44-year-old Castro Valley resident who describes herself as "a third-generation nag" with a low tolerance for procrastinators. "I get things done. The truth is, I'm organized, they're not. I can see the big *picture*. They can't. We're going on a trip to England. 'Did you call the travel agent?' 'No.' 'Well, *call* the travel agent . . . book the hotel . . . call *now*!' It's the same thing at work. Nagging can be a means to an end."

6   Professional Nags—people who do it for a living—have to disguise what they do to get what they want. "I have to nag all the time—but you have to be careful about using the word *nag*," says Ruth Holton, a lobbyist for Common Cause, the good-government advocacy group. "I have to ask [legislators] for the same thing over and over again, year in, year out. But if they perceive what you're doing as nagging, they'll say, 'I've heard this 100 times before,' and they'll shut down. There's a fine line between artful persistence and being perceived as a nag."

7   Social nags don't see themselves as naggers. The U.S. Surgeon General's office peppers us with health warnings and calls it education. Environmentalists harp on people to recycle and save the rain forest, all in the name of the Greater Good. "One person's nagger is another person trying to save the world," says Arthur Asa Berger, a popular culture critic at San Francisco State University.

8   Then, somewhere beyond the limits of social convention, lies the dangerous world of the good old-fashioned Domestic Nag. Observers of the human condition, from the Roman poets to the purveyors of prime-time TV, have mined domestic nagging's quirkiness for laughs. But behavioral experts say that's where nagging can run amok. At best, domestic nagging is irritating. In Neil Simon's *The Odd Couple*, Felix wanted Oscar to clean up his act. Oscar liked being a slob. Felix nagged, nothing changed, and Felix finally moved out. At its worst, domestic nagging is murderous. In England last May, a 44-year-old businessman strangled his wife after 15 years of her nagging finally made him snap. In January, a judge ruled that the wife's verbal abuse justifiably provoked him and gave the husband an 18-month suspended sentence.

9   What causes this dynamic of domestic demolition? At the root of nagging, behavioralists say, lies a battle for control. It begins with a legitimate request: "I need you to hear me . . . to be with me . . . to be around, to do things like take out the garbage." But the person being asked doesn't want to change and sees the request as a threat to his or her control of the status quo. So the request is ignored.

10 "From the nagger's point of view, the naggee isn't listening," says Andrew Christensen, a UCLA psychology professor who has studied nagging for four years. "From there, it escalates. The further you withdraw, the more I nag. The naggee's point of view is, 'If I don't respond, maybe you'll shut up.'" The original request gets lost in the power struggle. The nagging takes on a life of its own. The desperate refrain of "Take out the garbage!" can stand for a whole universe of complaints, from "You never do anything around here" to "I hate your stupid brown shoes!" "Sometimes I go through the house saying, 'Dammit, close the cupboards! Don't leave the towels on the floor! What's so hard about moving a vacuum cleaner across the hall. . . .' Bang! Bang! Bang! The list goes on," says a 40-year-old Mill Valley mother of two schoolchildren. "It's like the tape is stuck on replay and nobody's listening."

11 UCLA's Christensen calls it the "demand-withdraw pattern." In 60% of the couples he's studied,

women were in the demanding, or nagging, role. In 30% of the cases, men were the demanders. In 10%, the roles were equal. "It may be that, traditionally, women have been more interested in closeness and sharing feelings, and men have been more interested in privacy," he says.

12   The scenario of the man coming home from work and the woman spending the day with the kids feeds the gender stereotype of the female nag. "He wants to sit in front of the TV, she's primed to have an empathetic listener," Christensen says. "The reverse is true with sex. There, men tend to be in the nagging role. Either way, one feels abandoned, neglected and deprived, the other feels intruded upon. It's a stalemate."

13   Communications experts say there is a way to end the nagging. Both people have the power to stop. What it takes is earnest willingness to step out of the ritual. The naggee could say: "You keep bringing up the issue of the garbage. I'd like to sit down and talk about it." But the gesture would have to be heartfelt, not an exercise in lip service. The nagger could write a note instead of carping. "People tend to react differently to written communication," says Zilbergeld. In either case, the effect is paradoxical: When the nagger stops, it leaves room for the naggee to act. When the naggee listens, there's nothing to nag about.

14   And if it doesn't stop? "It gets more and more robotic," says Gahan Wilson, the *New Yorker* magazine artist who explored the fate of the Nag Eternal in a recent cartoon. "We spend much of our lives on automatic pilot."

APPLICATIONS FOR CRITICAL READING AND DISCUSSION

1. Circle the subject (what is being classified) the first time it appears in the piece of writing. Write it here.

2. What is the principle of the classification (on what basis is the classifying being done)?

3. Underline the classes the first time each appears.

4. State the topic sentence or thesis (the author's exact words or your own phrasing).

5. Translate the basic parts of the classification into a brief topic outline. Each roman-numeral part will be a class.

6. Is the main purpose to inform or to persuade?

EXERCISE 7

We know that certain kinds of instruments are grouped in orchestras. What is the basis for that grouping, and what are the subgroups?

Musical Instruments: Blowing, Bowing, and Beating
LOUISE DUDLEY AND AUSTIN FARICY

Musical instruments may be classified roughly according to the way the vibrator is set in motion, by bowing, blowing, or beating. Those in which the sound is made by beating are called the *instruments of percussion*: drum, xylophone, cymbals. Those in which the sound is made by blowing are *wind instruments*: horn, trumpet, flute. Those in which the sound is made by bowing are stringed instruments: violin, cello. The last name is the least satisfactory because certain of the stringed instruments, the harp, for example, are not bowed. Therefore, they are called stringed instruments, not *bowed instruments*. This is the usual classification of instruments: percussion, wind, strings. It is supposed that instruments of percussion came first, then wind instruments, and last, strings. A child follows this order in his natural development; at first he likes rattles and other toys that make noise by beating. Later he learns to whistle, and he likes the wind instruments, pipes of all kinds. Still later he begins to play on the strings, violin or cello.

2   Wind instruments are further subdivided into *wood winds:* piccolo, flute, oboe, clarinet, English horn, and bassoon; and *brasses*: trumpet, horn, trombone, and tuba. The names originally corresponded to the materials of which the instruments were made; most of the instruments of the brass family are still made of brass, but the name *wood winds* has stuck though the flute and piccolo are now always made of metal.

3   Thus we have four families of instruments: (1) Strings, (2) Wood winds, (3) Brasses, (4) Percussion. For obvious reasons the human voice, the organ, and the piano are not usually classed in one of these groups but are put in a separate section by themselves.

4   The instruments of percussion include all those in which the vibrator is struck or hit. These can be divided into two classes: those of indefinite pitch and those of definite pitch. Instruments of indefinite pitch include rattles, gongs, triangles, cymbals, tambourines, and castanets. Rattles are often gourds in which are placed pebbles and gravel to make sound when they are shaken. The tambourine is a small drum with metal disks or bangles in the rim. Gongs, cymbals, and triangles are metal pieces that sound when struck. Castanets, which are much used by Spanish dancers, are small, spoonshaped shells of hardwood or ivory; usually a pair is used in each hand. The drum has a piece of tightly stretched skin as its vibrator. All drums are of indefinite pitch except the timpani or kettledrums, which can be tuned. Other instruments of definite pitch are the xylophone, marimba, orchestral bells, and celesta. In these instruments small bars of metal or wood are hit with wooden hammers. In the xylophone and the marimba the bars are of wood; they are struck by two hammers held in the hands of the performer. In the orchestral bells and the celesta the bars are of metal and are struck by hammers which are manipulated from a keyboard.

5   The brasses are so named because the instruments are of brass. In the brass family the lips are the vibrators. A simple illustration of the lips as vibrators is found in whistling. In a brass instrument the lips are pressed tightly against the mouthpiece, and the sound is made as the air is blown through them. To the group of brasses belong the various members of the horn family: trumpet, French horn, trombone, and tuba.

6   In the wood-wind family there are two types of vibrator: air and reed. Of the air as vibrator one may have a very simple example by blowing across the top of a bottle or jug. If he uses bottles of different sizes he can get different sounds and, as the various jug bands have demonstrated, can play a tune by blowing first on one bottle and then on another. The sound is made because the air is set vibrating, and the stream of air thus becomes the vibrator. Instruments in which air is

the vibrator are the flute and the piccolo, which is a small flute.

7   The principle of the reed as vibrator is demonstrated by the small boy who whistles by blowing on a leaf or blade of grass held tightly across his mouth. The reed, which is a very elastic tongue of wood or metal, is placed in or upon an opening through which the air passes; the player, by blowing, sets the reed to vibrating and produces sound. Reeds may be single or double. In the single-reed instruments, the clarinet and saxophone, a single reed flutters back and forth between the air in the player's mouth and the air in the instrument. In the double-reed instruments, the oboe, English horn (contralto oboe), and bassoon, the air passes between two reeds, causing them to vibrate.

APPLICATIONS FOR CRITICAL READING AND DISCUSSION

1. Circle the subject (what is being classified) the first time it appears in the piece of writing. Write it here.

2. What is the principle of the classification (on what basis is the classifying being done)?

3. Underline the classes the first time each appears.

4. State the topic sentence or thesis (the author's exact words or your own phrasing).

5. Translate the basic parts of the classification into a brief topic outline. Each roman-numeral part will be a class.

6. Is the main purpose to inform or to persuade?

The Reading Connection from Classroom Sources

EXERCISE 8

Jerry Lopez calls himself an observer type in nightclubs—a person who looks around and groups the other patrons according to their behavior.

```
                Types of Nightclubbers
                      Jerry Lopez
     Dancers aren't the only men who go to nightclubs.
Having worked in and attended various clubs, I've come to
realize they attract about four different types of guys,
who can be grouped by the way they act. First there are
the dancers. They are out on the floor most of the night.
They aren't concerned with their appearance. They usually
wear jeans or shorts and a t-shirt. They're there to dance
and sweat. Then there are the posers. They go to model and
show off their clothes and hair. They won't dance for fear
of messing up their appearance, or even worse, sweating!
The third group is the scammers. Scammers go to pick up
women. They usually stand around and check out the body
parts of other people as they pass by. A person close to
them can see the lust in their eyes. Last, there are the
boozers or druggies. They can be seen stumbling around,
falling down, or lying in some corner where they have
passed out. Nightclubs attract those four types of men. At
times I am a member of a fifth: the observers.
```

APPLICATIONS FOR CRITICAL READING AND DISCUSSION

1. Circle the subject (what is being classified) the first time it appears in the piece of writing. Write it here.

2. What is the principle of the classification (on what basis is the classifying being done)?

3. Underline the classes the first time each appears.

4. State the topic sentence or thesis (the author's exact words or your own phrasing).

5. Translate the basic parts of the classification into a brief topic outline. Each roman-numeral part will be a class.

6. Is the main purpose to inform or to persuade?

EXERCISE 9

Successful sitcom characters have traits that we recognize—in ourselves, in others—and that's why we remember them so easily. Angela DeSarro, knowing that her audience will recall the reputations of certain characters, uses that common knowledge to classify sibling relationships.

```
                Three Kinds of Siblings
                     Angela DeSarro
     After eighteen years of having a brother of my own, and
having friends with brothers and sisters, I have concluded
that there are three types of siblings, based on
relationships. They can be classified as the Beaver and
Wally Cleaver siblings, the Brandon and Brenda Walsh
siblings, and the Bud and Kelly Bundy siblings. The Beaver
and Wally Cleaver siblings are the ones who don't really
have any trouble getting along. They usually have
something nice to say to each other. And when it comes to
sharing the toys, or later items such as clothing, that's
no problem for these siblings. Their lives are so
insulated, and their luck is so good that they never seem
to have big problems to confront. The next group is made
up of Brandon and Brenda Walsh siblings. Most people I
know can identify with them. These are the siblings who
have their share of both good and bad times. But no matter
what their differences are and even though at times they
argue, they will always return to mutual love and respect.
Finally, there are the Bud and Kelly Bundy siblings. These
are the ones who are always competing in a self-interested
way and never have anything nice to say to one another.
They're always exchanging insults. Even their jokes are
```

hurtful. With them life in the family is "survival of the meanest and the most greedy." Most siblings are inclined toward one of those three groups. At times we may feel we can identify with all three groups. But whether we get along with our siblings or not, they're the only ones "we're gonna get," so we had better learn to live with them.

APPLICATIONS FOR CRITICAL READING AND DISCUSSION

1. Circle the subject (what is being classified) the first time it appears in the piece of writing. Write it here.

2. What is the principle of the classification (on what basis is the classifying being done)?

3. Underline the classes the first time each appears.

4. State the topic sentence or thesis (the author's exact words or your own phrasing).

5. Translate the basic parts of the classification into a brief topic outline. Each roman-numeral part will be a class.

6. Is the main purpose to inform or to persuade?

EXERCISE 12

Demonstration Using the DCODE Worksheet

Marge Tanner describes the fly infestation well. At times the pesky insects darken the windows of facilities, and they enter through the doorways of the Village Cafeteria (formerly called the Central Feeding Unit) despite the strategic placement of a high-powered fan facing downward over each doorway. Once inside, the flies largely ignore the electronic fly zappers and make for the food on the tables. How do eaters fight the flies? Marge says there are three techniques for combating them.

WORKSHEET
Writing in DCODE

NAME: Marge Tanner

SECTION: _____ CHAPTER: _____ DATE: _____

Delve   Generate your topic, or ideas for your topic, by delving into your subject area through:

- *Freewriting*—writing sentence after sentence, nonstop and spontaneously.
- *Brainstorming*—jotting down answers to Who? What? Where? When? Why? and How? and then listing words and phrases in relation to those answers.
- *Clustering*—connecting bubbled ideas with lines to show strings of relationships, producing each new bubble item in response to the question, What comes to mind?
- *Combining* any of these approaches, as directed by your instructor.

Freewriting:
    People have all kinds of problems around this prison, but the one thing that everyone has in common is flies. They're everywhere. You walk thru the grass and they come at you in waves. Sometimes they're so thick on windows you can hardly seed thru. Then the worst of places for flies is wherever someone is eating. If you're eating, you compete with the flies for your food. You can look around the dining halls and see people fighting flies everywhere. What's really interesting is to see how different people fight the flies. Some of them shoo the flies by waving their hands. Others try to hide their food and then the third group tries to distract the flies by dropping some food on the table. That's called baiting.

Brainstorming:
    Who? fly fighters
    What? fly fighting
    Where? prison
    Why? Flies are pests.
    When? especially at meals
    How? by shooing, hiding and baiting

Clustering:

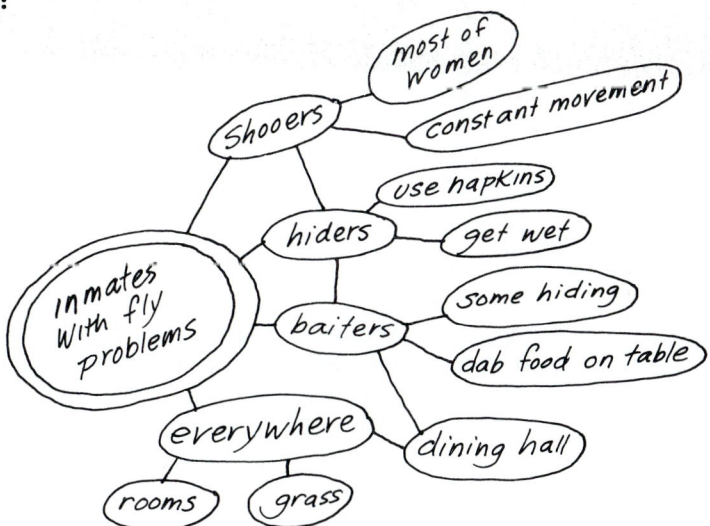

261

Concentrate Concentrate your work by stating your topic in one sentence that is not too broad, narrow, or vague to be developed. Base this sentence (which may become the topic sentence for your paragraph or the thesis for your essay) on an idea emerging from the **Delve** stage. You may have to try several statements here before you formulate one that is best for your writing task. Be sure that your final statement covers your assignment or intent and specifies both your subject (what you are writing about) and treatment (what aspect you will focus on). Label the *subject* and *treatment* parts.

```
                      subject                           treatment
There are three kinds of fly fighters around here: the shooers, the hiders,
and the baiters.
```

Organize Complete an outline or a cluster, as directed by your instructor. The cluster should be a section from, or a refined version of, the **Delve** clustering. Regardless of the strategy you use, the organizational pattern should indicate a division of your topic into parts that will, in turn, be further subdivided for support as necessary to address a particular audience on your concentrated topic.

```
        I.   Shooers
             A. Wave their hands
             B. Always in motion
        II.  Hiders
             A. Use napkins to cover
             B. Scoop food from under napkins
        III. Baiters
             A. Also hide
             B. Drop food on table
             C. Let flies eat
             D. Scoop and eat
```

Draft On separate paper, write and then revise your assignment as many times as necessary for **c**oherence, **l**anguage (usage, tone, and diction), **u**nity, **e**mphasis, **s**upport, and **s**entence structure (**cluess**).

Edit Correct problems in fundamentals such as **c**apitalization, **o**missions, **p**unctuation, and **s**pelling (**cops**). Before writing the final draft, read your paper aloud to discover oversights and awkwardness of expression.

First Draft

                        Types of Fly Fighters

   One of the ~~main problems~~ (major annoyances) here at the women's prison is ~~the fly situation.~~ (flies.) ~~Here~~ (Situated as it is) in the middle of an agricultural zone where ~~fly~~ breeding ~~goes on,~~ (sites for flies abound,) the prison attracts flies by the millions. Inmates, even the ones ~~that come from high class backgrounds,~~ (who have seldom dealt with fly infestations,) ~~have to~~ (must) learn how to ~~deal~~ (cope) with ~~flies. It happens mainly at eating time~~ (the problem, especially at eating time) when the flies want to share our meals. ~~You can look around~~ (In observing what goes on) at different tables in the dining hall, ~~and see~~ (I have discovered) that there are three kinds of fly fighters: the shooers, the hiders, and the baiters.

   The shooers are the most unimaginative. They wave their hands at the flies ~~like a bunch of wind mills~~, shooing ~~flies~~ (them) after they have landed, or by constant waving trying to keep them from landing. This technique requires an almost constant movement, ~~it~~ (one which) is contrary to the movements asociated with eating and is almost as difficult as patting ~~your~~ (one's) head while rubbing ~~your~~ (one's) stomach. At any time ~~you~~ (one) can look around the dining room and see the women waving their hands and the flies waving their wings as if they are ~~sending signals~~ (all communicating). (If so, the flies have the last word.)

   The hiders, the second class, ~~are sneaky~~ (practice stealth), figuring that any human being should be intelligent enough to hide food from a small(-)brained creature like a fly. Several napkins ~~are used~~ (After using several) to ~~hide~~ (enshroud) the ~~portion of~~ food, (the hiders,) and head bent forward to close space, ~~shovells it in.~~ (scoop food from under the cover and "chow down.") Unfortunately, the food often satUrates the napkin, (or) ~~sometimes the~~ flies manage to crawl under the covering. Overall, this technique is fairly succesSful and it is probably the most popular.

   The baiters, the third class, while being the most clever, ~~and they're~~ (are) probably the most cynical. They have ~~decided~~ (concluded) that flies will succeed in some ~~way~~ (fashion). The baiters offer a self-serving deal to the flies. Upon taking a seat at the table, they will immediately deposit a spoonful of food near the end of the tray or even on the table itself. The next step is to use the hiders' technique of covering the ~~main parts~~ major portion of food. While flies swarm to the exposed portion--the bait--the baiters, often with a smug look of superiority, carry the bait away to the dump zone.

Although t~~T~~he baiting method is probably the most successful, ~~but~~ it is used the least. Most women shoo flies or hide food ~~because they like to look good.~~ as an expression of their good manners and dignity. If you believe that last statement, I have an entertaining fly farm kit I am selling for only $29.95.

Final Draft

Types of Fly Fighters
Marge Tanner

One of the major annoyances here at the women's prison is flies. Situated as it is in the middle of an agricultural zone where breeding sites for flies abound, the prison attracts them by the millions. Inmates, even those who have seldom dealt with fly infestation, must learn to cope with the problem, especially at eating time, when the flies want to share our meals. In observing what goes on at different tables in the dining hall, I have discovered that there are three kinds of fly fighters: the shooers, the hiders, and the baiters.

The shooers are the most unimaginative. They wave their hands at the flies, shooing them after they have landed, or by constant waving trying to keep them from landing. This technique requires an almost constant movement, one which is contrary to the movements associated with eating and is almost as difficult as patting one's head while rubbing one's stomach. At any time one can look around the dining room and see the women waving their hands and the flies waving their wings as if they are all communicating. If so, the flies have the last word.

The hiders, the second class, practice stealth, figuring that any human being should be intelligent enough to hide food from a small-brained creature like a fly. After using several napkins to enshroud food, the hiders, head bent forward to close space, scoop food from under the covering and "chow down." Unfortunately, the food often saturates the napkin, or flies manage to crawl under the covering. But overall, this technique is fairly successful and is probably the most popular.

The baiters, the third class, while being the most clever, are probably the most cynical. They have concluded that flies will succeed in some fashion. The baiters offer a self-serving compromise to the flies. Upon taking a seat at the table, they will immediately deposit a spoonful of food near the edge of the tray or even on the table itself. The next step is to use the hiders' technique of

covering the major portion of food. While flies swarm to
the exposed portion--the bait--the baiters, often with a
smug look of superiority, eat and then carry the bait away
to the dump zone.
   Although the baiting method is probably the most
successful, it is used the least. Most women shoo flies or
hide food as an expression of their good manners and
dignity. If you believe that last statement, I have a very
entertaining fly farm kit I am selling for only $29.95.

APPLICATIONS FOR CRITICAL READING AND DISCUSSION

1. Circle the subject (what is being classified) the first time it appears in the piece of writing. Write it here.
   fly fighters

2. What is the principle of the classification (on what basis is the classifying being done)?
   behavior

3. Underline the classes the first time each appears.

4. State the topic sentence or thesis (the author's exact words or your own phrasing).
   "There are three kinds of fly fighters: the shooers, the hiders, and the baiters."

5. Translate the basic parts of the classification into a brief topic outline. Each roman numeral part will be a class.
   See the outline part of Organize on the **DCODE** Worksheet.

6. Is the main purpose to inform or to persuade?
   inform

Suggested Topics for Writing Classifications

Each of the following entries is plural and is to be divided into groups according to a single principle. Select one that interests you and proceed according to guidance from the "Writer's Checklist" and **DCODE**.

General Topics

1. Intelligence
2. Waitresses
3. Drinkers
4. Dates
5. Smokers
6. Flirts
7. Smiles
8. Sleepers in class
9. Gum chewers
10. Liars
11. Cheaters
12. Attention-getting devices
13. Gossips
14. Video game players
15. Customers
16. Crimes
17. Junk food
18. Siblings
19. TV watchers
20. Shoppers
21. Soap operas
22. Styles in clothing, talking, dancing
23. Attitudes toward careers, life
24. Bars, night clubs
25. Dopers
26. Marriages
27. Bosses
28. Sports fans
29. Parties
30. Advertisements
31. Churchgoers
32. Preachers
33. Disc jockeys
34. Doctors
35. Athletes
36. Singers
37. Comedians
38. Talk show hosts
39. Laughs
40. Bus drivers
41. Riders on buses or airplanes
42. Homeless people
43. Buildings
44. Ways of practicing religion
45. Junk food
46. Graffiti
47. Diets
48. Walkers or runners
49. Home computers
50. Mothers or fathers
51. Jazz
52. Rock music
53. Talkers on the telephone
54. Pick-up lines (as in a bar)
55. Running around the bases after hitting a home run
56. Ways of entering a classroom late
57. Chicken eaters
58. Surfers
59. Beards
60. Pet owners

Reading-Related Topics

"Maslow's Classification of Motives"

1. Write a paragraph or an essay in which you take one of Maslow's classes, such as "love needs" or "safety needs" and classify it at another level. You may use some of the stated subclasses. For example, "love needs" is already broken down into parts: "to belong, to be wanted, and to be loved."

"Listen Up!"

2. Using this paragraph as a model, write a classification of speakers or thinkers.

"Kinds of Book Owners"

3. Using this as a model, write about kinds of CD owners, pet owners, musical instrument owners, tool owners, or owners of art.

"Kinds of Scientific Findings"

4. In an extended classification, apply this to a body of subject material you have worked with in a science class.

"Why We Carp and Harp"

5. Pick one of the classes of naggers, and in a piece of writing show how the category can be divided into subclasses.

6. Write a paper in which you classify those who are nagged (the naggees).

"Musical Instruments: Blowing, Bowing, and Beating"

7. Write a paper in which you classify instruments according to how difficult they are to play.

8. Write a paper in which you classify instruments in terms of the moods they induce: warlike, romantic, nostalgic, excited, anxious, peaceful.

"Types of Nightclubbers"

9. Pick one of the types of nightclubber, such as the "scammers," and develop a set of classes based on the principle of techniques, appearance, or age.

"Three Types of Siblings"

10. Using this paragraph as a model, write about types of fathers, mothers, parents, or grandparents.

"Types of Fly Fighters"

11. Write a paper in which you classify other ways of combating bothersome insects, such as ants, mosquitoes, or cockroaches.

 **Writer's Checklist**

Apply the following ideas to your writing as you work with **DCODE**. Later, as a peer editor, apply the same ideas to the material you evaluate.

1. Clearly define your subject (what you are classifying) and consider your purpose (to inform or to persuade).

2. Classify your material on the basis of one principle. For example, if you classify community college students as vocational, academic, specialty, and serious, you would be mixing principles because the first three are based on main concerns and the last is based on attitude.

3. Consider whether you need subclasses. If you do, clearly distinguish the different levels.

4. Remember that the **Delve** stage of **DCODE** helps you find the principle, the **Concentrate** stage provides your topic sentence or thesis, and the **Organize** stage (with the outline and/or cluster) provides the classes, support, and sequence.

5. Avoid an unimaginative pattern, such as "good-average-bad" and "fast-medium-slow."

 **Journal-Entry Suggestions**

1. Select some of the unused "Reading-Related Topics" suggestions, and use them for journal topics.

2. Write a reaction to one or more "Reading Connection" selections. Agree, disagree, apply the statements to your own experiences, indicate the value of such statements, or explain why your were surprised, shocked, disgusted, pleased, or whatever, by the material.

3. Invent statements (using classification if appropriate) to support headlines from *Weekly World News*:

    "Noah's Ark Found in Pennsylvania!"
    "Kitty Survives Being Sucked into Vacuum Cleaner!"
    "Elvis' Ghost Is Spooking My Cows!"
    "Son's Pet Tarantula Saves Mom from Rapist!"
    "Newborn Baby Speaks in Morse Code!"
    "Blind Preacher Reads with His Glass Eye!"
    "Space Aliens Are Stupid!"
    "Waterskiing Squirrel Run Over by Toy Boat!"
    "Farmer Raises Giant Hamsters—3 Feet Tall!"
    "Two Villages Wiped Out by Giant Killer Snails!"

WORKSHEET
Writing in DCODE

NAME:_____

SECTION:_____ CHAPTER:_____ DATE:_____

Delve   Generate your topic, or ideas for your topic, by delving into your subject area through:

- *Freewriting*—writing sentence after sentence, nonstop and spontaneously.
- *Brainstorming*—jotting down answers to Who? What? Where? When? Why? and How? and then listing words and phrases in relation to those answers.
- *Clustering*—connecting bubbled ideas with lines to show strings of relationships, producing each new bubble item in response to the question, What comes to mind?
- *Combining* any of these approaches, as directed by your instructor.

WORKSHEET: Writing in DCODE

Concentrate   Concentrate your work by stating your topic in one sentence that is not too broad, narrow, or vague to be developed. Base this sentence (which may become the topic sentence for your paragraph or the thesis for your essay) on an idea emerging from the **Delve** stage. You may have to try several statements here before you formulate one that is best for your writing task. Be sure that your final statement covers your assignment or intent and specifies both your subject (what you are writing about) and treatment (what aspect you will focus on). Label the *subject* and *treatment* parts.

Organize   Complete an outline or a cluster, as directed by your instructor. The cluster should be a section from, or a refined version of, the **Delve** clustering. Regardless of the strategy you use, the organizational pattern should indicate a division of your topic into parts that will, in turn, be further subdivided for support as necessary to address a particular audience on your concentrated topic.

Draft   On separate paper, write and then revise your assignment as many times as necessary for **c**oherence, **l**anguage (usage, tone, and diction), **u**nity, **e**mphasis, **s**upport, and **s**entence structure (**cluess**).

Edit   Correct problems in fundamentals such as **c**apitalization, **o**missions, **p**unctuation, and **s**pelling (**cops**). Before writing the final draft, read your paper aloud to discover oversights and awkwardness of expression.

Comparison and Contrast: Showing Similarities and Dissimilarities

10

> My first draft usually has only a few elements worth keeping. I have to find what they are and build from them and throw out what doesn't work.
> — Susan Sontag

"Gee, Francine. You eat like a bird."

What are the two purposes of comparison and contrast?
What are the "4 P's" of writing comparison and contrast?
What is a good way of discovering points to apply to the two sides?
What are two patterns of comparison and contrast? What is an analogy?

Comparison and Contrast Defined

Comparison and contrast is a method of showing similarities and dissimilarities between subjects. *Comparison* is concerned with organizing and developing points of similarity, *contrast* has the same function for dissimilarity. In some instances a writing assignment may require that you cover only similarities or only dissimilarities. Occasionally, an instructor may ask you to separate one from the other. Usually, you will combine them within the larger design of your paragraph or essay. For convenience, the term *comparison* is often applied to both comparison and contrast, because both utilize the same techniques and are usually combined into one operation.

This chapter will help you deal with topics and choose strategies in writing comparison and contrast.

Generating Topics and Working with the 4 P's

Comparison and contrast is basic to your thinking. In your daily activities, you consider similarities and dissimilarities between persons, things, concepts, political leaders, doctors, friends, instructors, schools, nations, classes, movies, and so on. You naturally turn to comparison and contrast to solve problems and make decisions in your affairs and in your writing. Because you have had so many comparative experiences, finding a topic to write about is likely to be only a matter of choosing from a great number of appealing ideas. Freewriting, brainstorming, and clustering will help you generate topics that are especially workable and appropriate for particular assignments.

Many college writing assignments will specify a topic or ask you to choose one from a list. Regardless of the source of your topic, the procedure for developing your ideas by comparison and contrast is the same. That procedure can be appropriately called the "4 P's": *purpose, points, pattern,* and *presentation*.

Purpose

Two kinds of purposes exist: informative and persuasive.

Informative

If you want to explain something about a topic by showing each subject in relationship with the other, then your purpose will be informative. For example, you might be comparing two composers, Beethoven and Mozart. Both were musical geniuses, so you might decide that it would be senseless to argue that the work of one is superior to the other. Instead, you choose to reveal interesting information about both by showing them in relation to each other. The emphasis of your writing would be on insights into their characteristics, heightened by these characteristics' being placed alongside each other.

Persuasive

If you want to show that one actor, one movie, one writer, one president, one product, or one idea is better than another, your purpose will be persuasive. It will take shape as you write, beginning with emphasis in the topic sentence or thesis and being reinforced by repetition throughout your paper, in each case indicating that one side is superior.

Let's say for sake of an extended illustration that you are taking a course in twentieth-century European history and you are asked to write about two leaders. You have always been fascinated by the dictators Mussolini and Hitler, and you decide to pursue that as a topic. In freewriting, you discover that you know quite a bit about the two leaders. By brainstorming you come up with some specific information about the two.

Who? Mussolini and Hitler

What? fascist leaders, racists—with Hitler being more extreme

Where? in Italy and Germany, respectively

When? the decade before and during World War II

Why? greed, morals, possible psychological problems, with Hitler being more extreme

How? setting up totalitarian states

You tentatively decide that your purpose will be to persuade readers that, although both men were fascists, Hitler was more extreme in all important respects. If you need more information, you will have to consult your textbooks, your lecture notes, or sources in the library.

Points

The points are the ideas that will be applied somewhat equally to both sides of your comparison and contrast. They begin to emerge in freewriting, take on more precision in brainstorming, acquire a main position in further brainstorming, and assume the major part of the framework in the outline.

Especially when writing on an assigned topic based on lectures and reading, you will be able to decide on these points quickly. The subject material itself may dictate the points. For example, if you were comparing the federal governments of the United States and Great Britain, you would probably use these three points: executive, legislative, and judicial.

Using Clustering as a Technique for Finding Points

If you need to search for points (ideas that will be applied to both sides in your comparative study), the next **Delve** strategy, clustering, can serve you well. You might want to try this approach:

Step 1: Begin your first cluster on the left side of a page in which you double-bubble the side of the comparison you know better, and then to the right of that add bubbles for points based on your tentative purpose. For the second bubble in each chain, add a particular fact about the point.

Step 2: Repeat Step 1 for the second cluster. Draw this one on the right side of the page, and develop the bubbles to the left, making the ideas parallel to those in the first cluster.

Step 3: Add other divisions as they occur to you.

Step 4: Select the divisions that will serve you best in developing your tentative thesis or topic sentence, and connect those points from the two sides with double lines.

See Figure 10.1 for an example of a cluster on the Mussolini-Hitler topic.

FIGURE 10.1 Sample Cluster on the Mussolini-Hitler Topic

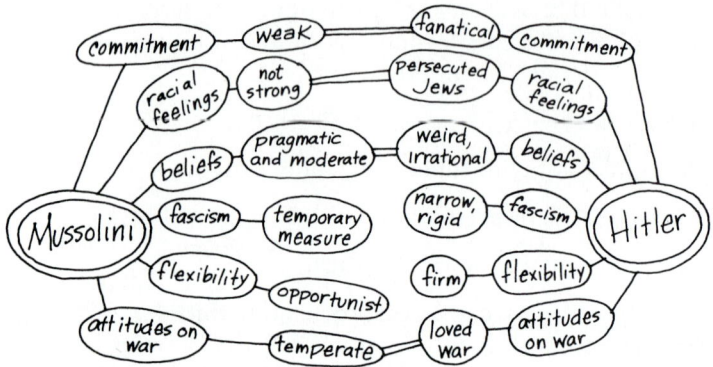

With this much organized information, you are ready to decide if you wish to modify the tentative topic sentence or thesis that has directed your use of the first three strategies.

In this instance, the information supports your controlling idea, which you can then enter in the **Concentrate** section of your **DCODE** Writing Worksheet:

Topic sentence or thesis:
Although Mussolini and Hitler were both fascist dictators, they were also significantly different, and Hitler was more extreme.

At this time you have a purpose and points. The final preparation stage, **Organize**, will help you select and develop a pattern for your comparison.

Pattern

Now you will choose between two basic patterns of organization: (1) subject by subject (opposing) or (2) point by point (alternating). In long papers you may mix them, but in the shorter pieces associated with most college assignments, you will almost certainly select one and make it your basic organizational plan.

In comparison and contrast, the outline works especially well in indicating relationships and sequence. As with most other writing forms we have worked with, the sequence of a comparison-and-contrast essay can be based on time, space, or emphasis. Emphasis is the most likely order.

The following illustrations will show you the two patterns as they are applied to both the paragraph (on the left) and the essay (on the right).

In the *subject-by-subject* approach, organize your material around the subjects—the sides of the comparative study, as shown in Figure 10.2.

FIGURE 10.2 Subject-by-Subject Organization

For Paragraph

Topic sentence
I. Mussolini
    A. Nature of beliefs
    B. Racial views
    C. Commitment
    D. Militaristic designs
II. Hitler
    A. Nature of beliefs
    B. Racial views
    C. Commitment
    D. Militaristic designs

For Essay

Introduction with thesis
I. Mussolini
    A. Nature of beliefs
    B. Racial views
    C. Commitment
    D. Militaristic designs
II. Hitler
    A. Nature of beliefs
    B. Racial views
    C. Commitment
    D. Militaristic designs
Conclusion

In the *point-by-point approach,* organize your paper mainly around the points that you will apply to the two subjects as shown in Figure 10.3.

FIGURE 10.3 Point-by-Point Organization

For Paragraph

Topic sentence
I. Nature of beliefs
    A. Mussolini
    B. Hitler
II. Racial views
    A. Mussolini
    B. Hitler
III. Commitment
    A. Mussolini
    B. Hitler
IV. Militaristic designs
    A. Mussolini
    B. Hitler

For Essay

Introduction with thesis
I. Nature of beliefs
    A. Mussolini
    B. Hitler
II. Racial views
    A. Mussolini
    B. Hitler
III. Commitment
    A. Mussolini
    B. Hitler
IV. Militaristic designs
    A. Mussolini
    B. Hitler
Conclusion

Presentation

The two patterns of organization—subject by subject and point by point—are equally valid, and each has its strengths for presentation of ideas.

As shown in Figure 10.2, the subject-by-subject pattern presents material in large blocks, which means the reader can see a body of material that is complete. However, if the body of material is complex, the reader has the burden of remembering ideas in going from one part to the next. Parallel development of ideas and cross-references in the second portion of the paragraph or essay can often offset that potential problem.

The point-by-point pattern shown in Figure 10.3 provides an immediate and direct relationship of points to subject. Therefore, it is especially useful in arguing that one side is superior to the other, in dealing with complex topics, and in working with longer compositions. But because of its direct applications, if development is not sufficient, it can appear mechanical and monotonous. You can avoid that appearance by developing each idea thoroughly.

Of the two patterns of development, the point-by-point is used more frequently in college writing assignments in both the paragraph and the essay forms.

In the following examples, the topic of Mussolini and Hitler is presented first in the final draft stage of the paragraph form and then in the essay form. Note that the paragraph (often, as here, the essay in miniature) is expanded into an essay by developing the topic sentence, the supporting points, and the restated topic sentence into separate paragraphs: introduction, middle paragraph, middle paragraph, middle paragraph, middle paragraph, and conclusion. Although both the paragraph and the essay make good observations and illustrate the use of pattern for presentation, for this topic the full essay would probably be more suitable in fulfilling the writer's purpose. Both the paragraph and the essay use a point-by-point arrangement.

Here is the paragraph:

Hitler and Mussolini have often been thought of as twin dictators, but there was considerable difference between the two men and their regimes, and Hitler was more extreme.	topic sentence
Both were fascists; however, the intensity of their beliefs	point 1: beliefs
varied. Until he fell under the influence of Hitler, Mussolini had tended to be pragmatic and often moderate. Hitler, *on*	transition
the contrary, carved out a series of weird, nihilistic goals near the beginning of his career and held to them unswervingly.	
Racism is justly associated with all fascism at that time, and,	point 2: racism
therefore, Mussolini is implicated. It should be pointed out,	transition
however, that the blatant racism by the Italians occurred after Mussolini's deep association with Hitler. *But* Hitler had held racist views from the beginning of his political movement, and it was a main motive in the Nazi movement.	
Their degree of commitment to act also varied. Mussolini	point 3: commitment
merely talked and strutted for the most part. He had few fixed doctrines and increasingly accommodated himself to	transition
circumstances. *But* Hitler meant every bit of his bellicosity, and was willing to wage the most frightful war of all time. A	
study of their involvement in that war, however, reveals	point 4: militaristic designs
striking dissimilarities. Italian fascism was comparatively restrained and conservative until the Nazi example spurred	transition
it to new activity. *In contrast*, the radical and dynamic pace of Hitler hardly flagged from January 1933 to April 1945. In the process, anti-Semitism, concentration camps, and total war produced a febrile and sadistic nightmare without any parallel in the Italian experience. Though both were fascist,	

history shows them to be different in all of these respects, and in each one Hitler was more radical.

restated topic sentence

Here is the essay:

> Hitler and Mussolini have often been thought of as twin dictators, but there were considerable differences between the two men and their regimes, and Hitler was more extreme. These differences become apparent when one considers the nature of their beliefs, their racial views, their commitment, and their militaristic designs.
>
> Both were fascists; however, the intensity of their beliefs varied. Until he fell under the influence of Hitler, Mussolini had tended to be pragmatic and often moderate. Though Italian fascism coined the concept of "totalitarianism," it allowed some nonfascist elements to enjoy partial liberty and never achieved a true totalitarian state. Hitler, on the contrary, carved out a series of weird, nihilistic goals near the beginning of his career and held to them unswervingly. Though he often showed a fine sense of tactics and timing, he was not so pragmatic and adjustable as Mussolini, but was bent on fixed, narrow ends. He was sexually perverted and his mind betrayed the marks of severe compulsive neurosis and emotional instability, conceiving irrational hatreds and enthusiasms of a thoroughly demonic nature which he was determined to see through to the end.
>
> Racism is justly associated with all fascism at that time, and, therefore, Mussolini, along with Hitler, is implicated. It should be pointed out, however, that the blatant racism by the Italians occurred after Mussolini's deep association with Hitler. Prior to that, for many years there had been no racial doctrine in Italian fascist ideology. But Hitler had held racist views from the beginning of his political movement, and it was a main motive in the Nazi movement. To resolve the "Jewish problem," he eventually slaughtered at least five million people.
>
> Their degree of commitment to act also varied. From a distance toward the end of the war, they may have seemed quite similar, but over the span of their reigns, they were different. Mussolini merely talked and strutted for the most part. He had few fixed doctrines and increasingly accommodated himself to circumstances. But Hitler meant every bit of his bellicosity, and was willing to wage the most frightful war of all time.
>
> A study of their involvement in that war, however, reveals striking dissimilarities. Italian fascism was comparatively restrained and conservative until the Nazi example spurred it to new activity. Mussolini talked of a militaristic policy, while he followed a more temperate course in practice and kept the peace for thirteen years, knowing that Italy could not gain from a major war. In contrast, the radical and dynamic pace of Hitler hardly flagged from January 1933 to April 1945. In the process, anti-Semitism, concentration camps, and total war produced a febrile and sadistic nightmare without any parallel in the Italian experience.
>
> Thus, though both were fascist, history shows them to be different in both ideas and action. Only at the end of their relationship, when Mussolini succumbed to Hitler's domination, do the two leaders appear as twin dictators, but beneath those appearances it is Hitler who is the pure true believer, the fascist dictator.

introduction with thesis

topic sentence

(middle paragraph)

topic sentence

(middle paragraph)

topic sentence

(middle paragraph)

topic sentence

(middle paragraph)

conclusion

Analogy

Analogy is a method of organizing and developing ideas by comparison. In an analogy, a writer explains or clarifies an unfamiliar subject by likening it to a familiar but strikingly different subject. Writers use analogy to make the new, different, complex, or difficult more understandable for the reader. Analogy, therefore, explains, clarifies, illustrates, and simplifies; it does not prove anything.

In the model analogy below, Emerson compares society to a wave. Most analogies, like this model, are part of a larger piece of writing.

> Society is a wave. The wave moves onward, but the water of which it is composed does not. The same particle does not rise from the valley to the ridge. Its unity is only phenomenal. The persons who make up a nation to-day, next year die, and their experience dies with them.

Ralph Waldo Emerson, "Self-Reliance"

Writers usually announce the analogy and then develop it. In addition, analogies, as a rule, rise spontaneously from the material as the writer's thoughts flow onward. Study the following model. Notice that the writer announces the comparison in the first sentence. To make the meaning clear, he compares the atmosphere of the earth to any window.

> The atmosphere of Earth acts like any window in serving two very important functions. It lets light in and it permits us to look out. It also serves as a shield to keep out dangerous or uncomfortable things. A normal glazed window lets us keep our houses warm by keeping out cold air, and it prevents rain, dirt, and unwelcome insects and animals from coming in. As we have already seen, Earth's atmospheric window also helps to keep our planet at a comfortable temperature by holding back radiated heat and protecting us from dangerous levels of ultraviolet light.
>
> Lately, we have discovered that space is full of a great many very dangerous things against which our atmosphere guards us. It is not a perfect shield, and sometimes one of these dangerous objects does get through. There is even some evidence that a few of these messengers from space contain life, though this has by no means been proved yet.

Lester Del Rey, *The Mysterious Sky*

The steps for writing the analogy are identical to those of comparison and contrast.

EXERCISE 1

Read the following model paragraph and answer the questions that follow.

Heavenly Father, Divine Goalie
CHARLES PREBISH

In *How We Play the Game*, Richard Lipsky tells us (of baseball), "The game takes place in an atmosphere of piety. In many ways the ballplayers themselves can be seen as priests who represent us in a liturgy (game) that is part of a sacred tradition." Lipsky's comment reveals that far too little has been said about the role of the player in sport religion. In other words, we need to reflect on the actors in sport religion. It would be incorrect, though, to suggest that it is only the actual players who fulfill the role of religious participants in sport. We must include the coaches and officials as well, in their role as functionaries in the religious process. They are not untrained, either. Sport, no doubt, has its own seminaries and divinity schools in the various minor leagues and training camps that school the participants in all aspects of the tradition, from theology to ritual. The spectators, as video viewers, radio listeners, or game-going die-hards, form the congregation of sport religion. Their attendance is not required for all religious observances, but they do attend at specified times to share in religious rites. And they bear the religious symbols of their faith: the pennants, emblems, hats, coats, gloves, and whatever other objects the media geniuses can promote to signify the glory of sport in general and the home team in particular. The sport symbol may not be the cross, rosary, mezuzah, but it is no less valuable to the owner, and likely considered to be just as powerful as its traditional counterpart, or more so.

APPLICATIONS FOR CRITICAL READING AND DISCUSSION

1. What is the basis of the analogy?

2. What are the points (there may be only one) in this study? State them here, and underline them in the selection.

Suggested Topics for Writing Analogy

1. Riding the merry-go-round and dating
2. Juggling and paying bills
3. Driving on the freeway and pursuing a career
4. Going fishing and looking for a job
5. Shopping in a supermarket and getting an education

6. Caring for a child and for a dog
7. Driving in traffic and fighting on a battlefield
8. Sleeping and watching television
9. Learning a new culture from an immigrant's viewpoint and learning an environment from an infant's viewpoint
10. Looking for Elvis and looking for truth (or the Holy Grail, an honest person, a unicorn, the Loch Ness monster, Bigfoot, or the Abominable Snowman)

 **The Reading Connection**

EXERCISE 2

Demonstration

We all know that life in nature is struggle. Here, famed literary critic, philosopher, and naturalist Joseph Wood Krutch shows that the struggle in nature has different combatants in different habitats.

The Desert and the Jungle
JOSEPH WOOD KRUTCH

The way of the desert and the way of the jungle represent the two opposite methods of reaching stability at two extremes of density. In the jungle there is plenty of everything life needs except mere *space,* and it is not for want of anything else that individuals die or that races have any limit set to their proliferation. Everything is on top of everything else; there is no cranny which is not both occupied and disputed. At every moment, *war* to the death rages fiercely. The place left vacant by any creature that dies is seized almost instantly by another, and life seems to suffer from nothing except too favorable an environment. In the desert, on the other hand, it is the *environment* itself which serves as the limiting factor. To some extent the *struggle* of creature against creature is mitigated, though it is of course not abolished even in the vegetable kingdom. For the plant which in the one place would be strangled to death by its neighbor dies a thirsty seedling in the desert because that same neighbor has drawn the scant moisture from the spot of earth out of which it was attempting to spring.

APPLICATIONS FOR CRITICAL READING AND DISCUSSION

1. Does this selection stress comparison or contrast?
    contrast

2. Is the purpose mainly to inform or to persuade?
    inform

3. What are the points (there may be only one) in this study? State them here, and underline them in the selection. *genders - condition*

4. Is the pattern mainly subject-by-subject or (point-by-point)? Make a simple outline of the pattern here.

   Brings out different in subject.

EXERCISE 4

Buildings do more than serve as shelter and objects of beauty. They also reflect a society's values and aspirations. Louise Dudley and Austin Faricy show that it is not a matter of chance that the Greek temple and the medieval cathedral have certain characteristics.

The Temple and the Cathedral
LOUISE DUDLEY AND AUSTIN FARICY

The Greek temple is classic and the medieval cathedral is romantic. Both are religious edifices, but they show a difference in the attitudes that created them, a difference far deeper than the dissimilarities of construction and mechanics. The Greek temple is hard, bright, exact, calm and complete; the walls and the columns are no higher than will stand of their own strength; the lintels and the roof are simple, sane, and sensible. Nothing more is attempted than can be accomplished, and the result is a perfect building, finished and finite. Anyone can understand its main construction at a glance. The Gothic cathedral, on the other hand, is built on the principle of balance. The openings are not made with lintels but are arched. One stone is held in place only by its relation to the other stones. The walls will not stand alone; they must be buttressed. As the walls go higher the arches become more pointed, the roof becomes steeper, and the buttresses are strengthened with pinnacles and flying buttresses, the whole so carefully and cleverly balanced that a fault in one stone might cause a wall or even the entire building to collapse. The whole cannot be grasped at a glance; one is conscious only of its great complexity, its infinite variety, its striving upward and beyond.

APPLICATIONS FOR CRITICAL READING AND DISCUSSION

1. Does this selection stress (comparison) or contrast?

2. Is the purpose mainly to inform or to (persuade)?

3. What are the points (there may be only one) in this study? State them here, and underline them in the selection.

   ```
   Life is a struggle for or with space.
   ```

4. Is the pattern mainly subject-by-subject or point-by-point? Make a simple outline of the pattern here.
   ```
   Subject-by-Subject
   I.  Jungle
       A. Space     } Points about the subject.
       B. Struggle
   II. Desert
       A. Space
       B. Struggle
   ```

EXERCISE 3

What are the sources of gender identity? In this passage from her book *The Language of Clothes,* Alison Lurie shows that people condition children from birth.

Pink Kittens and Blue Spaceships
ALISON LURIE

Sex-typing in dress begins at birth with the assignment of pale-pink layettes, toys, bedding and furniture to girl babies, and pale-blue ones to boy babies. Pink, in this culture, is associated with sentiment; blue with service. The implication is that the little girl's future concern will be the life of the affections; the boy's, earning a living. As they grow older, light blue becomes a popular color for girls' clothes—after all, women must work as well as weep—but pink is rare on boys: the emotional life is never quite manly.

2   In early childhood girls' and boys' clothes are often identical in cut and fabric, as if in recognition of the fact that their bodies are much alike. But the T-shirts, pull-on slacks and zip jackets intended for boys are usually made in darker colors (especially forest green, navy, red and brown) and printed with designs involving sports, transportation and cute wild animals. Girls' clothes are made in paler colors (especially pink, yellow and green) and decorated with flowers and cute domestic animals. The suggestion is that the boy will play vigorously and travel over long distances; the girl will stay home and nurture plants and small mammals. Alternatively, these designs may symbolize their wearers: the boy is a cuddly bear or a smiling tiger, the girl a flower or a kitten. There is also a tendency for boys' clothes to be fullest at the shoulders and girls' at the hips, anticipating their adult figures. Boys' and men's garments also emphasize the shoulders with horizontal stripes, epaulets or yokes of contrasting color. Girls' and women's garments emphasize the hips and rear through the strategic placement of gathers and trimmings.

APPLICATIONS FOR CRITICAL READING AND DISCUSSION

1. Does this selection stress comparison or contrast?

2. Is the purpose mainly to inform or to persuade?

   inform

3. What are the points (there may be only one) in this study? State them here, and underline them in the selection.

4. Is the pattern mainly (subject by subject) or point by point? Make a simple outline of the pattern here.

EXERCISE 5

The Natural Superiority of Women
ASHLEY MONTAGU

Physically and psychically women are by far the superior of men. The old chestnut about women being more emotional than men has been forever destroyed by the facts of two great wars. Women under blockade, heavy bombardment, concentration camp confinement, and similar rigors withstand them vastly more successfully than men. The psychiatric casualties of civilian populations under such conditions are mostly masculine, and there are far more men in our mental hospitals than there are women. The steady hand at the helm is the hand that has had the practice at rocking the cradle. Because of their greater size and weight, men are physically more powerful than women—which is not the same thing as saying that they are stronger. A man of the same size and weight as a woman of comparable background and occupational status would probably not be any more powerful than a woman. As far as constitutional strength is concerned, women are stronger than men. Many diseases from which men suffer can be shown to be largely influenced by their relation to the male Y-chromosome. More males die than females. Deaths from almost all causes are more frequent in males of all ages. Though women are more frequently ill than men, they recover from illnesses more easily and more frequently than men.

APPLICATIONS FOR CRITICAL READING AND DISCUSSION

1. Does this selection stress comparison or contrast?

2. Is the purpose mainly to inform or to persuade?

3. What are the points (there may be only one) in this study? State them here, and underline them in the selection.

4. Is the pattern mainly subject by subject or point by point? Make a simple outline of the pattern here.

EXERCISE 6

In this essay from her book *Show and Tell,* Suzanne Britt discusses two kinds of people: the neat and the sloppy. Wouldn't the world be a better place if we were all a bit neater? If you think so, prepare to argue with Suzanne Britt.

Vocabulary Preview: Write in short definitions for these words as they are used in the context of the following passage. (The paragraph numbers are given in parentheses.) Be prepared to use the words in your own sentences.

rectitude (2)

stupendous (2)

métier (3)

tentative (3)

excavation (5)

meticulously (5)

scrupulously (5)

cavalier (6)

heirlooms (6)

swath (12)

Neat People Vs. Sloppy People
SUZANNE BRITT

1 I've finally figured out the difference between neat people and sloppy people. The distinction is, as always, moral. Neat people are lazier and meaner than sloppy people.

2 Sloppy people, you see, are not really sloppy. Their sloppiness is merely the unfortunate consequence of their extreme moral rectitude. Sloppy people carry in their mind's eye a heavenly vision, a precise plan, that is so stupendous, so perfect, it can't be achieved in this world or the next.

3 Sloppy people live in Never-Never Land. Someday is their métier. Someday they are planning to alphabetize all their books and set up home catalogs. Someday they will go through their wardrobes and mark certain items for tentative mending and certain items for passing on to relatives of similar shape and size. Someday sloppy people will make family scrapbooks into which they will put newspaper clippings, postcards, locks of hair, and the dried corsage from their senior prom. Someday they will file everything on the surface of their desk, including the cash receipts from coffee purchases at the snack shop. Someday they will sit down and read all the back issues of *The New Yorker*.

4 For all these noble reasons and more, sloppy people never get neat. They aim too high and wide. They save everything, planning someday to

file, order, and straighten out the world. But while these ambitious plans take clearer and clearer shape in their heads, the books spill from the shelves onto the floor, the clothes pile up in the hamper and closet, the family mementos accumulate in every drawer, the surface of the desk is buried under mounds of paper and the unread magazines threaten to reach the ceiling.

5 Sloppy people can't bear to part with anything. They give loving attention to every detail. When sloppy people say they're going to tackle the surface of the desk, they really mean it. Not a paper will go unturned; not a rubber band will go unboxed. Four hours or two weeks into the excavation, the desk looks exactly the same, primarily because the sloppy person is meticulously creating new piles of papers with new headings and scrupulously stopping to read all the old book catalogs before he throws them away. A neat person would just bulldoze the desk.

6 Neat people are bums and clods at heart. They have cavalier attitudes toward possessions, including family heirlooms. Everything is just another dust-catcher to them. If anything collects dust, it's got to go and that's that. Neat people will toy with the idea of throwing the children out of the house just to cut down on the clutter.

7 Neat people don't care about process. They like results. What they want to do is get the whole thing over with so they can sit down and watch the rasslin' on TV. Neat people operate on two unvarying principles: Never handle any item twice, and throw everything away.

8 The only thing messy in a neat person's house is the trash can. The minute something comes to a neat person's hand, he will look at it, try to decide if it has immediate use and, finding none, throw it in the trash.

9 Neat people are especially vicious with mail. They never go through their mail unless they are standing directly over a trash can. If the trash can is beside the mailbox, even better. All ads, catalogs, pleas for charitable contributions, church bulletins and money-saving coupons go straight into the trash can without being opened. All letters from home, postcards from Europe, bills and paychecks are opened, immediately responded to, then dropped in the trash can. Neat people keep their receipts only for tax purposes. That's it. No sentimental salvaging of birthday cards or the last letter a dying relative ever wrote. Into the trash it goes.

10 Neat people place neatness above everything, even economics. They are incredibly wasteful. Neat people throw away several toys every time they walk through the den. I knew a neat person once who threw away a perfectly good dish drainer because it had mold on it. The drainer was too much trouble to wash. And neat people sell their furniture when they move. They will sell a La-Z-Boy recliner while you are reclining in it.

11 Neat people are no good to borrow from. Neat people buy everything in expensive little single portions. They get their flour and sugar in two-pound bags. They wouldn't consider clipping a coupon, saving a leftover, reusing plastic non-dairy whipped cream containers or rinsing off tin foil and draping it over the unmoldy dish drainer. You can never borrow a neat person's newspaper to see what's playing at the movies. Neat people have the paper all wadded up and in the trash by 7:05 A.M.

12 Neat people cut a clean swath through the organic as well as the inorganic world. People, animals, and things are all one to them. They are so insensitive. After they've finished with the pantry, the medicine cabinet, and the attic, they will throw out the red geranium (too many leaves), sell the dog (too many fleas), and send the children off to boarding school (too many scuff marks on the hardwood floors).

APPLICATIONS FOR CRITICAL READING AND DISCUSSION

1. Does this selection stress comparison or contrast?

2. Is the purpose mainly to inform or to persuade?

3. What are the points (there may be only one) in this study? State them here, and underline them in the selection.

4. Is the pattern mainly subject by subject or point by point? Make a simple outline of the pattern here.

EXERCISE 7

The title suggests that this essay is about a job search, but it is actually about an identity search. In it, Gary Soto, award winning writer and university professor, tells of his attempts to place himself among the different kinds of people of his childhood. This passage is from Soto's *Living up the Street* (1985).

Vocabulary Preview: Write in short definitions for these words as they are used in the context of the following passage. (The paragraph numbers are given in parentheses.) Be prepared to use them in your own sentences.

mimicked (2)

muu-muu (5)

contagious (10)

feigned (12)

chavalo (25)

Looking for Work
GARY SOTO

One July, while killing ants on the kitchen sink with a rolled newspaper, I had a nine-year-old's vision of wealth that would save us from ourselves. For weeks I had drunk Kool-Aid and watched morning reruns of *Father Knows Best*, whose family was so uncomplicated in its routine that I very much wanted to imitate it. The first step was to get my brother and sister to wear shoes at dinner.

2 "Come on, Rick—come on, Deb," I whined. But Rick mimicked me and the same day that I asked him to wear shoes he came to the dinner table in only his swim trunks. My mother didn't notice, nor did my sister, as we sat to eat our beans and tortillas in the stifling heat of our kitchen. We all gleamed like cellophane, wiping the sweat from our brows with the backs of our hands as we talked about the day: Frankie our neighbor was beat up by Faustino; the swimming pool at the playground would be closed for a day because the pump was broken.

3 Such was our life. So that morning, while doing-in the train of ants which arrived each day, I decided to become wealthy, and right away! After downing a bowl of cereal, I took a rake from the garage and started up the block to look for work.

4 We lived on an ordinary block of mostly working class people: warehousemen, egg candlers, welders, mechanics, and a union plumber. And

there were many retired people who kept their lawns green and the gutters uncluttered of the chewing gum wrappers we dropped as we rode by on our bikes. They bent down to gather our litter, muttering at our evilness.

5   At the corner house I rapped the screen door and a very large woman in a muu-muu answered. She sized me up and then asked what I could do.

6   "Rake leaves," I answered, smiling.

7   "It's summer, and there ain't no leaves," she countered. Her face was pinched with lines; fat jiggled under her chin. She pointed to the lawn, then the flower bed, and said: "You see any leaves there—or there?" I followed her pointing arm, stupidly. But she had a job for me and that was to get her a Coke at the liquor store. She gave me twenty cents, and after ditching my rake in a bush, off I ran. I returned with an unbagged Pepsi, for which she thanked me and gave me a nickel from her apron.

8   I skipped off her porch, fetched my rake, and crossed the street to the next block where Mrs. Moore, mother of Earl the retarded man, let me weed a flower bed. She handed me a trowel and for a good part of the morning my fingers dipped into the moist dirt, ripping up runners of Bermuda grass. Worms surfaced in my search for deep roots, and I cut them in halves, tossing them to Mrs. Moore's cat who pawed them playfully as they dried in the sun. I made out Earl whose face was pressed to the back window of the house, and although he was calling to me I couldn't understand what he was trying to say. Embarrassed, I worked without looking up, but I imagined his contorted mouth and the ring of keys attached to his belt—keys that jingled with each palsied step. He scared me and I worked quickly to finish the flower bed. When I did finish Mrs. Moore gave me a quarter and two peaches from her tree, which I washed there but ate in the alley behind my house.

9   I was sucking on the second one, a bit of juice staining the front of my T-shirt, when Little John, my best friend, came walking down the alley with a baseball bat over his shoulder, knocking over trash cans as he made his way toward me.

10 Little John and I went to St. John's Catholic School, where we sat among the "stupids." Miss Marino, our teacher, alternated the rows of good students with the bad, hoping that by sitting side-by-side with the bright students the stupids might become more intelligent, as though intelligence were contagious. But we didn't progress as she had hoped. She grew frustrated when one day, while dismissing class for recess, Little John couldn't get up because his arms were stuck in the slats of the chair's backrest. She scolded us with a shaking finger when we knocked over the globe, denting the already troubled Africa. She muttered curses when Leroy White, a real stupid but a great softball player with the gift to hit to all fields, openly chewed his host when he made his First Communion; his hands swung at his sides as he returned to the pew looking around with a big smile.

11 Little John asked what I was doing, and I told him that I was taking a break from work, as I sat comfortably among high weeds. He wanted to join me, but I reminded him that the last time he'd gone door-to-door asking for work his mother had whipped him. I was with him when his mother, a New Jersey Italian who could rise up in anger one moment and love the next, told me in a polite but matter-of-fact voice that I had to leave because she was going to beat her son. She gave me a homemade popsicle, ushered me to the door, and said that I could see Little John the next day. But it was sooner than that. I went around to his bedroom window to suck my popsicle and watch Little John dodge his mother's blows, a few hitting their mark but many whirring air.

12 It was midday when Little John and I converged in the alley, the sun blazing in the high nineties, and he suggested that we go to Roosevelt High School to swim. He needed five cents to make fifteen, the cost of admission, and I lent him a nickel. We ran home for my bike and when my sister found out that we were going swimming she started to cry because she didn't have the fifteen cents but only an empty Coke bottle. I waved for her to come and three of us mounted the bike—Debra on the cross bar, Little John on the handle bars and holding the Coke bottle which we would cash for a nickel and make up the difference that would allow all of us to get in, and me pumping up the crooked streets, dodging cars and pot holes. We spent the day swimming under the afternoon sun, so that when we got home our mom asked us what was darker, the floor or us? She feigned a stern posture, her hands on her hips and her mouth puckered. We played along. Looking down, Debbie and I said in unison, "Us."

13   That evening at dinner we all sat down in our bathing suits to eat our beans, laughing and chewing loudly. Our mom was in a good mood, so I took a risk and asked her if sometime we could have turtle soup. A few days before I had watched a television program in which a Polynesian tribe killed a large turtle, gutted it, and then stewed it over an open fire. The turtle, basted in a sugary sauce, looked delicious as I ate an afternoon bowl of cereal, but my sister, who was watching the program with a glass of Kool-Aid between her knees, said "Caca."

14   My mother looked at me in bewilderment. "Boy, are you a crazy Mexican. Where did you get the idea that people eat turtles?"

15   "On television," I said, explaining the program. Then I took it a step further. "Mom, do you think we could get dressed up for dinner one of these days? David King does."

16   "*Ay, Dios,*" my mother laughed. She started collecting the dinner plates, but my brother wouldn't let go of his. He was still drawing a picture in the bean sauce. Giggling, he said it was me, but I didn't want to listen because I wanted an answer from Mom. This was the summer when I spent the mornings in front of the television that showed the comfortable lives of white kids. There were no beatings, no rifts in the family. They wore bright clothes; toys tumbled from their closets. They hopped into bed with kisses and woke to glasses of fresh orange juice, and to a father sitting before his morning coffee while the mother buttered his toast. They hurried through the day making friends and gobs of money, returning home to a warmly lit living room, and then dinner. *Leave It to Beaver* was the program I replayed in my mind:

17   "May I have the mashed potatoes?" asks Beaver with a smile.

18   "Sure, Beav," replies Wally as he taps the corners of his mouth with a starched napkin.

19   The father looks on in his suit. The mother, decked out in earrings and a pearl necklace, cuts into her steak and blushes. Their conversation is politely clipped.

20   "Swell," says Beaver, his cheeks puffed with food.

21   Our own talk at dinner was loud with belly laughs and marked by our pointing forks at one another. The subjects were commonplace.

22   "Gary, let's go to the ditch tomorrow," my brother suggests. He explains that he has made a life preserver out of four empty detergent bottles strung together with twine and that he will make me one if I can find more bottles. "No way are we going to drown."

23   "Yeah, then we could have a dirt clod fight," I reply, so happy to be alive.

24   Whereas the Beaver's family enjoyed dessert in dishes at the table, our mom sent us outside, and more often than not I went into the alley to peek over the neighbor's fences and spy out fruit, apricots or peaches.

25   I had asked my mom and again she laughed that I was a crazy *chavalo* as she stood in front of the sink, her arms rising and falling with suds, face glistening from the heat. She sent me outside where my brother and sister were sitting in the shade that the fence threw out like a blanket. They were talking about me when I plopped down next to them. They looked at one another and then Debbie, my eight-year-old sister, started in.

26   "What's this crap about getting dressed up?"

27   She had entered her profanity stage. A year later she would give up such words and slip into her Catholic uniform, and into squealing on my brother and me when we "cussed this" and "cussed that."

28   I tried to convince them that if we improved the way we looked we might get along better in life. White people would like us more. They might invite us to places, like their homes or front yards. They might not hate us so much.

29   My sister called me a "craphead," and got up to leave with a stalk of grass dangling from her mouth. "They'll never like us."

30   My brother's mood lightened as he talked about the ditch—the white water, the broken pieces of glass, and the rusted car fenders that awaited our knees. There would be toads, and rocks to smash them.

31   David King, the only person we knew who resembled the middle class, called from over the fence. David was Catholic, of Armenian and French descent, and his closet was filled with toys. A bear-shaped cookie jar, like the ones on television, sat on the kitchen counter. His mother was remarkably kind while she put up with the racket we made on the street. Evenings, she often watered the front yard and it must have upset her

to see us—my brother and I and others—jump from trees laughing, the unkillable kids of the very poor, who got up unshaken, brushed off, and climbed into another one to try again.

32 David called again. Rick got up and slapped grass from his pants. When I asked if I could come along he said no. David said no. They were two years older so their affairs were different from mine. They greeted one another with foul names and took off down the alley to look for trouble.

33 I went inside the house, turned on the television, and was about to sit down with a glass of Kool-Aid when Mom shooed me outside.

34 "It's still light," she said. "Later you'll bug me to let you stay out longer. So go on."

35 I downed my Kool-Aid and went outside to the front yard. No one was around. The day had cooled and a breeze rustled the trees. Mr. Jackson, the plumber, was watering his lawn and when he saw me he turned away to wash off his front steps. There was more than an hour of light left, so I took advantage of it and decided to look for work. I felt suddenly alive as I skipped down the block in search of an overgrown flower bed and the dime that would end the day right.

APPLICATIONS FOR CRITICAL READING AND DISCUSSION

Racial prejudice against Hispanics underlies the basic meaning of this piece, but the comparative study is presented mainly as a study of classes, with the lower class represented by the narrator's family and the middle class represented by the families on *Leave It to Beaver* and *Father Knows Best* and by the family of David King.

1. Does this selection stress comparison or contrast?

2. Is the purpose mainly to inform or to persuade?

3. What are the points (there may be only one) in this study? State them here, and underline them in the text.

4. Is the pattern mainly subject by subject or point by point? Make a simple outline of the pattern here.

EXERCISE 8

Even if you know only one language, you use more than one variety of that language. You speak differently in public and in private. Richard Rodriguez spoke differently, but his public and private varieties were different languages. In this passage from *Hunger of Memory*, he discusses the languages of his childhood.

Vocabulary Preview: Write in short definitions for these words as they are used in the context of the following passage. (The paragraph numbers are given in parentheses.) Be prepared to use the words in your own sentences.

intimidated (7)	falsetto (14)
counterpoint (8)	feigned (14)
consoling (8)	exubcrance (14)
polysyllabic (10)	gradations (19)
guttural (13)	cloistered (22)
syntax (13)	lacquered (22)

Private Language, Public Language
RICHARD RODRIGUEZ

1 I remember to start with that day in Sacramento—a California now nearly thirty years past—when I first entered a classroom, able to understand some fifty stray English words.

2 The third of four children, I had been preceded to a neighborhood Roman Catholic school by an older brother and sister. But neither of them had revealed very much about their classroom experiences. Each afternoon they returned, as they left in the morning, always together, speaking in Spanish as they climbed the five steps of the porch. And their mysterious books, wrapped in shopping-bag paper, remained on the table next to the door, closed firmly behind them.

3 An accident of geography sent me to a school where all my classmates were white, many the children of doctors and lawyers and business executives. All my classmates certainly must have been uneasy on that first day of school—as most children are uneasy—to find themselves apart from their families in the first institution of their lives. But I was astonished.

4 The nun said, in a friendly but oddly impersonal voice, "Boys and girls, this is Richard Rodriguez." (I heard her sound out: *Rich-heard Road-ree-guess.*) It was the first time I had heard anyone name me in English. "Richard," the nun repeated more slowly, writing my name down in her black leather book. Quickly I turned to see my mother's face dissolve in a watery blur behind the pebbled glass door.

5 Many years later there is something called bilingual education—a scheme proposed in the late 1960s by Hispanic-American social activists, later endorsed by a congressional vote. It is a program that seeks to permit non-English-speaking children, many from lower-class homes, to use their family language as the language of school. (Such is the goal its supporters announce.) I hear them and am forced to say no: It is not possible for a child—any child—ever to use his family's language in school. Not to understand this is to misunderstand the public uses of schooling and to trivialize the nature of intimate life—a family's "language."

6 Memory teaches me what I know of these matters; the boy reminds the adult. I was a bilingual child, a certain kind—socially disadvantaged—the son of working-class parents, both Mexican immigrants.

7   In the early years of my boyhood, my parents coped very well in America. My father had steady work. My mother managed at home. They were nobody's victims. Optimism and ambition led them to a house (our home) many blocks from the Mexican south side of town. We lived among *gringos** and only a block from the biggest, whitest houses. It never occurred to my parents that they couldn't live wherever they chose. Nor was the Sacramento of the fifties bent on teaching them a contrary lesson. My mother and father were more annoyed than intimidated by those two or three neighbors who tried initially to make us unwelcome. ("Keep your brats away from my sidewalk!") But despite all they achieved, perhaps because they had so much to achieve, any deep feeling of ease, the confidence of "belonging" in public was withheld from them both. They regarded the people at work, the faces in crowds, as very distant from us. They were the others, *los gringos*. That term was interchangeable in their speech with another, even more telling, *los americanos*....

8   In public, my father and mother spoke a hesitant, accented, not always grammatical English. And they would have to strain—their bodies tense—to catch the sense of what was rapidly said by *los gringos*. At home they spoke Spanish. The language of their Mexican past sounded in counterpoint to the English of public society. The words would come quickly, with ease. Conveyed through those sounds was the pleasing, soothing, consoling reminder of being at home.

9   During those years when I was first conscious of hearing, my mother and father addressed me only in Spanish; in Spanish I learned to reply. By contrast, English (*inglés*), rarely heard in the house, was the language I came to associate with *gringos*. I learned my first words of English overhearing my parents speak to strangers. At five years of age, I knew just enough English for my mother to trust me on errands to stores one block away. No more.

10   I was a listening child, careful to hear the very different sounds of Spanish and English. Wide-eyed with learning, I'd listen to sounds more than words. First, there were English (*gringo*) sounds. So many words were still unknown that when the butcher or the lady at the drugstore said something to me, exotic polysyllabic sounds would bloom in the midst of their sentences. Often the speech of people in public seemed to me very loud, booming with confidence. The man behind the counter would literally ask, "What can I do for you?" But by being so firm and so clear, the sound of his voice said that he was a *gringo*; he belonged in public society.

11   I would also hear then the high nasal tones of middle-class American speech. The air stirred with sound. Sometimes, even now, when I have been traveling abroad for several weeks, I will hear what I heard as a boy. In hotel lobbies or airports, in Turkey or Brazil, some Americans will pass, and suddenly I will hear it again—the high sound of American voices. For a few seconds I will hear it with pleasure, for it is now the sound of my society—a reminder of home. But inevitably—already on the flight headed for home—the sound fades with repetition. I will be unable to hear it anymore.

12   When I was a boy, things were different. The accent of *los gringos* was never pleasing nor was it hard to hear. Crowds at Safeway or at bus stops would be noisy with sound. And I would be forced to edge away from the chirping chatter above me.

13   I was unable to hear my own sounds, but I knew very well that I spoke English poorly. My words could not stretch far enough to form complete thoughts. And the words I did speak I didn't know well enough to make into distinct sounds. (Listeners would usually lower their heads, better to hear what I was trying to say.) But it was one thing for *me* to speak English with difficulty. It was more troubling for *me* to hear my parents speak in public: their high-whining vowels and guttural consonants; their sentences that got stuck with "eh" and "ah" sounds; the confused syntax; the hesitant rhythm of sounds so different from the way *gringos* spoke. I'd notice, moreover, that my parents' voices were softer than those of *gringos* we'd meet....

14   There were many times like the night at a brightly lit gasoline station (a blaring white memory) when I stood uneasily, hearing my father. He was talking to a teenaged attendant. I do not recall what they were saying, but I cannot forget

---

*Spanish for "foreigners," especially Americans and the English

the sounds my father made as he spoke. At one point his words slid together to form one word—sounds as confused as the threads of blue and green oil in the puddle next to my shoes. His voice rushed through what he had left to say. And, toward the end, reached falsetto notes, appealing to his listener's understanding. I looked away to the lights of passing automobiles. I tried not to hear anymore. But I heard only too well the calm, easy tones in the attendant's reply. Shortly afterward, walking toward home with my father, I shivered when he put his hand on my shoulder. The very first chance that I got, I evaded his grasp and ran on ahead into the dark, skipping with feigned boyish exuberance.

15   But then there was Spanish. *Español:* my family's language. *Español:* the language that seemed to me a private language. I'd hear strangers on the radio and in the Mexican Catholic church across town speaking Spanish, but I couldn't really believe that Spanish was a public language, like English. Spanish speakers, rather, seemed related to me, for I sensed that we shared—through our language—the experience of feeling apart from *los gringos*. It was thus a ghetto Spanish that I heard and I spoke. Like those whose lives are bound by a barrio, I was reminded by Spanish of my separateness from *los otros* [the others], *gringos* in power. But more intensely than for most barrio children—because I did not live in a barrio—Spanish seemed to me the language of home. (Most days it was only at home that I'd hear it.) It became the language of joyful return.

16   A family member would say something to me and I would feel myself specially recognized. My parents would say something to me and I would feel embraced by the sounds of their words. Those sounds said: *I am speaking with ease in Spanish. I am addressing you in words I never use with los gringos. I recognize you as someone special, close, like no one outside. You belong with us. In the family.*

17   (Ricardo.)

18   At the age of five, six, well past the time when most other children no longer easily notice the difference between sounds uttered at home and words spoken in public, I had a different experience. I lived in a world magically compounded of sounds. I remained a child longer than most; I lingered too long, poised at the edge of language—often frightened by the sounds of *los gringos*, delighted by the sounds of Spanish at home. I shared with my family a language that was startlingly different from that used in the great city around us.

19   For me there were none of the gradations between public and private society so normal to a maturing child. Outside the house was public society; inside the house was private. Just opening or closing the screen door behind me was an important experience. I'd rarely leave home all alone or without reluctance. Walking down the sidewalk, under the canopy of tall trees, I'd warily notice the—suddenly—silent neighborhood kids who stood warily watching me. Nervously, I'd arrive at the grocery store to hear there the sounds of the *gringo*—foreign to me—reminding me that in this world so big, I was a foreigner. But then I'd return. Walking back toward our house, climbing the steps from the sidewalk, when the front door was open in summer, I'd hear voices beyond the screen door talking in Spanish. For a second or two, I'd stay, linger there, listening. Smiling, I'd hear my mother call out, saying in Spanish (words), "Is that you, Richard?" all the while her sounds would assure me: *You are home now; come closer; inside. With us.*

20   "*Sí*," I'd reply.

21   Once more inside the house I would resume (assume) my place in the family. The sounds would dim, grow harder to hear. Once more at home, I would grow less aware of that fact. It required, however, no more than the blurt of the doorbell to alert me to listen to sounds all over again. The house would turn instantly still while my mother went to the door. I'd hear her hard English sounds. I'd wait to hear her voice return to soft-sounding Spanish, which assured me, as surely as did the clicking tongue of the lock of the door, that the stranger was gone.

22   Plainly, it is not healthy to hear such sounds so often. It is not healthy to distinguish public words from private sounds so easily. I remained cloistered by sounds, timid and shy in public, too dependent on voices at home. And yet it needs to be emphasized: I was an extremely happy child at home. I remember many nights when my father would come back from work, and I'd hear him call out to my mother in Spanish, sounding relieved. In Spanish, he'd sound light and free notes he never could manage in English. Some nights I'd jump up just at hearing his voice. With *mis hermanos* [my brothers] I would come running

into the room where he was with my mother. Our laughing (so deep was the pleasure!) became screaming. Like others who know pain of public alienation, we transformed the knowledge of our public separateness and made it consoling—the reminder of intimacy. Excited, we joined our voices in a celebration of sounds. *We are speaking now the way we never speak out in public. We are alone—together,* voices sounded, surrounded to tell me. Some nights, no one seemed willing to loosen the hold sound had on us. At dinner, we invented new words. (Ours sounded Spanish, but made sense only to us.) We pieced together new words by taking, say, an English verb and giving it Spanish endings. My mother's instructions at bedtime would be lacquered with mock-urgent tones. Or a word like *si* would become, in several notes, able to convey added measures of feeling. Tongues explored the edges of words, especially the fat vowels. And we happily sounded that military drum roll, the twirling roar of the Spanish *r*. Family language: my family's sounds. The voices of my parents and and sisters and brothers. Their voices insisting: *You belong here. We are family members. Related. Special to one another. Listen!* Voices singing and sighing, rising straining, then surging, teeming with pleasure that burst syllables into fragments of laughter. At times it seemed there was steady quiet only when, from another room, the rustling whispers of my parents faded and I moved closer to sleep.

APPLICATIONS FOR CRITICAL READING AND DISCUSSION

1. Does this selection stress comparison or contrast?

2. Is the purpose mainly to inform or to persuade?

3. What are the points (there may be only one) in this study? State them here, and underline them in the selection.

4. Is the pattern mainly subject by subject or point by point? Make a simple outline of the pattern here.

294 CHAPTER 10

The Reading Connection from Classroom Sources

EXERCISE 9

Demonstration Using the DCODE Worksheet

From the several types of love, Jennifer Jeffries picked two and set out to find the relationship between them. She manages to answer the questions of what the two have in common and whether one can become the other.

WORKSHEET
Writing in DCODE

NAME: Jennifer Jeffries

SECTION: _____ CHAPTER: _____ DATE: _____

Delve Generate your topic, or ideas for your topic, by delving into your subject area through:

- *Freewriting*—writing sentence after sentence, nonstop and spontaneously.
- *Brainstorming*—jotting down answers to Who? What? Where? When? Why? and How? and then listing words and phrases in relation to those answers.
- *Clustering*—connecting bubbled ideas with lines to show strings of relationships, producing each new bubble item in response to the question, What comes to mind?
- *Combining* any of these approaches, as directed by your instructor.

Freewriting:
    Love is one of the most common words in the English language. It is one of the first words a person hears when coming into this world and it is one of the last a person hears when leaving the world. There are many kinds of love, the two that we are likely to remember the best are the first love and the last love. Those two are puppy love and true love. That is true if everything works out all right. I guess it's difficult to tell what kind of love one is in when one is in it, but later one can look at the love and figure out what kind it was, or in the case of true love that may last for a long time and even to the end of life you can figure out what it is while you are still experiencing it. These are two good ideas to compare and contrast because they are similar but mostly dissimilar.

Brainstorming:
    Who?   people in love
    What?   puppy love and true love
    Where? everywhere where people are free to fall in love
    When?   throughout life
    Why?   because all human beings of sound mind want to love and be loved
    How?   by using their own qualities and responding to the situation

Clustering:

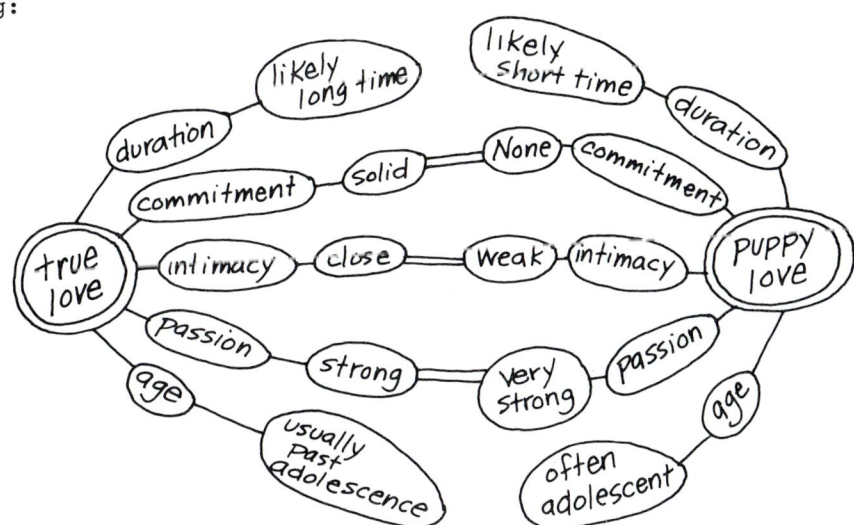

WORKSHEET: Writing in DCODE

Concentrate Concentrate your work by stating your topic in one sentence that is not too broad, narrow, or vague to be developed. Base this sentence (which may become the topic sentence for your paragraph or the thesis for your essay) on an idea emerging from the **Delve** stage. You may have to try several statements here before you formulate one that is best for your writing task. Be sure that your final statement covers your assignment or intent and specifies both your subject (what you are writing about) and treatment (what aspect you will focus on). Label the *subject* and *treatment* parts.

        subject   *treatment*

<u>True love and puppy love</u> are <u>mainly different when compared and contrasted in terms of passion, intimacy, and commitment.</u>

Organize Complete an outline or a cluster, as directed by your instructor. The cluster should be a section from, or a refined version of, the **Delve** clustering. Regardless of the strategy you use, the organizational pattern should indicate a division of your topic into parts that will, in turn, be further subdivided for support as necessary to address a particular audience on your concentrated topic.

```
    I.   Passion
         A. Puppy love
              1. Consuming
              2. Intense
         B. True love
              1. Present
              2. Proportional
    II.  Intimacy
         A. Puppy love
              1. Lots of talking
              2. Superficial
         B. True love
              1. Good communication
                   a. Feelings
                   b. Ideas
              2. Deep
    III. Commitment
         A. Puppy love
              1. Not tested
              2. Weak, if at all
         B. True love
              1. Proven
              2. Profound
```

Draft On separate paper, write and then revise your assignment as many times as necessary for **c**oherence, **l**anguage (usage, tone, and diction), **u**nity, **e**mphasis, **s**upport, and **s**entence structure (**cluess**).

Edit Correct problems in fundamentals such as **c**apitalization, **o**missions, **p**unctuation, and **s**pelling (**cops**). Before writing the final draft, read your paper aloud to discover oversights and awkwardness of expression.

First Draft

Two Loves: Puppy and True

~~Love can come in many forms, and it can change, but two forms that we are all familiar with are~~ true love and puppy love. ~~Most people experience the last one, and just about everyone wants to experience the first. The last one, true love, has three parts to it: passion, intimacy, and commitment. By applying the same to the first one you can see just how different the two forms are.~~ Passion is something that both ~~have~~. Puppy love couldn't exist without passion, ~~that's what a puppy is. Just~~ jumping around licking somebody's face ~~and staying~~ in a constant state of excitement. The person in puppy love is attracted physically to someone and is constantly aroused. The person in true love is also passionate, but it isn't ~~likely to be so constant and persistent.~~ The passion is based on more than ~~just the~~ physical ~~parts of the other~~ person. It is with the intimacy ~~part of love~~ that puppy love begins to really differ from true love. Puppy love may promote a lot of talk, but most of it can be attributed to the arousal factor. There's no closeness and depth of shared experience. But with true love there is a genuine ~~communications about feelings and ideas. There is~~ a closeness and concern for each other that is supportive and reassuring. That closeness usually comes from years of shared experience, which also proves commitment. And it is just that, the commitment, that is ~~maybe~~ the main difference between puppy love and true love. The people in puppy love may talk about eternity, but their love hasn't really gotten outside the physical realm. Their love has not been tested, but those in true love have a proven and profound commitment. True love has survived troubles and ~~come out~~ stronger. And it survived because it ~~had~~ more than the one dimension. ~~Therefore,~~ the two loves are very different. ~~That doesn't mean that~~ puppy love ~~can never be~~ true love, ~~or that the true love didn't grow from puppy~~

Annotations (handwritten):
- Of the many forms of love, the two opposite extremes are
- If love in its fullest form has three parts — passion, intimacy, and commitment — then true love and puppy love could be called complete and incomplete, respectively.
- Common to
- hence, the word puppy — an immature animal that excitedly
- A
- the passion is proportional to other parts of love — and life. True love attraction, though that should not be discounted factor
- but
- a
- factor
- Probably
- in this imperfect world of troubled lives become has has
- These considerations show that
- though
- may, with time, become

~~love. It also~~ That possibility doesn't mean that age ~~is necessarily linked to one of these. A so called dirty old man or even a dirty old woman may be just someone with an extreme case of puppy love.~~ corresponds with one form of love. And ~~a very young~~ A person of any age may, by knowing passion, intimacy, and commitment, experience true love, but true love is more likely to develop ~~and grew~~ over a period of time.

Final Draft

                Two Loves: Puppy and True
                    Jennifer Jeffries

    Of the many forms of love, the two opposite extremes are puppy love and true love. If love in its fullest form has three parts--<u>passion</u>, <u>intimacy</u>, and <u>commitment</u>--then puppy love and true love could be called <u>incomplete</u> and <u>complete</u>, respectively. Passion's common to both. Puppy love couldn't exist without *passion,* hence the word puppy--an immature animal that jumps around excitedly licking somebody's face. A person in puppy love is attracted physically to someone and is constantly aroused. A person in true love is also passionate, but the passion is proportional to other parts of love--and life. True love passion is based on more than physical attraction, though that should not be discounted. It is with the intimacy factor that puppy love really begins to differ from true love. Puppy love may promote a lot of talk, but most of it can be attributed to the arousal factor. There's no closeness and depth of shared experience. But with true love there is a genuine closeness and shared concern for each other that is supportive and reassuring. That closeness usually comes from years of shared experience, which also proves commitment. And it is just that factor, the <u>commitment</u>, that is probably the main difference between puppy love and true love. The people in puppy love may talk about eternity, but their love hasn't really gotten outside the physical realm. Their love has not been tested, whereas those in true love have a proven commitment. True love has survived troubles in this imperfect world of troubled lives and become stronger. And it has survived because it has more than the one dimension. These considerations show that these two loves are very different, though puppy love may, with time, become true love. That possibility doesn't mean that age necessarily corresponds with one form of love. A person of any age can, by knowing passion, intimacy, and commitment, experience true love, but true love is more likely to develop over a period of time.

APPLICATIONS FOR CRITICAL READING AND DISCUSSION

1. Does this selection stress comparison or contrast?
   ```
   contrast
   ```

2. Is the purpose mainly to inform or to persuade?
   ```
   to inform
   ```

3. What are the points (there may be only one) in this study? State them here, and underline them in the selection.
   ```
   commitment, intimacy, passion
   ```

4. Is the pattern mainly subject by subject or point by point? Make a simple outline of the pattern here.
   ```
   point-by-point

   See the DCODE Worksheet.
   ```

EXERCISE 10

Ray Sinclair is an avid fan of "Cheers," the long-running television sitcom, now in syndication. In reflecting on the success of the show, he has concluded that much of its strength is derived from its depiction of different sides of human nature. One pair of opposites is Sam and Woody.

```
                    Sam and Woody
                    Ray Sinclair
     One of the strengths of the show "Cheers" is the use of
opposites. Those of us who have watched the show for about
ten years, first as a prime-time show and then in
syndication, know the pairs well: Cliff and Norm, Frazier
and Lilith, Sam and Diane, Sam and Rebecca, Sam and Coach,
Diane and Carla, and my two favorites, Sam and Woody. The
astonishing differences between the characters in regards
to relationships and morality is quite noticeable, and
their personal backgrounds are as far apart as a sweet-
talking city guy on the make and a country bumpkin.
     We can understand why they are so different because
their backgrounds are so different. Sam was always one of
the popular guys. Before he was a bar owner, he was a
professional baseball pitcher for the Boston Red Sox. Sam
spent most of his days in the limelight, with the
television sports fans of America watching his every move.
As his baseball career skidded, he turned to drinking. His
drinking eventually led to alcoholism, now controlled. In
direct contrast, Woody came from a small farm town in
Indiana. His exposure to the big city was minimal at best.
Woody's idea of greatness is being a bartender at Cheers,
and he has never had a big problem because "big problem"
```

involves complications, and Woody is simple in every respect. But if he did a big problem, we know he would not turn to drink.

Their attitudes toward women and relationships define them as characters. Though not completely devoid of sincerity, Sam is a pompous man, who rates his car higher than any human being. As a self-proclaimed ladies' man, he has acquired a well-deserved reputation for being a womanizer. Sam treats each of his women as a challenge or test. The women whom Sam dates are young and stunningly beautiful, while maintaining an IQ of about twice their age. Sam also has a definite aversion to marriage or commitment. His dates not only come in second to his Corvette; they also are subjected to his star rating system. Occasionally he will approach a prospective date who is bright and knowledgeable, a person who has heard his lines and holds him in contempt. Forever vain, he cannot understand why he is being rejected. Of course, just the right situation or the right comment by a person, even Woody, may bring the "good Sam" to the surface, but in a flash the old "skirt-chaser" will return. Woody, on the other hand, values his family and friends, even those in the bar. His love life is meager, but then he, unlike Sam, is not preoccupied with sex and he doesn't have a constant need to be flattered and pampered. Woody is ready to have a conventional courtship with a woman, and when his childhood sweetheart hits town, he does just that. Although he and Sam have many conversations, Woody usually doesn't understand what Sam is talking about, which provides much opportunity for droll humor, and if he does understand, he will not be corrupted anyway. Good-natured, sweet, and engagingly naive, he is often Sam's foil. Woody is not judgmental about Sam, but we know he would not rate women with stars.

The differences between Sam and Woody are quite obvious. One is a lovable rogue and the other a wide-eyed country boy. Occasionally the silver-tongued Sam comes to the aid of Woody and once in a while--and not always deliberately--Woody will help Sam. We remember them for being themselves, and getting along like the other opposite pairs, going back and forth with their one-liners, never having physical fights, never being mean deep down. Instead, they have just found a place where the world doesn't seem to be so rough, a place called Cheers, "where everybody knows your name."

APPLICATIONS FOR CRITICAL READING AND DISCUSSION

1. Does this selection stress comparison or contrast?

2. Is the purpose mainly to inform or to persuade?

3. What are the points (there may be only one) in this study? State them here, and underline them in the selection.

4. Is the pattern mainly subject by subject or point by point? Make a simple outline of the pattern here.

EXERCISE 11

Women and men are often discussed in terms of their differences, but Vanessa Capili suggests that the word that should be stressed is *equal*. Here, she uses factual information and well-reasoned statements to express her views on the "woman-man" issue.

Men and Women: More Equal Than the Same
Vanessa Capili

For hundreds of years people have considered women inferior to men. As a result of that kind of thinking, women have been mistreated and discriminated against. In England until less than a century ago, husbands could beat wives, if the stick was no thicker than the beater's thumb, hence the "rule of thumb." Women were not supposed to read when pregnant because they might take brain power away from the fetus. Today thinking people hold different views about gender differences because they have information available in areas such as physicality, longevity, and maternal feelings (instincts).

Physically, men and women have different characteristics that give them advantages in particular areas. If a woman wants to challenge a man for a test in strength, sit-ups or leg wrestling would be the best activity for her to choose. Women have a larger pelvis, one that gives them plenty of room for muscle attachments and leverage in leg wrestling. Pound for pound, women can be as strong in the abdominal and leg muscles as men. Not only do women have a larger pelvis, but they also have more flexible and less tightly hinged joints than men, which is why in figure skating and ballet, women get thrown about more by men, while men use their upper body strength in lifting, holding, and throwing them.

In endurance events, like swimming and running, both men and women again have different characteristics that help them perform in these kinds of sports. Women, for instance, have higher body fat percentage than men, providing for both buoyancy and insulation against the cold in swimming and long-distance running; however, men usually perform better than women because they have larger hearts and lungs than women, meaning they have more oxygen-carrying hemoglobin in their blood. Muscles depend on oxygen to work; the more oxygen one can get to one's muscles, the more energy one has.

Now we know that physical differences between men and women balance out. But why do women live longer than men? Women live longer than men because women are less vulnerable than men. Women have two X chromosomes, which include genes that control the immune system; women with two X chromosomes have a "backup" set of genes and maybe a greater protection against diseases. Men, on the other hand, are more prone to diseases but also to accidents. Starting from birth, baby boys experience more birth defects and birth traumas than baby girls. They also are more likely to have autism, stuttering, dyslexia, and hyperactivity. Violent deaths in childhood, digestive disorders and kidney diseases in middle age, and viral infection in old age all contribute to men's being more vulnerable than women. Men's susceptibility to diseases may be caused by their having only one X chromosome. The other, the Y chromosome, determines their sex and is the most basic difference between men and women. The Y chromosome includes genes that produce testosterone and other hormones that produce the male body, so they only have a single X chromosome to control the immune system.

Longevity then makes women different from men. But another interesting area makes the two sexes equal or balance out: both men and women develop maternal feelings. Women, although physiologically and hormonally prepared to bear and nurse infants, are not better in mothering infants than men. Women can produce milk that responds to an infant's cry and go through a monthly hormonal cycle which prepares the body for conception. But studies show that men, however, can have a high level of maternal feelings (also applying to adoptive mothers who didn't go through monthly cycles for conception). Maternal feelings, therefore, develop through closeness and caretaking rather than through biological programming.

We see that men and women are indeed different, but each gender has strengths and weaknesses. What does this mean? It means that women and men should be considered mainly in terms of equality. Then we would say that men and women are equal--not the same--but equal.

APPLICATIONS FOR CRITICAL READING AND DISCUSSION

1. Does this selection stress comparison or contrast?

2. Is the purpose mainly to inform or to persuade?

3. What are the points (there may be only one) in this study? State them here, and underline them in the selection.

4. Is the pattern mainly subject by subject or point by point? Make a simple outline of the pattern here.

Suggested Topics for Writing Comparison and Contrast

After you limit your topic, personalize it or do some research so you will have specific support.

General Topics

1. Two generations of college students
2. Two automobiles, airplanes, bicycles, motorcycles, snowmobiles, computers
3. Two types of (or specific) police officers, doctors, teachers, preachers, students, athletes
4. Two magazines, newspapers
5. Two cultures, languages, social classes
6. Two famous persons—authors, generals, actors, athletes
7. Two kinds of love, hatred, revenge, compassion
8. Two sports
9. Two philosophies, religions, ideologies
10. Two foods, restaurants
11. Snow skiing and water skiing
12. London and Paris (or Los Angles and San Francisco, or any other pair of cities)
13. Living at college and living at home
14. Small college and large college/four-year college and community college
15. Fraternities or sororities: high school and college
16. Two gangs or two kinds of gangs
17. Weapons: today and yesterday
18. Christmas: today and yesterday, mine and my friend's

19. Two roommates, neighbors, friends, dates
20. Two movies, television shows, commercials, songs, singers
21. Luxury and necessity
22. Family: today and yesterday, mine and my friend's
23. College and high school: teachers, courses, facilities, sports, school spirit
24. Dating and going steady, living together and being married, a person before and after marriage
25. Apples and oranges
26. Batman and the Joker (or any other two characters from movies or television shows)
27. Two jobs, bosses, co-workers
28. Two views of the same incident
29. Two parties
30. Two (or two sets of) parents, grandparents
31. Two approaches to dealing with a problem
32. Shopping malls and neighborhood stores
33. Two views on materialism
34. Two ways of studying
35. Two political candidates or office holders

Reading-Related Topics

"The Desert and the Jungle"

1. Using this as a model, write about people living in a sparsely populated area (country) and in a densely populated area (city).

"Pink Kittens and Blue Spaceships"

2. Write a comparison and contrast based on the toys traditionally given to boys and girls.
3. Write a comparison and contrast based on games or recreation generally made available to girls and boys.

"The Temple and the Cathedral"

4. Write about two churches or temples as their structures reflect different religious views.
5. Write about a mall versus neighborhood stores as their structures reflect attitudes of different societies.
6. Write about an old stadium such as Soldiers' Field in Chicago or the Coliseum in Los Angeles versus an enclosed stadium such as the Superdome in New Orleans.

"Neat People vs. Sloppy People"

7. Write a comparative study on people with good table manners and those with bad table manners. Explain the causes and effects of their behavior.

8. Using this essay as a model, write a comparative study about one of the following:
   - people who exercise a lot and those who hardly exercise
   - people who diet and those who do not
   - men with beards and those without
   - women with extremely long fingernails and those with short fingernails
   - people who dye their hair and those who do not
   - people who take care of their yards and those who do not
   - people who take care of their children (or pets) and those who do not

"Looking for Work"

9. Following the lead of this essay, write a comparative study based on your own experiences with discrimination at work, play, or school.

10. Compare and/or contrast your experiences in growing up with those of Gary Soto.

"Private Language, Public Language"

11. If you speak a community dialect, compare and contrast it with mainstream English.

12. Compare and contrast the use of language by different generations within your family or within a family with which you are familiar.

13. If English is not your first language, or if your family spoke a community dialect, write a comparison-and-contrast piece based on:
    - when your family used each
    - what kinds of subjects were likely to be used by each
    - what feelings were likely to be expressed by each

"Two Loves: Puppy and True"

14. Using the terms and the pattern shown in this essay, write a comparison-and-contrast piece on two people you know.

15. Write a comparative study of two other kinds of love, such as those based mostly on companionship and those based mostly on romance. You could use the same points that Jennifer does: passion, intimacy, and commitment.

"Sam and Woody"

16. Write a comparative study of any two other characters from this show or another. Try to establish that the relationship of characters you select is central to the success of the show.

"Men and Women: More Equal Than the Same"

17. Write another comparative study based on points (such as intelligence, emotional stability, common sense, and sense of humor) not covered in this essay.

# Writer's Checklist

Apply these ideas to your writing of comparison and contrast or analogy as you work with **DCODE**. Later as a peer editor, apply the same ideas to the material you evaluate.

1. Purpose: At some point during the exploration of your topic, define your purpose clearly, answering these questions:
   a. Am I writing a work that is mainly comparison, mainly contrast, or balanced?
   b. Is my main purpose to explain or to persuade?
2. Points
   a. List your points of comparison and/or contrast, perhaps in your clustering.
   b. Eliminate irrelevant points.
3. Pattern
   a. Select the subject-by-subject or the point-by-point pattern after considering your topic and planned treatment. The point-by-point is usually preferred. Only in long papers is there likely to be a mixture of patterns.
   b. Compose an outline reflecting the pattern you select.
4. Presentation
   a. Be sure to give somewhat equal treatment to each application of a point to the subject. Attention to each part of the outline will usually ensure balanced development.
   b. Use transitional words and phrases to indicate comparison and contrast and to establish coherence.
   c. Note that the paragraph should have a carefully stated topic sentence; the essay should have a clear thesis and each developmental paragraph should have a topic sentence broad enough to embrace its content.

# Journal-Entry Suggestions

1. Select some of the unused "Reading-Related Topics" suggestions, and use them for journal topics.
2. Write a reaction to one or more "Reading Connection" selections. Agree, disagree, apply the statements to your own experiences, indicate the value of such statements, or explain why you were surprised, shocked, disgusted, pleased, or whatever, by the material.
3. Invent statements (using comparison and contrast if appropriate) to support headlines from *Weekly World News:*

    "Magician's Trick Backfires—and Three People Float Away!"
    "Boxing Kangaroo Runs Off with Loser's Wife!"
    "Judge Orders Psychic: 'Stop Reading People's Minds'!"
    "Wolf-like Mutant Captured in Ruins of Nuclear Plant!"
    "Mysterious Songs of the Whales Are Really '50s Rock 'n' Roll Hits!"
    "Haunted Honda for Sale!"
    "Pet Gator Dies of a Broken Heart!"
    "1st Bigfoot Captured!"
    "Wacky Inventor Makes Love Potion out of Toenails!"

WORKSHEET
Writing in DCODE

NAME:_____

SECTION:_____ CHAPTER:_____ DATE:_____

Delve   Generate your topic, or ideas for your topic, by delving into your subject area through:

- *Freewriting*—writing sentence after sentence, nonstop and spontaneously.
- *Brainstorming*—jotting down answers to Who? What? Where? When? Why? and How? and then listing words and phrases in relation to those answers.
- *Clustering*—connecting bubbled ideas with lines to show strings of relationships, producing each new bubble item in response to the question, What comes to mind?
- *Combining* any of these approaches, as directed by your instructor.

WORKSHEET: Writing in DCODE

Concentrate   Concentrate your work by stating your topic in one sentence that is not too broad, narrow, or vague to be developed. Base this sentence (which may become the topic sentence for your paragraph or the thesis for your essay) on an idea emerging from the **Delve** stage. You may have to try several statements here before you formulate one that is best for your writing task. Be sure that your final statement covers your assignment or intent and specifies both your subject (what you are writing about) and treatment (what aspect you will focus on). Label the *subject* and *treatment* parts.

Organize   Complete an outline or a cluster, as directed by your instructor. The cluster should be a section from, or a refined version of, the **Delve** clustering. Regardless of the strategy you use, the organizational pattern should indicate a division of your topic into parts that will, in turn, be further subdivided for support as necessary to address a particular audience on your concentrated topic.

Draft   On separate paper, write and then revise your assignment as many times as necessary for **c**oherence, **l**anguage (usage, tone, and diction), **u**nity, **e**mphasis, **s**upport, and **s**entence structure (**cluess**).

Edit   Correct problems in fundamentals such as **c**apitalization, **o**missions, **p**unctuation, and **s**pelling (**cops**). Before writing the final draft, read your paper aloud to discover oversights and awkwardness of expression.

Definition: Clarifying Terms

11

> " A definition is the enclosing of a wilderness of idea within a wall of words.
>
> — Samuel Butler

"We are neither hunters nor gatherers. We are accountants."

What is the difference between a simple definition and an extended definition? Why is a synonym often inadequate as a definition? How does definition relate to the other forms of discourse already covered? What are the parts of the analytical or formal definition? What are three common, effective ways of introducing an extended definition?

309

Definition Defined

Definition is a method of identifying and making the meaning of a term clear. By defining, you answer the question, What is the meaning of this? In establishing the meaning, you put limits on the term in the form of characteristics that distinguish it from other entities. For example, in the sentence that follows, the writer defines *incursion:*

> The German *incursion,* a sudden, hostile invasion into Polish territory, was the beginning of World War II.

Here, the writer places limits on *incursion.* It is a certain kind of movement into another's territory that is characterized as being a "sudden hostile invasion." It differs from a visit, a migration to settle land, and even an invasion that is not sudden and, in some cases, not hostile.

Most definitions, like the one in the example sentence, are short, usually a synonymous word, a phrase, or a sentence. Some definitions, however, are a paragraph or an entire essay covering several pages. The short definition is called a *simple definition;* the longer one (a paragraph or essay) is known as an *extended definition.*

Simple Definition

It is likely that, at some point when speaking or writing, you have needed a simple definition, so you went to a dictionary. But you faced two problems. You did not know which definition to use, and you did not know how to introduce the term without just dropping it in abruptly and mechanically with something such as *"The Random House Dictionary* says . . . ." Both problems can be remedied easily.

Dictionary Entries

Concentrate on the term in italics:

> That kind of cactus is *indigenous* to the Mojave Desert.
>
> **in•dig•e•nous** \in-'dij-ə-nes\ *adj* [LL *indigenus,* fr. L *indigena,* n., native, fr. OL *indu, endo* in, within (akin to L *in* and to L *de* down) + L *gignere* to beget — more at DE-, KIN] (1646) **1:** having originated in and being produced, growing, living, or occurring naturally in a particular region or environment **2:** INNATE, INBORN **syn** see NATIVE — **in•dig•e•nous•ly** *adv* — **in•dig•e•nous•ness** *n*

Webster's Ninth New Collegiate Dictionary

As you consider the term in context, you look at the dictionary definitions. The first one seems to offer an insight. *Produced* doesn't work, but *growing* and *living naturally in a particular region or environment* seem to fit. Yet *growing* and *living* are not precisely the same. Then you look at the second set of definitions: INBORN, INNATE **syn** see NATIVE. The words are synonyms—words or phrases that mean about the same as the subject word. You can see that of the three words, only *Native* fits. To provide more information for the reader, the dictionary also presents *native* with a special treatment of synonyms (hence the *syn*) in its own place. Looking under the word *native,* you find this definition:

¹na•tive \\'nāt-iv*adj* [ME *natif,* fr. MF, fr. L *nativus,* fr. *natus,* pp. of *nasci* to be born — more at NATION] (14c) **1**: INBORN, INNATE <~ talents> **2**: belonging to a particular place by birth <~ to Wisconsin> **3**: *archaic*: closely related **4**: belonging to or associated with one by birth **5**: NATURAL, NORMAL **6a**: grown, produced or originating in a particular place or in the vicinity: LOCAL **b**: living or growing naturally in a particular region: INDIGENOUS **7**: SIMPLE, UNAFFECTED **8a**: constituting the original substance or source **b**: found in nature esp. in an unadulterated form <mining ~ silver> **9**: *chiefly Austral:* having a usu. superficial resemblance to a specified English plant or animal — **na•tive•ly** *adv* — **na•tive•ness** *n*

syn NATIVE, INDIGENOUS, ENDEMIC, ABORIGINAL mean belonging to a locality. NATIVE implies birth or origin in a place or region and may suggest compatibility with it <*native* tribal customs> INDIGENOUS applies to species or races and adds to NATIVE the implication of not having been introduced from elsewhere <maize is *indigenous* to America> ENDEMIC implies being peculiar to a region <edelweiss is *endemic* in the Alps> ABORIGINAL implies having no known race preceding in occupancy of the region <the *aboriginal* peoples of Australia>

Webster's Ninth New Collegiate Dictionary

In the synonyms at the close of the entry, did you observe the various shades of meaning, especially the meaning of *indigenous* and *native*? A dictionary is an invaluable aid to definition but must be used with care if you want to express yourself clearly and precisely. No two words have exactly the same meaning, and a word may have many meanings, some that extend to very different concepts.

Techniques for Conveying Simple Definition

If you want to define a term without being abrupt and mechanical, you have several alternatives. All of the following allow you to blend the definition into your developing thought.

- Basic Dictionary Meaning
  You can quote the dictionary's definition, but if you do, you are obliged to indicate your source, which you should do directly and explicitly. Always give the complete title of the dictionary, not simply "Webster says." Noah Webster has been dead for more than a hundred and fifty years, and dozens of dictionaries use the "Webster" designation.

- Synonyms
  Keep in mind that no two words have exactly the same meaning, and use synonymous words parenthetically.

    EXAMPLE: He was guilty of the ancient sin of *hubris*, of excessive ambition.

- Direct Explanation
  You can state the definition.

    EXAMPLE: This spontaneous and loyal support of our preconception—this process of finding "good" reasons to justify our routine beliefs—is known to modern psychologists as *rationalizing*—clearly a new name for a very ancient thing.

James Harvey Robinson, "On Various Kinds of Thinking"

- Indirect Explanation
  You can imply the definition.

  EXAMPLE: Trance is a similar abnormality in our society. Even a mild mystic is *aberrant* in Western civilization.

  > Ruth Benedict, *Patterns of Culture*

- Analytical or Formal Definition
  In using this method, you define by placing the term (the subject) in a class (genus) and then identifying it with characteristics that show how it differs from other members of the same class, as the following examples show:

Subject	Class	Characteristics
A republic	is a form of government	in which power resides in the people (the electorate).
A wolf	is a large, doglike, carnivorous mammal	yellowish or brownish gray with coarse fur, erect, pointed ears, and a bushy tail.
Jazz	is a style of music	that features improvisation and performance.

EXERCISE 1

Completing Definitions   Complete the following formal definitions.

Subject	Class	Characteristics
1. Rock	is a style of music	
2. Rap	is a style of music	
3. Psychology	is a field of study	
5. Capitalism	is an economic system	
6. Racism		
7. Family		
8. An elephant		
9. A bicycle		
10. Happiness		

Avoiding Common Problems

- Do not use the expressions *is where* and *is when* in beginning the main part of the definition. The verb *is* (a linking verb) should be followed by a noun, a pronoun, or an adjective.

    WEAK: A stadium is where they hold sports spectaculars.
    BETTER: A stadium is a structure in which sports spectaculars are held.

    WEAK: Socialism is when the ownership and operation of the means of production and distribution and vested in the community as a whole.
    BETTER: Socialism is a theory or system of community organization that advocates the vesting of the ownership and control of the means of production, capital, land, and so forth, in the community as a whole.

- Do not use the *circular definition*, a practice of defining a term with the term itself.

    CIRCULAR: An aristocracy is a form of government based on rule by the aristocrats.
    DIRECT: An aristocracy is a form of government in which the power resides in the hands of the best individuals or a small privileged class.

- Do not define the subject in more complicated language than the original.

    MURKY: *Surreptitious* means "clandestine."
    CLEAR: *Surreptitious* means "secret."

- Do not substitute the example for the definition; the example is excellent for clarification, but it does not define.

    WEAK: Political conservatives are people like William F. Buckley, Jr., and Pat Robertson.
    BETTER: Political conservatives are people who are dedicated to preserving the existing conditions. Examples of conservatives are William F. Buckley, Jr., and Pat Robertson.

EXERCISE 2

Study of a Dictionary Definition Study the dictionary entry below, and answer the questions that follow it.

¹**na•tive** \'nāt-iv\ *adj* [ME *natif*, fr. MF, fr. L *nativus*, fr. *natus*, pp. of *nasci* to be born — more at NATION] (14c) **1**: INBORN, INNATE <~ talents> **2**: belonging to a particular place by birth <~ to Wisconsin> **3**: *archaic*: closely related **4**: belonging to or associated with one by birth **5**: NATURAL, NORMAL **6a**: grown, produced or originating in a particular place or in the vicinity: LOCAL **b**: living or growing naturally in a particular region: INDIGENOUS **7**: SIMPLE, UNAFFECTED **8a**: constituting the original substance or source **b**: found in nature esp. in an unadulterated form <mining ~ silver> **9**: *chiefly Austral*: having a usu. superficial resemblance to a specified English plant or animal — **na•tive•ly** *adv* — **na•tive•ness** *n*

> **syn** NATIVE, INDIGENOUS, ENDEMIC, ABORIGINAL mean belonging to a locality. NATIVE implies birth or origin in a place or region and may suggest compatibility with it <*native* tribal customs> INDIGENOUS applies to species or races and adds to NATIVE the implication of not having been introduced from elsewhere <maize is *indigenous* to America> ENDEMIC implies being peculiar to a region <edelweiss is *endemic* in the Alps> ABORIGINAL implies having no known race preceding in occupancy of the region <the *aboriginal* peoples of Australia>

Webster's Ninth New Collegiate Dictionary

1. How many meanings are given for the word *native*?

2. What are some synonyms for the word (words that have nearly the same meaning)?

3. When would you use meaning 3?

4. From what word in Middle English is *native* derived?

5. How does *indigenous* differ from *native*?

Extended Definition

An *extended definition* is the organization and development of the meaning of a term beyond the limits of the simple definition. It may be a paragraph or two or even an entire essay in length. Terms like *socialism, school spirit, correct English, democracy, power, personality, symbolism, prejudice, conformity, ethnocentrism,* and *affluent society* cannot be defined adequately for most assignments with just a synonym or a few lines of explanation. As with other forms of discourse, we are concerned with the purpose, techniques for development, and the organization of extended definitions.

Purpose

The definition can be used as a subordinate part of any one of the other forms of discourse, and it can be the main thrust of the paragraph or essay. Regardless of its stature within the framework of a piece of writing, it will attempt mainly to persuade or inform. Especially when subordinated to the patterns of argumentation, comparison and contrast, and causes and effects, the definition will serve to persuade. Terms such as *discrimination, racism, sexist,* and *punishment* almost always deal with attitudes in a persuasive manner. As always determine your purpose at the outset and match it with an appropriate tone for the anticipated audience.

Techniques for Development

Definitions can take many forms. In the discussion of the simple definition, you saw that terms can be defined in various ways—by synonyms, direct and indirect explanation, and analytical or formal definitions. They can also be defined by *etymology*, the history of the term. For example, in the definition of *indigenous* (as detailed in the dictionary entry in the "Simple Definition" section) gives *indigena*, meaning "native" in Latin, as the origin of the word. Another example is *hypocrite* which once meant "actor" (*hypokrites*) in the Greek. A hyprocite, in other words, is a person pretending to be someone else. The history of a word may be of no use in your extended definition because the meaning has changed so drastically, or it may be strikingly useful because it is colorful and incisive. Etymology as a technique for defining is simply one of several to be considered.

Among the more common techniques for defining are the forms of discourse we have previously worked with as chapter subjects. One useful approach is to consider each of the forms as part of your writing of the extended definition. For a particular term some forms will be more useful than others, and you will naturally use the material that best fulfills your purpose.

Each of the following questions takes an aspect of a form of discourse and directs it toward definition.

- Narration
  Can I tell an anecdote or story to define this subject (such as *jerk, humanitarian, patriot*)? This form may overlap with description and exemplification.

- Description
  Can I describe this subject (such as *a whale* or *the moon*)?

- Exemplification
  Can I give examples of this subject (such as naming individuals to provide examples of *actors, diplomats, comics, satirists*, or *racists*)?

- Functional Analysis
  Can I divide this subject into parts (for example, the parts of a *heart, cell*, or *carburetor*)? (This may also be the same as the analytical or formal definition discussed under "Simple Definition.")

- Process Analysis
  Can I define this subject (such as *lasagna, tornado, hurricane, blood pressure*, or any number of scientific processes) by describing how to make it or how it occurs? (Common to the methodology of communicating in science, this approach is sometimes called the "operational definition.")

- Analysis by Causes and Effects
  Can I define this subject (such as *a flood, a drought, a riot*, or *a cancer*) by its causes or effects?

- Classification
  Can I group this subject (such as kinds of *families, cultures, religions, governments*) into classes? (This, in a broad sense, is also related to formal definition in that the formal definition goes from the subject, to the class, to the characteristic[s] of the single member of the class.)

- Comparison and Contrast
  Can I define this subject (such as *extremist* or *patriot*) by explaining what it is similar to and different from? If you are defining *orangutan* to a person who has never heard of one but is familiar with the gorilla, then you could make comparison-and-contrast statements. If you want to define *patriot*, then you might want to stress what it is not (the contrast, also called negation) before you explain what it is: a patriot is not a one-dimensional flag waver, not someone who hates "foreigners" because America is always right and always best.

When writing, you can easily incorporate a consideration of these forms into your clustering by adding words to designate the forms of discourse at the first extension of bubbles from the double-bubbled subject to be defined. Figure 11.1 shows an example.

FIGURE 11.1 Sample Completed Bubble Cluster on Development Techniques

*See Exercise 11 for the development of this topic.

EXERCISE 3

Bubble-Clustering the Forms of Discourse

In the bubble cluster in Figure 11.2, fill in at least one bubble at the next extension of the clustering for each form of discourse. If the form does not apply (that is, it would not render useful information for definition), mark it NA ("not applicable"). Suggested topics are *airhead, cool, psychopath, gang, cult, racist, tagger, jock.*

Figure 11.2 Bubble Cluster on Development Techniques

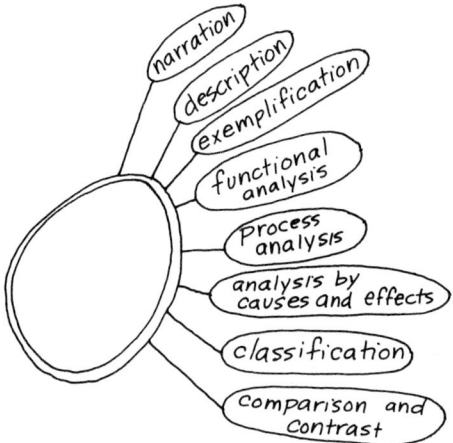

Order

The organization of your extended definition is likely to be one of emphasis, but it may be space or time, depending on the subject material. You may use one form of discourse for the overall pattern; if so, then you would employ the principles of organization discussed in previous chapters. The **Delve** stage (freewriting, brainstorming, and in particular, clustering) will provide you with material. **Concentrate** will give you the refined focus of the topic sentence or thesis, and the Outline part of **Organize** will establish the sequence. As you write drafts and revise, you may go back to modify parts of the writing, especially the outlining.

Introduction and Development

The three most common ways of introducing an extended definition are discussing why it is important to define the word, why it is difficult to define the word, and how the word is often misused.

Development, whether in the form of sentences for the paragraph or of paragraphs for the essay, is likely to represent one or more of the forms of discourse: narration, description, exposition (with its own subdivisions), and argumentation.

 # The Reading Connection

EXERCISE 4

Demonstration

When a term has a wide range of meanings, the meaning in a particular context becomes all the more important. Robert H. Dalton shows just how complicated a definition is for one term that is a part of virtually every English speaker's vocabulary.

Personality
ROBERT H. DALTON

 *EX* *EX*

 ETY mology

 EX

Historically, the term *personality* has many meanings, ranging from the popular phrase <u>"she has personality"</u> to the profound theological usage found in the expression <u>"personality of God"</u> as expounded in the doctrine of the Trinity. Personality, thus, has come to have a great variety of connotations. When we examine the word etymologically we see that our confusion is only increased; for the Latin word *persona*, from which our term personality comes, as it has been translated into various languages, may signify nobody or no one when used with a verb in the French language, or it may mean a representative of a great body, as *parson* in English. These varieties of usage only emphasize the fact that personality is a generic term which has no specific meaning, universally accepted. Even animals are referred to as "having personality"; here the connotation is *EX* <u>characteristic individuality</u>.

2   Of writers on the subject of personality, Allport has done the most adequate and comprehensive job of reviewing the historical meanings derived from the Latin *persona*. He distinguished fifty different definitions or meanings. Yet, as MacKinnon has pointed out, two opposed meanings stand out from the earliest to the latest of these definitions. On the one hand, <u>personality is thought of as a mask, a mere shield of outward and usually superficial appearance;</u> on the other hand, <u>it is conceived as the inner nature, the substance of an individual</u>. *contrast*

APPLICATIONS FOR CRITICAL READING AND DISCUSSION

1. Is the purpose mainly to persuade or to inform?
   `inform`

2. Underline definitions in the text.

3. In the left margin, annotate the text by indicating the form(s) of discourse used for defining: narration, description, exemplification (examples), functional analysis, process analysis, causes and/or effects, classification, and comparison and contrast.

4. If one form of discourse is used more than others, identify it here.
   ```
   exemplification
   ```

5. Write a one-sentence definition of the subject (word or term).
   ```
   Personality cannot be defined specifically, though the two leading
   definitions are "a mask, a mere shield of outward and usually superficial
   appearance" and "the inner nature, the substance of a man [person]."
   ```

EXERCISE 5

A tornado may be identified as a particular kind of whirling, highly destructive, wind storm. Morris Tepper extends that definition so that readers will have a good understanding of the many facets of this phenomenon.

Tornado
MORRIS TEPPER

What exactly is a tornado? The general picture is familiar enough. The phenomenon is usually brewed on a hot, sticky day with south winds and an ominous sky. From the base of a thundercloud a funnel-shaped cloud extends a violently twisting spout toward the earth. As it sucks in matter in its path, the twister may turn black, brown or occasionally even white (over snow). The moving cloud shows an almost continuous display of sheet lightning. It lurches along in a meandering path, usually northeastward, at 25 to 40 miles per hour. Sometimes it picks up its finger from the earth for a short distance and then plants it down again. The funnel is very slender: its wake of violence generally averages no more than 400 yards wide. As the tornado approaches, it is heralded by a roar of hundreds of jet planes or thousands of railroad cars. Its path is a path of total destruction. Buildings literally explode as they are sucked by the tornado's low-pressure vortex (where the pressure drop is as much as 10 percent) and by its powerful whirling winds (estimated at up to 500 miles per hour). The amount of damage depends mainly on whether the storm happens to hit populated areas. The worst tornado on record in the U.S. was one that ripped across Missouri, lower Illinois and Indiana in three hours on March 18, 1925, and killed 689 people.

2 The tornado's lifetime is as brief as it is violent. Within a few tens of miles (average: about 16 miles) it spends its force and suddenly disappears.

APPLICATIONS FOR CRITICAL READING AND DISCUSSION

1. Is the purpose mainly to persuade or to inform?

2. Underline definitions in the text.

3. In the left margin, annotate the text by indicating the form(s) of discourse used for defining: narration, description, exemplification (examples), functional analysis, process analysis, causes and/or effects, classification, and comparison and contrast.

4. If one form of discourse is used more than others, identify it here.

5. Write a one-sentence definition of the subject (word or term).

EXERCISE 6

In his famous essay "Self-Reliance," Ralph Waldo Emerson wrote "A man [person] must be a non-conformist." Paul Mussen, Mark Rosenzweig, and associates, writing as social scientists, disagree.

Conformity
PAUL MUSSEN AND MARK ROSENZWEIG ET AL.

Conformity can be defined as a change in a person's opinions or behavior as a result of real or imagined pressure from another person or a group. In common parlance, conformity usually has some negative connotations; to be called a conformist is to be called weak, a follower, a person who cannot or will not think for himself. This connotation is bolstered by the mass media; Hollywood, for example, consistently makes heroes of the nonconformist—the dashing figure who goes his own way in spite of tremendous group pressure. And yet, a moment's reflection should make it perfectly clear that if there is to be a society at all, there *must* be a significant degree of conformity to the laws and customs of that society. A society of nonconformists is a contradiction in terms. Conformity in certain cases may be weakness, but without a basic, underlying, and willing conformity to sensible laws and values, we would have chaos. There would not be enough policemen to protect us from the looters and the rapists; we could not trust our best friends. There are those who complain of the lack of law and order, but there is an interesting question on the other side too. Why is there any law and order in the first place?

APPLICATIONS FOR CRITICAL READING AND DISCUSSION

1. Is the purpose mainly to persuade or to inform?

2. Underline definitions in the text.

3. In the left margin, annotate the text by indicating the form(s) of discourse used for defining: narration, description, exemplification (examples), functional analysis, process analysis, causes and/or effects, classification, and comparison and contrast.

4. If one form of discourse is used more than others, identify it here.

5. Write a one-sentence definition of the subject (word or term).

EXERCISE 7

What was it like to be a white Southerner in the not-too-distant Old South? Ray Jenkins knows. As you read this selection, anticipate a reading-related writing topic asking you to indicate what it is like to live in your neighborhood or the neighborhood where your parents grew up.

Georgia on My Mind
RAY JENKINS

Unless a man has picked cotton all day in August; has sat in an outhouse in 20 degrees in January and passed this time of necessity by reading last year's Sears Roebuck catalogue; has eaten a possum and liked it; has castrated a live pig with a dull pocket knife and has wrung a chicken's neck with his own hands; has learned at least a few chords on a fiddle and guitar; has tried to lure a sharecropper's daughter into the woods for mischievous purposes; has watched a man who had succeeded in doing just that have his sins washed away in the Blood of the Lamb in a baptism in a muddy creek; has been kicked by a mean milch cow and kicked her back; has drunk busthead likker knowing full well it might kill him; has wished the next day it had killed him; has watched a neighbor's house burn down; has drawn a knife on an adversary in fear and anger; has half-soled his one pair of shoes with a tire repair kit; has gone into a deep dark well to get out a dead chicken that had fallen in; has waited beside a dusty road in the midday heat, hoping the R.F.D. postman would bring some long-coveted item ordered from the catalogue; has been in close quarters with a snake; has, in thirsty desperation, drunk water that worked alive with mosquito larvae called wiggletails; has eaten sardines out of a can with a stick; has killed a cat just for the hell of it; has felt like a [black] was mistreated but was afraid to say so; has stepped in the droppings of a chicken and not really cared; has been cheated by someone he worked hard for; has gone to bed at sundown because he could no longer endure the crushing isolation; has ridden a bareback mule three miles to visit a pretty girl who waited in a clean, flimsy cotton dress—unless he has done these things, then he cannot understand what it was like in my South.

2   It is a definition, I hasten to add, which conveys neither superiority nor inferiority; it is morally neutral. It is just that my experience was different from that of my children. Jimmy Carter will understand, but not my children.

APPLICATIONS FOR CRITICAL READING AND DISCUSSION

1. Is the purpose mainly to persuade or to inform?

2. Underline definitions in the text

3. In the left margin, annotate the text by indicating the form(s) of discourse used for defining: narration, description, exemplification (examples), functional analysis, process analysis, causes and/or effects, classification, and comparison and contrast.

4. If one form of discourse is used more than others, identify it here.

5. Write a one-sentence definition of the subject (word or term).

EXERCISE 8

Richard Rodriguez, a Mexican-American, has written widely about the clashing and comingling of cultures, especially in his home state of California. He challenges us to identify and acknowledge all we have borrowed from many cultures. After we have done that, how do we define *America*?

Vocabulary Preview: Write in short definitions for these words as they are used in the context of the following passage. (The paragraph numbers are given in parentheses.) Be prepared to use the words in your own sentences.

atriums (1)

nasal (1)

decipher (2)

assimilation (7)

orthodoxy (7)

paradoxical (7)

arrogance (11)

reciprocal (15)

deteriorated (16)

impertinence (18)

romanticism (20)

brandished (20)

proximity (22)

Does America Still Exist?
RICHARD RODRIGUEZ

For the children of immigrant parents the knowledge comes easier. America exists everywhere in the city—on billboards, frankly in the smell of French fries and popcorn. It exists in the pace: traffic lights, the assertions of neon, the mysterious bong-bong-bong through the atriums of department stores. American exists as the voice of the crowd, a menacing sound—the high nasal accent of American English.

2   When I was a boy in Sacramento (California, the fifties), people would ask me, "Where you from?" I was born in this country, but I knew the question meant to decipher my darkness, my looks.

3   My mother once instructed me to say, "I am an American of Mexican descent." By the time I was nine or ten, I wanted to say, but dared not reply, "I am an American."

4   Immigrants come to America and, against hostility or mere loneliness, they recreate a homeland in the parlor, tacking up postcards or calendars of some impossible blue—lake or sea or sky. Children of immigrant parents are supposed to perch on a hyphen between two countries. Relatives assume the achievement as much as anyone. Relatives are, in any case, surprised when the child begins losing old ways. One day at the family picnic the boy wanders away from their spiced food and faceless stories to watch other boys play baseball in the distance.

5   There is sorrow in the American memory, guilty sorrow for having left something behind—Portugal, China, Norway. The American story is the story of immigrant children and of their children—children no longer able to speak to grandparents. The memory of exile becomes inarticulate as it passes from generation to generation, along with wedding rings and pocket watches—like some mute stone in a wad of old lace. Europe. Asia. Eden.

6   But, it needs to be said, if this is a country where one stops being Vietnamese or Italian, this is a country where one begins to be an American. America exists as a culture and a grin, a faith and a shrug. It is clasped in a handshake, called by a first name.

7   As much as the country is joined in a common culture, however, Americans are reluctant to celebrate the process of assimilation. We pledge allegiance to diversity. America was born Protestant and bred Puritan, and the notion of community we share is derived from a seventeenth-century faith. Presidents and the pages of ninth-grade civics readers yet proclaim the orthodoxy: We are gathered together—but as individuals, with separate pasts, distinct destinies. Our society is as paradoxical as a Puritan congregation: We stand together, alone.

8   Americans have traditionally defined themselves by what they refused to include. As often, however, Americans have struggled, turned in good conscience at last to assert the great Protestant virtue of tolerance. Despite outbreaks of nativist frenzy, America has remained an immigrant country, open and true to itself.

9   Against pious emblems of rural America—soda fountain, Elks hall, Protestant church, and now shopping mall—stands the cold-hearted city, crowded with races and ambitions, curious laughter, much that is odd. Nevertheless, it is the city that has most truly represented America. In the city, however, the millions of singular lives have had no richer notion of wholeness to describe them than the idea of pluralism.

10 "Where you from" the American asks the immigrant child. "Mexico," the boy learns to say.

11 Mexico, the country of my blood ancestors, offers formal contrast to the American achievement. If the United States was formed by Protestant individualism, Mexico was shaped by a medieval Catholic dream of one world. The Spanish journeyed to Mexico to plunder, and they may have gone, in God's name, with an arrogance peculiar to those who intend to convert. But through the conversion, the Indian converted the Spaniard. A new race was born, the *mestizo*, wedding European to Indian. José Vasconcelos, the Mexican philosopher, has celebrated this New World creation, proclaiming it the "cosmic race."

12 Centuries later, in a San Francisco restaurant, a Mexican-American lawyer of my acquaintance says, in English, over *salade niçoise*, that he does not intend to assimilate into gringo society. His claim is echoed by a chorus of others (Italian-Americans, Greeks, Asians) in this era of ethnic pride. The melting pot has been relented, clanking, into the museum of quaint disgrace, alongside Aunt Jemima and the Katzenjammer Kids.* But resistance to assimilation is characteristically American. It only makes clear how inevitable the process of assimilation actually is.

13 For generations, this has been the pattern. Immigrant parents have sent their children to school (simply, they thought) to acquire the "skills" to survive in the city. The child returned home with a voice his parents barely recognized or understood, couldn't trust, and didn't like.

14 In Eastern cities—Philadelphia, New York, Boston, Baltimore—class after class gathered immigrant children to women (usually women) who stood in front of rooms full of children, changing children. So also for me in the 1950s. Irish-Catholic nuns. California. The old story. The hyphen tipped to the right, away from Mexico and toward a confusing but true American identity.

15 I speak now in the chromium American accent of my grammar school classmates—Billy Reckers, Mike Bradley, Carol Schmidt, Kathy O'Grady.... I believe I became like my classmates, became German, Polish, and (like my teachers) Irish. And because assimilation is always reciprocal, my classmates got something of me. (I mean sad eyes; belief in the Indian Virgin; a taste for sugar skulls on the Feast of the Dead.) In the blending, we became what our parents could never have been, and we carried America one revolution further.

16 "Does America still exist?" Americans have been asking the question for so long that to ask it again only proves our continuous link. But perhaps the question deserves to be asked with urgency now. Since the black civil rights movement of the 1960s, our tenuous notion of a shared public life has deteriorated notably.

17 The struggle of black men and women did not eradicate racism, but it became the great moment in the life of America's conscience. Water hoses, bulldogs, blood—the images, rendered black, white, rectangular, passed into living rooms.

18 It is hard to look at a photograph of a crowd taken, say, in 1890 or in 1930 and not notice the absence of blacks. (It becomes an impertinence to wonder if America *still* exists.)

19 In the sixties, other groups of Americans learned to champion their rights by analogy to the black civil rights movement. But the heroic vision

---

*Aunt Jemima—stereotypical black mammy; Katzenjammer Kids—stereotypical cartoon characters

faded. Dr. Martin Luther King, Jr., had spoken with Pauline eloquence of a nation that would unite Christian and Jew, old and young, rich and poor. Within a decade, the struggles of the 1960s were reduced to a bureaucratic competition for little more than pieces of a representational pie. The quest for a portion of power became an end in itself. The metaphor for the American city of the 1970s was a committee: one black,, one woman, one person under thirty. . . .

20   If the small town had sinned against America by too neatly defining who could be an American, the city's sin was a romantic secession. One noticed the romanticism in the antiwar movement—certain demonstrators who demonstrated a lack of tact or desire to persuade and seemed content to play secular Protestants. One noticed the romanticism in the competition among members of "minority groups" to claim the status of Primary Victim. To Americans unconfident of their common identity, minority standing became a way of asserting individuality. Middle-class Americans—men and women clearly not the primary victims of social oppression—brandished their suffering with exuberance.

21   The dream of a single society probably died with "The Ed Sullivan Show." The reality of America persists. Teenagers pass through big-city high schools banded in racial groups, their collars turned up to a uniform shrug. But then they graduate to jobs at the phone company or in banks, where they end up working alongside people unlike themselves. Typists and tellers walk out together at lunchtime.

22   It is easier for us as Americans to believe the obvious fact of our separateness—easier to imagine the black and white Americas prophesied by the Kerner report* (broken glass, street fires)—than to recognize the reality of a city street at lunch time. Americans are wedded by proximity to a common culture. The panhandler at one corner is related to the pamphleteer at the next who is related to the banker who is kin to the Chinese old man wearing an MIT sweatshirt. In any true national history, Thomas Jefferson begets Martin Luther King, Jr., who begets the Gray Panthers.† It is because we lack a vision of ourselves entire—the city street is crowded and we are each preoccupied with finding our own way home—that we lack an appropriate hymn.

23   Under my window now passes a little white girl softly rehearsing to herself a Motown obbligato.

* a federal government report on the causes of violence
† an aggressive group of elderly people advocating for their concerns

APPLICATIONS FOR CRITICAL READING AND DISCUSSION

1. Is the purpose mainly to persuade or to inform?

2. Underline definitions in the text.

3. In the left margin, annotate the text by indicating the form(s) of discourse used for defining: narration, description, exemplification (examples), functional analysis, process analysis, causes and/or effects, classification, and comparison and contrast.

4. If one form of discourse is used more than others, identify it here.

5. Write a one-sentence definition of the subject (word or term).

6. According to Rodriguez, does America still exist?

EXERCISE 9

We are all conditioned, directly and indirectly, to be members of our culture. Here, Polingaysi Qoyawayma writes of her Hopi culture—of how, much more than she had expected, she had absorbed "the Hopi way." In this excerpt from her book *No Turning Back* (told to Vada F. Carlson), she refers to herself in the third person (by name and as "she").

Vocabulary Preview: Write in short definitions for these words as they are used in the context of the following passage. (The paragraph numbers are given in parentheses.) Be prepared to use the words in your own sentences.

indignation (2)

contemptuous (3)

pagan (5)

temerity (7)

chasm (7)

kiva (10)

simulating (11)

mosaic (11)

din (13)

reprisals (18)

The Hopi Way
POLINGAYSI QOYAWAYMA (ELIZABETH Q. WHITE)

In the traditional Hopi pattern, children are advised, instructed, scolded, and sometimes punished, by their maternal uncles. Polingaysi's relations with her mother's brothers had been pleasant, but after she became a member of the Frey household, her old uncle in Moenkopi village began showing disapproval of her. Cousins repeated small remarks he had made about her and she became increasingly aware of his annoyance.

2   One day he sent word for her to come visit him. She went, to find him in a state of indignation. He began scolding at once.

3   "You proud and stubborn girl! Why are you straying from the Hopi way of life? Don't you know it is not good for a Hopi to be proud? Haven't I told you a Hopi must not pretend to hold himself above his people? Why do you keep trying to be a white man? You are a Hopi. Go home. Marry in the Hopi way. Have children."

His eyes were angry and his mouth contemptuous. "I have said you were Hopi, but you are no longer a true Hopi. You don't know the Hopi way. In a year or so, even if you do go back to Oraibi, you won't know anything. Leave these white people who are leading you away from your beliefs. Go. Go now."

4   Tears streamed down Polingaysi's cheeks as she listened to the man's bitter words. All her inner confusion, all her painful indecision, swelled in her breast until she could bear it no longer. She lashed back at him.

5   "I won't! I won't go back to the life of a pagan. Never, never again. I've worked for this education you ridicule. At Riverside, I scrubbed miles of dirty floors while I was learning a little about reading and writing and arithmetic. After I learned to sew, I made dresses for others, bending over the sewing machine while the other girls slept, to earn money for my own dresses.

6 "I've worked hard for everything I have. It has not been easy for me to learn this new way of living. Do you think I'll go back to sleeping on the floor and eating out of a single pot? Do you think I want to have a household of children who are always hungry and in rags, as I was in my childhood? No! I don't care what you think of me. I don't care what my Hopi people think. Not any more. I'm going to keep on learning, no matter how much you despise me for it."

7 Trembling violently, she turned on her heel and left his house, amazed at her temerity. How could she have dared talk in those defiant terms to an uncle? It frightened her. She could see the chasm between her two worlds widening; his words had stung like the lashes of the Whipper Kachina on the day of her initiation into the Kachina cult.

8 She had expected those initiatory lashes. Only Hopi children initiated into the Powamua fraternity escape them. She had looked forward to them as an opening of the door to wisdom.

9 As she walked swiftly toward the Frey home on the hillside, smarting under the injustice of her uncle's reproaches, she recalled the day of her initiation.

10 Feeling important and excited, she had walked between her ceremonial "parents" to the kiva, her shoulder blanket clutched close to shield her body from the February chill. The arms of the ladder had seemed to reach out to her, and she had gone into them and down the rungs into the dim warmth of the kiva.

11 Other initiates sat on the plastered stone bench between their sponsors, feet drawn up, simulating young eagles in the nest. Before she jointed them she saw the feathers dangling from a peg on the wall, and the beautiful little sand mosaic beneath them. It was only after she was seated that she saw the larger sandpainting on which she would later stand for whipping.

12 She began to be afraid. The other children also were fearful. Then an old man, naked except for a G-string, came down the ladder and began addressing the initiates. He spoke rapidly and in low tones. Although she listened intently, Polingaysi could not hear all of his words, but she realized that he was telling the ancient history of the Hopis and of their migrations from the beginning.

13 There was an air of expectancy on the part of the older people as the old man left the kiva, and suddenly there was a fearful din at the kiva opening, a sound of running feet, a beating of yucca lashes against the standard.

14 Hearts racing, the candidates for initiation stared at the kiva opening. Two Hu Kachinas, their bodies painted black with white spots, rushed down the ladder carrying armfuls of yucca lashes. They wore nothing except red moccasins, breech clout, mask, and foxskin ruff. The masks were black and bulging-eyed, with horns at each side, white spots on the cheeks, and a white turkey track in the center of each forehead.

15 Crow Mother, Ang-wu-sna-som-ta-qa, which is to say "Man With Crow Wings Tied To," followed, wearing a woman's dress and ceremonial robe with moccasins, and carrying additional pale green yucca lashes for the whippers. Her mask had great black crow wings at each side.

16 At once a little boy was led forward by his sponsors, his naked body trembling. Stepping into the large sandpainting, he raised one hand above his head and covered his genitals with the other. The lashes curled about his body, leaving welts, then his godfather pulled him aside and took the remainder of the whipping for him.

17 When her turn came, Polingaysi was grateful that she was a girl and was allowed to wear her blanket dress. The whipping she received was not painful, but the emotional strain sent her to the bench weeping and weak. It seemed cruel to her that Crow Mother should urge the whippers to strike harder. However, when the whippers whipped each other at the conclusion of the rites, she felt better. Justice had been done.

18 The Powamua chief then dismissed the Kachinas with gifts of breath feathers and cornmeal and began his lecture. The initiates were now at the threshold of knowledge, he told them. They would learn more secrets soon, but must not tell the younger, uninitiated children what had taken place. Telling, they were warned, would bring reprisals from the angry Kachinas.

19 Reaching the Freys' houseyard, Polingaysi looked down into the narrow streets of the old village of Moenkopi, the rock houses huddled on the lower slopes of the sand-dune-bordered wash.

20 "That initiation!" she thought angrily. "What was it but a pagan rite? I must forget it."

21 Not yet calm enough to talk with the Freys about her clash with the old uncle, she went to her room. Turning toward the mirror, she surveyed her solemn reflection unapprovingly.

22 "Maybe I'm not a true Hopi. But what am I? Am I a true anything? Am I sincere? Do I really want to waste my time in trying to bring the gospel to my stubborn, superstition-bound Hopi people? They will only despise me for it."

23 She began taking the pins from her long and heavy black hair, intending to wash it. Suddenly she realized how automatic the gesture had been, how Hopi. Wash the hair. Purify the life stream.

APPLICATIONS FOR CRITICAL READING AND DISCUSSION

1. Is the purpose mainly to persuade or to inform?

2. Underline definitions in the text.

3. In the left margin, annotate the text by indicating the form(s) of discourse used for defining: narration, description, exemplification (examples), functional analysis, process analysis, causes and/or effects, classification, and comparison and contrast.

4. If one form of discourse is used more than others, identify it here.

5. Write a one-sentence definition of the subject (word or term).

6. How do the author's experience at the initiation and her impulse to wash her hair collectively provide the parts of her definition of "the Hopi way"?

EXERCISE 10

Have you been poor? Read what Jo Goodwin Parker says about poverty before you answer.

What Is Poverty?
JO GOODWIN PARKER

You ask me what is poverty? Listen to me. Here I am, dirty, smelly, and with no "proper" underwear on and with the stench of my rotting teeth near you. I will tell you. Listen to me. Listen without pity. I cannot use your pity. Listen with understanding. Put yourself in my dirty, worn out, ill-fitting shoes, and hear me.

2   Poverty is getting up every morning from a dirt- and illness-stained mattress. The sheets have long since been used for diapers. Poverty is living in a smell that never leaves. This is a smell of urine, sour milk, and spoiling food sometimes joined with the strong smell of long-cooked onions. Onions are cheap. If you have smelled this smell, you did not know how it came. It is the smell of the outdoor privy. It is the smell of young children who cannot walk the long dark way in the night. It is the smell of the mattresses where years of "accidents" have happened. It is the smell of the milk which has gone sour

because the refrigerator long has not worked, and it costs money to get it fixed. It is the smell of rotting garbage. I could bury it, but where is the shovel? Shovels cost money.

3   Poverty is being tired. I have always been tired. They told me at the hospital when the last baby came that I had chronic anemia caused from poor diet, a bad case of worms, and that I need a corrective operation. I listened politely—the poor are always polite. The poor always listen. They don't say that there is no money for iron pills, or better food, or worm medicine. The idea of an operation is frightening and costs so much that, if I had dared, I would have laughed. Who takes care of my children? Recovery from an operation takes a long time. I have three children. When I left them with "Granny" the last time I had a job, I came home to find the baby covered with fly specks, and a diaper that had not been changed since I left. When the dried diaper came off, bits of my baby's flesh came with it. My other child was playing with a sharp bit of broken glass, and my oldest was playing alone at the edge of a lake. I made twenty-two dollars a week, and a good nursery school costs twenty dollars a week for three children. I quit my job.

4   Poverty is dirt. You can say in your clean clothes coming from your clean house, "Anybody can be clean." Let me explain about housekeeping with no money. For breakfast I give my children grits with no oleo or cornbread without eggs and oleo. This does not use up many dishes. What dishes there are, I wash in cold water and with no soap. Even the cheapest soap has to be saved for the baby's diapers. Look at my hands, so cracked and red. Once I saved for two months to buy a jar of Vaseline for my hands and the baby's diaper rash. When I had saved enough, I went to buy it and the price had gone up two cents. The baby and I suffered on. I have to decide every day if I can bear to put my cracked sore hands into the cold water and strong soap. But you ask, why not hot water? Fuel costs money. If you have a wood fire it costs money. If you burn electricity, it costs money. Hot water is a luxury. I do not have luxuries. I know you will be surprised when I tell you how young I am. I look so much older. My back has been bent over the wash tubs every day for so long, I cannot remember when I ever did anything else. Every night I wash every stitch my school age child has on and just hope her clothes will be dry by morning.

5   Poverty is staying up all night on cold nights to watch the fire knowing one spark on the newspaper covering the walls means your sleeping child dies in flames. In summer poverty is watching gnats and flies devour your baby's tears when he cries. The screens are torn and you pay so little rent you know they will never be fixed. Poverty means insects in your food, in your nose, in your eyes, and crawling over you when you sleep. Poverty is hoping it never rains because diapers won't dry when it rains and soon you are using newspapers. Poverty is seeing your children forever with runny noses. Paper handkerchiefs cost money and all your rags you need for other things. Even more costly are antihistamines. Poverty is cooking without food and cleaning without soap.

6   Poverty is asking for help. Have you ever had to ask for help, knowing your children will suffer unless you get it? Think about asking for a loan from a relative, if this is the only way you can imagine asking for help. I will tell you how it feels. You find out where the office is that you are supposed to visit. You circle that block four or five times. Thinking of your children, you go in. Everyone is very busy. Finally, someone comes out and you tell her that you need help. That never is the person you need to see. You go see another person, and after spilling the whole shame of your poverty all over the desk between you, you find that this isn't the right office after all—you must repeat the whole process, and it never is any easier at the next place.

7   You have asked for help, and after all it has a cost. You are again told to wait. You are told why, but you don't really hear because of the red cloud of shame and the rising cloud of despair.

8   Poverty is remembering. It is remembering quitting school in junior high because "nice" children had been so cruel about my clothes and my smell. The attendance officer came. My mother told him I was pregnant. I wasn't, but she thought that I could get a job and help out. I had jobs off and on, but never long enough to learn anything. Mostly I remember being married. I was so young then. I am still young. For a time, we had all the things you have. There was a little house in another town, with hot water and

everything. Then my husband lost his job. There was unemployment insurance for a while and what few jobs I could get. Soon, all our nice things were repossessed and we moved back here. I was pregnant then. This house didn't look so bad when we first moved in. Every week it gets worse. Nothing is ever fixed. We now had no money. There were a few odd jobs for my husband, but everything went for food then, as it does now. I don't know how we lived through three years and three babies, but we did. I'll tell you something, after the last baby I destroyed my marriage. It had been a good one, but could you keep on bringing children in this dirt? Did you ever think how much it costs for any kind of birth control? I knew my husband was leaving the day he left, but there were no goodbys between us. I hope he has been able to climb out of this mess somewhere. He never could hope with us to drag him down.

9   That's when I asked for help. When I got it, you know how much it was? It was, and is, seventy-eight dollars a month for the four of us; that is all I ever can get. Now you know why there is no soap, no needles and thread, no hot water, no aspirin, no worm medicine, no hand cream, no shampoo. None of these things forever and ever and ever. So that you can see clearly, I pay twenty dollars a month rent, and most of the rest goes for food. For grits and cornmeal, and rice and milk and beans. I try my best to use only the minimum electricity. If I use more, there is that much less for food.

10 Poverty is looking into a black future. Your children won't play with my boys. They will turn to other boys who steal to get what they want. I can already see them behind the bars of their prison instead of behind the bars of my poverty. Or they will turn to the freedom of alcohol or drugs, and find themselves enslaved. And my daughter? At best, there is for a her a life like mine.

11 But you say to me, there are schools. Yes, there are schools. My children have no extra books, no magazines, no extra pencils, or crayons, or paper and most important of all, they do not have health. They have worms, they have infections, they have pink-eye all summer. They do not sleep well on the floor, or with me in my one bed. They do not suffer from hunger, my seventy-eight dollars keeps us alive, but they do suffer from malnutrition. Oh yes, I do remember what I was taught about health in school. It doesn't do much good. In some places there is a surplus commodities program. Not here. The county said it cost too much. There is a school lunch program. But I have two children who will already be damaged by the time they get to school.

12 But, you say to me, there are health clinics. Yes, there are health clinics and they are in the towns. I live out here eight miles from town. I can walk that far (even if it is sixteen miles both ways), but can my little children? My neighbor will take me when he goes; but he expects to get paid, *one way or another*. I bet you know my neighbor. He is that large man who spends his time at the gas station, the barbershop, and the corner store complaining about the government spending money on the immoral mothers of illegitimate children.

13 Poverty is an acid that drips on pride until all pride is worn away. Poverty is a chisel that chips on honor until honor is worn away. Some of you say that you would do *something* in my situation, and maybe you would, for the first week or the first month, but for year after year after year?

14 Even the poor can dream. A dream of a time when there is money. Money for the right kinds of food, for worm medicine, for iron pills, for toothbrushes, for hand cream, for a hammer and nails and a bit of screening, for a shovel, for a bit of paint, for some sheeting, for needles and thread. Money to pay *in money* for a trip to town. And, oh, money for hot water and money for soap. A dream of when asking for help does not eat away the last bit of pride. When the office you visit is as nice as the offices of the other governmental agencies, when there are enough workers to help you quickly, when workers do not quit in defeat and despair. When you have to tell your story to only one person, and that person can send you for other help and you don't have to prove your poverty over and over and over again.

15 I have come out of my despair to tell you this. Remember I did not come from another place or another time. Others like me are all around you. Look at us with an angry heart, anger that will help you help me. Anger that will let you tell of me. The poor are always silent. Can you be silent too?

APPLICATIONS FOR CRITICAL READING AND DISCUSSION

1. Is the purpose mainly to persuade or to inform?

2. Underline definitions in the text.

3. In the left margin, annotate the text by indicating the form(s) of discourse used for defining: narration, description, exemplification (examples), functional analysis, process analysis, causes and/or effects, classification, and comparison and contrast.

4. If one form of discourse is used more than others, identify it here.

5. Write a one-sentence definition of the subject (word or term).

6. If you were the chair of a committee the author is addressing, what would you say to her?

The Reading Connection from Classroom Sources

EXERCISE 11

Almost every subculture has certain words that are understandable only to people who live in that culture. American prison slang has been around for more than a hundred years and is richly and colorfully complex, yet simple and direct. Prison student Jeri Linda White presents a brief language lesson.

```
                  Prison Slang
                 Jeri Linda White
     Prison slang is like other slang in that it is language
that is used in a special way for special reasons; like
conventional slang, some words have unusual, nonstandard
meanings, and some words are invented. Most slang is used
by people who want to conform to group language customs.
In prison it is used both by people who don't want others
to know what they are talking about and by those who are
seeking group identity. As a variety of language it is
like a dialect because it is just part of the culture of
that group. Prison slang covers many areas, but it
especially reflects prisoners' concerns: violence,
talking, and reputation. The very idea of violence is
strangely muted by the terms used to discuss brutal acts.
If a person is attacked by a group of people who throw a
blanket over her head before they beat her, she is said to
be the recipient of a "blanket party" given by a "rat
```

pack." If she "caught a cold" or they "took her wind," she died. They may have killed her with a sharp instrument called a "shank" or a "shiv." Perhaps she didn't know there was a "raven" (contract) out on her; she thought they were only "putting on a floor show" (pretending) or "selling wolf tickets" (bluffing). She should have listened to them talk more carefully. They said she had "snitched them off" (informed), and her friend had "pulled her coat" (told her something she should know), but then a cop came by and she said, "Radio it, dog-face it, dummy up" (all meaning shut up), and then she "put it on hold" (filed it away for future use). That was her mistake because the woman out to get her was a "die hard, hard core, cold piece" (each meaning career criminal), who was a "hog" (enforcer), "dancer" (fighter), and a "jive bitch" (agitator). These are only a few of the hundreds of slang words used by women behind bars. They are part of prison life.

APPLICATIONS FOR CRITICAL READING AND DISCUSSION

1. Is the purpose mainly to persuade or to inform?

2. Underline definitions in the text.

3. In the left margin, annotate the text by indicating the form(s) of discourse used for defining: narration, description, exemplification (examples), functional analysis, process analysis, causes and/or effects, classification, and comparison and contrast.

4. If one form of discourse is used more than others, identify it here.

5. Write a one-sentence definition of the subject (word or term).

EXERCISE 12

Demonstration Using the DCODE Worksheet

Would you like someone to love you or help you in an extreme fashion? Linda Wong thinks it would not be a good idea. Consider her definition of *extremist*.

NAME: Linda Wong

SECTION: _____ CHAPTER: _____ DATE: _____

Delve   Generate your topic, or ideas for your topic, by delving into your subject area through:

- *Freewriting*—writing sentence after sentence, nonstop and spontaneously.
- *Brainstorming*—jotting down answers to Who? What? Where? When? Why? and How? and then listing words and phrases in relation to those answers.
- *Clustering*—connecting bubbled ideas with lines to show strings of relationships, producing each new bubble item in response to the question, What comes to mind?
- *Combining* any of these approaches, as directed by your instructor.

Freewriting:

Some people think that extremists are good if they are involved in good things and bad if they are involved in bad things, but that is not true. The extremists are people that have lost their sense of balance and perspective. They don't have control over their own lives but they want to control the lives of others. The extremist in love is the person that loves too much. It reminds me of a guy down the street that is so extreme in love for this wife that he won't let her dress the way she wants to and won't let her go anywhere without him. He really loves her but he loves her too much. Some of the greatest villains in history were extremists. They may have even started with a good idea, but they became preoccupied with the idea, and they became extremists. Nobody likes to be around extremists. They're people that do a lot of damage.

Brainstorming:

Who?	people
What?	extremists
Where?	society
When?	all the time
Why?	insecurity
How?	losing sense of balance, going too far

Clustering:

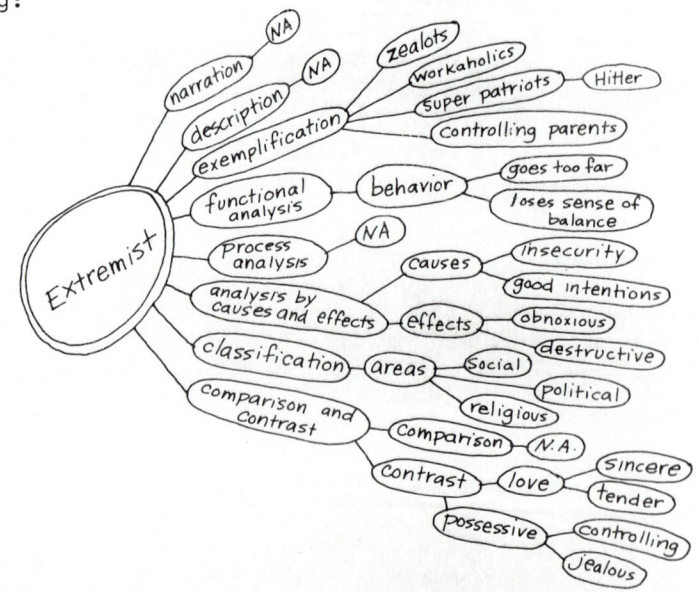

Concentrate Concentrate your work by stating your topic in one sentence that is not too broad, narrow, or vague to be developed. Base this sentence (which may become the topic sentence for your paragraph or the thesis for your essay) on an idea emerging from the **Delve** stage. You may have to try several statements here before you formulate one that is best for your writing task. Be sure that your final statement covers your assignment or intent and specifies both your subject (what you are writing about) and treatment (what aspect you will focus on). Label the *subject* and *treatment* parts.

<u>subject</u>   <u>treatment</u>
<u>Extremists are involved people who lose their sense of balance and go too far in concentrating on one thing</u>.

Organize Complete an outline or a cluster, as directed by your instructor. The cluster should be a section from, or a refined version of, the **Delve** clustering. Regardless of the strategy you use, the organizational pattern should indicate a division of your topic into parts that will, in turn, be further subdivided for support as necessary to address a particular audience on your concentrated topic.

```
    I.   Going too far
         A. Become preoccupied with one thing
         B. Lose sense of balance
    II.  Produce bad effect
         A. Are unpleasant to be around
         B. Are often destructive
    III. Become incomplete
         A. Are often thought of as one kind of person
            1. Workaholics
            2. Zealots
            3. Superpatriots
         B. Diminished by loss of perspective
```

Draft On separate paper, write and then revise your assignment as many times as necessary for **c**oherence, **l**anguage (usage, tone, and diction), **u**nity, **e**mphasis, **s**upport, and **s**entence structure (**cluess**).

Edit Correct problems in fundamentals such as **c**apitalization, **o**missions, **p**unctuation, and **s**pelling (**cops**). Before writing the final draft, read your paper aloud to discover oversights and awkwardness of expression.

First Draft

Going Too Far

Some people believe that it is good to be an extremist in some areas, but those people are actually changing the meaning of the word. ~~They are workaholics, the zealots, the superpatriots of the world.~~ According to the Random House Dictionary of the English Language, the word extreme itself mans "excessively biased ideas, intemperative conduct." ~~The~~ The person who is ~~an~~ extremist ~~is one who~~ goes too far. That means going too far in whatever the person is doing. I once heard someone say that it is good for ~~a person~~ people to be ~~an~~ extremist**s** in love. But that is not true. It is good to be enthusiastically and sincerely in love**,** but the people who are extremists in love ~~are those who~~ love excessively and intemperately. Some people who love well and may be tender and sensitive and attentive**,** but extremists are possessive or smothering. The same can be said of parents. We all want good parents**,** but Parental exremists involve themselves too much in the lives of their children, who, in turn, may find it difficult to develop as individuals and become independent. Even in patriotism, Good patriots are to be distinguished from extreme patriots. Good patriots love their country, but extreme patriots love their country so much that they think are inferior and suspect downgrade citizens from other countries. Extreme patriots may have Hitler like tendencies. Just what is wrong with extremists then? It is the loss of perspective. The extremists are so preoccupied with one concern that they lose their sense of balance. They may begin with a good objective, but they focus on it so much that they can become destructive, even obnoxious, and often pitiful. The worst effect is that extremists lose their completeness ~~wholeness~~ as human beings.

Final Draft

Going Too Far
Linda Wong

Some people believe that it is good to be an extremist in some areas, but those people are actually changing the meaning of the word. According to the Random House Dictionary of the English Language, the word extreme itself means "excessively biased ideas, intemperate

conduct." The extremist goes too far. That means going
too far in whatever the person is doing. I once heard
someone say that it is good for people to be extremists in *Example*
love. But that is not true. It is good to be enthusiasti- *Contrast*
cally and sincerely in love, but extremists in love love
excessively and intemperately. People who love well may be *Example*
tender and sensitive and attentive, but extremists are *Contrast*
possessive or smothering. The same can be said of parents.
We all want good parents, but parental extremists involve *Example*
themselves too much in the lives of their children, who,
in turn, may find it difficult to develop as individuals
and become independent. Even in patriotism, good patriots
are to be distinguished from extreme patriots. Good *Example*
patriots love their country, but extreme patriots love *Contrast*
their country so much that they think citizens from other
countries are inferior and suspect. Extreme patriots may
have Hitler-like tendencies. Just what is wrong with
extremists then? It is the loss of perspective. The
extremists are so preoccupied with one concern that they
lose their sense of balance. They are the workaholics, the *Examples*
zealots, the superpatriots of the world. They may begin
with a good objective, but they focus on it so much that
they can become destructive, obnoxious, and often pitiful. *Effect*
The worst effect is that these extremists lose their
completeness as human beings.

APPLICATIONS FOR CRITICAL READING AND DISCUSSION

1. Is the purpose mainly to persuade or to inform?
   to persuade

2. Underline definitions in the text.

3. In the left margin, annotate the text by indicating the form(s) of discourse used for defining: narration, description, exemplification (examples), functional analysis, process analysis, causes and/or effects, classification, and comparison and contrast.

4. If one form of discourse is used more than others, identify it here.
   exemplification

5. Write a one-sentence definition of the subject (word or term).
   The extremist is an involved person who goes too far in attitude or behavior and loses his or her sense of proportions.

EXERCISE 13

In her psychology and sociology classes, student Michelle Proctor discovered that *motivation* has been defined variously by social scientists with different perspectives.

Perspectives on Motivation
Michelle Proctor
What is motivation? It is basically defined as any
action or behavior that drives people to satisfy their
biological or psychological needs. There are three very

good theories that give different perspectives on motivation: Darwin's Instinct Theory, Hull's Drive Reduction Theory, and Maslow's Hierarchy of Needs Theory.

Charles Darwin's Instinct Theory explains that our basic instincts are what motivate us. The salmon's basic instincts tell it when to swim a thousand miles across an ocean to a river and up into the gravel bed where it was spawned years before and where it will spawn now. Instinct Theorists regard motivation in several ways. They believe our curiosity drives us to learn and acquire more. Our jealousy of others and yet our fearfulness of being alone motivates us to behave, while our needs of sociability lead us to do many things in order to be accepted. This theory seems to be good for defining much biological motivation, but it does not explain much of behavior.

The Drive Reduction Theory was brought forth in 1943 by Clark Hull. He believed motivation came from primary drives and secondary or acquired drives. Primary drives are the need for sleep, food, water, and other basic needs. Secondary needs would be our affiliation with others and our contact with them. If a person were dying of thirst and came to a town where he could find water, then the primary need would be to get water while his secondary need would be to socialize with the townspeople. The fault in Drive Reduction theory is that after our primary needs have been filled, our behavior does not stop. Our relationship with our environment is a good example of this. In earlier years we were motivated by a need to survive in our environment. Now that that need has been met, we still want to master our environment to the point that we may pollute it until no one will survive.

The third theory on motivation came from Abraham Maslow in 1970. Maslow's Hierarchy of Needs is explained in a pyramid of five steps, starting from the lowest need, the biological, to the highest need, self-actualization. Each step may be reached only by the completion of the previous step. In Maslow's pyramid the first need that must be met is biological. This contains our basic needs of food, water, and sleep. After that has been fulfilled, then safety must be met. We must be physically and psychologically secure in our environment and our surroundings to reach the next stage of love and belongingness. Here we must be able to love someone or something to receive love in return. This is where step four, self-esteem, comes into play, and self-esteem must be very high for us to reach the final step, self-actualization. Here we can accept our environment and work to help others learn and survive in their surroundings.

The first two theories define *motivation* primarily on the basis of our biological needs. Both contributed valuable insights into our understanding of why we behave as we do. Maslow was able to build on the ideas the other social scientists had developed. His Hierarchy of Needs is more comprehensive, offering a combination of biological and psychological needs. It represents the best definition we now have.

APPLICATIONS FOR CRITICAL READING AND DISCUSSION

1. Is the purpose mainly to persuade or to inform?

2. Underline definitions in the text.

3. In the left margin, annotate the text by indicating the form(s) of discourse used for defining: narration, description, exemplification (examples), functional analysis, process analysis, causes and/or effects, classification, and comparison and contrast.

4. If one form of discourse is used more than others, identify it here.

5. Write a one-sentence definition of the subject (word or term).

Suggested Topics for Writing Extended Definitions

The following topics are appropriate for extended development of definitions; most of them will also serve well for exercises in writing simple definitions.

1. Conservative
2. Hotdogger
3. Bonding
4. Sexist
5. Cult
6. Biker
7. Liberal
8. Workaholic
9. Surfer
10. Personal space
11. Clotheshorse
12. Educated
13. Gang
14. Freedom
15. Body language
16. Airhead
17. Druggie
18. Convict
19. Slang
20. Psychopath
21. School spirit
22. Feminist
23. Chicano
24. Jock
25. Hispanic
26. African American
27. Macho
28. Cool
29. Trendy
30. Jerk

Reading-Related Topics

"Personality"

1. Using this selection as a model, write an extended definition of one of the following terms that also has several different definitions: *character*, *instinct*, or *human nature*.

"Tornado"

2. Define another natural disaster, such as a flood, hurricane, earthquake, drought, or dust storm.

"Conformity"

3. If you disagree with the authors, provide your own definition of conformity. Define another term that is variously represented: *liberal*, *conservative*, or *radical*.

"Georgia on My Mind"

4. Ray Jenkins defines *traditional rural, white Southerner* by listing the unique and colorful experiences of that kind of person. Define one of the following persons by listing his or her experiences: dweller in a project, barrio, shantytown, streets, prison, juvenile hall, migrant worker camp, reservation, or refugee camp; someone who is a day care worker, security guard, police officer, preacher, nurse, firefighter, parent, or coach.

"Does America Still Exist?"

5. Richard Rodriguez shows that *America* is difficult to define. Try defining one of these terms that are equally difficult for reasons similar to the ones he gave: African American, Hispanic, Chicano(a), Latino(a), Native American, or Asian-American.

"The Hopi Way"

6. Every culture has its "way." The same can be said of people who live in certain areas or regions, of certain families, subcultures (drug, racket, cult), and of certain religions. Select one and, using "The Hopi Way" as a model, write a "The _____ Way" definition.

"What Is Poverty?"

7. Jo Goodwin Parker defines poverty in its "purest" or most extreme form. Select another term representing something that many have not experienced in its purest form and define it—for example, pain, hunger, loneliness, anger, jealousy, hurt, depression.

"Prison Slang"

8. Define another term for language usage such as jargon ("shop talk" by a group of people in a restricted activity, especially vocational or recreational), regional slang, age group slang, sign-language slang, or body language.

"Perspectives on *Motivation*"

9. Pick another term that has been defined by scholars with different perspectives, and summarize the various definitions. You may need to do a bit of research. Here are some terms: *instinct*, *human nature*, *free will*, and *sin*.

Writer's Checklist

Apply these ideas to your writing as you work with **DCODE**. Later, as a peer editor, apply the same ideas to the material you evaluate.

1. At the outset, determine your purpose as either persuasive or informative.
2. Match your tone to the purpose of the writing.
3. Use the clustering in **DCODE** to consider the other forms of discourse as sources of information for your definition.
4. Use the outline in the Organize stage of **DCODE** to establish the sequence in your main points of development.
5. Don't overlook word derivation, synonyms, direct explanations, indirect explanations.
6. Avoid "is where" and "is when," circular definitions, and the use of more difficult words in the definition than the one being defined.
7. For the extended formal or analytic definition, specify the term, class, and characteristic(s). Example: Capitalism is an economic system characterized by investment of money, private ownership, and free enterprise.
8. Consider these ways of introducing a definition: with a question, with a statement of what it is not, with a statement of what it originally meant, or with a discussion of why a clear definition is important. You may use a combination of these ways or all of them before you continue with your definition.
9. Whether you will personalize a definition depends on your purpose and your audience. Your instructor may ask you to write about a word within the context of your experience or to write about it from a detached, clinical view.

Journal-Entry Suggestions

1. Select some of the unused "Reading-Related Topics" suggestions, and use them for journal topics.
2. Write a reaction to one or more "Reading Connection" selections. Agree, disagree, apply the statements to your own experiences, indicate the value of such statements, or explain why your were surprised, shocked, disgusted, pleased, or whatever, by the material.
3. Invent statements (using definition if appropriate) to support headlines from *Weekly World News:*
    "World's First Potty-Trained Frog!"
    "Hero Chimp Lands Plane After Pilot Passes Out!"
    "42-lb. Grasshopper Captured—Alive!"
    "Grandma Hatches Bird Eggs with Her Own Body!"
    "Woman Jailed for Plant Abuse!"
    "Hero Pig Saves Farmer Trapped Under Tractor!"
    "Her Tongue Is 9 Inches Long!"
    "Man Turns Into a Werewolf at Planetarium Lunar Show!"
    "Bigfoot Stole My Wife!"
    "Man Makes Fortune Selling Fleas!"

NAME:_____

SECTION:_____ CHAPTER:_____ DATE:_____

Delve   Generate your topic, or ideas for your topic, by delving into your subject area through:

- *Freewriting*—writing sentence after sentence, nonstop and spontaneously.
- *Brainstorming*—jotting down answers to Who? What? Where? When? Why? and How? and then listing words and phrases in relation to those answers.
- *Clustering*—connecting bubbled ideas with lines to show strings of relationships, producing each new bubble item in response to the question, What comes to mind?
- *Combining* any of these approaches, as directed by your instructor.

WORKSHEET: Writing in DCODE

Concentrate   Concentrate your work by stating your topic in one sentence that is not too broad, narrow, or vague to be developed. Base this sentence (which may become the topic sentence for your paragraph or the thesis for your essay) on an idea emerging from the **Delve** stage. You may have to try several statements here before you formulate one that is best for your writing task. Be sure that your final statement covers your assignment or intent and specifies both your subject (what you are writing about) and treatment (what aspect you will focus on). Label the *subject* and *treatment* parts.

Organize   Complete an outline or a cluster, as directed by your instructor. The cluster should be a section from, or a refined version of, the **Delve** clustering. Regardless of the strategy you use, the organizational pattern should indicate a division of your topic into parts that will, in turn, be further subdivided for support as necessary to address a particular audience on your concentrated topic.

Draft   On separate paper, write and then revise your assignment as many times as necessary for **c**oherence, **l**anguage (usage, tone, and diction), **u**nity, **e**mphasis, **s**upport, and **s**entence structure (**cluess**).

Edit   Correct problems in fundamentals such as **c**apitalization, **o**missions, **p**unctuation, and **s**pelling (**cops**). Before writing the final draft, read your paper aloud to discover oversights and awkwardness of expression.

Literary Analysis: Reacting to Stories

12

> "Easy writing makes for hard reading.
> — Ernest Hemingway

Why do we read narrative literature? How is writing about narrative literature similar to other reading-related writing? What are conflict, plot, and theme in narrative literature?

Why We Read Fiction

Why do we read fiction? Among the proposed answers is one particularly intriguing theory by Robert Penn Warren. He said that we often find life disjointed and our own behavior beyond clear, reasonable explanation. But then we can study narrative literature, which has patterns of human life that we can contemplate from a distance. If the writers are good, we can see parallels with what we have experienced. We may see causes and effects that make sense. Fiction gives us little universes to ponder, to discuss with others, to marvel at, and to question.

Reading Literature

Because literature is a representation of life, it may be discussed from many perspectives. A single short story or poem may be a study in philosophy, psychology, history, or some other field. Prepare to engage your full intellect and complete knowledge in considering the literature you read. Keep in mind that no two people will interpret a piece of literature in precisely the same way because all of us are different in our experiences, ways of thinking, and values. However, we also have much in common, and we will usually be able to agree on one or more reasonable interpretations that can be explained using evidence found in the narrative without overlooking contradictory evidence.

Writing About Literature

In previous chapters, we have discussed how to write in relation to the essay or paragraph. In this chapter, we turn our attention to the short story and the narrative poem for subject material. The change is not significant. Stories and poems contain many of the forms emphasized in this book: narration, description, exemplification, functional analysis, causal analysis, classification, definition, comparison and contrast, and argumentation. Stories and poems also have raw materials that can be transformed into the same patterns of writing. Therefore, learning to write about literature extends what you are learning about writing while providing a new dimension of experience. This new dimension lays the groundwork for writing in more advanced composition classes, literature classes, and other humanities classes.

The forms of narrative we work with in this chapter are not complicated. Because both short stories and narrative poems tell stories, we can use the same principles to discuss them in a broad fashion. The following points will provide you with a good framework for basic reading for understanding, annotating your text, interpreting, and even generating topics for writing.

Setting

In its simplest form the *setting* is the environment for the literary work. It may be merely appropriate, without calling attention to itself. It may also be supportive, reinforcing the theme. For example, a story about death may occur in the winter, whereas a story about life or rediscovery of life may occur in springtime or early summer. Edgar Allan Poe uses this reinforcing technique in "The Fall of the House of Usher," a story about a disintegrating family living in a decrepit limestone house located in the midst of a swamp stewing with decaying plants. In this instance the setting is more than its descriptive details; certain aspects such as the house are *symbolic* (representing something in addition to itself). The house, poised precipitously above the water, is about to descend into its "grave." But in "The Lottery," an almost equally well-known story, the author, Shirley Jackson, sets her story of the barbaric execution of an innocent citizen in a bucolic village on a beautiful early summer day. The brutal act is all the more shocking because of the contrast between setting and event.

Conflict

Conflict is at the heart of each fictional work, whether it be a feature film or a prose story. In a short story the conflict is likely to relate mostly to the main character. That main character may be at odds with forces such as another character, something in the environment, or even something within himself or herself.

Characters

That main character, the one who deals most directly and most intimately with the conflict, is often called the *protagonist*. The opposition to the protagonist in dealing with his or her problem is often called the *antagonist*. In certain stories these terms may not fit well, but the principle of the main character dealing consciously or unconsciously with conflict is basic to fiction.

In dealing with conflict the central character or characters are likely to change, resist change, or make some self-discovery. This character or these characters will not necessarily be aware of the significance of what is occurring or even that it *is* occurring.

Plot

As the character or characters deal with conflict, a sequence of events will ensue. That sequence is called the *plot*. It begins with an *exposition*—an introduction to the situation and basic conflict. Then it continues through an event or series of events to the *climax*, or highest point in the struggle. Finally, it ends with the *resolution*—a final comment on the situation.

Theme

If the plot is basically "what happens," the *theme* is the significance of what happens. The theme is what the story means in terms of human nature, the human condition, one individual, or particular institutions. The theme is sometimes called the *fictional point*, and only in certain didactic stories will it be the same as the moral. In some contemporary stories that represent a fragmented, illogical reality, the theme may not be easily stated, because the depicted reality itself often defies clear comprehension.

Point of View

Each work will be told from a certain perspective, or in rare instances from more than one. That perspective is called *point of view*, which in most stories will be either *first-person* or *third-person*.

In the first-person story the reader hears the story from the narrator. That narrator may be the central character in the work; for example, Holden Caulfield, in *The Catcher in the Rye*, is both narrator and central character. The narrator can also be a minor character or merely an observer. Regardless of the role of the narrator, we get the freshness and directness of someone who is there; the "I" person speaks.

The other common point of view is third person. With this perspective we have a narrator who reports from a detached view, never using "I" to refer to himself or herself but instead using third-person pronouns such as "he" and "she." The author may choose to restrict himself or herself further by writing in *third-person objective*. This point of view presents characters and situations as we would ordinarily perceive them. We get to know people mainly by considering (1) how they look, (2) what they say, (3) how they act, (4) how others react to them, and (5) what others say about them.

The author may claim one other prerogative and reveal what a character or characters are thinking. Thus, the author becomes all-knowing. This enhanced point of view can be broadly called *third-person omniscient* (a term that may be qualified, depending on the author's self-imposed limitations or focus). The third-person omniscient point of view (with whatever limitation) is the most common in contemporary fiction. Most thrillers, for example, are told in the third-person omniscient point of view with a shifting or multiple approach to allow for a close scrutiny of several characters and their situations.

Analysis

The elements of narrative literature can be considered for emphasis in the analysis of a work, either separately or in combination. In other words, you can write a composition mainly about the use of setting in a particular work, or you can write an analysis that is equally concerned with character and theme. But regardless of the emphasis, since you are writing about a work that is made up of interdependent parts, you cannot easily write about one part and completely exclude the others. The theme of the work, the meaning of it, could scarcely be omitted in consideration of any of its parts, because each part is directed toward that fictional point.

Finding Topics for Literary Analysis

Analytical Analysis

Any one of the aspects of a narrative can serve as a good topic for a paragraph or essay. Here are some more specific ideas:

- *Setting:* Write about the appropriateness of the setting (with or without symbols) in supporting or even in representing the theme. You might employ your knowledge of the techniques of good descriptive writing by analyzing what the author has done with diction, images, and figurative language.

- *Conflict:* Discuss the extent to which the main character perceived and dealt with the conflict.

- *Character:* Write about the character's changing, not changing, or gaining self-knowledge. Or write a functional analysis based on a few of the central character's traits (such as honesty, dedication, insecurity, immaturity, cleverness, and low self-esteem); use **Delve** techniques to find these. You can also discuss characters in studies of comparison and contrast, definition (perhaps combined with functional analysis as in "Character X is a sexist"), or analysis of causes or effects (the whys or the results of a situation).

- *Plot:* Unless you are going to write about some idea such as irony or reversal, avoid this aspect because of the temptation to fall into the "plot summary" trap, which means merely telling what happens in the story rather than analyzing and interpreting.

- *Point of view:* An author selects a point of view that is advantageous to the story he or she wants to tell. Explain why a particular point of view is advantageous; for example, the first-person perspective may characterize, and the third-person objective may provide a sense of detachment or distance.

- *Theme:* Discuss how other aspects of the story (especially setting, conflict, character, and plot) support or establish the theme, the meaning of the story.

Speculative Analysis

There are also more imaginative ways of writing about literature. You can personalize aspects of plot, theme, or characterization by applying them to your own life. Or you can creatively alter stories by inventing new scenes for a character, projecting a character into the future in order to speculate about development, moving a character from one story to another, or fabricating flashbacks that would explain behavior found in a story. You can explore these and other imaginative ways of writing about fiction by trying some of the Imaginative Suggested Topics for Writing About Literature at the end of this chapter. Regardless of the type of assignment you do, you will need to support your ideas in a clear and logical manner.

Writing Literary Analysis with DCODE

As with other assignments, **DCODE** will serve you well in providing writing strategies. After you have read and annotated the story or poem, you will be ready to:

- *Freewrite*, to help you recollect your insights and knowledge;
- *Brainstorm*, to key in on specific information pertaining to the topic you have decided to explore;
- *Cluster*, to see some patterns;
- *Concentrate*, to frame a topic idea (a topic sentence or thesis);
- *Outline*, to establish sequence (probably by time, place, or emphasis);

- *Draft*, to present and revise your ideas; and
- *Edit*, to do the final polishing.

The first exercise contains a reading presented with completed Applications for Discussion. It is followed by student demonstrations: a student paragraph written with **DCODE**, another student paragraph, and a student essay.

The Reading Connection

EXERCISE 1

Demonstration with Annotations

On some occasions professionals have to use force for the best of reasons. But do the professionals maintain their objectivity when resistance occurs? In this story, William Carlos Williams, a medical doctor and a Pulitzer Prize–winning author, presents a doctor who struggles with his patient and, even more mightily, with himself.

Vocabulary Preview: Write in short definitions for these words as they are used in the context of the following passage. (The paragraph numbers are given in parentheses.) Be prepared to use the words in your own sentences.

photogravure (4)   apprehension (23)

diphtheria (11)   hysterically (25)

ensuing (22)   membrane (33)

The Use of Force
WILLIAM CARLOS WILLIAMS

They were new patients to me, all I had was the name, Olson. Please come down as soon as you can, my daughter is very sick.

2   When I arrived I was met by the mother, a big startled-looking woman, very clean and apologetic who merely said, Is this the doctor? and let me in. In the back, she added, You must excuse us, doctor, we have her in the kitchen where it is warm. It is very damp here sometimes.

3   The child was fully dressed and sitting on her father's lap near the kitchen table. He tried to get up, but I motioned for him not to bother, took off my overcoat and started to look things over. I could see that they were all very nervous, eyeing me up and down distrustfully. As often, in such cases, they weren't telling me more than they had to, it was up to me to tell them; that's why they were spending three dollars on me.

4   The child was fairly eating me up with her cold, steady eyes, and no expression to her face whatever. She did not move and seemed, inwardly, quiet; an unusually attractive little thing, and as strong as a heifer in appearance. But her face was flushed, she was breathing rapidly, and I realized that she had a high fever. She had magnificent blonde hair, in profusion. One of those picture children often reproduced in advertising leaflets and the photogravure sections of the Sunday papers.

5   She's had a fever for three days, began the father and we don't know what it comes from. My wife has given her things, you know, like

(annotations: "all uncomfortable"; "simple farm house")

people do, but it don't do no good. And there's been a lot of sickness around. So we tho't you'd better look her over and tell us what is the matter.

6   As doctors often do I took a trial shot at it as a point of departure. Has she had a sore throat?

7   Both parents answered me together, No . . . No, she says her throat don't hurt her.

8   Does your throat hurt you? added the mother to the child. But the little girl's expression didn't change nor did she move her eyes from my face.

9   Have you looked?

10 I tried to, said the mother, but I couldn't see.

11 As it happens we had been having a number of cases of diphtheria in the school to which this child went during that month and we were all, quite apparently, thinking of that, though no one had as yet spoken of the thing.

12 Well, I said, suppose we take a look at the throat first. I smiled in my best professional manner and asking for the child's first name I said, come on Mathilda, open your mouth and let's take a look at your throat.

13 Nothing doing.

14 Aw, come on, I coaxed, just open your mouth wide and let me take a look. Look, I said opening both hands wide, I haven't anything in my hands. Just open up and let me see.

15 Such a nice man, put in the mother. Look how kind he is to you. Come on, do what he tells you to do. He won't hurt you.

16 At that I ground my teeth in disgust. If only they wouldn't use the word "hurt" I might be able to get somewhere. But I did not allow myself to be hurried or disturbed but speaking quietly and slowly I approached the child again.

17 As I moved my chair a little nearer suddenly with one cat-like movement both her hands clawed instinctively for my eyes and she almost reached them too. In fact she knocked my glasses flying and they fell, though unbroken, several feet away from me on the kitchen floor.

18 Both the mother and father almost turned themselves inside out in embarrassment and apology. You bad girl, said the mother, taking her and shaking her by one arm. Look what you've done. The nice man . . .

19 For heaven's sake, I broke in. Don't call me a nice man to her. I'm here to look at her throat on the chance that she might have diphtheria and possibly die of it. But that's nothing to her. Look here, I said to the child, we're going to look at your throat. You're old enough to understand what I'm saying. Will you open it now by yourself or shall we have to open it for you?

20 Not a move. Even her expression hadn't changed. Her breaths however were coming faster and faster. Then the battle began. I had to do it. I had to have a throat culture for her own protection. But first I told the parents that it was entirely up to them. I explained the danger but said that I would not insist on a throat examination so long as they would take the responsibility.

21 If you don't do what the doctor says you'll have to go to the hospital, the mother admonished her severely.

22 Oh yeah? I had to smile to myself. After all, I had already fallen in love with the savage brat, the parents were contemptible to me. In the ensuing struggle they grew more and more abject, crushed, exhausted while she surely rose to magnificent heights of insane fury of effort bred of her terror of me.

23 The father tried his best, and he was a big man but the fact that she was his daughter, his shame at her behavior and his dread of hurting her made him release her just at the critical times when I had almost achieved success, till I wanted to kill him. But his dread also that she might have diphtheria made him tell me to go on, go on though he himself was almost fainting, while the mother moved back and forth behind us raising and lowering her hands in an agony of apprehension.

24 Put her in front of you on your lap, I ordered, and hold both her wrists.

25 But as soon as he did the child let out a scream. Don't, you're hurting me. Let go of my hands. Let them go I tell you. Then she shrieked terrifyingly, hysterically. Stop it! Stop it! You're killing me!

26 Do you think she can stand it, doctor, said the mother.

27 You get out, said the husband to the wife. Do you want her to die of diphtheria?

28 Come on now, hold her, I said.

29 Then I grasped the child's head with my left hand and tried to get the wooden tongue depressor between her teeth. She fought, with clenched teeth, desperately! But now I also had grown furious—at a child. I tried to hold myself down but I couldn't. I know how to expose a throat for

inspection. And I did my best. When finally I got the wooden spatula behind the last teeth and just the point of it into the mouth cavity, she opened up for an instant but before I could see anything she came down again and gripping the wooden blade between her molars <u>she reduced it to splinters before I could get it out again.</u> *she wins Round 3*

30. Aren't you ashamed, the mother yelled at her. Aren't you ashamed to act like that in front of the doctor? *strategy and weapon*

31. Get me a smooth-handled spoon of some sort, I told the mother. We're going through with this. The child's mouth was already bleeding. Her tongue was cut and she was screaming in wild hysterical shrieks. Perhaps I should have desisted and come back in an hour or more. No doubt it would have been better. But I had seen at least two children lying dead in bed of neglect in such cases, and feeling that I must get a diagnosis now or never I went at it again. <u>But the worst of it was that I too had got beyond reason. I could have torn the child apart in my own fury and enjoyed it. It was a pleasure to attack her. My face was burning with it.</u> *professional reasons and animal instincts*

32. The damned little brat must be protected against her own idiocy, one says to one's self at such times. Others must be protected against her. It is a social necessity. And all these things are true. But a blind fury, a feeling of adult shame, bred of a longing for muscular release are the operatives. One goes on to the end. *Dr wins in TKO in Round 4*

33. In a final unreasoning assault <u>I overpowered the child's neck and jaws. I forced the heavy silver spoon back of her teeth and down her throat till she gagged.</u> And there it was—both tonsils covered with membrane. She had fought valiantly to keep me from knowing her secret. She had been hiding that sore throat for three days at least and lying to her parents in order to escape just such an outcome as this.

34. Now truly she was furious. She had been on the defensive before but now she attacked. Tried to get off her father's lap and fly at me while tears of defeat blinded her eyes.

she's a bad loser. He's a winner with a bad conscience because, in his mind, he lost his professional integrity. He is his own harshest critic.

APPLICATIONS FOR CRITICAL READING AND DISCUSSION

1. Point out the significance of the setting, either stated or implied.

        Country farmhouse of a poor, uneducated family. In a simple, almost
        primitive setting, the doctor is stripped of his code of professional
        manner and descends to the level of a spoiled child.

2. Indicate the main conflict (and any secondary conflicts).

        Secondary: between the doctor and the little girl.
        Main: between the doctor and himself (the professional man versus the
        egotistical, emotional man).

3. Name the central character(s), and give his or her (their) traits.

        The doctor: honest--he admits his weakness
                    responsible--he feels guilty
                    egotistical--he wants to win

4. State the point of view (first or third person).

        First person—this is especially significant because the doctor is
        confessing his bad feelings, and his speaking directly makes the confession
        more poignant.

```
When force is used, two results are predictable.
  (1) the person being forced will resist and be resentful.
  (2) the enforcing person may get caught up in the act and lose sight of
      the real objective for using the force.
```

Consider these key points in the following models of student writing:

- *Development:* Study these examples, especially for their clear statements of purpose and for their development through the use of references to, summaries and paraphrases of, and quotations and explanations from, the story itself.

- *Verb tense:* As is customary in writing about literature, each student essay is written in the present tense. For example, the writers relate events in the story as "He *goes* to the farm house," "She *eyes* him with suspicion."

- *Quotations:* Quotations can effectively give the flavor of the original story while supporting the point the student writer is making. Use short quotations, and blend them in with your summary writing and commentary rather than using long passages.

Examine the three following student pieces for correct punctuation, and remember these main points about punctuating quotations:

- With a blend, you usually do not need commas:

    The girl looked at him "with cold steady eyes."
    He mounts the "final unreasoning assault."

- If you introduce a quotation with a statement that is grammatically complete (an independent clause), you must use a colon:

    The parents have little else to say because they want him to be the doctor: "That's why they were spending three dollars on me."

- With a conversational tag such as "he said," you have a choice of a comma or a colon, but a comma is more typical:

    He said, "It is a social necessity."

EXERCISE 1A

Student Demonstration Using the DCODE Worksheet

Many stories have more than one conflict. Here, Michael Fulton explains the difference between the primary and secondary conflicts in "The Use of Force."

WORKSHEET
Writing in DCODE

NAME: Michael Fulton

SECTION: _____ CHAPTER: _____ DATE: _____

Delve Generate your topic, or ideas for your topic, by delving into your subject area through:

- *Freewriting*—writing sentence after sentence, nonstop and spontaneously.
- *Brainstorming*—jotting down answers to Who? What? Where? When? Why? and How? and then listing words and phrases in relation to those answers.
- *Clustering*—connecting bubbled ideas with lines to show strings of relationships, producing each new bubble item in response to the question, What comes to mind?
- *Combining* any of these approaches, as directed by your instructor.

```
Freewriting:
        At first the story seems to be about the struggle of wills between the
        doctor and his patient--the little girl. But then it moves clearly to the
        doctor and the reader can see that he loses his self control. The first
        level of the story is like maybe what you would read in the newspaper or
        what you would hear about. That his doctor goes to tend to a patient and
        she won't let him see inside her mouth and she actually fights with him,
        but he does what he has to and forces her mouth open and sees the problem
        and takes care of it later you figure. But the real story is what goes on
        in his mind because he gets so worked up he loses control and feels like
        really hurting her. He learns something about himself that he doesn't like
        and that's the real story.

Brainstorming:
        Who?    the doctor
        What?   loses control
        Where?  farm house
        When?   1930s
        Why?    human beings are weak
        How?    goes through a struggle

Clustering:
```

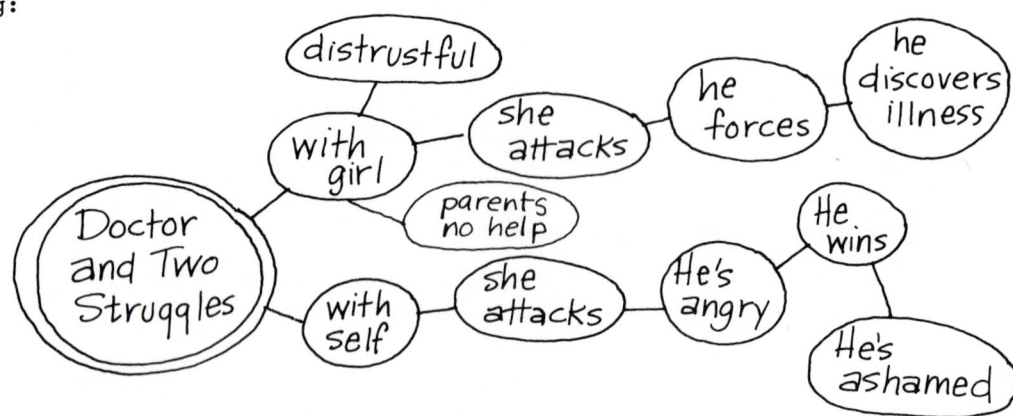

WORKSHEET: Writing in DCODE   **353**

Concentrate   Concentrate your work by stating your topic in one sentence that is not too broad, narrow, or vague to be developed. Base this sentence (which may become the topic sentence for your paragraph or the thesis for your essay) on an idea emerging from the **Delve** stage. You may have to try several statements here before you formulate one that is best for your writing task. Be sure that your final statement covers your assignment or intent and specifies both your subject (what you are writing about) and treatment (what aspect you will focus on). Label the *subject* and *treatment* parts.

<u>The story has two story lines based on two related conflicts</u>.
   subject   treatment

Organize   Complete an outline or a cluster, as directed by your instructor. The cluster should be a section from, or a refined version of, the **Delve** clustering. Regardless of the strategy you use, the organizational pattern should indicate a division of your topic into parts that will, in turn, be further subdivided for support as necessary to address a particular audience on your concentrated topic.

```
For literary analysis add short quotations here:
I.   The primary conflict
     A. Doctor-patient relationship
     B. Physical struggle
        1. Girl won't cooperate
        2. Doctor uses force
        3. Doctor examines her throat
     C. Job done
II.  The secondary conflict
     A. Doctor versus himself
        1. Tries to be professional
        2. Loses self control ("attractive little thing," "damned little
           brat," "furious")
        3. Loses sight of objective ("got beyond reason")
     B. Emotional (brutal) side wins ("It was a pleasure to attack her,"
        "blind fury")
```

Draft   On separate paper, write and then revise your assignment as many times as necessary for **c**oherence, **l**anguage (usage, tone, and diction), **u**nity, **e**mphasis, **s**upport, and **s**entence structure (**cluess**).

Edit   Correct problems in fundamentals such as **c**apitalization, **o**missions, **p**unctuation, and **s**pelling (**cops**). Before writing the final draft, read your paper aloud to discover oversights and awkwardness of expression.

First Draft

More Than Just a House Call

"The Use of Force" by William Carlos Williams has two story lines. One appears on the surface and moves the plot along. If the author had only written about it, the ~~story~~ account would be no more than ~~journalism~~ a news story. The doctor makes a house call because a little girl is sick. Her parents are self-conscious, and the doctor is out of his comfortable environment. The girl won't open her mouth ~~up~~ for an examination. The doctor insists, ~~and~~ After a scuffle ~~and some use of force~~ he uses and, he discovers that she has an infected throat. She will be treated. The story has a happy ending. But weave it in with the other part of the story, and the ending is not happy. The surface story is all between the girl and the doctor, but The ~~subterranean~~ deep story is between the doctor and himself, ~~and~~ I it's all about the use of force from the forcer's perspective. He's ~~mixed up~~ ambivalent about the experience at first. The girl is an "attractive little thing," ~~but is~~ who will soon become a "damned little brat." ~~obviously spoiled.~~ She struggles with such vigor that he is jolted out of his easy professional manner. He struggles with her, and she is a worthwhile opponent. He ~~gets~~ becomes "furious." ~~caught up in the combat.~~ He doesn't like what is happening, but he has "got beyond reason." ~~He~~ Although he struggles with himself, ~~and the~~ his bad side wins. He gets what he wants, and no one knows his secret: he has his own aggression ~~meanness~~ inside, just below the surface. His new role of forcing turns that aggression to even more savage feelings. ~~He has tasted the feeling of combat to win.~~ He remembers it was a pleasure to attack her. The struggle, which had nothing to do with medicine, and everything to do with passion for triumph, took the form of a "blind fury." He won the battle in ~~for~~ the first story, but he lost the battle in ~~for~~ the second. We may forgive him for being an imperfect human being, but he won't let himself off that easily.

Final Draft

More Than Just a House Call
Michael Fulton

"The Use of Force" by William Carlos Williams has two story lines. One appears on the surface and moves the plot along. If the author had written only about it, the account would be no more than a news story. The doctor

makes a house call because a little girl is sick. Her
parents are self-conscious, and the doctor is out of his
comfortable environment. The girl won't open her mouth for
an examination. The doctor insists. After a scuffle he
uses force and discovers that she has an infected throat.
She will be treated. The story has a happy ending. But
weave it in with the other part of the story, and the
ending is not happy. The surface story is all between the
girl and the doctor, but the deep story is between the
doctor and himself. It's all about the use of force from
the forcer's perspective. He's ambivalent about the
experience at first. The girl is an "attractive little
thing," who will soon become a "damned little brat." She
struggles with such vigor that he is jolted out of his
easy professional manner. He struggles with her, and she
is a worthwhile opponent. He becomes "furious". He doesn't
like what is happening, but he has "got beyond reason."
Although he struggles with himself, his bad side wins. He
gets what he wants, and no one knows his secret: he has
his own aggression inside, just below the surface. His new
role of forcing turns that aggression to even more savage
instincts. He remembers that "it was a pleasure to attack
her." The struggle, which had nothing to do with medicine,
and everything to do with passion for triumph, took the
form of a "blind fury." He won the battle in the first
story, but he lost the battle in the second. We may
forgive him for being an imperfect human being, but he
won't let himself off that easily.

EXERCISE 1B

Student Demonstration with Annotations

Setting is hardly mentioned in its physical properties, but as Gloria Mendez points out, it is a significant and highly revealing part of "The Use of Force."

Out of His Element
Gloria Mendez

<u>Setting in "The Use of Force" may at first appear to be insignificant, but it plays an important role in the story.</u> Most of what we perceive to be the setting must be imagined, for the author gives us little description. When the doctor arrives, the girl's mother says of her daughter, "We have her in the kitchen where it is warm. It is very damp here sometimes." The parents have little else to say because they want him to be the doctor: "That's why they were spending three dollars on me." The girl looks at him with "cold, steady eyes." From information such as that we infer setting. The family is poor; three dollars (in the 1930s) is a lot of money. Their home is simple—cold and damp. The girl is not accustomed to being around doctors, so she is fearful. But in this kitchen she is in her territory. The doctor, in this alien setting, is out of his element. He is dealing with people who have a different background from his, and they are self-conscious

topic sentence

setting as (1) physical properties

setting as (2) atmosphere

and distrustful. With no familiar setting and with no allies, he is vulnerable to the pressure that he faces. Maybe in his office, surrounded by his medical equipment and his staff, he would have retained his composure. In this setting he gives in to his most basic instincts and, for a brief period, becomes as emotional and self-centered as the child.

EXERCISE 1C

Student Demonstration with Annotations

This essay explains that the first-person point of view places the central character in "The Use of Force" in close focus, with all his strengths and weaknesses there on the surface for our analysis—and for his own.

The Use of Self-Analysis
Janet Peterson

One of the main thrusts in "The Use of Force" is point of view. <u>The narrator, a doctor, tells his own story, a story about his encounter with an uncooperative patient but also--and mainly--a story about the narrator's transformation from a mature, rational person to someone of a lower order who has lost considerable self-respect</u>. *[thesis]*

This transformation happens in stages of attitudinal change which occur during his arrival, his early attempt at obtaining cooperation, his losing his self-control, and his reflection on his behavior. *[parts of support]*

<u>When the doctor arrives at the small farmhouse, he feels like an outsider</u>. The family is self-conscious and not sure about how to act around a doctor. They are poor, and out of concern for the daughter, are spending some of their meager funds to get a diagnosis and possible treatment. The doctor observes that they are "all very nervous, eyeing me up and down distrustfully." They tell him very little, wanting to get their money's worth. *[topic sentence]*

<u>The doctor initially follows standard procedure</u>. He sees that she is feverish and panting. With concern about a local diphtheria epidemic, he asks the mother if she had looked at the girl's throat. In a foreshadowing that the doctor does not catch, the mother says, "I tried to . . . , but I couldn't see." Moving to the hands-on stage, he asks the girl to open her mouth. "Nothing doing." He tries a gentle approach, shows her he has no concealed weapons by opening his hands. But her mother mentions the word "hurt," and the doctor grinds his "teeth in disgust." He maintains his composure as he approaches her. She loses hers, as she tries to scratch his eyes out and succeeds in knocking his glasses to the floor. *[topic sentence]*

<u>Both his tact and his attitude change</u>. The parents are embarrassed; they apologize, threaten the daughter, and awkwardly try to help the doctor. He's disgusted with them, however; they've done all the wrong things. But he admires the girl, even saying he had "already fallen in love with the savage brat." He knows that her anger is *[topic sentence]*

caused by her fear of him. He decides to use force--for her own good. The possibility that she has diphtheria is there. The girl's resistance builds: she screams and struggles. He uses a "wooden tongue depressor," and she chews it "into splinters."

<u>It is during this phase of the incident that the doctor joins the struggle at her level</u>. As he admits, "But now I also had grown furious--at a child. I tried to hold myself down but I couldn't." He goes for heavier equipment--a metal spoon. He convinces himself that he must get the "diagnosis now or never." Whether his rationality or truth prevailed in that decision, he does know that he "had got beyond reason. I could have torn the child apart in my fury. It was a pleasure to attack her. My face was burning with it." He has truth and reason on his side, but his emotions as "a blind fury" are in control. He mounts the "final unreasoning assault" and wins. She has an infected throat, and he has exposed it, but she still tries to attack "while tears of defeat blinded her eyes." *[topic sentence]*

<u>The final stage, the recognition, is there throughout the last part of the story</u>. If the doctor had dismissed the incident, we would have thought him insensitive. If the doctor had savored the experience, we would have called him sadistic. But the doctor, with obvious regret, has admitted that he had "grown furious," lost restraint, "got beyond reason," felt a "longing for muscular release," and gone on "to the end." *[topic sentence]*

The "use of force" has two effects in this story. The girl resents the force and becomes alternately defensive and offensive. The doctor uses force and becomes so caught up in the physical and emotional conflicts that he is responding to the wrong motive for acting. It is the point of view that highlights the doctor's feelings of guilt in retrospect. This feeling comes across much more poignantly because this story is, after all, a confessional.

EXERCISE 2

Tough and streetsmart, Squeaky runs a race on an inner-city course, but curiously the title of the story refers to Raymond, her mentally disabled brother, who is her responsibility. This story comes from a collection entitled *Gorilla, My Love* by Toni Cade Bambara, a teacher and highly acclaimed author.

Raymond's Run
TONI CADE BAMBARA

I don't have much work to do around the house like some girls. My mother does that. And I don't have to earn my pocket money by hustling; George runs errands for the big boys and sells Christmas cards. And anything else that's got to get done, my father does. All I have to do in life is mind my brother Raymond, which is enough.

2   Sometimes I slip and say my little brother Raymond. But as any fool can see he's much bigger and he's older too. But a lot of people call him my little brother cause he needs looking after cause he's not quite right. And a lot of smart mouths got lots to say about that too, especially when George was minding him. But now, if any-

body has anything to say to Raymond, anything to say about his big head, they have to come by me. And I don't play the dozens* or believe in standing around with somebody in my face doing a lot of talking. I much rather just knock you down and take my chances even if I am a little girl with skinny arms and a squeaky voice, which is how I got the name Squeaky. And if things get too rough, I run. And as anybody can tell you, I'm the fastest thing on two feet.

3   There is no track meet that I don't win the first place medal. I used to win the twenty-yard dash when I was a little kid in kindergarten. Nowadays, it's the fifty-yard dash. And tomorrow I'm subject to run the quarter-meter relay all by myself and come in first, second, and third. The big kids call me Mercury cause I'm the swiftest thing in the neighborhood. Everybody knows that—except two people who know better, my father and me. He can beat me to Amsterdam Avenue with me having a two fire-hydrant headstart and him running with his hands in his pockets and whistling. But that's private information. Cause can you imagine some thirty-five-year-old man stuffing himself into PAL [Police Athletic League] shorts to race little kids? So as far as everyone's concerned, I'm the fastest and that goes for Gretchen, too, who has put out the tale that she is going to win the first-place medal this year. Ridiculous. In the second place, she's got short legs. In the third place, she's got freckles. In the first place, no one can beat me and that's all there is to it.

4   I'm standing on the corner admiring the weather and about to take a stroll down Broadway so I can practice my breathing exercises, and I've got Raymond walking on the inside close to the buildings, cause he's subject to fits of fantasy and starts thinking he's a circus performer and that the curb is a tightrope strung high in the air. And sometimes after a rain he likes to step down off his tightrope right into the gutter and slosh around getting his shoes and cuffs wet. Then I get hit when I get home. Or sometimes if you don't watch him he'll dash across traffic to the island in the middle of Broadway and give the pigeons a fit. Then I have to go behind him apologizing to all the older people sitting around trying to get some sun and getting all upset with the pigeons fluttering around them, scattering their newspapers and upsetting the waxpaper lunches in their laps. So I keep Raymond on the inside of me, and he plays like he's driving a stage coach which is O.K. by me so long as he doesn't run me over or interrupt my breathing exercises, which I have to do on account of I'm serious about my running, and I don't care who knows it.

5   Now some people like to act like things come easy to them, won't let on that they practice. Not me. I'll high-prance down 34th Street like a rodeo pony to keep my knees strong even if it does get my mother uptight so that she walks ahead like she's not with me, don't know me, is all by herself on a shopping trip, and I am somebody else's crazy child. Now you take Cynthia Proctor for instance. She's just the opposite. If there's a test tomorrow, she'll say something like, "Oh, I guess I'll play handball this afternoon and watch television tonight," just to let you know she ain't thinking about the test. Or like last week when she won the spelling bee for the millionth time, "A good thing you got 'receive,' Squeaky, cause I would have got it wrong. I completely forgot about the spelling bee." And she'll clutch the lace on her blouse like it was a narrow escape. Oh, brother. But of course when I pass her house on my early morning trots around the block, she is practicing the scales on the piano over and over and over and over. Then in music class she always lets herself get bumped around so she falls accidentally on purpose onto the piano stool and is so surprised to find herself sitting there that she decides just for fun to try out the ole keys. And what do you know—Chopin's† waltzes just spring out of her fingertips and she's the most surprised thing in the world. A regular prodigy. I could kill people like that. I stay up all night studying the words for the spelling bee. And you can see me any time of day practicing running. I never walk if I can trot, and shame on Raymond if he can't keep up. But of course he does, cause if he hangs back someone's liable to walk up to him and get smart, or take his allowance from him, or ask him where he got that great big pumpkin head. People are so stupid sometimes.

6   So I'm strolling down Broadway breathing out and breathing in on counts of seven, which is my lucky number, and here comes Gretchen and her sidekicks: Mary Louise, who used to be a friend of mine when she first moved to Harlem from Baltimore and got beat up by everybody till I took

---

*The players trade insults about a family member.
† Frédéric François Chopin (1810–1849), a Polish composer and pianist

up for her on account of her mother and my mother used to sing in the same choir when they were young girls, but people ain't grateful, so now she hangs out with the new girl Gretchen and talks about me like a dog; and Rosie, who is as fat as I am skinny and has a big mouth where Raymond is concerned and is too stupid to know that there is not a big deal of difference between herself and Raymond and that she can't afford to throw stones. So they are steady coming up Broadway and I see right away that it's going to be one of those Dodge City* scenes cause the street ain't that big and they're close to the buildings just as we are. First I think I'll step into the candy store and look over the new comics and let them pass. But that's chicken and I've got a reputation to consider. So then I think I'll just walk straight on through them or even over them if necessary. But as they get to me, they slow down. I'm ready to fight, cause like I said I don't feature a whole lot of chit-chat, I much prefer to just knock you down right from the jump and save everybody a lotta precious time.

7   "You signing up for the May Day races?" smiles Mary Louise, only it's not a smile at all. A dumb question like that doesn't deserve an answer. Besides, there's just me and Gretchen standing there really, so no use wasting my breath talking to shadows.

8   "I don't think you're going to win this time," says Rosie, trying to signify† with her hands on her hips all salty, completely forgetting that I have whupped her behind many times for less salt than that.

9   "I always win cause I'm the best," I say straight at Gretchen who is, as far as I'm concerned, the only one talking in this ventriloquist-dummy routine. Gretchen smiles, but it's not a smile, and I'm thinking that girls never really smile at each other because they don't know how and don't want to know how and there's probably no one to teach us how, cause grown-up girls don't know either. Then they all look at Raymond who has just brought his mule team to a standstill. And they're about to see what trouble they can get into through him.

10 "What grade you in now, Raymond?"

11 "You got anything to say to my brother, you say it to me, Mary Louise Williams of Raggedy Town, Baltimore."

12 "What are you, his mother?" sasses Rosie.

13 "That's right, Fatso. And the next word out of anybody and I'll be *their* mother too." So they just stand there and Gretchen shifts from one leg to the other and so do they. Then Gretchen puts her hands on her hips and is about to say something with her freckle-face self but doesn't. Then she walks around me looking me up and down but keeps walking up Broadway, and her sidekicks follow her. So me and Raymond smile at each other and he says, "Gidyap" to his team and I continue with my breathing exercises, strolling down Broadway toward the ice man on 145th with not a care in the world cause I am Miss Quicksilver herself.

14 I take my time getting to the park on May Day because the track meet is the last thing on the program. The biggest thing on the program is the May Pole dancing, which I can do without, thank you, even if my mother thinks it's a shame I don't take part and act like a girl for a change. You'd think my mother'd be grateful not to have to make me a white organdy dress with a big satin sash and buy me new white baby-doll shoes that can't be taken out of the box till the big day. You'd think she'd be glad her daughter ain't out there prancing around a May Pole getting the new clothes all dirty and sweaty and trying to act like a fairy or a flower or whatever you're supposed to be when you should be trying to be yourself, whatever that is; which is, as far as I am concerned, a poor Black girl who really can't afford to buy shoes and a new dress you only wear once a lifetime cause it won't fit next year.

15 I was once a strawberry in a Hansel and Gretel pageant when I was in nursery school and didn't have no better sense than to dance on tiptoe with my arms in a circle over my head doing umbrella steps and being a perfect fool just so my mother and father could come dressed up and clap. You'd think they'd know better than to encourage that kind of nonsense. I am not a strawberry. I do not dance on my toes. I run. That is what I am all about. So I always come late to the May Day

---

*the setting of the old television series "Gunsmoke." The episodes often contained showdown scenes between the marshal and the gunslingers.
†here, using gestures as a kind of insult

program, just in time to get my number pinned on and lay in the grass till they announce the fifty-yard dash.

16   I put Raymond in the little swings, which is a tight squeeze this year and will be impossible next year. Then I look around for Mr. Pearson, who pins the numbers on. I'm really looking for Gretchen if you want to know the truth, but she's not around. The park is jam-packed. Parents in hats and corsages and breast-pocket handkerchiefs peeking up. Kids in white dresses and light-blue suits. The parkees unfolding chairs and chasing the rowdy kids from Lenox as if they had no right to be there. The big guys with their caps on backwards, leaning against the fence swirling the basketballs on the tips of their fingers, waiting for all these crazy people to clear out the park so they can play. Most of the kids in my class are carrying bass drums and glockenspiels* and flutes. You'd think they'd put in a few bongos or something for real like that.

17   Then here comes Mr. Pearson with his clipboard and his cards and pencils and whistles and safety pins and fifty million other things he's always dropping all over the place with his clumsy self. He sticks out in a crowd because he's on stilts. We used to call him Jack and the Beanstalk to get him mad. But I'm the only one that can outrun him and get away, and I'm too grown for that silliness now.

18   "Well, Squeaky," he says, checking my name off the list and handing me number seven and two pins. And I'm thinking he's got no right to call me Squeaky, if I can't call him Beanstalk.

19   "Hazel Elizabeth Deborah Parker," I correct him and tell him to write it down on his board.

20   "Well, Hazel Elizabeth Deborah Parker, going to give someone else a break this year?" I squint at him real hard to see if he is seriously thinking I should lose the race on purpose just to give someone else a break. "Only six girls running this time," he continues, shaking his head sadly like it's my fault all of New York didn't turn out in sneakers. "That new girl should give you a run for your money." He looks around the park for Gretchen like a periscope in a submarine movie. "Wouldn't it be a nice gesture if you were . . . to ah . . ."

21   I give him such a look he couldn't finish putting that idea into words. Grownups got a lot of nerve sometimes. I pin number seven to myself and stomp away, I'm so burnt. And I go straight for the track and stretch out on the grass while the band winds up with "Oh, the Monkey Wrapped His Tail Around the Flag Pole," which my teacher calls by some other name. The man on the loudspeaker is calling everyone over to the track and I'm on my back looking at the sky, trying to pretend I'm in the country, but I can't, because even grass in the city feels hard as sidewalk, and there's just no pretending you are anywhere but in a "concrete jungle" as my grandfather says.

22   The twenty-yard dash takes all of two minutes cause most of the little kids don't know no better than to run off the track or run the wrong way or run smack into the fence and fall down and cry. One little kid, though, has got the good sense to run straight for the white ribbon up ahead so he wins. Then the second-graders line up for the thirty-yard dash and I don't even bother to turn my head to watch cause Raphael Perez always wins. He wins before he even begins by psyching the runners, telling them they're going to trip on their shoelaces and fall on their faces or lose their shorts or something, which he doesn't really have to do since he is very fast, almost as fast as I am. After that is the forty-yard dash which I use to run when I was in first grade. Raymond is hollering from the swings cause he knows I'm about to do my thing cause the man on the loudspeaker has just announced the fifty-yard dash, although he might just as well be giving a recipe for angel food cake cause you can hardly make out what he's sayin for the static. I get up and slip off my sweat pants and then I see Gretchen standing at the starting line, kicking her legs out like a pro. Then as I get into place I see that ole Raymond is on line on the other side of the fence, bending down with his fingers on the ground just like he knew what he was doing. I was going to yell at him but then I didn't. It burns up your energy to holler.

23   Every time, just before I take off in a race, I always feel like I'm in a dream, the kind of dream you have when you're sick with fever and feel all hot and weightless. I dream I'm flying over a sandy beach in the early morning sun, kissing the leaves off the trees as I fly by. And there's always the smell of apples, just like in the country when I was little and used to think I was a choo-choo train, running through the fields of corn and

---

*musical instruments played with small, light hammers

chugging up the hill to the orchard. And all the time I'm dreaming this, I get lighter and lighter until I'm flying over the beach again, getting blown through the sky like a feather that weighs nothing at all. But once I spread my fingers in the dirt and crouch over the Get on Your Mark, the dream goes and I am solid again and am telling myself, Squeaky you must win, you must win, you are the fastest thing in the world, you can even beat your father up Amsterdam if you really try. And then I feel my weight coming back just behind my knees then down to my feet then into the earth and the pistol shot explodes in my blood and I am off and weightless again, flying past the other runners, my arms pumping up and down and the whole world is quiet except for the crunch as I zoom over the gravel in the track. I glance to my left and there is no one. To the right, a blurred Gretchen, who's got her chin jutting out as if it would win the race all by itself. And on the other side of the fence is Raymond with his arms down to his side and the palms tucked up behind him, running in his very own style, and it's the first time I ever saw that and I almost stop to watch my brother Raymond on his first run. But the white ribbon is bouncing toward me and I tear past it, racing into the distance till my feet with a mind of their own start digging up footfuls of dirt and brake me short. Then all the kids standing on the side pile on me, banging me on the back and slapping my head with their May Day programs, for I have won again and everybody on 151st Street can walk tall for another year.

24 "In first place . . ." the man on the loudspeaker is clear as a bell now. But then he pauses and the loudspeaker starts to whine. Then static. And I lean down to catch my breath and here comes Gretchen walking back, for she's overshot the finish line too, huffing and puffing with her hands on her hips taking it slow, breathing in steady time like a real pro and I sort of like her a little for the first time. "In first place . . ." and then three of four voices get all mixed up on the loudspeaker and I dig my sneaker into the grass and stare at Gretchen who's staring back, we both wondering just who did win. I can hear old Beanstalk arguing with the man on the loudspeaker and then a few others running their mouths about what the stopwatches say. Then I hear Raymond yanking at the fence to call me and I wave to shush him, but he keeps rattling the fence like a gorilla in a cage like in them gorilla movies, but then like a dancer or something he starts climbing up nice and easy but very fast. And it occurs to me, watching how smoothly he climbs hand over hand and remembering how he looked running with his arms down to his side and with the wind pulling his mouth back and his teeth showing and all, it occurred to me that Raymond would make a very fine runner. Doesn't he always keep up with me on my trots? And he surely knows how to breathe in counts of seven cause he's always doing it at the dinner table, which drives my brother George up the wall. And I'm smiling to beat the band cause if I've lost the race, or if me and Gretchen tied, or even if I've won, I can always retire as a runner and begin a whole new career as a coach with Raymond as my champion. After all, with a little more study I can beat Cynthia and her phony self at the spelling bee. And if I bugged my mother, I could get piano lessons and become a star. And I have a big rep as the baddest thing around. And I've got a roomful of ribbons and medals and awards. But what has Raymond got to call his own?

25 So I stand there with my new plans, laughing out loud by this time as Raymond jumps down from the fence and runs over with his teeth showing and his arms down to the side, which no one before him has quite mastered as a running style. And by the time he comes over I'm jumping up and down so glad to see him—my brother Raymond, a great runner in the family tradition. But of course everyone thinks I'm jumping up and down because the men on the loudspeaker have finally gotten themselves together and compared notes and are announcing "In first place—Miss Hazel Elizabeth Deborah Parker." (Dig that.) "In second place—Miss Gretchen P. Lewis." And I look over at Gretchen wondering what the "P" stands for. And I smile. Cause she's good, no doubt about it. Maybe she'd like to help me coach Raymond; she obviously is serious about running, as any fool can see. And she nods to congratulate me and then she smiles. And I smile. We stand there with this big smile of respect between us. It's about as real a smile as girls can do for each other, considering we don't practice real smiling every day, you know, cause maybe we too busy being flowers or fairies or strawberries instead of something honest and worthy of respect . . . you know . . . like being people.

APPLICATIONS FOR CRITICAL READING AND DISCUSSION

1. Point out the significance of the setting, either stated or implied.

2. Indicate the main conflict (and any secondary conflicts).

3. Name the central character(s), and give his or her (their) traits. How does the main character change? Why?

4. State the point of view (first or third person).

5. Briefly discuss the theme (what the story means, what it says about an individual specifically or human nature generally). Consider why the narrator seems to change her goals and even include her rival at the end of the story.

EXERCISE 3

Michael looks at the girls, and his wife Frances becomes annoyed. Is Irwin Shaw writing about two individuals, or do they represent a long-standing division between the sexes?

Vocabulary Preview: Write in short definitions for these words as they are used in the context of the following passage. (The paragraph numbers are given in parentheses.) Be prepared to use the words in your own sentences.

cunning (12)

transparent (12)

battalions (52)

The Girls in Their Summer Dresses
IRWIN SHAW

1 Fifth Avenue was shining in the sun when they left the Brevoort. The sun was warm, even though it was February, and everything looked like Sunday morning—the buses and the well-dressed people walking slowly in couples and the quiet buildings with the windows closed.

2 Michael held Frances' arm tightly as they walked toward Washington Square in the sunlight. They walked lightly, almost smiling, because they had slept late and had a good breakfast and it was Sunday. Michael unbuttoned his coat and let it flap around him in the mild wind.

3 "Look out," Frances said as they crossed Eighth Street. "You'll break your neck."

4 Michael laughed and Frances laughed with him.

5 "She's not so pretty," Frances said. "Anyway, not pretty enough to take a chance of breaking your neck."

6 Michael laughed again. "How did you know I was looking at her?"

7 Frances cocked her head to one side and smiled at her husband under the brim of her hat. "Mike, darling," she said.

8 "O.K.," he said. "Excuse me."

9 Frances patted his arm lightly and pulled him along a little faster toward Washington Square. "Let's not see anybody all day," she said. "Let's just hang around with each other. You and me. We're always up to our neck in people, drinking their Scotch or drinking our Scotch; we only see each other in bed. I want to go out with my husband all day long. I want him to talk only to me and listen only to me."

10 "What's to stop us?" Michael asked.

11 "The Stevensons. They want us to drop by around one o'clock and they'll drive us into the country."

12 "The cunning Stevensons," Mike said. "Transparent. They can whistle. They can go driving in the country by themselves."

13 "Is it a date?"

14 "It's a date."

15 Frances leaned over and kissed him on the tip of the ear.

16 "Darling," Michael said, "this is Fifth Avenue."

17 "Let me arrange a program," Frances said. "A planned Sunday in New York for a young couple with money to throw away."

18 "Go easy."

19 "First let's go to the Metropolitan Museum of Art," Frances suggested, because Michael had said during the week he wanted to go. "I haven't been there in three years and there're at least ten pictures I want to see again. Then we can take the bus down to Radio City and watch them skate. And later we'll go down to Cavanaugh's and get a steak as big as a blacksmith's apron, with a bottle of wine, and after that there's a French picture at the Filmarte that everybody says—say, are you listening to me?"

20 "Sure," he said. He took his eyes off the hatless girl with the dark hair, cut dancer-style like a helmet, who was walking past him.

21 "That's the program for the day," Frances said flatly. "Or maybe you'd just rather walk up and down Fifth Avenue."

22 "No," Michael said. "Not at all."

23 "You always look at other women," Frances said. "Everywhere. Every damned place we go."

24 "No, darling," Michael said, "I look at everything. God gave me eyes and I look at women and men and subway excavations and moving pictures and the little flowers of the field. I casually inspect the universe."

25 "You ought to see the look in your eye," Frances said, "as you casually inspect the universe on Fifth Avenue."

26 "I'm a happily married men." Michael pressed her elbow tenderly. "Example for the whole twentieth century—Mr. and Mrs. Mike Loomis. Hey, let's have a drink," he said, stopping.

27 "We just had breakfast."

28 "Now listen, darling," Mike said, choosing his words with care, "it's a nice day and we both felt good and there's no reason why we have to break it up. Let's have a nice Sunday."

29 "All right. I don't know why I started this. Let's drop it. Let's have a good time."

30 They joined hands consciously and walked without talking among the baby carriages and the old Italian men in their Sunday clothes and the young women with Scotties in Washington Square Park.

31 "At least once a year everyone should go to the Metropolitan Museum of Art," Frances said after a while, her tone a good imitation of the tone she had used at breakfast and at the beginning of

their walk. "And it's nice on Sunday. There're a lot of people looking at the pictures and you get the feeling maybe Art isn't on the decline in New York City, after all—"

32. "I want to tell you something," Michael said very seriously. "I have not touched another woman. Not once. In all the five years."
33. "All right," Frances said.
34. "You believe that, don't you?"
35. "All right."
36. They walked between the crowded benches, under the scrubby city-park trees.
37. "I try not to notice it," Frances said, "but I feel rotten inside, in my stomach, when we pass a woman and you look at her and I see that look in your eye and that's the way you looked at me the first time. In Alice Maxwell's house. Standing there in the living room, next to the radio, with a green hat on and all those people."
38. "I remember the hat," Michael said.
39. "The same look," Frances said. "And it makes me feel bad. It makes me feel terrible."
40. "Sh-h-h, please, darling, sh-h-h."
41. "I think I would like a drink now," Frances said.
42. They walked over to a bar on Eighth Street, not saying anything, Michael automatically helping her over curbstones and guiding her past automobiles. They sat near a window in the bar and the sun streamed in and there was a small, cheerful fire in the fireplace. A little Japanese waiter came over and put down some pretzels and smiled happily at them.
43. "What do you order after breakfast?" Michael asked.
44. "Brandy, I suppose," Frances said.
45. "Courvoisier," Michael told the waiter. "Two Courvoisiers."
46. The waiter came with the glasses and they sat drinking the brandy in the sunlight. Michael finished half his and drank a little water.
47. "I look at women," he said. "Correct. I don't say it's wrong or right. I look at them. If I pass them on the street and I don't look at them, I'm fooling you, I'm fooling myself."
48. "You look at them as though you want them," Frances said, playing with her brandy glass. "Every one of them."
49. "In a way," Michael said, speaking softly and not to his wife, "in a way that's true. I don't do anything about it, but it's true."
50. "I know it. That's why I feel bad."
51. "Another brandy," Michael called. "Waiter, two more brandies."
52. He sighed and closed his eyes and rubbed them gently with his fingertips. "I love the way women look. One of the things I like best about New York is the battalions of women. When I first came to New York from Ohio that was the first thing I noticed, the million wonderful women, all over the city. I walked around with my heart in my throat."
53. "A kid," Frances said. "That's a kid's feeling."
54. "Guess again," Michael said. "Guess again. I'm older now. I'm a man getting near middle age, putting on a little fat and I still love to walk along Fifth Avenue at three o'clock on the east side of the street between Fiftieth and Fifty-seventh Streets. They're all out then, shopping, in their furs and their crazy hats, everything all concentrated from all over the world into seven blocks—the best furs, the best clothes, the handsomest women, out to spend money and feeling good about it."
55. The Japanese waiter put the two drinks down, smiling with great happiness.
56. "Everything is all right?" he asked.
57. "Everything is wonderful," Michael said.
58. "If it's just a couple of fur coats," Frances said, "and forty-five-dollar hats—"
59. "It's not the fur coats. Or the hats. That's just the scenery for that particular kind of woman. Understand," he said, "You don't have to listen to this."
60. "I want to listen."
61. "I like the girls in the offices. Neat, with their eyeglasses, smart, chipper, knowing what everything is about. I like the girls on Forty-fourth Street at lunchtime, the actresses, all dressed up on nothing a week. I like the salesgirls in the stores, paying attention to you first because you're a man, leaving lady customers waiting. I got all this stuff accumulated in me because I've been thinking about it for ten years and now you've asked for it and here it is."
62. "Go ahead," Frances said.
63. "When I think of New York City, I think of all the girls on parade in the city. I don't know whether it's something special with me or whether every man in the city walks around with the same feeling inside him, but I feel as though I'm at a picnic in this city. I like to sit near the women in the theatres, the famous beauties who've taken six hours to get ready and look it.

And the young girls at the football games, with the red cheeks, and when the warm weather comes, the girls in their summer dresses." He finished his drink. "That's the story."

64. Frances finished her drink and swallowed two or three times extra. "You say you love me?"
65. "I love you."
66. "I'm pretty, too," Frances said. "As pretty as any of them."
67. "You're beautiful," Michael said.
68. "I'm good for you," Frances said, pleading. "I've made a good wife, a good housekeeper, a good friend. I'd do any damn thing for you."
69. "I know," Michael said. He put his hand out and grasped hers.
70. "You'd like to be free to—" Frances said.
71. "Sh-h-h."
72. "Tell the truth." She took her hand away from under his.
73. Michael flicked the edge of his glass with his finger. "O.K.," he said gently. "Sometimes I feel I would like to be free."
74. "Well," Frances said, "any time you say."
75. "Don't be foolish." Michael swung his chair around to her side of the table and patted her thigh.
76. She began to cry silently into her handkerchief, bent over just enough so nobody else in the bar would notice. "Someday," she said, crying, "you're going to make a move."
77. Michael didn't say anything. He sat watching the bartender slowly peel a lemon.
78. "Aren't you?" Frances asked harshly. "Come on, tell me. Talk. Aren't you?"
79. "Maybe," Michael said. He moved his chair back again. "How the hell do I know?"
80. "You know," Frances persisted. "Don't you know?"
81. "Yes," Michael said after a while, "I know."
82. Frances stopped crying then. Two or three snuffles into the handkerchief and she put it away and her face didn't tell anything to anybody. "At least do me one favor," she said.
83. "Sure."
84. "Stop talking about how pretty this woman is or that one. Nice eyes, nice breasts, a pretty figure, good voice." She mimicked his voice. "Keep it to yourself. I'm not interested."
85. Michael waved to the waiter. "I'll keep it to myself," he said.
86. Frances flicked the corners of her eyes. "Another brandy," she told the waiter.
87. "Two," Michael said.
88. "Yes, Ma'am, yes sir," said the waiter, backing away.
89. Frances regarded Michael coolly across the table. "Do you want me to call the Stevensons?" she asked. "It'll be nice in the country."
90. "Sure," Michael said. "Call them."
91. She got up from the table and walked across the room toward the telephone. Michael watched her walk, thinking what a pretty girl, what nice legs.

APPLICATIONS FOR CRITICAL READING AND DISCUSSION

1. Point out the significance of the setting, either stated or implied.

2. Indicate the main conflict (and any secondary conflicts).

3. Name the central character(s), and give his or her (their) traits.

4. State the point of view (first or third person).

5. How does the behavior of both characters change after Michael starts looking at other women?

6. Would you say one is more at fault in this argument? Explain.

7. What is the significance of Michael's last observation of Frances?

8. What do you think will happen to their marriage? Why?

9. What would be your "Dear Abby" advice to them?

10. Briefly discuss the theme (what the story means, what it says about an individual specifically or human nature generally).

EXERCISE 4

This narrator has something to tell you: He's not crazy. Okay, he can hear things in heaven and hell, and there was this guy with an evil eye he wanted to smash, but really he's as normal—as—as a lot of other Edgar Allan Poe characters.

Vocabulary Preview: Write in short definitions for these words as they are used in the context of the following passage. (The paragraph numbers are given in parentheses.) Be prepared to use the words in your own sentences.

dissimulation (3)	anxiety (11)
profound (3)	audacity (15)
suppositions (7)	derision (17)
crevice (8)	dissemble (18)
stealthily (8)	

The Tell-Tale Heart
EDGAR ALLAN POE

True!—nervous—very, very dreadfully nervous I had been and am; but why *will* you say that I am mad? The disease had sharpened my senses—not destroyed—not dulled them. Above all was the sense of hearing acute. I heard all things in the heaven and in the earth. I heard many things in hell. How, then, am I mad? Hearken! and observe how healthily—how calmly I can tell you the whole story.

2   It is impossible to say how first the idea entered my brain; but once conceived, it haunted me day and night. Object there was none. Passion there was none. I loved the old man. He had never wronged me. He had never given me insult. For his gold I had no desire. I think it was his eye! yes, it was this! One of his eyes resembled that of a vulture—a pale blue eye, with a film over it. Whenever it fell upon me, my blood ran cold; and so by degrees—very gradually—I made up my mind to take the life of the old man, and thus rid myself of the eye for ever.

3   Now this is the point. You fancy me mad. Madmen know nothing. But you should have seen *me*. You should have seen how wisely I proceeded—with what caution—with what foresight—with what dissimulation I went to work! I was never kinder to the old man than during the whole week before I killed him. And every night, about midnight, I turned the latch of his door and opened it—oh, so gently! And then, when I had made an opening sufficient for my head, I put in a dark lantern, all closed, closed, so that no light shone out, and then I thrust in my head. Oh, you would have laughed to see how cunningly I thrust it in! I moved it slowly—very, very slowly, so that I might not disturb the old man's sleep. It took me an hour to place my whole head within the opening so far that I could see him as he lay upon his bed. Ha!—would a madman have been so wise as this? And then, when my head was well in the room, I undid the lantern cautiously—oh, so cautiously—cautiously (for the hinges creaked)—I undid it just so much that a single thin ray fell upon the vulture eye. And this I did for seven long nights—every night just at midnight—but I found the eye always closed; and so it was impossible to do the work; for it was not the old man who vexed me, but his Evil Eye. And every morning, when the day broke, I went boldly in to the chamber, and spoke courageously to him, calling him by name in a hearty tone, and inquiring how he had passed the night. So you see he would have been a very profound old man, indeed, to suspect that every night, just at twelve, I looked in upon him while he slept.

4   Upon the eighth night I was more than usually cautious in opening the door. A watch's minute hand moves more quickly than did mine. Never before that night had I *felt* the extent of my own powers—of my sagacity. I could scarcely contain my feelings of triumph. To think that there I was, opening the door, little by little and he not even to dream of my secret deeds or thoughts. I fairly chuckled at the idea; and perhaps he heard me; for he moved on the bed suddenly, as if startled. Now you may think that I drew back—but no. His room was as black as pitch with the thick darkness (for the shutters were close fastened, through fear of robbers), and so I knew that he could not see the opening of the door, and I kept pushing it on steadily, steadily.

5   I had my head in, and was about to open the lantern, when my thumb slipped upon the tin fastening, and the old man sprang up in the bed, crying out—"Who's there?"

6   I kept quite still and said nothing. For a whole hour I did not move a muscle, and in the meantime I did not hear him lie down. He was still sitting up in the bed listening;—just as I have done, night after night, hearkening to the death watches in the wall.

7   Presently I heard a slight groan, and I knew it was the groan of mortal terror. It was not a groan of pain or of grief—oh, no!—it was the low stifled sound that arises from the bottom of the soul when overcharged with awe. I knew the sound well. Many a night, just at midnight, when all the world slept, it has welled up from my own bosom, deepening, with its dreadful echo, the terrors that distracted me. I say I knew it well. I knew what the old man felt, and pitied him, although I chuckled at heart. I knew that he had

been lying awake ever since the first slight noise, when he had turned in the bed. His fears had been ever since growing upon him. He had been trying to fancy them causeless, but could not. He had been saying to himself—"It is nothing but the wind in the chimney—it is only a mouse crossing the floor," or "it is merely a cricket which has made a single chirp." Yes, he has been trying to comfort himself with these suppositions; but he had found all in vain. *All in vain;* because Death, in approaching him, had stalked with his black shadow before him, and enveloped the victim. And it was the mournful influence of the unperceived shadow that caused him to feel—although he neither saw nor heard—to *feel* the presence of my head within the room.

8   When I had waited a long time, very patiently, without hearing him lie down, I resolved to open a little—a very, very little crevice in the lantern. So I opened it—you cannot imagine how stealthily, stealthily—until, at length, a single dim ray, like the thread of the spider, shot from out the crevice and full upon the vulture eye.

9   It was open—wide, wide open—and I grew furious as I gazed upon it. I saw it with perfect distinctness—all a dull blue, with a hideous veil over it that chilled the very marrow in my bones; but I could see nothing else of the old man's face or person: for I had directed the ray as if by instinct, precisely upon the damned spot.

10   And now have I not told you that what you mistake for madness is but over-acuteness of the senses?—now, I say, there came to my ears a low, dull, quick sound, such as a watch makes when enveloped in cotton. I knew *that* sound well too. It was the beating of the old man's heart. It increased my fury, as the beating of a drum stimulates the soldier into courage.

11   But even yet I refrained and kept still. I scarcely breathed. I held the lantern motionless. I tried how steadily I could maintain the ray upon the eye. Meantime the hellish tattoo of the heart increased. It grew quicker and quicker, and louder and louder every instant. The old man's terror *must* have been extreme! It grew louder, I say, louder every moment!—do you mark me well? I have told you that I am nervous: so I am. And now at the dead hour of the night, amid the dreadful silence of that old house, so strange a noise as this excited me to uncontrollable terror.

Yet, for some minutes longer I refrained and stood still. But the beating grew louder, louder! I thought the heart must burst. And now a new anxiety seized me—the sound would be heard by a neighbor! The old man's hour had come! With a loud yell, I threw open the lantern and leaped into the room. He shrieked once—once only. In an instant I dragged him to the floor, and pulled the heavy bed over him. I then smiled gaily, to find the deed so far done. But, for many minutes, the heart beat on with a muffled sound. This, however, did not vex me; it would not be heard through the wall. At length it ceased. The old man was dead. I removed the bed and examined the corpse. Yes, he was stone, stone dead. I placed my hand upon the heart and held it there many minutes. There was no pulsation. He was stone dead. His eye would trouble me no more.

12   If still you think me mad, you will think so no longer when I describe the wise precautions I took for the concealment of the body. The night waned, and I worked hastily, but in silence. First of all I dismembered the corpse. I cut off the head and the arms and the legs.

13   I then took up three planks from the flooring of the chamber, and deposited all between the scantlings. I then replaced the boards so cleverly, so cunningly, that no human eye—not even *his*—could have detected any thing wrong. There was nothing to wash out—no stain of any kind—no blood-spot whatever. I had been too wary for that. A tub had caught all—ha! ha!

14   When I had made an end of these labors, it was four o'clock—still dark as midnight. As the bell sounded the hour, there came a knocking at the street door. I went down to open it with a light heart,—for what had I *now* to fear? There entered three men, who introduced themselves, with perfect suavity, as officers of the police. A shriek had been heard by a neighbor during the night; suspicion of foul play had been aroused; information had been lodged at the police office, and they (the officers) had been deputed to search the premises.

15   I smiled,—for *what* had I to fear? I bade the gentlemen welcome. The shriek, I said, was my own in a dream. The old man, I mentioned, was absent in the country. I took my visitors all over the house. I bade them search—search *well*. I led them, at length, to *his* chamber. I showed them his

treasures, secure, undisturbed. In the enthusiasm of my confidence, I brought chairs into the room, and desired them *here* to rest from their fatigues, while I myself, in the wild audacity of my perfect triumph, placed my own seat upon the very spot beneath which reposed the corpse of the victim.

16   The officers were satisfied. My *manner* had convinced them. I was singularly at ease. They sat, and while I answered cheerily, they chatted familiar things. But, ere long, I felt myself getting pale and wished them gone. My head ached, and I fancied a ringing in my ears: but still they sat and still chatted. The ringing became more distinct:—it continued and became more distinct: I talked more freely to get rid of the feeling: but it continued and gained definitiveness—until, at length, I found that the noise was *not* within my ears.

17   No doubt I now grew *very* pale;—but I talked more fluently, and with a heightened voice. Yet the sound increased—and what could I do? It was *a low, dull, quick sound—much such a sound as a watch makes when enveloped in cotton.* I gasped for breath—and yet the officers heard it not. I talked more quickly—more vehemently; but the noise steadily increased. I arose and argued about trifles, in a high key and with violent gesticulations, but the noise steadily increased. Why *would* they not be gone? I paced the floor to and fro with heavy strides, as if excited to fury by the observation of the men—but the noise steadily increased. Oh God! what *could* I do; I foamed—I raved—I swore! I swung the chair upon which I had been sitting, and grated it upon the boards, but the noise arose over all and continually increased. It grew louder—louder—*louder*! And still the men chatted pleasantly, and smiled. Was it possible they heard not? Almighty God!—no, no! They heard!—they suspected!—they *knew*!—they were making a mockery of my horror!—this I thought, and this I think. But any thing was better than this agony! Any thing was more tolerable than this derision! I could bear those hypocritical smiles no longer! I felt that I must scream or die!—and now—again!—hark! louder! louder! louder! *louder*!—

18   "Villains!" I shrieked, "dissemble no more! I admit the deed!—tear up the planks!—here, here!—it is the beating of his hideous heart!"

APPLICATIONS FOR CRITICAL READING AND DISCUSSION

1. Point out the significance of the setting, either stated or implied.

2. Indicate the main conflict (and any secondary conflicts).

3. Name the central character(s), and give his or her (their) traits, including, in this instance, the traits of mental illness.

4. State the point of view (first or third person).

5. What does the narrator say about reasoning, and how does he use reasoning?

6. Briefly discuss the theme (what the story means, what it says about an individual specifically or human nature generally).

EXERCISE 5

Frankie really loved this guy, but he "was doing her wrong," and, well, she took action. This song relates one of the best-known crimes of passion in folk literature.

Frankie and Johnny
ANONYMOUS

Frankie she was a good woman
As everybody knows,
Spent a hundred dollars
Just to buy her man some clothes.
5 He was her man, but he was doing her wrong.

Frankie went down to the corner
Just for a bucket of beer,
Said: "Mr. bartender
10 Has my loving Johnny been here?
"He was my man, but he's a-doing me wrong."

"Now I don't want to tell you no stories
And I don't want to tell you no lies
15 I saw your man about an hour ago
With a gal named Nellie Bligh
He was your man, but he's a-doing you wrong."

Frankie she went down to the hotel
20 Didn't go there for fun,
Underneath her kimona
She carried a forty-four gun.
He was her man, but he was doing her wrong.

25 Frankie looked over the transom
    To see what she could spy,
    There sat Johnny on the sofa
    Just loving up Nellie Bligh.
    He was her man, but he was doing her
30   wrong.

    Frankie got down from that high stool
    She didn't want to see no more;
    Rooty-toot-toot three times she shot
    Right through that hardwood door.
35 He was her man, but he was doing her
        wrong.

    Now the first time that Frankie shot
        Johnny
    He let out an awful yell,
40 Second time she shot him
    There was a new man's face in hell.
    He was her man, but he was doing her
        wrong.

    "Oh roll me over easy
45 Roll me over slow
    Roll me over on the right side
    For the left side hurts me so."
    He was her man, but he was doing her
        wrong.

50 Sixteen rubber-tired carriages
    Sixteen rubber-tired hacks
    They take poor Johnny to the graveyard
    They ain't gonna bring him back.
    He was her man, but he was doing her
55   wrong.

    Frankie looked out of the jailhouse
    To see what she could see,
    All she could hear was a two-string
        bow
60 Crying nearer my God to thee.
    He was her man, but he was doing her
        wrong.

    Frankie she said to the sheriff,
    "What do you reckon they'll do?"
65 Sheriff he said "Frankie,
    It's the electric chair for you."
    He was her man, but he was doing her
        wrong.

    This story has no moral
70 This story has no end
    This story only goes to show
    That there ain't no good in men!
    He was her man, but he was doing her
        wrong.

APPLICATIONS FOR CRITICAL READING AND DISCUSSION

1. Point out the significance of the setting, either stated or implied.

2. Indicate the main conflict (and any secondary conflicts).

3. Name the central character(s), and give his or her (their) traits.

4. State the point of view (first or third person).

5. Briefly discuss the theme (what the story means, what it says about an individual specifically or human nature generally).

EXERCISE 6

Poet Robert Browning creates a chilling character who tells about his "last duchess." According to the duke, she had a problem, and he fixed the problem in a way appropriate for a man of his station. She still hangs around, if you know what I mean, but she doesn't say anything.

My Last Duchess
ROBERT BROWNING

That's my last Duchess painted on the wall,
Looking as if she were alive. I call
That piece a wonder, now: Frà Pandolf's hands
Worked busily a day, and there she stands.
5   Will't please you sit and look at her? I said
"Frà Pandolf" by design, for never read
Strangers like you that pictured countenance,
The depth and passion of its earnest glance,
But to myself they turned (since none puts by
10 The curtain I have drawn for you, but I)
And seemed as they would ask me, if they durst,
How such a glance came there; so, not the first
Are you to turn and ask thus. Sir, 'twas not
Her husband's presence only, called that spot
15 Of joy into the Duchess' cheek: perhaps
Frà Pandolf chanced to say "Her mantle laps
Over my lady's wrist too much," or "Paint
Must never hope to reproduce the faint
Half-flush that dies along her throat": such stuff
20 Was courtesy, she thought, and cause enough
For calling up that spot of joy. She had
A heart—how shall I say?—too soon made glad,
Too easily impressed; she liked whate'er
She looked on, and her looks went everywhere.
25 Sir, 'twas all one! My favor at her breast,
The dropping of the daylight in the West,
The bough of cherries some officious fool
Broke in the orchard for her, the white mule
She rode with round the terrace—all and each
30 Would draw from her alike the approving
        speech,
Or blush, at least. She thanked men,—good! but
    thanked
Somehow—I know not how—as if she ranked
35 My gift of a nine-hundred-years-old name
With anybody's gift. Who'd stoop to blame
This sort of trifling? Even had you skill
In speech—which I have not—to make your
    will
Quite clear to such an one, and say, "Just this
40 Or that in you disgust me; here you miss,
Or there exceed the mark"—and if she let
Herself be lessoned so, nor plainly set
Her wits to yours, forsooth, and made excuse,
—E'en then would be some stooping; and I
45   choose
Never to stoop. Oh sir, she smiled, no doubt,
Whene'er I passed her; but who passed without
Much the same same smile? This grew; I gave
    commands
50 Then all smiles stopped together. There she
        stands
As if alive. Will't please you rise? We'll meet
The company below, then. I repeat,
The Count your master's known munificence
55 Is ample warrant that no just pretense
Of mine for dowry will be disallowed;
Though his fair daughter's self, as I avowed
At starting, is my object. Nay, we'll go
Together down, sir. Notice Neptune, though,
60 Taming a sea-horse, thought a rarity,
Which Claus of Innsbruck cast in bronze for me!

APPLICATIONS FOR CRITICAL READING AND DISCUSSION

1. Point out the significance of the setting, either stated or implied.

2. Indicate the main conflict (and any secondary conflicts).

3. Name the central character(s), and give his or her (their) traits.

4. State the point of view (first or third person).

5. What happened to the duchess? On what evidence or reasoning do you base your answer?

6. How does the portrait covered by a curtain represent the kind of control the duke wants?

7. Briefly discuss the theme (what the story means, what it says about an individual specifically or human nature generally).

EXERCISE 7

Richard Cory was a fancy man to the common folks—fancy in every way. Then one night he . . .

Richard Cory
EDWIN ARLINGTON ROBINSON

Whenever Richard Cory went down town,
We people on the pavement looked at him:
He was a gentleman from sole to crown,
Clean favored, and imperially slim.

5 And he was always quietly arrayed,
And he was always human when he talked;
But still he fluttered pulses when he said,
"Good morning," and he glittered when he walked.

10 And he was rich—yes, richer than a king—
And admirably schooled in every grace:
In fine, we thought that he was everything
To make us wish that we were in his place.

So on we worked, and waited for the light,
15 And went without the meat, and cursed the bread;
And Richard Cory, one calm summer night,
Went home and put a bullet through his head.

APPLICATIONS FOR CRITICAL READING AND DISCUSSION

1. Point out the significance of the setting, either stated or implied.

2. Indicate the main conflict (and any secondary conflicts).

3. Name the central character(s), and give his or her (their) traits. Explain how the word choice implies that Richard Cory is like an aristocrat and that the common people are common.

4. State the point of view (first or third person).

5. What separates Richard Cory from the common people?

6. Briefly discuss the theme (what the story means, what it says about an individual specifically or human nature generally).

EXERCISE 8

If we can have a tomb for the unknown soldier, why can't we have one for the unknown citizen? But then, how is he unknown? To his friends? his family? Was he unknown even to himself? And was he free and happy?

The Unknown Citizen
W. H. AUDEN

(To JS/07/M/378
This Marble Monument
Is Erected by the State)

He was found by the Bureau of Statistics to be
One against whom there was no official
    complaint,
And all the reports on his conduct agree
5 That, in the modern sense of an old-fashioned
    word, he was a saint,
For in everything he did he served the Greater
    Community.
Except for the War till the day he retired
10 He worked in a factory and never got fired

But satisfied his employers, Fudge Motors Inc.
Yet he wasn't a scab or odd in his views,
For his union reports that he paid his dues,
(Our report on his Union shows it was sound)
15 And our Social Psychology workers found
That he was popular with his mates and liked a drink.
The Press are convinced that he bought a paper every day
20 And that his reactions to advertisements were normal in every way.
Policies taken out in his name prove that he was fully insured,
And his Health-card shows he was once in
25 hospital but left it cured.
Both Producers Research and High-Grade Living declare
He was fully sensible to the advantages of the Installment Plan

30 And had everything necessary to the Modern Man,
A phonograph, a radio, a car and a frigidaire.
Our researchers into Public Opinion are content
That he held the proper opinions for the time of
35 year;
When there was peace, he was for peace; when there was war, he went.
He was married and added five children to the population,
40 Which our Eugenist says was the right number for a parent of his generation.
And our teachers report that he never interfered with their education.

Was he free? Was he happy? The question is
45 absurd:
Had anything been wrong, we should certainly have heard.

APPLICATIONS FOR CRITICAL READING AND DISCUSSION

1. Point out the significance of the setting, either stated or implied.

2. Indicate the main conflict (and any secondary conflicts).

3. Name the central character(s), and give his or her (their) traits. How does the author regard the central character—with admiration, scorn, compassion, or what?

4. State the point of view (first or third person).

5. How is the "Unknown Citizen" different from most of us?

6. What areas of the life of the "Unknown Citizen" are covered?

7. Briefly discuss the theme (what the story means, what it says about an individual specifically or human nature generally).

Suggested Topics for Writing About Literature

Although the first group of questions is listed as "Analytical" and the second as "Imaginative," those terms suggest only a tendency. Broadly speaking, both groups are both analytical and imaginative.

Analytical Topics

"Raymond's Run"

1. Write a functional analysis of Squeaky's traits.
2. Write a paper in which you discuss Squeaky's feelings for family and neighborhood.
3. Write a paragraph or a short essay that mainly explains the title of the selection.
4. Write a paper in which you explain how we get to know Squeaky from what she says, what she does, and how others react to her.
5. Write a paper that explains what Squeaky learns about herself and her values.

"The Girls in Their Summer Dresses"

6. Write a comparison and contrast of Michael and Frances. Use particular moments in their conversation (such as at the beginning, when she becomes annoyed, when they decide to have a drink, and when they decide to visit with friends) or character traits (such as honesty, loyalty, love, affection, lust, forgiveness) for points in your organization.
7. Write a functional analysis of Frances or Michael, using character traits such as those indicated in the previous question.
8. Write about the significance of setting.
9. State the theme that you think the author implies, and then agree or disagree with it.
10. Write a piece in which you show how the characters' behavior becomes more self-conscious, mechanical, and detached as the story progresses.
11. Develop a persuasive piece in which you argue that either Michael or Frances is primarily at fault.
12. Argue that neither Michael nor Frances is at fault because men and women simply have different views toward male-female relationships.

"The Tell-Tale Heart"

13. Discuss the importance of the use of point of view.
14. Discuss the story as a case study in mental illness.
15. Discuss the aspect of sound in relation to plot development.
16. Discuss the growing tension in the plot.
17. Discuss the stages of change in the narrator as he tells the tale. (Don't overlook the changes in sentence structure and punctuation.)
18. Discuss the references to the "eye," showing the narrator's preoccupation with it.

"Frankie and Johnny"

19. Write a paper on both the causes and effects of Frankie's shooting Johnny.
20. Write a paper in which you discuss the songwriter's techniques in using language and in developing a narrative account. You may want to refer to the instructions in this book on narration (Chapter 3) and description (Chapter 4).

"My Last Duchess"

21. Write a character study (using functional analysis) of the duke, drawing supporting information from the poem. His traits, such as intelligence, arrogance, and pride (try brainstorming and clustering for more), could provide a framework for your statement.
22. Write a character study of the duchess, drawing supporting information from the poem. If you speculate to round out your study, label your speculation as such.
23. Write a piece that explains what happened to the duchess. Use evidence from the poem.

"Richard Cory"

24. Write a paper in which you discuss how the poet's word choice indicates the kind of person Richard Cory was. Comment on the difference in word choice between lines 1–12 and lines 13–14.

"The Unknown Citizen"

25. Write a paper in which you establish that the range and depth of information was or was not adequate for your understanding this unknown citizen. Include a discussion of the specific facets of his life that were investigated.
26. Characterize the "unknown citizen" according to what we know about him. These questions may help you understand the author's purpose: How does the author regard him (contempt, pity, admiration, disinterest, affection, sympathy, or other)? Is he a conformist? What other traits does he have? Is he free? Is he happy?

Imaginative Topics

"Raymond's Run"

1. Write an account of the "run" from Raymond's point of view.
2. Write about Squeaky from Gretchen's point of view.

"The Girls in Their Summer Dresses"

3. Project the couple a year or so into the future, and write about them.
4. Pretend you are a marriage counselor or Abigail Van Buren ("Dear Abby"), and give some advice to this troubled couple.
5. Using the same stanzaic patterns in "Frankie and Johnny," write a ballad about "Frances and Michael."

"The Tell-Tale Heart"

6. Assume the identity of the old man, and write a diary about the narrator leading up to the fateful eighth night.
7. Assume the identity of a psychologist who has just interviewed the narrator. Write an account of that meeting.
8. Write a police report describing the investigation, arrest, and booking of the narrator.

"Frankie and Johnny"

9. Using the basic form and approach that Auden employed (a simple statement in sentences) in "The Unknown Citizen," write about Frankie's life (assuming she was not a conformist) in "The Known Citizen."
10. Alter Frankie's personality so that she would secretly get rid of Johnny for his wandering eye, and then install his portrait somewhere so that she could view it whenever she likes. She might call the picture "My Last Dude." Write a narrative account of that new Frankie.

"My Last Duchess"

11. Imagine that the duke has sent word to Frankie that he desires her for a bride, but he wants her to smile only for him. Write out her answer to him.
12. Assume that you are the duchess just before the duke took whatever steps he took, and write a diary entry about your life on his estate.
13. The person listening to the duke is an envoy for the leader of another city-state. The leader's daughter is the duke's prospective bride. Write out a statement about the duke that the envoy might deliver to the young woman. His report can either state the situation outright or be subtle and suggestive.

"Richard Cory"

14. Do an interview after the fashion of "Lifestyles of the Rich and Famous" with Richard Cory.
15. Write the suicide letter that Richard Cory left. Optional: include a whimsical development using the stages of **DCODE**.

"The Unknown Citizen"

16. Pick a point toward the end of the life of the unknown citizen, and ask him if he was happy and if he was free. His answer will be your paragraph or essay. You may, if you like, assume this poem was actually written before his death, and now he is writing a rebuttal.

Literary Analysis: Reacting to Stories

WORKSH
Writing in DCO

D**elve** Generate your
- *Freewriting*
- *Brainstorm*
  then listing
- *Clustering–*
  each new b
- *Combining*

 Writer's Checklist

Apply these ideas to your writing as you work with **DCODE**. Later, as a peer editor, apply the same ideas to the material you evaluate.

1. Identify the work you are discussing by title (and usually by author).
2. Use a clear thesis for your essay or topic sentence for your paragraph.
3. Do not use only the title of the work for your title.
4. Develop your ideas by explaining, referring to the story, summarizing, paraphrasing, and quoting.
5. Use quotation marks around the words you borrow.
6. Use short quotations, and blend them with your own comments, paraphrasing or summarizing instead of using long quotations.
7. Use present-tense verbs. If you change the tense of a verb in a quotation (in order to be consistent), enclose the changed word in brackets.

 **Journal-Entry Suggestions**

1. Select some of the unused "Reading-Related Topics" suggestions and use them for journal topics.
2. Write a reaction to the theme or subject material in one or more "Reading Connection" selections. Explain why you were surprised, shocked, disgusted, pleased, or whatever, by what you read.
3. Invent statements to support headlines from *Weekly World News:*

    "Baby Born with Angel Wings!"
    "2000-Year-Old Greek Statue Has Face of Elvis!"
    "Warning: Walking Trees Invading U.S.!"
    "Venus Flytrap Eats Kitten!"
    "My Houseplant Screamed and Saved My Life!"
    "Teacher Shoots Student to Death—for Misspelling a Word!"
    "Space Alien Sports Broadcast Picked Up on Satellite Dish!"
    "Dandruff Sets Man's Hair on Fire!"
    "Fly Like a Bird in Ten Easy Steps!" (Lessons by Swami Sudhanami Bundra)
    "My Garlic Breath Saved Me from a Vampire!"

Concentrate Concentrate your work by stating your topic in one sentence that is not too broad, narrow, or vague to be developed. Base this sentence (which may become the topic sentence for your paragraph or the thesis for your essay) on an idea emerging from the **Delve** stage. You may have to try several statements here before you formulate one that is best for your writing task. Be sure that your final statement covers your assignment or intent and specifies both your subject (what you are writing about) and treatment (what aspect you will focus on). Label the *subject* and *treatment* parts.

Organize Complete an outline or a cluster, as directed by your instructor. The cluster should be a section from, or a refined version of, the **Delve** clustering. Regardless of the strategy you use, the organizational pattern should indicate a division of your topic into parts that will, in turn, be further subdivided for support as necessary to address a particular audience on your concentrated topic.

Draft On separate paper, write and then revise your assignment as many times as necessary for **c**oherence, **l**anguage (usage, tone, and diction), **u**nity, **e**mphasis, **s**upport, and **s**entence structure (**cluess**).

Edit Correct problems in fundamentals such as **c**apitalization, **o**missions, **p**unctuation, and **s**pelling (**cops**). Before writing the final draft, read your paper aloud to discover oversights and awkwardness of expression.

Argumentation: Persuading, Arguing, and Thinking Critically

13

> "What a writer asks of his reader is not so much to *like* as to *listen*.
> — Henry Wadsworth Longfellow

What is the difference between persuasion and argumentation? What is a proposition in an argument? What is the difference between fact and opinion? What is the difference between inductive and deductive thought? What are logical fallacies?

Persuasion and Argumentation Defined

If you are writing a piece that has a thesis (an assertion), you are trying to convince your audience of its validity. That is *persuasion*. It is a much broader term than *argument*. You may, for example, be stating that exercise is good for most people. You would probably not expect your audience to disagree with that assertion, though the members of your audience may not be exercising enough for their good health. Your intent might be to move them to action—to exercise. Or you might be trying to sell a product—a good product such as wholesome bread. You would want to persuade your audience to purchase that product. In those cases, persuasion is there, but argument is absent because no contrary view exists.

Although persuasion can exist without argumentation, all argumentation is by its very nature persuasive. *Argumentation* begins with a debatable issue and attempts to persuade an audience. It differs from pure exposition, which attempts to explain, though in endeavoring to convince an audience that an assertion is valid, exposition can also be regarded as persuasive. Similarly, argumentation differs from narration and description. But it may use any of these other forms of discourse in developing its ideas; therefore, it can be regarded as the most complex form.

Specifically, an argument may begin with a controversy or disagreement. A friend may say that Magic Johnson was a better basketball player than Larry Bird. You disagree, stating your reasons for your view, refuting some of your friend's points, and perhaps accepting others. Spirited discussion ensues. Most arguments are that simple. However, in college writing assignments and in other situations, you will be expected to write out an argument in a systematic fashion designed to appeal to your audience's sense of reason and often, in a fair manner, to your audience's emotions. And you will be expected to examine the arguments of others. Argumentation as a form of discourse is the essence of critical thought.

Argumentation requires that you think clearly, organize your points skillfully, present your side honestly, cogently, and logically, and, if advantageous to your viewpoint, refute your opponent's claims. Opinions and generalizations must be supported with relevant evidence: facts, testimony, and valid reasons. You must control your biases and prejudices, omit any emotional and vehement outbursts, and discard any trivial, irrelevant, and false claims if you are to command the respect of your audience.

Purpose

The purpose of your argument will be to win the members of the audience to your view or modify their views.

The Problem and Your Proposition

The *proposition* (the main point or thesis) should be a clear, concise statement of your position on a problem that is subject to argument. Good propositions are statements of policy, value, or belief. A *question of policy* calls for action by the reader. The writer of the proposition "The United States should not give military aid to Central American countries" advocates action in relation to diplomatic problems between the United States and Central American countries. A *question of value or belief* calls for acceptance by the reader. The proposition "Future historians will praise the Clinton administration's program on environmental protection" implies that the writer, within the context of divided opinion, will offer proof to try to persuade the reader to accept a view.

Your Audience

Your audience may be uninformed, informed, biased, hostile, receptive, apathetic, sympathetic, empathetic—any one, a combination, or something else. The point is that you should be intensely concerned about who will read your composition. If your readers are likely to be uninformed about the social and historical background of the issue, then you need to set the issue in its context. The discussion of background should lead to the problem for which you have a proposition or solution. If your readers are likely to be biased or even hostile to your view, take special care to refute the opposing view in a thoughtful, incisive way that does not further antagonize them. If your readers are already receptive and perhaps even sympathetic, and you wish to move them to action, then you might appeal to their conscience and the need for commitment.

Components of Your Paper

All arguments will include a *proposition* and *support* (the evidence or the reasons for a view being valid). In addition to those components you may want to include *definitions, background,* and *refutation.* Always take care to define terms that may be obscure or ambiguous. Arguments often break down or are misguided because terms are left undefined. For example, terms such as "liberal" and "conservative" mean different things to different people and should be defined within the specific context. The need for background and the extent of that background will depend on the knowledge of the audience. Refutation is a common feature in argumentation because you usually have to show that the other side is wrong in order to advance you own view. However, given a sympathetic audience that needs only to be moved, refutation may be unnecessary.

Organizational Plan

You can organize your composition of argumentation in various ways. You may wish to start with a brief introduction, such as a short history of the controversy, an analysis of the situation, policy, problem, or plan, or a condition that is the source of disagreement. You may start by presenting your case, saving the statement of the main issue for your conclusion. You may state the main issue, refute your opponent's claims, and then follow with a confirmation of your position. You may present your case and follow with a refutation of your opponent's. You may also use any of the methods that have proved effective in the organization and development of the other kinds of discourse, especially exposition. Below are some possible patterns.

- main issue—support
- main issue—refutation—support
- main issue—support—refutation

There are, of course, other variants, and there are also several methods of developing the material within each pattern. You may organize the supporting facts by comparison, one side at a time or one issue at a time (present an issue favoring your position, then refute one of your opponent's claims). You may develop the argument by a method such as cause and effect, or contrast, or by any combination of methods.

Appropriate Kinds of Evidence

In order to appeal to those with different viewpoints, you must prove your claims are valid. Your proof must consist of evidence and sound reasons forcefully and logically interwoven into an effective pattern of organization and development. Supporting the individual issues, then, is the most important part of writing a good argument.

What kinds of evidence make up proof?

First, you can offer facts. John F. Kennedy, who took office on January 20, 1961, and was assassinated in Dallas, Texas, on November 22, 1963, was the youngest person and the first Catholic ever elected president. Since an event that has happened is true and can be verified, these statements about President Kennedy are facts. But that Lee Oswald killed Kennedy is to some a questionable fact. That Kennedy was a great president is opinion because it cannot be verified.

Some facts are readily accepted because they are a part of general knowledge—you and your reader know them to be true, for they can be or have been verified. Other "facts" are based on personal observation and are often reported in various publications. You should always be concerned about the reliability of the source for both the information you use and that used by those of other viewpoints.

Second, you can cite examples. Keep in mind that you must present a sufficient number of examples and that the examples must be relevant.

Third, you can present statistics. Statistics, as defined in *Webster's New World Dictionary,* are facts and data of a numerical kind that are classified and tabulated in order to present significant information about a given subject.

Avoid presenting a long list of figures; select statistics carefully and use them with things familiar to your reader. The millions of dollars spent on a war in a single week, for example, become more comprehensible when expressed in terms of what the money would purchase in education, highways, or urban renewal.

To test the validity of statistics, either yours or your opponent's, ask: Who gathered them? Under what conditions? For what purpose? How are they used?

Fourth, you can cite evidence from and opinions of authorities. Most readers accept facts from recognized, reliable sources—governmental publications, standard reference works, books and periodicals published by established firms. In addition, they will accept evidence and opinions from individuals who, because of their knowledge and experience, are recognized as experts.

In using authoritative sources as proof, keep these points in mind:

1. Select authorities who are generally recognized as experts in their field.

2. Use authorities who qualify in the field pertinent to your argument.

3. Select authorities whose views are not biased.

4. Try to use several authorities.

5. Identify the authority's credentials clearly in the essay.

Inductive and Deductive Reasoning

The two basic forms of reasoning are *inductive* and *deductive*.

Inductive reasoning moves from particulars to the conclusion. In inductive thinking, you infer a conclusion from having studied a number of instances; you assume that what is true for one or more members of a class is true for all, most, or some other members of the class. You have been making conclusions according to this kind of reasoning all your life. As a child you may have touched a hot stove, thereby concluding that all stoves were hot and to be avoided. Or in selecting a college, you may have gathered facts and data about several schools, even visiting three or four, and, finding a college with an excellent faculty, modern facilities, and a distinguished and prosperous alumni, decided to go to that college.

Inductive reasoning usually follows four steps: (1) gathering evidence of a number of particulars or instances, (2) observing certain characteristics, (3) noting that they point toward a probable conclusion, and (4) making the so-called *inductive leap to* a useful generalization.

However, inductive thinking gives at best only a probability. Not all stoves are hot; not all colleges with the above commendable points are good. Nevertheless, if you use care in the process, this reasoning will produce a valid inductive leap in enough cases to make the method useful.

To test whether inductive reasoning—yours or your opponent's—is valid, ask: Have enough instances been investigated? Are the instances typical? Have the negative instances been explained satisfactorily? Is the generalization properly qualified by words such as *probably, usually,* and *most?*

Analogy is a popular form of inductive reasoning, and because it is vivid and interesting, it can be valuable in argumentation. However, in using analogy you assume that if two things are similar in several respects, they are also alike in the aspect important to your argument; therefore, you must be sure to use the analogy fairly and not force similarities where none exist. If differences exist, they should be explained satisfactorily. Moreover, keep in mind that analogy is effective for clarification or emphasis but not for proof. Weak analogies can be easily turned into an opponent's advantage by his or her pointing out that you have stressed similarities that do not exist and ignored the differences; thus the soundness of your reasoning in other parts of the argument may be questioned. (See Chapter 10 for more discussion of analogies.)

Another form of inductive reasoning involves the use of causes and effects. In fact, the basic principles of cause and effect analysis will often dictate the pattern of argumentation. If, for example, you are arguing that the current grading system should be abolished, you will very naturally explain that the weaknesses of the current system produce unfavorable results, which clearly illustrates causal analysis. (See Chapter 8 for an extended discussion of this form.)

Of course, exemplification is basic to inductive thinking, because, from the examples, one draws a generalization.

Deductive reasoning moves from the generalization to the particulars and instances. One concludes that what is true for all the members of a class of persons or things is true for each member of the class. Consider the following example:

> John and Bill are discussing the possibility of a strike at their factory. John says, "I'm certain that Jim Powers will join the strikers." Bill wonders how he can be so sure that Powers, a thirty-year employee and a foreman respected by both labor and management, will go on strike.

Such a conclusion, however, is more than a guess on John's part; he has reasoned deductively. In the past twenty-five years, there have been several strikes at the factory, some before it became a union shop. In each strike, all union members went on strike. Jim Powers, though a good friend of management, is a union member. Thus, John concludes that union members will strike and that Jim Powers will strike with the others.

This type of reasoning may be expressed in the form of a *syllogism*—the basic pattern of the deductive argument. There are three principal forms of the syllogism. The one used below is the categorical syllogism, by far the most common. The syllogism contains three statements:

- *Major premise*: All union members will strike.
- *Minor premise*: Jim Powers is a union member.
- *Conclusion*: Therefore, Jim Powers will strike.

If we let the letters, A, B, and C represent the terms of the syllogism, it looks like the following:

- All A's are B's.
- C is an A.
- Therefore, C is a B.

In ordinary thinking, our deductive thought patterns may be less precise than the formal syllogism. Our everyday reasoning is likely to have qualifications or limitations. We can represent our typical thought process as follows:

- Almost all union members will strike.
- Jim Powers is a union member
- Therefore, Jim Powers will probably strike.

The important point about this informal syllogism is that if we qualify the major premise *(almost all),* then we must also qualify the conclusion *(probably).*

In arguing deductively, you do not express yourself in the formal syllogism; instead you omit one of the premises. You would write: "When the union strikes, Jim Powers will be sure to strike." Expressions of this type are called *enthymemes*. When you read this form of argument, you should seek out the unstated premise, set up a formal syllogism in your mind or on paper, and test its validity.

Although inductive logic and deductive logic can be separated for discussion, the two are inextricably bound together, with one easily leading to the other.

Because inductive thinking suggests independence of thought and because it is a method frequently used to discover new ideas, we may wish to think that we are more inductive than deductive in conducting the affairs of our everyday lives. After all, isn't the purest expression of inductive thought the scientific principle in which we proceed from a hunch to collecting data to the formation of a hypothesis? But careful inductive thought is hard, time-consuming, and complicated. As a result we may do much less inductive thought than the typical person believes.

The most purely inductive thinker is the infant. Born without information, the infant responds to stimuli. Soon after birth, the infant uses *inference* (reaches conclusions based on available evidence) in order to discover which people are reliable or responsive while discovering what produces pain and pleasure within the environment. A few instances may be enough to produce a generalization. Grabbing a rose bush one time may be enough to convince a child that although roses are enticingly attractive, the rose bushes will cause pain if clutched. The child might even associate the flowers themselves with the pain caused by the thorns. That is inductive thought in its simplest form, a form that, though part of one's basic learning process, also has potential for flawed reasoning.

While that inductive process develops, the child's protectors are busily teaching the child how to behave. "Don't play in the street." "Don't poke your brother in the eye." "Don't pick up the puppy by its tail." There are consequences to performing all of those acts. The child could learn by experimenting and forming generalizations, but the protectors want to prevent unpleasantness and, therefore, will provide generalizations that can be applied to specific situations in deductive thought. The implications of the above commands go beyond the specific. The loved ones would be clearly implying, "Don't play in *any* streets." "Don't poke *anyone* in the eye." "Don't pick up *any* puppies by the tail." At home, at school, while watching television, and when reading, the child will receive many admonitions.

In time the child will be introduced to a system of laws, most all of which are to be applied deductively, with an occasional inductive interlude. For example, the driver who sees a steady red traffic light does not collect evidence and form a generalization about whether to stop. Instead, the driver makes this deductive application." "Drivers should almost always stop at red traffic lights. This is a red traffic light and I am a driver. Therefore, I should almost certainly stop." In most cases the driver does simply stop. But the driver might notice that other drivers are behaving strangely: that some are driving to the curb, that others are looking around, that some are staring back. Our driver might put these observations together and decide that this is a special situation and on closer scrutiny discover that an emergency rescue vehicle is approaching from behind. The driver might even cautiously edge out into the intersection to allow room for the emergency vehicle to pass.

Thus, we continually go back and forth from inductive to deductive reasoning, with a greater dependence on the latter. Unfortunately, many major premises are based on poor use of the inductive process or are passed down through acts of ignorance, mental laziness, or prejudice and become the foundation of much of our behavior.

Logical Fallacies

Certain flawed patterns in inductive and deductive thought, commonly called *logical fallacies,* are of primary concern in argumentation. You should be able to identify these patterns in the arguments of those on the other side of an issue and to avoid them in your own writing.

These eight are among the most common fallacies:

1. *Post hoc, ergo propter hoc* ("after this, therefore, because of this"): When one happening precedes another in time, the first is assumed to cause the other.

    EXAMPLES: "I knew I'd have a day like this when I saw that black cat run across my driveway this morning."

    "See what I told you! We elected him president, and now we have high inflation."

2. *False analogy:* False analogies ignore differences and stress similarities, often in an attempt to prove something.

   EXAMPLES: "People have to get a driver's license because unqualified people could have bad effects on society. Therefore, couples should also have to get a license to bear children because unqualified parents can produce delinquent children."

   "The leader of that country is a mad dog dictator, and you know what you do with a mad dog. You get a club and kill it."

3. *Hasty generalization:* This is a conclusion based on too few reliable instances.

   EXAMPLES: "Everyone I've met this morning is going to vote for the incumbent. The incumbent is going to win."
   "How many people did you meet?"
   "Three."

4. *False dilemma:* This fallacy presents the reader with only two alternatives from which to choose. The solution may lie elsewhere.

   EXAMPLES: "Now, only two things can be done with the savings and loan places. You either shut them down now or let them go bankrupt."

   "The way I see it, you either bomb them back into the Stone Age or let them keep on pushing us around."

5. *Argumentum ad hominem* (arguing against the person): This is the practice of abusing and discrediting your opponent rather than keeping to the main issues of the argument.

   EXAMPLES: "Who cares what he has to say? After all, he's a wild-eyed liberal who has been divorced twice."

   "Let's put aside the legislative issue for a moment and talk about the person who proposed it. For one thing he's a Southerner. For another he's Catholic. Enough said."

6. *Begging the question:* This fallacy assumes something is true without proof, and occurs when a thinker assumes a position is right before offering proof.

   EXAMPLES: "Those savages can never be civilized."

   "I have one simple question. When is he going to stop ripping off his customers? Case closed."

7. *Circular reasoning:* This form asserts proof that is no more than a repetition of the initial assertion.

   EXAMPLE: "You can judge good art by reading what good critics say about it."
   "But who are good critics?"
   "The people who spend their time judging good art."

8. *Non sequitur:* This fallacy draws a conclusion that does not follow.

   EXAMPLES: "Sue Jones has been an excellent school principal, so she will make an excellent mayor for our city."

   "If the equal rights amendment passes, men and women will all be using the same rest rooms."

EXERCISE 1:

Inductive and Deductive Reasoning

Identify the logical fallacy in the following sentences.

1. "If politicians can hire ghostwriters, why can't a little student like me be allowed to do the same thing?"

2. " 'Stamp out dirty books,' I say. Just look at all the crime we have since they started allowing this stuff."

3. "I was starting to have my doubts about the accuracy of newspapers until I read a newspaper editorial last week saying how reliable newspapers actually are."

4. "Before you start investigating subversion, let me remind you of the old farmer who burned his barn down when he tried to smoke out a nest of wasps."

5. "Blaming a company for making big profits is like blaming a cow for giving too much milk."

6. "Okay, so my spouse left me. Who cares? They're like buses; you miss one, and another one'll come along in a minute or two."

7. "I used to think Hemingway was a great writer until I read about his life. The guy was a self-centered, pompous jerk, and I'll never read any of his stuff again."

8. "I was really shocked until she told me it happened in New York, and then I just said, 'What's new?' "

9. "Like I say, you either fish or you cut bait. Will you marry me or won't you? Take your choice." (Two fallacies here)

10. "Mark my words. If they start controllin' hand guns, it's just a matter of time 'til we'll be back to defendin' ourselves with clubs and rocks against criminals with bazookas."

EXERCISE 2

Inductive and Deductive Reasoning

Provide examples for the following logical fallacies either in a group or individually, as directed by your instructor.

1. *Post hoc:*

2. False analogy:

3. Hasty generalization:

4. False dilemma:

5. *Argumentum ad hominem:*

6. Begging the question:

7. Circular reasoning:

8. *Non sequitur:*

The Reading Connection

EXERCISE 3

Demonstration

According to Louis Nizer, if we want to win the war against drugs, we should change the strategy and, instead, sell drugs to addicts.

Vocabulary Preview: Write in short definitions for these words as they are used in the contexts of the following passage. (The paragraph numbers are given in parentheses.) Be prepared to use them in your own sentences.

nominal (2)

discrepancies (2)

perpetrators (6)

pittance (6)

tribute (8)

macabre (9)

diminish (9)

sordid (9)

salutary (11)

consign (12)

How About Low-Cost Drugs for Addicts?
LOUIS NIZER

1. We are losing the war against drug addiction. Our strategy is wrong. I propose a different approach.

2. The Government should create clinics, manned by psychiatrists, that would provide drugs for nominal charges or even free to addicts under controlled regulations. It would cost the Government only 20 cents for a heroin shot, for which the addicts must now pay the mob more than $100, and there are similar price discrepancies in cocaine, crack and other such substances.

3. Such a service, which would also include the staff support of psychiatrists and doctors, would cost a fraction of what the nation now spends to maintain the land, sea and air apparatus necessary to interdict illegal imports of drugs. There would also be a savings of hundreds of millions of dollars from the elimination of the prosecutorial procedures that stifle our courts and overcrowd our prisons.

4. We see in our newspapers the triumphant announcements by Government agents that they have intercepted huge caches of cocaine, the street prices of which are in the tens of millions of dollars. Should we be gratified? Will this achievement reduce the number of addicts by one? All it will do is increase the cost to the addict of his illegal supply.

5. Many addicts who are caught committing a crime admit that they have mugged or stolen as many as six or seven times a day to accumulate the $100 needed for a fix. Since many of them need two or three fixes a day, particularly for crack, one can understand the terror in our streets and homes. It is estimated that there are in New York City alone 200,000 addicts, and this is typical of cities across the nation. Even if we were to assume that only a modest percentage of a city's addicts engage in criminal conduct to obtain the money for the habit, requiring multiple muggings and thefts each day, we could nevertheless account for many of the tens of thousands of crimes each day in New York City alone.

6. Not long ago, a Justice Department division issued a report stating that more than half the perpetrators of murder and other serious crimes were under the influence of drugs. This symbolizes the new domestic terror in our nation.

EX. This is why our citizens are unsafe in broad daylight on the most traveled thoroughfares. This EX. is why typewriters and television sets are stolen from offices and homes and sold for a pittance. EX. This is why parks are closed to the public and why murders are committed. This is why homes need multiple locks, and burglary systems, and why store windows, even in the most fashionable areas, require iron gates.

7   The benefits of the new strategy to control this terrorism would be immediate and profound.

8   First, the mob would lose the main source of its income. It could not compete against a free supply for which previously it exacted tribute estimated to be hundreds of millions of dollars, perhaps billions, from hopeless victims.

9   Second, pushers would be put out of business. There would be no purpose in creating addicts who would be driven by desperate compulsion to steal and kill for the money necessary to maintain their habit. Children would not be enticed. The mob's macabre public-relations program is to tempt children with free drugs in order to create customers for the future. The wave of street crimes in broad daylight would diminish to a trickle. Homes and stores would not have to be fortresses. Our recreational areas could again be used. Neighborhoods would not be scandalized by sordid street centers where addicts gather to obtain their supply from slimy merchants.

10 Third, police and other law-enforcement authorities, domestic or foreign, would be freed to deal with traditional nondrug crimes.

11 There are several objections that might be raised against such a salutary solution.

12 First, it could be argued that by providing free drugs to the addict we would consign him to permanent addiction. The answer is that medical and psychiatric help at the source would be more effective in controlling the addict's descent than the extremely limited remedies available to the victim today. I am not arguing that the new strategy will cure everything. But I do not see many addicts being freed from their bonds under the present system.

13 In addition, as between the addict's predicament and the safety of our innocent citizens, which deserves our primary concern? Drug-induced crime has become so common that almost every citizen knows someone in his immediate family or among his friends who has been mugged. It is these citizens who should be our chief concern.

14 Another possible objection is that addicts will cheat the system by obtaining more than the allowable free shot. Without discounting the resourcefulness of the bedeviled addict, it should be possible to have Government cards issued that would be punched so as to limit the free supply in accord with medical authorization.

15 Yet all objections become trivial when matched against the crisis itself. What we are witnessing is the demoralization of a great society: the ruination of its school children, athletes and executives, the corrosion of the workforce in general.

16 Many thoughtful sociologists consider the rapidly spreading drug use the greatest problem that our nation faces—greater and more real and urgent than nuclear bombs or economic reversal. EX. In China, a similar crisis drove the authorities to apply capital punishment to those who trafficked in opium—an extreme solution that arose from the deepest reaches of frustration.

17 Free drugs will win the war against the domestic terrorism caused by illicit drugs. As a strategy, it is at once resourceful, sensible and simple. We are getting nowhere in our efforts to hold back the ocean of supply. The answer is to dry up demand.

APPLICATIONS FOR CRITICAL READING AND DISCUSSION

1. Circle the proposition in the text. If it is not presented in one sentence, state it in a sentence of your own here.
    ```
    The government should create clinics, staffed by psychiatrists, that would
    provide drugs for nominal fees or even free to addicts.
    ```

2. Underline the main points of support.

major TV network recently aired a preview of a soap opera rape scene during a morning game show.

6   The newest craze in horror movies is something called the "teen slasher" film, and it typically depicts the killing, torture and sexual mutilation of women in sickening detail. Several rock groups now simulate sexual torture and murder during live performances. Others titillate youthful audiences with strippers confined in cages on stage and with half-naked dancers, who often act out sex with band members. Sexual brutality has become the common currency of America's youth culture and with it the pervasive degradation of women.

7   Why is this graphic violence dangerous? It's especially damaging for young children because they lack the moral judgment of adults. Many children are only dimly aware of the consequences of their actions, and, as parents know, they are excellent mimics. They often imitate violence they see on TV, without necessarily understanding what they are doing or what the consequences might be. One 5-year-old boy from Boston recently got up from watching a teen-slasher film and stabbed a 2-year-old girl with a butcher knife. He didn't mean to kill her (and luckily he did not). He was just imitating the man in the video.

8   Nor does the danger end as children grow older. National health officials tell us that children younger than teen-agers are apt to react to excessive violence with suicide, satanism, drug and alcohol abuse. Even grown-ups are not immune. One series of studies by researchers at the University of Wisconsin found that men exposed to films in which women are beaten, butchered, maimed and raped were significantly desensitized to the violence. Not only did they express less sympathy for the victims, they even approved of lesser penalties in hypothetical rape trials.

9   Sado-masochistic pornography is a kind of poison. Like most poisons, it probably cannot be totally eliminated, but it certainly could be labeled for what it is and be kept away from those who are most vulnerable. The largest record companies have agreed to this—in principle at least. In November 1985, the Recording Industry Association of America adopted my proposal to alert parents by having producers either put warning labels on records with explicitly sexual lyrics or display the lyrics on the outside of the record jackets. Since then, some companies have complied in good faith, although others have not complied at all.

10   This is where we parents must step in. We must let the industry know we're angry. We must press for uniform voluntary compliance with labeling guidelines. And we must take an active interest at home in what our children are watching and listening to. After all, we can hardly expect that the labels or printed lyrics alone will discourage young consumers.

11   Some parents may want to write to the record companies. Others can give their support to groups like the Parent Teacher Association, which have endorsed the labeling idea. All of us can use our purchasing power. We have more power than we think, and we must use it. For the sake of our children, we simply can't afford to slip back into apathy.

12   My concern for the health and welfare of children has nothing to do with politics: It is addressed to conservatives and liberals alike. Some civil libertarians believe it is wrong even to raise these questions—just as some conservatives believe that the Government should police popular American culture. I reject both these views. I have no desire to restrain artists or cast a "chill" over popular culture. But I believe parents have First Amendment rights, too.

13   The fate of the family, the dignity of women, the mental health of children—these concerns belong to everyone. We must protect our children with choice, not censorship. Let's start working in our communities to forge a moral consensus for the 1990's. Children need our help, and we must summon the courage to examine the culture that shapes their lives.

3. Draw a box around the refutation, if any.

4. Annotate the following kinds of evidence or proof in the left margin: facts, examples, statistics, and authoritative statements.

EXERCISE 4

Movies are rated. Music disks are not. Tipper Gore, author of *Raising PG Kids in an X-Rated Society* (1987), believes that the representation of sex and violence can have bad effects on children, and has a proposal for a labeling system.

Vocabulary Preview: Write in short definitions for these words as they are used in the contexts of the following passage. (The paragraph numbers are given in parentheses.) Be prepared to use them in your own sentences.

apathetic (4)

titillate (6)

pervasive (6)

degradation (6)

graphic (7)

immune (8)

desensitized (8)

hypothetical (8)

compliance (10)

consensus (13)

Curbing the Sexploitation Industry
TIPPER GORE

1 I can't even count the times in the last three years, since I began to express my concern about violence and sexuality in rock music, that I have been called a prude, a censor, a music hater, even a book burner. So let me be perfectly clear: I detest censorship. I'm not advocating censorship but rather a candid and vigorous debate about the dangers posed for our children by what I call the "sexploitation industry."

2 We don't need to put a childproof cap on the world, but we do need to remind the nation that children live in it, too, and deserve respect and sensitive treatment.

3 When I launched this campaign in 1985 . . . I went to the source of the problem, sharing my concerns and proposals with the entertainment industry. Many producers were sympathetic. Some cooperated with my efforts. But others have been overtly hostile, accusing me of censorship and suggesting, unfairly, that my motives are political. This resistance and hostility has convinced me of the need for a two-pronged campaign, with equal effort from the entertainment industry and concerned parents. Entertainment producers must take the first step, by labeling sexually explicit material.

4 But the industry cannot be expected to solve the problem on its own. Parents should encourage producers to cooperate and praise them when they do. Producers need to know that parents are aware of the issue and are reading their advisory labels. Above all, they need to know that somebody out there cares, that the community at large is not apathetic about the deep and lasting damage being done to our children.

5 What's at issue is not the occasional sexy rock lyric. What troubles—indeed, outrages—me is far more vicious: a celebration of the most gruesome violence, coupled with the explicit message that sado-masochism is the essence of sex. We're surrounded by examples—in rock lyrics, on television, at the movies and in rental videos. One

APPLICATIONS FOR CRITICAL READING AND DISCUSSION

1. Circle the proposition in the text. If it is not presented in one sentence, state it in a sentence of your own here.

2. Underline the main points of support.

3. Draw a box around the refutation, if any.

4. Annotate the following kinds of evidence or proof in the left margin: facts, examples, statistics, and authoritative statements.

EXERCISE 5

Weekly World News readers eagerly await Ed Anger's solutions to the world's problems, and he obliges every week. Ed has never met a problem he couldn't solve—quickly and simply. For him it's as easy as 1, 2, 4.

Make Docs Wheel and Deal Like Used Car Salesmen!
ED ANGER

1 I'm madder than a doctor with a dent in his Ferrari over all this crap about skyrocketing health care costs.

2 Let's face it. The solution to this medical mess is easy as pie and would provide EVERY American with top-dollar care.

3 Doctors and hospitals should do business like car dealerships, for Pete's sake.

4 Here are just a few examples of the way medicine oughta work under The Ed Anger Health Care Plan.

5 1. Every sawbones and every hospital should be forced to advertise in the classified section of the newspaper right next to those flashy new car ads.

6 THIS WEEKEND ONLY! TWO HEART BYPASSES FOR THE PRICE OF ONE! *That's right, folks! Get your ticker in tip-top shape at Mad Mike's Surgery Outlet!*

7 *Super Doc Mike Sullivan can put you in a luxury double bypass for the low, low price of just $925.00—and a friend or relative gets one free!*

8 *Nurses, hospital gowns, anesthetic and meals are optional. Second bypass must be done same day. No rain checks.*

9 2. Doctors ought to go on the radio like those nutty stereo and tire salesmen.

10 GOTTA BRAIN TUMOR? *Blown liver? Heart look like a hunk of lard? No problem! At Doctor Larry's Body Shop, we'll have you running like a top in no time flat. Our factory trained medical staff can get you back to being a party animal fast! Why be an invalid when you can throw away that wheelchair? We'll beat any competitor's price and we have the longest spinal surgery warranties in the business! Factory rebates of up to $5,000 on all transplants! We want to save, Save,* SAVE YOU MONEY!

11 3. Every hospital and doctor oughta have a staff of salesmen that greet you at the door with the hottest medical deals of the week. Then you could wheel and deal and get a rock-bottom price on big-buck operations like brain transplants and plastic surgery.

12 These high-pressure salesmen could even duck out and check with the doctor if you won't budge on a price. And you could start to walk out the door if they wouldn't take your final offer.

13 4. Every hospital should take organ trade-ins for transplants. A 40-year-old liver that was leaking bile might bring in a trade-in price of a thousand bucks, or instance. A bum ticker should still be worth a few hundred bucks even with high mileage.

14 These trade-ins could then be used for research or foisted off on poor people who can't afford any better.

15 5. Doctors and hospitals oughta have slogans like car dealers.
16 Bad Credit? No Job? Divorced? Noooooooo problem at Harry's Hospital Heaven—where nobody walks!
17 Or *Sal's Discount Surgery—We cut for less bucks! Buy here, pay here.*

APPLICATIONS FOR CRITICAL READING AND DISCUSSION

1. Circle the proposition in the text. If it is not presented in one sentence, state it in a sentence of your own here.

2. Underline the main points of support.

3. Draw a box around the refutation, if any.

4. Annotate the following kinds of evidence or proof in the left margin: facts, examples, statistics, and authoritative statements.

The Reading Connection from Classroom Sources

Most arguments require at least a long paragraph and usually a substantial essay for adequate development. This section contains two student essays and a paragraph based on one of the essays.

EXERCISE 6

Demonstration

Eric Miller isn't asking people to stop smoking; he's only asking them to stop smoking in public places.

              A New Wind Blowing
                  Eric Miller

     One of the most common complaints heard in restaurants
and work places pertains to smoking. In all crowded public
places, when a smoker lights up, people get upset. Three
reasons make this proposition right. <u>One is the discomfort.</u>
Most people don't like to breathe secondhand smoke. It
smells bad. <u>That reason is coupled with the health reason.</u>   *authoritative*
Studies indicate (as reported by Joseph Califano, former   *statement*
Secretary of Health, Education and Welfare) that 5,000

Americans die each year from secondhand smoke and that *statistics*
people living with smokers are 80 percent more likely to *statistics*
get lung cancer than those who do not live with smokers. In
1993 the Environmental Protection Agency formally *authoritative statement*
classified secondhand smoke as a potent carcinogen--in a
class with asbestos. <u>Connected with this health problem is
the matter of cost.</u> The last five surgeons general have *authoritative statement*
agreed that secondhand smoke is a significant health
problem with a huge cost to society in medical bills and
lost job productivity. Although many smokers agree with the
proposal for restriction, others feel that they are losing
their rights. They shouldn't. They can continue to smoke,
but only if they do not jeopardize the health of others in
public places. Discomfort, bad health, and bills for
taxpayers are too much for society to pay in order to live
without restriction.

APPLICATIONS FOR CRITICAL READING AND DISCUSSION

1. Circle the proposition in the text. If it is not presented in one sentence, state it in a sentence of your own here.

2. Underline the main points of support.

3. Draw a box around the refutation, if any.

4. Annotate the following kinds of evidence or proof in the left margin: facts, examples, statistics, and authoritative statements.

EXERCISE 7

Demonstration Using the DCODE Worksheet

This is an essay version of the previous paragraph, by the same student author.

WORKSHEET
Writing in DCODE

NAME: Eric Miller

SECTION:_____ CHAPTER:_____ DATE:_____

Delve Generate your topic, or ideas for your topic, by delving into your subject area through:

- *Freewriting*—writing sentence after sentence, nonstop and spontaneously.
- *Brainstorming*—jotting down answers to Who? What? Where? When? Why? and How? and then listing words and phrases in relation to those answers.
- *Clustering*—connecting bubbled ideas with lines to show strings of relationships, producing each new bubble item in response to the question, What comes to mind?
- *Combining* any of these approaches, as directed by your instructor.

Freewriting:

    Like many people I am bothered by smokers. I don't mind if they smoke, but I don't want to breathe their smoke. Some smokers think their rights are being violated, but that is not the main issue. I am in favor of individual rights, but I think this issue is different from most issues of individual rights because it is a health issue. I will admit I don't like the smell of tobacco smoke, but there are other smells I also don't like. The main thing here is that the breathing secondary or secondhand smoke is bad for your health. If you are around a smoker, your chances of getting cancer are greater. Then there is the expense. People around smokers get sick more often and miss work and have to go to the doctor and pay bills. All of these things suggest that we would all be better off if they smokers didn't smoke in public places. It would even be better for the smokers because they would know what the boundaries are and fewer people would be complaining and fighting.

Brainstorming:

    Who?s   smokers
    What?   restricting smoking
    Where? public places
    When?   all the time
    Why?   discomfort, health cost
    How?   national law

Clustering:

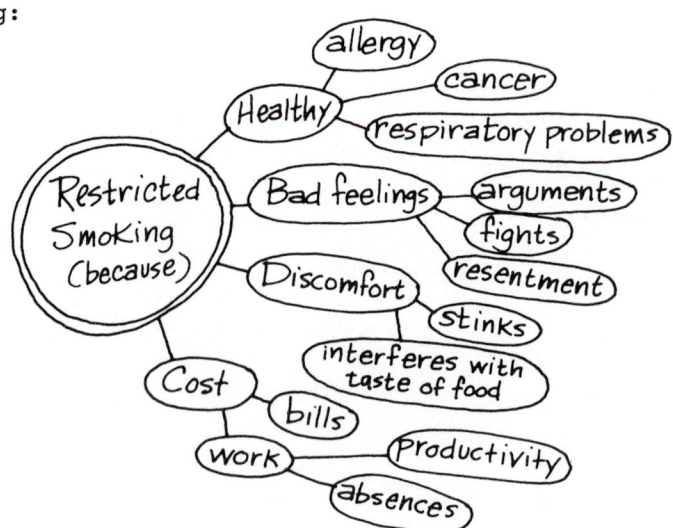

WORKSHEET: Writing in DCODE   **401**

Concentrate   Concentrate your work by stating your topic in one sentence that is not too broad, narrow, or vague to be developed. Base this sentence (which may become the topic sentence for your paragraph or the thesis for your essay) on an idea emerging from the **Delve** stage. You may have to try several statements here before you formulate one that is best for your writing task. Be sure that your final statement covers your assignment or intent and specifies both your subject (what you are writing about) and treatment (what aspect you will focus on). Label the *subject* and *treatment* parts.

<u>Smoking in public places</u> <u>should be restricted by a national law</u>.
        subject   treatment

Organize   Complete an outline or a cluster, as directed by your instructor. The cluster should be a section from, or a refined version of, the **Delve** clustering. Regardless of the strategy you use, the organizational pattern should indicate a division of your topic into parts that will, in turn, be further subdivided for support as necessary to address a particular audience on your concentrated topic.

```
    I.   Disturbed smokers
         A. Belief of violation of their rights
         B. But could benefit
    II.  Main reason to restrict smoking: health
         A. Illness and death from secondhand smoke
            1. Many people with respiratory illness
            2. Califano estimates 5,000 deaths a year
         B. Cancer from secondhand smoke
            1. Secondary smoke listed as a carcinogen
            2. Nonsmokers with smokers, 80% more likely to get cancer
    III. Second reason: discomfort
         A. Disagreeable odor
         B. Must be seen in relation to whole problem
    IV.  Third reason: cost
         A. Medical bills
         B. Lost productivity
```

Draft   On separate paper, write and then revise your assignment as many times as necessary for **c**oherence, **l**anguage (usage, tone, and diction), **u**nity, **e**mphasis, **s**upport, and **s**entence structure (**cluess**).

Edit   Correct problems in fundamentals such as **c**apitalization, **o**missions, **p**unctuation, and **s**pelling (**cops**). Before writing the final draft, read your paper aloud to discover oversights and awkwardness of expression.

First Draft

A New Wind Blowing

Confusion prevails on the issue of smoking in public places. Both smokers and nonsmokers are confused and would like the problem solved. It is time to pass a national law restricting smoking in public places. On the one side are many who, because of preference or addiction, desire to smoke. On the other side are primarily those who do not smoke and do not want to breathe the smoke of those who do. Laws vary from community to community; business persons wonder what is morally right and what price they may eventually have to pay in relation to this issue. For all the right reasons, the solution has become quite clear.

Smokers may be disturbed by this proposition. They may feel that their rights would be violated both at work and elsewhere. They shouldn't because a national law restricting them can also benefit them. No one will be fired, and no one will be deprived of the privilege of visiting public places; the only restriction is on smoking. The smokers can continue to puff away—as along as they do not imperil the health of others. This law would eliminate the hostility felt by a large percentage of the nonsmokers and therefore, improve relationships between smokers and nonsmokers.

The main reason that smoking should be restricted is the issue of health, the health of those who breathe secondary smoke. Joseph Califano, former Secretary of Health, Education, and Welfare, reports that more than 5,000 Americans die each year because of secondary-hand smoke, and that nonsmokers who live with smokers are 80 percent more likely to get lung cancer than those who are married to nonsmokers. Moreover, some people are allergic to tobacco smoke, and some have respiratory illnesses that are made worse by the tobacco smoke. In 1993, the Environmental Protection Agency classified tobacco smoke as a carcinogen and placed it in a group with asbestos. The study by the EPA discovered that all people tested—and many were non-smokers—had nicotine in their blood.

A second reason is the discomfort factor. Tobacco smoke has a disagreeable odor stinks to most nonsmokers. The smell also clings to the clothes

insert sentence from next page

and hair of nonsmokers. In a restaurant, the ~~good smell~~ *pleasing aroma* of food is ~~made bad~~ *altered if not destroyed* by tobacco smoke, and because the senses of smell and taste are so close*ly related*, tobacco smoke interferes with the pleasure of eating. There are, of course, other unpleasant clinging odors created by human beings, and were it not for the fact that secondary smoke is a health issue the discomfort factor might not be enough to ~~ask for this new law.~~ *warrant the proposed restriction.*

Another idea is the cost involved. The last five surgeons general have agreed that secondhand smoke is a significant problem with huge costs to the entire nation. Nonsmokers and all taxpayers pay huge sums to take care of problems caused by secondhand smoke. People who are made ill by second~~ary~~*hand* tobacco smoke miss work, *losing time and money,* and their employers lose productivity. Some may argue that creating nonsmoking areas, installing signs, and enforcing the rules *would* cost money, but the bill for these adjustments is nowhere close to what we *are* pay*ing* in the absence of a national law.

Powerful lobbies for tobacco companies line up on the other side. But on the side of restriction is logic, honest, and a lot of scientific information. On the side of restriction is also a large group of smokers who can't quit smoking and see the rightness of such a proposal. A new wind is blowing across the nation--and it is smoke-free, at least in public places.

Final Draft

A New Wind Blowing
Eric Miller

Confusion prevails on the issue of smoking in public places. Both smokers and nonsmokers are confused and would like the problem solved. On one side are many who, because of preference or addiction, desire to smoke. On the other side are primarily those who do not smoke and do not want to breath the smoke of those who do. Laws vary from community to community; businesspersons wonder what is morally right and what price they may eventually have to pay in relation to this issue. For all the right reasons, the solution has become quite clear. It is time to pass a national law restricting smoking in public places.

fact

> Smokers may be disturbed by this proposition. They may feel that their rights would be violated both at work and elsewhere. They shouldn't, because a national law restricting them can benefit them also. This law would eliminate the hostility felt by a large percentage of the nonsmokers and, therefore, improve relationships between smokers and nonsmokers. Moreover, no one will be fired, and no one will be deprived of the privilege of visiting public places; the only restriction is on smoking. The smokers can continue to puff away--as long as they do not imperil the health of others.

<u>The main reason that smoking should be restricted is the issue of health, the health of those who breathe secondhand smoke</u>. Joseph Califano, former Secretary of Health, Education, and Welfare, reports that more than 5,000 Americans die each year because of secondhand smoke, and that nonsmokers who live with smokers are 80 percent more likely to get lung cancer than those who are married to nonsmokers. Moreover, some people are allergic to tobacco smoke, and some have respiratory illnesses that are made worse by the tobacco smoke. In 1993, the Environmental Protection Agency classified tobacco smoke as a carcinogen and placed it in a group with asbestos. The study by the EPA discovered that all people tested-- and many were nonsmokers--had nicotine in their blood.   *authoritative statement*   *statistics*   *statistics*   *examples*   *fact*

<u>A second reason is the discomfort factor</u>. Tobacco smoke has a disagreeable odor to most nonsmokers. In a restaurant, the pleasing aroma of food is altered if not destroyed by tobacco smoke, and because the senses of smell and taste are so closely related, tobacco smoke interferes with the pleasure of eating. The smell also clings to the clothes and hair of nonsmokers. There are, of course, other unpleasant clinging odors created by human beings, and were it not for the fact that secondhand smoke is a health issue the discomfort factor might not be enough to warrant the proposed restriction.

<u>Another factor is the cost involved</u>. The last five surgeons general have agreed that secondhand smoke is a significant problem with huge costs to the entire nation. Nonsmokers and all taxpayers pay huge sums to take care of problems caused by secondhand smoke. People who are made ill by secondhand tobacco smoke miss work, losing time and money, and their employers lose productivity. Some may argue that creating nonsmoking areas, installing signs, and enforcing the rules would cost money, but the bill for these adjustments is nowhere close to what we are paying in the absence of a national law.   *authoritative statement*   *fact*

Powerful lobbies for tobacco companies are on the other side. But on the side of restriction is logic, honesty, and an abundance of scientific information. On the side of restriction is also a large group of smokers who are unable or unwilling to quit smoking and see the rightness of such a proposal. A new wind is blowing across the nation--and it is smoke free, at least in public places.

APPLICATIONS FOR CRITICAL READING AND DISCUSSION

1. Circle the proposition in the text. If it is not presented in one sentence, state it in a sentence of your own here.

2. Underline the main points of support.

3. Draw a box around the refutation, if any.

4. Annotate the following kinds of evidence or proof in the left margin: facts, examples, statistics, and authoritative statements.

EXERCISE 8

In this well-reasoned essay, Angela DeSarro argues that every person should have the right to die.

```
                   Right to Die
                  Angela DeSarro
```
    Debbie, 20, was dying of ovarian cancer. Racked with pain, nauseous, emaciated, she sought the ultimate relief and found it in euthanasia. A doctor administered a drug and she died. This scenario is repeated frequently across this land as hidden, illegal acts, but this particular incident was written up by the attending physician in the *Journal of the American Medical Association* (Jan. 8, 1988). Some readers approved; others wanted the doctor identified and arrested. Surely it is time for this society to properly address the question underlying this controversy: If patients are terminally ill, should they have the right to die? The answer is yes for three good reasons: the pain and suffering caused by the illness may be excruciating, the patients may want to die with dignity, and the patients, as individuals, should be allowed to choose what is best for them, including death in certain circumstances.

    First, the individuals may fear the pain or the suffering that would take place near the end, just before death. There may come a time when the pain-killing medication no longer works. In addition to enduring terrible pain, Debbie had reached the point that she was vomiting constantly and could not sleep. Some patients would rather end life peacefully and painlessly and not go through all the suffering that will eventually end only in death anyway.

    The second reason that patients should be allowed to choose death is that they may want to die with some dignity. They may want to die at least looking somewhat healthy rather than emaciated with tubes coming out of their nose, throat, and urinary tract, and with their body hooked up to machines. Each person should be allowed to decide just what "dignity" means.

Finally, shouldn't it be up to the individual to decide when he or she is to die? Only that individual knows when the time has come to die. Many people believe that, and legally or illegally, many people will follow their beliefs. People will make the decision to take their lives. Some doctors will assist them, while maintaining that it is not immoral or unethical to aid terminally ill people who make a rational decision to take their lives.

Laws in most places prohibit terminally ill patients from choosing death and physicians from assisting them. Laws that exist tend to cut black and white when it comes to matters of the heart. The gray area between those extremes is the area that needs attention. A contract that avoids abuse could be drawn up between the doctor and patient, giving the doctor permission to administer a lethal dose of a drug such as morphine. Euthanasia should be legal.

APPLICATIONS FOR CRITICAL READING AND DISCUSSION

1. Circle the proposition in the text. If it is not presented in one sentence, state it in a sentence of your own here.

2. Underline the main points of support.

3. Draw a box around the refutation, if any.

4. Annotate the following kinds of evidence or proof in the left margin: facts, examples, statistics, and authoritative statements.

Suggested Topics for Writing Argumentation

General Topics

Following are subject ideas. In order to turn a subject into a proposition, compose a sentence that proclaims a policy, value, or belief in order to address a problem.

EXAMPLE:
Subject idea: gun control
Proposition: In order to curtail the problem of violence in our country, the federal government should pass a law requiring the registration of all guns.

1. Abortion
2. Advertising
3. AIDS
4. Animal experiments
5. Birth control
6. Capital punishment
7. Censorship
8. Child rearing
9. Child support
10. Collective bargaining
11. Crime
12. Drugs
13. Education
14. Evolution
15. Federal deficit
16. Foreign trade
17. Gun control
18. Homosexuality
19. Marriage
20. Media
21. Minimum wage
22. National debt
23. Political scandals
24. Pornography
25. Prayer in public schools
26. Speed limit
27. Sports and drugs
28. Sports and racism
29. Surrogate mothers
30. Welfare/workfare

Reading-Related Topics

"How About Low-Cost Drugs for Addicts?"

1. Write an argument on the other side of this issue. The author provides some of the opposing views in his refutation toward the end of his essay.

"Curbing the Sexploitation Industry"

2. Take the opposing view on one or several of the proposals the author makes and write a paper of argumentation.

"Make Docs Wheel and Deal Like Used Car Salesmen!"

3. Argue against Ed Anger in a cool, well-reasoned rebuttal. Discuss Anger's approach, use of evidence, and style, if you like.

4. Use Anger's implied proposition, modify it to suit your thinking, and develop it into a thoughtful paragraph or essay.

"A New Wind Blowing"

5. Take the other side of this argument, and write a paper of argumentation.

"Right to Die"

6. Take the other side of this argument, and write a paper of argumentation.

Writer's Checklist

Apply these ideas to your writing as you work with **DCODE**. Later, as a peer editor, apply the same ideas to the material you evaluate.

1. State the problem and your proposition.

2. Consider your audience.

3. Determine the components of your paper such as definitions, background, and refutation.

4. Decide on your organizational plan. The main patterns are these:

   main issue—support

   main issue—refutation—support

   main issue—support—refutation

5. Consider the most commonly used pattern as presented here:

Background	Discussion of the problem, reason for concern, historical development, etc.
Proposition	
Refutation	The other view and its fundamental inadequacy.
Support	
Support	The evidence — why your solution is valid.
Support	
Emphatic restatement of proposition	The clinching statement, often with generalization based on evidence.

6. Select the appropriate kinds of evidence such as these to use with your explanations:

   Facts

   Examples

   Statistics

   Data from and opinions of authorities

   Products of inductive and deductive reasoning

7. Avoid logical fallacies.

 **Journal-Entry Suggestions**

1. Select some of the unused "Reading-Related Topics" suggestions and use them for journal topics.

2. Write a reaction to one or more "Reading Connection" selections. Agree, disagree, apply the statements to your own experiences, indicate the value of such statements, or explain why you were surprised, shocked, disgusted, pleased, or whatever, by the material.

3. Invent statements (using argumentation if appropriate) to support headlines from *Weekly World News:*

   "Mongoose Attacks Man's Snakeskin Boots!"
   "Baby Geese Adopt Airplane as Their New Mom!"
   "War Chicken Awarded Medal for Bravery!"
   "4-year-old Singer Is Elvis Reborn!"
   "Vampire Sues Airline Over Busted Coffin!"
   "29-year-old Beauty Marries Giraffe!"
   "Singing Kitty Knows 26 Songs by Heart!"
   "Titanic Captain Found in Lifeboat!"
   "Scientists Breed Pet Dinosaurs!"
   "Elvis' Secret Diary Found!"
   "Screwy Swami Flies Magic Carpet into Power Lines!"
   "Farmer Puts Sneakers on All His Barnyard Animals!"
   "Man Fries Eggs on His Bald Head!"

WORKSHEET
Writing in DCODE

NAME:_____

SECTION:_____ CHAPTER:_____ DATE:_____

Delve   Generate your topic, or ideas for your topic, by delving into your subject area through:

- *Freewriting*—writing sentence after sentence, nonstop and spontaneously.
- *Brainstorming*—jotting down answers to Who? What? Where? When? Why? and How? and then listing words and phrases in relation to those answers.
- *Clustering*—connecting bubbled ideas with lines to show strings of relationships, producing each new bubble item in response to the question, What comes to mind?
- *Combining* any of these approaches, as directed by your instructor.

WORKSHEET: Writing in DCODE

Concentrate Concentrate your work by stating your topic in one sentence that is not too broad, narrow, or vague to be developed. Base this sentence (which may become the topic sentence for your paragraph or the thesis for your essay) on an idea emerging from the **Delve** stage. You may have to try several statements here before you formulate one that is best for your writing task. Be sure that your final statement covers your assignment or intent and specifies both your subject (what you are writing about) and treatment (what aspect you will focus on). Label the *subject* and *treatment* parts.

Organize Complete an outline or a cluster, as directed by your instructor. The cluster should be a section from, or a refined version of, the **Delve** clustering. Regardless of the strategy you use, the organizational pattern should indicate a division of your topic into parts that will, in turn, be further subdivided for support as necessary to address a particular audience on your concentrated topic.

Draft On separate paper, write and then revise your assignment as many times as necessary for **c**oherence, **l**anguage (usage, tone, and diction), **u**nity, **e**mphasis, **s**upport, and **s**entence structure (**cluess**).

Edit Correct problems in fundamentals such as **c**apitalization, **o**missions, **p**unctuation, and **s**pelling (**cops**). Before writing the final draft, read your paper aloud to discover oversights and awkwardness of expression.

Using Textbook and Library Sources: Writing the Documented Paper

14

> "Some books leave us free, and some books make us free."
> — Ralph Waldo Emerson

"The cards say you've been dead for two and a half years."

What are the two types of documented writing presented here? How do you determine the appropriate form(s) of discourse in a textbook-based documented paper? How can **DCODE** be used in writing the documented paper? What form of documentation is used in this book? What is plagiarism?

The documented paper, a common assignment in college writing especially, will probably be one of two types: the textbook-based paper or the library-based paper. Both will be discussed in this chapter.

The Textbook-Based Documented Paper

Instruction in this type of writing is correlated with selections in this text through cross-references, a Thematic Table of Contents, and a list of suggested reading-related topics. Whereas the library research paper is likely to be many pages long, the textbook-based paper can be as short as a paragraph or as long as an assignment requires. Therefore, you may see it as a extension of conventional reading-related writing but with the acknowledged borrowing of ideas from the model paragraphs and essays.

Those readings have been selected to stimulate thought, to provide examples for parallel ideas in writing, and to provide examples for form in writing. Even a cursory glance will reveal that although each has a dominant form—narration, description, exposition, or argumentation—none uses a single form exclusively.

Moreover, perhaps you have noticed that several thematic ideas have been presented from different perspectives by both student and professional writers. These themes provide an opportunity for expanding your writing experiences. By grouping some of the essays according to subject and by releasing the restriction of writing with a specific dominant form throughout a piece, this chapter provides opportunities to combine subjects and forms. The resulting paper—a textbook-based documented paragraph or essay—will be mainly your thinking, but it will use ideas from essays in this book for support, and it will give credit to those sources.

The form or forms of discourse you use in your documented paper will depend on what you are trying to do in addressing your subject, your assignment, and your audience. One form may dominate, or several may share preeminence (especially in the longer paper). Let us review the forms here by examining the chapter titles:

    Narration: Moving Through Time
    Description: Moving Through Space
    Exemplification: Illustrating Ideas
    Functional Analysis: Examining the Components
    Process Analysis: Writing About Doing
    Analysis by Causes and Effects: Determining Reasons and Results
    Classification: Establishing Groups
    Comparison and Contrast: Showing Similarities and Dissimilarities
    Definition: Clarifying Terms
    Literary Analysis: Reacting to Stories
    Argumentation: Persuading, Arguing, and Thinking Critically

Working with the Thematic Table of Contents

The alternate listing of the readings in the Thematic Table of Contents of this textbook arranges titles by themes. If you see a thematic area that interests you, you can decide whether you could write a paragraph or essay on some aspect of it; then you can consider the subject material from two or more of the pieces of writing for that theme to see if you can find information that will illustrate your points and help you fulfill your writing purpose. Or you can first read the works listed under a topic and then invent a topic sentence for a paragraph or a thesis for an essay to cover an aspect that interests you. In your final draft, the work will be yours, but you will have borrowed some ideas and credited the sources.

Suggested Topics Related to Areas in the Thematic Table of Contents

Sexism
- Discrimination against women
- Women as victims
- Men as victims
- Women as survivors
- Strength of women

Exploitation
- Discrimination against minorities
- Exploitation in business
- Class discrimination

Cultural Issues
- Cultural adjustments
- Compromises by immigrants
- Important learning experiences by immigrants
- Cultural identity: divided or single?

Violence
- Causes
- Effects
- Experiences

Show Business
- Ways to succeed
- Show business as business
- Experiences

Prison Life
- Convicts as human beings
- Prison: punishment or rehabilitation?
- Prison life and street life

Education
- Different forms
- Self-esteem and education
- Value
- Effects

Environment and Health
- Environmental effects on health
- Habits/addiction and health
- Health care

Psychology
- Difficulty of really knowing another's mind
- Loneliness
- Why we do what we do

Love
- Love and sexual attraction
- Love and hatred
- Love and communication

Sports
- Great players
- Sports and violence
- Sports and values
- Sports and business

DCODE Application

The same systematic process you have used throughout this book will work well for you in writing a documented paper. The only adjustment you need make is for incorporating ideas from textbook sources into your work. At what point you will consult your sources will depend on your knowledge of the subject you are writing about. If you already have a good command of your topic, you might proceed all the way to the **Organize** stage of the writing process before reading intensely, copying out quotations, and paraphrasing ideas for use. You can simply attach your short quotations and references to your outline and work them into your first draft. However, if you are less confident with your subject material and you are looking for some rather extensive support, you might want to begin the reading and note taking during the **Delve** stage, perhaps after freewriting. For that larger undertaking, you might need to use note cards (see the next part of this chapter).

Basic Documentation

Documenting sources for papers based on textbook material is usually quite simple. One documentation method is MLA (Modern Language Association) style, which is discussed thoroughly in the next section of this chapter. Here are its most common principles, with some examples for application:

- If you use material from a secondary source, identify that source so the reader will recognize it or be able to find it.

- Any idea borrowed, whether it is quoted, paraphrased, or summarized, should be documented, and there are three basic situations:
    Normally, you need give only the author's name and a page number: (Rivera 45).
    If you state the author's name in introducing the quotation or idea, then give only the page number: (45)
    If the author has written more than one piece in the book, then a title or shortened form of the title is also required: (Rivera, *The Land* 45).

- Borrowing words or ideas without giving credit to the originators constitutes plagiarism (see pp. 430–431).

Examples of documenting a quotation by an author mentioned only once in the textbook are:

- Using the author's name to introduce:

    Suzanne Britt says that "neat people are bums and clods at heart" (285).

- Not using the author's name to introduce:

    Another author says that "neat people are bums and clods at heart" (Britt 285).

Examples of documenting an idea borrowed from an author but not quoted are:

- Using the author's name to introduce:

    Suzanne Britt believes that neat people are weak in character (285).

- Not using the author's name to introduce:

    Although some maintain that neat people also are likely to have high values, at least one other well-known author and social critic says that neat people are weak in character (Britt 284–285).

The Presentation

Writing a textbook-based documented paragraph or essay is not difficult. You simply write a piece of material as you usually would but include some ideas from other sources. You can even use ideas from other sources to contrast with your own. For example, you can say, "Unlike Richard Rodriguez in 'Private Language, Public Language' (342), I think that bilingual education is highly desirable." Do not feel that each point you make must be directly related to sources.

Here is a paragraph illustrating how to incorporate ideas and document them:

> Sexist men are victims of their own bias against females. Because they cannot accept women as full human beings, they themselves are smaller in dimension. In Irwin Shaw's "The Girls in Their Summer Dresses," Michael looks at his wife, but he doesn't see a full human being; he just sees a sexual object: "what a pretty girl, what nice legs" (365). Because he sees her and other women that way, he cannot ever have the relationship with her that she deserves and that he would find fulfilling. Of course, thinking of women as just soft and cuddly has its effects on men in other ways. The man as father who thinks that way may very well regard his own daughter as one limited in her ranges of activities and limited in her potential. He may be one of those fathers who immediately stereotype their daughters as headed for a "life of the affections," not like a son's, "earning a living" (Lurie 281). Unfortunately, these men cannot accept females as their equals in any important respect, and, in doing so, they deprive themselves, as well as others.

Jackie Malone, "Sexist Men as Victims"

The Library-Based Documented Paper

The library-based documented paper, sometimes called the research paper, will probably be longer and more complex than the other type, involving a set of procedures ranging from library usage to the completion of a formal work. It will be discussed systematically with examples in the last part of this chapter.

Using the Library

Although some research topics require interviews, surveys, or the study of documents in off-campus archives, the center for most academic research is the college library. There you will find *primary sources* (examples of the actual subjects being investigated, such as literary works, letters, and the texts of speeches and interviews); *secondary sources* (biographies, scholarly books and monographs, periodical articles, and other works about the subject); and the various reference tools needed to identify and obtain these sources.

If your library uses a computerized indexing system, you can obtain lists of probable sources by going to the computer terminal and typing in a user code plus an author, title, or subject description. Libraries differ in the systems offered. The following material pertains to the noncomputerized library system. Always work with the best system available and obtain help from librarians.

The Library Catalog

One indispensable research tool is the card catalog or its equivalent, the computer catalog, which indexes all the books and bound periodicals in the library's collection. The catalog is usually divided into three sections: (1) an author file, which contains entries for all books arranged alphabetically by author; (2) a title file, which consists of entries for all books and bound periodicals arranged alphabetically; and (3) a subject file, which includes entries for all books arranged alphabetically by subject. The entries in this catalog provide several kinds of information that will aid you in your research:

1. A Library of Congress or Dewey Decimal system call number that indicates the exact location of the work in the library.
2. Author, title, and publication data for the book.
3. Brief notes about the book's contents.
4. Cross-references to other headings under which each book is listed.

   Figures 14.1 through 14.3 show examples of the three types of cards.

General Encyclopedias and Biographical Dictionaries

Articles in encyclopedias and other general reference works usually treat their subject so briefly and superficially that there is seldom any need to cite them in a formal research paper. However, they do often provide useful background information, as well as bibliographical references that may lead you to more promising sources.

- General Encyclopedias

    Collier's Encyclopedia. 24 vols. 1991.
    The Encyclopedia Americana. International Edition. 32 vols. 1993.
    Encyclopedia Britannica. 32 vols. 1993.
    The Random House Encyclopedia. Revised ed. 1990.

- Biographical Dictionaries

    American Men and Women of Science. 1971– .
    Who's Who in America. 1899– .

Specialized Reference Works

Many of the subjects covered in general reference works are treated in greater detail in books such as the ones listed below. For additional titles consult such works as Eugene Sheehy's *Guide to Reference Books*, Gavin Higgens's *Printed Reference Material*, or G. Chandler's *How to Find Out: Printed and On-Line Sources*.

The Sciences

McGraw-Hill Encyclopedia of Science and Technology. 15 vols. 1975.
   Supplemented by *McGraw-Hill Yearbook of Science and Technology*, 1971– .

FIGURE 14.1 Author Card

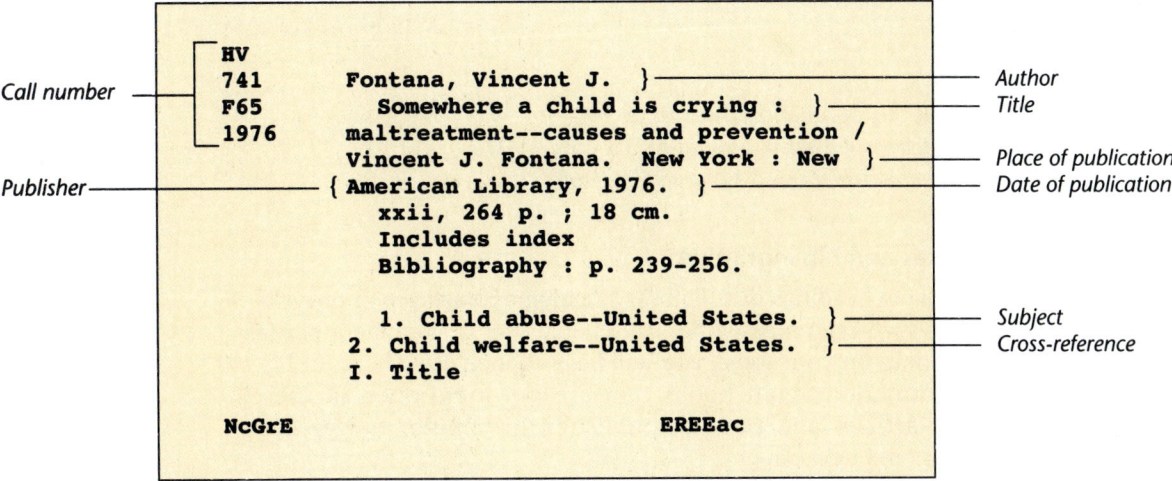

FIGURE 14.2 Title Card

```
                Somewhere a child is crying
HV
741      Fontana, Vincent J.
F65          Somewhere a child is crying :
1976     maltreatment--causes and prevention /
         Vincent J. Fontana.  New York : New
         American Library, 1976.
             xxii, 264 p. ; 18 cm.
             Includes index
             Bibliography : p. 239-256.

             1. Child abuse--United States.
             2. Child welfare--United States.

NcGrE                                  EREEtc
```

FIGURE 14.3 Subject Card

```
                CHILD ABUSE--UNITED STATES
HV
741      Fontana, Vincent J.
F65          Somewhere a child is crying :
1976     maltreatment--causes and prevention /
         Vincent J. Fontana.  New York : New
         American Library, 1976.
             xxii, 264 p. ; 18 cm.
             Includes index
             Bibliography : p. 239-256.

             1. Child abuse--United States.
             2. Child welfare--United States.

NcGrE                                  EREEsc
```

The Social Sciences

International Encyclopedia of the Social Sciences. 18 vols. 1968.

The Humanities

Cambridge History of American Literature. 1943.
Cambridge History of English Literature. 15 vols. 1907–.
Encyclopedia of World Art. 15 vols. 1959–1968.

Periodical Indexes and Bibliographies

Although the subject headings of the library catalog and articles in encyclopedias and other such reference works will enable you to compile a partial bibliography of books on your topic, you will have to look elsewhere for bibliographical information about books that are not mentioned in these sources and for articles and reviews published in popular magazines, scholarly journals, and newspapers.

Indexes to Articles and Reviews in Popular Magazines

Book Review Digest. 1905– .
Nineteenth Century Reader's Guide to Periodical Literature. 1890–1899.
Poole's Index to Periodical Literature. 1802–1906.
Reader's Guide to Periodical Literature. 1900– .

How to Use the *Reader's Guide to Periodical Literature*

This is an index to about 185 popular U.S. magazines, representing the important scientific and humanistic subject fields.

Look up your topic alphabetically. If you are unable to find the topic you are looking for, ask for assistance from a reference librarian. The items listed under each subject heading are titles of magazine articles. If the title is not explanatory, it is followed by a short clarification in brackets.

After the title, these items follow:

Author (if available), last name, first initial
Abbreviated description of article features (see page headed "Abbreviations")
Title of magazine, sometimes abbreviated (see page headed "Abbreviations of Periodicals Indexed")
Volume number (if any)
Page number(s)
Date

Figure 14.4 labels the various parts of a *Reader's Guide* entry.

FIGURE 14.4 Explanation of an Entry

Microfilm Resources and Computerized Information Services

Much of the information in written reference works is now stored also on microfilm or in computer files. Microfilm indexes such as *Magazine Index*, which lists articles in over 300 popular magazines, are useful because the researcher can easily scan hundreds of items in a few minutes. Even faster are computerized research systems such as Dialog Information Services, which can search thousands of entries for material pertinent to the researcher's interest. Although computer searches are expensive, they are also a convenient and reliable means of gathering bibliographical data on subjects in all academic areas.

The Research Paper

Research is a systematic process of exploration and discovery—a means of attaining new knowledge and gaining fresh insights to previously held values and beliefs. Thus it is both an essential human activity and an indispensable scholarly tool.

Some research activities involve laboratory experimentation. Others require field investigations such as interviews, surveys, and observations of natural phenomena. Still others lead researchers into libraries and archives to explore published and unpublished sources of information.

Although specific aims and methods may vary from one research activity to another, most nonexperimental research tasks will depend on these basic steps:

1. Choose a subject that interests you, and narrow it until it becomes a topic that you can investigate thoroughly and write about convincingly.

2. Find out what style of documentation is appropriate for this piece of research writing, and familiarize yourself with the conventions for preparing a bibliography or list of works cited and for documenting sources.

3. Use the resources in your college library to identify books, articles, and other materials pertaining to your topic.

4. Compile a preliminary bibliography of the sources referred to above, following the documentation style appropriate to your discipline.

5. Locate, read, and take notes on the sources listed in the preliminary bibliography.

6. Develop a thesis statement and an outline or some other tentative organizational plan based on the evidence you have accumulated.

7. Present results and conclusions in systematic, accurately documented written form.

8. Prepare a list of works cited from the preliminary bibliography.

In the remainder of this chapter, these steps will be illustrated with a student research project, written by a student in a second-semester composition class. Based on the conventions of the *MLA Handbook for Writers of Research Papers*, 3d ed., this essay—together with the introductory notes and annotations that accompany it—provides a practical guide to parenthetical documentation style, techniques for using sources, methods of organization, revision strategies, and other important aspects of the research writing process.

Background: The Research Assignment

The assignment on which the sample paper was based required students to choose a researchable subject and limit it to manageable proportions, gather information from at least six different sources, and present results and conclusions in an expository paper of 5–8 pages.

> **Step 1.** Choose a subject that interests you, and narrow it until it becomes a topic that you can investigate thoroughly and write about convincingly.

Circumstances of Composition

Sarah Johnson, the author of the sample paper, decided almost immediately that she wanted to investigate the problem of child abuse—partly because she had already read several magazine and newspaper articles on the subject but even more so because her own close family ties made her sympathetic to the plight of abused children and curious to learn more about the victims.

> **Step 2.** Find out what style of documentation is appropriate for this piece of research writing, and familiarize yourself with the conventions for preparing a bibliography or list of works cited and for documenting sources.

Preliminary Bibliography and Works Cited

As you find references to books and articles that seem pertinent to your topic, record each citation on a separate index card or piece of paper (most researchers use 3 x 5 inch cards for this purpose because cards are easier to file and rearrange).

Each of the cards in this preliminary bibliography should include a call number (see p. 418), which will enable you to find the book or periodical (if your library has it), plus all the bibliographical information you need to document the work in your research paper.

The most efficient method of recording this information is to use the appropriate form for each citation in the preliminary bibliography so that you can later prepare a list of **works cited** simply by alphabetizing the cards and typing them as a single list, skipping two spaces after periods and one space after other punctuation.

Listed below are sample bibliographical entries for the kinds of sources you are most likely to use in a research paper. To determine the format for a reference, first identify the type of source you are citing (e.g., a book by a single author, an article in a journal, etc.) and find the matching heading. Then use the sample reference as a model for your own entry.

Books

- **A Book by One Author**

    Adeler, Thomas L. In a New York Minute. New York: Harper, 1990.

- **An Anthology**
    List the name of the editor, followed by a comma, a space, and "ed."

    Gunn, Giles, ed. New World Metaphysics. New York: Oxford UP, 1981.

- **Two or More Books by the Same Author**
  In the preliminary bibliography, record information for each book on a separate card, and cite the author's name both times. When incorporating such entries into the list of works cited, follow these procedures: Give the name in the first entry; in successive entries, substitute three hyphens for exactly the same name; alphabetize the works by title.

    Walter, Alice. The Color Purple: A Novel. New York: Harcourt, 1982.
    - - -. Meridian. New York: Harcourt, 1976.

- **A Book by Two or More Authors**
  To cite a book with two or three authors, list them in the sequence they appear on the title page, giving the first author's name in reverse order. If there are more than three authors, cite only the name of the person listed first on the title page and use the abbreviation "et al." ("and others") in place of the other authors' names.

    Berry, Mary Frances, and John W. Blassingame. Long Memory: The Black Experience in America. New York: Oxford UP, 1981.
    Danziger, James N., et al. Computers and Politics: High Technology in American Local Governments. New York: Columbia UP, 1982.

- **A Book with a Corporate Author**

    Detroit Commission on the Renaissance. Toward the Future. Detroit: Wolverine, 1989.

Articles in Periodicals

The usual pattern for citing articles in periodicals is as follows: author's name followed by a period and two spaces; title of article followed by a period and two spaces; name of periodical, volume number, date, and inclusive page numbers separated by a single space. If no author is given, cite the title first and alphabetize the title.

- **Article in a Weekly or Biweekly Magazine**

    "How to Stop Crib Deaths." Newsweek 6 Aug. 1973: 79.

- **Article in a Monthly or Bimonthly Magazine**

    Browne, Malcolm W. "Locking Out the Hackers: There Are Ways to Keep Trespassers Out of Computer Systems." Discover Nov. 1983: 30–40.

- **Newspaper Article**

    Gregory, Tina. "When All Else Fails." Philadelphia Inquirer 2 Apr. 1990: C12.

If the city of publication is not part of the name of the newspaper, include it in square brackets after the name. If the city is part of the newspaper's name but is not widely known, include the state in brackets.

- **Editorial**

    "The President's Failure." Editorial. Charlotte [N.C.] Observer 20 Nov. 1987: 14A.

A Work in an Anthology

Give the author and title of the work you are citing. Then cite the title of the anthology. After the title, give the name of the editor or translator, preceded by the abbreviation "Ed." or "Trans." Follow with city, publisher, and date. Skip two spaces and cite the inclusive page numbers. If the work has been published elsewhere before its inclusion in the anthology, give full information for the original publication and for the anthology. Use the abbreviation "Rpt. in" before the citation for the anthology.

> Booth, Wayne C. "The Scholar in Society." Introduction to Scholarship in Modern Languages and Literatures. Ed. Joseph Gibaldi. New York: MLA, 1981. 116–143.
>
> Tolkien, J.R.R. "Children and Fairy Stories." Tree and Leaf. By Tolkien. London: Allen, 1964. 102–110. Rpt. in Only Connect: Readings on Children's Literature. Ed. Sheila Egoff, G. T. Stubbs, and L. F. Ashley. 2nd ed. Toronto: Oxford UP, 1980. 111–120.

An Article in an Encyclopedia

Treat an encyclopedia article or dictionary entry as a piece in a collection. For familiar reference books, do not cite the editor's name or give publication information other than the year. If the articles are arranged alphabetically, omit the page numbers.

> Schmitt, Barton D., and C. Henry Kempe. "Child Abuse." The Encyclopedia Americana. International ed. 1980.

Government Publications

Usually the writer of a government publication is not named, so treat the issuing government agency as the author. Abbreviations are acceptable if they are clear. Most federal publications come from the Government Printing Office (GPO) in Washington, D.C.

> United States. Dept. of Transportation. National Highway Traffic Safety Admin. Driver Licensing Laws Annotated 1980. Washington: GPO, 1980.

Citations from the *Congressional Record* require only a date and page number.

> Congressional Record. 11 Sept. 1992: 12019–24.

Published Proceedings of a Conference

> Proceedings of the 34th Annual International Technical Communication Conference. Denver, 10–13 May 1987. San Diego: Univelt, 1987.

Treat particular presentations in the proceedings as you would pieces in a collection.

> Wise, Mary R. "The Main Event Is Desktop Publishing." Proceedings of the 34th International Technical Communication Conference. Denver, 10–13 May 1987. San Diego: Univelt, 1987.

A Lecture, Speech, or Address

> Kosinski, Jerzy. Address. Opening General Session. NCTE Convention. Louisville, KY, 26 March 1987.

A Personal Interview

> Thomas, Carolyn. Personal interview. 5 Jan. 1993.

Documenting

Although you need not acknowledge a source for generally known information such as the dates of the Civil War or the names of the ships that carried Columbus and his followers to the New World, you must identify the exact source and location of each statement, fact, or idea you borrow from another person or work.

There are many ways to acknowledge sources, but one of the simplest and most efficient is the documentation system given in the *MLA Handbook for Writers of Research Papers,* 3d ed. (1988). MLA requires only a brief parenthetical reference in the text of the paper keyed to a complete bibliographical entry in the list of works cited at the end of the essay.

For most parenthetical references, you will need to cite only the author's last name and the number of the page from which the statement or idea was taken, and if you mention the author's name in the text, the page number alone is sufficient. This format also allows you to include within the parentheses additional information, such as title or volume number, if it is needed for clarity. Documentation for some of the most common types of sources is discussed in the sections below, and additional examples of documentation in the context of a student research paper can be found at the end of this chapter.

References to Articles and Single-Volume Books

Articles and single-volume books are the two types of works you will be referring to most often in your research paper. When citing them, either mention the author's name in the text and note the appropriate page number in parentheses immediately after the citation or acknowledge both name and page number in the parenthetical reference, leaving a space between the two. If punctuation is needed, insert the mark outside the final parenthesis.

- Author's Name Cited in the Text

    Marya Mannes has defined euthanasia as "the chosen alternative to the prolongation of a steadily waning mind and spirit by machines that will withhold death or to an existence that mocks life" (61).

- Author's Name Cited in Parentheses

    Euthanasia has been defined as "the chosen alternative to the prolongation of a steadily waning mind and spirit by machines that will withhold death or to an existence that mocks life" (Mannes 61).

- Corresponding Bibliographic Entry

    Mannes, Marya. <u>Last Rights.</u> New York: Morrow, 1973.

References to Works in an Anthology

When referring to a work in an anthology, either cite in the text the author's name and indicate in parentheses the page number in the anthology where the source is located, or acknowledge both name and page reference parenthetically.

- Author's Name Cited in Text

    One of the most widely recognized facts about James Joyce, in Lionel Trilling's view, "is his ambivalence toward Ireland, of which the hatred was as relentless as the love was unfailing" (153).

- Author's Name Cited in Parentheses

    One of the most widely recognized facts about James Joyce "is his ambivalence toward Ireland, of which the hatred was as relentless as the love was unfailing" (Trilling 153).

- Corresponding Bibliographic Entry

    Trilling, Lionel, "James Joyce in His Letters." <u>Joyce: A Collection of Critical Essays</u>. Ed. William M. Chace. Englewood Cliffs: Prentice-Hall, 1974.

References to Works of Unknown Authorship

If you borrow information or ideas from an article or book for which you cannot determine the name of the author, cite the title instead, either in the text of the paper or in parentheses, and include the page reference as well.

- Title Cited in the Text

    According to an article entitled "Going Back to Booze," surveys have shown that most adult alcoholics began drinking heavily as teenagers (42).

- Title Cited in Parentheses

    Surveys have shown that most adult alcoholics began drinking heavily as teenagers ("Going Back to Booze" 42).

- Corresponding Bibliographic Entry

    "Going Back to Booze." <u>Time</u> 31 Nov. 1979; 41–46.

References in Block Quotations

Quotations longer than four typewritten lines are indented ten spaces without quotation marks, and their references are put outside end punctuation.

> Implicit in the concept of Strange Loops is the concept of infinity, since what else is a loop but a way of representing an endless process in a finite way? And infinity plays a large role in many of Escher's drawings. Copies of one single theme often fit into each other, forming visual analogues to the canons of Bach. (Hofstadter 15)

- Corresponding Bibliographic Entry

    Hofstadter, Douglas. <u>Gödel, Escher, Bach: An Eternal Golden Braid</u>. New York: Vintage, 1980.

> **Step 3.** Use the resources in your college library to identify books, articles, and other materials pertaining to your topic.

Because Sarah already had some familiarity with her subject, she decided that there was no need to consult encyclopedias or other general reference works, so she began her research by compiling a selected bibliography of books listed in the library catalog under the subject heading "child abuse." For each source, she recorded the call number plus pertinent bibliographical information on a 3 x 5 inch card. Then she went to the reference room, checked under the same subject heading in recent volumes of the *Reader's Guide to Periodical Literature* and several other periodical indexes, made additional bibliography cards for ten articles that seemed especially promising, and looked up the call number of each periodical in another reference room resource—the serials catalog.

> **Step 4.** Compile a preliminary bibliography of the sources referred to above, following the documentation style appropriate to your discipline.

Several entries from the preliminary bibliography are shown in Figures 14.5 through 14.10. Note that the writer has taken the time to convert the publication data for each book or article into the format appropriate for that source.

FIGURE 14.5 Entry for an Unsigned Article in a Weekly Magazine

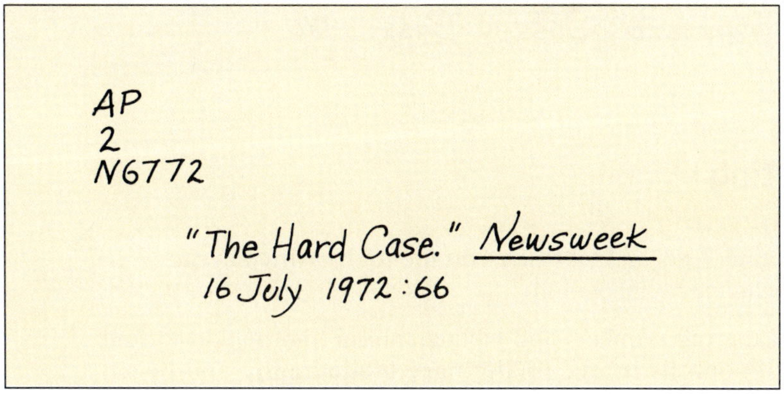

```
AP
2
N6772

    "The Hard Case." Newsweek
    16 July 1972: 66
```

FIGURE 14.6 Entry for a Book by a Single Author

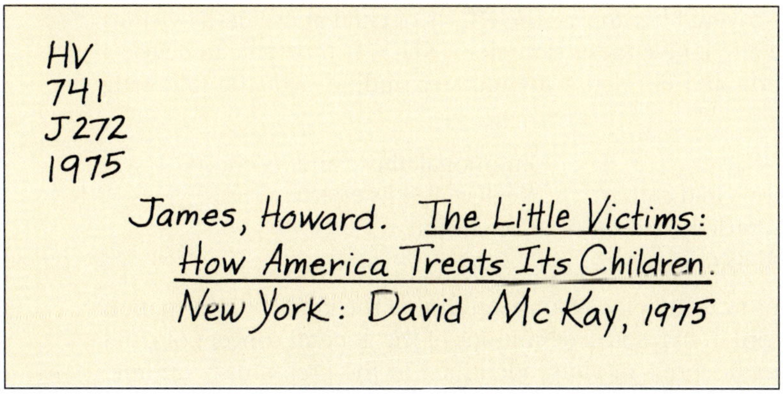

```
HV
741
J272
1975

    James, Howard. The Little Victims:
    How America Treats Its Children.
    New York: David McKay, 1975
```

FIGURE 14.7 Entry for an Essay Collection with More than Three Editors

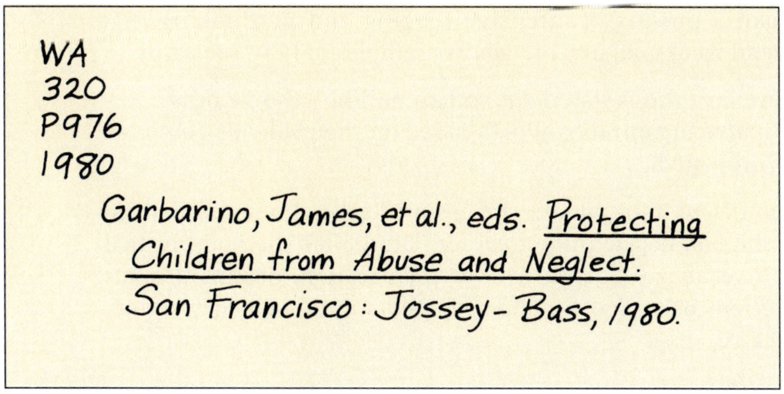

```
WA
320
P976
1980

    Garbarino, James, et al., eds. Protecting
    Children from Abuse and Neglect.
    San Francisco: Jossey-Bass, 1980.
```

After reading the essay collection edited by Garbarino, Sarah made additional bibliography cards for each of the essays on which she expected to take notes. Notice that in the example below the author's name and the title of the essay are cited first:

FIGURE 14.8 Entry for an Essay in an Edited Collection

> Gottlieb, Benjamin. "The Role of the Individual and Social Support in Preventing Child Maltreatment." In <u>Protecting Children from Abuse and Neglect</u>. Eds. James Garbarino, et al. San Francisco: Jossey-Bass, 1980.

Researching and Writing

Step 5. Locate, read, and take notes on the sources listed in the preliminary bibliography.

Next, Sarah used the call numbers and bibliographical information to find the books and periodicals in her preliminary bibliography and began reading. At first, she skimmed quickly over each work, noting major ideas and reflecting on how she might restrict her subject. Through this process, she eventually discovered her topic—the effects of child abuse on its victims—and formulated a tentative thesis statement. She was then able to devise a plan of organization and develop a preliminary outline with the following subdivisions:

Introduction	Emotional abuse and its effects
Profile of the typical child abuser	Neglect and its effects
Characteristics of abused children	Conclusion
Physical abuse and its effects	

These decisions in turn helped Sarah determine the kinds of information she needed to record in her notes: definitions of the general concept of child abuse and the specific forms of abuse identified in the preliminary outline, statistical data indicating the scope and seriousness of the problem, and explanations and examples of the effects of abuse. With these considerations in mind, she began a process of intensive reading and note taking that continued for several weeks. Figure 14.9 shows samples of her note cards.

Step 6. Develop a thesis statement and an outline or some other tentative organizational plan based on the evidence you have accumulated.

As Sarah accumulated information, she grouped related notes under the outline headings she had decided upon earlier; later, after she had finished her research, she rearranged material within each section, discarded notes that seemed repetitious or irrelevant, and prepared a more detailed outline, shown in Figure 14.10.

FIGURE 14.9 Samples of Note Cards

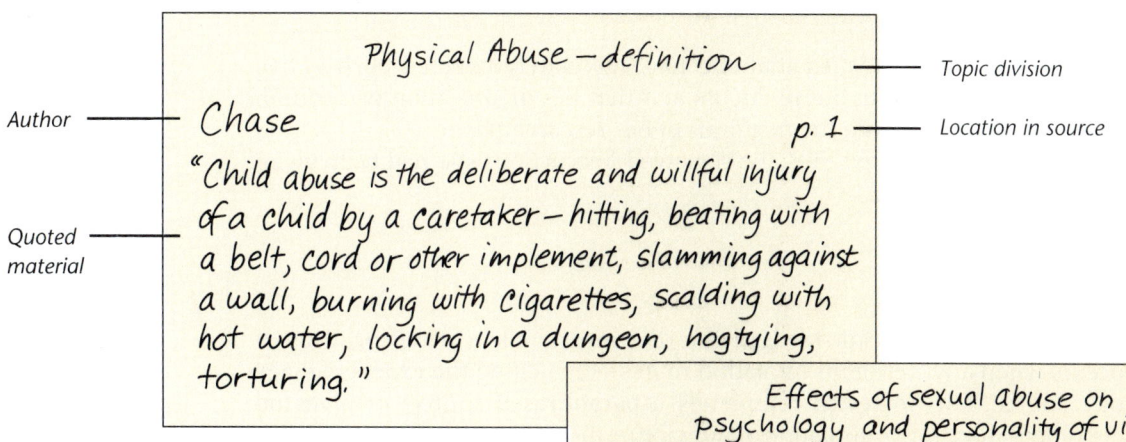

FIGURE 14.10 Sarah's Outline

Outline

Thesis Statement: For the survivors, child abuse is more than the momentary pain and humiliation of a blow or an insult or even a sexual attack; it is a lifelong trauma.

Introduction
I. Types of child abusers
   A. People who take pleasure in inflicting pain on others
   B. People who have difficulty coping with stress
   C. People with various types of personality problems
   D. People who were themselves abused children
II. Typical victims of child abuse
   A. Infants
   B. School-age children
III. Major forms of child abuse and their effects on the victim
   A. Physical abuse
      1. Definition
      2. Effects
   B. Emotional abuse
      1. Definition
      2. Effects
   C. Sexual abuse
      1. Definition
      2. Effects
   D. Neglect
      1. Definition
      2. Effects
Conclusion

> **Step 7.** Present results and conclusions in systematic, accurately documented written form.

When she was satisfied that she had adequately covered each of the main points she had set out to discuss and that her organization was sound, Sarah was ready to write the first draft of her research paper.

Before she began to write, she reviewed instructions she had been given on avoiding plagiarism.

Plagiarism

Plagiarism is the unacknowledged use of someone else's words or ideas. It occurs when a writer omits quotation marks when citing the exact language of a source, fails to revise completely a paraphrased source, or gives no documentation for a quotation or paraphrase. The best way to avoid this problem is to be attentive to the following details.

When you copy a quotation directly into your notes, check to be sure that you have put quotation marks around it. If you forget to include them when you copy, you might omit them in the paper as well.

When you paraphrase, keep in mind that it is not sufficient to change just a few words or rearrange sentence structure. You must completely rewrite the passage. One of the best ways to accomplish this is to read the material you want to paraphrase; then cover the page so that you cannot see it, and write down the information as you remember it. Then, compare your version with the original and make any necessary changes in the note. If you cannot successfully rewrite the passage, quote it instead.

The difference between legitimate and unacceptable paraphrases an be seen in the following examples:

- Source

    "What is unmistakably convincing and makes Miller's theatre writing hold is its authenticity in respect to the minutiae of American life. He is a first-rate reporter; he makes the details of his observation palpable."

    From Harold Clurman's introduction to The Portable Arthur Miller

- Unacceptable paraphrase

    What is truly convincing and makes Arthur Miller's theatrical writing effective is its authenticity. He is an excellent reporter and makes his observation palpable.

- Legitimate paraphrase

    The strength of Arthur Miller's dramatic art lies in its faithfulness to the details of the American scene and in its power to bring to life the reality of ordinary experience.

The differences between these two versions of Clurman's statement are enormous. The first writer has made some token changes, substituting a few synonyms (*truly* for *unmistakably, excellent* for *first-rate*), deleting part of the first sentence, and combining the two parts of the second sentence into a single clause. Otherwise, this is a word-for-word copy of the original, and if the note were copied into the paper in this form, the writer would be guilty of plagiarism. The second writer, on the other hand, has changed the vocabulary of the original passage and completely restructured the sentence so that the only similarity between the note and the source is the ideas.

Check to see that each note has the correct name and page number so that when you use this information in your paper, you will be able to credit it to the right source.

If you have any doubts about the way in which you have handled material from printed sources, confer with your teacher before you submit your paper.

Keeping those points in mind, Sarah proceeded to complete her preliminary draft, which consisted mainly of the quotations and paraphrases recorded in her notes. Next she started revising. First, she concentrated on the large elements of composition. She rearranged sentences to achieve emphasis, inserted transitional words and phrases to improve coherence within and between paragraphs, and added her own comments to explain or interpret her sources.

Turning next to smaller details, she varied her word choice to eliminate unnecessary repetition, revised several weak passive voice constructions, consulted a dictionary to confirm the spelling of several words that were not part of her usual vocabulary, and checked for possible errors in grammar and punctuation.

Step 8. Prepare a list of works cited from the preliminary bibliography.

When she finished, she compiled a list of works cited from her preliminary bibliography, made a few minor adjustments in her outline, and typed the final copy of the manuscript. Then she proofread the paper once more to ensure that it was free of typographical errors and submitted it for evaluation.

Sample Research Paper

Use and Documentation of Sources

Sarah Johnson's research paper begins on p. 432. The first paragraph exemplifies several characteristics of effective research writing:

- Quotations and paraphrases are skillfully intermixed with original statements.

- Passages quoted verbatim are varied in length and unobtrusively embedded in the writer's own sentences.

- Quotations are transcribed exactly as they appear in their sources and enclosed by quotation marks.

- Each source is clearly identified by a parenthetical reference.

Paragraphs 2 and 3 illustrate a wide range of techniques for using sources. In paragraph 2, for example, the writer uses information from five different sources. Some she quotes or summarizes in a few words; others she treats at greater length.

Note, too, the use of the ellipsis mark to indicate the omission of words in two of the quotations in paragraph 2. In citing the passage from Garbarino and Stocking, the writer omits three words—"a parent's own"—to make the first element of the series parallel with the ones following it. In the indented quotation, she eliminates a substantial amount of the original text to enhance the dramatic effect of the informant's self-revelations.

Content and Organization

Paragraphs 2 and 3 treat points I and II in the outline. Note in particular the specificity of the topic sentence that begins each paragraph and the fullness of the supporting evidence.

The Effects of Child Abuse

by

Sarah Jo Johnson

English 1200

April 14, 1993

Outline

Thesis Statement: For the survivors, child abuse is more than the momentary pain and humiliation of a blow or an insult or even a sexual attack; it is a lifelong trauma.

Introduction
- I. Types of child abusers
    - A. People who take pleasure in inflicting pain on others
    - B. People who have difficulty coping with stress
    - C. People with various types of personality problems
    - D. People who were themselves abused children
- II. Typical victims of child abuse
    - A. Infants
    - B. School-age children
- III. Major forms of child abuse and their effects on the victim
    - A. Physical abuse
        1. Definition
        2. Effects
    - B. Emotional abuse
        1. Definition
        2. Effects
    - C. Sexual abuse
        1. Definition
        2. Effects
    - D. Neglect
        1. Definition
        2. Effects

Conclusion

Sarah J. Johnson
Professor Parsons
English 1200
14 April 1993

The Effects of Child Abuse

One of the most serious but least reported crimes in the United States is child abuse, a term which "denotes a situation ranging from the deprivation of food, clothing, shelter and paternal love to incidences where children are physically abused and mistreated by an adult, resulting in obvious physical trauma to the child and not infrequently leading to death" (Fontana, <u>The Maltreated Child</u> 10). The number of child abuse incidents in a given year cannot be determined exactly because only about one case in eight is reported ("Abused Child" 41). But according to David Walters, "Child abuse is pandemic in the United States" (3). Most of these cases involve one or more of the following types of maltreatment: physical abuse, sexual abuse, emotional abuse, or neglect. All have serious immediate consequences--especially physical abuse, which frequently results in death--but for the survivors, child abuse is more than the momentary pain and humiliation of a blow or an insult of even a sexual attack; it is a lifelong trauma.

To understand the effects of child abuse, we must first understand what motivates or provokes it. Some abusers are sadists or psychopaths who inflict pain on others "for the joy of it" (Fontana, <u>Somewhere a Child Is Crying</u> 70). Most, however, are otherwise normal people who have difficulty coping with stress (Friedman and D'Agostino 31) or overcoming the effects of "emotional deprivation in . . . childhood, low levels of empathy, low self-esteem, social aloofness, and a variety of other personal characteristics" (Garbarino and Stocking 7). The one

Johnson 2

characteristic that most child abusers have in common is their family history. According to a 1976 article in <u>U.S. News and World Report</u>, "80% of all abusive parents were themselves abused as children" ("Authorities Face Up" 84), but even more revealing than the bare statistical data are the sentiments expressed by one child abuser in an interview with Brandt F. Steele:

> Our defense mechanisms make it difficult to read us, but look to see what went into our lives to make us this way. It's true that we are socially alienated, most of us with good reason. Ninety percent of us were abused as children. . . . Since most of us grew up viewing others as part of negative, harmful relationships, why should we form more relationships now? . . . Child abusers are going through hell. (3)

These parents in turn pass on their legacy of bitterness and hostility to their own children. Often this abuse is directed at infants, especially babies who require expensive medical services at birth; unwanted or unplanned children; and infants who for one reason or another fail to measure up to their parents' expectations. Older children also suffer abuse. Of the reported incidents of child abuse each year, approximately half involve schoolage children (Steele and Pollock 130). "At this age," Vladimir de Lissovoy observes, "the child must make a transition from the primary group of the family to the world outside" (12), a transition that brings changes in attitudes and behavior which may provoke acts of parental abuse.

One of the most common forms of child abuse, as well as the most frequently reported, is physical maltreatment such as "hitting, beating with a belt, cord or other implement, slamming against a wall, burning with cigarettes, scalding with hot water, locking in a dungeon, hogtying, torturing" (Chase 1). For children who survive these brutal attacks, the effects range from bruises and other minor injuries to permanent disabilities. Among the most serious complications are the ones cited by Elizabeth Elmer in <u>Children in Jeopardy</u>:

> Multiple fractures of the extremities, if not properly treated, may result in some permanent disability, such as a limp or limitation of motion, while subdural hematomas, suffered by a number of the children, may prevent the brain from growing normally and thereby cause permanent mental retardation. (44)

In the long run, physical abuse may also lead to attitudinal or behavioral problems, as in the case of a twelve year old, seventh grade classmate of my younger sister Valerie Johnson. In a recent personal interview, Valerie informed me that in 1985 this young adolescent was beaten with a broom handle, which left his arms red, scraped, and bruised. The year before, his mother had burned him with an iron. Thus far, he has suffered no debilitating injuries, but each instance of abuse provokes him to misbehave at school by throwing temper tantrums or refusing to obey his teacher--actions that bring additional parental punishment and start the cycle all over again.

When children have caring parents and a warm home environment, they will most likely become parents their children will love also. Exactly the opposite is true of children living in homes where love is seldom or never shared (Rogers 57). Robert Bates aptly characterizes these children as "emotionally abused" individuals who "feel unwanted, angry, and bad" (53).

Emotional abuse includes not providing attention, normal living opportunities, and necessary supervision (Rogers 48). People who abuse children in this way constantly belittle them by calling them names, saying

"I hate you," or telling them they were never wanted. Abuse such as this often causes children to see themselves as worthless. Furthermore, most children suffering from emotional abuse see their situation as hopeless because they know they cannot fight back and win (Rogers 48). Emotionally abused children can be helped, but in most cases they must be placed in foster homes while the parents undergo counseling (Bates 53).

Another serious form of child abuse is sexual exploitation or assault. Because the offender is usually a close relative of the child, many families are reluctant to report such cases ("The Hard Case" 32), but according to one source, sexual abuse may occur even more frequently than physical abuse (James 39). In fact, the two are difficult to distinguish in cases involving sexual assault in which "the offender may directly confront the child with sexual demands in the context of verbal threats . . . intimidation with a weapon, . . . or direct physical assault" (Burgess and Groth 81). More commonplace are non-violent incidents of abuse, which usually involve "exhibition of sexual organs, genital and nongenital petting or fondling, mouth-genital contacts, and attempted penetration without force" (Bates 51).

The long-range effects of sexual molestation are difficult to assess because little data is currently available (Bates 51), but many authorities agree that such abuse may adversely affect children's sense of self-confidence and self-respect. It may also interfere with what Ann Burgess and Nicholas Groth refer to as the "subsequent psychological development" of the victims, their "personality formation, attitudes and values, identity issues, and the like" (79).

More difficult to document are the effects of neglect, the fourth main type of child abuse. Unlike physical, emotional, or sexual abuse, child neglect is, in the words

Johnson 5

of Dale Rogers, a "passive negative treatment characterized by a parent or custodian's lack of care and interest, and includes not feeding, not clothing, not looking after, not nurturing" (41). Therefore, only the most extreme cases are likely to be publicized. An especially graphic example of neglect is the case in which a mother left her young child unattended in a car with all the windows closed. She had intended to be gone for only a short time, but she was delayed, and by the time she returned, the child had died from the extreme heat (Walters 12). Usually, however, neglect has a more subtle influence, affecting not just the child's physical well-being, but also his or her ability to function normally in later life.

In this sense, neglected children are much like those who have been subjected to other types of abuse. All of them must seek comfort, love, and acceptance in the outside world, but they are poorly equipped to make this transition, as Janice Zemdegs convincingly demonstrates in an essay entitled "Outrage: What It Feels Like to Be an Abused Child." Especially informative are the words of the young woman whose experiences are the focus of Zemdegs's study.

> I remember when I finally left home to attend nursing school... my main purpose in life was to be released from the war mentally and physically intact. ... What I never realized was I didn't know how to cope in a normal environment. (104)

Child abuse, then, is a complex and far-reaching problem. Abused children obviously have a disadvantage in life from the beginning, for the physical and psychological pain they experience in their childhood remains in their memories. It blights their adult lives and dooms many of them to continue the destructive cycle in which the abused child of one generation becomes the abusive parent of the next.

Johnson 6

Works Cited

"Abused Child." *Today's Education* Jan. 1974: 40–42.

"Authorities Face Up to the Child-Abuse Problem." *U.S. News* 3 May 1976: 83–84.

Bates, Robert. "Child Abuse and Neglect: A Medical Priority." Volpe, Breton, and Mitton 45–57.

Burgess, Ann W., and Nicholas Groth. "Sexual Victimization of Children." Volpe, Breton, and Mitton 79–89.

Chase, Naomi. *A Child Is Being Beaten*. New York: Holt, 1975.

de Lissovoy, Vladimir. "The Behavioral and Ecological Syndrome of the High-Risk Child." Volpe, Breton, and Mitton 11–17.

Elmer, Elizabeth. *Children in Jeopardy: A Study of Abused Minors and Their Families*. Pittsburgh: U of Pittsburgh P, 1967.

Fontana, Vincent. *The Maltreated Child: The Maltreatment Syndrome in Children*. 2nd ed. Springfield: Thomas, 1971.

———. *Somewhere a Child Is Crying: Maltreatment Causes and Prevention*. New York: Macmillan, 1973.

Friedman, Robert M., and Paul D'Agostino. "The Effects of Schools upon Families: Toward a More Supportive Relationship." Volpe, Breton, and Mitton 27–41.

Garbarino, James, and S. Holly Stocking. "The Social Context of Child Maltreatment." *Protecting Children from Abuse and Neglect: Developing and Maintaining Effective Support Systems for Families*. Ed James Garbarino, et al. San Francisco: Jossey, 1980.

"The Hard Case." *Newsweek* 16 July 1973: 32.

James, Howard. *The Little Victims: How America Treats Its Children*. New York: McKay, 1975.

Johnson, Valerie. Personal interview. 5 Mar. 1990.

Rogers, Dale E. *Hear the Children Crying*. Old Tappan: Revell, 1978.

Steele, Brandt F. "Working with Abusive Parents: A Psychiatrist's View." <u>Children Today</u> May–June 1975: 3.

Steele, Brandt F., and Carl B. Pollock. "A Psychiatric Study of Parents Who Abuse Infants and Small Children." <u>The Battered Child</u>. Ed. Ray E. Helfer and C. Henry Kempe. 2nd ed. Chicago: U of Chicago P, 1974.

Volpe, Richard, Margo Breton, and Judith Mitton, ed. <u>The Maltreatment of the School-Aged Child</u>. Lexington: Heath, 1980.

Walters, David R. <u>Physical and Sexual Abuse of Children: Causes and Treatment</u>. Bloomington: Indiana UP, 1975.

Zemdegs, Janice. "Outraged: What It Feels Like to Be an Abused Child." Volpe, Breton, and Mitton 91–107.

EXERCISE 1

Short Documented Paper Using Library Sources

1. Select one of these subject areas for further consideration.

Drugs	Entertainment
A politician	An athlete
A governmental program	Crime
Alcohol	Abortion
Tobacco	Pollution

2. Narrow it to a workable topic for a hypothetical paper of a length designated by your instructor. If possible present this topic as a thesis.

3. Find and record in correct form two sources listed in *Reader's Guide to Periodical Literature.* (Your instructor may require more.)

4. Find and record in correct form two book sources. Use the subject catalog or the electronic system, if available. (Your instructor may require more.)

Optional

5. After skimming some of your sources, list the natural divisions of your topic.

6. Put your sources on note cards. Make sure to use the correct form of notation.

7. Complete a topic outline on a separate piece of paper.

8. Complete a rough draft.

9. Edit and revise your rough draft.

10. Submit your documented paper.

    This complete documented paper may be only five or six paragraphs long, or it may extend to many pages. The basic procedure is the same regardless of length. A short documented paper might utilize only periodical sources.

 **Writer's Checklist**

Apply these ideas to your writing during both the planning and writing stages. Use **Delve** from **DCODE** to explore your subject area, **Concentrate** to formulate your thesis, and **Organize** to divide your material and establish its sequence.

1. Choose a subject that interests you, and narrow it until it becomes a topic that you can investigate thoroughly and write about convincingly.

2. Find out what style of documentation is appropriate for this piece of research writing, and familiarize yourself with the conventions for preparing a bibliography or list of works cited and for documenting sources.

3. Use the resources in your college library to identify books, articles, and other materials pertaining to your topic.

4. Compile a preliminary bibliography of the sources referred to above, following the documentation style appropriate to your discipline.

5. Locate, read, and take notes on the sources listed in the preliminary bibliography.

6. Develop a thesis statement and an outline or some other tentative organizational plan based on the evidence you have accumulated.

7. Present results and conclusions in systematic, accurately documented written form.

8. Revise carefully. To identify potential problems as you develop your ideas and synthesize material from your sources, ask yourself questions such as these:

    Have I expressed my ideas clearly and organized them coherently?
    Have I included enough information from my sources to support the thesis?
    Are all paragraphs relevant to the thesis and consistent with the intended arrangement?
    Have I accurately quoted or paraphrased all ideas and information I have drawn from my sources?
    Have I acknowledged each source in the text through parenthetical documentation as recommended earlier in this chapter?
    Have I made my own judgments an integral part of the essay?
    Do my conclusions follow logically from the evidence presented?

9. Prepare a list of works cited from the preliminary bibliography.

WORKSHEET
Writing in DCODE

NAME:_____

SECTION:_____ CHAPTER:_____ DATE:_____

Delve   Generate your topic, or ideas for your topic, by delving into your subject area through:

- *Freewriting*—writing sentence after sentence, nonstop and spontaneously.
- *Brainstorming*—jotting down answers to Who? What? Where? When? Why? and How? and then listing words and phrases in relation to those answers.
- *Clustering*—connecting bubbled ideas with lines to show strings of relationships, producing each new bubble item in response to the question, What comes to mind?
- *Combining* any of these approaches, as directed by your instructor.

WORKSHEET: Writing in DCODE

Concentrate   Concentrate your work by stating your topic in one sentence that is not too broad, narrow, or vague to be developed. Base this sentence (which may become the topic sentence for your paragraph or the thesis for your essay) on an idea emerging from the **Delve** stage. You may have to try several statements here before you formulate one that is best for your writing task. Be sure that your final statement covers your assignment or intent and specifies both your subject (what you are writing about) and treatment (what aspect you will focus on). Label the *subject* and *treatment* parts.

Organize   Complete an outline or a cluster, as directed by your instructor. The cluster should be a section from, or a refined version of, the **Delve** clustering. Regardless of the strategy you use, the organizational pattern should indicate a division of your topic into parts that will, in turn, be further subdivided for support as necessary to address a particular audience on your concentrated topic.

Draft   On separate paper, write and then revise your assignment as many times as necessary for **c**oherence, **l**anguage (usage, tone, and diction), **u**nity, **e**mphasis, **s**upport, and **s**entence structure (**cluess**).

Edit   Correct problems in fundamentals such as **c**apitalization, **o**missions, **p**unctuation, and **s**pelling (**cops**). Before writing the final draft, read your paper aloud to discover oversights and awkwardness of expression.

A Handbook: Revising and Editing

15

> " It's not wise to violate rules until you know how to observe them.
> — T. S. Eliot

What is the difference between revising and editing ? What, if anything, is wrong with slang ? What is the difference between standard and nonstandard language ? What does the acronym **cluess** stand for ? What does the acronym **cops** stand for ?

CHAPTER 15

This chapter covers all matters pertaining to the **Draft** and **Edit** stages of **DCODE**, with emphasis on **cluess** (**c**oherence, **l**anguage, **u**nity, **e**mphasis, **s**upport, and **s**entence structure) and **cops** (**c**apitalization, **o**missions, **p**unctuation, and **s**pelling). The part of the chapter on fundamentals emphasizes sentence structure. Half of the exercises have answers in the back of the book, so after reading the directions and examples, you can work independently on your problems. The Correction Symbols and Abbreviations chart on the inside back cover is keyed mainly to items in this chapter.

Revising

Draft is the part of the writing process in which your work begins to assume its final form. You should write as many drafts as necessary, revising as you go. How extensively and in what order you apply the following principles will depend on your topic and audience. Cross-references indicate where many of these matters are also discussed in other chapters and in another section of this chapter.

One approach to revision is to use the **cluess** acronym as a checklist to make sure that you are not overlooking some techniques for improving your work. Because writing is a recursive process, you will work and rework your material numerous times, thus applying and reapplying these principles. A set of questions at the end of this section will also help you to focus your attention on the main points of drafting and revising.

Coherence

Coherence is a technique for connecting ideas smoothly and logically. You must weave your ideas together so skillfully that the reader can easily see the relationship of one idea to another and to the central thought (the topic sentence for the paragraph and the thesis for the essay). You can effectively achieve **c**oherence by using

- an overall plan.
- transitional words and expressions.
- repetition of key words and ideas.
- pronoun reference.
- a consistent point of view.

Overall Plan

Each of the preceding chapters of instruction in writing the forms of discourse discusses strategies for an overall plan, or organization. (See the "Order" or "Organization" sections in Chapters 3–13.) Three basic patterns prevail: *time* (chronological), *space* (spacial), and *emphasis* (moving toward the idea you want to stress). Sometimes you will combine patterns. The coherence of each can be strengthened by using transitional words such as:

- For *time*: first, then, soon, later, following, after
- For *space*: up, down, right, left, beyond, behind, above, below, before
- For *emphasis*: first, second, third, most, more

Transitional Words and Expressions

By using *transitional words and expressions*, you gain coherence. Some of the most frequently used words and expressions for coherence are:

- *To indicate addition:* again, also, and, and then, besides, equally important, finally, first, further, furthermore, in addition, indeed, in fact, in the second place, likewise, moreover, next, too, secondly, other

- *To indicate comparison (likenesses):* at the same time, in the same way, in like manner, likewise, similarly

- *To indicate concession:* although this may be true, at the same time, after all, certainly, doubtless, granted that, I admit, I concede, naturally, no doubt, surely

- *To indicate consequences or result:* all in all, accordingly, after all, and so, as a consequence, as a result, at last, consequently, finally, hence, in conclusion, so, therefore, then, thus

- *To indicate condition:* as if, if, as though, even if

- *To indicate contrast:* and yet, although true, at the same time, but, conversely, for all that, however, in contrast, nevertheless, notwithstanding, on the one hand, on the other hand, rather, still, whereas, yet

- *To indicate examples:* especially, for example, for instance, for one thing, frequently, in general, in particular, in this way, namely, occasionally, specifically, that is, to illustrate, thus, usually

- *To indicate reason:* because, since, for

- *To indicate repetition:* and so again, as has been said, in fact, indeed, in other words, to recapitulate, to repeat, I repeat

- *To indicate summary:* in brief, in short, to sum up, to summarize, in conclusion, to conclude

- *Relative pronouns, demonstrative adjectives, and other pronouns:* this, that, these, those, who, whom, whose, which, what, that, it, they, them, few, many, most, several, he, she, and so forth.

Repetition of Key Words and Ideas

Repeat key words and phrases to keep the dominant subject in the reader's mind and maintain the continuity necessary for a smooth flow of logical thought.

Pronoun Reference

Use pronouns as substitutes for their noun antecedents to carry your reader back to the thought in a previous sentence. Pronouns provide a natural connecting link.

Consistent Point of View

Gain coherence by maintaining a consistent point of view. Unnecessary, sudden, and illogical shifts in point of view—that is, in subject, person, number, tense, voice, and mood—affect sentence and paragraph relationships, thus obscuring meaning.

In the paragraph that follows, notice that frequent shifts in the subject and person cause confusion. Observe also the shifts in tense and voice.

> Good study habits are necessary for success in college. The art of studying must be learned in order to excel in anything. Two hours for each hour of class time is required but is not enough if you are careless and haphazard in your study habits. He is just putting in time that is of little or no use. A student must have much self-discipline and motivation to learn to the best of their ability.

Study how the paragraph below illustrates a consistent point of view. Observe the ways in which the writer achieves a consistent point of view: a dominant subject, the verbs in the same tense and voice, and correct pronoun reference.

> If you as a student are going to be successful in college, you must acquire good study habits. You should put in approximately two hours work outside of class for every hour in class. You must find a place to study that is free from noise and visitors who will disturb you once you get going. You must learn the skills and techniques of efficient reading so that you can use your study time effectively. You must take care of your health by eating properly, getting enough exercise, and sleeping sufficiently. Above all, you must have the self-discipline and motivation to keep you at the job for the next four years of your life.

The next paragraph is written in a consistent point of view and also demonstrates the other four techniques for achieving coherence.

What is masculinity? One dictionary defines it as: manly; virile; robust; *therefore*, a composite of *these* definitive terms would be: One *who* is resolute, dignified, honorable, sexually potent, sturdy, healthy, lusty, and most important, male. It is immediately obvious that all of *these* qualities are not visible to the naked eye: *moreover*, social mores would play an important part in interpretation. *For example*, Tchambuli tribesmen of New Guinea, reformed head-hunters, are *artists who* enjoy painting, music, and drama. *They* spend much of *their* time ornamenting *themselves*, conducting neighborhood plays, and gossiping. Certainly not the type of conduct *we* consider *masculine*. During the early expansion of this country, the Eastern man, with *his* powdered wig, ruffled shirt, ornamented breeches, and jeweled snuffbox regarded the frontiersman as not far above an animal; for *his* part, the frontiersman looked upon *his* Eastern counterpart as a soft, unreliable Fop; *nevertheless*, this country could not have endured without *both*. Today such distinctions are often blurred, and younger people are more androgynous. Previously conditioned by two wars, the older generation has firm convictions as to what constitutes *masculinity*. Permed hair, ring bedecked fingers, perfume, gold chains, and earrings do not meet their established specifications. *However*, all of these ornamentations and embellishments are widely accepted by the young.	[italics mine] transitional words pronoun reference transitional words pronoun reference repetition of key words transitional words repetition of key word transitional word

> *Role* playing is necessary to any *society*. But man's role does not possess a fixed image. The role has, is, and will be modified by *society*.

repetition of "role"

repetition of "society"

EXERCISE 1

Underline the methods used for achieving coherence, and label them in the margins.

The Chain of Reason vs. the Chain of Thumbs
STEPHEN JAY GOULD

The *Weekly World News,* most lurid entry in the dubious genre of shopping mall tabloids, shattered all previous records for implausibility with a recent headline: "Siamese Twins Make Themselves Pregnant." The story recounted the sad tale of a conjoined brother-sister pair from a remote Indian village (such folks never hail from Peoria, where their nonexistence might be confirmed). They knew that their act was immoral, but after years of hoping in vain for ordinary partners, and in the depths of loneliness and frustration, they finally succumbed to an ever-present temptation. The story is heart-rending, but faces one major obstacle to belief: all Siamese twins are monozygotic, formed from a single fertilized egg that failed to split completely in the act of twinning. Thus, Siamese twins are either both male or both female.

2 I will, however, praise the good people at *Weekly World News* for one slight scruple. They did realize that they had created a problem with this ludicrous tale, and they did not shrink from the difficulty. The story acknowledged that, indeed, Siamese twins generally share the same sex, but held that this Indian pair had been formed, uniquely and differently, from two eggs that had fused! Usually, however, *Weekly World News* doesn't even bother with minimal cover-ups. Last fall, . . . they ran a screaming headline about a monster from Mars, recently sighted in a telescope and now on its way to earth. The accompanying photo of the monster showed a perfectly ordinary chambered nautilus (an odd-looking and unfamiliar creature to be sure). I mean, they didn't even bother to retouch the photo or to hide in any way their absurd transmogrification of a marine mollusk into an extraterrestrial marauder!

Language

Language takes on a special meaning here, referring to usage, tone, and diction.

Usage

Many people confuse grammar and usage. *Grammar* is the way we put words together. If English is your first language, then you knew English grammar fairly well by the time you were three or four years old. By now you know English grammar thoroughly. Of course, you may not know the terms and understand the theory, but you know the grammar and use it for communication.

Usage is of more concern here, because it pertains to kinds of language presentation. Usage can be standard or nonstandard. *Standard usage* pertains to the language of the educated person. If you write a letter to the editor of a good newspaper, and that editor publishes it without changing it substantially in word choice or structure, you are probably using standard usage. If you cannot do that, you are probably writing *nonstandard English*. Neither level should be saddled with a value judgment. Both are varieties of the English language. In fact, both contain good grammar, but if you write nonstandard English in your college assignments, you will have trouble. If you speak nonstandard English in certain vocations, you will not prosper. Saying *ain't* and *he don't* are examples of nonstandard usage. Some people who use those expressions are articulate speakers who can think well, explain carefully, and tell a good story. Nevertheless, the ideas of those people may be discredited in certain situations because of the nonstandard English.

We can take our consideration of language further. Language can be divided into varieties that depend on function. The function pertains to the social situation of the communication. Some situations call for formal presentation and others for informal presentation. The point is that we talk differently and write differently in different situations. Over a period of a day, I might (going from formal to informal) give a formal speech, talk to a group of students, talk to my long-time colleagues, talk to a neighbor, and talk to my family. In each situation, I change my language. If I were to speak the same way in each situation, I would not be an effective communicator. The same is true for writing. We all, whether we use mostly standard or nonstandard English, have different ways of speaking and writing. If I were to use the same language in the formal speech that I use in talking to my family, I would draw unfavorable attention.

We all, or almost all, operate on the principle of appropriateness. If I used *ain't* as part of my explanations in this textbook, you would be surprised and probably disappointed, and you would think about my word choice rather than what I have to say. Why would you be surprised? Because it is not appropriate for this situation. If you write an essay that contains slang as part of your expression, you will be understood, but if it is not appropriate, you will draw unfavorable attention to your words. That reaction does not mean that slang does not have its place. It does; it can be imaginative and colorful. Often, though, it is only a weak substitute for a precise vocabulary.

One variety of English is called community dialect, or black English. It differs from conventional English mainly in verb patterns and is discussed in detail in the Verbs section of this chapter.

Usage is an important part of writing and revising. Judge what is appropriate for your audience and your purpose. What kind of language is anticipated? What kind of language is best for accomplishing your purpose?

Much of the material in this chapter is grammatical explanation of standard, mostly formal English. Using standard verb tenses and pronoun case will help you to write effectively. The material is easily accessible, with explanations and exercises supported by answers in the Answer Key. As you apply those principles in drafting and revision, you will master them.

Tone

Have you ever heard someone say, "Don't talk to me in that tone of voice"? or "I accepted what she was saying, but I didn't like the tone she used when she told me"? *Tone* in those contexts means that the sound of the speaker's voice and maybe the language choices have conveyed disrespect to the listener. The tone could have represented any number of feelings about the subject material and the audience. Tone can have as many parts as you can have feelings: it can, for example, be sarcastic, humorous, serious, cautionary, objective, groveling, angry, bitter, sentimental, or loving.

Let's say you are getting a haircut, and, looking in those omnipresent mirrors bordered with pictures of people with different styles of haircuts, you see that the barber is cutting off too much hair. You could use different tones in giving him or her some timely how-to-do-it instructions.

> OBJECTIVE: "If you don't mind, what I meant to say was that I would like a haircut proportioned just like that one there on the picture of Tom Cruise from *The Rain Man*."
>
> HUMOROUS: "I hesitate to make suggestions to someone who is standing at my back and holding a sharp instrument near my throat, but I'm letting my hair grow out a bit, and I don't want you to take off a lot in the back and on the sides."
>
> ANGRY AND SARCASTIC: "Look, man, when I sat down, I said I wanted my hair cut in the design of Tom Cruise in *The Rain Man*. The way you're hacking at it, you must've thought I said, *Top Gun*."
>
> SERVILE: "I really like the way you cut my hair, and I can see that you are proportioning it with great care, but I would like my hair to be a bit longer than the style that I think you're working on. Do you remember how I used to get my hair cut about a year ago, a little longer on the sides and more bushy on top? You came up with a great style that everyone liked. Could you give me one similar to that?"
>
> OVERBEARING: "Damn it, buddy. Will you watch what you're doing! I asked for a hair cut, not a shave. If God had wanted me to have bare skin above my shoulders, he would've put the hair on my feet."

In speech, feelings and attitudes are represented by inflection, loudness, word choice, and language patterns. In writing, tone is conveyed mainly by word choice and order; it is closely related to style—the variations of the way you write, depending on your purpose. Your purpose is simply to present a particular idea in a particular context. The context implies the audience; it is important to employ the tone appropriate to your audience.

Usually your tone will be consistent throughout your presentation, although in the fairly typical college assignment of the informal essay, you may choose to begin in a light-hearted, amusing tone before switching to the more serious, objective mode.

Diction

Diction is word choice. Both usage and tone, of course, use diction as their main vehicle. Pervasive in writing and speaking, diction relates directly as a major factor to several forms of discourse, and is covered specifically in several places in this book. Chapter 4, "Description," discusses denotation and connotation, general and specific, and abstract and concrete, and Chapter 12, "Definition," covers dictionary use; see also the "Modifiers" section in this chapter. The important point to remember is that diction is more than just looking in the dictionary to find a word with a certain dictionary definition (denotation), although it is that, too. It is also finding the best word for a particular purpose in addressing a particular audience.

Unity

A main idea, stated or implied, is the unifying point around which the support revolves. For a paragraph, the elements are the topic sentence and the supporting sentences. For the essay, the elements are the thesis and the supporting developmental paragraphs. If you correlate all, you will have **u**nity. Unity can be strengthened and made all the more apparent by restating the topic sentence or thesis at the end of the unit and by repeating key words and phrases.

Like other parts of this "Draft/Revision" section, unity is also covered elsewhere in the book, especially in Chapter 1, "Topic Sentence," and Chapter 2, "Thesis."

Emphasis

Emphasis can be achieved in several ways but mainly through placement of idea and by repetition.

Placement

The most emphatic part of any passage, from sentence to book, is the last part, because we usually remember most easily what we read last. The second most emphatic part is the first because our mind is uncluttered when we read it. For these reasons, among others, the topic sentence or thesis is usually at the beginning of a piece and is often restated at the end, in an echoing statement in the paragraph, or in a conclusion in the essay.

Repetition

Repetition is one of the simplest devices to apply. It can involve words, phrases, slightly altered sentences, and synonyms. Examine the following passage for skillful use of placement and repetition. The italicized words are repetitions.

To the uninitiated, the term "*adobe* house" may evoke an image of a small, ill lit mud shack with dirt floors and bugs. That image may have been true in the past and may still be true in many under-developed countries. But modern, western *adobe* structures can be well designed, airy, well lit, and integrated with solar collector features.	placement
Although *adobe* is associated with the Southwest, there are few places in the world where some form of *adobe* has not been used. One of the most easily obtained materials, sun-dried earth blocks have been used for thousands of years. Residential *adobe* ruins in Egypt predate the Great Pyramid of Giza. The ruins of Tyre and Nineveh are structurally related to the still-occupied pueblos at Taos and Acoma in New Mexico. One of the seven wonders of the ancient world, the Hanging Gardens of Babylon, was probably built of *adobe* bricks. The arid lands of the world, where sand and clay are found, and where the sunshine is bountiful, have long histories of *earth construction*. Because of this construction in highly populated areas such as India, Africa, and the Middle East, about eighty percent of all residential structures in the world today are of *adobe*.	topic idea; placement repeated topic idea; placement within the sentence and paragraph James Maurer, "Adobe: Mud for Castles and Hovels"

Support

How much support does a piece of writing need? A good developmental paragraph fulfills its function by fully developing the topic sentence. An essay is complete when it fulfills its function of developing a thesis. Obviously, you will have to judge what is complete. With some subjects, you will need little supporting and explanatory material. With others, you will need much more. Incompleteness, not overdevelopment, is more common among beginning writers.

Consider the following paragraph for completeness of support. Is it complete? Does the writer make the main idea clear and provide adequate support for it?

> A cat's tail is a good barometer of its intentions. By various movements of its tail a cat will signal many of its wants. Other movements indicate its attitudes. An excited or aggressively aroused cat will whip its entire tail back and forth.

At first glance, it would appear that this paragraph is complete. The writer begins with a concise topic sentence telling us that a cat's tail is a good barometer of its intentions. He adds additional information of a general nature in the following two sentences. Then, he presents a supporting example concerning the aggressively aroused cat. But the paragraph is not explicit; the writer has insufficient supporting material for the opening generalizations. He leaves us with too much information to fill in. What are some other ways that cats communicate their intentions with their tails? How do they communicate specific wishes or desires? Is such communication effective? If he is to answer these questions that come into the reader's mind, he must present more supporting material for his beginning generalizations. The original paragraph that follows begins with a concise topic sentence that is supported with particulars.

> A cat's tail is a good barometer of its intentions. An excited or aggressively aroused cat will whip its entire tail back and forth. When I talk to Sam, he holds up his end of the conversation by occasionally flicking the tip of his tail. Mother cats move their tails back and forth to invite their kittens to play. A kitten raises its tail perpendicularly to beg for attention; older cats may do so to beg for food. When your cat holds its tail aloft while crisscrossing in front of you, it is trying to say, "Follow me"—usually to the kitchen, or more precisely, to the refrigerator. Unfortunately, many cats have lost their tails in refrigerator doors as a consequence.

Michael W. Fox, "What Is Your Pet Trying To Tell You"

Let us now strengthen our understanding of paragraph structure by analyzing the structure of our model paragraph, putting to use the information we have assimilated to this point in the discussion. The writer of the model paragraph begins with the highest generalization (the main idea in the topic sentence): "A cat's tail is a good barometer of its intentions." He follows immediately with six major supporting statements and ends with a final sentence to add humor to the writing. If we place this material in outline form, we can easily see the recurrent pattern in the flow of thought from general to particular.

A cat's tail is a good barometer of its intentions.	topic sentence (highest generalization)
A. An excited or aggressively aroused cat will whip its entire tail back and forth.	major support
B. When I talk to Sam, he holds up his end of the conversation by occasionally flicking the tip of his tail.	major support
C. Mother cats move their tails back and forth to invite their kittens to play.	major support
D. A kitten raises its tail perpendicularly to beg for attention;	major support
E. Older cats may do so to beg for food.	major support
F. When your cat holds its tail aloft while criss-crossing in front of you, it is trying to say, "Follow me"—usually to the kitchen, or more precisely, to the refrigerator.	major support
Unfortunately, many cats have lost their tails in refrigerator doors as a consequence.	added for humor

Sentence Structure

Sentence structure is an important concern throughout this chapter; therefore, more cross-references are in order. See later sections of this chapter for treatments of sentence correctness (fragments, comma splices, and run-togethers), sentence types (simple, compound, complex, and compound-complex), sentence combining, and parallel structure.

Here are some additional ways to use emphasis and variety in the sentence. The first aspect also pertains to the "Emphasis" section of this unit.

Emphasis is a rhetorical and syntactical means of giving importance to words and ideas. Emphasis may be achieved in a variety of ways:

- **Position**. In general, the beginning and the end of the sentence are its most important parts. The center is for detail rather than for emphasis. Although grammatically correct, the first sentence in each of the following pairs is unclearly focused because important parts contain unimportant material.

UNCLEAR:	The first prize in the contest was an overwhelmingly large one, I remember.
IMPROVED:	The first prize in the contest, I remember, was an overwhelmingly large one.
UNCLEAR:	In this room, old magazines, dress forms, and many trunks were piled.
IMPROVED:	In this room were piled books, old magazines, dress forms, and many trunks.
UNCLEAR:	However, he could not redeem himself, in my opinion.
IMPROVED:	In my opinion, however, he could not redeem himself.

- **Periodic structure.**

  When he [Johnson] felt like saying that oats is food for men in Scotland and [for] horses in England, he said so.

  Bertrand Russell, "The Unhappy American Way"

- **Use of active and passive voices.** The *active voice* is more forceful than the passive voice. By placing the emphasis on the doer of the action, the writer creates a sense of movement and life; he or she gives action to the happening.

PASSIVE VOICE: The circus tent was destroyed by fire.
IMPROVED: Fire destroyed the circus tent.

The *passive voice* is used if the writer wishes to emphasize the receiver of the action or if the doer of the action is not definitely known. Read the following sentence; notice how emphasis is given to Roman homes by use of the passive voice.

> Roman homes were decorated by Greek artists.
>
> Gilbert Highet, *The Migration of Ideas*

- **Climactic order.** Elements arranged in order of increasing importance are in climactic order of sentence structure.

  > The Romans first appear in history as a single people, brave, conservative, uneducated, peripheral, and rather unpromising.
  >
  > Gilbert Highet, *The Migration of Ideas*

By climactic order of arrangement of the elements in the series describing the Romans, the writer stresses *rather unpromising*.

POOR EMPHASIS: The flood killed hundreds of people, swept away all communication lines, and destroyed innumerable homes.
IMPROVED: The flood swept away all communication lines, destroyed innumerable homes, and killed hundreds of people.

- **Inversion.**

  > Happy is the man who sees good in all people.
  > What a piece of work is man!
  >
  > William Shakespeare

  > Hardly more than two generations ago Americans first woke up to the fact that their land was not inexhaustible.
  >
  > Joseph Wood Krutch, *The Voice of the Desert*

- **Hyperbole.** Hyperbole is deliberate exaggeration or overstatement.

  > Nothing can keep him out of that game.
  > He sat alone with a hundred frustrations of his own creation.

- **Punctuation.** Punctuation is a means of pointing out constructions designed for emphasis. Study the uses of the dash and comma in the following sentences.

  > Certainly one of the striking—some would say one of the inevitable—characteristics of our society is its penchant for making widely and easily accessible either substitutes for, or inferior versions of, a vast number of good things, like the vile substitute for bread available at any grocer's.
  >
  > Joseph Wood Krutch, "Is Our Common Man Too Common?"

  > They believed in guns, not butter.
  > It is time for a change, isn't it?

Note: For emphasis, commas may separate items in a series joined by conjunctions:

> At the present time I have no energy, or desire, or money to run for public office.

Variety is a characteristic of good writing. A series of simple sentences or a series of complicated sentences may become monotonous, dull reading. In addition, a series of sentences beginning with a noun subject, or with a noun cluster as a subject introduced by a determiner like *the*, may produce the same result.

To gain variety, vary sentence length, structure, and even word order. Vary the basic patterns with modifying phrases and clauses. Begin sentences with adverbs, conjunctions, phrases, and clauses.

- Vary the beginnings of your sentences with introductory phrases or clauses.

This is a compound sentence introduced by a participial phrase—the past participle, *written:*

> Written in short lengths for newspaper serialization, the autobiography is not a literary masterpiece, but it is the more impressive because of the commonplaceness of much of its material.
>
> George Orwell, "Reflections on Gandhi"

This sentence is introduced by a prepositional phrase modifying the subject, *science fiction:*

> In a crude and fumbling fashion, science fiction is trying to fill this gap.
>
> Arthur Koestler, "The Boredom of Fantasy"

A clause is used as an introductory modifier in this sentence:

> Where the tradition would have used the wide screen to encompass mighty spectacles, *The Robe* is roundabout and casual.
>
> Eric Larrabee, "The Big Picture"

> When we reach out for the stars, our limitations become grotesquely apparent. [a clause]
>
> Arthur Koestler, "The Boredom of Fantasy"

> From a sociological point of view, the most significant of the somatotonic traits is lust for power. [a phrase]
>
> Aldous Huxley, "Who Are You?"

> In the West, for more than two thousand years, men were content with a classification system devised by the Greek physician, Hippocrates. [a phrase]
>
> Aldous Huxley, "Who Are You?"

- Vary the beginnings of your sentences with introductory adverbs and conjunctions.

> However, Gandhi's pacifism can be separated to some extent from his other teachings.
>
> George Orwell, "Reflections on Gandhi"

> Perhaps, when they read about the latest hydrogen bomb tests, people are more aware than they admit even to themselves of the possibility that human civilization may be approaching its end. [adverb *perhaps* and adverbial clause]
>
> Arthur Koestler, "The Boredom of Fantasy"

> But while in the past such exercises [writings in science fiction] were isolated literary extravaganzas, they are now mass-produced for a mass audience. [conjunction]
>
> Arthur Koestler, "The Boredom of Fantasy"

> But these great decisions only made thrift and circumspection more imperative. [conjunction]
>
> Winston Churchill, *Marlborough, His Life and Times*

- Vary the internal structure of your sentences with phrases, clauses, and sentence interrupters.

  > We have tried, however painful it may be, to set this out with naked candour. [sentence interrupter]
  >
  > Winston Churchill, *Marlborough*

  > There are, on the other hand, a few mitigating features which may also be mentioned. [sentence interrupter]
  >
  > Winston Churchill, *Marlborough*

  > The splendid silver wine-flasks, or pilgrim bottles—as big as small barrels—which have been so much admired travelled with him in his campaigns; but they and other luxurious trappings were used only on State occasions when it was his duty to entertain the princes and generals of the Grand Alliance, or some special rejoicing. [modifier enclosed in dashes, and clauses]
  >
  > Winston Churchill, *Marlborough*

- Vary the kinds of sentences.

  > Nor did he [Gandhi], like most Western pacifists, specialize in avoiding awkward questions.
  >
  > George Orwell, "Reflections on Gandhi"

  > I have painted easel pictures, not frescoes.
  >
  > W. Somerset Maugham, *The Summing Up*

  > Is it possible that science fiction, now in its infancy, will grow up and one day become the literature of the future?
  >
  > Arthur Koestler, "The Boredom of Fantasy"

  > Yet the dynamo, next to the steam-engine, was the most familiar of exhibits.
  >
  > Henry Adams, *The Education of Henry Adams*

- Vary the sentence length. In the paragraph that follows, observe the many uses of variety: kinds of sentences, shifting of words out of their normal position, short and long sentences, and modification within the sentences:

  > Certainly, style is not affectation. Conscious though it may be, when self-conscious it is an obstruction. Its purpose, to my way of thinking, is to give the reader pleasure by sparing him the works which the writer is duty bound to have done for him. Writers, notwithstanding their hopes or ambitions, may or may not be artists. But there is no excuse for their not being artisans. The style is the man, we are told. True in the final and spiritual sense as this is, style is more than that. It is the writing man *in print*. It is, so to speak, his written voice and, if it is truly his voice, even in

print it should be his and his alone. The closer it comes to the illusion of speech, perhaps the better. Yet the closeness of the written word to the spoken can, and in fact should, never be more than an illusion. For the point of the written word is planning, as surely as the charm of the spoken one is its lack of it.

John Mason Brown, "Pleasant Agony"

- **Use periodic sentences.** The periodic principle is used effectively in this sentence:

> When I think of the one-legged kittens that land on my pages; when I remember the false starts, illegible scribblings, unfinished sentences, discarded drafts, changed constructions, and altered words which mark my beginnings, my continuings, my endings, I blush with shame and, like the voyagers in Dante's realm, abandon all hope.

John Mason Brown

Writer's Revision Checklist

Coherence

1. Are the ideas clearly related, each one to the others and to the central idea?
2. Is coherence enhanced by the use of transitional words, pronoun reference, repetition, and a consistent point of view?
3. Is there a clear pattern of organization (time, space, or emphasis)?
4. Should the points of support be placed in a different order?
5. Is the pattern supported by key words that suggest the basis of that organization (time: *now, then, later*; space: *above, below, up, down*; emphasis: *first, second, last*)?

Language

1. Is the language appropriate (properly standard and formal or informal) for the purpose of the piece and for the intended audience?
2. Is the tone (language use showing attitude toward material and audience) appropriate?
3. Is the word choice effective? Are the words precise in conveying meaning? Are there problems with denotative or connotative, general or specific, aspects of diction?

Unity

1. Is there a clear, well-stated topic sentence or thesis, one that indicates both subject and treatment?
2. Are all points of support clearly related to and subordinate to that topic sentence or thesis?

Emphasis

1. Are ideas properly placed (especially near the beginning and end) for emphasis?
2. Are important words and phrases repeated for emphasis?

Support

1. Is there adequate supporting information, such as evidence and reasoning, to explain the topic sentence or thesis?

Sentence Structure

1. Are there problems with sentence structure (fragments, comma splices, run-togethers)?
2. Are the sentences varied in beginnings?
3. Are the sentences varied in pattern (simple, compound, complex, and compound-complex)?
4. Do the sentences properly emphasize ideas?

EXERCISE 2

Using the "Writer's Revision Checklist," rework the following student first draft. Then check for the points of **Edit—cops: c**apitalization, **o**missions (oversights or grammar problems), **p**unctuation, and **s**pelling. Space is provided for you to add, delete, move, and correct material. (See the Answer Key for a revised and edited version.)

Neglected Children

The neglect of children by their parents can have many harmful effects. Three important ones are discussed here. Neglect affects a childs choices, a childs future, and a childs feelings. These effects overlap adding to the confusion he is already experiencing. A childs choices are effectd by the parents neglect. If a child does not get the healthy attention and affection from his parents he may withdraw socially or seek it elsewhere and all too often unhealthy choices are made. The future of the child is shaped by neglect and may set him on a long road of addictions and dysfunctional relationships in the future. There is a large percentage of abused children which become parents and pass their neglect on their children. A parents attitude around the child gives him many messages. You can get feelings of being unloved and unworthy of love that way. Instead of seeing this as a fault of the parent the child can get all bummed out and can internalize these feelings and see himself as bad, as faulty and as being different than other children.

EXERCISE 3

Using the "Writer's Revision Checklist," rework the following student first draft. Then check for the points of **Edit—cops: c**apitalization, **o**missions (oversights or grammar problems), **p**unctuation, and **s**pelling. Space is provided for you to add, delete, move, and correct material.

```
                         Quitting School
    Quitting school was not a big deal for me until I
realize all the effects of quitting would bring to my
life. At that time I didn't care. I plan to marry a few
months later after my high school graduation. I was happy
at the time.
    Quitting school was a big mistake because when I went
out to look for a job I couldn't qualify for any of the
good positions because of my lack of education. Instead I
took a job as in a fast foods place where I had no future.
Then I went to work in a big company just doing simple
office work. When it came time for promotions I couldn't
pass the tests they gave. That was not all. As a result of
quitting school later. I couldn't even help my children
with their homework or buy the special things for them.
    I started my family when I was not even eighteen years.
The first year of my marriage was fine, then things started
to fall apart. My husband had quit school too, and he
didn't make much money, and as I mentioned, I didn't make
much either. We argued a lot mainly over money. We couldn't
get a big enough house for our family so that we could have
the privacy we needed. I quit work to raise my kids and
that when I really got in deep. My car was getting old and
money was not enough to make big payments I had to buy
another old car, which broke down all the time. I started
freaking out. The fighting got worse and we had a divorce.
    I was lucky that my parents decided to help me, and now
I am dedicated to getting a good education. I will work
hard to learn so me and my children can have a better life.
```

(The remainder of this chapter applies to both revising and editing.)

Parts of Speech

Words are classified as parts of speech according to two simple principles: (1) a word does not become a part of speech until it is in the context of communication, which usually means in a sentence, and (2) words are grouped as nouns, pronouns, adjectives, verbs, adverbs, prepositions, conjunctions, and interjections on the basis of similar characteristics.

The first principle is important because some words can be any of several parts of speech. The word *round,* for example, can function as five:

1. I watched the potter *round* the block of clay. (verb)
2. I saw her go *round* the corner. (preposition)
3. She has a *round* head. (adjective)
4. The astronauts watched the world go *round.* (adverb)
5. The champ knocked him out in one *round.* (noun)

Nouns

- ***Nouns are naming words.*** Nouns may name persons, animals, plants, places, things, substances, qualities, or ideas—for example, *Bart, armadillo, Mayberry, tree, rock, cloud, love, ghost, music, virtue.*

- ***Nouns can have a plural form.*** The most common plurals are formed by adding *-s* or *-es.* Some examples are *trees, rocks, clouds, ghosts.* But some nouns change to plural in other ways: *mouse–mice, ox–oxen.* Only a few, such as *deer–deer,* have the same form for both singular and plural.

- ***Nouns are often pointed out by noun indicators.*** These noun indicators—*the, a, an*—signal that a noun is ahead, though there may be words between the indicator and the noun itself.

the slime	*a* werewolf	*an* aardvark
the green slime	*a* hungry werewolf	*an* angry aardvark

Pronouns

A pronoun is a word that is used in place of a noun.

- Some pronouns may represent persons:

I	him	himself	me
her	herself	we	they
itself	us	them	ourselves
you	who	themselves	she
whom	yourselves	he	myself
that	it	yourself	

- Some pronouns refer to nouns (persons, places, things) in a general way:

each	everyone	nobody	somebody

- Other pronouns point out particular things:

  SINGULAR: *this, that*
  This is my treasure.
  That is your junk.

  PLURAL: *these, those*
  These are my children.
  Those are your brats.

If words like *this* and *these* modify nouns rather than replace them, as in the above example, they become adjectives:

> *This* treasure delights me.   *These* children are adorable.
> *That* junk disgusts me.   *Those* brats are obnoxious.

- Still other pronouns introduce questions.

    Which is the best CD player?
    What are the main ingredients of a Twinkie?

Verbs

Verbs are words with certain forms that show action or express being. They occur in set positions in sentences. The action should make them easy for you to identify.

> The aardvark *ate* the crisp, tasty ants. (action verb)
> The aardvark *washed* them down with a snoutful of water. (action verb)

The **being** verbs are few in number and are also easy to identify. The most common being verbs are *is, was, were, are,* and *am.* These words are always verbs.

> Gilligan *is* on an island in the South Pacific. (being verb)
> I *am* his enthusiastic fan. (being verb)

The form of a verb refers to its tense, meaning the time of the action or being. The time may be in the present or past.

> Roseanne *sings* "The Star-Spangled Banner." (present)
> Roseanne *sang* "The Star-Spangled Banner." (past)

A **helping** verb or verbs may be used with the main verb to show other tenses.

> She *had sung* the song many times in the shower. (helping verb and main verb to show a certain time in the past)
> She *will be singing* the song no more in San Diego. (helping verbs and main verb to show a certain time in the future)

Some helping verbs can be used alone as main verbs: *has, have, had, is, was, were, are, am.* Certain other helping verbs function only as helpers: *will, shall, should, could.*

The most common position for the verb is directly after the subject or after the subject and its modifiers.

> At high noon only two men (subject) *were* on Main Street.
> The man with the faster draw (subject and modifiers) *walked* away alone.

Adjectives

Adjectives are words that modify nouns and pronouns. Most adjectives answer the questions What kind? Which one? and How many?

- Adjectives answering the **What kind?** question are descriptive. They tell the quality, kind, or condition of the nouns or pronouns they modify.

    red convertible   *noisy* muffler   *dirty* fork   *wild* roses

- Adjectives answering the **Which one?** question narrow or restrict the meaning of the modifier. Some of these are pronouns used as adjectives.

    my money   *our* ideas   *their* house   *this* reason   *these* apples

- Adjectives answering the **How many?** question are, of course, numbering words.

    some people   *each* pet   *few* goals   *three* dollars   *one* glove

- The words *a, an,* and *the* are **article adjectives.** They point out persons, places, and things.

Adverbs

Adverbs are words that modify verbs, adjectives, and other adverbs. Adverbs answer the questions How? Where? When? and How much?

MODIFYING VERBS: They <u>did</u> their work <u>quickly</u>.
                                          v   adv

                                 He <u>replied</u> <u>angrily</u>.
                                        v   adv

MODIFYING ADJECTIVES: They were <u>somewhat</u> <u>happy</u>.
                                              v   adv

- Adverbs that answer the **How?** question are concerned with manner or way.

    She ate the snails *hungrily.*   He snored *noisily.*

- Adverbs that answer the **Where?** question show location.

    They drove *downtown.*   She climbed *upstairs.*   He stayed *behind.*

- Adverbs that answer the **When?** question indicate time.

    The ship sailed *yesterday.*   I expect an answer *soon.*

- Those that answer the **How much?** question express degree.

    She is *entirely* correct.   He was *somewhat* happy.

Most words ending in -ly are adverbs.

He completed the task <u>skillfully</u>.
                                     adv

She answered him <u>courteously</u>.
                                 adv

However, there are a few exceptions.

The house provided a <u>lovely</u> view of the valley.
                                      adj

Your goblin mask is <u>ugly</u>.
                                adj

Prepositions

A preposition is a word or words that function as a connective. The preposition connects its **object(s)** to some other word(s) in the sentence. A preposition and its object(s)—usually a noun or pronoun—with modifiers make up a **prepositional phrase.**

Bart worked <u>against</u> great <u>odds</u> and completed the fourth grade.
      prep   object
       prepositional phrase

Everyone <u>in</u> his <u>household</u> cheered his effort.
     prep object
      prepositional phrase

Some of the most common prepositions are the following:

about	above	across	after	against
among	around	before	behind	below
beneath	beside	between	beyond	but
by	despite	down	for	from
in	into	like	near	of
off	on	over	past	to
toward	under	until	upon	with

Some prepositions are composed of more than one word and are made up from other parts of speech:

according to	ahead of	along with	as far as
as well as	aside from	back of	because of
in spite of	instead of	in front of	together with

Caution: Do not confuse adverbs with prepositions.

I went *across* slowly. (without an object—adverb)
I went *across* the field. (with an object—preposition)
We walked *behind* silently. (without an object—adverb)
We walked *behind* the mall. (with an object—preposition)

Conjunctions

A conjunction is a word that connects and shows a relationship between words, phrases, or clauses. A phrase is two or more words acting as a part of speech; we have discussed verb phrases and prepositional phrases. A clause is a group of words with a subject and a verb. An independent clause can stand by itself: *She plays bass guitar.* A dependent clause cannot stand by itself: *When she plays bass guitar.*
 There are two kinds of conjunctions: coordinating and subordinating:

Coordinating conjunctions connect words, phrases, and clauses of equal rank: noun with noun, adjective with adjective, verb with verb, phrase with phrase, main clause with main clause, and subordinate clause with subordinate clause. The seven common coordinating conjunctions are *for, and, nor, but, or, yet,* and *so.* One simple way to remember them is to think of the acronym FANBOYS; each letter in that word is the first letter of one of the common coordinating conjunctions. The coordinating conjunctions will take on special significance in our discussion of compound and compound-complex sentences.

TWO NOUNS: Bring a <u>pencil</u> <u>and</u> some <u>paper</u>.
         noun conj noun

TWO PHRASES: Did she go <u>to the store</u> <u>or</u> <u>to the game</u>?
          phrase conj phrase

Paired conjunctions such as *either/or, neither/nor,* and *both/and* are usually classed as coordinating conjunctions.

<u>Neither</u> the coach <u>nor</u> the manager was at fault.
  conj   conj

Subordinating conjunctions connect dependent clauses with main clauses. These conjunctions will be important in our discussion of complex and compound-complex sentences. The most common subordinating conjunctions are:

after	although	as	as if
as long as	as soon as	because	before
besides	but that	if	in order that
notwithstanding	provided	since	so that
till	until	when	whenever
where	whereas	wherever	

Sometimes the dependent clause comes *before* the main clause and is set off by a comma.

<u>Although</u> <u>she</u> <u>was</u> in pain, she still stayed in the game.
  conj   sub   v
      dependent clause

Sometimes the dependent clause comes *after* the main clause and is *not* set off by a comma.

She stayed in the game <u>because</u> <u>she</u> <u>was needed.</u>
                     conj   sub   v
                         dependent clause

Caution: Certain words can function as either conjunctions or prepositions. It is necessary to look ahead to see if the word introduces a clause with a subject and verb—conjunction function—or takes an object—preposition function. Some of the words with two functions are these: *after, for, since, until.*

After the concert was over, we went home. (clause follows—conjunction)
After the concert, we went home. (object follows—preposition)

Interjections

An interjection is one or more words used to convey strong emotions or surprise. When an interjection is used alone, it is usually punctuated with an exclamation mark.

    Wow!   Curses!   Kawabunga!   Yabba dabba doo!

When it is used as part of a sentence, an interjection is usually followed by a comma.

    Oh, I did not consider that problem.

The interjection presents no significant structural problem and is seldom used in college writing.

CHAPTER 15

EXERCISE 4

Identify the part of speech of each italicized word or group of words by placing the appropriate abbreviations in the blanks. (See the Answer Key for answers.)

N	noun	PRO	pronoun
V	verb	ADJ	adjective
ADV	adverb	PREP	preposition
CONJ	conjunction		

1. I could *never* do *that* hard work at my age.
2. We *must leave* for the seashore at once *before* the shower.
3. *Until* Steve signs the checks, *we* must remain here.
4. *These* men are anxiously awaiting your *instructions*.
5. What is the *price* of those new *foreign* cars?
6. Your *sister* is later than *you* this time.
7. The coach is always *nervous before* the game begins.
8. The *Norwegian* people protested the visit *of* the alleged terrorist.
9. *I* shall have been absent a week *tomorrow*.
10. That *reckless* driver hurt only *himself* in the accident.
11. Her attitude *toward* the suspension of the students was *somewhat* cool.
12. We *found* the answer to those difficulties *since* he was last present.
13. Joan is much *wiser* now, *and* she will never forget the lesson.
14. We saw the ship *that* was in the *collision*.
15. *Behind* the store is a *winding* road which leads to the farms.
16. *If* you wish, I *will take* down his message for you.
17. A *group* of students *asked* to see those new paintings earlier.
18. When Kristin had finished talking, she came *over* to *my* side of the room.
19. *Certainly*, you may see *his* answers.
20. I will *not* agree to *your* criticism.

EXERCISE 5

Identify the part of speech of each italicized word or group of words by placing the appropriate abbreviations in the blanks.

N	noun	PRO	pronoun
V	verb	ADJ	adjective
ADV	adverb	PREP	preposition
CONJ	conjunction		

1. *According to* legend, silk *was discovered* by Empress Hsi Ling-shi. _____ _____

2. Empress Hsi Ling-shi *lived around* 2500 B.C. _____ _____

3. *One* day while walking, *she* saw a mulberry tree covered with caterpillars. _____ _____

4. The *caterpillars* were eating the *mulberry* leaves. _____ _____

5. A few days *later* she saw the branches filled *with* the caterpillars' cocoons. _____ _____

6. She plucked a cocoon *from* a branch and *took* it home. _____ _____

7. *There* she placed *it* in a pot of water. _____ _____

8. She *watched as* it loosened into a web. _____ _____

9. She picked the *web apart*. _____ _____

10. She discovered that *it* was a *long* thread of silk. _____ _____

11. The process of making silk *became* China's *best-kept* secret. _____ _____

12. The *secret lasted* for the next 3,000 years. _____ _____

13. Foreign gold poured *into* China from the *silk* trade. _____ _____

14. To pass on the secret of silk-making *to* the *outside* world was forbidden. _____ _____

15. Betraying the secret was punishable *by death*. _____ _____

16. *Anyone* who has ever seen or worn a garment of pure silk knows why the Chinese had to guard *their* invention so jealously. _____ _____

17. Silk is *petal* soft and lighter than the *sheerest* cotton. _____ _____

18. It is *stronger* than *some* kinds of steel thread of equal thickness. _____ _____

19. Silk *drapes* and flows *gracefully*. _____ _____

20. It can be dyed to *richer* hues than any other natural *fabric*. _____ _____

Verbs and Subjects

It is appropriate to consider subjects and verbs together, because each subject is identified by its relationship to its companion verb, and each verb is identified by its relationship to its companion subject. Keep in mind that the word *verb* is used in two ways in this book. First, it is a part of speech. Second, it is a part of sentence structure. Put simply, a word is first a part of speech, then a part of a larger structure. Therefore, a noun or pronoun part of speech can become a subject part of sentence structure, and a verb part of speech can become a verb part of sentence structure.

Verbs

Basic Principles

It makes sense to begin with the verb because verbs are usually more easily recognized than subjects. The simple verb as a part of sentence structure is the main verb part of speech without modifiers. The verb is a part of speech with certain forms. It shows action or expresses being and occurs in set positions in sentences. The **action words** are those such as *ate* and *washed*. The **being words**, few in number, include *is, was, were, are,* and *am;* these words are always verbs. A verb's **form** refers to its tense, meaning time of the action or being. Words that show the element of time, such as *see, saw,* and *seen,* can be verbs as parts of speech and, therefore, verbs as sentence structure. The **set position** means verbs will usually occur in a sentence after the subject and always in relationship to it. The verb usually occurs in a sentence after the subject, which in turn is usually near the beginning of the sentence.

By using these principles, you can identify many verbs even when you do not know their meaning. Consider this nonsense sentence:

The zonkomore floggled in the zotter.

Of course, we recognize *floggled* as the verb. Why? Certainly not because it is a familiar action word, though we can see it is not a being word. We recognized it because (1) it follows the subject, a noun head word pointed out by the noun indicator *the,* and (2) it has an *-ed* ending, which suggests past tense, and only verbs have tense forms.

Other Considerations

Verbs may occur as single words or as phrases. A **verb phrase** is made up of a main verb and one or more helping verbs such as the following:

be	is	was	were
are	am	will	shall
could	has	have	had

Here are some examples of sentences containing verb phrases:

Pat Sajak *has performed* on television for years.
His fans *have admired* him for his many roles.

Verbs that are joined by a coordinating conjunction such as *and* and *or* are called **compound verbs**:

Pat Sajak *created* and *hosted* his own talk show.
He *told* jokes and *asked* his guests provocative questions.

Verbs should not be confused with their modifiers:

Pat Sajak *does* not *sing* opera and *can* hardly *dance*.

The modifier *not* is always an adverb, never a verb. One cannot *not* something; the same can be said of *hardly*. Although most verbs occur after the subject, some occur in other positions:

There *are* many assistants on game shows but only one Vanna White.

The word *there* is an adverb and can't be a subject. The subject is *assistants*.

Sentences that are questions often divide verb phrases, placing one verb on each side of the subject, as in "Where *did* Pat *find* Vanna?" If you have trouble finding the verb, recast the question, making it into a statement form: "Pat *did find* Vanna where." That change will usually reposition the subject first and the verb parts together. The result will not necessarily be a smooth or complete statement, but you will be able to see the basic elements more easily. Here are some more examples:

CHANGE: What <u>would</u> Pat <u>have done</u> without Vanna?
            v   sub   v

TO: <u>Pat</u> <u>would have done</u> what without Vanna?
   sub   v

CHANGE: <u>Can</u> <u>you</u> <u>turn</u> letters gracefully?
           v sub v

TO: <u>You</u> <u>can turn</u> letters gracefully.
   sub   v

A verb-like word with an *-ing* ending is not part of the main verb unless it has a helping verb:

Getting ready for the show, Vanna *practiced* spelling and *limbered* up her wrists and lips.

Getting is not a verb because you would not say, "She getting ready," in standard English. If you said, "She is getting ready," then *is getting* would be the verb phrase.

Subjects

The **simple subject** is usually the main noun or pronoun occurring before the verb. It is what the sentence is about. You can recognize the simple subject by asking Who? or What? causes the action or expresses the state of being found in the verb.

The <u>Skipper</u> <u>commanded</u> the Minnow.
     sub   action v

Who commanded? The Skipper (subject).

<u>Gilligan</u> <u>was</u> his first mate.
 sub   being v

Who was? Gilligan (subject).

Variations in Type and Location

The subject may be simple (as in previous examples) or compound:

The <u>Skipper</u> and <u>Gilligan</u> <u>worked</u> together.
    sub   sub   v

<u>Mary Anne</u> and <u>Ginger</u> <u>were</u> companions by circumstance.
  sub   sub   v

Although the subject usually occurs before the verb, it may follow the verb:

Up onto the shore of an uncharted desert isle <u>washed</u> the <u>Minnow</u>.
                                                       v   sub

There <u>is</u> much <u>reason</u> for hope.
     v   sub

Be careful not to confuse subjects with objects of prepositions. The object of a preposition cannot be a main part of sentence structure:

The <u>captain</u> <u>of the Minnow</u> <u>lost</u> his way <u>in the storm</u>.
     sub   prep phrase   v   prep phrase

The <u>brains</u> <u>of the group</u> <u>was</u> the professor.
    sub   prep phrase v

The command, or directive, sentence has a "you" implied subject:

(<u>You</u>) <u>Read</u> the passage well.
 sub

(<u>You</u>) <u>Go</u> left at the next corner.
 sub

EXERCISE 6

Write the simple subject, without modifiers, in the first blank; write the verb in the second blank. Some sentences may have compound subjects, compound verbs, or both; and some sentences may have an implied ("you") subject. (See the Answer Key for answers.)

1. Early in the morning Kathy usually dug clams down on the beach. _____ _____

2. Never again will I be able to trust him on a mission. _____ _____

3. Berlin and London were bombed heavily during World War II. _____ _____

4. Perhaps Linda and you will decide to join us on the cruise to Bermuda. _____ _____

5. Over by the bench stand the captain and the coach. _____ _____

6. Several students are applying for that position. _____ _____

7. Please tell Barbara not to be late again for school. _____ _____

8. William Faulkner, a Nobel Prize winner, wrote mostly about the South. _____ _____

9. For a long time now I have waited and thought about speaking to him. _____ _____

10. Whom can we find to take his place as quarterback? _____ _____

11. There are no longer any customers for that line of goods. _____ _____

12. Where will we find a drugstore open at this late hour? _____ _____

13. The players, after losing the game, assembled in the coach's office and elected Robert captain. _____ _____

14. By this time next year, we shall be living in Mexico. _____ _____

15. A very few of those orders may be delayed until tomorrow. _____ _____

16. Did you ever wish to remain at the beach all summer? _____ _____

17. Please buy me that gold pin in the store window. _____ _____

18. His immediate reaction to the unfair proposals was to leave the room. _____ _____

19. Deep in the Maine woods lies an old cabin built long ago. _____ _____

20. Leave the papers on the desk. _____ _____

EXERCISE 7

Write the simple subject, without modifiers, in the first blank; write the verb in the second blank. Some sentences may have compound subjects, compound verbs, or both; and some sentences may have an implied ("you") subject.

1. The earliest evidence of Chinese writing comes from the Shang dynasty. _____ _____

2. Archaeologists have found and studied hundreds of animal bones and tortoise shells with written symbols on them. _____ _____

3. These strange objects are known as oracle bones. _____ _____

4. Priests used them in fortune telling. _____ _____

5. People 3,500 years ago developed part of the culture existing in China today. _____ _____

6. Some of the characters are very much like those in a modern Chinese newspaper. _____ _____

7. In the Chinese method of writing, each character stands for an idea, not a sound. _____ _____

8. On the other hand, many of the Egyptian hieroglyphs stood for sounds in their spoken language. _____ _____

9. But there were practically no links between China's spoken language and its written language. _____ _____

10. One might read Chinese and not speak it. _____ _____

11. The Chinese system of writing had one great advantage. _____ _____

12. People with different dialects in all parts of China could learn the same system of writing and communicate with it. _____ _____

13. Thus, the Chinese written language aided the unification of a large and diverse land. _____ _____

14. The disadvantage of the Chinese system is the enormous number of written characters. _____ _____

15. A barely literate person needs at least 1,000 characters. _____ _____

16. A true scholar needs about 10,000 characters. _____ _____

17. For centuries, this requirement severely limited the number of literate, educated Chinese. _____ _____

18. A noble's children learned to write. _____ _____

19. A peasant's children did not. _____ _____

20. Consider these ideas as a background to modern educational systems. _____ _____

Sentence Problems

Sentence writing is plagued with three recurring problems: the fragment, the comma splice, and the run-together. All three are structural problems that confuse the reader because they give false signals. If you encounter a false signal, you may be able to figure out what the writer intended to say, but you will have to expend extra effort in order to do so. You will have to work without the true signals that the author should have given. A good sentence should not draw that unfavorable attention. It should be easy on the eye and easy on the mind.

Fragments

A correct sentence offers signals of completeness. The structure and punctuation provide those signals. For example, if I say to you, "She left in a hurry," you do not necessarily expect me to say anything else, but if I say, "In a hurry," you do. If I say, "Tomorrow I will give you a quiz on the reading assignment," and I leave the room, you will merely take note of my words. But if I say, "Tomorrow when I give you a quiz on the reading assignment," and leave the room, you will probably be annoyed, and you may even chase after me and ask me to finish my sentence. Those examples illustrate the difference between completeness and incompleteness, between a correct sentence and a fragment.

In short, we can say that a sentence is a word or a group of words—usually with a subject and a verb—that makes sense. However, there are many one-word sentences and many arrangements of words that lack a subject and a verb but still make sense. You must then be able to distinguish between effective, or acceptable, fragments and the vague, unintentional fragments (usually phrases, incomplete structures, and dependent clauses) that do not make sense standing alone.

Among the commonly used acceptable fragments are the following:

Interjections: Great! Hooray! Whoa!
Exclamations: What a day! How terrible! What a bother!
Greetings: Hello. Good morning. Good night. Good evening.
Questions: What for? Why not? Where to?
Informal Conversation: (What time is it?) Eight o'clock. Really.

You will notice that most of these acceptable fragments are conversational and would seldom appear in college writing. Other fragments that you may see in books are unconventional and are used for special effects.

Your main concern is with the unacceptable fragment, commonly called simply the fragment. A **fragment** is a word or group of words without either a subject or verb ("He going to town.") or without both ("Going to town."), or it is a group of words with a subject and verb that cannot stand alone ("When he left."). Although its punctuation signals a sentence, the structure of a fragment signals incompleteness. If you were to say it or write it to someone, that person would expect you to go on and finish the idea.

Other specific examples of common unacceptable fragments are:

Dependent clause only: When she came.
No subject in main clause: Went to the library.
No verb in main clause: She being the only person there.
Phrase(s) only: Waiting there for some help.

Exercises 9 and 10 will give you an opportunity to work with each of the various types of unacceptable fragments.

Dependent Clauses as Fragments

Although a dependent clause has a subject and verb, it cannot stand by itself because it begins with a subordinating word. The dependent clause as a fragment can be corrected by removing the subordinating word or by attaching the dependent clause to an independent clause. Some of the most common subordinating words are these:

*B*ecause (he left)
*A*lthough (he left)
*T*hat (he left)
*W*hen (he left)
*A*fter (he left)
*S*ince (he left)
*H*ow (he left)
*T*ill (he left)
*U*nless (he left)
*B*efore (he left)

He left is a sentence (an independent clause), but placing any one of these ten words before it turns it into a dependent clause and, by itself, a fragment. Note that the first letters of the words spell out BAT WASHTUB. Using that acronym to remember these common subordinating words, you will be able to spot many fragments easily. Following are some examples:

INCORRECT: They continued to dance. *While the ship was sinking.*
CORRECT: While the ship was sinking, they continued to dance.
CORRECT: The ship was sinking. They continued to dance.

INCORRECT: I knew the senator. *Who led the fight for civil rights.*
CORRECT: I knew the senator who led the fight for civil rights.

Phrases as Fragments

Although a phrase may carry an idea, it is fragmentary because it is incomplete in structure. It lacks a subject and verb. A phrase fragment can usually be corrected by connecting it to a complete sentence (independent clause). An appositive phrase is usually set off by a comma or commas. A verbal or prepositional phrase is usually set off by a comma at the beginning of a sentence.

- **Verbal phrase**

    INCORRECT: *Having studied hard all evening.* John decided to retire.
    CORRECT: Having studied hard all evening, John decided to retire.

    The italicized part of the incorrect example is a verbal phrase. A **verbal** is verb-like without being a verb in sentence structure. Verbals include verb parts of speech ending in *-ed* and *-ing*. They function as nouns (called **gerunds**) or adjectives and adverbs (called **participles**). They also include the infinitive, a construction made up of the preposition *to* and a verb—for example, *to leave*.

- **Prepositional phrase**

    INCORRECT: *After the last snow.* The workers built the road.
    CORRECT: After the last snow, the workers built the road.

- **Appositive phrase**

    INCORRECT: He lived in the small town of Whitman. *A busy industrial center near Boston.*
    CORRECT: He lived in the small town of Whitman, a busy industrial center near Boston.

    In this example, the fragment is an appositive phrase—a group of words following a noun or pronoun and renaming it.

Fragments as Word Groups Without Subjects or Verbs

Each conventional sentence must have an independent clause, meaning a word or a group of words that contains a subject and a verb and that can stand alone. A command or direction sentence, such as "Think," has an understood subject of *you*. For example:

    INCORRECT: John studied many long hours. And received the highest grade in the class. (without subject)
    CORRECT: John studied many long hours and received the highest grade in the class.

    INCORRECT: Few children living in that section of the country. (without verb)
    CORRECT: Few children live in that section of the country.

Comma Splices and Run-Togethers

The comma splice and the run-together are two other kinds of faulty "sentences" that give false signals to the reader. In each instance the punctuation suggests that there is only one sentence, but there is material for two.

The **comma splice** consists of two independent clauses with only a comma between them.

The weather was disappointing, we canceled the picnic. (A comma by itself cannot join two independent clauses.)

The **run-together** differs from the comma splice in only one respect: it has no comma. Therefore, the run-together is two independent clauses with *nothing* between them.

The weather was disappointing we canceled the picnic. (Independent clauses must be connected by something.)

Because an independent clause can stand by itself as a sentence and because two independent clauses must be properly linked, you can use a simple technique to identify the comma splice and the run-together. If you see a sentence that you think may contain one of these two errors, ask yourself this question: "Can I insert a period at some place in the word group and still have a sentence on each side?" If the answer is yes and there is no coordinating conjunction, then you have a comma splice or a run-together to correct. In our previous examples of the comma splice and the run-together, we could insert a period after the word *disappointing* in each case, and we would still have an independent clause—therefore, a sentence—on each side.

Once you identify a comma splice or a run-together in your writing, you need to correct it. There are four different ways to fix these common sentence problems.

1. Use a Comma and a Coordinating Conjunction.

INCORRECT: We wanted to go to the beach the weather was bad. (run-together)

CORRECT: We wanted to go to the beach, but the weather was bad. (Here we inserted a comma and the coordinating conjunction *but*.)

Knowing the seven coordinating conjunctions will help you in writing sentences and correcting sentence problems. The acronym FANBOYS should aid you in remembering them:

*F*or
*A*nd
*N*or
*B*ut
*O*r
*Y*et
*S*o

2. Make One of the Clauses Dependent.

INCORRECT: The weather was disappointing, we canceled the picnic.

CORRECT: *Because* the weather was disappointing, we canceled the picnic.

By inserting the subordinating conjunction *because*, we transform the first independent clause into a dependent clause and correct the comma splice. Knowing the common subordinating conjunctions will help you in writing sentences and correcting sentence problems. Use the acronym BAT WASHTUB to recall them:

Because
After
That
When
Although
Since
How
Till
Unless
Before

Other subordinating words are *if, besides, until, whereas, as, as if, whenever, wherever*.

3. Use a Semicolon.

INCORRECT: The weather was disappointing, we canceled the picnic.
CORRECT: The weather was disappointing; therefore, we canceled the picnic.

This comma splice was corrected by a semicolon. *Therefore*, the transitional connective, is optional. The most common transitional connectives are these:

However
Otherwise
Therefore
Similarly
Hence
On the other hand
Then
Consequently
Also
Thus

Did you pick out the phrase HOTSHOT CAT, made up of the first letters of each of these common transitional connectives? The acronym will help you remember them. Others include *in fact* and *for example*.

4. Make Each Clause a Separate Sentence.

INCORRECT: The weather was disappointing, we canceled the picnic.
CORRECT: The weather was disappointing. We canceled the picnic.

To correct the comma splice, replace the comma with a period and begin the second sentence (clause) with a capital letter. After identifying a comma splice or run-together word group, this method is quite easy. You simply complete the procedure shown in the example. This method is at once the simplest and most common method of correcting comma-splice and run-together problems.

EXERCISE 8

Write the appropriate identification in each blank. (See the Answer Key for answers.)

OK   correct
CS   comma splice
RT   run-together
FRAG   fragment

_____ 1. Romance seems to be a glamorous necessity for American writers who succeed in this generation.

_____ 2. A dog's eyes show a blankness of mind, therefore a dog's eyes are not a good indication of whether a dog can be trained.

_____ 3. Those who say American schools are inferior to European schools and provide only entertainment.

_____ 4. Jazz can express pain and sorrow if played by a skillful musician.

_____ 5. The faculty is not perfect, the administration is weak.

_____ 6. "Commuting is good," Ann said, "it gives you time to think."

_____ 7. Her mother was well-educated and came from Nebraska, where I lived.

_____ 8. An instrument of manual operation for shaping metal, wood, or plastics, and holding the work.

_____ 9. Some taxpayers panic when told of the fantastic increase in college enrollment.

_____ 10. You present real content instead of circling around the topic.

_____ 11. Fast driving is dangerous he can prove it because his father was a highway patrolman in Utah where his brother drove an ambulance.

_____ 12. Words can be studied in several ways, the etymology of words reveals their history.

_____ 13. Birds singing in the sycamore trees.

_____ 14. The silent letter in some words that changes the way the word sounds when it's pronounced.

_____ 15. If Frank went to sleep and woke up in the year 2000 and heard about the 1992 election.

_____ 16. The Danish invasion of England changed the language, another factor was the Norman Conquest.

_____ 17. Football is essentially a spectator sport.

_____ 18. Russia won first place and we took second we have to step up our athletic programs.

_____ 19. My favorite author is John Steinbeck his best books are about common people.

_____ 20. The problem is a legal one; it is also an ethical one that touches every member of the community.

EXERCISE 9

Write the appropriate identification in each blank.

    OK   correct
    CS   comma splice
    RT   run together
    FRAG   fragment

_____ 1. The male newt glows during the courting season, the human male has no such attraction.

_____ 2. I think many Americans regard etiquette in terms of morality or social ethics.

_____ 3. Although there has been an alarming increase in heart disease among men.

_____ 4. Their tremendous success in helping other adult illiterates to read.

_____ 5. Billie traveled with the Artie Shaw band, in the North she was not allowed to sing.

_____ 6. They said his mother was interested in the money, he refused to believe them.

_____ 7. She went fishing with her uncle who owned the store where we got the presents they were lost because of the rush.

_____ 8. Keith completed his report, his friends were envious.

_____ 9. Authorities disagree on what makes a car safe; it's more than seat belts.

_____ 10. The problem difficult to locate.

_____ 11. To read carefully or write clearly if you really want to communicate with the class.

_____ 12. I can't wait that long, I'm moving out today.

_____ 13. People's survival seems to hang upon their ability to use their wits; being half-educated won't do.

_____ 14. Joanne needs an automobile she lives a mile from her work, and the bus service is bad.

_____ 15. Your high sales resistance and your critical mind.

_____ 16. José said, "You're the person I need for my project you want to work, and you don't expect to be paid."

_____ 17. The television industry patronizes the intellectual life of America, and it succeeds while it insults.

_____ 18. In order to be colorful and vivid, and to ensure concrete images by being specific.

_____ 19. Janelle said that she considered the movie inferior to others on that topic.

_____ 20. Although they were not pleased with his work as he learned how to operate the machine.

EXERCISE 10

Write the appropriate identification in each blank. Rewrite the incorrect sentences.

    OK   correct
    CS   comma splice
    RT   run together
    FRAG fragment

_____ 1. A total institution is a behavior setting, it has certain unique characteristics.

_____ 2. A total institution completely encompassing the individual.

_____ 3. Forming barriers to the types of social intercourse that occur outside such a setting.

_____ 4. Monasteries, jails, homes for the aged, boarding schools, and military academies being a few examples of total institutions.

_____ 5. In total institutions the individuals must sleep, play, and work within the same setting.

_____ 6. These are generally segmented spheres of activity in the lives of most individuals, within a total institution one sphere of activity overlaps with others.

_____ 7. Each phase of life taking place in the company of a large group of others.

_____ 8. Frequently, sleeping is done in a barracks, food is served in a cafeteria.

_____ 9. In such activities everyone being treated alike and must perform certain essential tasks.

CHAPTER 15

_____ 10. Activities in an institution tightly scheduled according to a master plan.

_____ 11. With set times to rise, to eat, to exercise, and to sleep.

_____ 12. These institutional characteristics result in a bureaucratic society it requires the hiring of other people for surveillance.

_____ 13. What often results is a split in the groups within an institution into a large, managed group (inmates) and a small supervisory staff.

_____ 14. There tends to be great social distance between the groups, they perceive each other according to stereotypes and have severely restricted communications.

_____ 15. The world of the inmate differing greatly from the outside world.

_____ 16. When one enters a total institution, all previous roles, such as father or husband, are disrupted.

_____ 17. The individual is further depersonalized.

_____ 18. The effects of an institutional setting so all-encompassing, one can meaningfully speak of an "institutional personality."

_____ 19. A persistent manner of behaving compliantly and without emotional involvement.

_____ 20. Individual adaptations can be as extreme as psychosis, childlike regression, and depression or as mild as resigned compliance.

Types of Sentences

You may be pleased to discover that there are only four kinds of conventional sentences in English writing: simple, compound, complex, and compound-complex. The terms may be new to you, but the concepts are simple. If you can recognize subjects and verbs, distinguish between independent clauses and dependent clauses, and count to four, you should be able to identify and write these forms with a little instruction and practice. On the basis of number and kinds of clauses, sentences may be classified as simple, compound, complex, and compound-complex.

Clauses

A **clause** is a group of words with a subject and a verb that functions as a part or all of a complete sentence. There are two kinds of clauses: (1) independent (main) and (2) dependent (subordinate).

> INDEPENDENT CLAUSE: I have the money.
> DEPENDENT CLAUSE: When you are ready

An **independent (main) clause** is a group of words with a subject and verb that can stand alone and make sense. An independent clause expresses a complete thought by itself and can be written as a separate sentence.

A **dependent clause**, on the other hand, is a group of words with a subject and verb that depends on a main clause to give it meaning. The dependent clause functions in the common sentence patterns as a noun, adjective, or adverb.

> that fell last night (no meaning alone)
> The snow *that fell last night* is nearly gone. (dependent adjective clause modifying the noun *snow*)
>
> Since Helen came home (no meaning alone)
> *Since Helen came home*, her mother has been happy. (dependent adverbial clause answering the question *when* and modifying the verb *has been*)
>
> that he would win (no meaning alone)
> *That he would win* seemed certain. (dependent noun clause acting as the subject of the verb *seemed*)

Simple Sentences

A **simple sentence** consists of an independent clause and no dependent clauses. It may contain phrases and have more than one subject and/or verb.

> The *lake looks* beautiful in the moonlight. (one subject and one verb)
> The *Army, Navy,* and *Marines sent* men to the disaster area. (three subjects and one verb)
> *We sang* the old songs and *danced* happily at their wedding. (one subject and two verbs)
> My *father, mother,* and *sister came* to the school play, *applauded* the performers, and *attended* the party afterwards. (three subjects and three verbs)

Compound Sentences

A **compound sentence** consists of two or more independent clauses with no dependent clauses.

> *He opened the door,* and *he found the missing paper.*
> *He opened the door; he found the missing paper.*
> *He opened the door;* however, *he did not find the missing paper.*

Independent clauses in a compound sentence are usually connected by either a coordinating conjunction or a semicolon. Sometimes independent clauses are joined by conjunctions in pairs. At other times, independent clauses are joined by a semicolon and marked by one of the transitional connectives (conjunctive adverbs). The coordinating conjunctions are *for, and, nor, but, or, yet, so* (FANBOYS). Conjunctions in pairs include *either/or, neither/nor, not only/but also*. Among the most common transitional connectives are **h**owever, **o**therwise, **t**herefore, **s**imilarly, **h**ence, **o**n the other hand, **t**hen, **c**onsequently, **a**lso, **t**hus (HOTSHOT CAT).

Notice the punctuation in the following examples. Commas precede coordinating conjunctions; semicolons precede transitional connectives and commas follow them.

> Neither is the battle over, nor the victory won.
> He is not only the best athlete, but he is also the best student in our class.
> We were late; therefore, we missed the first act.
> I am very tired, and I wish to rest for a few minutes.
> John is a very able politician; he should win the election.

Complex Sentences

A **complex sentence** consists of one independent clause and one or more dependent clauses.

> When lilacs are in bloom, we love to visit friends in the country. (one dependent clause and one independent clause)
> Although it rained last night, we decided to take the path that led through the woods. (one independent clause and two dependent clauses)

At times, the complex sentence is written with a noun clause as subject, object, or complement (sentence completer):

> *That he continues to try* is praiseworthy. (noun clause as subject)
> I know *who will win*. (noun clause as object)
> His difficulty was *how he should approach the matter*. (noun clause as complement)

Compound-Complex Sentences

A **compound-complex sentence** consists of two or more independent clauses and one or more dependent clauses.

> Albert enlisted in the Army, and Robert, who was his older brother, joined him a day later.
>
> INDEPENDENT CLAUSES: Albert enlisted in the Army; Robert joined him a day later.
> DEPENDENT CLAUSE: who was his older brother
>
> Because Mr. Roberts was a talented teacher, he was voted teacher of the year, and his students prospered.
>
> INDEPENDENT CLAUSES: he was voted teacher of the year; his students prospered
> DEPENDENT CLAUSE: Because Mr. Roberts was a talented teacher

Punctuation Tips

1. Use a comma before a coordinating conjunction (FANBOYS) between two independent clauses.

    The movie was good, but the tickets were expensive.

2. Use a comma after a dependent clause (usually beginning with a subordinating word from the BAT WASHTUB list) that occurs before the main clause.

    When the bus arrived, we quickly boarded.

3. Use a semicolon between two independent clauses in one sentence if there is no coordinating conjunction.

    The bus arrived; we quickly boarded.

4. Use a semicolon before and a comma after a transitional connective (HOTSHOT CAT) between two independent clauses.

    The bus arrived; however, it was full of passengers.

Summary

This table gives you the basic sentence-type information. The dependent clauses are italicized; the independent clauses are underlined.

Type	Definition	Example
Simple	One independent clause	She did the work.
Compound	Two or more independent clauses	She did the work, and she was paid.
Complex	One independent clause and one or more dependent clauses	*Because she did the work*, she was paid.
Compound-complex	Two or more independent clauses and one or more dependent clauses	*Because she did the work*, she was paid, and she was satisfied.

EXERCISE 11

Indicate the kind of sentence by writing the correct letters in the blank. (See the Answer Key for answers.)

```
S     simple
CP    compound
CX    complex
CC    compound-complex
```

_____ 1. I left early in the afternoon; I wanted to reach Fresno before dark.

_____ 2. If you wish to see him, you must make an appointment date weeks in advance.

_____ 3. Before the opening game of the season, the Boston Celtics had played the Los Angeles Lakers two games.

_____ 4. Before you study the plays of that dramatist, you should read some comments by Edith Hamilton.

_____ 5. The shrubs are beginning to grow, but the trees that our neighbor gave to us are dead.

_____ 6. After visiting friends in Albany, we drove on to Pembroke, Massachusetts, and stayed that night in a motel on the east shore of Oldham Pond.

_____ 7. This is the school from which many famous leaders of our country graduated.

_____ 8. Although our campus covers many acres, we do not have sufficient parking areas.

_____ 9. You must be there early in the morning, or you will lose the job to someone else.

_____ 10. I saw the last game that he played in college.

_____ 11. The character delineation in that novel was excellent, but the plot was weak and confusing.

_____ 12. The coach who gave you those suggestions is one of the best ball players with the New York Yankees.

_____ 13. You must return those books to the library at once, or you will be fined.

_____ 14. When I look at the calendar, I realize with a shock that Christmas is only a few weeks away.

_____ 15. The lady entered the store, walked directly to the dress department, handed the waiting clerk a torn dress, and demanded her money back.

_____ 16. Patricia visited her family in Iowa, and I attended school in New York.

_____ 17. It would be unwise for you to demand his resignation before discussing the matter with his superior.

_____ 18. After our glorious stay in Rome, we flew to Egypt and spent the summer studying at the University of Cairo.

_____ 19. They were very late in arriving home; nevertheless, we stayed up and greeted them.

_____ 20. He would not agree to all the proposals.

EXERCISE 12

Indicate the kind of sentence by writing the appropriate letter in the blanks.

    S   simple
    CP   compound
    CX   complex
    CC   compound-complex

_____ 1. Throughout history there have been truth tests for the innocent and the guilty.

_____ 2. Many of these methods relied (unknowingly) on the basic physiological principles that also guided the creation of the polygraph.

_____ 3. For example, one method of lie detection involved giving the suspect a handful of raw rice to chew.

_____ 4. After the suspect chewed for some time, he or she was instructed to spit out the rice.

_____ 5. An innocent person was expected to do this easily, but a guilty person was expected to have grains of rice sticking to the roof of the mouth and tongue.

_____ 6. This technique relied on the increased sympathetic nervous system activity in the presumably fearful and guilty person.

_____ 7. This activity would result in the drying up of saliva.

_____ 8. That, in turn, would cause grains of rice to stick in the mouth.

_____ 9. A similar but more frightening technique involved placing a heated knife blade briefly against the tongue.

_____ 10. An innocent person would not be burned, but the guilty person would immediately feel pain, again because of the relative dryness of the mouth.

_____ 11. A more primitive but functional technique for detecting liars was supposedly used by a Persian king.

_____ 12. He was presumed to have a very special donkey, one that had the ability to tell an innocent person from a guilty one.

_____ 13. When a crime was committed, the suspects would be gathered in a hall next to the room that held the donkey.

_____ 14. According to directions, each suspect entered the room alone, found the donkey in the dark, and pulled its tail.

_____ 15. The donkey did the rest.

_____ 16. If an innocent person pulled the tail, the donkey was said to remain silent.

_____ 17. If a guilty person pulled the tail, the donkey would bray loudly.

_____ 18. In fact, the donkey's tail was dusted with graphite.

_____ 19. The guilty person emerged with clean hands because he or she wanted to avoid detection.

_____ 20. The king knew that the person with clean hands was guilty, and he proceeded with punishment.

Sentence Combining

The simple sentence, the most basic sentence in the English language, can be exceptionally useful and powerful. Some of the greatest statements in literature have been presented in this form. Its strength is in its singleness of purpose. However, a piece of writing made up of a long series of simple sentences is likely to be monotonous. Moreover, the form may suggest a separateness of ideas that does not serve your purpose well. If your ideas are closely related, some equal in importance and some not, you can work with patterns of sentence combining to show those relationships between ideas. These patterns are simply structures of coordination and subordination.

Coordination

If you want to communicate two ideas that are equally important and closely related, you certainly will want to place them close together, in a **compound sentence**. Consider this arrangement.

> (1) Looking forward to the play-off games of the National League West, we find a few surprises. (2) The Los Angeles Dodgers have not played well in August. (3) The San Francisco Giants have now won ten games in a row. (4) These two teams are tied for the lead. (5) Atlanta and Cincinnati are only a few games back.

The paragraph contains five sentences. All are related and the sequence of ideas is sound. But notice that the connection between ideas seems closer at two points. Sentences 2 and 3 stand in contrast. The writer can show that relationship by combining the sentences in either of two ways.

> The Los Angeles Dodgers have not played well in August, but the San Francisco Giants have now won ten games in a row.

or

> The Los Angeles Dodgers have not played well in August; however, the San Francisco Giants have now won ten games in a row.

In each instance the period is dropped and the two sentences are combined into one. The first sentence uses a comma and the coordinating conjunction *but*. The second uses the transitional connective *however*, preceded by a semicolon and followed by a comma.

Sentences 4 and 5 have an almost identical contrasting relationship and can be similarly combined. The revised paragraph might look like this:

> Looking forward to the playoff games in the National League West, we find a few surprises. The favored Los Angeles Dodgers have not played well in August, but the San Francisco Giants have now won ten games in a row. These two teams are tied for the lead; however, Atlanta and Cincinnati are only a few games back.

Obviously, not all sentences can be or should be combined. Notice what happens when we combine sentences 3 and 4:

> ILLOGICAL COMBINATION: The San Francisco Giants have now won ten games in a row, and these two teams are tied for the lead.

Sentences 1 and 2 also could not be combined effectively.

You, the writer, must make the choice. These are the questions to ask yourself: Are the ideas closely and logically related? Are the ideas of somewhat equal importance?

Relevant Punctuation

When you combine two sentences by using a coordinating conjunction, drop the period, change the capital letter to a small letter, and insert a comma before the coordinating conjunction (one of the seven words, the first letters of which comprise the acronym FANBOYS).

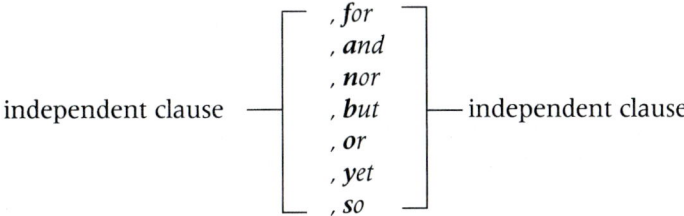

When you combine two sentences by using a semicolon, replace the period with a semicolon and change the capital letter to a small letter. If you wish to use a transitional connective, insert it after the semicolon and follow it with a comma. (Usually no comma follows *then, now, thus,* and *soon.*) The first letters of ten common transitional connectives comprise the acronym HOTSHOT CAT.

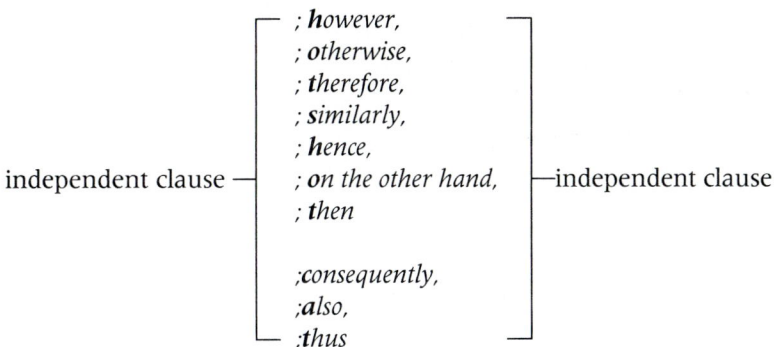

Other transitional connectives are *moreover, nevertheless,* and *in fact.*

Subordination

Whereas a compound sentence contains independent clauses that are equally important and closely related, a **complex sentence** combines ideas of unequal value in close relationship. The following two sentences can be combined as either a compound sentence or a complex sentence, depending on whether the writer thinks the ideas are of equal value.

>My neighbors are considerate.
>They never play loud music.

Combined as a compound sentence, suggesting that the ideas are of equal value, the new sentence looks like this:

>*My neighbors are considerate*, and *they never play loud music*.
>   independent clause   independent clause
>   (main idea)   (main idea)

Here are the same two ideas combined as a complex sentence, suggesting that the ideas are of unequal value:

<u>*Because my neighbors are considerate*</u>, <u>they never play loud music</u>.
        dependent clause   **independent clause**
     (less-important idea)   **(main idea)**

Although both of these forms, compound and complex, are correct, we are likely to believe that the complex form conveys the ideas more precisely in this sentence because one idea does seem to be more important—one idea depends on the other.

Thus if you have two sentences with closely related ideas and one is clearly more important than the other, you may want to consider combining them in a complex sentence. Compare these two paragraphs:

Version 1 contains six simple sentences, implying that the ideas are of equal value:

> (1) I was very upset. (2) The Fourth of July fireworks were especially loud. (3) My dog ran away. (4) The animal control officer made his morning rounds. (5) He found my dog in another part of town. (6) I am relieved.

Version 2, on the other hand, consists of two simple sentences and two complex sentences, showing that some ideas are more important than others:

> (1) I was very upset. (2) Because the Fourth of July fireworks were especially loud, my dog ran away. (3) When the animal control officer made his morning rounds, he found my dog in another part of town. (4) I am relieved.

You will probably consider Version 2 superior to Version 1. Sentences 2 and 3 are closely related, but 3 is more important. And sentences 4 and 5 are closely related, but 5 is more important. The revision made each pair into a complex sentence.

Although you could combine sentences 1 and 2, the result would be illogical because the wrong idea would be conveyed:

> ILLOGICAL COMBINATION: I was upset because the Fourth of July fireworks were especially loud.

The person is upset because the dog ran away, not because the fireworks were especially loud.

A complex sentence is composed of one independent clause and one or more dependent clauses. In combining two independent clauses in order to write a complex sentence, your first step is to decide on a subordinating word that will best show the relationship between the clauses. Among the most common are those represented by the now-familiar BAT WASHTUB acronym; they are shown here in context in complex sentences. Consider the meaning as well as the placement of each subordinating word.

> *Because* the storm hit, the game was canceled.
> *After* the storm passed, the clown dogs began to bark.
> *That* the incident occurred was a fact.
> *When* she read her poem, they were moved to fits of hysterics.
> He did not volunteer to work on the holiday, *although* the pay was good.
> No one has visited her *since* she moved into town.
> *How* they would abscond with the baked Alaska, he didn't know.
> They decided to wait *till* the cows came home.
> They refused to work *unless* they were allowed to wear chef hats.
> *Before* the session ended, all the "hep cats" blew some sweet sounds.

Other subordinating words are:

once	until	whenever	while
as	in order that	so that	if
even if	provided that	even though	where
wherever	rather than	than	whether
who	whoever	whom	whomever
which	whichever		

Relevant Punctuation

If the dependent clause comes *before* the main clause, set it off with a comma (as is done in this sentence):

Before you dive, be sure there is water in the pool.

If the dependent clause comes *after* or *within* the main clause, set if off only if the clause is not necessary to the meaning of the main clause or if the dependent clause begins with the word *although* or *though*:

Everyone *who tries* will pass this class.
(The dependent clause is necessary because one would not say, "Everyone will pass this class.")

John, *who tries,* will pass this class.
(The dependent clause is not necessary because one can say, "John will pass this class.")

He continued, *although* he was tired.

Coordination and Subordination

At times you may want to show the relationship of three or more ideas within one sentence. If that relationship involves two or more main ideas and one or more supporting ideas, the combination can be stated in a **compound-complex sentence** (two or more independent clauses and one or more dependent clauses).

<u>*Before he learned how to operate a word-processor,*</u>
    dependent clause

<u>*he had trouble with his typewritten assignments,*</u>
    independent clause

but now <u>*he produces clean, attractive material.*</u>
    independent clause

In our previous discussion of the complex sentence, we presented this group of six sentences:

I was very upset. The Fourth of July fireworks were especially loud. My dog ran away. The animal control officer made his morning rounds. He found my dog in another part of town. I am relieved.

We then converted the group of six sentences to four:

I was very upset. Because the Fourth of July fireworks were especially loud, my dog ran away. When the animal control officer made his morning rounds, he found my dog in another part of town. I am relieved.

But what if we wanted to show an even closer relationship of ideas? One solution would be to use coordination and subordination and to combine the two complex sentences in this way (the italicized sentence is compound-complex):

I was very upset. *Because the Fourth of July fireworks were especially loud, my dog ran away; but when the animal control officer made his morning rounds, he found my dog in another part of town.* I am relieved.

Relevant Punctuation

If the compound or compound-complex sentence has one or more commas in the first clause, you may want to use a semicolon before the coordinating conjunction between the two clauses. Its purpose is to show the reader very clearly the division between the two independent clauses. The preceding example illustrates this use of the semicolon.

Other Methods of Combining Ideas

You have learned how to combine simple sentences into compound, complex, and compound-complex sentences that show the coordination and subordination of ideas. There are numerous other methods of combining ideas, too. Here are two that you are likely to use in your own writing:

- Use an appositive, a noun phrase that immediately follows a noun or pronoun and renames it.

    Susan is the leading scorer on the team.
    Susan is a quick and strong player.
    Susan, *a quick and strong player,* is the leading scorer on the team.

- Use a prepositional phrase.

    Dolly Parton wrote a song about a coat.
    The coat has many colors
    Dolly Parton wrote a song about a coat *of many colors.*

EXERCISE 13

Combine each group of sentences into a single sentence by using a pattern of coordination. (See the Answer Key for answers.)

1. Cobras are among the most feared of all snakes.
   They are not the deadliest of all snakes.

   Cobras do not coil before they strike.
   They cannot strike for a long distance.

2. Cobras do not have a hood.
   They flatten their neck by moving their ribs when they are nervous or frightened.

   Cobras use their poison in two ways.
   One way is by injecting venom with their fangs.
   Another way is by spitting venom at their victims.

3. Human beings will not die from the venom that has been spit.
   It can cause blindness if it is not washed from the eyes.

   A person can die from a cobra bite.
   Death may come in only a few hours.

4. Snake charmers have long worked with cobras.
   They use a snake, a basket, and a flute.

   The snakes cannot *hear* the music.
   They respond to the rhythmic movements of the charmers.

   The snake charmers are hardly ever in danger of being bitten.
   They defang the cobras or sew their mouths shut.

5. Most cobras will flee from people.
   They attack if they are cornered or if they are guarding their eggs.

   The tiny mongoose is the enemy of the cobra.
   It uses its quickness and sharp teeth to kill the cobra.

EXERCISE 14

Combine each group of sentences into a single sentence by using a pattern of coordination or subordination.

1. Henry David Thoreau grew tired of living in society.
   He wanted to face his essential self.

   He built a cabin in the woods.
   He lived there for more than a year.

2. Gilligan had a plan.
   He would float in a shipping crate to Hawaii.

   It would be a surprise.
   He would send help to his friends on the island.

3. A storm came up.
   Gilligan's craft sank in three feet of water in the lagoon.
   The skipper cried bitter tears over the loss of his little buddy.

   The professor made a submarine out of coconut shells, Mrs. Howell's corset,
     Ginger's jewelry, and fish bones.
   Gilligan was rescued.

4. Captain Ahab set sail for the South Seas.
   Captain Ahab had an obsession.

   He wanted to kill the great white whale.
   The name of the great white whale was Moby Dick.

   The captain and the whale had their encounter.
   Moby Dick was easily the victor.

5. Hamlet was sad.
   His father was dead.
   His mother had married his uncle.

   Hamlet believed that his uncle had killed his father.
   Hamlet plotted to kill his uncle.

6. Romeo and Juliet were young.
   They fell in love.

   Their families were feuding.
   Romeo and Juliet decided to run away.

   They tried to trick their families.
   Their plans turned sour.
   They both died.

7. The contestant spun the wheel one more time.
   Vanna White clapped her hands with glee.

   Pat Sajak made a wry joke about greed.
   Only one letter remained.

8. The wheel stopped.
   The contestant lost his turn.

   The audience groaned.
   Vanna White slumped, and Pat Sajak comforted her sad heart.

9. Several tabloids have reported that Elvis has not left us.
   He has been sighted in several parts of the country and even on other planets.

   The tabloids report that the King is just tired and wants privacy.
   They give credit to unnamed reliable sources.

10. Ernest Hemingway wrote *The Old Man and the Sea.*
    His central character is Santiago.
    Santiago is a fisherman with a string of bad luck.

    He catches a fish.
    He loses most of it to sharks.

    He struggles courageously.
    He achieves a moral victory.

    Santiago is true.
    He obeys his code.

Balance in Sentence Writing

Parallel structure is based on repeated or balanced elements. The unbalanced sentence is awkward at best and misleading at worst.

Basic Principles of Parallelism

In simple terms, **parallelism** is a balancing of one structure with another of the same kind. When that balance is anticipated but the structures are different, the result is an awkward nonparallelism.

NONPARALLEL: Larry Bird's reputation is based on his ability in *passing, shooting,* and *to rebound.*

PARALLEL: Larry Bird's reputation is based on his ability in *passing, shooting,* and *rebounding.*

The words *passing* and *shooting* are of the same kind (verb-like words used as nouns, called gerunds), but the next two words in the nonparallel example, *to rebound,* are a preposition and verb (called an infinitive). You don't have to know terms in order to realize that there is a problem in smoothness and emphasis. Just read the material aloud. Then compare it with the parallel statement; *to rebound* is changed to the gerund *rebounding* to make a sentence that's easy on the ear.

Parallelism as it relates to sentence structure may be achieved by joining words with similar words: nouns with nouns, adjectives with adjectives, adverbs with adverbs, and so forth:

> *Men, women,* and *children* enjoy the show. (nouns)
> The players are *excited, eager,* and *enthusiastic.* (adjectives)
> The author wrote *skillfully* and *quickly.* (adverbs)

Parallel structure may also be gained by joining groups of words with other similar groups of words: prepositional phrase with prepositional phrase, clause with clause, sentence with sentence:

> She fell *in love* and *out of love* in a few minutes. (prepositional phrases)
> *Who he was* and *where he came from* did not matter. (clauses)
> *He came in a hurry. He left in a hurry.* (sentences)

Signal Words

Some words signal parallel structure. If you use *and,* the items joined by this word will almost always be of the same form; if they aren't, then *and* is probably inappropriate.

> The weather is hot *and* humid. (*and* joins adjectives)
> The car *and* trailer are parked in front of the house. (*and* joins nouns)

The same principle is true for *but,* though it implies a direct contrast. Where contrasts are being drawn, parallel structure is essential to clarify those contrasts.

> He purchased a Dodger Dog, *but* I chose the Stadium Peanuts. (*but* joins contrasting clauses)
> She made an A in math *but* failed her art class. (*but* joins contrasting verbs)

You should regard all of the coordinating conjunctions (FANBOYS) as signals for parallel structure.

Combination Signal Words

The words *and* and *but* are the most common individual signal words used with parallel constructions. Sometimes, however, **combination words** signal the need for parallelism or balance. The following are the most common combination conjunctions used in making comparisons: *either/or, neither/nor, not only/but also, both/and, whether/or.* Now consider this faulty sentence and two possible corrections:

> NONPARALLEL: *Either* we will win this game *or* go out fighting. (After *either* we have a clause; after *or* we have a verb.)
>
> PARALLEL: We will *either* win this game *or* go out fighting. (The correction is made by moving the word *either,* thereby balancing a verb, *win,* with a verb, *go.*)
>
> PARALLEL: *Either* we will win this game, *or* we will go out fighting. (The correction is made by inserting a comma and the words *we will,* thereby balancing a clause with a clause.)

EXERCISE 15

Mark each sentence as P (parallel) or NP (not parallel). Rewrite the sentences with non-parallel structure. (See Answer Key for answers.)

_____ 1. They push education aside if it interferes with love or the moment it is no longer fun.

_____ 2. She has to assume responsibility for her own decisions and has her own duties.

_____ 3. Reading the assignment and to take lecture notes are equally important.

_____ 4. Benjamin Franklin was a statesman, a writer, and he was also an inventor.

_____ 5. Jeanne's methods were using puns, homonyms, and to tell jokes.

_____ 6. The prime minister recommended an increase in taxes and that several fees be increased.

_____ 7. Mr. Roberts found teaching in the classroom more inspiring than to manage the school.

_____ 8. To give is as important as receiving.

_____ 9. The ghouls tried to gain entrance first by persuasion and then to force.

_____ 10. The new governor has already shown herself to be not only charming but also a person of political sophistication.

_____ 11. Brooke is not only captain of the softball team but also of the fencing team.

_____ 12. She was disappointed both in their performance and their attitude.

_____ 13. The conscientious objectors came to listen and with questions.

_____ 14. Taking the oral examination is usually harder than to write the dissertation.

_____ 15. His trouble was that he regarded every foreigner as ignorant and a liar.

_____ 16. The General Assembly understood neither the speaker's words nor what his purpose was.

_____ 17. Tarzan explained both the causes of the deaths and his plan to save the village.

_____ 18. General Eisenhower was not only commander of the American forces but of all the Allied armies in Europe.

_____ 19. Martin Luther King, Jr., was both a preacher and he was a powerful political influence.

_____ 20. The psychologist recommended plenty of work, friends, and eating good food.

EXERCISE 16

Mark each sentence as P (parallel) or NP (not parallel). Rewrite the sentences with non-parallel structure.

_____ 1. Where he had been and his experiences did not matter to the monsignor.

_____ 2. The students, classified employees, and those who teach all bear responsibility.

_____ 3. She had two ambitions: to learn and advancing.

_____ 4. He wrote the essay swiftly and with skill.

_____ 5. John decided that either he must go to work or quit eating.

_____ 6. Jill arrived with happiness. She left sadly.

_____ 7. The weather is hot and it feels muggy.

_____ 8. Neither snow, sleet, nor the raining will stop me.

_____ 9. To know her is loving her.

_____ 10. This country is known as one of the people, for the people, and run by the people.

_____ 11. José Canseco is a famous baseball player and who went from Oakland to Texas.

_____ 12. Jazz is a music form based on improvisation, performance, and it uses African rhythms.

_____ 13. Ruthanne decided to either play the saxophone or the clarinet.

_____ 14. Charley gave not only thanks to his parents but also his fellow students.

_____ 15. Jannel used both her wits and her courage to survive the ordeal.

_____ 16. To go or not going—that was the question.

_____ 17. Who would go and the mission of the person were major concerns.

_____ 18. The integrity of the whole program depended on what she would say and her reaction.

_____ 19. He intended to go to work, mind his own business, and then he would go home.

_____ 20. He shouted, "Who are you and do you want something?"

Verbs

Community Dialects and Standard Usage

"Nonstandard" usage may be part of what we call a community dialect, one that serves a person well within a given community of speakers. However, outside that community it may bring unfavorable attention to itself.

Consider this hypothetical situation. I am your teacher. At our first class meeting, I say to you, "I be your educational leader in here." At that moment, the English department head bursts into the room and shouts, "Don't listen to him. He don't know his verbs, and he ain't qualified to learn you." Chances are, you would rightly question the quality of teaching in that department. The problem would not be one of understanding—you would know what the speakers meant. The problem instead involves appropriate use of language. Both the chairperson and I would be using verbs that are not customarily used by people in our roles and situations. Even if *you* sometimes use some of those words in those ways, you might be bothered and disappointed by *our* doing so.

If, however, in a certain community of speakers, one person says, "He don't look good today," and that person's companion says, "She don't either," then there is no problem, because there the word *don't*, used with the third-person-singular subject, draws no unfavorable attention and understanding is clear.

Community dialects may be highly expressive and colorful. Popular songs and many television programs often use them well. Some people who use only a community dialect are much more gifted in communicating—explaining things, telling a story, getting to the point—than those who use only the standard dialect. And some people can use either the standard or the community dialect with equal skill. Those people are, in a limited sense, bilingual.

That said, we turn to our concern in this chapter, the standard use of language—and specifically in this section, the standard use of verbs. Standard usage is advantageous because it is appropriate for the kind of writing and speaking you are likely to do in pursuing your college work and future career.

Verbs can be divided into categories labeled *regular* and *irregular*, depending on their forms. The **regular verbs** use an *-ed* ending to indicate past tense (meaning time). For example, you would say, "I *need* this instruction now," for present tense and "I *needed* this instruction last year" for past tense. In **irregular verbs**, the past tense forms vary widely. The following patterns will show the difference between a community dialect and the standard dialect for a regular verb (*walk*) and three irregular verbs (*do*, *be*, and *have*).

Regular Verb: walk	Community Dialect	Standard English
Present Tense	I, you, we, they — walks he, she, it — walk	I, you, we, they — walk he, she, it — walks
Past Tense	I, you, we, they, he, she, it — walk	I, you, we, they, he, she, it — walked

Regular Verb: do	Community Dialect	Standard English
Present Tense	I, you, we, they — does he, she, it — do	I, you, we, they — do he, she, it — does
Past Tense	I, you, we, they, he, she, it — done	I, you, we, they, he, she, it — did

Irregular Verb: be	Community Dialect		Standard English	
Present Tense	I		I	am
	you, we, they	be, is, or no verb	you, we, they	are
	he, she, it		he, she, it	is
Past Tense	I, he, she, it	were	I, he, she, it	was
	we		we	
	you, they	was	you, they	were

Irregular Verb: have	Community Dialect		Standard English	
Present Tense	I, you, we, they	has	I, you, we, they	have
	he, she, it	have	he, she, it	has
Past Tense	I, you, we, they	have or has	I, you, we, they	had
	he, she, it		he, she, it	

Regular and Irregular Verbs

Whereas regular verbs are predictable—having an *-ed* ending for past and past-participle forms—irregular verbs, as we have seen and as the term suggests, follow no definite pattern. Some similar-sounding irregular verbs pattern differently.

shake	shook	shaken
make	made	made
ring	rang	rung
swing	swung	swung
bring	brought	brought

The following lists give you the basic forms for both regular and irregular verbs. We suggest that you go through the list of irregular verbs systematically and discover which ones you do not know; then master them. The words *be, is, am, are, were, have, has,* and *had* were covered in the preceding section.

The **present tense** form of most regular and irregular verbs fits *I, you,* and *they* as it is. For *he, she,* and *it,* add an *-s,* an *-es,* or if the present tense form ends in *-y,* drop the *-y* and add *-ies:*

I *drink* a gallon of Kool-aid each day.
She *drinks* two gallons of Kool-aid each day.

The **past tense** of regular verbs is formed by adding *-ed* to the base or by dropping the ending *-y* and adding *-ied* to a verb like *marry*. Past-tense forms of irregular verbs vary:

We *drank* Kool-aid at the pool.

The **past participle** form is used with a helping verb or verbs such as *has, have, had,* or *will have:*

He *has drunk* Kool-aid since he was three.

The **present participle** form is the present-tense form plus *-ing*. It must be used with helping verbs such as *is, am, are, was,* or *were:*

I *am drinking* Kool-aid while I write this sentence.

Because this form presents no significant problems for most writers, it is not included in the list. You should note, however, that the present participle used as a verb without a helping verb will make a fragment, not a sentence. No word ending in *-ing* can be a verb all by itself:

He *going* to town. (fragment)
He *is going* to town. (correct)

Regular Verbs

- **Present Tense** For *he, she,* and *it,* add an *-s* or an *-es*. For some words ending in *-y*, drop the *-y* and add *-ies*. This base form can also be used with the words *do, does, did, may, shall, will, could, might, should, would,* and *must*.

- **Past Tense** Add *-ed* to the base form, or if the word ends in *-y* preceded by a consonant, drop the *-y* and add *-ied*.

- **Past Participle** Use the past tense form with helping words such as *have, has,* or *had*.

Present	*Past*	*Past Participle*
ask	asked	asked
answer	answered	answered
cry	cried	cried
decide	decided	decided
enjoy	enjoyed	enjoyed
finish	finished	finished
happen	happened	happened
learn	learned	learned
like	liked	liked
love	loved	loved
need	needed	needed
open	opened	opened
start	started	started
suppose	supposed	supposed
walk	walked	walked
want	wanted	wanted

Irregular Verbs

- **Present Tense** For *he, she,* and *it,* add an *-s* or an *-es*. For some words ending in *-y*, drop the *-y* and add *-ies*. This base form can also be used with the words *do, does, did, may, shall, will, could, might, should, would,* and *must*.

- **Past Tense** Use the form shown below.

- **Past Participle** Use the form shown below with helping words such as *have, has,* or *had*.

Present	Past	Past Participle
arise	arose	arisen
awake	awoke (awaked)	awaked
become	became	become
begin	began	begun
bend	bent	bent
blow	blew	blown
break	broke	broken
bring	brought	brought
buy	bought	bought
catch	caught	caught
choose	chose	chosen
cling	clung	clung
come	came	come
creep	crept	crept
deal	dealt	dealt
dive	dived (dove)	dived
drink	drank	drunk
drive	drove	driven
eat	ate	eaten
feel	felt	felt
fight	fought	fought
fling	flung	flung
flow	flowed	flowed
fly	flew	flown
forget	forgot	forgotten
freeze	froze	frozen
get	got	got
go	went	gone
grow	grew	grown
kneel	knelt	knelt
know	knew	known
lead	led	led
leave	left	left
lose	lost	lost
mean	meant	meant
read	read	read
ride	rode	ridden
ring	rang	rung
seek	sought	sought
shine	shone	shone
shoot	shot	shot
sing	sang	sung
sink	sank	sunk
slay	slew	slain
sleep	slept	slept
slink	slunk	slunk
speak	spoke	spoken
spend	spent	spent
spring	sprang	sprung
steal	stole	stolen
stink	stank (stunk)	stunk
sweep	swept	swept
swim	swam	swum

Present	Past	Past Participle
swing	swung	swung
take	took	taken
teach	taught	taught
tear	tore	torn
think	thought	thought
throw	threw	thrown
weep	wept	wept
wring	wrung	wrung
write	wrote	written

"Problem" Verbs

The following pairs of verbs are especially troublesome and confusing: *lie* and *lay, sit* and *set,* and *rise* and *raise.* One way to tell them apart is to remember that the words *lay, set,* and *raise* take objects and the others do not. In the examples, the italicized words are objects.

Present Tense	Meaning	Past Tense	Past Participle	Example
lie	to rest	lay	lain	I lay down to rest.
lay	to place something	laid	laid	I laid the *book* on the table.
sit	to rest	sat	sat	I sat in the chair.
set	to place something	set	sat	I set the *basket* on the floor.
rise	to go up	rose	risen	The smoke rose quickly.
raise	to lift	raised	raised	She raised the *question*.

EXERCISE 17

In each sentence, the last verb is in the wrong tense. Cross it out and write the correct form above it. (See the Answer Key for answers.)

1. Francis Bacon said that reading made a full man.

2. The tutor had gone over the metaphors many times before Lisa take the test.

3. Sydney was always surprised that only a few students in every class knew what an iambic foot was.

4. After having worked in the shoe store for twelve years Kristin quits to take up computer programming.

5. We heard a crash in the kitchen, but the embarrassed hostess doesn't explain it.

6. Janet has only the bibliography page to type before the lights went out.

7. No one who has a full-time job got a fellowship this year.

8. Jorgensen proposes in the first act, but he will marry another woman in the second act.

9. The reporter didn't know that *Prudence* was a female's name.

10. Whitehead, the philosopher and mathematician, said that imagination was a contagious disease.

11. The minister offered to heal anyone of any illness; then he asks for a love offering.

12. He gives her a beautiful diamond; then she breaks the engagement and kept the diamond.

13. As Pam lectures, she had the habit of twitching her nose.

14. The guide liked our group because jokes were passed back and forth and are really enjoyed.

15. When little Lizzie went to bed crying, Bob comes up to comfort her.

16. Bruce thought we added Alaska because we need more people in the United States.

17. Frank fell asleep before he finishes the last page of the manuscript.

18. The thing we wanted most was to have told him we will always be his friends.

19. Pat thinks he is seeing things when a man handed him the money.

20. We drove past the church where the people were milling around and the minister is shaking everybody's hand.

EXERCISE 18

Cross out the incorrect verb form.

1. Keith (knew, knowed) he could not finish the term paper that semester.

2. They (dragged, drug, drugged) the cart into the back yard.

3. I was sure that I hadn't (ate, eaten) the lobster.

4. When we arrived, the windows were (broke, broked, broken).

5. Robin (dive, dived) from the high board and swam over to us.

6. Margie had (spread, spreaded) the maps out on the table before the meeting.

7. Have they (began, begun) to gather that material this early?

8. Gloria (swimmed, swam, swum) that distance twice last week.

9. The water pipes have (burst, busted, bursted) again.

10. I (ran, run) over to Colleen's house for help.

11. Sharon (saw, seen) us come in and ran out the back door.

12. Philip has (grew, growed, grown) three inches since last summer.

13. Before Keith (came, come) in to supper, he mowed the grass.

14. After he had (throwed, thrown) the javelin, he walked over to the stands and talked with Linda.

15. If Pat had (wore, worn) a tie, it would have been a surprise to all of us.

16. When we (awoke, awaked), we found the presents under the tree.

17. I (done, did) him a favor many years ago.

18. Liz (drank, drunk) the water and hurried back to the field.

19. Holly (fling, flung) the papers in all directions and rushed out of the meeting.

20. We (use, used) to cross his lawn before he put up a fence.

EXERCISE 19

Cross out the incorrect verb form.

1. The book is (lying, laying) on top of the bureau.

2. Will you (receive, received) this offer of assistance at this late date?

3. His recent decision will certainly (change, changed) drastic changes in our policy.

4. When he heard her call, he (rose, raised) and left the room.

5. That dog can (sit, set) in the yard for hours and bark constantly.

6. Marcia (done, did) many chores before she left for school.

7. Why are you (sitting, setting) those plants in the hot sun?

8. My mother (don't, doesn't) understand why Victor takes so long to come home from kindergarten.

9. Two little boys (drowned, drownded) in the river yesterday.

10. The spy (fool, fooled) his captor by disguising himself as a workman.

11. My cousins will (left, leave) from Europe soon.

12. We (learn, learned) from his conversation that he did not wish to go again.

13. Jean hasn't been able to (taught, teach) those boys anything.

14. Why don't you (try and, try to) come over for a few minutes this evening?

15. The police officers would not (see, saw) us cross the bridge during the heavy rainstorm.

16. You (lie, lay) down here and rest for a few minutes before class.

17. The cost of those articles has (raised, risen) considerably since the first of the year.

18. Pam (rose, raised) the window and waved to me as I passed.

19. My brother (lay, laid) the money on the table and looked hopefully at Mother.

20. Please (sit, set) the shoes down on the rack and come over here.

Subject-Verb Agreement

This section is concerned with **number agreement** between subjects and verbs. The basic principle of subject-verb agreement of number is that if the subject is singular, the verb should be singular, and if the subject is plural, the verb should be plural. There are ten major problem areas. In the following examples, the true subjects and verbs are italicized.

1. *Do not let words that come between the subject and verb affect agreement.*

   - Modifying phrases and clauses frequently come between the subject and verb:

     The various *types* of drama *were* not *discussed*.
     Henry, who is hitting third, *is* the best player.
     The *price* of those shoes *is* too high.

   - Certain unfamiliar prepositions cause trouble. The following words are prepositions, not conjunctions: *along with, as well as, besides, in addition to, including, together with*. The words that function as objects of prepositions cannot also be subjects of the sentence.

     The *coach*, along with the players, *protests* the decision.

   - In compound subjects in which one subject is positive and one subject is negative, the verb agrees with the positive subject.

     Phillip, not the other boys, *was* the culprit.

2. *Do not let inversions (verb precedes subject, not the normal order) affect the agreement of subject and verb.*

   - Verbs and other words may come before the subject. Do not let them affect the agreement. To understand subject-verb relationships, recast the sentence in normal word order.

     Are *Juan* and his *sister* at home? (question form)
     Juan and his *sister are* at home. (normal order)

   - A sentence filler is a word that is grammatically independent of other words in the sentence. The most common fillers are *there* and *here*. Even though it precedes the verb, it should not be treated as the subject.

     There are many *reasons* for his poor work.
     (Using *is* as a verb in this sentence would have been faulty subject-verb agreement.)

3. ***A singular verb agrees with a singular indefinite pronoun.***

- Most indefinite pronouns are singular.

  Each of the women *is* ready at this time.
  Neither of the women *is* ready at this time.
  One of the children *is* not paying attention.

- Certain indefinite pronouns do not clearly express either a singular or plural number. Agreement, therefore, depends on the meaning of the sentence. These pronouns are *all, any, none,* and *some*.

  All of the melon *was* good.
  All of the melons *were* good.
  None of the pie *is* acceptable.
  None of the pies *are* acceptable.

4. ***Two or more subjects joined by* and *usually take a plural verb.***

   The *captain* and the *sailors were* happy to be ashore.
   The *trees* and *shrubs need* more care.

- If the parts of a compound subject mean one and the same person or thing, the verb is singular.

  The *secretary* and *treasurer is* not present.

- When *each* or *every* modify singular subjects joined by *and,* the verb is singular.

  Each *boy* and each *girl brings* a donation.
  Each *woman* and *man has asked* the same questions.

5. ***Alternate subjects—that is, subjects joined by* or, nor, either/or, neither/nor, not only/but also—*should be handled in the following manner:***

- If the subjects are both singular, the verb is singular.

  Rosa or *Alicia is* responsible.

- If the subjects are plural, the verb is plural.

  Neither the *students* nor the *teachers were* impressed by his comments.

- If one of the subjects is singular and the other subject is plural, the verb agrees with the nearer subject.

  Either the Garcia *boys* or their *father goes* to the hospital each day.

6. ***Collective nouns—*team, family, group, crew, gang, class, *and the like—take a singular verb if the verb is considered a unit, a plural verb if the group is considered as a number of individuals.***

   The *jury are voting* on a verdict.
   (Here the individuals are acting not as a unit but separately. If you don't like the way this sounds, substitute "The members of the jury are voting on a verdict.")

7. ***Titles of books, essays, short stories, and plays, a word spoken of as a word, and the names of businesses take a singular verb.***

   Canterbury Tales was written by Geoffrey Chaucer.
   Markle Brothers has a sale this week.

8. ***Sums of money, distances, and measurements are followed by a singular verb when a unit is meant, a plural verb when the individual elements are considered separately.***

> *Three dollars was* the price. (unit)
> *Three dollars were* lying there. (individual)
> *Five years is* a long time. (unit)
> The *first five years were* difficult ones. (individual)

9. ***Be careful of agreement with nouns ending in -s. Several nouns ending in -s take a singular verb—for example,* aeronautics, civics, economics, ethics, measles, mumps.**

> *Mumps is* an extremely unpleasant disease.
> *Economics is* my major field of study.

10. ***Some nouns have only a plural form and so take only a plural verb—for example,* clothes, fireworks, headquarters, scissors, trousers.**

> His *trousers are* badly wrinkled.
> Marv's *clothes were* stylish and expensive.

EXERCISE 20

Cross out the incorrect verb form. (See Answer Key for answers.)

1. Where can you go to find a place where there (is, are) no tin cans to spoil the view?

2. We have no case if neither the police nor the detectives (has, have) produced a suspect.

3. (Has, Have) either of the winners admitted cheating?

4. Every child who camps in the woods (eat, eats) more there than at home.

5. We wanted to be sure all of the dishes (were, was) tasted by everyone.

6. Several, not just one, of his answers (is, are) right.

7. On one occasion, a husband and wife (was, were) elected co-presidents.

8. Macaroni and cheese (is, are) the regular chef's special on Fridays.

9. A photographer knows that each pose and each lighting shift (change, changes) the subject's appearance.

10. Every pen and pencil in the office (has, have) a clip attached.

11. The captain said either the mates or the lieutenant (was, were) able to guide the ship.

12. It looks as if neither the treasury nor the miscellaneous funds (is, are) enough to cover expenses.

13. Old Mt. Triton (attracts, attract) artists every fall.

14. That lawyer always (want, wants) to defend the underdog.

15. The students wait until the faculty (get, gets) in line.

16. *Knots and Splices* (tell, tells) about the way to make a hammock from cord.

17. Three months (seem, seems) like a long vacation to a businessperson.

18. Aesthetics (is, are) often as much a philosophical consideration as artistic.

19. At the end of the conference two hours (is, are) spent on reviewing and summarizing.

20. John asked if mathematics (was, were) different from arithmetic.

EXERCISE 21

Cross out the incorrect verb form.

1. The many kinds of poetry (is, are) included.

2. Jane, one of the best players, (are, is) lost for the season.

3. The cost of those victories (is, are) not soon forgotten.

4. My neighbor, along with fifteen of his rowdy friends, (are, is) noisy almost every night.

5. Cindy Jenkins, not the other Cindys, (is, are) the one I am talking about.

6. (Is, Are) Bill and Joan coming to the party?

7. There (is, are) many questions and few answers.

8. Each of the students (are, is) prepared for the challenge.

9. Neither of the workers (cares, care) who takes the first break.

10. One of the professors (talk, talks) louder than the other.

11. Some of the apple pie (was, were) edible.

12. Some of the apples (was, were) edible.

13. Do your car or your shoes (need, needs) polishing?

14. Neither my shoes nor my car (need, needs) polishing.

15. Make certain that every adult and child (get, gets) the message.

16. The manager and coach (is, are) sitting in the dugout.

17. *Microbe Hunters* (is, are) a famous book about biology.

18. Penneys (celebrate, celebrates) its annual Blue Moon Sale this week.

19. Civics (is, are) my favorite class.

20. The fireworks (explode, explodes) on the stadium infield.

Consistency in Tense

Consider this statement:

> We went (1) downtown, and then we watch (2) a movie. Later we met (3) some friends from school, and we all go (4) to the mall. For most of the evening, we play (5) video games in arcades. It was (6) a typical but rather uneventful summer day.

Does the shifting verb tense bother you (to say nothing about with the lack of development of ideas)? It should! The writer makes several unnecessary changes. Verbs 1, 3, and 6 are in the past tense and verbs 2, 4, and 5 are in the present tense. Changing all verbs to past tense makes the statement much smoother:

> We went downtown, and then we watched a movie. Later we met some friends from school, and we all went to the mall. For most of the evening, we played video games in arcades. It was a typical but rather uneventful summer day.

In other instances you might want to maintain a consistent present tense. There are no inflexible rules about selecting a tense for a certain kind of writing, but you should be consistent, changing tense only for a good reason.

It is worth noting that the present tense will usually serve you best in writing about literature, even if the literature was written long in the past:

> *Moby Dick* is a novel about Captain Ahab's obsession with a great white whale. He *sets* sail with a full crew of sailors who *think* they *are going* on merely another whaling voyage. Most of the men *are* experienced seamen.

The past tense is likely to serve you best in writing about your personal experiences and about historical events (though the present tense can often be used effectively to establish the feeling of intimacy and immediacy):

> In the summer of 1991, Hurricane Bob *hit* the Atlantic coast region. It *came* ashore near Cape Hatteras and *moved* north. The winds *reached* a speed of more than ninety miles per hour on Cape Cod but then *slackened* by the time Bob reached Maine.

Active and Passive Voice

Which of these sentences sounds better to you?

>Don Mattingly slammed a home run.
>A home run was slammed by Don Mattingly.

They both carry the same message, but the first expresses it more effectively. The subject *(Don Mattingly)* is the actor. The verb *(slammed)* is the action. The direct object *(home run)* is the receiver of the action. The second sentence lacks the vitality of the first because the receiver of the action is the subject and the doer is embedded in the prepositional phrase at the end of the sentence.

The first sentence demonstrates the **active voice.** It has an active verb (one that accepts a direct object), and the action moves from the beginning to the end of the sentence. The second exhibits the **passive voice** (with the action reflecting back on the subject). When given a choice, you should usually employ the active voice. It promotes energy and directness.

The passive voice, though not usually the preferred form, does have its uses:

- When the doer of the action is unknown or unimportant

>My car was stolen.   (The doer, a thief, is unknown.)

- When the receiver of the action is more important than the doer

>My neighbor was permanently   (The neighbor's suffering
>disabled by an irresponsible   is the focus, not the
>drunk driver.   drunk driver.)

As you can see, the passive construction places the doer at the end of a prepositional phrase (as in the second example) or does not include the doer in the statement at all (as in the first example). Instead, passive voice places the receiver of the action in the subject position, and presents the verb in its past-tense form preceded by a *to be* helper. The transformation is a simple one:

>She read the book.   (active)
>The book was read by her.   (passive)

Because most voice-related problems involve the unnecessary and ineffective use of the passive form, the exercises will concentrate on identifying passive voice and changing it to active.

EXERCISE 22

Rewrite these sentences to convert the verbs from passive to active voice.

1. A letter has been written by me to you.

2. An honest dollar was never made by his ancestors, and now he is following in their fingerprints.

3. Her tongue is so long a letter can be sealed by her after she puts it in the mailbox.

4. The instructor was given a much-deserved medal of valor by the president of the school.

5. Few people noticed that most of the work was done by the quiet students.

6. The ballgame was interrupted by the bats catching flies in the outfield.

7. The commotion at the apathy convention was caused by a person who attended.

8. The air was filled with speeches by him.

9. He doesn't have an enemy, but he is hated by all his friends.

10. His lips are never passed by a lie—he talks through his nose.

Strong Predication

The verb is an extremely important part of any sentence. Therefore, the verb (often called the predicate) should be chosen with care. Some of the most widely used verbs are the "being" verbs: *is, was, were, are, am*. We couldn't get along in English without them, but often because of their commonness, writers use them when more forceful and effective words are available. Revising and editing for better verbs is sometimes called "strengthening predication."

Consider these examples:

WEAK PREDICATION: He is the leader of the people.
STRONG PREDICATION: He leads the people.

WEAK PREDICATION: She was the first to finish.
STRONG PREDICATION: She finished first.

EXERCISE 23

Rewrite the following sentences to strengthen the weak verbs (predicates).

1. He is the writer of that essay.

2. She was the driver of the speeding car.

3. He was the player of the guitar.

4. They were the leaders of the entire region in sales.

5. The medicine was a cure for the cold.

6. The last entertainer was the winner of the award.

7. The yowling cat was the cause of my waking up last night.

8. The mechanic is the fixer of my car.

9. He is in the process of tying his shoes.

10. She is a shoe salesperson.

Pronouns

All that you have studied so far in grammar and sentence structure will help you to work on the problems of pronoun case, pronoun-antecedent agreement, and pronoun reference.

Case

Case is the form a pronoun takes as it fills a position in a sentence. Words such as *you* and *it* do not change, but others do, and they change in predictable ways. For example, *I* is a subject word and *me* is an object word. As you refer to yourself, you will select a pronoun that fits a certain part of sentence structure. You say, "*I* will write the paper," not "*Me* will write the paper," because *I* is in the subject position. But you say, "She will give the apple to *me*," not "She will give the apple to *I*," because *me* is in the object position. These are pronouns that do change:

Subject (Subjective)	*Object (Objective)*
I	me
he	him
she	her
we	us
they	them
who	whom

Subjective Case

Subjective pronouns can fill two positions in a sentence.

1. Pronouns in the subjective case may fill subject positions.
   Some will be easy to identify because they are at the beginning of the sentence.

   I dance in the park.
   He dances in the park.
   She dances in the park.
   We dance in the park.
   They dance in the park.
   Who is dancing in the park?

   Others will be more difficult to identify because they are not at the beginning of a sentence and may not appear to be part of a clause. The words *than* and *as* are signals for these special arrangements, which can be called incompletely stated clauses.

   He is taller than *I* (am).
   She is faster than *we* (are).
   We work as hard as *they* (do).

   The words *am, are,* and *do,* which by understanding complete the clauses, have been omitted. We are actually saying, "He is taller than *I* am," "She is faster than *we are,*" and "We work as hard as *they do.*" The italicized pronouns are subjects of "understood" verbs.

2. Pronouns in the subjective case may refer back to the subject. They may follow a form of the verb *to be*, such as *was, were, are, am,* and *is*.

> I believe it is *he*.
> It was *she* who spoke.
> The victims were *they*.

Some will not refer back through a verb:

> The leading candidates—Juan, Darnelle, Steve, Kimlieu, and *I*—made speeches.

Objective Case

Objective pronouns can also fill two positions in sentences.

1. Pronouns in the objective case may fill object positions. They may be objects after the verb.

   > I gave *him* the message. (indirect object)
   > We saw *her* in the library. (direct object)

   They may be objects after prepositions.

   > The problem was clear to both of *us*.
   > I offered the opportunity to *him*.

2. They may refer back to object words.

   > They gave the results to us—Steve and *me*.
   >   (referring back to an object of preposition)
   > The judge addressed the defendants—Judy and *him*.
   >   (referring back to a receiver of the action, the direct object)

In short, some pronouns are subjects or refer to subjects and, therefore, are subject words *(I, we, he, she, they, who)*; these pronouns are in the subjective case. Others are objects or refer to objects and therefore are object words *(me, us, him, her, them, whom)*; those pronouns are in the objective case.

Techniques for Determining Case

Here are three techniques that will help you decide which pronoun to use when the choice is more difficult:

1. If you have a compound element (such as a subject or object of a preposition), consider only the pronoun part. The sound alone will probably tell you the answer.

   > She gave the answer to Marie and *(I, me)*.

   Marie and the pronoun make up a compound object of the preposition *to*. Having *Marie* there may be confusing; disregard *Marie* and ask yourself, "Would I say, 'She gave the answer *to me* or *to I*'?" The way it sounds would tell you the answer is *to me*. Of course, if you immediately notice that the pronoun is in an object position, you need not bother with sound.

2. If you are choosing between *who* (subject word) and *whom* (object word), look to the right to see if the next verb has a subject. If it does not, the pronoun probably is the subject, but if it does, the pronoun probably is an object.

Another related technique works the same way. Almost always, if the next important word after *who* or *whom* in a statement is a noun or pronoun, the word choice will be *whom*. However, if the next important word is something other than a noun or pronoun, the word choice will be *who*.

In order to apply these techniques, you must disregard qualifier clauses such as "I think," "it seems," and "we hope."

> The person (*who*, whom) works the hardest will win. (*Who* is the correct answer because it is the subject of the verb *works*.)
> The person (who, *whom*) we admire most is Jose. (*Whom* is the correct answer because the next verb, *admire*, already has a subject, *we*. *Whom* is an object.)
> Tom is the person (*who*, whom), we hope, has won. (*We hope* is a qualifier clause, so we disregard it here and concentrate on the other words. Since we need a subject for the verb *has won*, we select the subject word *who*.)

3. *Let's* is made up of the word *let* and *us* and means "you *let us*"; therefore, when you select a pronoun to follow it, consider the two original words and select another object word—*me*.

> Let's you and (I, *me*) take a trip to Westwood. (Think of "You let us, you and me, take a trip to Westwood." *Us* and *me* are object words.)

EXERCISE 24

Cross out the incorrect pronoun form. (See the Answer Key for answers.)

Compounds

1. José, William, and (she, her) were asked to wait on tables.

2. Did you and (she, her) go to the movies last Saturday evening?

3. They bought those Christmas presents for Christine and (he, him).

4. Her mother also sent Alicia and (they, them) additional announcements.

Appositives

5. Let's you and (I, me) do the homework together tomorrow afternoon.

6. Three members of the sophomore class—Kyoko, you, and (she, her)—were chosen to attend the fall conference.

7. They classified two students as incompetent—Lionel and (he, him).

8. (We, Us) married people must be willing to make some compromises to preserve our relationships.

9. Will they ask (we, us) women to join their club?

Comparisons

10. My brother is much shorter than (I, me).

11. Kim runs as fast as (she, her).

12. Alkie is not as sensible about such things as (they, them).

13. Sam is as reliable as (I, me).

Who, Whom

14. (Who, Whom) do you know at my school?

15. Syd is one person, I believe, (who, whom) we can depend on.

16. (Who, Whom) was to blame for that accident?

17. The young man (who, whom) we met last week is Phil's brother.

18. (Who, Whom) do you believe will win the contest?

19. Give the glasses to (whoever, whomever) is staying for the last race.

Predicate Pronoun

20. It is (I, me) to whom they gave the books.

EXERCISE 25

Cross out the incorrect pronoun form.

1. She did not realize that you and (I, me) would be asked to testify.

2. Give the award to (whoever, whomever) is voted most valuable player.

3. We need one person (who, whom) we can rely on.

4. Would you support (her, she) in the election?

5. Let's you and (I, me) take that trip next year.

6. Everybody but (he, him) was ready for the test.

7. Only two were chosen, Kathy and (he, him).

8. Every person must bring (their, his or her) book to class.

9. Distribute the cards among John, Joe, and (he, him).

10. Gilligan knows the answer better than (we, us).

11. The person (which, who) came will call on you again.

12. You know that much better than (I, me).

13. The police believed (they, them) to be us.

14. The court found (us, we) to be responsible.

15. (Whoever, Whomever) they choose will receive the promotion.

16. I would have liked to be (she, her).

17. Each person must evaluate (his or her, their) own progress.

18. Just between you and (I, me), I think we should go.

19. It could have been (he, him) whom you saw.

20. The dogs (who, which) were trained were sent to the hunt.

Pronoun-Antecedent Agreement

A pronoun agrees with its antecedent in person, number, and gender.

- **Person**—first, second, or third—indicates perspective.
- **Number** indicates singular or plural.
- **Gender** indicates sex: masculine, feminine, or neuter.

	Person	Singular	Plural
Subject Words	First	I	we
	Second	you	you
	Third	he, she, it	they
Object Words	First	me	us
	Second	you	you
	Third	him, her, it	them

Agreement in Person

Avoid needless shifting in person, which means shifting of point of view. The following paragraph is an example of an inconsistent point of view. See if you can tell where the shifts occur.

INCONSISTENT: The wedding did not go well. It was a disaster. *You* could see the trouble develop when the caterers started serving drinks before the ceremony. Then the bride started arguing with her future mother-in-law. *I* was ready to leave right away. Then the sound system went out and the band canceled. *You* wished *you* hadn't come, but *you* had to stay. *I* will never forget that day.

The word *you* is second person; the word *I* is first person. When the writer switches back and forth, the results is reader confusion and annoyance. The following revision corrects the problem by making the point of view consistently first person.

CONSISTENT: The wedding did not go well. It was a disaster. *I* could see the trouble develop when the caterers started serving drinks before the ceremony. Then the bride started arguing with her future mother-in-law. *I* was ready to leave right away. After that, the sound system went out and the band canceled. *I* wished *I* hadn't come, but *I* had to stay. *I* will never forget that day.

Agreement in Number

Most problems with pronoun-antecedent agreement involve number. The principles are simple: If the antecedent (the word the pronoun refers back to) is singular, use a singular pronoun. If the antecedent is plural, use a plural pronoun.

- A singular antecedent requires a singular pronoun.

    Jim forgot *his* notebook.

- A plural antecedent requires a plural pronoun.

    Many *students* cast *their* votes today.

- A singular indefinite pronoun as an antecedent takes a singular pronoun.

    Each of the girls brought *her* book.

- A plural indefinite pronoun as an antecedent takes a plural pronoun.

    Few knew *their* assignments.

- Two or more antecedents, singular or plural, take a plural pronoun. Such antecedents are usually joined together by *and* or by commas and *and*.

    Howard and his *parents* bought *their* presents early.

- Alternate antecedents—that is, antecedents joined by *or, nor, whether/or, either/or, neither/nor, not only/but also*—require a pronoun that agrees with the nearer antecedent.

    Neither John nor his *friends* lost *their* way.
    Neither his friends nor *John* lost *his* way.

- In sentence constructions with the expressions *one of*, the antecedent is usually the plural noun immediately before it.

    He is one of those *people who* want *their* money now.

- In sentence constructions with the expression *only one of*, the antecedent is usually the singular word *one*.

    She is the only *one* of the members *who* wants *her* money now.

- Collective nouns such as *team, jury, committee*, and *band* used as an antecedent will take a singular pronoun if they are considered as units.

    The *jury* is doing *its* best. (not *their*)

- Collective nouns with meaning suggesting individual behavior would usually take a plural form.

    The *jury* are putting on *their* coats.

Agreement in Gender

The pronoun should agree with its antecedent in gender, if the gender of the antecedent is specific. Masculine and feminine pronouns are gender specific: *he, him, she, her*. Others are neuter: *who, whom, I, we, me, us, it, they, them, who, whom, that, which*. The words *who* and *whom* refer to people. *That* can refer to ideas, things, and people but usually not to people. *Which* refers to ideas and things but never to people.

   My *girlfriend* gave me *her* best advice. (feminine)
   Mighty *Casey* tried *his* best. (masculine)
   The *people whom* I work with are loud. (neuter)

Indefinite singular pronouns used as antecedents require, of course, singular pronouns. Handling the gender of these singular pronouns is not as obvious; opinion is divided.

- Traditionally, writers have used the masculine form of pronouns to refer to the indefinite singular pronouns when the gender is unknown.

    Everyone should work until *he* drops.

- In order to avoid a perceived sex bias, most writers and speakers now prefer to use *he or she* or *his or her* instead of just *he* or *his*.

    Everyone should work until *he or she* drops.
    Everyone should mind *his or her* own business.

- Although option 1 is more direct, it is offensive to many listeners and readers. Option 2, if used several times in a short passage, can be awkward. In order to avoid those possible problems, writers and speakers often simply reword the sentence to avoid the use of the indefinite singular pronoun, often going to a plural usage.

    People should mind *their* own business.

- In any case, avoid using a plural pronoun with a singular indefinite pronoun; such usage violates the basic principle of number agreement.

    WRONG: *Everyone* should do *their* best.

EXERCISE 26

Cross out the incorrect pronoun form. (See the Answer Key for answers.)

1. Before a person can leave this camp, (he or she, they) must get permission from the director.

2. Our high school band gave (their, its) first concert of the season last Friday.

3. Will anyone who has seen that television show please raise (his or her, their) hand?

4. The team won (its, their) first game yesterday.

5. Everyone who was contacted should leave (his or her, their) reports on the president's desk.

6. Frank is one of those workers who want (his or her, their) jobs changed.

7. Christine was among the passengers (who, which) were lost at sea during the big storm.

8. Richard was afraid of anybody and anything (who, that, which) might interfere with his completing the government work.

9. Juan is the only one of that group who keeps (himself or herself, themselves, himself) in good condition.

10. Neither of the women felt that it was (her, their) fault the new machine did not work properly.

11. The sales division has (its, their) offices in Glendora, California.

12. The instructor was determined that both of the boys be punished for (his, their) part in the hazing of the younger boys.

13. Neither Mary nor her sisters could finish (her, their) project in time for the exhibition.

14. A student must not be late for class very often if (you, he or she, they) wants a good grade.

15. Either of the women will lend you (her, their) history book to study that assignment.

16. The manager and the owner of the store left (his or her, their) offices open last evening.

17. Either his family or Jung must pay (his, their) semester bills before next week.

18. All students have a right to vote for these candidates, but will (he or she, they) exercise that right in the coming election?

19. A photographer must use the best film in that light if (you, he or she, they) wishes to get good pictures.

20. It is often difficult for someone in that position to justify (himself or herself, themselves).

EXERCISE 27

Cross out the incorrect pronoun form.

1. The music was so bad that I wished (I, you) hadn't come.

2. He is the only one of the seven candidates who says that (he, they) will support a tax increase.

3. Concord is a famous historical town; just seeing the Old North Bridge can cause (you, one) to recreate the days of the patriots in your mind.

4. Each of the students brought (their, his or her) registration cards to the first class meeting.

5. Neither Mark nor the other players would admit it was (his, their) fault.

6. She is one of those people who is always trying to put (her, their) life in balance.

7. He is the only one of all the staff who will not do (their, his) share of work.

8. The members of the team are now leaving the stadium under (its, their) own power.

9. Everyone should work until (they, he or she) drops.

10. Going into battle, few seemed to care about (their, his or her) well-being.

11. Everyone should mind (their, his or her) own business.

12. On days like that, (you want, one wants) to be somewhere else.

13. When I was in France, I discovered that (you, one) can't find many fried chicken restaurants.

14. Each of the dogs strained at (its, his or her) leash.

15. She is the only one of the administrators who speaks (her, their) mind.

16. A politician must be responsive to (his or her, their) constituents or lose the next election.

17. Either of the examiners will give you (his or her, their) patient consideration.

18. The secretary and the treasurer must do (their, his or her) best work.

19. The jury voted on (their, its) first case after two hours of deliberation.

20. Every immigrant is faced with dealing with the problem of cultural adjustment, as well as (his or her, their) own personal problems.

Pronoun Reference

A pronoun must refer clearly to its antecedent. Because a pronoun is a substitute word, it can express meaning clearly and definitely only if its antecedent is easily identified.

In some sentence constructions, gender and number make the reference clear.

> Thomas and Jane discussed *his* absences and *her* good attendance. (gender)
> If the three older boys in the *club* carry out those plans, *it* will break up. (number)

Word order can also make reference clear. A pronoun should be placed as close to its antecedent as possible. An antecedent is preferably the first noun or indefinite pronoun before the pronoun.

The following are additional guidelines for making pronoun reference clear in your writing.

- When using a pronoun to refer to a general idea, make sure that the reference is clear. The pronouns used frequently in this way are *this, that, which,* and *it*. The best solution may be to recast the sentence to omit the pronoun in question.

    UNCLEAR: She whistled the same tune, *which* irritated me.
    CLEAR: She whistled the same tune, a *habit* that irritated me.
    RECAST: Her whistling the same tune irritated me.

    UNCLEAR: They treated him like a criminal, and *that* angered him.
    CLEAR: They treated him like a criminal, and *that kind* of treatment angered him.
    RECAST: Their treating him like a criminal angered him.

Confusion caused by vague reference of a pronoun to its antecedent can be eliminated by repeating the word intended as the antecedent or by using a synonym for the word. Confusion may also be eliminated by rephrasing the sentence.

> UNCLEAR: You could defend his position, but *it* would be weak.
> CLEAR: You could defend his position, but *your defense* would be weak.
> RECAST: Your defense of his position would be weak.

- Avoid ambiguous reference. The following sentences illustrate the kind of confusion that results from structuring sentences with more than one possible antecedent for the pronoun.

> UNCLEAR: John gave David *his* money and clothes.
> CLEAR: John gave his own money and clothes to David.

> UNCLEAR: Mary told her sister that *her* car has a flat tire.
> CLEAR: Mary said to her sister, "Your car has a flat tire."

- Avoid implied reference. Implied reference occurs when the antecedent is not stated; it may be a related word, a modifier, or a possessive form.

> VAGUE: We put mosquito netting over the opening, but *some* of *them* still got into the tent. (a modifier)
> CLEAR: We put mosquito netting over the opening, but some of the mosquitoes still got into the tent.

> VAGUE: This is my brother's boat, *whom* you met yesterday. (possessive)
> CLEAR: This boat belongs to my brother, whom you met yesterday.

- Usually avoid the indefinite use of *it, they,* and *you.*

> VAGUE: They say the Republican party needs new leadership.
> CLEAR: The editor of the *London Times* says the Republican party needs new leadership.

> VAGUE: In the army, you make few decisions.
> CLEAR: In the army, privates make few decisions.

Indefinite forms have their place, however, and are part of well-established expression.

> It is cool today.
> It is a certainty that he will lose.
> It is late.

EXERCISE 28

Some of the following sentences contain pronouns that are examples of faulty reference; underline these pronouns and correct them. If the sentence is correct, write OK. (See the Answer Key for answers.)

1. In small classes, the student is often able to receive individual assistance.

2. Ibsen's *Hedda Gabler* is a play that still has a powerful dramatic impact.

3. If the leader is permitted to carry out his so-called policy of security, he will become a dictator.

4. In large classes, you are often unable to receive individual help.

5. The professor told Shan-ting that his short story would soon be published.

6. In order to run effectively for office, one needs a great deal of money.

7. That is Cynthia's house that we visited yesterday.

8. Although Andrew respected the teaching profession, he did not want to be a teacher.

9. In that college, they have excellent science laboratories.

10. According to the magazine, one is more likely to encounter drunk drivers on the highway after midnight.

11. There is a message on the table that anyone can see.

12. Marge told her mother that her ideas were good.

13. That was one of Larry's poems which we read yesterday.

14. Julian implied that he should buy the property.

15. Pam whistled too often and too loud, which constantly irritated me.

16. Many people do not visit their doctor at least once a year. This may lead to unnecessary serious illnesses.

17. My brother enjoys studying law. For that reason, I want to be one.

18. As a traveler approaches that corner, you should slow down and take great care.

19. In this pamphlet, it says that campers should bring their own tents and blankets.

20. Edward loves his older brother and admires him also.

EXERCISE 29

The following sentences contain pronouns that are examples of faulty reference. Underline those pronouns, and correct them.

1. They treated him like a child and that angered him.

2. He talked while he was eating, which annoyed his companions.

3. You could disagree with the idea, but it would not be easy.

4. Marcus handed Jim his keys.

5. Jannis told Jannel that her hair was too long.

6. We installed mud flaps, but some of it still got on the fenders.

7. The instructor told the student that his deadline was tomorrow.

8. This is my sister's house, whom you met yesterday.

9. They say the unemployment is causing social problems.

10. He never looked at me when he talked, which made me distrust him.

11. He often interrupted other people, which I found annoying.

12. They regarded him as incompetent, which embarrassed him.

13. You could come to her aid, but would it be appreciated?

14. Franklin told Jeff that his car needed to be repaired.

15. They say that the big bands are coming back.

16. In the prison, you have little freedom.

17. This is my uncle's dog, who has a hundred-acre farm.

18. You could build a baseball field, but would it be worth the bother?

19. They say on television that anyone can buy a new car.

20. He put his finger into a hole in the dike at the edge of the ocean, but some of it still came in.

Modifiers

Adjectives and adverbs can often be used to strengthen communication. If you have a thought, you know what it is, but when you deliver that thought to someone else in the form of words, you might not say or write what you mean. Your thought may be eloquent and your word choice weak. Keep in mind that no two words have the same meaning. Further, some words are very vague and general. If you use a common word such as *good* or a slang word such as *neat* to characterize something that you like, you will be limiting your communication. Of course, those who know you most intimately will understand fairly well; after all, certain people who are really close may be able to convey ideas using only grunts and gestures.

But what if you want to write to someone you hardly know and explain how you feel about an important issue? In that situation, the more precise the word, the better the communication. By using modifiers, you may be able to add significant information about the words being modified—the nouns, pronouns, adjectives, adverbs, and verbs. Keep in mind that anything can be overdone; therefore, use adjectives and adverbs wisely and economically.

<u>Without adjectives and adverbs</u>, <u>even</u> John Steinbeck, <u>the</u>
      adv phrase   adv   adj

<u>famous Nobel Prize–winning</u> author, <u>surely</u> could <u>not</u> have
       adj   adv   adv

described <u>the crafty</u> octopus <u>very well</u>.
         adj   adv adv

Adjectives and Adverbs

Adjectives modify (describe) nouns and pronouns and answer the questions *Which one? What kind?* and *How many?* They may be words, phrases, or clauses.

Which one? The <u>new</u> <u>car</u> is mine.
             adj n

What kind? <u>Mexican</u> <u>food</u> is my favorite.
            adj   n

How many? A <u>few</u> <u>friends</u> are all one needs.
              adj n

Adverbs modify verbs, adjectives, or other adverbs and answer the questions *Where?, When?, Why?,* and *How?* They may be words, phrases, or clauses. Most words ending in *-ly* are adverbs.

Where? The cuckoo <u>flew</u> <u>south</u>.
              v   adv

When? The cuckoo <u>flew</u> <u>yesterday</u>.
             v   adv

Why? The cuckoo <u>flew</u> <u>because of the cold weather</u>.
             v   adv phrase

How? The cuckoo <u>flew</u> <u>swiftly</u>.
            v   adv

We have two concerns regarding the use of adjectives and adverbs in writing. One is a matter of diction, or word choice—in this case, selecting adjectives and adverbs that will strengthen the writing. The other is common problems with modifiers—how to identify and correct them.

Selecting Adjectives and Adverbs

If you want to finish the sentence, "She danced _____ ," you have quite a list of adverbs to select from, including these:

bewitchingly	angelically	quaintly	zestfully
gracefully	grotesquely	carnally	smoothly
divinely	picturesquely	serenely	unevenly
exquisitely	seductively	mirthfully	happily
vivaciously	gleefully	skillfully	obediently
solemnly	weirdly	awkwardly	

If you want to finish the sentence, "She was a(n) _____ speaker," you have another large list, this time one of the adjectives such as the following:

distinguished	dependable	effective	sly
influential	impressive	polished	astute
adequate	boring	abrasive	humorous
fluent	eloquent	finished	funny
brilliant	scared	handicapped	witty
liberal	hardy	unintelligible	satirical
adroit	flippant	scintillating	aggressive
inspiring	principal	crafty	deft

Identifying and Correcting Common Problems with Adjectives and Adverbs

The form of certain adjectives and adverbs will change according to the meaning of the statement, depending on which one out of how many are being modified.

Adjectives: The following table shows how some adjectives change following a regular pattern.

Positive (one)	*Comparative (two)*	*Superlative (three or more)*
nice	nicer	nicest
rich	richer	richest
big	bigger	biggest
tall	taller	tallest
lonely	lonelier	loneliest
terrible	more terrible	most terrible
beautiful	more beautiful	most beautiful

These are usually the rules:

- Add an *-er* to short adjectives (one or two syllables) to rank units of two:

    Julian is *nicer* than Sam.

- Add an *-est* to short adjectives to rank units of three or more:

    Of the fifty people I know, Julian is the *nicest.*

- Add the word *more* to long adjectives (three or more syllables) to rank units of two:

    My home town is *more beautiful* than yours.

- Add the word *most* to long adjectives to rank units of three or more:

    My home town is the *most beautiful* in all America.

Some adjectives are irregular in the way they change to show comparison.

Positive (one)	*Comparative (two)*	*Superlative (three or more)*
good	better	best
bad	worse	worst

Adverbs: For most adverbs, use the word *more* before the comparative form (two) and the word *most* before the superlative form (three or more).

Joan performed *skillfully.*
Jim performed *more skillfully* than Joan.
But Tom performed *most skillfully* of all.

Avoid double negatives. Words such as *not, none, nothing, never, hardly, barely,* and *scarcely* should not be combined.

DOUBLE NEGATIVE: I do *not* have *no* time for recreation. (incorrect)
SINGLE NEGATIVE: I have *no* time for recreation. (correct)
DOUBLE NEGATIVE: I've *hardly never* lied. (incorrect)
SINGLE NEGATIVE: I've *hardly* ever lied. (correct)

Do not confuse adjectives with adverbs. Among the most commonly confused adjectives and adverbs are *good/well, bad/badly,* and *real/really.* The words *good, bad,* and *real* are always adjectives. *Well* is sometimes an adjective. The words *badly* and *really* are always adverbs. *Well* is usually an adverb.

In order to distinguish these words, consider what is being modified. Remember that adjectives modify nouns and pronouns and that adverbs modify verbs, adjectives, and other adverbs.

WRONG: I feel *badly* today. (We're concerned with the condition of *I*.)
RIGHT: I feel *bad* today. (The adjective *bad* modifies the pronoun *I*.)

WRONG: I feel *well* about that choice.
RIGHT: I feel *good* about that choice. (We're concerned with the condition of *I*. But if the context is different, and we are concerned with the health of an individual, it is right to say, "I feel well" because we are saying "well person.")

WRONG: He did *real* well. (Here adjective *real* modifies the adverb *well*, but adjectives do not modify adverbs.)
RIGHT: He did *really* well. (The adverb *really* modifies the adverb *well*.)

Do not use an adverb such as *very, more,* or *most* before absolute forms of adjectives such as *perfect, round, unique, straight,* and *square.*

Do not confuse standard and nonstandard forms of adjectives and adverbs:

- **Accidently.** This is an incorrect spelling of *accidentally.*

- **All ready, already.** *All ready* means "completely prepared." *Already* means "previously."

    We are *all ready* to give the signal to move out. (*prepared*)
    When he arrived at the station, we had *already* left. (*previously*)

- **All right, alright.** *All right* (two words) means "correct," "yes," "certainly." *Alright* is an unacceptable spelling.

    Yes, I am *all right* now.

- **All together, altogether.** *All together* means "in a group." *Altogether* means "completely," "wholly," "entirely."

    The boys were *all together* at the end of the field.
    The manuscript is *altogether* too confusing.

Be careful to place such words as *also, almost, even, just, hardly, merely, only,* and *today* in the sentence to convey the intended meaning. As these words change position in the sentence, they may also change the meaning of the sentence.

I *only* advised him to act cautiously.
I advised *only* him to act cautiously.
Only I advised him to act cautiously.
I advised him *only* to act cautiously.

EXERCISE 30

Cross out the mistake in each sentence, and write in the correction above it. (See Answer Key for answers.)

1. He thought his teacher had a most unique method of lecturing.

2. Some jobs are done easier by blind men than by those with sight.

3. It was up to the parents to decide if this kind of movie is real bad for children.

4. The adventure of life is too impossible to discuss.

5. Joseph felt badly about rejection slips, but worse about his bank account.

6. Victor was not the stronger of the pair, but he was the best boxer.

7. The whole class thought Robin's sunglasses the most perfect they had seen.

8. The suspect became violenter as the police drew nearer.

9. Of all the potential winners, the judges agreed that Miss Idaho was more beautiful.

10. The United States has no central educational authority, but overall it does good.

11. An unambiguous word only can mean one thing.

12. It is real easy to forget that "liquor" used to mean "liquid."

13. Hurtful experiences of childhood don't fade out easy.

14. She said he had all ready ruined his reputation by making her buy her own flowers.

15. The trembling voice may indicate that the speaker does not feel alright.

16. Julian had two ways of starting a speech: one way was with a definition, but the easiest way was with a joke.

17. Frank choked as if the very words tasted badly to him.

18. Julie made a real good decision..

19. Jeanne didn't say the food was terrible; only she said it was bad.

20. On controversial topics, he was all together too easily offended.

EXERCISE 31

Cross out the mistake in each sentence, and write in the correction above it.

1. I remember one real good experience.

2. It left me feeling alright.

3. Of the two cars I have owned, the '48 Chevrolet was the best.

4. It was also the beautifulest car I have ever seen.

5. When I drove it, I felt like the most rich person in town.

6. For a year I didn't have no time for anything except polishing my car.

7. I had it painted green so it was real handsome.

8. My name for it was the "Hornet," and when people gave me glances as I drove it, I felt well.

9. I hardly never abused that vehicle.

10. When I finally traded it in, I didn't never look back for fear I would cry.

11. All I can say is that it was most perfect.

12. Later I went back to the dealer, but I was all ready too late.

13. The Hornet had been bought by a young man who thought it was the better of all the cars on the lot.

14. He said he couldn't find no better car anywhere.

15. I could see he felt real good.

16. He and his family were standing altogether.

17. It was no time for me to feel badly.

18. In fact, as I said, I felt alright about the transaction.

19. I didn't shed no tears.

20. That experience is a real happy memory for me.

Dangling and Misplaced Modifiers

Modifiers should clearly relate to the word or words they modify. A modifier that gives information but fails to make clear which word or group of words it refers to is called a **dangling modifier.**

>DANGLING: *Walking down the street,* a snake startled me. (The snake was not walking.)
>CORRECT: *Walking down the street, I* was startled by a snake.
>CORRECT: As I walked down the street, I was startled by a snake.

>DANGLING: *At the age of six,* my uncle died. (The uncle was not six.)
>CORRECT: *When I was six,* my uncle died.

A modifier that is placed so that it modifies the wrong word or words is called a **misplaced modifier.** The term also applies to words that are positioned so as to unnecessarily divide closely related parts of sentences such as infinitives or subjects and verbs.

>MISPLACED: The sick man went to a doctor *with a high fever.*
>CORRECT: The sick man *with a high fever* went to a doctor.

>MISPLACED: I saw a great movie *sitting in my pickup.*
>CORRECT: *Sitting in my pickup,* I saw a great movie.

>MISPLACED: I saw many new graves *walking through the cemetery.*
>CORRECT: *Walking through the cemetery,* I saw many new graves.

>MISPLACED: I forgot all about my sick dog *kissing my girlfriend.*
>CORRECT: *Kissing my girlfriend,* I forgot all about my sick dog.

>MISPLACED: I tried to *earnestly and sincerely* complete the task. (splitting of the infinitive *to complete*)
>CORRECT: I tried *earnestly and sincerely* to complete the task.

>MISPLACED: My neighbor, *while walking to the store,* was mugged. (unnecessarily dividing the subject and verb)
>CORRECT: *While walking to the store,* my neighbor was mugged.

Try this procedure in working with the following exercises.

1. Circle the modifier.
2. Draw an arrow from the modifier to the word or words it modifies.
3. If the modifier does not relate directly to anything in the sentence, it is dangling, and you must recast the sentence.
4. If the modifier does not modify the nearest word or words, or if it interrupts related sentence parts, it is misplaced and you need to reposition it.

EXERCISE 32

In the blank, write "D" for dangling modifier, "M" for misplaced modifier, and "C" for correct sentences. Correct the sentences with modifier problems. (See the Answer Key for the answers.)

_____ 1. Interested in my studies, there was no time for romance at school.

_____ 2. Falling throughout the night, the snow blocked major highways.

CHAPTER 15

_____ 3. The radio announced that a hundred cars were stranded approximately in the snow.

_____ 4. The radio announced approximately that a hundred cars were stranded in the snow.

_____ 5. My computer never worked properly in spite of following the instructions carefully.

_____ 6. Working at the computer all night, the work was still not completed.

_____ 7. The students gossiping noisily left the room.

_____ 8. Noisily, the gossiping students left the room.

_____ 9. By practicing every day, French can be learned in two weeks.

_____ 10. While working in the factory, much money was made.

_____ 11. The doctor told him to stop smoking last week.

_____ 12. While returning from shopping, Debra's promise was remembered and she stopped.

_____ 13. Walking to school, the rain came down heavily.

_____ 14. In our English classes, we only studied grammar on rare occasions.

_____ 15. To be correct, infinitive phrases should never dangle.

_____ 16. To protect their hands, gloves were worn by the astronauts.

_____ 17. When only eight years old, my mother took me to Europe.

_____ 18. I only drank a glass of milk.

_____ 19. Jill tried to carefully and constantly avoid making her date jealous.

_____ 20. While recovering in the hospital, my friends brought me flowers.

EXERCISE 33

In the blank, write "D" for dangling modifier, "M" for misplaced modifier, and "C" for correct sentences that are correct. Correct the sentences with modifier problems.

_____ 1. When I was only ten years old, my father died.

_____ 2. When ten years old, my father died.

_____ 3. After the game was over, Jean went to the banquet.

_____ 4. Jean went after the game was over to the banquet.

_____ 5. Traveling over the mountain road, the inn was reached.

_____ 6. To climb mountains, one needs strength and equipment.

_____ 7. Driving through the forest, many deer were seen from our car.

_____ 8. Many deer were seen as we drove through the forest.

_____ 9. The plan, after study, was discontinued.

_____ 10. After giving it considerable study, the plan of action was discontinued.

_____ 11. Traveling over the mountain road, Ron reached the inn.

_____ 12. The moon cast its spell rising over the mountain on the lovers.

_____ 13. Rising over the mountain, the moon cast its spell on the lovers.

_____ 14. Ms. Prank wanted to buy a car for her husband with a large trunk.

_____ 15. To miss the construction, a detour was taken.

_____ 16. To miss the construction, Ginny took a detour.

_____ 17. Ginny took to miss the construction, a detour.

CHAPTER 15

_____ 18. To play basketball well, good eyes and stamina are needed.

_____ 19. After playing all the game, the coach knew that Jean was tired.

_____ 20. It is desirable to usually avoid splitting an infinitive.

Punctuation and Capitalization

Understanding punctuation usage will also give you the knowledge of how to use patterns of written expression not available to the uninformed. If you aren't sure of how to punctuate a compound or compound-complex sentence, then you probably will not write one. If you don't know how to show that some of the words you use come from other sources, you may mislead your reader. And if you misuse punctuation, you force your readers to struggle, and you invite unfavorable opinions of your work; worse, your readers may not get your message.

End Punctuation

Periods

- Place a period after a complete statement.

    The weather is beautiful today.
    Leave your coat in the hall.

- Place a period after common abbreviations (but not after acronyms, such as FBI, NAACP, and NATO).

    Dr., Mr., Mrs., Dec., B.C., A.M.

- Use an ellipsis—three periods within a sentence and three periods plus punctuation at the end of a sentence—to indicate that words have been omitted from quoted material.

    He stopped walking and the buildings . . . rose up out of the misty courtroom. . . . (James Thurber, "The Secret Life of Walter Mitty")

Question Marks

- Place a question mark at the end of a direct question.

    Will you go to the country tomorrow?

- Use a single question mark in sentence constructions that contain a double question—that is, a quoted question following a question.

    Did he say, "Are you going?"

- Do *not* use a question mark after an indirect question.

    She asked me what caused the slide.

Exclamation Points

- Place an exclamation point after a word or a group of words that express strong feeling.

    Oh! What a night!
    Help!
    Gadzooks!

- Do not overwork the exclamation point. Do not use double exclamation points. Use the period or comma for mild exclamatory words, phrases, or sentences.

    Oh, we can leave now.

Commas

The comma is the most frequently used punctuation mark. It is used essentially to separate and to set off sentence elements.

Commas to Separate

- Use a comma to separate main clauses joined by one of the coordinating conjunctions—*for, and, nor, but, or, yet, so*. The comma may be omitted if the clauses are brief and parallel.

    We traveled many miles to see the game, but it was canceled.
    Mary left and I remained. (brief and parallel clauses)

- Use a comma after long introductory modifiers. The modifiers may be phrases or dependent clauses.

    Before the arrival of the shipment, the boss had written a letter protesting the delay. (two prepositional phrases)
    If you don't hear from me, assume that I am lost. (introductory clause, an adverbial modifier)
    In winter we skate on the river. (short modifier, no comma)

- Use a comma to separate words, phrases, and clauses in a series.

    Red, white, and *blue* were her favorite colors. (words)
    He ran *down the street, across the park,* and *into the arms of his father.* (phrases)
    When John was asleep, when Mary was at work, and *when Bob was studying,* Mother had time to relax. (clauses)

- However, when coordinating conjunctions connect all the elements in a series, the commas are omitted.

    He bought apples and pears and grapes.

- When words, phrases, and clauses make up a series without a conjunction, use a comma between all series elements.

    He bought us *paper, pencils, crayons, books.* (words)
    She went west *by car, by train, by ship.* (phrases)
    Lupe is a person *who is fair, who is honest, who is sincere.* (clauses)

- Use a comma to separate coordinate adjectives not joined by *and* that modify the same noun.

    I need a *sturdy, reliable* truck.

    Do not use the comma to separate adjectives that are not coordinate. Use this technique to determine if the adjectives are coordinate: Put *and* between the adjectives. If it fits naturally, the adjectives are coordinate; if it does not, they are not, and you do not need a comma.

    | She is a kind, beautiful person. | kind *and* beautiful (natural, hence the comma) |
    | I built a red brick wall. | red *and* brick wall (not natural, no comma) |

- Use a comma to separate sentence elements that might be misread.

    Inside the dog scratched his fleas.
    Inside, the dog scratched his fleas.

    Without benefit of the comma, the reader might initially misunderstand the relationship among the first three words.

Commas to Set Off

- Use commas to set off (enclose) adjectives in pairs that follow a noun.

    The scouts, *tired and hungry,* marched back to camp.

- Use commas to set off nonessential (unnecessary for meaning of the sentence) words, phrases, and clauses.

    My brother, *a student at Ohio University,* is visiting me. (If you drop the phrase, the basic meaning of the sentence remains intact.)
    Marla, *who studied hard,* will pass. (The clause is not essential to the basic meaning of the sentence.)
    All students *who studied hard* will pass. (Here the clause *is* essential. If you remove it, you would have *All students will pass,* which is not necessarily true.)
    I shall not stop searching *until I find the treasure.* (A dependent clause at the end of a sentence is usually not set off with a comma. However, a clause beginning with the word *though* or *although* will be set off regardless of where it is located.)
    I felt unsatisfied, *though we had won the game.*

- Use commas to set off parenthetical elements such as mild interjections (*oh, well, yes, no,* and others), transitional connectives (*however, otherwise, therefore, similarly, hence, on the other hand, then, consequently, also, thus*) quotation indicators, and special abbreviations (*etc., i.e., e.g.,* and others).

    Oh, what a silly question! (mild interjection)
    It is necessary, *of course,* to leave now. (transitional connective)
    "When I was in school," *he said,* "I read widely." (quotation indicators)
    Books, papers, pens, *etc.,* were scattered on the floor. (The abbreviation *etc.,* however, should be used sparingly.)

- Use commas to set off nouns used as direct address.

    Play it again, Sam.
    Jane, I didn't hear your answer.

- Use commas to separate the numbers in a date.

    May 4, 1993, is a day I will remember.

    Do not use commas if the day of the month is not specified, or if the day is given before the month.

    May was my favorite time.
    One day I will never forget is 4 May 1993.

- Use commas to separate the city from the state. No comma is used between the state and the zip code.

    Walnut, California 91789

- Use a comma following the salutation and the complementary closing in a letter:

    Dear John,
    Sincerely,

- Use a comma in numbers to set off groups of three digits. However, omit the comma in dates, serial numbers, page numbers, years, and street numbers.

    The total assets were $2,000,000.
    I look forward to the year 2000.

EXERCISE 34

Insert all necessary commas in the following sentences. (See the Answer Key for answers.)

1. Commas are used to separate words phrases and clauses in a series.

2. A strong assertive comma separates coordinate adjectives.

3. After introductory modifiers a comma is used to mark the start of the main clause.

4. A comma is used between independent clauses and a period is usually found at the end of a sentence.

5. After all the meaning of the sentence is often clarified by a comma.

6. Inside the car smelled new and clean.

7. In the beginning there was nothing but noise and chaos.

8. The crazy-looking car was painted pink black green and lavender.

9. Liz worked at her desk all night but the job was not finished in time.

10. The sharp gleaming rays of the sun would soon be hidden by the trees.

11. The banquet having been finished the diners moved to the living room.

12. Bach and Handel both born in 1685 were the two greatest baroque composers.

CHAPTER 15

13. Motor racing not horse racing is the more popular sport.

14. "When I was a boy" Joe said "one dollar a week was enough!"

15. Dwight Jones the salesperson will take your order now.

16. Well that's the way it's going to be!

17. The new car all sleek and shiny was nowhere to be found.

18. He arrived in Tribbey Oklahoma on February 21 1934.

19. The old boxer was only down not out.

20. The Eiffel Tower which is located in Paris is no longer the highest tower in the world.

EXERCISE 35

Insert all necessary commas in the following sentences.

1. Dwight Eisenhower a former president spent his winters in Palm Springs.

2. "The fault dear Brutus is not in our stars, but in ourselves. . . ."

3. The ship tall and stately sailed into the harbor.

4. Many writers I believe have died tragic deaths.

5. Percy Shelley a romantic poet drowned off the west coast of Italy.

6. Will Rogers said "I never met a man I didn't like."

7. It is however not up to me to decide your fate.

8. The puppy wet and bedraggled crept under the porch.

9. You will of course have prepared your case ahead of time.

10. My English class coming as it does early in the morning often finds me barely awake.

11. After the game was discussed by the coaches.

12. We must trust each other or we cannot be friends.

13. Outside the house did not appear to be occupied.

14. Lincoln called this country "of the people by the people and for the people."

15. If you should not hear from me send the police to this address.

16. Because Cary had opened the package there were no surprises to anticipate.

17. A high rugged brick wall surrounded the manor on all sides.

18. The angel told them to fear not for she brought them good news.

19. Larry wrapped Frank labeled and Liz addressed each package.

20. The fast steady goat reached the top before we did.

Semicolons

The semicolon indicates a longer pause and stronger emphasis than the comma. It is used principally to separate main clauses within a sentence.

- Use a semicolon to separate main clauses not joined by a coordinating conjunction.

    You must buy that car today; tomorrow will be too late.

- Use a semicolon between two main clauses joined by a transitional connective such as one of the HOTSHOT CAT words (*however, otherwise, therefore, similarly, hence, on* the other hand, *then, consequently, accordingly, thus*).

    It was very late; therefore, I remained at the hotel.

- Use a semicolon to separate main clauses joined by a coordinating conjunction if these clauses contain commas.

    Byron, the famous English poet, was buried in Greece; and Shelley, who was his friend and fellow poet, was buried in Italy.

- Use a semicolon in a series between items that contain commas.

    He has lived in Covina, California; Reno, Nevada; Shawnee, Oklahoma; and Bangor, Maine.

- Do *not* use the semicolon to separate elements of unequal grammatical rank, before a direct question, before a listing, or in place of a dash in a list.

    WRONG: If I were sure of the answer; I would raise my hand. (unequal grammatical rank)
    RIGHT: If I were sure of the answer, I would raise my hand.

    WRONG: He said; "I will go home now." (direct question)
    RIGHT: He said, "I will go home now."

    WRONG: We bought the following supplies; sugar, flour, bread, butter, and eggs. (listing)
    RIGHT: We bought the following supplies: sugar, flour, bread, butter, and eggs.

EXERCISE 36

Each sentence needs one or more semicolons or commas. Insert the appropriate marks. (See the Answer Key for answers.)

1. The Bohemians clustered together on Telegraph Hill they shared it with the Italian fishermen.

2. Washington's death was mourned in many countries indeed, his image was actually worshiped by many in the United States.

3. It is one thing to dig but it is another thing to live underground.

4. The advertisements show rugged males, all smoking beautiful females, all in bathing suits and luxury cars, all with only two seats.

5. Keith intended to buy only a pair of shoes, a prosaic enough errand, he thought but he actually bought each sibling a gift, one an ivory figurine and the other a delicate fan.

6. Ginny found one page of Ruskin a pleasure but twenty she found a bore.

7. Spring was full of the promise of apples, now only pink-white, sweet blossoms pumpkins, still just tiny green marbles and corn, barely showing above the brown earth.

8. Gertrude Stein knew about the people in Paris for she lived there.

9. Professor Anne Parker told us that the life of Joseph was a foreshadowing of the life of Jesus in fact, in comparing their lives he pointed out thirteen literal and symbolic similarities.

10. One author bases the story on his or her own life, and it need not be an unusual one another analyzes relationships among others, imaginary or real still another concentrates on historical events, commenting as he or she records.

11. F. Scott Fitzgerald was interested in the power of money to buy status in fact he, himself, bought status.

12. Paperwork makes different demands on different people otherwise Parkinson's law would not work in our office.

13. The critic called Pamela Johnson's novel a shallow romance but she insisted it was a penetrating psychological study.

14. It is impossible to make predictions about a grown dog by studying a mongrel puppy however, a purebred puppy is almost sure to be a duplicate of its parents.

15. Many children are afraid of their grandfathers and I was one of them.

16. Cows will find their way out of a fire but horses will run into it.

17. He believed he was responsible for me, and he told me so I was determined to do things my way, even if it meant failing or humiliating him.

18. The judge had an avid interest in nature and often lived in the open for weeks at a time it cost him his marriage.

19. They were poor people and they lived in the damp chill of an inhospitable island.

20. Thoreau did not want to become a recluse he wanted only to lead a simple life.

EXERCISE 37

Each sentence needs one or more semicolons or commas. Insert the appropriate marks.

1. He was the person I met on the subway I never forget a face.

2. That melon looks fresh but it costs too much.

3. We gave the book to Wanda however, she never opened it.

4. He became king after the abolition of the Parliament but his days of power were numbered.

5. Please remain quiet while Stanley reads the announcement you may nap if you like.

6. The best part of the trip was our stay at Yosemite the worst part was the traveling.

7. I found them another house it was similar to the first one they saw.

8. Alicia looks somewhat tired I wonder if she is really well.

9. The apple Sam gave me is very sour but it is the thought that counts.

10. Our instructor gave a lecture on constitutional law it was brilliant in expression and content.

11. I did not recommend that novel to Judy she discovered it herself.

12. Will it be our turn next or will we have to wait longer?

13. It was not the whale that destroyed Captain Ahab it was Captain Ahab that destroyed Captain Ahab.

14. I do not feel responsible he had a clear choice in the matter.

15. No one could be wiser than the Zen master we could only study his principles.

16. Henry is the only person who could be so ruthless George comes in a close second.

17. Debra smiled sweetly as she handed the president the message but he was suspicious.

18. She was only the messenger however he attacked her instead of the message.

19. It was a long, cold winter and I was fortunate to work indoors.

20. We sent members notice of the meeting well in advance yet some said they received nothing.

Quotation Marks

Quotation marks are used principally to set off direct quotations. A direct quotation consists of material taken from the written work or the direct speech of others; it is set off by double quotation marks. Single quotation marks are used to set off a quotation within a quotation.

> Double quotation marks: He said, "I don't remember."
> Single quotation marks: He said, "I don't remember if she said, 'Wait for me.' "

- Use double quotation marks to set off direct quotations.

    John said, "Give me the book."
    Socrates said, "Know thyself."
    As Edward McNeil writes of the Greek achievement: "To an extent never before realized, mind was supreme over faith, logic and science over superstition."

- Use double quotation marks to set off titles of shorter pieces of writing such as magazine articles, essays, short stories, short poems, one-act plays, chapters in books, songs, and separate pieces of writing published as part of a larger work.

    The book *Literature: Structure, Sound, and Sense,* contains a deeply moving poem entitled "On Wenlock Edge."
    Poe's story "The Tell-Tale Heart" is about an insane narrator.
    My favorite Elvis song is "Don't Be Cruel."

- Do *not* use quotation marks for the title on the title page or first page of your own written work.

    WRONG: "Struggling with Math"
    RIGHT: Struggling with Math

- Use double quotation marks to set off slang, technical terms, and special words.

    There are many aristocrats, but Elvis is the only true "King." (special word)
    The "platoon system" changed the game of football. (technical term)
    Everyone knows that Michael Jackson is "bad." (slang)

- Use double quotation marks in writing dialogue (conversation). Write each speech as a separate paragraph and set it off with double quotation marks.

    "Will you go with me?" he asked.
    "Yes," she replied. "Are you ready now?"
    "Of course. How about you?"
    "Certainly," she answered. "When do we leave?"
    "At once."

- Use single quotation marks to set off a quotation with a quotation.

    Professor Baxter said, "You should remember Shakespeare's words, 'All the world's a stage.' "

- Do *not* use quotation marks for indirect quotations.

    WRONG: He said that "he would bring the supplies."
    RIGHT: He said that he would bring the supplies.
    RIGHT: He said, "I will bring the supplies."

Punctuation with Quotation Marks

- A period or comma is always placed *inside* the quotation marks.

  Our assignment for Monday was to read Poe's "The Raven."
  "I will read you the story," he said. "It is a good one."

- A semicolon or colon is always placed *outside* the quotation marks.

  He read Robert Frost's poem "Design"; then he gave the examination.

- A question mark, exclamation point, or dash is placed *outside* the quotation marks when it applies to the entire sentence and *inside* the quotation marks when it applies to the material in quotation marks.

  He asked, "Am I responsible for everything?" (quoted question within a statement)
  Did you hear him say, "I have the answer"? (statement within a question)
  Did she say, "Are we ready?" (question within a question)
  She shouted, "Impossible!" (exclamation)
  "I hope—that is, I—" he began. (dash)

Italics

Italics (slanting type) are used to call special attention to certain words or groups of words. In handwriting or typing, such words are underlined.

- Italicize (underline) foreign words and phrases that are still listed in the dictionary as foreign.

  nouveau riche   Weltschmerz

- Italicize (underline) titles of books (except the Bible), long poems, plays, magazines, motion pictures, musical compositions, newspapers, and works of art.

  I think Hemingway's best novel is *A Farewell to Arms*.
  His source material was taken from *Time, Newsweek,* and the London *Times*. (Sometimes the name of the city in titles of newspapers is italicized, also—for example, *The New York Times*.)
  The *Mona Lisa* is my favorite painting.

- Italicize (underline) the names of ships, airplanes, spacecraft, and trains.

  SHIPS: *Queen Mary   Lurline   Stockholm*
  SPACECRAFT: *Challenger   Voyager 2*

- Italicize (underline) to differentiate letters, figures, and words when they refer to themselves rather than to the ideas or things they usually represent.

  Do not leave the *o* out of *sophomore*.
  Your *3*'s look like *5*'s.

Dashes

The dash is used when a longer pause than the comma indicates is desired. The dash is typed as two hyphens with no space before or after them (—).

- Use a dash to indicate a sudden change in sentence construction or an abrupt break in thought.

  Here is the true reason for his failing—but maybe you don't care.

- Use a dash after an introductory list. The words *these, those, all,* and occasionally *such* introduce the summarizing statement.

  > English, French, history—these are the subjects I like.
  > Dodgers, Giants, Yankees—such names bring back memories of exciting World Series games.

- Use a dash for emphasis to set off material that interrupts the flow of an idea, sets off material for emphasis, or restates an idea as an appositive.

  > You are—I am certain—not serious. (interrupting)
  > Our next decision is—how much money did we raise? (emphasis)
  > Dione has one talent—playing the kazoo. (restatement)

- Use a dash to indicate an unfinished statement or word or an interruption. Such interruptions usually occur in dialogue.

  > Susan said, "Shall we—" (no period)
  > "I only wanted—" Jason remarked. (no comma)

- Do *not* use a dash in places in which other marks of punctuation would be more appropriate.

  > WRONG: Lupe found the store—and she shopped.
  > RIGHT: Lupe found the store, and she shopped.
  >
  > WRONG: I think it is too early to go—
  > RIGHT: I think it is too early to go.

Colons

The colon is a formal mark of punctuation used chiefly to introduce something that is to follow, such as a list, a quotation, or an explanation.

- Use a colon after a main clause to introduce a formal list, an emphatic or long restatement (appositive), an explanation, an emphatic statement, or a summary.

  > The following automobiles were in the General Motors show: Cadillac, Chevrolet, Buick, Oldsmobile, and Pontiac. (list)
  > He worked toward one objective: a degree. (restatement or appositive)
  > Let me emphasize one point: I do not accept late papers. (emphatic statement)

- Use a colon to introduce a formal quotation or a formal question.

  > Shakespeare's Polonius said: "Neither a borrower nor a lender be." (formal quotation)
  > The question is this: Shall we surrender? (formal question)

- Use a colon in the following conventional ways: to separate a title and subtitle, a chapter and verse in the Bible, and hours and minutes; after the salutation in a formal business letter; and between the act and the scene of a play.

  > Title and subtitle: *Korea: A Country Divided*
  > Chapter and verse: Genesis 4:12
  > Hour and minutes: 8:25 P.M.
  > Salutation: Dear Members: Dear Ms. Johnson:
  > Act and scene: *Hamlet* III:ii

Parentheses

Parentheses are used to set off material that is of relatively little importance to the main thought of the sentence. Such material—numbers, parenthetical material, figures, supplementary material, and sometimes explanatory details—merely amplifies the main thought.

- Use parentheses to set off material that is not part of the main sentence but is too relevant to omit altogether. In this category are numbers that designate items in a series, amplifying references, explanations, directions, and qualifications.

    > He offered two reasons for his losing: (1) he was tired; (2) he was out of condition. (numbers)
    > Review the chapters on the Civil War (6, 7, and 8) for the next class meeting. (references)
    > Her husband (she had been married about a year) died last week. (explanation)

- In business writing, parentheses are often employed to enclose a numerical figure that repeats and confirms a spelled-out number.

    > I paid twenty dollars ($20) for the book.

- Correctly punctuate sentences with parentheses. Use the comma, semicolon, and colon after the parentheses when the sentence punctuation requires their use. Use the period, question mark, and exclamation point in positions depending on whether they go with the material within the parentheses or with the entire sentence.

    > The greatest English poet of the seventeenth century was John Milton (1608–1674).

Brackets

Brackets are used within a quotation to set off editorial additions or corrections made by the person who is quoting.

> Churchill said: "It [the Yalta Agreement] contained many mistakes."

Capitalization

In English, there are many conventions concerning the use of capital letters. However, because style and use of capital letters may vary, certain established rules for capitalization will prove helpful to you.

- Capitalize the first word of a sentence.
- Capitalize proper nouns and adjectives derived from proper nouns.

    > Names of persons:
    >   Edward Jones
    >
    > Adjectives derived from proper nouns:
    >   a Shakespearean sonnet, a Miltonic sonnet
    >
    > Countries, nationalities, races, languages:
    >   Germany, English, Spanish, Chinese

States, regions, localities, other geographical divisions:
California, the Far East, the South

Oceans, lakes, mountains, deserts, streets, parks:
Lake Superior, Fifth Avenue, Sahara Desert

Educational institutions, schools, courses:
Rancho Santiago College, Spanish 3, Joe Hill School, Rowland High School

Organizations and their members:
Boston Red Sox, Boy Scouts, Audubon Society

Corporations, governmental agencies or departments, trade names:
U.S. Steel Corporation, Treasury Department, White Memorial Library

Calendar references such as holidays, days of the week, months:
Easter, Tuesday, January

Historic events such as eras, periods, documents, laws:
Declaration of Independence, Geneva Convention, First Crusade, Romantic Age

- Capitalize words denoting family relationships when they are used before a name or substituted for a name.

  He walked with his nephew and Aunt Grace.
  but
  He walked with his nephew and his aunt.

  Grandmother and Mother are away on vacation.
  but
  Grandmother and my mother are away on vacation.

- Capitalize abbreviations after names.

  Henry White, Jr.
  William Green, M.D.

- Capitalize titles of themes, books, plays, movies, poems, magazines, newspapers, musical compositions, songs, and works of art. Do not capitalize short conjunctions and prepositions unless they come at the beginning of the title.

  Desire Under the Elms
  Last of the Mohicans
  "Blueberry Hill"
  Terminator
  Of Mice and Men

- Capitalize any title preceding a name or used as a substitute for a name. Do not capitalize a title following a name.

Judge Stone	Alfred Stone, a judge
General Clark	Raymond Clark, a general
Professor Fuentes	Harry Jones, the former president

Apostrophes

The apostrophe is used with nouns and indefinite pronouns to show possession, to show the omission of letters and figures in contractions, and to form the plurals of letters, figures, and words referred to as words.

- Use an apostrophe and -s to form the possessive of a noun, singular or plural, that does not end in -s.

    man's coat
    women's suits
    child's toy

- Use an apostrophe alone to form the possessive of a plural noun ending in -s.

    girls' clothes
    dogs' food
    the Browns' house

- Use an apostrophe and -s or the apostrophe alone to form the possessive of singular nouns ending in -s. Use the apostrophe and -s only when you would pronounce the s.

    James' hat or (if you would pronounce the s) James's hat

- Use an apostrophe and -s to form the possessive of certain indefinite pronouns.

    everybody's
    one's
    another's

- Use an apostrophe to indicate that letters or figures have been omitted.

    I can't stop now.
    six o'clock
    in the '80s

- Use an apostrophe to indicate the plural of letters, figures, and words used as words.

    five 8's
    and's
    Dot your i's.

- Use an apostrophe with pronouns only when you are making a contraction. Problems in understanding this rule account for a large percentage of errors in mechanics.

    WRONG: The dog bit it's tail. (not a contraction)
    RIGHT: The dog bit its tail.

    WRONG: The problem is your's. (not a contraction)
    RIGHT: The problem is yours.

    WRONG: The problem is also their's. (not a contraction)
    RIGHT: The problem is also theirs.

    WRONG: Whose the leader now?
    RIGHT: Who's the leader now? (a contraction of *who is*)

    WRONG: Its a big problem.
    RIGHT: It's a big problem. (a contraction of *it is*)

Hyphens

The hyphen is used for the purpose of bringing two or more words together into a single compound word. Hyphenation, therefore, is essentially a spelling problem rather than one of punctuation. Because the hyphen is not used with any degree of consistency, it is advisable to consult your dictionary to learn current usage. Study the following uses as a beginning guide.

- Use a hyphen to separate the parts of many compound words.

    brother-in-law
    go-between
    about-face

- Use a hyphen between prefixed and suffixes and proper names.

    all-American
    neo-Nazi
    mid-Atlantic

- Use a hyphen with spelled-out compound numbers up to ninety-nine and with fractions.

    twenty-six
    one hundred eighty-one
    two-thirds

- Use a hyphen to join two or more words used as a single adjective modifier of a noun.

    bluish-gray eyes
    first-class service
    hard-fought game
    sad-looking mother

EXERCISE 38

One punctuation mark or capital letter is omitted in each of the following sentences. Insert them as needed. Pairs of quotation marks are considered one unit. (See the Answer Key for answers.)

1. Wyatt Earp said, In two years at Wichita, my deputies and I arrested more than 800 men.

2. It was all in a days work.

3. "We really have no satisfactory synonym for Lebensraum," Cary said.

4. "Its like a miracle of God," Ginny said; "I can rest now."

5. "Just say Stop when you've had enough," she teased.

6. The wind carried its murmur through the trees, and we listened to the crickets chirping louder and louder as the birds chirping softened into silence.

7. In a trite way its true that the best things are free.

8. Melville's novel Billy Budd was published posthumously.

9. What does Keats mean by "Darkling I listen" in his poem Ode to a Nightingale?

10. Jack Londons books are still widely read in this country and abroad.

11. Will couldn't see the connection between Oxford and Walnut—or could he.

12. Every one of the miners was lost in the cave in.

13. The boy from Germany crossed his 7s.

14. Joe Louis, Art Aragon, and Rocky Marciano these were my father's favorite fighters.

15. The following citizens in Hiroshima were interviewed a town official, a housewife, a farmer, a mechanic, and a doctor.

16. Marx and Engels you know who they were understood dialectical materialism much better than the working class did.

17. The romantic period is not as difficult to teach to this generation as I thought it would be.

18. Those who believed in the Declaration of independence thought that Madison's *Federalist* was too conservative.

19. It's not difficult to think of C. P. Snow as an english major, although his field was science.

20. The doctor, Ralph Berger, called aunt Helen to hold his son's head while he stitched it up.

EXERCISE 39

There are twenty punctuation marks needed in the following paragraph; the locations are indicated by the numbers. Pairs such as quotation marks and parentheses are considered one unit. Insert the marks as needed.

Shakespeares¹ age was like ours² it³ was full of change and turmoil"⁴ the old gentleman said.⁵ New ideas were not confined exclusively to one social class⁶ one religion⁷ or one political party. Outer space stirred the imaginations of most of the people⁸ not just the astronomers. They went to see Troilus and Cressida⁹ for fun¹⁰ and they bought all the books available on the strange customs of other cultures. And whos¹¹ to say that when Hamlets¹² father says¹³ ¹⁴I am thy fathers¹⁵ spirit¹⁴ he is any less visible than the ghosts¹⁶ some people say they see today. There wasnt¹⁷ much Shakespeare didnt¹⁸ know about us. Thats¹⁹ why we still quarrel about the meaning of his plays²⁰ we are still discovering the truth about ourselves in them.⁵

1. _____
2. _____
3. _____
4. _____
5. _____
6. _____
7. _____
8. _____
9. _____
10. _____
11. _____
12. _____
13. _____
14. _____
15. _____
16. _____
17. _____
18. _____
19. _____
20. _____

Spelling

Some people are born good spellers. They see a word and can spell it correctly forever; others struggle. If you are not a great speller, you probably never will be, but the good news is that you can be a competent speller—with work. This unit offers you a systematic approach and several separate strategies to spelling well in a language that is inconsistent to a significant degree. Some words just don't look like the way they sound; in other words, they are not phonetic, and they do not pattern in ways parallel with other words of the same spelling. This anonymous poem shows some of the problems:

>When in the English language we speak
>Why is *break* not rhymed with *freak*?
>Will you tell me why it's true
>That we *sew*, but we also saw *few*?
>And why cannot makers of verse
>Rime the word *horse* with *worse*?
>*Beard* sounds much different from *heard*.
>*Cord* is so different from *word*.
>*Cow* is *cow*, but *low* is *low*.
>*Shoe* never rhymes with *foe*;
>And think of *hose*, and *dose*, and *lose*.
>And think of *goose* and yet of *choose*.
>*Doll* and *roll*, and *home* and *some*.
>And since *pay* is rimed with *say*,
>Why *paid* and *said*, I pray?
>*Mould* is not pronounced like *could*
>And *done* is not like *gone* and *lone*.
>If there is one *tooth* and a whole set of *teeth*
>Why shouldn't the plural of *booth* be *beeth*?
>If the singular is *this* and the plural is *these*
>Should the plural of *kiss* be *kese*?
>We speak of masculine pronouns *he, his, him*,
>Why not *She, shis,* and *shim*?
>If the plural of *box* is *boxes*
>Why is it *oxen* instead of *oxes*?
>If the plural of *mouse* is *mice*
>Why doesn't *house* become *hice*?
>If the plural of *man* is *men*
>Why is it *pans* instead of *pen*?
>If the plural of *foot* is *feet*,
>Why is it *boots* instead of *beet*?
>To sum it all up, it seems to me
>That sounds and letters just do not agree.

Despite these problems inherent in our language, you can be an effective speller. Unfortunately, for those who are not, there are unhappy consequences. In a society as literate as ours, if you are a poor speller, you will find yourself with a serious handicap. The professions and trades, as well as the schools, demand that individuals spell well and write effectively. If you write *thier* for *their* or *definately* for *definitely* in compositions, term reports, examinations, letters of application, or business reports, you will draw unfavorable attention from your audience. Use these steps as a guide to efficient spelling:

1. Make up your mind that you are going to spell well.
2. Keep a list of the words you misspell; work on spelling them correctly.
3. Get into the habit of looking up new words in the dictionary for correct spelling as well as for meaning.
4. Look at each letter in the word carefully and pronounce each syllable; that is, *change-a-ble, con-tin-u-ous, dis-ap-pear-ance.*
5. Visualize how the word is made up.
6. Write the word correctly several times. After each writing, close your eyes and again visualize the word.
7. Set up frequent recall sessions with problem words. Become aware of the reasons for your errors.

The following tips will help you become a better speller:

- Do not omit letters.
  Many errors occur because of mispronunciations of words in which certain letters are omitted. Observe the omissions in the words below. Then concentrate on learning the correct spellings.

Incorrect	*Correct*	*Incorrect*	*Correct*
agravate	aggravate	ajourned	adjourned
aproved	approved	aquaintance	acquaintance
artic	arctic	comodity	commodity
efficent	efficient	envirnment	environment
familar	familiar	irigation	irrigation
libary	library	paralell	parallel
parlament	parliament	paticulaly	particularly
readly	readily	sophmore	sophomore
stricly	strictly	unconsious	unconscious

- Do not add letters.

Incorrect	*Correct*	*Incorrect*	*Correct*
atheIete	athlete	comming	coming
drownded	drowned	folkes	folks
occassionally	occasionally	ommission	omission
pasttime	pastime	priviledge	privilege
similiar	similar	tradgedy	tragedy

- Do not substitute incorrect lettters for correct letters.

Incorrect	*Correct*	*Incorrect*	*Correct*
benefisial	beneficial	bullitins	bulletins
sensus	census	discription	description
desease	disease	dissention	dissension
itims	items	offence	offense
peculier	peculiar	resitation	recitation
screach	screech	sustansial	substantial
surprize	surprise	technacal	technical

- Do not transpose letters.

Incorrect	Correct	Incorrect	Correct
alu*nm*i	alumni	child*er*n	children
dup*il*cate	duplicate	irre*ve*lant	irrelevant
kind*el*	kindle	p*re*haps	perhaps
pe*rf*er	prefer	pe*rs*cription	prescription
princip*el*s	principles	ye*i*ld	yield

  Note: Whenever you notice other words that fall into any one of these categories, add them to the list.

- Apply the spelling rules for spelling *ei* and *ie* words correctly.

  Remember the poem?

  > Use *i* before *e*
  > Except after *c*
  > Or when sounded as *a*
  > As in *neighbor* and *weigh*.

  i* Before *e

achieve	belief	believe	brief
chief	field	grief	hygiene
niece	piece	pierce	relief
relieve	shield	siege	variety

  Except After *c*

ceiling	conceit	conceive	deceit
deceive	perceive	receipt	receive

  Exceptions: either, financier, height, leisure, neither, seize, species, weird.

  When Sounded as *a*

deign	eight	feign	feint
freight	heinous	heir	neigh
neighbor	rein	reign	skein
sleigh	veil	vein	weigh

- Apply the rules for dropping the final *e* or retaining the final *e* when a suffix is added.

  Words ending in a silent *e* usually drop the e before a suffix beginning with a vowel; for example, *accuse + -ing = accusing*. Some common suffixes beginning with a vowel are the following: *-able, -al, -age, -ary, -ation, -ence, -ing, -ion, -ous, -ure.*

  admire + *-able* = admirable
  plume + *-age* = plumage
  explore + *-ation* = exploration
  come + *-ing* = coming
  fame + *-ous* = famous

  arrive + *-al* = arrival
  imagine + *-ary* = imaginary
  precede + *-ence* = precedence
  locate + *-ion* = location
  please + *-ure* = pleasure

  Exceptions: *dye + -ing = dyeing* (to distinguish it from *dying*), *acreage, mileage.*

Words ending in a silent *-e* usually retain the *e* before a suffix beginning with a consonant; for example: *arrange + -ment = arrangement*. Some common suffixes beginning with a consonant are the following: *-craft, -ful, -less, -ly, -mate, -ment, -ness, -ty.*

state + *-craft* = statecraft
hope + *-less* = hopeless
stale + *-mate* = stalemate
like + *-ness* = likeness

hate + *-ful* = hateful
safe + *-ly* = safely
manage + *-ment* = management
entire + *-ty* - entirety

Exceptions: Some words taking the *-ful* or *-ly* suffixes drop the final *e*:

awe + *-ful* = awful
true + *-ly* = truly

due + *-ly* = duly
whole + *-ly* = wholly

Some words taking the suffix *-ment* drop the final *e*; for example:

acknowledgment   argument   judgment

Words ending in silent *-e* after *c* or *g* retain the *e* when the suffix begins with the vowel *a* or *o*. The final *-e* is retained to keep the *c* or *g* soft before the suffixes.

advantag*e*ous   courag*e*ous
notic*e*able   peac*e*able

- Apply the rules for doubling a final consonant before a suffix beginning with a vowel.

Words of one syllable:

blot	blotted	brag	bragging	cut	cutting
drag	dragged	drop	dropped	get	getting
hop	hopper	hot	hottest	man	mannish
plan	planned	rob	robbed	run	running
sit	sitting	stop	stopped	swim	swimming

Words accented on the last syllable:

acquit	acquitted	admit	admittance	allot	allotted
begin	beginning	commit	committee	concur	concurring
confer	conferring	defer	deferring	equip	equipped
occur	occurrence	omit	omitting	prefer	preferred
refer	referred	submit	submitted	transfer	transferred

Words that are not accented on the last syllable, or words that do not end in a single consonant preceded by a vowel, do not double the final consonant (whether or not the suffix begins with a vowel).

Frequently Misspelled Words

a lot	absence	across	actually
all right	among	analyze	appearance
appreciate	argument	athlete	athletics
awkward	becoming	beginning	belief
benefit	buried	business	certain
college	coming	committee	competition
complete	consider	criticism	definitely

dependent	develop	development	difference
disastrous	discipline	discussed	disease
divide	dying	eighth	eligible
eliminate	embarrassed	environment	especially
etc.	exaggerate	excellent	exercise
existence	experience	explanation	extremely
familiar	February	finally	foreign
government	grammar	grateful	guarantee
guard	guidance	height	hoping
humorous	immediately	independent	intelligence
interest	interfere	involved	knowledge
laboratory	leisure	length	library
likely	lying	marriage	mathematics
meant	medicine	neither	ninety
ninth	nuclear	occasionally	opinion
opportunity	parallel	particular	persuade
physically	planned	pleasant	possible
practical	preferred	prejudice	privilege
probably	professor	prove	psychology
pursue	receipt	receive	recommend
reference	relieve	religious	repetition
rhythm	ridiculous	sacrifice	safety
scene	schedule	secretary	senior
sense	separate	severely	shining
significant	similar	sincerely	sophomore
speech	straight	studying	succeed
success	suggest	surprise	thoroughly
though	tragedy	tried	tries
truly	unfortunately	unnecessary	until
unusual	using	usually	
Wednesday	writing	written	

Confused Spelling/Confusing Words

The following are more words that are commonly misspelled or confused with one another. Some have similar sounds, some are often mispronounced, and some are only misunderstood.

a: An article adjective that is used before a word beginning with a consonant or a consonant sound, as in "I ate *a* donut."

an: An article adjective that is used before a word beginning with a vowel sound (*a, e, i, o, u*) or with a silent *h*.

and: A coordinating conjunction, as in "Sara *and* I like Johnny Cash."

accept: A verb meaning "to receive," as in "I *accept* your explanation."

except: A preposition meaning "to exclude," as in "I paid everyone *except* you."

advice: A noun meaning "guidance," as in "Thanks for the *advice.*"

advise: A verb meaning "to give guidance," as in "Will you please *advise* me of my rights?"

all right: An adjective meaning "correct" or "acceptable," as in "It's *all right* to cry."
alright: Misspelling.

all ready: An adjective that can be used interchangeably with *ready*, as in "I am *all ready* to go to town."
already: An adverb meaning "before," which cannot be used in place of *ready*, as in "I have *already* finished."

a lot: An adverb meaning "much," as in "She liked him *a lot*," or a noun meaning "several," as in "I had *a lot* of suggestions."
alot: Misspelling.

altogether: An adverb meaning "completely," as in "He is *altogether* happy."
all together: An adverb meaning "as one," which can be used interchangeably with *together*, as in "The group left *all together*."

choose: A present-tense verb meaning "to select," as in "Do whatever you *choose*."
chose: The past-tense form of the verb *choose*, as in "They *chose* to take action yesterday."

effect: Usually a noun meaning "result," as in "That *effect* was unexpected."
affect: Usually a verb meaning "change," as in "Ideas *affect* me."

hear: A verb indicating the receiving of sound, as in "I *hear* thunder."
here: An adverb meaning "present location," as in "I live *here*."

it's: A contraction of *it is*, as in "*It's* time to dance."
its: Possessive pronoun, as in "Each dog has *its* day."

know: A verb usually meaning "to comprehend" or "to recognize," as in "I *know* the answer."
no: An adjective meaning "negative," as in "I have *no* potatoes."

led: The past-tense form of the verb *lead*, as in "I *led* a wild life in my youth."
lead: A present-tense verb, as in "I *lead* a stable life now" or a noun referring to a substance, such as "I sharpened the *lead* in my pencil."

loose: An adjective meaning "without restraint," as in "He is a *loose* cannon."
lose: A present-tense verb from the pattern *lose, lost, lost*, as in "I thought I would *lose* my senses."

paid: The past-tense form of *pay*, as in "He *paid* his dues."
payed: Misspelling.

passed: The past-tense form of the verb *pass,* meaning "went by," as in "He *passed* me on the curve."
past: An adjective meaning "formerly," as in "That's *past* history now."

patience: A noun meaning "willingness to wait," as in "Job was a man of much *patience.*"
patients: A noun meaning "people under care," as in "The doctor had fifty *patients.*"

peace: A noun meaning "calm" or "without strife," as in "The guru was at *peace* with the world."
piece: A noun meaning "particle," as in "I gave him a *piece* of my mind."

quiet: An adjective meaning "silent," as in "She was a *quiet* child."
quit: A verb meaning "to cease" or "to withdraw," as in "I *quit* my job."
quite: An adverb meaning "very," as in "The clam is *quite* happy."

receive: A verb meaning "to accept," as in "I will *receive* visitors now."
recieve: Misspelling.

stationary: An adjective meaning "not moving," as in "Try to avoid running into *stationary* objects."
stationery: A noun meaning "paper material to write on," as in "I bought a box of *stationery* for Sue's birthday present.

than: A conjunction, as in "He is taller *than* I am."
then: An adverb, as in "She *then* left town."

their: An adjective, as in "They read *their* books."
there: An adverb, as in "He left it *there,*" or a filler word as in "*There* is no time left."
they're: A contraction of *they are,* as in "*They're* happy."

to: A preposition, as in "I went *to* town."
too: An adverb meaning "having exceeded or gone beyond what is acceptable," as in "You are *too* late to qualify for the discount," or "also," as in "I have feelings, *too.*"
two: An adjective of number, as in "I have *two* jobs."

thorough: An adjective, as in "He did a *thorough* job."
through: A preposition, as in "She went *through* the yard."

truly: An adverb meaning "sincerely" or "completely," as in "He was *truly* happy."
truely: Misspelling

weather:	A noun meaning "condition of the atmosphere," as in "The *weather* is pleasant today."
whether:	A conjunction, as in "*Whether* he would go was of no consequence."
write:	A present-tense verb, as in "Watch me as I *write* this letter."
writen:	Misspelling.
written:	A past-participle verb, as in "I have *written* the letter."
you're:	A contraction of *you are*, as in "*You're* my friend."
your:	A possessive pronoun, as in "I like *your* looks."

Brief Guide for ESL Students

If you came to this country knowing little English, you probably acquired vocabulary first; then you began using that vocabulary within the basic patterns of your own language. If your native language had no articles, you probably used no articles; if your language had no verb tenses, you probably used no verb tenses, and so on. Using the grammar of your own language with your new vocabulary may have initially enabled you to make longer and more complex statements in English, but eventually you learned that your native grammar and your adopted grammar were different. You may have even learned that no two grammars are the same, and that English has a bewildering set of rules and an even longer set of exceptions to those rules. Chapter 15 presents grammar (the way we put words together) and rhetoric (the way we use language effectively) that can be applied to your writing. The following are some definitions, rules, and references that are of particular concern to writers who are learning English as a second language.

Using Articles in Relation to Nouns

Articles: Articles are either indefinite (*an, a*) or definite (*the*). Because they point out nouns, they are often called noun determiners.

Nouns: Nouns can be either singular (*book*) or plural (*books*) and are either count nouns (things that can be counted, such as "book") or noncount nouns (things that cannot be counted, such as "homework"). If you are not certain whether a noun is a count noun or a noncount noun, try placing the word *much* before the word. You can say, "much homework," so *homework* is a noncount noun.

Rules:

- **Use an indefinite article** (*a* or *an*) **before singular count nouns and not before noncount nouns.** The indefinite article means "one," so you would not use it before plural count nouns.

CORRECT:	I saw a book. (count noun)
CORRECT:	I ate an apple. (count noun)

INCORRECT:	I fell in a love. (noncount noun)
CORRECT:	I fell in love. (noncount noun)
INCORRECT:	I was in a good health. (noncount noun)
CORRECT:	I was in good health. (noncount noun)

- **Use the definite article** (*the*) **before both singular and plural count nouns that have specific reference.**

CORRECT:	I read the book. (a specific one)
CORRECT:	I read the books. (specific ones)
CORRECT:	I like to read a good book. (nonspecific, therefore the indefinite article)
CORRECT:	A student who works hard will pass. (any student, therefore nonspecific)
CORRECT:	The student on my left is falling asleep. (a specific student)

- **Use the definite article with noncount nouns only when they are specifically identified.**

CORRECT:	Honesty (as an idea) is a rare commodity.
CORRECT:	The honesty of my friend has inspired me. (specifically identified)
INCORRECT:	I was in trouble and needed the assistance. (not specifically identified)
CORRECT:	The assistance offered by the paramedics was appreciated. (specifically identified)

- **Place the definite article before proper nouns** (*names*) **of:**

  oceans, rivers, and deserts. (for example, *the Pacific Ocean* and the *Red River*)

  countries, if the first part of the name indicates a division. (*the United States of America*)

  regions. (*the South*)

  plural islands. (*the Hawaiian Islands*)

  museums and libraries. (*the Los Angeles County Museum*)

  colleges and universities when the word *college* or *university* comes before the name. (*the University of Oklahoma*)

These are the main rules. For a more detailed account of rules for articles, see a comprehensive ESL book in your library.

Sentence Patterns

This chapter (see the Types of Sentences section) defines and illustrates the patterns of English sentences. Some languages include patterns not used in standard English. The following principles are well worth remembering:

- Unlike patterns in certain other languages, the conventional English sentence is based on one or more clauses, each of which must have a subject (sometimes with the implied "you") and a verb.

INCORRECT:	Saw the book. (subject needed even if it is obvious)
CORRECT:	I saw the book.

- English does not repeat a subject, even for emphasis.

    INCORRECT: The book that I read it was interesting.
    CORRECT: The book that I read was interesting.

Verb Endings

- *English indicates time through verbs.* Learn the different forms of verb tenses and the combinations of main verbs and helping verbs.

    INCORRECT: He watching the game. (A verblike word ending in *-ing* cannot be a verb all by itself.)
    CORRECT: He is watching the game. (Note that a helping verb such as *is, has, has been, will,* or *will be* always occurs before the main verb.)

- *Take special care in maintaining consistency in tense.* (These points are covered with explanations, examples, and exercises in the Verbs section of this chapter.)

    INCORRECT: I went to the mall. I watch a movie there. (verb tenses inconsistent)
    CORRECT: I went to the mall. I watched a movie there.

Idioms

Some of your initial problems with writing English are likely to arise from trying to adjust to a different and difficult grammar. If the English language employed an entirely systematic grammar, your learning would be easier, but English has patterns that are both complex and irregular. Among them are idioms, word groups that often defy grammatical rules and mean something other than what they appear to mean on the surface.

The expression "He kicked the bucket," does not mean that someone struck a cylindrical container with his foot; instead, it means that someone has died. That example is one kind of idiom. Because the expression suggests a certain irreverence, it would not be the choice of most people who want to make a statement about death; but if it is used, it must be used with its own precise wording, not "He struck the long cylindrical container with his foot," or "He did some bucket-kicking." Like other languages, the English language has thousands of these idioms. "Gee, Francine, you eat like a bird," the caption of the cartoon for Chapter 10, contains one. Expressions such as "the more the merrier" and "on the outs" are ungrammatical. They are also very informal expressions and, therefore, would seldom be used in college writing, though they are an indispensable part of a flexible, effective, all-purpose vocabulary. Because of their twisted meanings and illogic, idioms are likely to be among the last parts of language that a new speaker learns well. A speaker must know the culture thoroughly in order to understand when, where, and how slang and other idiomatic expressions work.

If you listen carefully and read extensively you will learn idioms. Your library will have dictionaries that explain them.

Suggestions for ESL Writers

1. Read your material aloud and try to detect the inconsistencies and awkward phrasing.

2. Have others read your material aloud for the same purposes.

3. If you have severe problems with grammatical awkwardness, try composing shorter, more direct sentences until you become more proficient in phrasing.

4. Keep a list of problems you have (such as articles, verb endings, clause patterns), review relevant parts of this chapter, and concentrate on your problem areas during your drafting, revising, and editing.

EXERCISE 40

Make corrections in the use of articles, verbs, and phrasing. (See the Answer Key for answers.)

```
                    George Washington at Trenton
     One of most famous battles during War of Independence
occur at Trenton, New Jersey, on Christmas Eve of the
1776. The colonists outmatched in supplies and finances
and were outnumbered in troop strength. Most observers in
other countries think rebellion would be put down soon.
British overconfident and believe there would be no more
battles until spring. But George Washington decide to
fight one more time. That Christmas, while large army of
Britishers having party and thinking about the holiday
season, Americans set out for surprise raid. They loaded
onto boats used for carrying ore and rowed across Delaware
River. George Washington stood tall in lead boat.
According to legend, drummer boy floated across river on
his drum, pulled by rope tied to boat. Because British did
not feel threatened by the ragtag colonist forces, they
unprepared to do battle. The colonists stormed living
quarters and the general assembly hall and achieved
victory. It was good for the colonists' morale, something
they needed, for they would endure long, hard winter
before they fighting again.
```

Appendix

Taking Tests

Good test-taking begins with good study techniques. These techniques involve, among other things, how to read, think, and write effectively. Those skills have been covered in this book. Here we will deal only with a few principles that apply directly and immediately to the test situation.

As the beginning of the semester, you should discover how you will be tested in each course. Match your note-taking and underlining of texts to the kind or kinds of tests you will take. Objective tests will usually require somewhat more attention to details than will subjective or essay tests.

For both types of tests—and you will probably have a combination—you should carefully apportion your time, deciding how much to spend on each section or essay, and allowing a few minutes for a quick review of answers. For both, you should also read the directions carefully, marking key words (if you are permitted to do so) as a reminder to you for concentration.

Objective Tests

Here are some tips on taking objective tests:

- Find out whether you will be graded on the basis of the number of correct answers or on the basis of right-minus-wrong. This is the difference: If you are graded on the basis of the number of correct answers, there is no penalty for guessing; therefore, if you want the highest possible score, you should leave no blanks. But if you are graded on the basis of right-minus-wrong (meaning one or a fraction of one is subtracted from your correct answers for every miss), then answer only if the odds of being right are in your favor. For example, if you know an answer is one of two possibilities, you have a 50 percent chance of getting it right; consequently, guess if the penalty is less than one because you could gain one by getting it right and lose less than one by getting it wrong. Ask your teacher to explain if there is a right-minus-wrong factor.

- If you are going to guess and you want to get some answers correct, you should pick one column and fill in the bubbles. By doing that, you will almost certainly get some correct.

- Studies show that in a typical four-part multiple choice test section, more answers are B and C than A and D.

- Statements with absolutes such as *always* and *never* are likely to be false, whereas statements with qualifications such as *usually* and *probably* are more likely to be true.

- If you don't know the answer, instead of fixating on it and getting frustrated, mark it with what seems right, put a dot alongside your answer, and go back later for a second look if time permits.

- When (and if) you go back to check your work, do not make changes unless you discover that you obviously marked one incorrectly. Studies have shown that first hunches are usually more accurate.

Subjective or Essay Tests

Here are some tips on taking subjective test:

- Consider the text, the approach taken by the instructor in lectures, and the overall approach in the course outline, and try to anticipate essay questions. Then, in your preparation, jot down and memorize simple outlines that will jog your memory during the test if you have anticipated correctly.

- Remember to keep track of time. A time-consuming A+ essay that does not allow you to finish the second half of the exam will result in a failing grade.

- Study the essay questions carefully. Underline key words. Each essay question will have two parts: the subject part and the treatment part. It may also have a limiting part. If you are required, for example, to compare and contrast President Carter and President Bush on their environmental programs, you should be able to analyze the topic immediately in this fashion:

    The *subject* is President Carter and President Bush.
    The *limitation* is their environmental programs.
    The *treatment* is comparison and contrast.

    EXAMPLE: Compare and contrast the environmental programs
                  treatment   *limitation*

    of President Carter and President Bush.
         subject

    The treatment part (here "compare and contrast") may very well be one of the forms of discourse such as definition, classification, or analysis, or it may be something like "evaluate" or "discuss," in which a certain form or forms would be used. Regardless of what the treatment word is, the first step is to determine the natural points of division and to prepare a simple outline or outline substitute for organization.

- In writing the answer, be sure that you include specific information as support for your generalizations.

Making Application

Two forms of practical writing that you may need even before you finish your college work are the letter of application and the résumé. They will often go together as requirements by an employer. In some instances the employer will suggest the form and content of the letter and résumé; in others, you will receive no directions and should adjust your letter and résumé to match the requirements and expectations as you perceive them. The models that follow are typical of what job applicants commonly submit.

Letter of Application

Write your letter of application with extreme care. You can even adapt **DCODE** for the process. Moving from **Delve** to **Concentrate** and then to **Organize** will generate ideas, focus your attention on a particular job opportunity, and establish order. ***Drafting*** with the revision will sharpen your presentation, and ***Editing*** will rid your paper of errors.

A few basic guidelines will serve you well:

- Use standard letter-size paper and type.
- Do not apologize, and do not brag.
- Do not go into tedious detail, but do relate your education, work experience, and career goals to the available job.
- Begin your letter with a statement indicating why you are writing the letter and how you heard about the job opening.
- End the letter by stating how you can be contacted for an interview.

Résumé

Employers are especially concerned about your most recent work experiences and education, so include them first, as indicated in the example. The heading "College Activities" can be replaced with "Interests and Activities." Your main concern is presenting relevant information in a highly readable form. Always end with a list of references.

Letter of Application

203 Village Center Avenue
Glendora, California 91740
July 11, 1993

Mr. Roy Ritter
Computers Unlimited
1849 N. Granada Avenue
Walnut, California 91789

Dear Mr. Ritter:

I am responding to your advertisement in the Los Angeles *Times* for the position of salesperson for used computers. Please consider me as a candidate.

In one more semester I will have completed my A.A. degree at Mt. San Antonio College with a major in Business Management and a minor in Computer Technology.

My experience relates directly to the job you offer. As a result of my part-time work for two years as lab technician at Mt. San Antonio College, I have come to know the operations of several different computers. I have also learned to explain the operations to people who have very little knowledge of computers. In my business classes, I have studied the practical approaches to advertising and sales while also learning theory. Each semester for the past two years, I have worked in the college bookstore, where I helped customers who were buying various products, including computers.

This job would coincide perfectly with my work in school, my work experience, and even my goal of being a salesperson with a large company.

Enclosed is my résumé with several references to people who know me well. Please contact them if you want information or if you would like a written evaluation.

I am available for an interview at your request.

Sincerely yours,

Benjamin Johanson

```
                          RÉSUMÉ

                    Benjamin Johanson
                    203 Village Center Avenue
                    Glendora, California 91740
                    (818) 987-5555
```

WORK EXPERIENCE:
  1990—93   Lab Assistant in the Mt. San Antonio College Computer Lab

  1990—93   Sales and Stock Technician in the Mt. San Antonio College Bookstore

EDUCATION:
  1990—93   Full-time student at Mt. San Antonio College

  1987—90   High school diploma from Glendora High School

COLLEGE ACTIVITIES:
        Hackers' Club (1992—1993)
        Chess Club (1992—1993)
        Forensics Club (1992—1993) —twice a regional debate champion

REFERENCES:
  Stewart Hamlen
  Chairperson, Business Department
  Mt. San Antonio College
  Walnut, California 91789
  (714) 594-5611, ext. 4707

  Bart Grassmont
  Personnel Director, Book Store
  Mt. San Antonio College
  Walnut, California 91789
  (714) 594-5611, ext. 4706

  Howard McGraw
  Coach, Forensics Team
  Mt. San Antonio College
  Walnut, California 91789
  (714) 594-5611, ext. 4575

Answer Key

Chapter 1

Exercise 4

1. Students cheat in school to release certain pressures. (E)
2. Shakespeare is an Elizabethan writer. (I)
3. The quarterback in football and the general of an army are alike in significant ways. (E)
4. Animals use color chiefly for protection. (E)
5. Portland is a city in Oregon. (I)
6. The life of the ocean is divided into distinct realms. (E)
7. Rome has a glorious and tragic story. (I)
8. Boston is the capital of Massachusetts. (I)
9. The word "macho" has a special meaning to the Hispanic community. (E)
10. The history of plastics is exciting. (I)

Exercise 7

Answers will vary. Possible answers:

I.
   A.
      1. Loud and fast
      2. Louder and faster
   B.
      3. Death
      4. Destruction

II.
   A.
      1. Electronic hissing
      2. Screams
   B. Props
   C. Lighting effects

III.
   A. Costumes
   B. Stage business
      1.
      2. Throwing fake buzzard eggs at audience
   C.
      1. Singing
      2.
         a. Guitars
         b. Drums
   D.
      1. Dancing
      2. Prancing
      3. Bungee jumping over audience

Chapter 15

Exercise 2

Neglected Children

~~The neglect of children by their parents can have many harmful effects. Three important ones are~~ discussed here. ~~Neglect affects a childs choices, a childs future, and a childs feelings.~~ *[Edited: Parents who neglect their children produce harmful effects in three areas: making choices, future relationships, and low self-esteem.]* These effects overlap adding to the confusion ~~he is~~ *they are* already experiencing. ~~A childs~~ *First, their* choices are ~~effected~~ *affected* by the parents' neglect. If ~~a child does~~ *children do* not get the healthy attention and affection from ~~his~~ *their* parents ~~he~~ *they* may withdraw socially or seek ~~it~~ *nurturing* elsewhere ~~and~~, all too often ~~unhealthy choices are made~~ *they make unhealthy choices*. The future of ~~the child~~ *children* is also shaped by neglect ~~and~~ *which* may set ~~him~~ *them* on a long road of addictions and dysfunctional relationships ~~in the future~~. ~~There is a large percentage of~~ *Moreover, many* abused children ~~which~~ *who* become parents and pass their neglect on ~~to~~ their children. ~~A parents'~~ *Third, children's* attitude around ~~the child~~ *them* gives ~~him many~~ *mixed* messages. ~~You~~ *Children* can get feelings of being unloved and unworthy of love ~~that way~~ *and they develop low self-esteem*. Instead of seeing ~~this~~ *the neglect* as a fault of ~~the parent~~ *the parents, children* can ~~get all bummed out~~ *become despondent* and can internalize these feelings ~~and see himself~~ *seeing themselves* as bad, as faulty ~~and as being different than other children~~, *and inadequate.*

Exercise 4

1. adv, adj
2. v, prep
3. conj, pro
4. adj, n
5. n, adj
6. n, pro
7. adj, conj
8. adj, prep
9. pro, adv
10. adj, pron
11. prep, adv
12. v, conj
13. adj, conj
14. pro, n
15. prep, adj
16. conj, v
17. n, v
18. adv, adj
19. adv, adj
20. adv, adj

Exercise 6

1. Kathy, dug
2. I, will be
3. Berlin/London, were bombed
4. Linda/you, will decide
5. captain/coach, stand
6. students, are applying
7. (you) tell
8. William Faulkner, wrote
9. I, have waited/thought
10. we, can find
11. customers, are
12. we, will find
13. players, assembled/elected
14. we, shall be living
15. few, may be delayed
16. you, did wish
17. (you) buy
18. reaction, was
19. cabin, lies
20. (you) leave

Exercise 8

1. OK	2. CS	3. FRAG	4. OK	5. CS
6. CS	7. OK	8. FRAG	9. OK	10. OK
11. RT	12. CS	13. FRAG	14. FRAG	15. FRAG
16. CS	17. OK	18. RT	19. RT	20. OK

Exercise 11

1. CP	2. CX	3. S	4. CX	5. CC
6. S	7. CX	8. CX	9. CP	10. CX
11. CP	12. CX	13. CP	14. CX	15. S
16. CP	17. S	18. S	19. CP	20. S

Exercise 13

1. Although cobras are among the most feared of all snakes, they are not the deadliest of all snakes.
   Cobras do not coil before they strike; therefore, they cannot strike for a long distance.
2. Cobras do not have a hood, but they flatten their neck by moving their ribs when they are nervous or frightened.
   Cobras use their poison in two ways: by injecting venom with their fangs and by spitting venom at their victims.
3. Although human beings will not die from the venom that has been spit, it can cause blindness if it is not washed from the eyes.
   A person can die from a cobra bite, and death may come in only a few hours.
4. Snake charmers have long worked with cobras; they use only a snake, a basket, and a flute.
   The snakes cannot *hear* the music, but they respond to the rhythmic movements of the charmers.
   The snake charmers are hardly ever in danger of being bitten because they defang the cobras or sew their mouths shut.
5. Most cobras flee from people, but they attack if they are cornered or if they are guarding their eggs.
   The tiny mongoose, the enemy of the cobra, uses its quickness and sharp teeth to kill the cobra.

Exercise 15

1. NP / or if it is no longer fun.
2. NP / and for his own behavior
3. NP / taking lecture notes
4. NP / Delete "he was also"
5. NP / to tell jokes
6. NP / and an increase in several fees
7. NP / than managing
8. NP / Giving
9. NP / and then by force.
10. NP / but also politically sophisticated
11. NP / captain not only of
12. NP / in both their
13. NP / and to ask questions.
14. NP / than writing
15. NP / and untruthful
16. NP / nor his purpose
17. P
18. NP / commander not only
19. NP / and a powerful
20. NP / and good food.

Exercise 17

1. makes	2. took	3. is	4. quit	5. didn't
6. go	7. will get	8. marries	9. is	10. is
11. asked	12. keeps	13. has	14. were	15. came
16. needed	17. finished	18. would	19. hands	20. was

Exercise 20

1. are	2. have	3. Has	4. eats	5. were
6. are	7. were	8. is	9. changes	10. has
11. was	12. are	13. attract	14. want	15. get
16. tells	17. seems	18. is	19. are	20. was

Exercise 24

1. she	2. she	3. him	4. them	5. me
6. she	7. him	8. We	9. us	10. I
11. she	12. they	13. I	14. Whom	15. whom
16. Who	17. whom	18. Who	19. whoever	20. I

Exercise 26

1. he or she	2. its	3. his or her	4. its	5. his or her
6. their	7. who	8. that	9. himself	10. her
11. its	12. their	13. their	14. he or she	15. her
16. their	17. his	18. they	19. he or she	20. himself or herself

Exercise 28

	From	To
1.	OK	
2.	OK	
3.	OK	
4.	you	students
5.	his	"Your short story . . . ."
6.	OK	
7.	that	This house belongs to Cynthia, whom we visited yesterday.
8.	OK	
9.	they	That college has
10.	OK	
11.	that	There on the table is a message that
12.	her (second)	mother, "Your ideas are good."
13.	OK	
14.	OK	
15.	which	a practice
16.	This	This infrequency

17. one   to be a lawyer.
18. you   he or she
19. it   This pamphlet says
20. he   and Edward admires

Exercise 30

1. a unique   2. more easily   3. really bad   4. is impossible
5. bad   6. better   7. were perfect.   8. more violent
9. the most   10. but overall   11. can mean only one   12. really
13. easily   14. already   15. all right   16. easier
17. bad   18. really   19. she only said   20. altogether

Exercise 32

1. D   Interested in my studies, I had
2. OK
3. M   that approximately a hundred
4. M   that approximately a hundred
5. D   in spite of my
6. D   night, I still had not completed
7. M   Gossiping noisily, the students
8. M   Gossiping noisily, the students
9. D   By practicing every day, one can learn
10. D While working in the factory, we made
11. M Last week, the doctor told him
12. D While returning from shopping, Debra remembered her promise and stopped.
13. D As we walked to school
14. M we studied grammar only on rare occasions
15. D To be correct, one should never write dangling infinitive phrases.
16. M To protect their hands, astronauts wore gloves.
17. D When I was only eight years old,
18. M I drank only a glass of milk.
19. M Jill tried carefully and constantly to avoid
20. D While I was recovering

Exercise 34

1. words, phrases,
2. strong,
3. modifiers,
4. clauses,
5. all,
6. Inside,
7. beginning,
8. pink, black, green,

9. night,
10. sharp,
11. finished,
12. Handel, both born in 1685,
13. Motor racing, not horse racing,
14. boy," Joe said,
15. Jones, the salesperson,
16. Well,
17. car, all sleek and shiny,
18. Tribbey, Oklahoma, on February 21, 1934.
19. down,
20. Tower, which is located in Paris,

Exercise 36

1. Hill;
2. countries;
3. dig, but
4. smoking; beautiful females, all in bathing suits; and luxury cars
5. thought;
6. pleasure,
7. pink-white, sweet blossoms; pumpkins, still just tiny green marbles;
8. Paris, for
9. Jesus; in fact, in comparing their lives,
10. an unusual one; another analyzes relationships among others, imaginary or real;
11. status; in fact,
12. people;
13. romance,
14. a mongrel puppy;
15. grandfathers, and
16. fire, but
17. told me so;
18. at a time;
19. people, and they
20. become a recluse;

Exercise 38

1. "In . . . men."
2. day's
3. *Lebensraum*
4. It's
5. 'Stop' or stop
6. birds'
7. it's
8. *Billy Budd*
9. "Ode . . . Nightingale"?
10. London's
11. he?
12. cave-in
13. 7's
14. Marciano—
15. interviewed:
16. Engels—were—
17. Romantic period
18. Independence
19. English
20. Aunt

Exercise 40

George Washington at Trenton

One of **the** most famous battles during the War of Independence occur**red** at Trenton, New Jersey, on Christmas Eve of ~~the~~ 1776. The colonists **were** outmatched in supplies and finances and **were** outnumbered in troop strength. Most observers in other countries **thought the** rebellion would be put down soon. **The** British **were** overconfident and believe**d** there would be no more battles until spring. But George Washington decide**d** to fight one more time. That Christmas, while **a** large army of Britishers **were** having party and thinking about the holiday season, **The** Americans set out for **a** surprise raid. They loaded onto boats used for carrying ore and rowed across **the** Delaware River. George Washington stood tall in **the** lead boat. According to legend, **the** drummer boy floated across **the** river on his drum, pulled by **a** rope tied to **a** boat. Because **the** British did not feel threatened by the ragtag colonist forces, they **were** unprepared to do battle. The colonists stormed **the** living quarters and the general assembly hall and achieved victory. It was good for the colonists' morale, something they needed, for they would endure **a** long, hard winter before ~~they~~ fighting again.

Text Credits

Maya Angelou   From *I Know Why The Caged Bird Sings*. Copyright © 1969 by Maya Angelou. Reprinted by permission of Random House, Inc.

Ed Anger   "Make Docs Wheel & Deal Like Used Car Salesmen," an editorial, January 19, 1993, from *Weekly World News*. Reprinted by permission.

W. H. Auden   "The Unknown Citizen" by W. H. Auden from *W. H. Auden: Collected Poems* ed. by Edward Mendelson. Copyright 1940 and renewed 1968 by W. H. Auden. Reprinted by permission of Random House, Inc.

Toni Cade Bambara   From *Gorilla, My Love* by Toni Cade Bambara. Copyright © 1970 by Toni Cade Bambara. Reprinted by permission of Random House, Inc.

Sharon Bernstein   "Multiculturalism: Building Bridges or Burning Them?" by Sharon Bernstein. Published November 30, 1992. Copyright, 1992, Los Angeles Times. Reprinted by permission.

Suzanne Britt   "Neat People Vs. Sloppy People" by Suzanne Britt from *Show and Tell*, 1983. Published by Contemporary Books Inc. Reprinted by permission of the author.

Norman Cousins   "Who Killed Benny Paret?" *Saturday Review*, May 5, 1962. Used by permission.

Michael Fox   From "What Is Your Pet Trying to Tell You?" Excerpted from *The World Book Year Book*. © 1981 World Book-Childcraft International, Inc. By permission of World Book, Inc.

Frankie and Johnny   "Frankie and Johnny" from *America's Favorite Ballads* by Pete Seeger. Copyright © 1961 (Renewed) by Oak Publications, a division of Music Sales Corporation (ASCAP). International Copyright Secured. All Rights Reserved. Used by Permission of Music Sales Corporation.

Bruce Jay Friedman   "Eating Alone in Restaurants" by Bruce Jay Friedman from *The Lonely Guy's Book of Life*, McGraw-Hill 1979. Reprinted by permission of McGraw-Hill Book Co.

Tipper Gore   "Curbing the Sexploitation Industry" from *The New York Times* March 14, 1988, OP-ED. Copyright © 1988 by The New York Times Company. Reprinted by permission.

Lewis Grossberger   "Triumph of the Wheel" from *Rolling Stone*, December 4, 1986. By Straight Arrow Publishers, Inc. All rights reserved. Reprinted by permission.

Ted Gup   "Foul" from *Time*, April 3, 1989. Copyright 1989 by The Time, Inc. Magazine Company. Reprinted by permission.

Doug Harbrecht   From "Beauty or the Beast" by Doug Harbrecht. Copyright 1992 by the National Wildlife Federation. Reprinted from the July/August issue of *International Wildlife*.

William Helmreich   "Optimism, Tenacity Lead Way Back to Life" from the *Los Angeles Times* November 25, 1992. Reprinted by permission of the author.

Mary Ann Hogan   "Why We Carp and Harp" from the *Los Angeles Times* 3/10/92. Copyright © 1992 by Mary Ann Hogan. Reprinted by permission of the author.

David Levine   "I'm Outta Here" from *Seventeen*, March 1992 issue. Reprinted by permission of the author.

Malcolm X   From *The Autobiography of Malcolm X* by Malcolm X, with Alex Haley. Copyright © 1964 by Alex Haley and Malcolm X. Copyright © 1965 by Alex Haley and Betty Shabazz. Reprinted by permission of Random House, Inc.

W. S. Merwin   "Unchopping a Tree" from *The Miner's Pale Children*, Atheneum, Copyright © 1969, 1970 by W. S. Merwin. Reprinted by permission of Georges Borchardt, Inc.

Louis Nizer   "How About Low-cost Drugs for Addicts?" from *The New York Times* June 8, 1986. Copyright © 1986 by The New York Times Company. Reprinted by permission.

Kesaya E. Noda   "Growing Up Asian in America" from *Making Waves* by Asian Women United of California. Reprinted by permission of Beacon Press.

Polinagaysi Ooyawayma   "No Turning Back" from *No Turning Back* Copyright © 1964. Reprinted by permission of The University of New Mexico Press.

Jo Goodwin Parker   "What is Poverty?" from *America's Other Children: Public Schools Outside Suburbia*, edited by George Henderson. Copyright © 1971 by the University of Oklahoma Press.

Judith Ramsey   "Guide to Recognizing and Handling Mental Illness," *Family Circle* (October 1974). Reprinted by permission of the author.

Richard Rodriguez   "Private Language, Public Language" and "Does America Still Exist?" from *Hunger of Memory*. Copyright © 1982 by Richard Rodriguez. Reprinted by permission of David R. Godine, Publisher.

Tim Rutten   "Face to Face with Guns and the Young Men Who Use Them" by Tim Rutten. Published April 2, 1992. Copyright, 1992, Los Angeles Times. Reprinted by permission.

Irwin Shaw   "The Girls in Their Summer Dresses" from *Five Decades* by Irwin Shaw. Copyright © 1978 by Irwin Shaw. Used by permission of Dell Books, a division of Bantam, Doubleday, Dell Publishing Group, Inc.

Gary Soto   "Looking for Work" from *Living Up the Street*, Copyright © 1985 by Gary Soto. Used by permission of Strawberry Hill Press, Portland, Oregon.

Amy Tan   "The Rules of the Game," reprinted by permission of The Putnam Publishing Group from *The Joy Luck Club* by Amy Tan. Copyright © 1989 by Amy Tan.

Luis Torres   "Los Chinos Discover el Barrio," May 11, 1989. Reprinted by permission of Luis Torres, a Los Angeles-based journalist.

Anastasia Toufexis   "Struggling for Sanity," *Time*, January 30, 1989. Copyright 1989 The Time, Inc. Magazine Company. Reprinted by permission.

Nancy Traver   "Children without Pity" *Time*, October 26, 1992. Copyright 1992 The Time, Inc. Magazine Company. Reprinted by permission.

Webster's Ninth New Collegiate Dictionary   Extract reprinted by permission. From *Webster's Ninth New Collegiate Dictionary* © 1991 by Merriam-Webster, Inc. publisher of the Merriam-Webster ® dictionaries.

Carl G. Wilgus   From "Conserving Energy as You Ski" *Skiing* (February 1981). Reprinted by permission.

William Carlos Williams   "The Use of Force" from *The Farmers Daughters*. Copyright 1938 by William Carlos Williams. Reprinted by permission of New Directions Publishing Corporation.

Elizabeth Wong   "The Struggle to Be an All-American Girl" reprinted by permission of the author.

Name and Title Index

Adams, Henry, *Education of Henry Adams, The*, H13
Adler, Mortimer J., "Kinds of Book Owners," 251
"Adobe: Mud for Castles and Hovels" (Maurer), H8
Angell, Roger, "On the Ball," 89
Anger, Ed, "Make Docs Wheel and Deal Like Used Car Salesmen!," 397–398
Angelou, Maya, "Cotton-Picking Time," 63, 70–71
Anonymous, "Frankie and Johnny," 370–371
"Arsenic for Everyone" (Carson), 215
Ashen, Frank, "Why Not 'Ms. and Mr.'?," 125
Auden, W. H., "Unknown Citizen, The," 374–375
"Autobiography of Malcolm X, The" (Malcolm X and Haley), 190–191

"Babe Ruth" (Gallico), 89
"Baby Nag-a-Lot" (*Time* Magazine), 124
"Back of the Bus" (King), 214
Bambara, Toni Cade, "Raymond's Run," 357–361
Barrio, Raymond, "Shack of Misery, A," 97–98
"Ben Franklin, Renaissance Man" (Udell), 165–166
Benedict, Ruth, *Patterns of Culture*, 312
Bernstein, Sharon, "Multiculturalism: Building Bridges or Burning Them?," 217–219
"Big Picture, The" (Larrabee), H12
"Big Wheel, A" (Grossberger), 151–152
"Birth of an Island, The" (Carson), 181–182
"Blue Winds Dancing" (Whitecloud), 96
"Blues Abroad, The" (Lee), 62–63
"Boredom of Fantasy, The" (Koestler), H12
"Boss Observed, The" (Ford), 149
Britt, Suzanne, "Neat People vs. Sloppy People," 284–285
Brooks, John, "Effects of the Telephone, The," 212
Brown, John Mason, "Pleasant Agony," H13
Browning, Robert, "My Last Duchess," 372

Campos, Maria, 36
"Cancer Puzzle, The" (Weaver), 147–148
"Cannibalism in Sibling Rivalry" (Morris), 123
Capili, Vanessa, "Men and Women: More Equal Than the Same," 301–302
Capp, Glenn R., "Listen Up!," 250

Carson, Rachel
  "Arsenic for Everyone," 215
  "Birth of an Island, The," 181–182
"Cat, The" (Twain), 95
"Causes of Mental Illness" (Ramsay), 23–24
"Causes of World War II" (Taylor), 213
"Chain of Reason vs. the Chain of Thumbs, The" (Gould), H5
"Cheating Is Not Worth the Bother" (Olivas), 134–139
"Children Without Pity" (Traver), 129–131
Churchill, Winston, *Marlborough, His Life and Times*, H12, H13
Clurman, Harold, *Portable Arthur Miller, The*, 430
"Conformity" (Mussen and Rosenzweig), 320
"Conserving Energy as You Ski" (Wilgus), 185–186
"Cops Can Be Human" (Larue), 132
"Cotton-Picking Time" (Angelou), 63, 70–71
Cousins, Norman, 37
  "Who Killed Benny Paret?," 224–225
Cuber, John, "Kinds of Scientific Findings," 252
"Curbing the Sexploitation Industry" (Gore), 395–396
"Customer Is Always Right, The" (Mullins), 78

Dalton, Robert H., "Personality," 318
"Death by Gangbanging" (Gonzales), 225–226
Del Rey, Lester, "Mysterious Sky, The," 278
Del Turco, A., "Popping the Cork," 197–198
DeSarro, Angela
  "No Secrets to Her Success: Reba McEntire," 226–227
  "Right to Die," 405–406
  "Rosanne," 164–165
  "Three Kinds of Siblings," 259–260
"Desert and the Jungle, The" (Krutch), 280
Dillard, Anne, "Strangers to Darkness," 93–94
"Does America Still Exist?" (Rodriguez), 322–324
Dudley, Louise
  "Musical Instruments: Blowing, Bowing, and Beating," 256–257
  "Temple and the Cathedral, The," 282

Eardley, A. J., "Glaciers: Types and Subtypes," 248

"Eating Alone in Restaurants" (Friedman), 183–184
Education of Henry Adams, The (Adams), H13
"Effects of Child Abuse, The" (Johnson), 432–440
"Effects of the Telephone, The" (Brooks), 212
Emerson, Ralph Waldo, "Self-Reliance," 278

"Face to Face with Guns and the Young Men Who Use Them" (Rutten), 72–73
Faricy, Austin
  "Musical Instruments: Blowing, Bowing, and Beating," 256–257
  "Temple and the Cathedral, The," 282
Fee, Ed, "Underwater Paradise," 108
"Fighting, Founding Mothers, The" (Johnson), 133
Ford, Richard, "Boss Observed, The," 149
"Foul" (Gup), 117
Fox, Michael W.
  "What Is Your Pet Trying to Tell You?," 38, H9
Frank, Francine, "Why Not 'Ms. and Mr.'?," 125
"Frankie and Johnny" (Anonymous), 370–371
"Freeze-Dried Memories" (Jordan), 122
Friedman, Bruce Jay, "Eating Alone in Restaurants," 183–184
Fulton, Michael, "More Than Just a House Call," 351–355

Gallico, Paul, "Babe Ruth," 89
"Georgia on My Mind" (Jenkins), 321
"Girls in Their Summer Dresses, The" (Shaw), 363–365
"Glaciers: Types and Subtypes" (Eardley), 248
"Going Too Far" (Wong), 331–335
"Gonna Rock To-o-N-i-i-ight!" (Young), 178
Gonzales, Aida, "Death by Gangbanging," 225–226
"Good King Elvis" (Miller), 32–33
Gore, Tipper, "Curbing the Sexploitation Industry," 395–396
Gould, Stephen Jay, "Chain of Reason vs. the Chain of Thumbs, The," H5
Grossberger, Lewis, 37
  "Big Wheel, A," 151–152
"Growing Up Asian in America" (Noda), 155–159
Gup, Ted, "Foul," 117

Haley, Alex, "Autobiography of Malcolm X, The," 190–191
Hall, Holly, "Scaled Slaves," 118
"Heavenly Father, Divine Goalie" (Prebish), 279
"Hefty Burger" (Scott), 90
Helmreich, William, "Optimism, Tenacity Lead Way Back to Life," 153–154
Highet, Gilbert
    "Migration of Ideas, The," H11
    "Subway Station," 101
Hills, L. Rust, "How to Eat an Ice-Cream Cone," 180–181
Hogan, Mary Ann, "Why We Carp and Harp," 253–255
"Hopi Way, The" (Qoyawayma [White]), 325–327
"How About Low-Cost Drugs for Addicts?" (Nizer), 393–394
"How to Eat an Ice-Cream Cone" (Hills), 180–181
"How to Sharpen a Knife" (Pettit), 177
Humphries, Daniel, 37
Hutchinson, James, "Pain Unforgettable," 74–77
Huxley, Aldous, "Who Are You?," H12

"I'm Outta Here!" (Levine), 220–223
"Is Our Common Man Too Common?" (Krutch), H1

Jackson, Byron, "Make Me a Traffic Cop," 17–22
Jasper, Shontel, "She Came a Long Way," 109
Jeffries, Jennifer, "Two Loves: Puppy and True," 294–298
Jenkins, Ray, "Georgia on My Mind," 321
Johnson, Maxine, "Fighting, Founding Mothers, The," 133
Johnson, Sarah Jo, "Effects of Child Abuse, The," 432–440
Jordan, Pat, "Freeze-Dried Memories," 122

Keller, Helen
    "Language Set Me Free," 65
    Story of My Life, The, 62
Kendall, Raymond, "Sonata, The," 150
"Kick Me!" (Morgan), 227–233
"Kinds of Book Owners" (Adler), 251
"Kinds of Scientific Findings" (Cuber), 252
King, Martin Luther, Jr., "Back of the Bus," 214
Knight, Frederick B., "Maslow's Classification of Motives," 249
Koestler, Arthur, "Boredom of Fantasy, The," H12
Krutch, Joseph Wood
    "Desert and the Jungle, The," 280
    "Is Our Common Man Too Common?," H11
    "Voice of the Desert, The," H11

"Language Set Me Free" (Keller), 65
Larrabee, Eric, "Big Picture, The," H12
Larue, Janet, "Cops Can Be Human," 132
Leah, "Razor Wire Sweat Lodge," 42–54
Lee, Andrea, "Blues Abroad, The," 62–63
Levine, David, "I'm Outta Here!," 220–223
"Listen Up!" (Capp), 250
"Living Cell, The" (Rubenstein), 148
"Looking for Work" (Soto), 286–289
Lopez, Jerry, "Types of Nightclubbers," 258
"Los Chinos Discover el Barrio" (Torres), 63, 66
"Love Happened" (Pei), 79
Lurie, Alison, "Pink Kittens and Blue Spaceships," 281

"Magic Johnson" (Norton), 160–164
"Make Docs Wheel and Deal Like Used Car Salesmen!" (Anger), 397–398
"Make Me a Traffic Cop" (Jackson), 17–22
"Making a Perfect Paper Airplane" (Tillman), 199–200
Malcolm X, "Autobiography of Malcolm X, The," 190–191
Malone, Jackie, "Sexist Men as Victims," 417
Marlborough, His Life and Times (Churchill), H12, H13
"Maslow's Classification of Motives" (Knight), 249
Maugham, W. Somerset, "Summing Up, The," H13
Maurer, James, "Adobe: Mud for Castles and Hovels," H8
Maxwell, Brian, 37
"Medieval Society" (Wallbank), 247
"Men and Women: More Equal Than the Same" (Capili), 301–302
Mendez, Gloria, "Out of His Element," 355–356
Merwin, W. S., "Unchopping a Tree," 187–189
"Migration of Ideas, The" (Highet), H11
Miller, Eric, "New Wind Blowing, A," 398–404
Miller, Jim, "Good King Elvis," 32–33
Mondegaran, Maysim, "Sabsi Polo Mahi," 192–197
Montagu, Ashley, "Natural Superiority of Women, The," 283
"More Than Just a House Call" (Fulton), 351–355
Morgan, Jamie, "Kick Me!," 227–233
Morris, Desmond
    "Cannibalism in Sibling Rivalry," 123
    "Personal Space," 120
Mullins, James, "Customer is Always Right, The," 78
"Multiculturalism: Building Bridges or Burning Them?" (Bernstein), 217–219
"Musical Instruments: Blowing, Bowing, and Beating" (Dudley and Faricy), 256–257

Mussen, Paul, "Conformity," 320
"My Last Duchess" (Browning), 372
"Mysterious Sky, The" (Del Rey), 278

"Natural Superiority of Women, The" (Montagu), 283
"Nature on the Rampage" (Sutton and Sutton), 179
"Neat People vs. Sloppy People" (Britt), 284–285
"New Wind Blowing, A" (Miller), 398–404
Nizer, Louis, "How About Low-Cost Drugs for Addicts?," 393–394
"No Secrets to Her Success: Reba McEntire" (DeSarro), 226–227
Noda, Kesaya A., "Growing Up Asian in America," 155–159
Norton, Cyrus, "Magic Johnson," 160–164

Olivas, Zara, "Cheating Is Not Worth the Bother," 134–139
"On the Ball" (Angell), 89
"On Various Kinds of Thinking" (Robinson), 311
"Optimism, Tenacity Lead Way Back to Life" (Helmreich), 153–154
Orwell, George, "Reflections on Gandhi," H12, H13
"Out of His Element" (Mendez), 355–356

"Pain Unforgettable" (Hutchinson), 74–77
Parker, Jo Goodwin, "What Is Poverty?," 327–329
Patterns of Culture (Benedict), 312
Pei, Sandra, "Love Happened," 79
"Personal Space" (Morris), 120
"Personality" (Dalton), 318
"Perspectives on Motivation" (Proctor), 335–336
Peterson, Janet, "Use of Self-Analysis, The," 356–357
Pettit, Florence H., "How To Sharpen A Knife," 177
"Pink Kittens and Blue Spaceships" (Lurie), 281
"Pleasant Agony" (Brown), H13
Poe, Edgar Allan, "Tell-Tale Heart, The," 367–369
"Popping the Cork" (Del Turco), 197–198
Portable Arthur Miller, The (Clurman), 430
Prebish, Charles, "Heavenly Father, Divine Goalie," 279
"Prison Slang" (White), 330–331
"Private Language, Public Language" (Rodriguez), 290–293
Proctor, Michelle, "Perspectives on Motivation," 335–336

Qoyawayma, Polingaysi (Elizabeth Q. White), "Hopi Way, The," 325–327

Ramsay, Judith, "Causes of Mental Illness," 23–24

"Raymond's Run" (Bambara), 357–361
"Razor Wire Sweat Lodge" (Leah), 42–54
"Reflections on Gandhi" (Orwell), H12, H13
"Richard Cory" (Robinson), 373
"Right to Die" (DeSarro), 405–406
Rivera, Juanita, "Santa Anas, The," 105–107
Robinson, Edwin Arlington, "Richard Cory," 373
Robinson, James Harvey, "On Various Kinds of Thinking," 311
Rodriguez, Richard
    "Does America Still Exist?," 322–324
    "Private Language, Public Language," 290–293
"Rosanne" (DeSarro), 164–165
Rosen, Ruth, "Search for Yesterday," 3
Rosenzweig, Mark, "Conformity," 320
Rubenstein, Irwin, "Living Cell, The," 148
"Rules of the Game" (Tan), 99–100
Russell, Bertrand, "Unhappy American Way, The," H10
Rutten, Tim, "Face to Face with Guns and the Young Men Who Use Them," 72–73

"Sabzi Polo Mahi" (Mondegaran), 192–197
"Sam and Woody" (Sinclair), 299–300
"Santa Anas, The" (Rivera), 105–107
"Scaled Slaves" (Hall), 118
Scott, Dale, "Hefty Burger," 90
"Search for Yesterday" (Rosen), 3
"Self-Reliance" (Emerson), 278
"Sexist Men as Victims" (Malone), 417
"Shack of Misery, A" (Barrio), 97–98
Shakespeare, William, H11
Shaw, Irwin, "Girls in Their Summer Dresses, The," 363–365
"She Came a Long Way" (Jasper), 109
Sinclair, Ray, "Sam and Woody," 299–300
"Sonata, The" (Kendall), 150
Soto, Gary, "Looking for Work," 286–289
"Sounds of the City, The" (Tuite), 102–103

Story of My Life, The (Keller), 62
"Strangers to Darkness" (Dillard), 93–94
"Struggle to Be an All-American Girl, The" (Wong), 64, 68–69
"Struggling for Sanity" (Toufexis), 126–128
"Subway Station" (Highet), 101
"Summing Up, The" (Maugham), H13
Sutton, Ann, "Nature on the Rampage," 179
Sutton, Myron, "Nature on the Rampage," 179

Tan, Amy, "Rules of the Game," 99–100
Tanner, Marge, "Types of Fly Fighters," 260–265
Taylor, A. J. P., "Causes of World War II," 213
"Tell-Tale Heart, The" (Poe), 367–369
"Temple and the Cathedral, The" (Dudley and Faricy), 282
Tepper, Morris, "Tornado," 319
"Three Kinds of Siblings" (DeSarro), 259–260
Tillman, John L., "Making a Perfect Paper Airplane," 199–200
"Tornado" (Tepper), 319
Torres, Luis, "Los Chinos Discover el Barrio," 63, 66
Toufexis, Anastasia
    "Struggling for Sanity," 126–128
    "What Happens to Steroid Studs?," 216
Traver, Nancy, "Children Without Pity," 129–131
Tuite, James, "Sounds of the City, The," 102–103
Twain, Mark, "Cat, The," 95
"Two Loves: Puppy and True" (Jeffries), 294–298
"Types of Fly Fighters" (Tanner), 260–265
"Types of Nightclubbers" (Lopez), 258

Udell, Allison, "Ben Franklin, Renaissance Man," 165–166

"Unchopping a Tree" (Merwin), 187–189
"Underwater Paradise" (Fee), 108
"Unhappy American Way, The" (Russell), H10
"Unknown Citizen, The" (Auden), 374–375
"Use of Force, The" (Williams), 348–350
"Use of Self-Analysis, The" (Peterson), 356–357

"Voice of the Desert, The" (Krutch), H11

Wallbank, T. Walter, "Medieval Society," 247
Weaver, Robert F., "Cancer Puzzle, The," 147–148
"What Happens to Steroid Studs?" (Toufexis), 216
"What Is Poverty?" (Parker), 327–329
"What Is Your Pet Trying to Tell You?" (Fox), 38, H9
White, Elizabeth Q. (Polingaysi Qoyawayma), "Hopi Way, The," 325–327
White, Jeri, "Prison Slang," 330–331
Whitecloud, Thomas S., "Blue Winds Dancing," 96
"Who Are You?" (Huxley), H12
"Who Killed Benny Paret?" (Cousins), 224–225
Why Not 'Ms. and Mr.'? (Frank and Ashen), 125
"Why We Carp and Harp" (Hogan), 253–255
Wilgus, Carl, "Conserving Energy as You Ski," 185–186
Williams, William Carlos, "Use of Force, The," 348–350
Wong, Elizabeth, "Struggle to Be an All-American Girl, The," 64, 68–69
Wong, Linda, "Going Too Far," 331–335

Young, Jennifer McBride, "Gonna Rock To-o-N-i-i-ight!," 178

Subject Index

a, H109
  as article adjective, H18
  with count nouns, H112–H113
  as noun indicator, H17
a lot/alot, H110
Abbreviations
  in bibliographical entries for government publications, 424
  after names, capitalization of, H100
  punctuation with, H88, H90
Abstract words, 91
accept/except, H109
accidently, H82
Action words. *See* Verbs
Active voice, H10–H11, H66
Adams, Henry, *Education of Henry Adams, The*, H13
Addition, transitional words and expressions to indicate, H3
Addresses (locations), punctuation with, H91
Addresses (speeches), bibliographical entries for, 424
Adjectives, H18, H80. *See also* Modifiers
  adverbs compared with, H82
  article, H18
  capitalization of, H99
  coordinate, H90
  demonstrative, as transitional words and expressions, H3
  problems with, H81
  punctuation with, H90, H102
  selecting, H80
  showing comparison, H81
  this and *these* as, H17
  two or more words used as, H90, H102
  verbals as, H30
Adverbs, H19, H80. *See also* Modifiers
  adjectives compared with, H82
  conjunctive. *See* Transitional connectives
  introductory, H12
  prepositions compared with, H20
  problems with, H81–H82
  selecting, H80
  showing comparison, H81
  standard and nonstandard usage of, H82
  verbals as, H30
advice/advise, H109
After this, therefore, because of this (*post hoc, ergo propter hoc*) fallacy, 210, 389
Airplane names, H97
all, subject-verb agreement and, H62
all ready/already, H82, H110

all right/alright, H82, H110
all together/altogether, H82, H110
Alphabetical order, in bibliographies, 423
Alternate antecedents, pronoun-antecedent agreement and, H73
Alternate subjects, subject-verb agreement and, H62
altogether/all together, H82, H110
an, H109
  as article adjective, H18
  with count nouns, H112–H113
  as noun indicator, H17
Analogy, 278
  false, 390
  in inductive reasoning, 387
  suggested topics for writing, 279–280
Analytical analysis, of literature, 346–347
Analytical definition, 312
and, H109. *See also both/and*
Anecdotes, 37, 61
Antagonist, 345
Antecedents
  agreement with pronouns. *See* Pronouns, agreement with antecedents
  pronoun reference and, H76–H77
Anthologies
  bibliographical entries for, 422, 424, 426
  MLA documentation style for, 425
any, subject-verb agreement and, H62
Apostrophes, H101
Application letters, A2–A3, A4
Appositives, H46
  punctuation with, H30, H98
Arguing against the person (*argumentum ad hominem*) fallacy, 390
Argumentation
  audience and, 385
  components of, 385
  definition of, 384
  definitions in, 385
  inductive and deductive reasoning and, 387–389
  logical fallacies and, 389–390
  organization of, 385–386
  proof for, 386
  proposition and, 384–385
  purpose of, 384
  suggested topics for writing, 406–407
Argumentum ad hominem (arguing against the person) fallacy, 390
Article adjectives, H18
Articles (in periodicals). *See* Periodicals
Articles (parts of speech), H109, H112
  as article adjectives, H18

  with count nouns, H112–H113
  definite, H17, H113
  indefinite, H17, H18, H109, H112–H113
  as noun indicators, H17
as, pronouns in subjective case as subject and, H68
Attitudes
  of audience, process analysis and, 176
  tone and, H6–H7
Audience
  argumentation and, 385
  attitude of, 176
  knowledge of, 176
  process analysis and, 176
  usage and, H6
Author file, in libraries, 418, 419
Authoritative sources, in argumentation, 386
Authors, citing. *See* Bibliographical entries; Documented writing; MLA style; Research papers

Background
  in argumentation, 385
  in introductory paragraph, 35
bad/badly, H82
Balance, H49
  basic principles of, H49–H50
  in sentence structure, H49–H50
  signal words for, H50
BAT WASHTUB, H31–H32
Begging the question, 390
Being verbs, H18, H24
Belief, questions of, 384–385
Bible, punctuation of chapters and verses of, H98
Bibliographical entries
  for books
    anthologies, 422, 424, 426
    with corporate author, 423
    encyclopedias, 424
    multiple books by same author, 423
    by one author, 422, 427
    single-volume, 425
    by two or more authors, 423
    with unknown author, 426
  for conference proceedings, 424
  for government publications, 424
  for lectures, speeches, and addresses, 424
  for periodicals
    editorials in, 423
    monthly or bimonthly magazines, 423
    newspaper articles, 423

unsigned articles in, 427
weekly or biweekly magazines, 423, 427
for personal interviews, 424
Bibliographies. *See also* Bibliographical entries
for periodicals, 420
preliminary, 422–424
Biographical dictionaries, 418
Black English. *See* Community dialect
Books
bibliographical entries for. *See* Bibliographical entries, for books
MLA style for. *See* MLA style
titles of. *See* Titles (of works)
both/and, H20
as signal for parallel structure, H50
Brackets, 423, H98
Brainstorming, 4, 5, 42, 245–246
Business names
capitalization of, H100
subject-verb agreement and, H63
Business writing
letters, punctuating, H98
parentheses in, H99

Calendar references
capitalization of, H100
punctuation in, H91
Call numbers, in libraries, 418, 419, 422
Capitalization, H99–H100
Card catalog, in libraries, 418, 419
Case, of pronouns. *See* Pronouns, case of
Categorical syllogism, 388
Cause and effect, in inductive reasoning, 387
Cause-and-effect analysis
definition and, 315
definition of, 208
immediate and remote, 209
introducing, 210–211
patterns in, 211
primary and secondary, 209
with process analysis, 175
purpose of, 208–209
sequence in, 210
topic sentence or thesis for, 209
Central character, in literature, 346
Characters, in literature, 345
central characters, 346
literary analysis and, 347
choose/chose, H110
Chronological order. *See* Order, time
Circular definition, 313
Circular reasoning, 390
Classification, 116
avoiding overlap in, 243
complex, 248
definition and, 315

definition of, 242–244
effectiveness of, 243–244
principles that fit purpose of, 243
simple, 247
suggested topics for writing, 266–267
writing with DCODE, 245–247
Clauses, H37
dependent. *See* Dependent clauses
independent, H30, H37, H38
combining in complex sentences, H44–H45
connecting, H37–H38
introductory, H12
main, punctuation with, H89, H93, H98
making into separate sentences, H32
nonessential, commas to set off, H90
noun, in complex sentences, H38
subject-verb agreement and, H61
varying sentence structure with, H13
Climactic order, of sentence structure, H11
Climax, in literature, 345
cluess, 3, 16, 45. *See also* Coherence; Emphasis; Language; Sentences, structure of; Support; Unity
Clustering, 4–5, 6, 10, 43, 246
finding points for comparison and contrast with, 273–274
Coherence
overall plan and, H2
point of view and, H4–H5
pronoun reference and, H3
repetition of key words and phrases and, H3
in revising, 16, H2–H5
transitional words and expressions and, H2–H3
Collective nouns
pronoun-antecedent agreement and, H73
subject-verb agreement and, H62
Colons, H98
Combination signal words, H50
Comma splices, H30–H31
correcting, H31–H32
identifying, H31
Commas
in addresses, H91
in compound-complex sentences, H46
with coordinating conjunctions, H38, H39, H89
correcting comma splices and run-togethers with, H31
in dates, H91
with dependent clauses, H39, H45
for emphasis, H11
after introductory modifiers, H89
in numbers, H91
with quotation marks, H97
in salutations and closings of letters, H91

to separate coordinate adjectives, H90
to separate main clauses, H89
to separate sentence elements that might be misread, H90
in series, H11, H89
to set off adjectives in pairs following nouns, H90
to set off nonessential words, phrases, and clauses, H90
to set off nouns used as direct address, H90
to set off parenthetical elements, H90
Community dialect, H6, H53–H55
adjectives and adverbs and, H82
verbs and, H54–H55
Comparative adjectives, H81
Comparative adverbs, H81
Comparison and contrast, 116
"4 P's" of, 273
analogy and, 278
suggested topics for writing, 279–280
definition and, 317
definition of, 272
generating topics for, 273
patterns for, 274–277
points in, 273–274
clustering as technique for finding, 273–274
presentation of, 276–277
purpose of, 273
suggested topics for writing, 303–305
transitional words and expressions to indicate, H3
Complement, noun clauses as, H38
Complex classification, 248
Complex sentences, H38, H39
combining sentences to make, H43–H45
punctuating, H45
Compound-complex sentences, H38, H39, H45–H46
punctuating, H45
Compound numbers, hyphens in, H102
Compound sentences, H37–H38, H39
combining sentences to make, H42–H43
punctuating, H43
Compound subjects, H25
subject-verb agreement and, H61, H62
Compound verbs, H24
Compound words, hyphens in, H102
Computer catalog, in libraries, 418, 419
Computerized indexing systems, in libraries, 417, 421
Concentrate stage, in DCODE process, 3, 8, 43–44, 246
Concession, transitional words and expressions to indicate, H3
Concluding paragraphs, 32, 36–38
ineffective, 37–38

Concrete examples, 119
Concrete words, 91
Condition, transitional words and expressions to indicate, H3
Conference proceedings, bibliographical entries for, 424
Conflict
  in literature, 345, 347
  in narratives, 60
Conjunctions, H20–H21
  coordinating. *See* Coordinating conjunctions
  introductory, H12
  objects of prepositions compared with, H21
  paired, H20, H38
  subordinating, H21, H31–H32
Conjunctive adverbs. *See* Transitional connectives
Connectives, transitional. *See* Transitional connectives
Consequences, transitional words and expressions to indicate, H3
Contractions, H101
Contrast. *See* Comparison and contrast
Conversation
  in narratives, 61
  punctuating, H97
Coordinate adjectives, punctuation with, H90
Coordinating conjunctions, H20
  correcting comma splices and run-togethers with, H31
  independent clauses joined by, H37–H38
  punctuation with, H38, H39, H43, H89, H93
  as signals for parallel structure, H50
  verbs joined by, H24
Coordination, combining sentences and, H42–H43, H45–H46
cops, 3, 18, 48. *See also* Capitalization; Punctuation
Count nouns, H112
  rules for, H112–H113
Countries, capitalization of, H99
Courses, capitalization of, H100
Critical reading, thinking, and writing, 23–24

Dangling modifiers, H85
Dashes, H11, H97–H98
Dates
  capitalization of, H100
  punctuation with, H91
Days of the week, capitalization of, H100
DCODE process, 3–19
  Concentrate stage of, 3, 8, 43–44, 246
  Delve stage of, 3, 4–6, 42–43, 245–246
  Draft stage of, 3, 16–18, 45–47, 247, H2–H4

Edit stage of, 3, 18–19, 48–50
flexibility of, 41
Organize stage of, 3, 10–11, 44–45, 247
writing classification using, 245–247
writing essays using, 41–50
writing literary analysis using, 347–348
writing reaction statements using, 27
writing research papers using, 416
writing summaries using, 25–26
Deductive reasoning, 387–388, 389
  logical fallacies in, 389–390
Definite article, H113
Definition, 116
  analytical, 312
  in argumentation, 385
  circular, 313
  definition of, 310
  examples contrasted with, 312
  extended, 314–317
    developing, 315–316, 317
    introduction of, 317
    order of, 317
    purpose of, 314
    suggested topics for writing, 337–338
  formal, 312
  in introductory paragraph, 35–36
  position of words in sentence and, H82
  with process analysis, 175
  simple, 310–314
    avoiding common problems in, 313
    blending into writing, 311–312
    in dictionary entries, 310–311
Delve stage, in DCODE process, 3, 4–6, 42–43, 245–246
Demonstrative adjectives, as transitional words and expressions, H3
Dependent clauses, H37, H38
  correcting comma splices and run-togethers with, H31–H32
  punctuation with, H39, H45
  as sentence fragments, H29
  subordinating conjunctions and, H21
Description
  definition and, 315
  definition of, 88
  in narratives, 63–64
  objective, 88–89, 91
  subjective, 89, 91
  writing, 89–92
    suggested topics for, 110–112
Deserts, capitalization of, H100
Detached position. *See* Third-person point of view
Details, in description, 90
  order of, 92
Developmental paragraph, definition of, 2–3
Dewey Decimal System call number, 418, 419

Dialect. *See* Community dialect
Dialogue
  in narratives, 64
  punctuating, H97
Diction, 16, H7
  in description, 90, 91
  modifiers and, H80
  tone and, H7
Dictionary, biographical, 418
Dictionary entries, 310–311
Dilemma, false, 390
Direct questions, punctuating, H88
Directive process analysis, 174, 175
Distances, subject-verb agreement and, H63
Documented writing
  DCODE for, 416
  ideas not quoted and, 416–417
  library-based, 414. *See also* Library research
  MLA style for. *See* MLA style
  plagiarism and, 416, 430–431
  presentation of, 417
  quotations and, 416
  research papers and. *See* Research papers
  textbook-based, 414
  thematic table of contents and, 415
  when to document sources and, 416, 425
Dominant impression, in description, 89–91, 92
Double negatives, H81
Double questions, punctuating, H88
Draft stage, in DCODE process, 3, 16–18, 45–47, 247, H2–H14
Drafts, 16–18
  editing, 18–19, 48–50
  of essays, 45–50
  number of, 17, H2
  revising. *See* Revising

-e, silent, suffixes with words ending in, H107–H108
each, subject-verb agreement and, H62
-ed ending, H30, H54, H55
Edit stage, in DCODE process, 3, 18–19, 48–50
Editing, 18–19
  of essays, 48–50
  revising compared with, 17
Editor
  of anthology, bibliographical entries and, 424
  of essay collection, MLA style and, 427, 428
Editorials, bibliographical entries for, 423
Education of Henry Adams, The (Adams), H13
ei words, spelling, H107

either/or, H20
   pronoun-antecedent agreement and, H73
   as signals for parallel structure, H50
   subject-verb agreement and, H62
Ellipsis, 431, H88
Emphasis
   active and passive voices and, H10–H11
   colons for, H98
   dashes for, H98
   examples ordered by, 121
   functional analysis ordered by, 147
   placement and, H8
   repetition for, H8
   in revising, 16
   sentence structure and, H10–H11
Encyclopedias, 418
   bibliographical entries for, 424
English language
   black. *See* Community dialect
   nonstandard. *See* Community dialect
   as second language. *See* ESL students
   spelling problems in, H105
   standard, H5–H6, H54–H55, H82
Entertaining, as purpose of narratives, 60
Enthymemes, 388
-er ending, H81
-es ending, H55
ESL students
   guide for, H112–H115
      articles in relation to nouns, H112–H113
      idioms, H114
      sentence patterns, H113–H114
      verb endings, H114
   writing suggestions for, H115
Essay tests, A2
Essays
   collections of, MLA style and, 427, 428
   concluding paragraph of, 32, 36–38
   definition of, 32–34
   editing, 48–50
   introductory paragraph of, 32, 34–36
   main parts of, 32
   paragraphs and, 32–33
   patterns in, 34
   titles of, subject-verb agreement and, H63
   writing, DCODE process for, 41–50
-est ending, H81
Etymology, 315
every, subject-verb agreement and, H62
Evidence, in argumentation, 385, 386
Examples. *See* Exemplification
except/accept, H109
Exclamation points, H89, H97
Exemplification, 116–118
   in argumentation, 386

   connecting examples with purpose and, 118
   definition and, 315
   definition of, 116–117
   definitions contrasted with, 312
   hypothetical examples and, 119–120
   in inductive reasoning, 387
   number of examples and, 121
   order of examples and, 121
   sources of examples and, 118
   specific examples and, 119
   typical examples and, 119
   writing, suggested topics for, 140–142
Experiences. *See* Personal experiences
Explanations
   direct, in simple definitions, 311
   indirect, in simple definitions, 312
   punctuation with, H98
Exposition, 116. *See also* Classification; Comparison and contrast; Definition; Exemplification; Functional analysis; Process analysis
   in literature, 345
Extended definition. *See* Definition, extended

Facts, in argumentation, 386
Fallacies, logical, 389–390
False analogy, 390
False dilemma, 390
Family relationship words, capitalization of, H100
FANBOYS, H31
Feelings
   exclamation points and, H89
   interjections and, H21
   tone and, H6–H7
Fiction. *See* Literary analysis; Literature
Fictional point, in literature, 345
Figures. *See* Numbers
Figures of speech, 90
First-person point of view
   in literature, 346
   for personal experiences, 62, 91
Foreign words and phrases, H97
Formal definition, 312
Fractions, hyphens in, H102
Fragments. *See* Sentence fragments
Freewriting, 4, 5, 42, 245
Functional analysis, 116
   approaches to, 146–147
   definition and, 315
   definition of, 146–148
   mixing principles of, 146
   order for, 147
   with process analysis, 175
   writing, suggested topics for, 167–168

Gender
   agreement in, of pronouns and antecedents, H73–H74
   pronoun reference and, H76
General encyclopedias, 418
General words, 91
Generalizations
   hasty, 390
   inductive and deductive reasoning and, 387–390
   unsupported, 116–117
Geographical divisions, capitalization of, H100
Gerunds, H30
good/well, H82
Government publications, bibliographical entries for, 424
Governmental agencies or departments, capitalization of, H100
Grammar, usage compared with, H5
grammar/grammer, H110

Hasty generalization, 390
hear/here, H110
Helping verbs, H18, H25, H56
here/hear, H110
Historical events
   capitalization of, H100
   past tense for writing about, 62, H65
HOTSHOT CAT, H32
Humanities, reference works in, 420
Hyperbole, H11
Hyphens, H102
Hypothetical examples, 119–120

Ideas
   combining
      with complex sentences, H43–H45
      with compound-complex sentences, H45–H46
      with compound sentences, H42–H43
   developing with examples. *See* Exemplification
   of others. *See also* Documented writing; Research papers
      borrowed but not quoted, documenting, 416–417
      plagiarism and, 416, 430–431
   progression of, 16, 92
   relationships among, outlining and, 10–11
   repeating, coherence and, H3
Idioms, H114
ie words, spelling, H107
-ied ending, H55
-ies ending, H55
Imagery, 63–64, 90
Immediate causes and effects, 209
Impression, dominant, in description, 89–91, 92

Indefinite articles, H112–H113
Indefinite pronouns
    possessive of, H101
        pronoun-antecedent agreement and, H73–H74
        pronoun reference and, H77
        subject-verb agreement and, H62
Indenting
    in developmental paragraphs, 2–3
    in outlines, 11
Independent clauses, H30, H37, H38
    combining in complex sentences, H44–H45
    connecting, H37–H38, H39
Index cards, for research papers, 422–424, 429
Indexes
    microfilm, 421
    to periodicals, 420, 421
Indirect questions, punctuating, H88
Inductive leap, 387
Inductive reasoning, 387, 388–389
    logical fallacies in, 389–390
Inference, 388–389
Infinitive, H30
Informative process analysis, 174–175
Informing
    as purpose of comparison and contrast, 273
    as purpose of narratives, 60
-ing ending, H25, H30, H56
Interjections, H21, H90
Interruptions, dashes to indicate, H98
Interviews, bibliographical entries for, 424
Introduction
    of cause-and-effect analysis, 210–211
    of extended definition, 317
Introductory clauses, H12
Introductory conjunctions, H12
Introductory lists, punctuation with, H98
Introductory modifiers, punctuation with, H89
Introductory paragraphs, 32, 34–36
    ineffective, 36
    length of, 36
Introductory phrases, H12
Inversion, in sentences, H11
    subject-verb agreement and, H61–H62
is when, avoiding in definitions, 313
is where, avoiding in definitions, 313
Isolation, for emphasis, 16
Italics, H97
it's/its, H110

Journals, 27–28

know/no, H110
Knowledge, of audience, process analysis and, 176

Lakes, capitalization of, H100
Language. *See also* Diction; English language; ESL students; Tone; Usage; Words
    capitalization of name of, H99
    in definitions, 313
    in revising, 16
lay/lie, H58
Lectures, bibliographical entries for, 424
led/lead, H110
Length
    of introductory paragraphs, 36
    of narratives, 60
    of sentences, varying, H13
let's, pronouns following, H70
Letters (correspondence)
    of application, A2–A3, A4
    salutation and closing of, punctuation with, H91, H98
Letters (of alphabet)
    capitalizing, H99–H100
    omitted, H101
    used as letters, H97, H101
Library of Congress call number, 418, 419
Library research, 414
    biographical dictionaries and, 418
    card catalog and, 418, 419
    computerized indexing systems and, 417
    general encyclopedias and, 418
    primary and secondary sources and, 417
    specialized reference works and, 418, 420–421
lie/lay, H58
Lists, punctuation with, H98
Literary analysis, 346
    analytical, 346–347
    finding topics for, 346–347
    speculative, 347
    suggested topics for, 376–378
    writing with DCODE, 347–348
Literature
    analysis of. *See* Literary analysis
    characters in, 345
    conflict in, 345
    plot in, 345
    point of view in, 346
    reasons for reading, 344
    setting and, 344–345
    theme in, 345
    writing about, 344–346
        present tense for, H65
Localities, capitalization of, H100
Logic. *See* Reasoning
Logical fallacies, 389–390
loose/lose, H110
-ly ending, H19

Magazines. *See* Periodicals
Main clauses, punctuation with, H89, H93, H98
Main point. *See* Thesis
Mapping. *See* Clustering
Meaning. *See also* Definition
    in narratives, 60
Measurements, subject-verb agreement and, H63
Microfilm indexes, 421
Misplaced modifiers, H85
MLA Handbook for Writers of Research Papers, 421. *See also* MLA style
MLA style, 425–428
    for anthologies, 425–426
    for articles, unknown author and, 427
    for articles in periodicals, 425, 426
    for block quotations, 426
    for books by single author, 427
    for essay collections, edited, 427, 428
    principles of, 416–417
    for single-volume books, 425
    unknown author and, 426, 427
Modifiers, H79. *See also* Adjectives; Adverbs
    dangling, H85
    introductory, punctuation with, H89
    misplaced, H85
    precision of, H79
    verbs compared with, H25
Money amounts, subject-verb agreement and, H63
Mountains, capitalization of, H100

Names
    capitalization of, H97, H99
    proper, hyphens with, H102
Narratives
    in conversation, 61
    definition and, 315
    definition of, 60
    description in, 63–64
    dialogue in, 64
    length of, 60
    order in, 61
    point of view in, 62–63, 91
    with process analysis, 175
    properties of, 60
    purposes and forms of, 60–61
    verb tense in, 61–62
Nationalities, capitalization of, H99
Negatives, double, H81
neither/nor, H20
    pronoun-antecedent agreement and, H73
    as signal for parallel structure, H50
    subject-verb agreement and, H62
Newspapers. *See* Periodicals
no/know, H110
Non sequitur, 390

Noncount nouns, H112
    rules for, H113
none, subject-verb agreement and, H62
Nonstandard English. *See* Community dialect
nor. *See also* neither/nor
    pronoun-antecedent agreement and, H73
    subject-verb agreement and, H62
not only/but also
    pronoun-antecedent agreement and, H73
    as signal for parallel structure, H50
    subject-verb agreement and, H62
Note cards, for research papers, 422–424, 429
Noun clauses, in complex sentences, H38
Noun indicators, H17
Noun phrases, as appositives, H46
Nouns, H17, H112
    collective
        pronoun-antecedent agreement and, H73
        subject-verb agreement and, H62
    count, H112
        rules for, H112–H113
    as direct address, commas to set off, H90
    noncount, H112
    plural, H17, H101
        pronoun-antecedent agreement and, H73
        subject-verb agreement and, H61–H63
    possessive of, H101
    proper, definite article with, H113
    singular, ending in -s, subject-verb agreement and, H63
    verbals functioning as, H30
Number, agreement in, of pronouns and antecedents, H72–H73
Numbers
    compound, hyphens in, H102
    omitted, H101
    pronoun reference and, H76
    punctuation with, H91
    used as numbers, H97, H101

Objective case, pronouns in, H69
Objective description, 88–89, 91
Objective tests, A1
Objects
    noun clauses as, H38
    of prepositions, H19
        conjunctions compared with, H21
        pronouns in objective case as, H69
        subjects compared with, H26
    pronoun-antecedent agreement and, H72

pronouns referring back to, objective case and, H69
of verbs, pronouns in objective case as, H69
Oceans, capitalization of names of, H100
one of, pronoun-antecedent agreement and, H73
only one of, pronoun-antecedent agreement and, H73
Opinions, in argumentation, 386
or. *See also* either/or; whether/or
    pronoun-antecedent agreement and, H73
    subject-verb agreement and, H62
Order. *See also* Organization
    in cause-and-effect analysis, 210
    chronological. *See* Order, time
    climactic, in sentences, H11
    coherence and, H2
    for comparison and contrast, 274
    in description, 92
    emphasis, H2, H8
        in cause-and-effect analysis, 210
        examples in, 121
        for functional analysis, 147
    emphasis and, 16
    of examples, 121
    for extended definition, 317
    in narratives, 61
    in process analysis, 176
    references to space for, 61
    of sentences, emphasis and, H10
    space, 61, 92, H2
        in cause-and-effect analysis, 210
        examples in, 121
        for functional analysis, 147
    time, 61, 92, H2
        in cause-and-effect analysis, 210
        examples in, 121
        for functional analysis, 147
        in process analysis, 176
    of verbs in sentences, H18, H24, H25
Organization. *See also* Order; Patterns
    of argumentation, 385–386
    of examples, 121
Organizations, capitalization of, H100
Organize stage, in DCODE process, 3, 10–11, 44–45, 247
Outcome, in narratives, 60
Outlines, 10
Outlining, 10–11
    of reading material, 24–25
    for research papers, 428–429

paid/payed, H110
Paired conjunctions, H20, H38
Paragraph unit, 2–3
    introductory, 34

Paragraphs
    concluding, 32, 36–38
    developmental, 2–3
        definition of, 2–3
    essays and, 32–33
    introductory, 32, 34–36
        ineffective, 36
        length of, 36
    reaction, 26–27
    structure of, support and, H9–H10
    summary, 25–26
    topic sentences of, 8
    writing
        DCODE process for, 3–19, 25, 27
        types of, 23–27
Parallelism, H49
    basic principles of, H49–H50
    signal words for, H50
Paraphrasing, 430
Parentheses, H98, H99
Parenthetical elements, commas to set off, H90
Parenthetical references, 425–426
Parks, capitalization of names of, H100
Participles, H30
    past
        of irregular verbs, H56–H58
        of regular verbs, H56
    present, H56
Parts of speech, H16–H21
passed/past, H110
Passive voice, H10–H11, H66
past/passed, H110
Past tense. *See* Verb tense, past
patience/patients, H110
Patterns. *See also* Organization
    in cause-and-effect analysis, 211
    for comparison and contrast, 274–277
    in essays, 34
    in writing, 10–11
payed/paid, H110
peace/piece, H110
Periodic sentence structure, H10, H13
Periodicals
    bibliographical entries for. *See* Bibliographical entries
    computerized research systems for, 421
    indexes to articles and reviews in, 420
    microfilm indexes to, 421
    MLA style for articles in, 425
        unknown author and, 426, 427
    Reader's Guide to Periodical Literature and, how to use, 420
    titles of, H97
Periods, H88, H97
Person, agreement in, of pronouns and antecedents, H72

Personal experiences
    examples from, 118, 119
    past tense for, 62, H65
    person point of view for, 91
    point of view for, 62
Personal interviews, bibliographical entries for, 424
Persuasion
    definition of, 384
    with process analysis, 175
    as purpose of comparison and contrast, 273
    as purpose of narratives, 60
Phrases
    appositive, punctuation with, H30
    foreign, H97
    introductory, H12
    nonessential, commas to set off, H90
    noun, as appositives, H46
    prepositional, H19
        combining ideas with, H46
        punctuation with, H30
    repeating. *See* Repetition
    as sentence fragments, H30
    subject-verb agreement and, H61
    verb, H24–H25
        in questions, H25
    verbal, punctuation with, H30
piece/peace, H110
Plagiarism, 416, 430–431
Plays
    colons separating acts and scenes of, H98
    titles of, subject-verb agreement and, H63
Plot, in literature, 345
    literary analysis and, 347
Plurals, H17, H101
    apostrophes in, H101
    pronoun-antecedent agreement and, H73
    subject-verb agreement and, H61–H63
Point-by-point patterns, for comparison and contrast, 275, 276–277
Point of view
    coherence and, H4–H5
    in description, 91–92
    in essays, 62–63
    first person
        in literature, 346
        for personal experiences, 62, 91
    in literature, 346
        literary analysis and, 347
    in narratives, 62–63
    shifts in, H4
    third person, 62–63, 92, 346

Points. *See also* Ideas
    in comparison and contrast, 273–274
        clustering as technique for finding, 273–274
    main. *See* Thesis
Policy, questions of, 384
Position. *See* Order; Organization
Positive adjectives, H81
Possessives, H101
Post hoc, ergo propter hoc (after this, therefore, because of this) fallacy, 210, 389
Predicates. *See* Verbs
Predication, strong, H67
Prefixes, hyphens with, H102
Preparation stage, in process analysis, 176
Prepositional phrases, H19
    combining ideas with, H46
    punctuation with, H30
Prepositions, H19–H20
    adverbs compared with, H20
    objects of. *See* Objects, of prepositions
    subject-verb agreement and, H61
Present tense. *See* Verb tense, present
Primary causes and effects, 209
Primary sources, 417
Process analysis, 116
    audience and, 176
    with cause and effect, 175
    definition and, 315
    definition of, 174
    with definitions, 175
    directive, 174, 175
    with functional analysis, 175
    informative, 174–175
    with narration, 175
    with persuasion, 175
    stages in, 176
    suggested writing topics for, 200–203
Pronoun reference, H76–H77
    ambiguous, H77
    coherence and, H3
    implied, H77
    indefinite pronouns and, H77
Pronouns, H17. *See also* Pronoun reference
    agreement with antecedents, H72
        in gender, H73–H74
        in number, H72–H73
        in person, H72
    apostrophes in, H101
    case of, H68–H70
        determining, H69–H70
        objective, H69
        subjective, H68–H69
    indefinite. *See* Indefinite pronouns
    relative, as transitional words and expressions, H3
    as transitional words and expressions, H3
Proof, in argumentation, 385, 386

Proper names, hyphens with, H102
Proposition, in argumentation, 384–385
Protagonist, 345
Punctuation. *See also* Commas; Quotation marks; Semicolons
    apostrophes, H101
    in bibliography, 422, 423
    brackets, 423, H98
    colons, H98
    correcting sentence fragments with, H30
    dashes, H11, H97–H98
    emphasis, H11
    end, H88
    exclamation points, H89, H97
    hyphens, H102
    parentheses, H98, H99
    of parenthetical references, 425
    periods, H88
    of phrases, H30, H90
    question marks, H88, H97
Purpose, connecting examples to, 118

Question marks, H88, H97
Questions
    answered by adjectives, H18, H80
    answered by adverbs, H19, H80
    with definitions, in introductory paragraph, 35–36
    direct, H88
    double, H88
    indirect, H88
    in introductory paragraph, 35–36
    of policy, 384
    pronouns introducing, H17
    punctuation with, H88, H98
    of value or belief, 384–385
    verb phrases in, H25
quiet/quit/quite, H110
Quotation marks, 430
    double, H96
    punctuation with, H97
    to set off quotations, H96
    to set off titles, H96
    single, H96
    when not to use, H96
Quotations
    block quotations and, 426
    in concluding paragraph, 37
    copying directly, 430
    direct, H97
    documenting in paper, 416, 426
    ellipsis marks in, 431, H88
    indicators of, commas to set off, H90
    indirect, H97
    in introductory paragraph, 35
    omitting words in, 431, H88
    punctuation with, H90, H97, H98
    within quotations, H96

Races, capitalization of, H99
raise/rise, H58
Reaction, 23
Reaction paragraph, 26–27
Reader's Guide to Periodical Literature, how to use, 420
Reading
    critical, 23–24
    of literature, 344
Reading material, outlining, 24–25
real/really, H82
Reason, transitional words and expressions to indicate, H3
Reasoning
    circular, 390
    deductive, 387–388, 389–390
    inductive, 387, 388–390
    logical fallacies in, 389–390
receive/recieve, H110
Reference works
    biographical dictionaries, 418
    dictionary entries and, 310–311
    general encyclopedias, 418
    specialized, 418, 420–421
Refutation, in argumentation, 385
Regions, capitalization of, H100
Relative pronouns, as transitional words and expressions, H3
Remote causes and effects, 209
Repetition
    for coherence, H2, H3
    for emphasis, 16, H8
    pronoun reference and, H76
    transitional words and expressions to indicate, H3
    for unity, 16
Rephrasing, pronoun reference and, H76–H77
Research. *See also* Library research; Research papers
    process of, 421
    as source of examples, unsupported, 118
Research papers. *See also* Library research
    assignment and, 422
    bibliographical entries for, 422–424
    circumstances of composition and, 422
    DCODE process for writing, 416
    documentation style for, 425–428
    plagiarism and, 416, 430–431
    preliminary bibliography and works cited for, 422–424
    research process for, 428–430
    sample, 431–440
    steps in research for, 421
Resolution, in literature, 345
Results, transitional words and expressions to indicate, H3
Résumé, A3, A5
Revising, H2–H14
    checklist for, H14
    coherence in, 16, H2–H5
    editing compared with, 17
    emphasis in, 16, H8
    language in, 16, H5–H7
    sentence structure in, 17, H10–H13
    support in, 16–17, H9–H10
    unity in, 16, H8
rise/raise, H58
Run-togethers, H31
    correcting, H31–H32
    identifying, H31

-s ending, H55, H101
Schools, capitalization of, H100
Sciences, reference works in, 418
Secondary causes and effects, 209
Secondary sources, 417
Semicolons
    combining sentences with, H43
    in compound-complex sentences, H46
    correcting comma splices and run-togethers with, H32
    independent clauses joined by, H37, H39
    with quotation marks, H97
    to separate main clauses, H93
    in series, H93
    where not to use, H93
Sensory impressions. *See* Imagery
Sentence completers, H38
Sentence fillers, subject-verb agreement and, H61–H62
Sentence fragments, H28–H30
    acceptable, H28–H29
    dependent clauses as, H29
    phrases as, H30
    unacceptable, H28, H29
    word groups without subjects or verbs as, H30
Sentence interrupters, varying sentence structure with, H12
Sentence outline, 10
Sentences, H36–H39. *See also* Clauses; Phrases
    combining, H42–H46
        appositive for, H46
        coordination and, H42–H43
        coordination and subordination and, H45–H46
        prepositional phrases for, H46
        subordination and, H43–H45
    complex, H38
        combining sentences to make, H43–H45
        punctuating, H45
    compound, H37–H38, H39
        combining sentences to make, H42–H43
        punctuating, H43
    compound-complex, H38, H39, H45–H46
        punctuating, H45
    introductory adverbs in, H12
    introductory clauses in, H12
    introductory conjunctions in, H12
    introductory phrases in, H12
    length of, varying, H13
    patterns used in, H113–H114
    position of, emphasis and, H10
    problems with. *See* Comma splices; Run-togethers; Sentence fragments
    punctuating, H39
    questions. *See* Questions
    simple, H37, H39
    structure of, 17
        balance in, H49–H50
        climactic order of, H11
        dashes to indicate sudden change in, H97
        emphasis and, H10–H11
        inversion and, H11
        periodic, H10, H13
        varying, H11–H13
    topic. *See* Topic sentences
    varying kinds of, H13
Sequence. *See* Order; Organization; Patterns
Series, punctuating, H11, H89, H93
Set position, of verbs, H24
set/sit, H58
Setting, in literature, 344–345
    literary analysis and, 346–347
Setup, in narratives, 60
Sex bias, avoiding, H74
Ship names, H97
Shocking statements, in introductory paragraph, 35
Signal words, for parallelism, H50
Simple classification, 247
Simple definition. *See* Definition, simple
Simple sentences, H37, H39
Simple subject, H25
sit/set, H58
Slang, H6, H97
Social sciences, reference works in, 420
some, subject-verb agreement and, H62
Sources
    authoritative, in argumentation, 386
    documenting. *See* Documented writing; MLA style
    primary and secondary, 417
Spacecraft names, H97
Spatial order. *See* Order, space
Specific examples, 119
Specific information, in narratives, 63–64
Specific words, 91
Speculative analysis, of literature, 347
Speeches, bibliographical entries for, 424

Spelling, H105–H112
    misspelled and confused words and, H108–H112
    tips for, H106–H108
    words frequently misspelled and, H108–H109
Spin-off, 23, 27
Standard usage, H5–H6, H54
    adjectives and adverbs and, H82
    verbs and, H54–H55
States, capitalization of, H100
stationary/stationery, H110
Statistics, in argumentation, 386
Stories. *See also* Literary analysis; Literature
    titles of, subject-verb agreement and, H63
Streets, capitalization of, H100
Strong predication, H67
Struggle, in narratives, 60
Study techniques, for tests, A1
Subject (of sentence)
    agreement with verbs, in number, H61–H63
    alternate, subject-verb agreement and, H62
    compound, H25
        subject-verb agreement and, H61, H62
    noun clauses as, H38
    order in sentence, H26
    pronoun-antecedent agreement and, H72
    pronouns as, subjective case and, H68
    pronouns referring back to, subjective case and, H68–H69
    simple, H25
Subject (topic). *See* Ideas; Points; Thesis; Topic sentences; Topics
Subject-by-subject pattern, for comparison and contrast, 274–275, 276
Subject file, in libraries, 418, 419
Subjective case, pronouns in, H68–H69
Subjective description, 89, 91
Subjective tests, A2
Subordinating conjunctions, H21, H31–H32
Subordinating words, H44–H45
Subordination, combining sentences and, H43–H46
Suffixes
    hyphens with, H102
    spelling rules for, H107–H108
Summary, 23, 25–26
    in concluding paragraph, 37
    transitional words and expressions to indicate, H3
    writing, 25–26
Superlative adjectives, H81
Superlative adverbs, H81
Support, H9–H10

    in argumentation, 385, 386
    completeness of, H9
    concluding paragraphs that function as part of, 36
    in essays, 32
    examples for. *See* Exemplification
    generalizations without, 116–117
    paragraph structure and, H9–H10
    in revising, 16
Surprise, interjections and, H21
Syllogism, 388
Symbolic aspects, in literature, 345
Synonyms
    for emphasis, H8
    pronoun reference and, H76
    in simple definitions, 311

Table of contents, thematic, 415
Technical terms, H97
Temporal order. *See* Order, time
Tense. *See* Verb tense
Test taking
    objective tests and, A1
    study techniques and, A1
    subjective or essay tests and, A2
Textbook, documented papers based on, 414
than, pronouns in subjective case as subject and, H68
than/then, H110
that, pronoun-antecedent agreement and, H73
the
    with count nouns, H113
    with noncount nouns, H113
    as noun indicator, H17
    with proper nouns, H113
their/there/they're, H110
Thematic table of contents, 415
Theme, in literature, 345
    literary analysis and, 347
then/than, H110
there/they're/their, H110
these, as adjective, H17
Thesis, 34. *See also* Ideas; Points; Topic sentences; Topics
    anecdotes related to, in concluding paragraph, 37
    in argumentation, 384–385
    for cause-and-effect analysis, 209
    direct statement of, 35
    in exemplification, 118
    restatement of, in concluding paragraph, 37
    supporting, 16–17
    topic sentences compared with, 34
they're/their/there, H110
Thinking, critical, 23–24
Third-person point of view, 62–63, 92

    in literature, 346
    objective, 346
    omniscient, 346
this, as adjective, H17
thorough/through, H110
Time. *See also* Order, time; Verb tense
    colons in, H98
    phrases specifying change in, 61
Title file, in libraries, 418, 419
Titles (of works)
    foreign, H97
    punctuating, H97
    punctuation with, H98
    subject-verb agreement and, H63
Titles (of people), after names, H100
to/too/two, H110
Tone, 16, H6–H7
Topic outline, 10
Topic sentences, 8
    for cause-and-effect analysis, 209
    in exemplification, 118
    supporting, 16–17
    thesis compared with, 34
Topics. *See also* Ideas; Points; Thesis
    for comparison and contrast, generating, 273
    introducing, in cause and effect analysis, 210–211
Trade names, H100
Train names, H97
Transition, in essays, 32
Transitional connectives, H32, H37–H38, H43
    punctuation with, H39, H43, H90, H93
Transitional words and expressions
    chronological order and, 61
    coherence and, H2–H3
truly/truely, H110
two/to/too, H110
Typical examples, 118, 119

Underlined type, H97
Unity, H8
    in revising, 16
Usage, 16, H5–H6
    diction and, H7
    grammar compared with, H5
    nonstandard. *See* Community dialect
    social situation and, H6
    standard, H5–H6, H54
        adjectives and adverbs and, H82
        verbs and, H54–H55

Value, questions of, 384–385
Verb phrases, H24–H25
    in questions, H25
Verb tense, H114
    change in, 62, H65

consistency of, H65, H114
in narratives, 61–62
past, H55
    for historical events and personal experiences, 62, H65
    of irregular verbs, H56–H58
    of regular verbs, H56
    standard and nonstandard usage and, H54–H55
past participle, H56
    of irregular verbs, H56–H58
    of regular verbs, H56
present, H55
    of irregular verbs, H56–H58
    in narratives, 61
    of regular verbs, H56
    standard and nonstandard usage and, H54–H55
    for writing about literature, H65
present participle, H56
shifting, H65
Verbal phrases, punctuation with, H30
Verbals, H30
Verbs, H17–H18, H24–H26
    action, H24
    agreement with subjects, in number, H61–H63
    being, H18, H24
    compound, H24
    endings of, H114
    form of, H24
    helping, H18, H25, H56
    infinitive, H30
    irregular, H55–H58
        standard and nonstandard usage and, H54, H55
    objects of, pronouns in objective case as, H69
    order in sentence, H18, H24, H25
    plural, subject-verb agreement and, H61–H63
    "problem," H58
    regular, H55–H56
        standard and nonstandard usage and, H54
    set position of, H24
    standard and nonstandard usage of, H53–H55
    strong predication and, H67
    verbals and, H30
Viewpoint. *See* Point of view

weather/whether, H112
well/good, H82
whether/or
    pronoun-antecedent agreement and, H73
    as signals for parallel structure, H50
whether/weather, H112
which, pronoun-antecedent agreement and, H73
who/whom, choosing between, H69–H70
Word choice. *See* Diction
Words. *See also* Adjectives; Adverbs; Articles (parts of speech); Language; Nouns; Prepositions; Verbs
    abstract, 91
    action. *See* Verbs
    classification as parts of speech, H16–H21
    compound, hyphens in, H102
    concrete, 91
    foreign, H97
    general and specific, 91
    meanings of. *See* Definition
    nonessential, commas to set off, H90
    omitting in quotations, 431
    order of, pronoun reference and, H76
    position in sentence, meaning and, H82
    to promote coherence in process analysis, 176
    repeating. *See* Repetition
    signaling parallel structure, H50
    special, quotation marks for, H97
    spelling, H105–H112
        misspelled and confused words and, H108–H112
        tips for, H106–H108
    subordinating, H44–H45
    transitional, H2–H3
    used as words, H97
        plurals of, H101
        subject-verb agreement and, H63
Works cited list, 422–424
write/writen/written, H112
Writing
    about literature, 344–346. *See also* Literary analysis
    critical, 23–24
    DCODE process for. *See* DCODE process
    of description, 89–92
    documented. *See* Documented writing
    drafts in, 16–18
    of journal entries, 27–28
    patterned, 10–11
    reading related, 23–27
    of research papers, 428–431
    sentence variety in, H11–H12
    of summaries, 25–26
written/write/writen, H112

you're/your, H112